CW01669541

THE SKILLFUL TEACHER

The Comprehensive Resource for Improving Teaching and Learning

7TH EDITION

Jon Saphier

Mary Ann Haley-Speca

Robert Gower

RBT

Research for Better Teaching, Inc. • One Acton Place, Acton, MA 01720 • 978.263.9449 • www.RBTeach.com

Library of Congress Cataloging-in-Publication Data

Names: Saphier, Jon, author. | Haley-Speca, Mary Ann, author. | Gower, Robert, author.
Title: The skillful teacher : the comprehensive resource for improving teaching and learning / Jon Saphier, Mary Ann Haley-Speca, Robert Gower.
Description: Seventh Edition. | Acton, MA : Research for Better Teaching, Inc., [2018] | Includes bibliographical references and index.
Identifiers: LCCN 2017046882 | ISBN 9781886822610 (Paperback : alk. paper)
Subjects: LCSH: Teaching. | Learning.
Classification: LCC LB1025.3 .S27 2018 | DDC 371.102--dc23
LC record available at https://lccn.loc.gov/2017046882

Printed in the United States of America.
10 9 8 7 6 5 4 3 2 1

Published and distributed by:
Research for Better Teaching, Inc.
One Acton Place
Acton, MA 01720
978-263-9449 voice
978-263-9959 fax
info@RBTeach.com
www.RBTeach.com

Contents

Preface v
Acknowledgments vii
About the Authors ix

1. Skillful Teaching: The Missing Element in School Reform 1
2. The Skillful Teacher Framework 9

PART ONE:
INTRODUCTION TO ESSENTIAL BELIEFS 19

3. Schooling 21
4. Cultural Proficiency and Anti-Racism 29

PART TWO:
INTRODUCTION TO MANAGEMENT 41

5. Attention 43
6. Momentum 59
7. Space 71
8. Time 81
9. Routines 105
10. Discipline 121

PART THREE:
INTRODUCTION TO INSTRUCTION 193

11. Clarity 195
12. Principles of Learning 267
13. Models of Teaching 291

PART FOUR:
INTRODUCTION TO MOTIVATION **313**

14. Expectations **315**
15. Personal Relationship Building **389**
16. Classroom Climate **407**

PART FIVE:
INTRODUCTION TO CURRICULUM **441**

17. Curriculum Design **443**
18. Lesson Objectives **461**
19. Planning **487**
20. Differentiated Instruction **521**
21. Assessment **549**
22. Overarching Objectives **621**

Reference List **633**

Subject Index **653**

Preface

We wrote this book to assist teachers in their efforts to build greater competence in teaching skills. Our values are obvious. We believe that many things—good curriculum, parental involvement, a clean and safe building—are important for good schools. But of all the things that are important to having good schools, nothing is as important as the teacher and what he or she knows, believes, and can do. A teacher's skill makes a difference in student performance, not only in achievement scores on tests (as important as that might be) but also in students' sense of fulfillment in school and their feelings of well-being.

Our exploration of teaching is guided by three key concepts: (1) comprehensiveness, (2) repertoire, and (3) matching. Comprehensiveness refers to our efforts to understand teaching as a whole. Repertoire challenges teachers to develop a variety of strategies and behaviors for dealing with teaching situations. Matching directs teachers to think about what behavior to pick from their expanding repertoires in light of the situation, group, or characteristics of individual students. Throughout, we revisit these three ideas again and again. As we define and describe each area of teaching, we take the reader through the range of options we have uncovered for handling it. And then, we address matching for that area.

We propose that the skills of teaching include anything a person does that influences the probability of intended learning. That definition broadens the field for application of skill beyond classroom management and good delivery of instruction. Teaching skill includes motivating students and teaching them how to translate that motivation into effective effort. It includes analyzing content for possible misconceptions. It includes error analysis and the planning of reteaching for those who didn't get it the first time around.

In the first chapter, we argue that skillful teaching is the missing element in school reform efforts, and we outline the seven complex knowledge areas we believe are required for skillful teaching. *The Skillful Teacher* addresses one of those complex knowledge areas: generic pedagogy. The second chapter describes The Skillful Teacher Framework, an intuitive structure for organizing this knowledge and capturing future new knowledge. It is a framework that provides educators with a common language and concept system for enabling this complex and critical work in classrooms across the country. The remaining chapters step through each component of The Skillful Teacher Framework. You can read this book sequentially, chapter by chapter, or go straight to a chapter on a particular component of skillful teaching you want to focus on.

We hope, through this book, to build a common language and concept system for talking about teaching—not a dictionary of jargon, but a set of important and meaningful concepts about teaching that all educators can begin to use in common. Having language and shared vocabulary to describe what one does creates more conscious awareness of the most subtle aspects of practice, expands one's lenses for noticing causal relationships, and illuminates opportunities to constructively and creatively adjust and modify practice to achieve our goals. Furthermore, if we can better understand each other—speaking and writing in clear, meaningful terms—then we can expect observation write-ups and evaluations of teaching to be more useful, supervision conferences to be more specific and productive, and staff development programs to be more focused.

We might also expect some of the barriers of isolation and loneliness between teachers to come down. We might expect conversation in teachers' rooms and other meeting places to be more open, more mutually helpful, and more about instruction. With a common professional knowledge base, discussing problems with each other might seem less an admission of personal inadequacy and more a matter of a professional challenge to tackle with knowledge and skills.

In undergraduate teacher education courses, student teaching, and graduate seminars, this same focus on skills and the development of common technical understandings should find a place. Technical understanding of teaching casts no aspersions on the importance of humanism, child development, or detailed knowledge of age- and grade-specific content, methods, and materials. Student teachers in the primary grades, for example, would do well to know about unifix cubes and how to use them to teach place value. Similarly, student teachers in high school social studies would do well to know about TCI's "History Alive" units (www.teachtci.com) and the excellent units of the DBQ Project (www.dbqproject.com). But teacher training (and in-service training) already deals with these things. In our development as a profession, it is time to deal with teaching itself.

This 7th edition of *The Skillful Teacher* has been updated and revised to reflect our knowledge of successful new practices and recent research. Enhanced content for each chapter, such as videos, additional reference materials, and practice exercises, is available for registered readers on *The Skillful Teacher* website at www.RBTeach.com/TST7. These resources are indicated throughout the book by icons in the margins. A lightbulb highlights a "truth" about skillful teaching and a check mark suggests a skillful practice. Please visit the website regularly, as we will be updating the content with new material of interest to our readers.

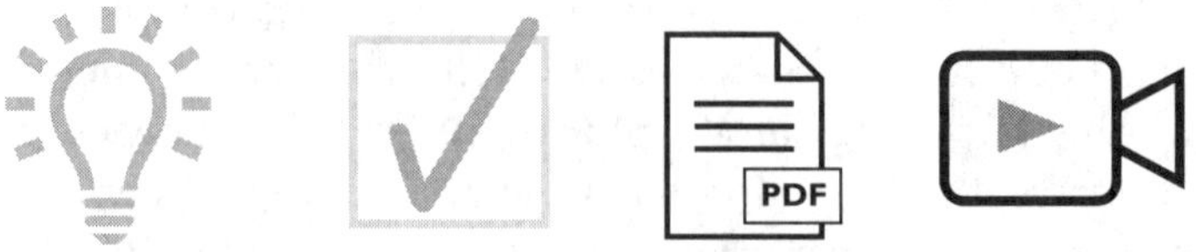

We hope you will find this new edition of *The Skillful Teacher* both instructive and inspiring.

Acknowledgments

A book that attempts to synthesize as much information as this one is obviously indebted to a host of practitioners, researchers, and thought leaders. The reference list at the end of the book reflects the range of authors who have influenced our thinking.

First and foremost, we extend our gratitude to the team of Research for Better Teaching, Inc. (RBT) colleagues and consultants, some of whom have dedicated more than half of their careers to studying, teaching, contributing to, and disseminating this body of work and continue with us today (Deb Reed, Alexander Platt, Marcia Booth, Ken Chapman, Ann Stern, Caroline Tripp, Jim Warnock), others who have joined RBT more recently as valued consultants (Jan Burres, Laura Cooper, Renee DeWald, Reena Freedman, Elizabeth Imende, Nancy Love, Sue McGregor, Harriet Scarborough, Ruth Sernak, Kathy Spencer, Aminata Umoja, DeNelle West), and still others who have either retired from RBT or continued to work in the field in other capacities (Greg Ciardi, Maxine Minkoff, Ned Paulsen, Laura Porter, Fran Prolman, Paula Rutherford, Mary Sterling, Louise Thompson, and Bruce Wellman).

Over the course of more than 40 years, we and these RBT consultants have had the privilege of working with hundreds of thousands of practitioners who have opened their classrooms to us, shared their practice and their insights, bravely explored and experimented with concepts within The Skillful Teacher Framework, and openly shared their successes and their struggles. We are indebted to each of them for the ways in which they contributed to the growth of this professional knowledge base. And in this edition, in particular, we appreciate the contributions by classroom teachers Danielle Berwick, Meghan Conley, Danielle Conway, and Michael Scalise, who were kind enough to share with us some of their classroom routines.

In addition, Dr. Tiffany Pogue of Albany State University provided subtle and valuable suggestions for the new chapter on cultural proficiency. We're very grateful to her.

We thank the many educators in Brookline, Cambridge, Carlisle, Concord, and Newton, Massachusetts, whose participation in our early observational studies contributed to the original conceptual framework for this book. Specifically, Ginny Chalmers, Susan-Jo Russell, Suzanne Stuart, and Risa Whitehead opened their classrooms to us and held many important discussions with us about teaching. Peggy McNeill MacMullen was an invaluable part of the early brain trust that developed The Skillful Teacher Framework.

Ann Ballantine brought to the project a rare combination of editing, book production skills, and project management. Her commitment to our mission was responsible for great work above and beyond the call of duty.

Leah Conn's editing and additions to the exercises and videos associated with each chapter will be prized by those who use these online resources on *The Skillful Teacher* website.

Suzanne Peterman of Top Dog Design brought new graphics and refined formatting skills to the book design.

Ivy Schutt managed permissions and editing work with diligence and excellence.

Carole Fiorentino was a skilled detective in tracking down hard-to-find references to be sure we were accurate and up to date.

Finally, we especially want to thank our spouses and families for their continuing support and understanding of the often demanding schedules of our work to advance the professionalization of teaching.

About the Authors

Jon Saphier founded Research for Better Teaching, Inc. (RBT) in 1979, after 10 years as a teacher, instructional coach, and administrator. RBT is an educational consulting organization dedicated to improving classroom teaching and school leadership throughout the United States and internationally. He has led large-scale district improvement projects and has forged working alliances among superintendents, teacher union leaders, and school boards in school districts such as Montgomery County, Maryland; Eugene, Oregon; and Brockton, Revere, and Attleboro in Massachusetts. He is an annual guest instructor for The Harvard Graduate School of Education's Achievement Gap Institute and is a well-known keynote speaker on high-expertise teaching, school leadership, and related education topics. Dr. Saphier is an author of eight books on education, including *The Skillful Teacher,* now its 7th edition. Other publications include *High Expectations Teaching, How to Bring Vision to School Improvement*, and *John Adams' Promise*. Dr. Saphier holds an Ed.D. from Boston University, M.Ed. from University of Massachusetts, M.S. from London School of Economics, and a B.A. from Amherst College.

Mary Ann Haley-Speca is a founding consultant and former director of training with Research for Better Teaching, Inc. (RBT). During her tenure with RBT, Ms. Haley-Speca worked with teachers and administrators in urban, suburban, and rural public school districts and private institutions throughout the world, focusing on the study of instruction, school, and organizational culture; coaching, supervision, and evaluation practices; and professional development planning. She is the co-author of two other popular RBT publications: *Activators* and *Summarizers*. She has served as a classroom teacher, staff developer, and program supervisor in the Hudson and Concord, Massachusetts, public schools. She is currently working as a full-time consultant with RBT on long-term projects in several urban and suburban school districts throughout the United States.

Robert Gower is retired as Professor Emeritus at the University of Massachusetts–Lowell (UML) where he helped develop the doctoral program in Leadership in Schooling and was on the Advisory Board of the Graduate School of Education. He still teaches The Skillful Teacher online course at UML. Bob's distinguished career includes being an elementary teacher, a principal, a researcher, a pioneer in the study of teaching, and a standout instructor and mentor for generations of graduate students. In 2007, he received the Faculty Excellence & Service Award and was recognized as a 2007 Honors Fellow by the University of Massachusetts.

CHAPTER 1

Skillful Teaching

The Missing Element in School Reform

Skillful Teaching:

The Missing Element in School Reform

Since the last edition of *The Skillful Teacher*, published in 2008, we have witnessed many new initiatives aimed at improving what schools offer children: The No Child Left Behind (NCLB) Federal Law, the U.S. Department of Education's Race to the Top competitive program, the Gates Foundation–funded Measures of Effective Teaching (MET) project, the Common Core curriculum standards, and the passing of the Every Student Succeeds Act (ESSA) by Congress.

We hope to build a common language and concept system for talking about teaching—not a dictionary of jargon, but a set of important and meaningful concepts that all educators can begin to use in common.

However, during this period and, in fact, since the 1990s progress narrowing the achievement gap has actually plateaued nationwide and deteriorated markedly in urban schools (Reardon, 2013). Why is this the case? Let's look at each of these school-improvement initiatives:

▲ NCLB created a nationwide focus on testing with both positive and negative effects. The positive effect was to focus attention on student gain scores, especially for underserved students. The negative effect was to drive teaching toward test-centered skill work and away from responsiveness to students' interests and creativity, critical thinking, and deep understanding.

▲ Race to the Top generated intensive development of materials for teacher evaluation and employment regulations that made teacher ratings give weight to student gain scores for a large proportion of the rating. The benefits were rubrics that attempted to capture the range of categories in which teacher performance mattered. The minuses, which in our view far outnumber the pluses, were overreliance on unreliable measures of student gains, superficial and ineffective training of evaluators, reduction of rubrics to checklists, and neglect of the *improvement of teaching* in favor of the evaluation of teachers.

▲ The MET project attempted to correlate five observation protocols with measured student gain scores. The highest correlation went not to an observation protocol, but to a highly developed student questionnaire, the Tripod Survey. Student evaluations of teachers were far more accurate than observation instruments. The benefit was to validate student evaluations and highlight the factors they identify (Ferguson et al., 2015).

- ▲ The Common Core curriculum standards brought a spotlight onto critical thinking, deep understanding, and students' capacity to articulate their thinking and support their positions with evidence. This focus has, unfortunately, been sidetracked by erroneous assumptions that the standards are a national curriculum. Common Core standards are not a curriculum; they are competency targets to shoot for. They originated from the governors of 50 states, not the U.S. Department of Education. The Council of Chief State School Officers decided to contract with experts to write them; there was no federal participation at all. These erroneous assumptions were compounded by fear that the tests derived from the standards would be harder than the current ones states use, because they require more thinking and writing. Thus state scores would go down.

- ▲ The enactment of ESSA has given us a breather from the testing mania still abroad in the land, but it has done nothing about the central issue—creating the required conditions to support a highly skilled teaching profession based on sophisticated expertise and deep collaboration.

Although these programs have had some positive effects, they have not led to enough progress in raising the quality of our schools overall because none of them systematically or consistently addressed the most important variable in student achievement: skillful teaching. The valuable work of the last two decades on other aspects of school improvement has not been in vain or off target. It was necessary but insufficient. We needed standards. We needed accountability and a focus on results for students. We needed data systems to track student learning at a fine grain. But these hallmark reforms of the 1990s and 2000s have still not budged student achievement significantly because we left off the third leg of the stool in school reform—standards and accountability for the *expertise* of our teacher corps in the complex knowledge and skill of good teaching.

THE WORK WE STILL NEED TO DO

Several days each week, we are in classrooms in one of our major cities—New York, Memphis, Washington D.C., San Diego, and others—providing coaching and support to teachers and principals. What we see sometimes exhilarates us and, at other times, breaks our hearts. The best classrooms are uplifting places that deliver skillful teaching and convey belief and hope to all their students about the promise of education and the capacity of each child to achieve at high levels. All our children could learn in such places, but they do not.

There are many outstanding professional teachers at work in our schools, including those serving our most economically disadvantaged children. They

Figure 1.1 Seven Knowledge Bases for High-Expertise Teaching

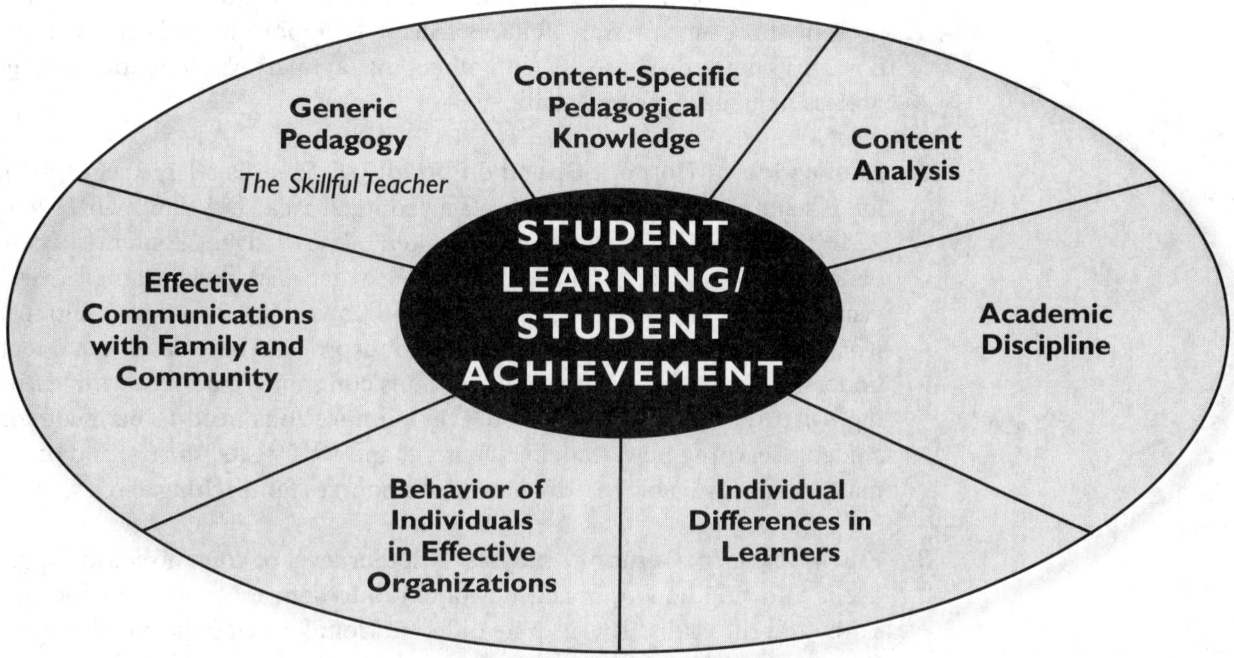

had to acquire their expertise over many years and usually alone through their own initiative and perseverance. But there are simply not enough of them. The stark fact is that there are larger numbers of underprepared teachers. And blaming them for skills they don't have is unfair. There is a massive gap between the knowledge and skills they bring to the classroom and the knowledge and skills they should and could have with proper training and support. The fundamentals of high-expertise teaching have not been provided to or expected of large portions of our teacher corps.

The Skillful Teacher provides a detailed roadmap for anyone seeking to master generic pedagogy.

There are seven kinds of professional knowledge (Figure 1.1) that are central to high-expertise teaching (Saphier, 2017). In addition to Generic Pedagogy (the focus of *The Skillful Teacher*) and Content-Specific Pedagogy, five other important knowledge bases bear on the success of teaching and learning. Five of them—Content Analysis, Academic Discipline, Individual Differences in Learners, Behavior of Individuals in Effective Organizations, Effective Communications with Family and Community—are seldom found in teacher preparation programs or other systems that influence teacher capacity.

1. **Knowledge of Generic Pedagogy:** *The Skillful Teacher* tackles the vast and complex field of generic pedagogical knowledge. Without solid

skills in this area, many people entering teaching, who are experts at their content and are mature individuals transferring from successful careers in other walks of life, quickly fail. We hope *The Skillful Teacher* can help prevent those unnecessary failures. But it is important to keep in mind how this knowledge base fits with others that are part of a fully functioning professional teacher's repertoire.

2. **Knowledge of Content-Specific Pedagogy:** There is a large set of tools for teaching that are specific to each content area. Lee Shulman (1986) described these as pedagogical content knowledge. Content-specific pedagogical knowledge includes knowing what analogies, examples, and visual representations best capture key ideas of the academic discipline; what experiments, equipment, models, and projects best develop student understanding; what prior misconceptions commonly interfere with learning; what real-world, culturally relevant connections need to be made for students learning new academic content; and what texts, stories, and other materials are available that are powerful resources for teaching and learning.

3. **Knowledge of Content Analysis:** Another level of content-based expertise is knowing how to break the content into concepts and sub-concepts, skills, and sub-skills. This is quite different from knowing the content itself. It means that the teacher understands how the concepts and skills are connected to one another and how to bring these relationships to the attention of students. Every teacher must understand the network of concepts "that relate to the specific concept to be taught and how that network is connected to the content in the year-long curriculum as well as to the curricula of the previous and following years" (West & Staub, 2003, p. 19). Liping Ma (1999) gives clear examples of how this kind of knowledge empowers good lesson and unit planning.

   Curriculum materials cannot be relied on to hold these connections, much less make them explicit for students. Curriculum materials are resources for teachers to draw on to create the best lessons for their students. Skillful teachers are wary of curricula that prescribe a script that allows only one way of teaching. Such materials are marginally appropriate for para-professionals and provisional teachers who have no pedagogical knowledge of their own. But they ensure that a large proportion of students will not learn because their learning style is not matched to that one way of teaching.

4. **Knowledge of the Academic Discipline:** Teachers must, of course, have knowledge of their academic discipline and of the standards in the discipline that their state has adopted. Most states have raised standards for teachers' content knowledge and require a college major for secondary teachers in the

field they will be teaching. This is a necessary, but insufficient, condition for developing successful teachers.

5. **Knowledge of Individual Differences in Learners:** Teachers must be aware of their students' cultural, developmental, and learning characteristics and how to include those differences in instructional decisions. This is a vast field. Cognitive developmental differences, for example, can cause unrealistic expectations in mathematics of primary students who are still in the Piagetian concrete operations stage or who haven't yet achieved conservation of number. Quite differently, but equally important, knowledge of a student's culture can have a profound effect on a teacher's ability to interpret student behavior or to make culturally relevant connections between academic content and student experience.

6. **Knowledge of the Behavior of Individuals in Effective Organizations:** This kind of knowledge relates to effective teams, effective meetings, good communication, and problem-solving skills with other adults and the awareness of one's role as a teacher in building a strong "Adult Professional Culture" among colleagues.

7. **Knowledge of How to Communicate Effectively with Families and Community:** This knowledge enables teachers to find multiple access channels to communicate to families what they most want to know—that the teacher knows their child and wants the best for him or her. Beyond that is knowledge of how to connect families and their children around homework and how to enlist hard-to-reach families in supporting the education of their children.

What steps can we each take in our own schools and districts to bring high-expertise teaching skills into the mainstream practice of all teachers? If you are a new or experienced teacher, an administrator, a coach, or a central office administrator and are concerned about the future of our children, this book is for you, because it explains the what and how of generic pedagogy, a fundamental component of high-expertise teaching. We seek to explain it in all its range and complexity. *The Skillful Teacher* provides a detailed roadmap for anyone seeking to master generic pedagogy.

THE PROFESSIONAL KNOWLEDGE AND SKILL REQUIRED

What do teachers need to know and be able to do to bring all our students to high levels of achievement? The ten jobs of teaching, listed in Table 1.1 and explained in separate chapters of this book, represent just a sample of the com-

Table 1.1 Ten Jobs of Teaching

1. Make sure *all* students have to explain their thinking frequently in class by talking, writing, or interacting, in some way, in response to the ideas or skills in each lesson.

2. Make sure you have a way of knowing (i.e., some *evidence*) at the end of the lesson what each of the students has learned or can do relative to the objective.

3. Make sure the students have exemplars of good work to model and that they receive detailed information/feedback, frequently, about how they are doing relative to the learning targets.

4. Make sure the examples, illustrations, and materials used to make new ideas accessible to students are drawn from the best craft knowledge of the field and deepened by strategies from cognitive science like "modeling thinking aloud" and "mental imagery."

5. Work actively to make it safe for students to make mistakes and learn from them.

6. Work actively to communicate to students your belief that they are able, that ability can be increased, and that effective effort, the most significant determinant of achievement, can be learned.

7. Make sure students feel known and valued, and have some ownership and choices in how the business of classroom life proceeds.

8. Make sure the rules and consequences are clearly understood by students and facilitate learning. Respond promptly with the "body language of meaning business" when students are off task (Jones, 2013). Ensure that backup management structures for routines, procedures, and arrangements of space and time are clearly understood by the students and facilitate learning.

9. Make sure the learning objective for the lesson/unit is appropriate, clearly thought out, and that the students can say what it is with understanding. Draw on a diagnostic analysis of the gaps in students' prior knowledge to make sure the objective of the day is the most important one for these students.

10. Make sure each night that student products or other forms of student work are analyzed to focus detailed lesson planning and reteaching for the next day. Align learning experiences logically with objectives, and plan how to stitch those learning experiences together with questions, cues, and directions that guide student cognition and stimulate higher-level thinking for all, not just some, students.

plex and sophisticated skill sets required for successful teaching. These are not options. They are not choices according to style. They are bottom-line essentials needed by every teacher. These are known, validated elements of successful teaching and learning in the classroom. They are also not easy to do. They require deep, sophisticated knowledge to carry out well; far more than we acknowledge in either our requirements to enter teaching or our support systems for teachers once they are employed. Each job can be accomplished by drawing on known repertoires of skills.

These are known, validated elements of successful teaching and learning in the classroom.

Wonderful schools in the most challenging circumstances can be found all over the country in any year, though there are far too few of them. Their examples, however, never seem to generalize to the schools around them. Typically, they don't last more than a decade before declining. Why is this? School institutions with excellent practice do not have staying power because the knowledge and expertise behind those practices does not carry forward to those who succeed the reformers. It is not built into the personnel systems that produce and support the teachers and leaders who succeed the inspired and dedicated people who make the initial transformations happen. To learn more about how to restructure the personnel system see *John Adams' Promise* (Saphier, 2005) and "Growing Lilies in the Desert," both available on *The Skillful Teacher* website at www.RBTeach.com/TST7.

If we are serious about the promises of democracy and freedom, then we owe every child a chance at a good life through education. It is time to unite around this missing leg of education reform and find a way to build professional knowledge into every stage of the teacher and leader development process. This book is designed to make clear and accessible, with detailed examples, the full range and complexity of this knowledge base for

- ▲ teachers who want to improve their own practice,
- ▲ coaches who want to help teachers solve students' learning problems,
- ▲ administrators who want to be sure they are looking for the most important aspects of good teaching to inform their feedback,
- ▲ central office leaders who want to design systems for continuous improvement, and
- ▲ policy makers who want resources aimed at the key lever—skillful teaching.

CHAPTER QUICK GUIDE

Seven Kinds of Professional Knowledge Central to High-Expertise Teaching:

1. Generic Pedagogy (*The Skillful Teacher*)
2. Content-Specific Pedagogy
3. Content Analysis
4. Academic Discipline
5. Individual Differences in Learners
6. Behavior of Individuals in Effective Organizations
7. Effective Communications with Family and Community

Ten Jobs of Teaching (Table 1.1):

- ▲ Represent a sample of the complex and sophisticated skill sets required for successful teaching.
- ▲ They are known, validated elements of successful teaching and learning in the classroom.
- ▲ They are not easy to do.
- ▲ They require deep, sophisticated knowledge to carry out well.

CHAPTER 2

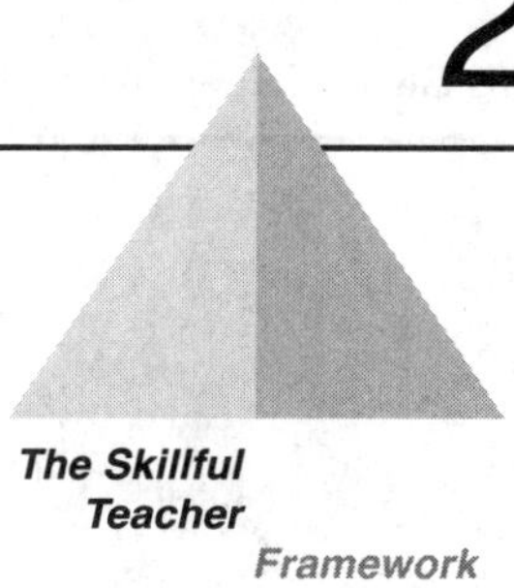

The Skillful Teacher Framework

Skillful Teachers are made, not born.

The Skillful Teacher Framework is different from other frameworks. First, it is based on a theory of knowledge grounded in sound epistemology (Polanyi, 1966). Second, it is practical and specific. It uses numerous classroom examples and plain language, without jargon, to spell out the details of what a skill looks like and sounds like. Third, it is written to assist in classroom problem-solving and asserts that successful teaching is inherently problem-solving and decision-making from repertoires. Fourth, it supports building strong "Adult Professional Culture" based on constant learning and non-defensive examination of practice in relation to student learning. Finally, it is inclusive. Teaching skill is defined to include anything a person does that influences the probability of intended learning.

WHAT IS SKILLFUL TEACHING?

Skillful teachers are made, not born. They have learned the skills they use, and others can look at what they are doing in the classroom and say what is skillful about it. Some skillful teachers do not have the vocabulary or the concepts for describing what they already do. They just "know" what to do and do it effortlessly and naturally—intuitively, some might say. This effortlessness is an unconscious, automatic kind of knowing—tacit knowledge, Polanyi calls it. The limitation of this kind of knowing is that it is acquired only by a few (not given at birth, we want to repeat) and unpredictably learned over time, in many different ways. These teachers cannot pass this "knowing" on to others because they can't describe in detail what they do.

Being skillful in teaching is the core theme of this book. As we explain this theme, we want to be clear that we are not "walling out" from our conception of good teaching certain other important things. We value teachers who are sensitive, know how to laugh, and know how to love. Being skillful is not in competition with being a thinking, feeling person. But we are focusing in this book on the skillful part of being a good teacher. There is more to good teaching than skill, but there is no good teaching without it.

How do we define a skillful teacher?

1. Skillful teachers are aware of the complexity of their job and work to be conscious and deliberate about what they do. They don't do what they do just because that is the way it has always been done or because that's the cultural expectation of how it shall be done. They do what they do because they have thought about it and made choices from a repertoire of options that seem best.

2. Skillful teachers want to control and regulate their teaching to have a positive effect on their students. They monitor what they do, get feedback, and try different things. Skillful teachers are determined that their students will succeed. When that isn't happening, they examine their practices.

3. Skillful teachers are clear about what is to be learned, what achievement means, and what they are going to do to help their students attain it. If one thing doesn't work, they make another plan that is also technically clear and well thought out.

4. Skillful teachers are learners—always a student of teaching, as Joyce, Clark, and Peck (1981) said long ago. Skillful teachers constantly reach out to their colleagues with an assertive curiosity that says, "I don't know it all. No one does or ever will, but I am always growing, adding to my knowledge and skills and effectiveness." To skillful teachers, that openness and reaching out is an important element of professionalism.

THE ELEMENTS OF THE FRAMEWORK

The tasks of skillful teaching can be grouped according to their function—Management, Instructional Strategies, Motivation, and Curriculum—and their associated areas of performance, as illustrated in Figure 2.1. Altogether, these areas of performance delineate teaching. Teaching is all of them.

▲ One of the Essential Beliefs is that all students can learn rigorous academic materials at high standards. We believe that the presence of this belief is what drives a teacher to increase their repertoire of teaching skills. Other important beliefs in this foundation include the role of interdependence among educators in getting the job done for students, acknowledgment of the importance of collegial behavior for strong school culture, the belief that professional knowledge is based on repertoires and matching, and the belief in the need for constant learning. It includes

Figure 2.1 The Skillful Teacher Framework

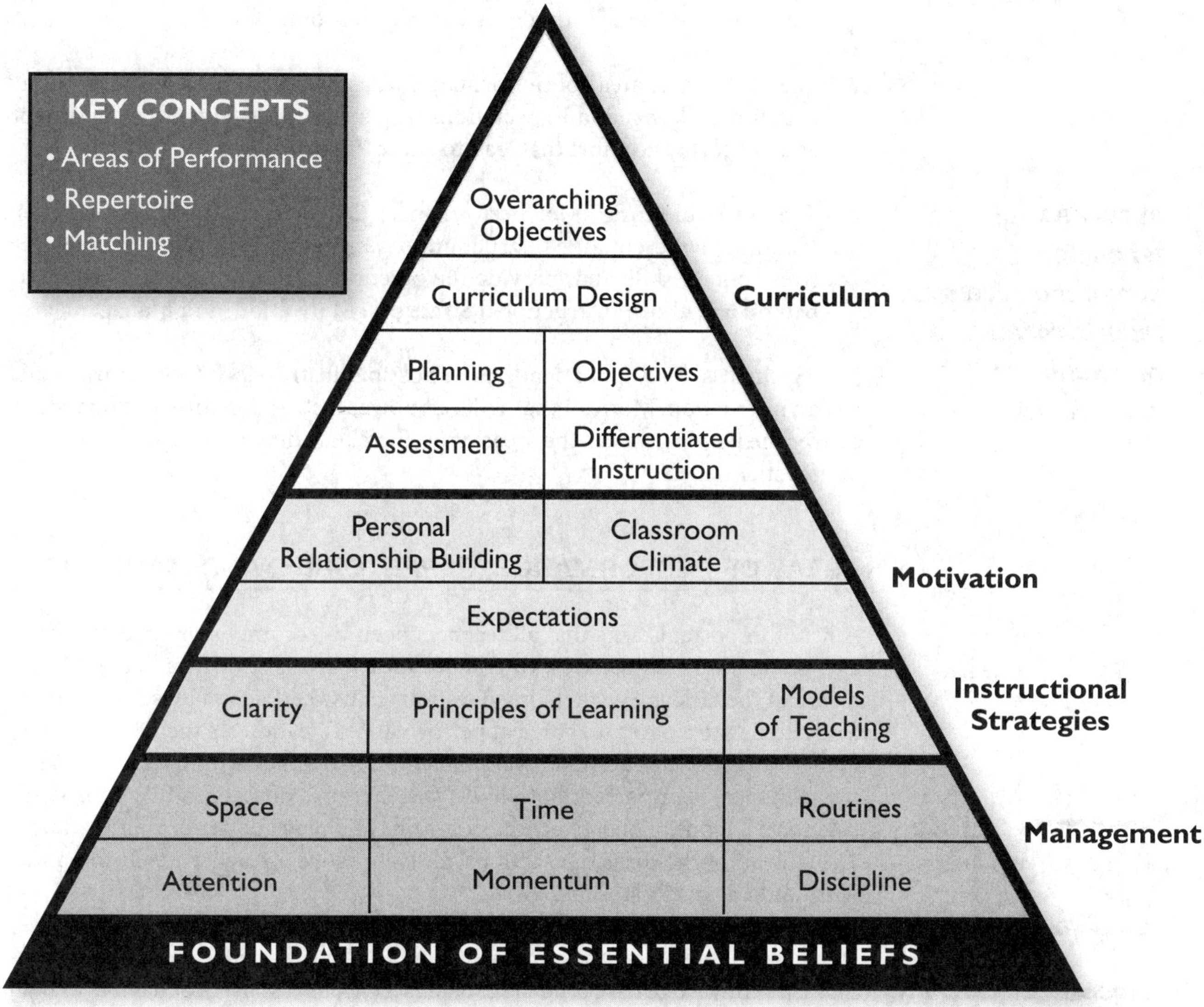

teacher beliefs about the important positive effects that cultural proficiency and anti-racism have on learning in the classroom.

▲ The Management areas of performance: Attention, Momentum, Space, Time, Routines, and Discipline are the foundation of teaching. If these jobs aren't being handled, no learning can take place. They contain the prerequisite skills for good teaching.

- ▲ The Instructional Strategies areas of performance: Clarity, Models of Teaching, and Principles of Learning deliver the goods. These skills come to life during interactive learning time in the classroom.

- ▲ The Motivation areas of performance: Classroom Climate, Personal Relationship Building, and Expectations help students generate the investment and put forth the effort that lead to successful learning.

- ▲ The Curriculum areas of performance: Curriculum Design, Objectives, Planning, Differentiated Instruction, Assessment, and Overarching Objectives contain skills that provide the blueprints for instruction. They stand behind and above Instructional Strategies, Motivation, and Management.

In successful teaching, comprehensiveness, repertoire, and matching are what count.

Management skills support and make possible instruction. Curriculum skills design instruction. Motivational skills empower instruction. Instructional skills deliver the goods. And all the areas of performance depend on the Foundation of Essential Beliefs.

AREAS OF PERFORMANCE, REPERTOIRES, AND MATCHING

A list of important tasks that all teachers need to accomplish regardless of the age, grade level, subject area, or courses they teach is shown in Table 2.1. We have cast the task as a challenging question to answer. Each of these questions is associated with a particular area of performance. We indicate the area of performance next to each question. Every one of these questions (and related areas of performance) is important unto itself, and there is a chapter in this book dedicated to each one. Collectively the questions and areas of performance address virtually all of the decisions, actions, and situations a teacher needs to handle with students in classrooms.

Video: Repertoire and Matching

We answer these questions by drawing on the rich knowledge base about teaching. This knowledge base is not a set of prescriptions or a list of behaviors known to produce effective learning (though there are a few of these). Rather, it offers options, or repertoires, for dealing with each area. It also asserts that effective teaching lies in choosing appropriately from among the options to match given students, situations, or curricula.

Conceptualizing our knowledge base as repertoires for accomplishing tasks rather than as "effective behaviors" legitimizes professional conversations and healthy debates about choices. In contrast, the "effectiveness" paradigm implies there are singularly effective ways of performing tasks, thus discouraging dis-

Table 2.1 The Important Questions of Teaching and Areas of Performance

Essential Questions	Areas of Performance
1. How do I get students to pay attention and stay on task?	Attention
2. How do I keep the flow of events moving smoothly and minimize downtime, delays, and distractions?	Momentum
3. How do I get the most out of my space and furniture?	Space
4. How do I time events and regulate schedules so that students get the most productive learning time?	Time
5. What procedural routines are important and how do I get maximum mileage out of them?	Routines
6. How do I eliminate disruptions while building responsibility and ownership?	Discipline
7. How do I make concepts and skills clear and accessible to students?	Clarity
8. How do I design more efficient and effective learning experiences?	Principles of Learning
9. How do I create learning experiences that develop the mind as well as the content?	Models of Teaching
10. How do I communicate to students that what we're doing is important, that they can do it well, and that I won't give up on them?	Expectations
11. How do I build good personal relationships with students and make them feel truly known and valued?	Personal Relationship Building
12. How do I build a climate of inclusion, risk-taking, and personal efficacy?	Classroom Climate
13. What do I need to know about my curriculum?	Curriculum Design
14. How should I frame objectives so they precisely guide my planning and are on-target for my students' learning?	Lesson Objectives
15. How do I plan lessons that will reach all my students?	Planning
16. What choices do I have for differentiating learning experiences?	Differentiated Instruction
17. How can I use assessment to inform instruction and improve student performance?	Assessment
18. How do my personal passions show up in a "test-driven" world?	Overarching Objectives

agreement and debate—at least if we don't want to damage friendships with peers. (If there is only one effective way of doing things and we disagree, we can't both be right.) Thus the repertoire and matching model of professional knowledge is a foundation for strong "Adult Professional Culture" where we need each other to think through difficult matching choices.

In successful teaching, comprehensiveness, repertoire, and matching are what count: comprehensive awareness of all of the areas of performance involved in running a successful classroom; repertoire so that one has options to work with and draw on when addressing a given aspect of classroom life; and matching: making decisions about which tool will be most effective to use in a given situation. Ultimately, matching is the name of the game.

This is the foundation for successful differentiation. We are conceptualizing our knowledge base as a large set of repertoires to accomplish a range of purposes. Purposes that are different but interactive and that are simultaneously present in the complex human environment that all classrooms are. This position honors the design and problem-solving nature of what teaching is. A similar point is made by Mary Kennedy (2016) in her analysis of the nature of teaching.

To illustrate this, consider a simple management concern: dealing with intrusions. A teacher is instructing a small group when a student outside of the group (Jimmy) is stuck on an item on a worksheet and approaches the teacher for help. The challenge for the teacher is maintaining the momentum of the instructional group while simultaneously addressing Jimmy's needs. There are several options for how the teacher can handle this: (1) wave Jimmy off, (2) wave Jimmy in but signal him to be silent until there is an appropriate pause to give help, (3) redirect Jimmy to another student for help, or (4) proactively teach students what to do when the teacher is engaged in an instructional group. No one of these options is inherently better teaching. Each could be an effective and most appropriate response in a particular situation. For instance, if Jimmy doesn't have the confidence or social skills to approach another student for help, then waving him in may be better than redirecting. But if Jimmy is overly dependent on the teacher, waving him off may be the best choice, especially if the teacher believes Jimmy can do it himself if he tries again. The teacher's success in handling Jimmy will depend on whether she knows the options available for dealing with the situation and can choose the best response by matching the options to the specific situation.

There are many ways of dealing with each of the major areas of teaching identified in our list of questions, and skillful teaching involves continually broadening one's repertoire in each area and picking from it appropriately to match given students, groups, situations, or curricula. The knowledge base about teaching identifies choices available in each of these performance areas, available for anyone to learn, refine, and do skillfully. This book presents options for each performance area, illustrates them with examples, and offers what is known about how to choose which is best for the moment.

Figure 2.2 Moves

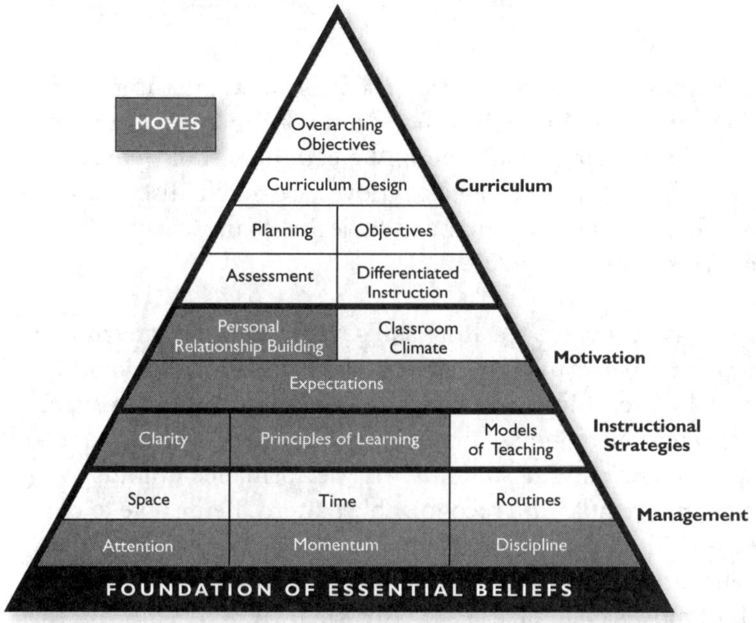

Figure 2.3 Patterns

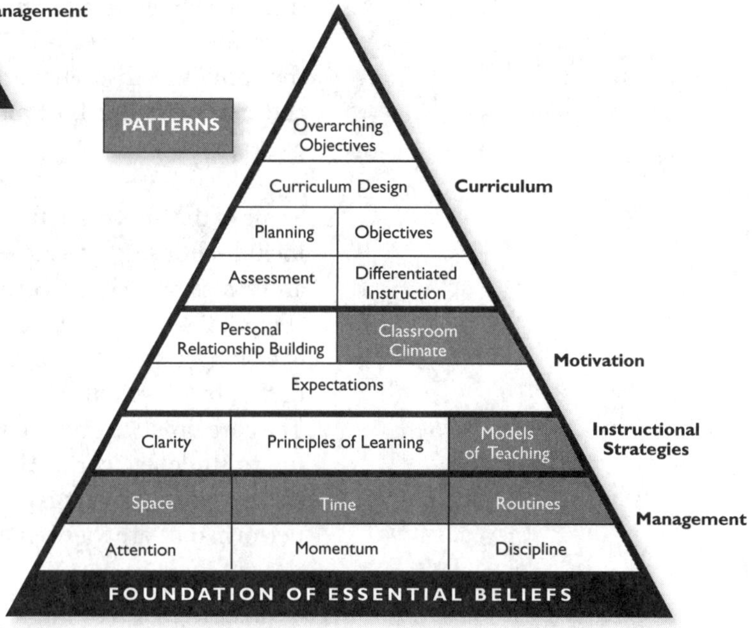

Figure 2.4 Abstractions

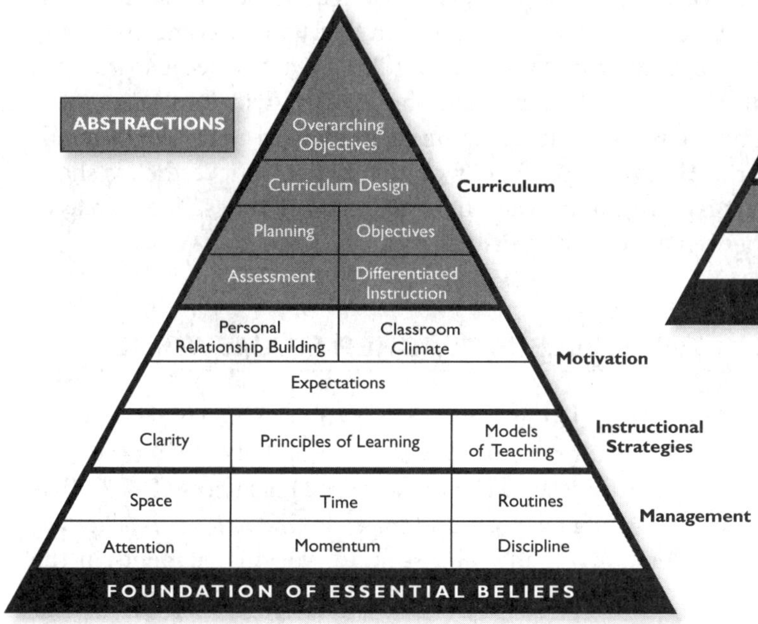

Three kinds of knowledge—moves, patterns, and abstractions—comprise skillful teaching.

MOVES, PATTERNS, AND ABSTRACTIONS

Because teaching combines these eighteen areas of performance, it is important to recognize how they are related to each other. Some of the areas of performance have specific skills associated with them. We call these skills *moves* because they represent a brief action or a remark. Moves are quick, discrete, and observable behaviors. They can be counted if you so desire. Many teaching skills can be explained in terms of moves (Figure 2.2).

Other areas of performance involve teaching skills that are more pattern like (Figure 2.3). They can't be performed or seen quickly. An example would be implementing a model of teaching. For instance, a teacher skilled in using Taba's (1962) nine-step inductive model orchestrates a series of events and follows certain principles for reacting to students. The performance unfolds over time according to a certain regular and recognizable pattern. Being able to perform the pattern is the skill. It's a cohesive, planned package that is greater than the sum of its discrete parts. Skillful teachers understand moves as stand-alone actions and patterns of moves that make sense only when viewed as purposeful packages.

Some of the important things teachers do skillfully are hard to see at all. These skills include choosing objectives, designing learning experiences, organizing curricula, and assessing student learning. These areas of knowledge and skill are abstractions (Figure 2.4). The connections between actions and decisions become clear only over longer stretches of time or in conversation with a teacher because they are driven by big-picture blueprints (overarching objectives, curriculum maps, etc.). They are practiced before school, during planning, or after school while responding to students' work. Although not directly observable, they nevertheless shape and account for what is going on in a classroom at almost all times. These areas of performance are found in Curriculum Planning.

CROSSWALKING THE SKILLFUL TEACHER FRAMEWORK

Readers wishing to know the relationship of The Skillful Teacher Framework to widely used teacher evaluation rubrics can download detailed crosswalk documents from *The Skillful Teacher* website (www.RBTeach.com/TST7). The following crosswalks show which chapters and pages in *The Skillful Teacher* describe behaviorally the looks-like and sounds-like of various elements in the rubrics:

- ▲ Crosswalk aligned to Charlotte Danielson's Framework for Teaching
- ▲ Crosswalk aligned to Kim Marshall's Teacher Evaluation Rubrics
- ▲ Crosswalk aligned to Robert Marzano's Teacher Evaluation Model
- ▲ Crosswalk aligned to the Massachusetts Model System for Teacher Evaluation
- ▲ Crosswalk aligned to David Rose's Universal Design for Learning

Crosswalk Rubrics

THE DETAILS OF THE SKILLFUL TEACHER FRAMEWORK

Part One of *The Skillful Teacher* explores the Foundation of Essential Beliefs. Part Two addresses the Management areas of performance—those most pressing and immediate needs for many teachers. Part Three addresses Instructional Strategies. Part Four tackles Motivation. Part Five examines Curriculum—the design skills for decisions about what education is for, what shall be taught, and how to know if it has been learned. Thus the chapters move from the specific and discrete to the complex; from those parts of teaching that are moves, to patterns of moves, to decisions about design. Each chapter addresses a different area of performance. We frequently start by describing why the area of performance is important and how it relates to the bigger picture of teaching and learning. Then, we define concepts and categories useful for understanding the area of performance and look at each category to lay out the repertoire of ways teachers handle pertinent situations. We do this with examples as often as possible. Next, we usually examine what is known about matching teacher choices to students, situations, or curricula.

Video: All areas of performance impact learning

It is not absolutely necessary to read the chapters in order, but there are certain cumulative benefits that make that desirable. Good discipline, for example, builds on a foundation of teacher skills with Attention, Momentum, Expectations, and Personal Relationship Building. A teacher who is struggling with a difficult class can turn to the chapter on discipline, which has references back to specific management, instructional, and motivational areas of performance, and are the first places to check when working with very challenging students.

Even experienced teachers should check their skills against the repertoires available in each area of performance to see if there are ways to add to their range, effectiveness, and ability to match the diverse needs of students in their classrooms.

CHAPTER QUICK GUIDE

How Do We Define a Skillful Teacher?

- ▲ Skillful teachers are aware of the complexity of their job and work to be conscious and deliberate about what they do.
- ▲ Skillful teachers want to control and regulate their teaching to have a positive effect on their students.
- ▲ Skillful teachers are clear about what is to be learned, what achievement means, and what they are going to do to help their students attain it.
- ▲ Skillful teachers are learners.

The Skillful Teacher Framework Encompasses These Areas of Performance:

1. A Foundation of Essential Beliefs: School, Cultural Proficiency, and Anti-Racism
2. Management: Attention, Momentum, Space, Time, Routines, and Discipline
3. Instructional Strategies: Clarity, Models of Teaching, and Principles of Learning
4. Motivation: Classroom Climate, Personal Relationship Building, and Expectations
5. Curriculum: Curriculum Design, Lesson Objectives, Planning, Differentiated Instruction, Assessment, and Overarching Objectives

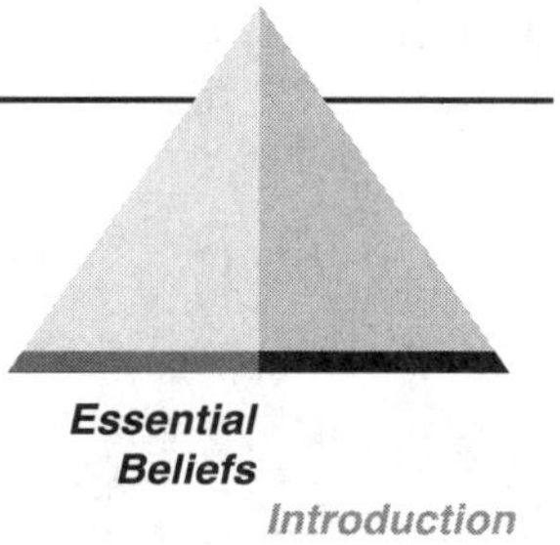

Part 1

Introduction to Essential Beliefs

The Skillful Teacher is a book about how to make the knowledge base of teaching more accessible. It is also about teacher learning and is a resource for it. There are certain beliefs about children, about professional learning, and about schools that bear heavily on a teacher's willingness to learn, and what it is he or she feels impelled to *seek* to learn. Without these beliefs, teachers are not committed to stretching themselves to acquire the expertise that none of us starts with. Beliefs drive behavior, are often unexamined, and are resistant to change. Without understanding one's beliefs, it is impossible to understand one's attitude and motivation to learn new skills and approaches to teaching.

Beliefs drive behavior, are often unexamined, and are resistant to change.

> **Chapter 3:** "Schooling" takes on beliefs about the nature of professional teaching knowledge and describes how this view influences the way "Adult Professional Culture" develops. Also in this chapter are essential beliefs about the learning environments we create for students, and the impact those environments have on student learning. Finally, we discuss teacher efficacy and how important our own beliefs are about what is possible for us to accomplish, even with students who are discouraged and far behind academically.
>
> **Chapter 4:** "Cultural Proficiency and Anti-Racism" separates out, for special treatment, our beliefs about the need for culturally proficient instruction in our classrooms and active anti-racism in our stance. In this chapter, we trace the similarities and important differences between cultural proficiency and anti-racism.

In these two chapters, we push back against beliefs that stand in the way of teacher learning. In particular, we push against the beliefs that there is no established knowledge base on teaching, that improving schools requires nothing more than recruiting superior people who know their content, and that teaching knowledge consists of a prescribed set of effective behaviors. These beliefs devalue the complexity of the profession and hobble teacher learning. Unfortunately, they are widespread and articulated frequently from pulpits of high visibility.

CHAPTER 3

Essential Beliefs
Schooling

Essential Beliefs: Schooling

There are certain beliefs about children, about professional learning, and about schools that bear heavily on a teacher's willingness to learn, and what it is he or she feels impelled to seek to learn.

BELIEFS ABOUT TEACHING KNOWLEDGE AND SKILL

> ***1. Belief**: Teaching is intellectually complex, difficult, and demanding work. The knowledge and skills required to teach successfully are on a par with that required for proficient practice in architecture, engineering, or law.*

Teaching is intellectually complex, difficult, and demanding work.

For those who believe that teaching is intellectually complex, difficult, and demanding and that, like any other true profession, its knowledge is based on repertoires and matching, then the doors of professional dialogue are opened wide. The need to learn with colleagues by examining situation specific questions comes to the fore, as does the need to reach out for new strategies and ways of thinking in the public knowledge base (Saphier, 2005).

Think about why it is so difficult to get teachers to share their good ideas and successful practices openly at faculty meetings and other forums. Teachers who believe in the effectiveness paradigm assume there are right ways and wrong ways of doing things—effective and ineffective (or at least less effective). Suppose you share a successful practice that is different from what I do. The tacit inference, based on my effectiveness belief system, is that either you are right or I am. You are either showing me up or trying to tell me how to do it right, which I'm not doing now. But if a school culture has internalized the belief in the complexity of teaching and the view of professional knowledge posed in this book, then I can hear your successful practice as an interesting alternative for my consideration, not a prescription for how to do it instead of the way I employ. Thus one belief essential to fruitful teacher learning and a strong professional community is about the nature of professional knowledge itself; it is based on repertoires and matching, not effective behaviors.

Professional knowledge is based on repertoires and matching, not effective behaviors.

> ***2. Belief:*** *The nature of professional knowledge is defined by areas of performance, repertoires, and matching, not effective behaviors.*

Skillful teaching requires informed and continuous decision-making based on an understanding of multiple and interconnected areas of performance, repertoires, and matching versus learning a prescribed set of behaviors. Consequently, teachers are never finished learning. They must constantly enlarge their repertoires, stretch their comfort zones, and develop their ability to match particular situations to reach more students with appropriate instruction.

Skillfulness in teaching derives from having large repertoires so that you are equipped to make choices in the major areas of performance that affect student learning. Once you have the repertoires, skillfulness means making choices thoughtfully based on reason, experience, and knowledge that are appropriate for a given student, situation, or curriculum.

This is the nature of professional knowledge and its use in any profession. In a profession, you have to have knowledge of your clients, your content, and the array of tools particular to your craft in order to act with expertise and get good results. So it is with teaching.

> ***3. Belief:*** *The knowledge bases of a professional teacher are many, diverse, and complex; skillful teaching requires systematic and continual study of these knowledge bases.*

The seven knowledge bases, described in Chapter 1, include continuing development in knowledge about content, generic pedagogy, content-specific pedagogy, children and their differences, behaviors of individuals in effective organizations, and communications with family and community. For purposes of the category system here, pedagogy includes the study of curriculum design and planning. All of these are important areas of teacher knowledge in addition to interactive teaching skill. Teachers must broaden their concept of professional development to include these domains and find ways to build repertoires in them.

> ***4. Belief****: The development of skillful teaching requires deep collaboration and non-defensive self-examination of practice in relation to student results.*

We need each other in this profession. The complexity of the work requires high-functioning teams that design lessons and common formative assessments together, who do error analysis of student work, and who help each other with the design and implementation of reteaching. This kind of deep collaboration requires more than structures and protocols. It requires skillful leadership and the interpersonal skills to build trust, safety, risk-taking, and determination to reach all the children. "All the children belong to us" is the mantra of such teams.

BELIEFS ABOUT THE LEARNING ENVIRONMENT WE CREATE

> ***5. Belief**: The total environment of a school has a powerful effect on students' learning.*

Teachers must participate actively with their colleagues to shape the school as a learning environment. They must learn how to play a role in strengthening the institution and see themselves as players beyond the classroom, responsible for the system of the school. For this to happen, interdependence and collegiality need to be built into the fabric of their working relationships. Interdependence requires that they function as both leaders and team players and that they support a balance of autonomy and cohesion in curriculum and teaching practices.

Skillful teachers are leaders who take the initiative to influence colleagues toward ideas they value and move the school toward practices they believe will strengthen everyone. They are team players, collaborating with colleagues to improve the school and help individual students, and willing to give up some autonomy for actions implied by common visions and agreements.

The connection between teacher learning and this belief in interdependence and collegiality is that only teachers who have regular interaction with their colleagues through joint work can experience the benefit of their knowledge and the synergy of creating new knowledge with others.

> ***6. Belief**: Learning is constructed as learners assimilate new experience with prior knowledge.*

Teachers who accept this belief must construct learning experiences where learners are active, applying knowledge, and reflecting on its meaning out loud or in writing. It is their responsibility to create a balance between students' time receiving new information and practicing skills and their time actively constructing, assimilating, and applying that information in real contexts. This implies that teachers learn a variety of models of teaching and take it on themselves to learn how to develop the influence strand of classroom climate described in Chapter 16. It particularly moves them to learn skills for making students' thinking visible and find ways to activate students' knowledge in relation to new concepts (see Chapter 11, "Clarity").

__7. Belief:__ Learning varies with the degree to which a learner's needs for inclusion, influence, competence, and confidence are met.

The psychological and cognitive milieu that teachers create has an enormous impact on what and how children learn. It is a teacher's professional responsibility to design an environment in which each child can succeed. Such an environment is characterized by community, mutual support, risk-taking, and higher-level thinking for all. It is also characterized by explicit attention to students' social and emotional learning.

It is a teacher's professional responsibility to design an environment in which each child can succeed.

Teachers cannot narrow their self-definition to being representatives of academic disciplines only. They must think of themselves as teachers of students as well as teachers of a particular discipline. Influencing student motivation becomes part of their job description, as well as teaching social skills. And they become particularly interested in the skills for getting students to exert effective effort (see Chapter 14, "Expectations").

BELIEFS ABOUT TEACHER EFFICACY

__8. Belief:__ Children's learning is primarily determined by their effective effort and use of appropriate strategies. "Intelligence," or the ability to learn, is not a fixed, inborn trait. All children have the raw material to learn rigorous academic material at high standards.

Most Americans believe that intelligence is a fixed, innate trait that is endowed at birth, is unevenly distributed, and determines how well a student can do. This belief in the bell curve of intelligence—that only a few students are smart enough to learn sophisticated academic material at high standards—has huge implications for teaching and learning.

"You can get smart" (Howard, 1990, p. 12). Teachers who have internalized this belief believe it is their responsibility to give their students

- ▲ the belief that ability can be grown,
- ▲ the confidence that it applies to them,
- ▲ the tools to accomplish it, and
- ▲ the desire to want to.

Teachers who believe that almost all of their students can achieve at a high level given the right conditions—that students can increase their ability through application, focus, and good strategies—are almost driven to rethink their role as a teacher. That new conceptualization would include being a teacher of strategies as well as a teacher of an academic discipline. And it would include an implied obligation for the teacher to diversify his or her teaching to match different student learning styles. When a student isn't learning, it would drive the teacher to ask, "How might I approach this differently or alter the conditions?" And it would certainly imply developing the commitment to—and repertoire for—conveying high-expectation messages to students.

Effective effort and good strategies are the principal determinants of academic success.

Others (Gould, 1996) have documented the history of the bell curve's limiting view of intelligence, with its sad consequences for students. We present this history in Chapter 14, "Expectations," and we make the case that intelligence can indeed be developed and that effective effort and good strategies are the principal determinants of academic success (Howard, 1990; Resnick, 1995; Dweck, 2007). Our point is that a teacher's belief about the nature of intelligence and its limits (or limitlessness) forms a powerful frame around the motivation to expand his or her teaching repertoires. Anyone serious about professional development must address this belief system to unleash the full energy of adults to expand their capacity to reach all students.

> *9. Belief: We can get underperforming, low confidence students to believe in themselves. We really can change their attributions so that they outperform their own internalized stereotypes.*

This is a belief about teacher efficacy. It means that not only do we believe that all students can learn and that effective effort is the key to academic success, we also believe we can get our students to believe it too and act from that belief. Furthermore, we believe it is our job to do so. Chapter 14, "Expectations," describes in some detail how we carry out that commitment. These how-to's are further elaborated on in *High Expectations Teaching* (Saphier, 2017).

Having completed over seven decades of desegregation since *Brown v Board of Education*, we are experiencing the de facto resegregation of schools through socioeconomic, racial, and ethnic neighborhood stratification. We are faced with significant achievement gaps for African American, Latino, and other students of color in our society. Communicating positive expectations and dissolving persistent negative stereotypes—perhaps, even internalized (Howard & Hammond, 1985)—is especially important. The roots of what students will do are planted firmly in their beliefs about what they can do. What are we, as educators, doing to help students, especially students of color, become believers in themselves as achievers? Avoiding the negative Pygmalion behaviors which we describe in the Expectations chapter will be a good start, but what's next? A steady stream of authors and researchers are telling us that new curricula and new, tougher standards are not enough.

"First, without a doubt, the indispensable characteristic of successful teachers in low-income-area schools is a positive attitude. It is not enough for a teacher to use the right words. The critical question is, what implicit and explicit messages are students getting from the teacher about their ability to learn?" (Frick, 1987, p. 20). No wonder Hattie (2009) finds that teacher efficacy has the highest effect size of all the behaviors he reviews. The more teachers can press for and attribute success to ability and effort as students go through school (rather than luck or easy work), the more success we will have with all students. "If you have a C average or below, you should spend three hours studying for this test" means, "That's what it will take to get an A, and you can do it." This conviction about student capacity makes it incumbent on teachers to teach students how to exert effective effort; many come to school not knowing how to do so. That adds a new dimension to the job of teaching.

Maybe, each school needs a person to shepherd that new job, a person in charge of "exceeding expectations," someone who shakes us up and goes around periodically reminding us to re-examine what we are expecting and demanding of students in the way of performance. Perhaps, that will be one effect of this chapter on you. In the end, the hope and the promise of this area of performance is that it will elicit better performance from students and give them more equal and fair school experiences.

> ***10. Belief****: Racism in our society and a dearth of cultural proficiency in our classrooms exert a downward force on the achievement of students of color that must be met with active countermeasures. To achieve our espoused goal of educating all children to a high level, we need to become culturally proficient and anti-racist.*

Due to the importance of this belief in The Skillful Teacher Framework, we explore it in a separate chapter, Chapter 4, "Cultural Proficiency and Anti-Racism."

CHAPTER QUICK GUIDE

Essential Beliefs About Teaching Knowledge and Skill:

- ▲ Teaching is intellectually complex, difficult, and demanding work. The knowledge and skills required to teach successfully are on a par with that required for proficient practice in architecture, engineering, or law.
- ▲ The nature of professional knowledge is defined by "areas of performance," "repertoire," and "matching," not effective behaviors.
- ▲ A professional teacher's knowledge bases are many, diverse, and complex. Skillful teaching requires systematic and continual study of these knowledge bases.
- ▲ The development of skillful teaching requires deep collaboration and non-defensive self-examination of practice in relation to student results.

Essential Beliefs About the Learning Environment We Create:

- ▲ The total environment of a school has a powerful effect on students' learning.
- ▲ Learning is constructed as learners assimilate new experience with prior knowledge.
- ▲ Learning varies with the degree to which a learner's needs for inclusion, influence, competence, and confidence are met.

Essential Beliefs About Teacher Efficacy:

- ▲ Children's learning is primarily determined by their effective effort and use of appropriate strategies. "Intelligence," or the ability to learn, is not a fixed, inborn trait. All children have the raw material to learn rigorous academic material at high standards.
- ▲ We can get underperforming, low-confidence students to believe in themselves.

To check your knowledge about Beliefs About Schooling, see the exercises on *The Skillful Teacher* website at www.RBTeach.com/TST7.

NOTES

CHAPTER 4

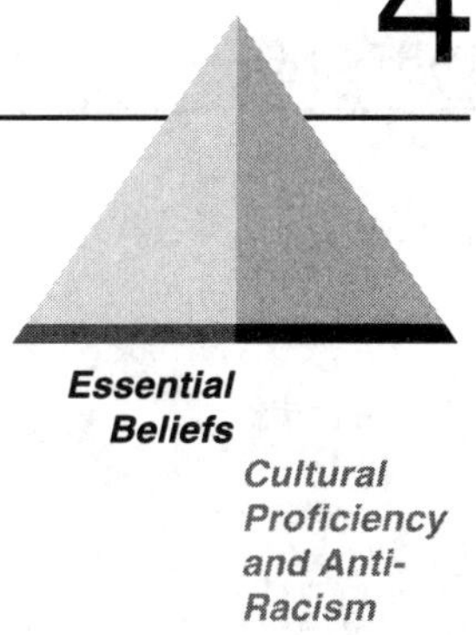

Essential Beliefs: *Cultural Proficiency and Anti-Racism*

Racism in our society and a dearth of cultural proficiency in our classrooms exert a downward force on the achievement of students of color that must be met with active countermeasures. To achieve our espoused goal of educating all children to a high level, we need to become culturally proficient and anti-racist.

This belief is of such significance that we have devoted an entire chapter to it. The topic invites us all to climb a big hill. It is foreign territory for many of us, confusing and intimidating for others, and a long overdue social justice mission for still others. But it is inevitably a vital part of our work as educators. Our goal in this chapter is to urge teachers and school communities to have important and often difficult conversations about cultural diversity and race. These conversations can and should lead to action that creates a more inclusive and productive school experience for everyone. Although this can be difficult work, the rewards are well documented (Ladson-Billings, 1995). An important literature, many decades old, goes into depth on this topic far beyond what we can accomplish in this short chapter. We did, however, want to put a stake in the ground.

Let us start with a couple of postulates: cultural proficiency is not the same as anti-racism, and racism is not the same as cultural improficiency. It is important for us, as teachers, to understand what is similar and what is different across these two concepts, for both have profound implications for our teaching and our ability to reach our students.

CULTURAL PROFICIENCY/IMPROFICIENCY

Cultural Proficiency is first a mindset that says, "I have to be curious about my students' cultures and learn about them. If I don't, my students can't make adequate connections to the content I am attempting to teach because I won't be able to embed the learning in culturally relevant examples." Zaretta Hammond (2015) is not just saying: "I will create an environment of respect for your culture." She is saying: "I will take the chains off your capacity to process information." The incongruence between a student's home culture and the culture of the school is the issue to be resolved by *knowing* the home culture of students of color. This mindset then provokes the use of skills to apply that knowledge in the design of culturally relevant lessons. These are vital skills for American teachers, even those who teach predominantly white students. It cannot be omitted from any text that attempts to profile the full range of generic pedagogy as we do here.

There is a scene in the French movie *The Class* in which a language arts teacher is trying to get his students to write a personal essay about their lives. These 8th graders, who are a very mixed group from Africa, Asia, Europe, and the Middle East, are resisting him. At one point, a student says, "There might be things we're ashamed to write about." The teacher asks for an example. A Senegalese Muslim student says, referring to his Tunisian buddy in the back, "You can be ashamed of a friend's Mom."

Teacher: "So Boubacar, why? She isn't pretty enough for you?"

Student: "No, no. For instance, Raba's mom, she offered me a sandwich. But I refused because I was ashamed."

Teacher: "Ashamed to eat with Raba's mother?"

Student: "No, it's not that."

Teacher: "It doesn't make sense. Explain it to me."

Student: "There's nothing to explain. I just don't want to eat with her out of respect."

Teacher: "You never eat with people you respect, out of respect!?"

Student: "I mean, c'mon. She's not my girlfriend!"

Teacher: "You can only eat lunch with your girlfriend? Or "a" girlfriend? Tell my why, Boubacar, I am interested."

Student: "I can't even explain it to you. Anyway, I'm ashamed even to talk about it. I hang out with Raba. He's my boy! So I respect his mom. I'm not going to eat in front of her."

Teacher: "So now we'll know that if Boubacar eats in front of us, he is demonstrating an utter lack of respect."

Student: "No, it's not like that. Oh God. Look, you just can't understand."

Teacher: "So I'm not smart enough to understand the great Boubacar?"

Student: "No, it's just that you're not going to get it."

Teacher: "All right." [He moves on.]

This teacher is Eurocentric in interpreting what his student says. He never thinks that cultural differences could account for different behaviors or opinions. In this same scene, he goes on to interact this way with two more students who speak respectively from a Chinese and Tunisian cultural frame.

Even without knowing anything about Boubacar's culture, a *culturally aware* teacher might suspect there was a cultural reason and inquire into it. Why might it be that Boubacar respects Raba's mom, and therefore he says, "I'm not going to eat in front of her"? Could there be a norm in Boubacar's culture that children do not eat in the presence of adults? Would eating at her kitchen table violate a cultural norm? A teacher proceeding from this insight might instead respond as follows:

Teacher: "Can you say more about what you mean by ashamed of a friend's mother?"

Student: "Raba's mom, she offered me a sandwich. But I refused because I was ashamed."

Teacher: "So there was something you felt ashamed about because she offered you something to eat."

Student: "No, I would be ashamed to eat in front of her."

Teacher: "Oh, and so I'm guessing that would violate an important norm in your culture. What is it in your culture, Boubacar, that makes it disrespectful to eat in the presence of adults?"

Student: "Well, you just don't do that!"

> **Teacher**: "...because it's a sign of respect for children not to, is that right?"
>
> **Student** : "Yes."
>
> **Teacher** : "Thanks, it's important for us to know that so we can avoid putting anyone in an embarrassing situation when we're in the company of folks from Senegal."

With a culturally proficient teacher, students feel included, that they have a place in the classroom because their culture is acknowledged, and recognized as having value.

With a culturally proficient teacher, students feel included and that they have a place in the classroom because their culture is present, acknowledged, and recognized as having value in the artifacts of the class and the examples that are used in lessons. At the very least, they experience curiosity and respect for their cultural norms and values.

Cultural *improficiency* is about a lack in one's understanding of people from cultures other than one's own. It makes students feel misunderstood and alien, like strangers in a strange land. The opposite, cultural proficiency, enables behaviors in the classroom that acknowledge and value the culture of those different from oneself.

WORKING ON CULTURAL PROFICIENCY

Consider that over half of the children in American schools today are children of color. Some of their families have come from central and south America, Asia, eastern Europe, Africa, the Middle East, and the Caribbean. Like all children in all schools, they need to feel known and valued to have their energy available for learning. Zaretta Hammond (2015) argues that culturally proficient teaching allows children to process information.

Nuri-Robbins and colleagues (2012) describe six stages of cultural proficiency illustrated in Figure 4.1. They define these points as follows:

1. Cultural destructiveness is any policy, practice, or behavior that effectively eliminates all vestiges of another peoples' culture (p. 79).

2. Cultural incapacity is any policy, practice, or behavior that presumes one's culture is superior to that of others (p. 83).

3. Cultural blindness is any policy, practice, or behavior that ignores existing cultural differences or that considers such differences inconsequential (p. 87).

Figure 4.1 Six Stages of Cultural Proficiency

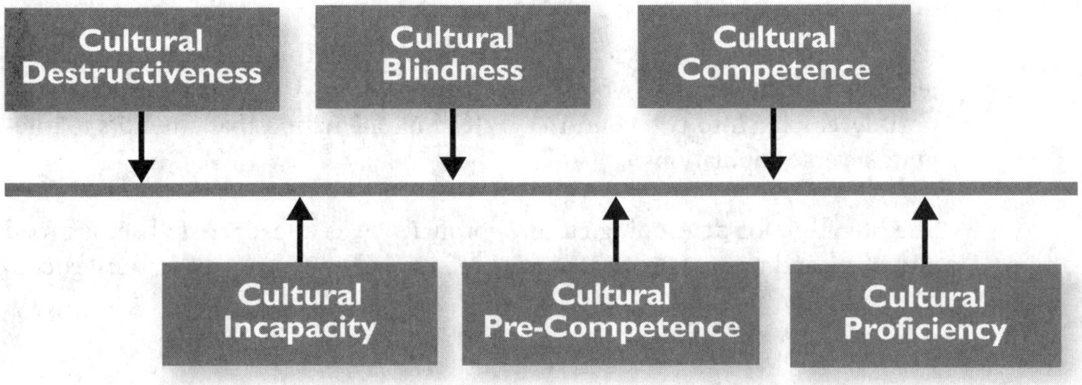

Based on Nuri-Robbins, Lindsey, & Lindsey (2012)

4. People or organizations that are culturally pre-competent recognize that their skills and practices are limited when interacting with other cultural groups (p. 90).

5. Cultural competence is any policy, practice or behavior that uses the essential elements of cultural proficiency as the standard for the individual or the organization (p. 94).

6. Cultural proficiency is manifest in people and organizations who esteem culture, who know how to learn about individual and organizational cultures, and who interact effectively with a variety of cultural groups...not a destination but rather a way of being (p. 97).

When teachers' beliefs and practices are not culturally proficient, when children feel that they and their cultures are "the other," that they are outsiders, unwelcome, or that their cultures are ignored, absent, or "less than," their learning is seriously compromised. The message is received as, "I am treated as an outsider and less worthy. Less is demanded and less is expected of me in school. My very identity is devalued. Therefore, school is not for me. It's an alien environment."

As teachers of *all* children, committed to equality of opportunity and raising capable and involved citizens, we must figure out how to make students from diverse cultural backgrounds believe that we, as individual teachers, and we, as a school community, know and value their cultures. Therefore each of us must

(1) learn about the cultures of our students and (2) find ways to make their cultures appear in validating ways in our curricula and our instructional examples. That is the starting point for cultural proficiency, and cultural proficiency is a new skill set that all American teachers must have. This is true even for those teaching in homogeneous white communities. Otherwise, we inadvertently support developing into two countries instead of one nation that attempts to integrate diverse populations.

The literature for developing cultural proficiency as a teacher skill set is broad and deep, and it must now enter our professional knowledge base, our lexicon, and our commitments.

BIAS AND RACISM

You can be moving toward cultural proficiency with actions such as visiting students' homes, and by studying other cultures, but still inadvertently act towards your students with implicit biases (see the "Implicit Bias" online assessment at www.implicit.harvard.edu). Sometimes messages based on implicit biases—that individuals of a particular gender, ethnicity, or race are "less than," less intelligent, less responsible, less motivated—can be sent subtly. Messages of this nature that students receive are even more damaging than those that flow from cultural improficiency. Beyond being perceived as less valuable (cultural improficiency), bias assumes someone is less able and less worthy because of a trait like gender, ethnicity, or race.

Video: Implicit Bias

Racism in the U.S. is not just about a void in one's ability to see beyond one's own race as the norm and acknowledge differences with respect. It is about stereotypes and oppression by a dominant racial group built into our institutions. Racism is a social construct that operates as a system of oppression based on race. By oppression we mean here the use of power to push down or deny advantages and access to certain groups. And it shows up in the behavior of members of marginalized groups toward themselves as internalized racism; it shows up in the behavior of individuals from the dominant group committing microaggressions as externalized racism (Sue, 2007); it shows up in the operation of structures like special education and the implementation of school procedures for student placement as structural racism (Frattura & Capper, 2007); and it shows up in public policies like mortgage red-lining, stop-and-frisk practices, and investment in where public transportation routes go and where infrastructure is built as institutional racism (Alexander, 2012).

Racism is certainly a first cousin of cultural blindness and cultural improficiency, but it is profoundly different. Almost all American immigrants came from ethnic groups who chose to come here. Not so with citizens descended from African slaves. American society harbors a heritage of enslavement that still lives on in the world that surrounds people of color, particularly black Americans. Ta-Nehisi Coates (2016) refers to it as the plundering of "the black body" to fuel the economy of the entire country (not just the South) for two centuries. This sense of blackness, however, is complicated by the diversity of dark-skinned Americans who may not identify as "African Americans" and are not descended from former slaves.

Videos: Microaggressions, Stereotype Threat

The presumed inferiority of African Americans shows up in a range of places unknown to any other group or for so long a time. We can see this bias in unequal distribution of governmental resources to schools, unequal access to health care, in drug laws and the mass incarceration of black men, in the militarization of police forces and the shooting of unarmed black men that has filled the news in recent years. While these shootings are not new as events, their being considered *newsworthy* events is new.

The American view of intelligence as innate, fixed, and deterministic compounds the problem. It is reinforced periodically in books declaiming the genetically inferior intelligence based on race (Jensen, 1969; Shockley, 1992; Herrnstein & Murray, 1994). It mingles with other angles of racism and creates the secret (and not so secret) belief that people of color, particularly African Americans, are less intelligent than white people. This implicit racism induces differential teacher behavior toward students of color (Torff, 2011; Rosen, 2017) and stereotype vulnerability (Steele, 2010) among the students themselves—lower performance in situations where race even subtly calls their ability into question. One consequence of this history is what Claude Steele identified 25 years ago as "stereotype threat." His book, *Whistling Vivaldi* (2010), summarizes his quarter of a century of research in engaging and nonjudgmental prose.

"Stereotype threat" is a psychic condition that inevitably, for people of color, induces a look around every room one enters to count how many people like you there are and to react to any social cue that identifies you as a person of color (like having to check your race on an application form or an exam header) with an unconscious loss of performance edge. All humans are vulnerable to stereotype threat, but because of widespread racist beliefs about who is intelligent and has the potential to become highly educated, students of color are more likely to experience stereotype threat on a daily basis in school.

While the all-black Rosenwald Schools in the Jim Crow South did not throw stereotype threat in the face of black children (though it was certainly triggered by the surround-sound messages by the rest of society), integrated schools inadvertently and inescapably do. This is not an argument for return to segrega-

Figure 4.2 Anti-Racism Continuum

tion. On the contrary, it is the reason why educators in integrated schools must have high expectations and actively push and encourage students of color, just as the best all-black schools did in the first half of the 20th century despite being underresourced. And it is certainly a reason why all the professional learning we advocate regarding cultural proficiency is applicable to the varieties of culture represented by students in our schools. These students have a very different immigrant history, but the impact of racism ensures that they too experience the macro- and microaggressions that African Americans experience.

Cultural and institutional manifestations of racism carry over into school and curriculum as the stereotypes, distortions, or omission of cultures other than white Western European. School and classroom audits of curriculum units for cultural proficiency and for racism can be most revealing (Frattura & Capper, 2007).

Working on Anti-Racism

All of us, but especially those of us who are members of the dominant white culture, need thorough education about these issues of race. We need information and experiences that will cause us to examine our tacit beliefs about people of color and the societal practices that reinforce these beliefs. And above all, we need to build culturally relevant instruction into our practice (see Chapter 16, "Classroom Climate").

The developmental continuum for anti-racism (illustrated in Figure 4.2) might be described using the following statements:

▲ Racism is any policy, practice, or behavior that effectively subjects a person to oppression by a member of a dominant racial group.

▲ Color Blindness is any policy, practice, or behavior that uses the power of the dominant racial group to deny recognition of differences to the oppressed group.

- ▲ Awareness of racial identity shows recognition and respect for those features of one's identity that are associated with race.

- ▲ Awareness of white privilege is recognition of the advantages in everyday life and in navigating the rules and practices of government and the economy that accrue automatically to whites.

- ▲ Active anti-racism means taking actions to interrupt cycles of oppression and end racism in society.

Video: White Privilege

As teachers, we can deepen our understanding of racism by studying the current manifestations of white privilege and the history of racism in our country and in other countries. Often, it is an unexamined history and one whose consequences for people of color, especially African Americans, can be hard for whites to comprehend deeply, at least deeply enough to begin to appreciate the experience of people of color in our society.

LEARNING MORE ABOUT RACISM AND WHITE PRIVILEGE

Waking Up White

Deepening white people's understanding of the actual experience of people of color within our country is fundamental to the forward motion we can and must make toward an integrated and fair society. This is particularly important for educators. Our teacher workforce is predominantly white, and our student population nationwide is majority non-white. Even for white educators in largely white school districts, this deepened understanding is essential, both now and even more in the future.

For readers for whom the points made in this chapter seem exaggerated or too far out of the mainstream for professional development, we recommend the readings from the bibliography on *The Skillful Teacher* website titled "Waking Up White," a title we borrow from Debby Irving's (2014) book of the same title. This is a sequence of readings which we believe can take a person to this deeper level of understanding. The sequence is important. If one is new to the journey to anti-racism, reading Ta-Nehisi Coates's (2016) profound book, *Between the World and Me,* too early might blunt that book's effect, because you won't be able to put his comments about the "black body" into proper context. Taking the Implicit Bias test (www.implicit.harvard.edu), referenced earlier, might be a motivator to undertake this reading.

Readers may disagree with the sequence and even the readings and films we have chosen. We look forward to suggestions you may offer. Together, we can

Video: How to Talk About Race

improve this list. However, we urge other organizations interested in improving schools and moving social justice forward in our country to begin this study and to do so in a sequence that does not overwhelm. We have to open our eyes to what we have created and what our possibilities are as a multi-racial society.

CHAPTER QUICK GUIDE

Essential Beliefs:

Racism in our society and a dearth of cultural proficiency in our classrooms exerts a downward force on the achievement of students of color that must be met with active countermeasures.

- ▲ With a culturally proficient teacher, students feel included and that they have a place in the classroom.
- ▲ Racism is a social construct that operates as a system of oppression based on race.
- ▲ Racism shows up in a variety of forms: internalized racism, externalized racism, institutionalized racism, and systemic racism.
- ▲ Manifestations of racism carry over into school and curriculum as stereotypes, distortions, or omission of non-white cultures.

Six Stages of Cultural Proficiency:

(1) Cultural Destructiveness, (2) Cultural Incapacity, (3) Cultural Blindness, (4) Cultural Pre-Competence, (5) Cultural Competence, and (6) Cultural Proficiency.

The Anti-Racism Continuum:

(1) Racism, (2) Color Blindness, (3) Awareness of Racial Identity, (4) Awareness of White Privilege, and (5) Active Anti-Racism.

To check your knowledge about Beliefs: Cultural Proficiency and Anti-Racism, see the exercises on *The Skillful Teacher* website at www.RBTeach.com/TST7.

NOTES

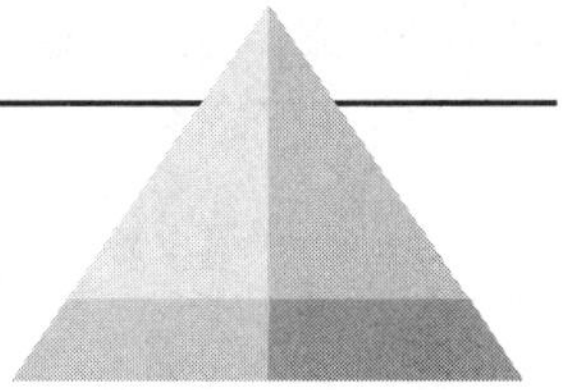

Part 2
Introduction to Management

The most important issue overall for teachers regarding management is to keep their eye on the prize: developing, monitoring, and adjusting their management systems in ways that clear obstacles to student learning and help students to develop their identities as capable, respected, and self-reliant high achievers. Fred Jones (2013) defines classroom management as a "system that includes instructional strategies focused on making students independent and resourceful, motivational strategies that help students be more conscientious and accountable, and discipline strategies that reduce goofing off, set limits, and train students to be responsible and cooperate with one another" (p. 22). We think that sums it up pretty well.

An effective management system paves the way for learning.

An effective management system paves the way for learning to occur with minimal interference and maximal nourishment. Thus Part 2 lays the groundwork for successful instruction. There are six important management areas, each of which has a chapter devoted to it:

Chapter 5: "Attention" addresses the question, How do teachers get student attention, keep it focused on learning, and refocus it when it drifts? This chapter explores recent brain research and relevant guidelines that emerge for focusing attention. It also offers a vast repertoire of interactive tools that serve this purpose.

Chapter 6: "Momentum" addresses the question, How do teachers anticipate, manage, or circumvent blocks to the smooth orderly flow of classroom life in order to preserve maximum time for learning? In this chapter, we identify eight categories of events teachers monitor to minimize disruptions to the learning environment.

Chapter 7: "Space" addresses the question, How is the classroom's physical space arranged and used to support instructional objectives and signal what is important? This chapter examines repertoire and flexibility in furniture and seating arrangements with an eye to matching them to different forms of learning and ensuring easy access, visual and physical, to every student in the room. It also explores the ways in which space allocation and location of materials and resources indicate awareness of (and responsiveness to) students' psychological needs to feel a sense of ownership, privacy, and self-sufficiency.

Chapter 8: "Time" addresses the question, What principles of time allocation do teachers need to use to guide the planning and implementation of successful learning experiences? The bottom line in this area of performance is maximizing student-engaged and high-success time. This requires effective management systems, attention to pacing and rhythm during instructional time, and structures for providing ongoing and meaningful feedback when students are engaged in independent work.

Chapter 9: "Routines" addresses the question, What routines are important in order to maximize smooth operations and minimize wasted time and energy for teacher and students? How do teachers ensure that students know what the routines are, why they are important, and how to carry them out? These questions are the primary focus of this chapter.

Chapter 10: "Discipline" addresses the question, How do I eliminate disruptions while building student responsibility and ownership? Vigilance in other management areas lays a solid foundation on which to build this sixth area of management. In this chapter, we highlight the interconnectedness of areas of performance other than management: personal relationship building, clarity of instruction, design of learning experiences, the appropriateness of objectives, and the need to establish, communicate, reinforce, and uphold clear standards and expectations for behavior in order to help students learn what is appropriate and inappropriate, acceptable and unacceptable in a communal environment. Teachers also need to be prepared for the small percentage of students who, for any number of complex reasons, require something more. The chapter explains models of discipline that teachers can add to their toolkits over time for use with the most resistant students.

Attention to each management area—and the conscious choices made within them—can have a positive impact on the climate and tone of day-to-day classroom operations. This in turn will create an environment conducive to learning and achievement.

CHAPTER 5

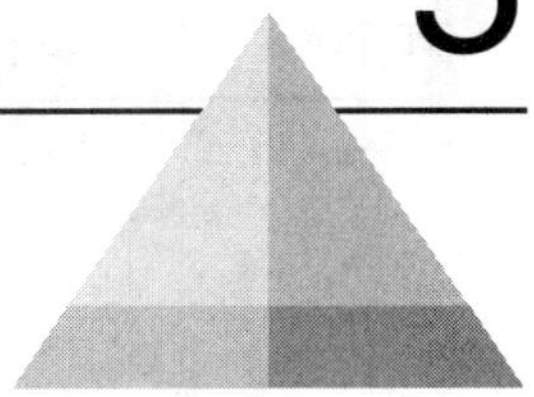

Management: Attention

Focusing student attention on learning experiences is perhaps the most fundamental management challenge a teacher faces daily, hourly, and moment to moment in any classroom. In many ways, "Attention" is the bellwether area of performance among the group of management areas. Unless students are paying attention to the instruction, it does not matter how good the lesson may be. Engaging and involving students on task in large-group, small-group, or individual learning experiences is what "Attention" is all about—indeed, what management is all about. It is the precondition for instruction, the *sine qua non* for curriculum implementation.

WHAT WE KNOW FROM BRAIN RESEARCH

To determine what works and how to gain and maintain student attention most effectively and efficiently, it is prudent to consider how some of the brain research of the past two decades informs thinking. Jensen (2000) states that the challenge for a teacher is knowing how to capitalize on the brain's attentional biases while also engaging students in meaningful learning. This challenge is twofold: (1) capturing students' attention and (2) sustaining their focus on what the teacher deems to be important.

Two generalizations derived from brain research have implications for classroom practice. The first is that "the human brain is designed to selectively attend to stimuli . . . has a built-in bias for certain types of stimuli . . . and a natural prioritization process is occurring all the time, consciously and unconsciously" (Jensen, 2000, p. 121). Second, key factors in the brain's initial filtering include novelty or contrast to what is familiar, intensity of stimuli, movement, and emotion (Wolfe, 2001; Jensen, 2000).

Zaretta Hammond (2015) adds a cultural perspective to all of this.

> Before we can be motivated to learn what is in front of us we must pay attention to it. Every brain's RAS (Reticular Activating System) is tuned to novelty, relevance, and emotion but each person interprets these three elements through his particular cultural lens. Cultures based on an oral

Teachers need to build a repertoire of ways to capture the brain's attention.

> tradition rely heavily on the RAS to activate learning using music, call and response, and other attention grabbing strategies to signal something important. (p. 48)

These imply the need to design learning experiences that are vivid, varied, and delivered with passion and enthusiasm for the subject matter. Learning experiences that begin with or incorporate an element of novelty or surprise grab attention. Examples would be the physics teacher who introduces Newton's first law by ripping a tablecloth from under a place setting without disturbing it, the math teacher who enters dressed as Cleopatra when she will be teaching about number systems and place value, or two teachers who stage an argument in front of the class to introduce a lesson on conflict and conflict resolution.

> Children are often criticized for "not paying attention." There is no such thing as not paying attention; the brain is always paying attention to something. What we really mean is that the child or student is not paying attention to what we think is relevant or important. Attention, as all of us know, is selective. (Wolfe, 2011, p. 80)

Jensen (2000) notes that the "brain is designed to attend selectively to stimuli, prioritizing on the basis of perceived importance and screening out that which seems to be less crucial to survival. The level of attention people apply to a learning situation is influenced or limited by their perception of its value" (p. 121). And Wolfe (2011) holds that "two factors strongly influence whether the brain initially attends to arriving information and whether this attention will be sustained" (p. 83). These two factors are meaning and emotion. Thus for students to want to attend, they need to know why something is important, personally relevant, and worthy of their attention.

In this chapter, we describe ways in which teachers keep students alert by

- ▲ doing things in the moment that are surprising or out of the ordinary (like breaking into song to give directions when student attention has drifted or randomizing calling-on patterns so a student never knows for sure when it will be her turn);
- ▲ enlisting interest in the content through the use of voice variety, gestures, challenges, and props; and
- ▲ winning students' attention with positive emotional overtones, such as praise, enthusiasm, humor, and dramatization.

BUILDING AN ATTENTION REPERTOIRE

> Attention level is determined by the interaction of various factors: sensory input (sources of information such as textbooks, videos, field trips, etc.); data's intensity or perceived importance; and the brain's "chemical flavor" of the moment. (Jensen, 2000, p. 123)

That teachers need to build a repertoire of ways to capture the brain's attention is the important consideration here. Wolfe (2011) points out that although novelty is an innate attention getter, it is also short lived. Repeated use of any particular strategy or format can result in habituation—the natural tendency of the brain to ignore a stimulus once it has become familiar.

"Emotion drives attention, and attention drives learning."

(Sylwester, 1995)

Teachers need to consider the types of input or explanatory devices to employ when presenting information and ensure that they enable students with different modality strengths (auditory, visual, kinetic, and kinesthetic) equal opportunity to absorb and process information. (This is discussed in more detail in Chapter 11, "Clarity" and Chapter 21, "Assessment.")

Optimal Emotional State

> All learning is state dependent: the physiological, emotional, postural, and psychological state learners are in will mediate content. And these states are related to the chemical "flavor of the moment" in the brain. Chemicals can be too high, resulting in hyper or stressed states; chemicals can be too low, yielding drowsiness. The learner's state can be influenced in the classroom with simple interventions. (Jensen, 2000, p. 125)

"Emotion drives attention and attention drives learning" (Sylwester, 1995). Teachers need to recognize and do something when students' emotional states are either too low or too high to enable them to focus. They need to develop a repertoire of ways to induce emotional state changes or bring them into balance when the need arises. To induce calm, for example, Jensen suggests calling up predictable, ritual activities such as routine openings, closings, and greetings. When the need is to energize or motivate, teachers might introduce novelty or unexpected change. The former (inducing calm) points to elements of classroom climate (Chapter 16), especially ways to create a sense of community and belonging. This also makes the case for strategic use of a principle of learning called "Similarity of Environment" (Chapter 12). "Vividness," another one of the principles of learning, highlights inducing surprise to energize. It underscores why doing something out of the ordinary to surprise or startle students can serve as an effective, in-the-moment, attention move.

Benefits of Laughter

> Laughter has been shown to boost the body's production of neurotransmitters critical for alertness and memory. Some studies have shown that having fun and pleasant experiences improve the functioning of the body's immune system for three days. (Fry, 1997, as cited in Jensen, 2000, p. 125)

Optimal learning occurs when there is a balance between the level of challenge and existing knowledge or skills.

Teachers, like everyone else, need to enjoy the work they do. They need to be able to laugh with students and see the humor in the everyday life of a classroom. We attended a presentation by a motivational speaker several years ago who put it this way: "If by 10 o'clock every morning, we haven't had ourselves a good belly laugh something is very wrong. It means we must be taking ourselves too seriously because working with a room full of children is very funny business!" Teachers need to give themselves permission to be silly or outrageous at times and draw the students into their light mood. This can be done through the use of props, costumes, dramatization, or telling funny stories. There needs to be a balance in designing learning experiences that are both enjoyable and challenging (see the "Feeling Tone" principle of learning in Chapter 12).

Balancing Challenge

Optimal learning occurs when there is a balance between the level of challenge and existing knowledge or skills. If the challenge is greater than the skills, it can create anxiety; if the skills are greater than the challenge, boredom is likely. This suggests that getting students into optimal learning states requires assessing the potential gap between the readiness level of the student and the challenge present in the learning experience. This sometimes calls for pre-assessment activities, analysis of the data, and differentiating the learning experience accordingly (see Chapters 20 and 21 for more on each of these).

Using Physical Movement

> When the brain is fully engaged it is more efficient and effective. Vigorous physical activity is believed to increase blood flow to the brain. Cross lateral movement that works both sides of the body evenly and involves coordinated motion of both eyes, both ears, both hands, and both feet activates both hemispheres and all four lobes of the brain. As a result, cognitive functioning is heightened and ease of learning increases. (Hannaford, 2005, p. 92)

Using physical movement can have dramatic effects on learning. Intermittent physical movement throughout a learning experience is powerful for maintaining the highest levels of attention. Jensen (2000) suggests starting a class period with two minutes of stretching to increase the overall alertness students bring to the learning experience. If learning experiences call for students to be sedentary for periods of time, the teacher needs to plan with movement in mind. The movement doesn't have to be a break from the focus of the lesson. If students have a reason to move periodically (for example, get together with a learning partner seated in some other part of the room for two or three minutes of stand-up processing time, a team relay race where students go to the board one team member at a time to build a proof to a problem, or groups working together to build a human sculpture representing the structure of an atom), chances are they will remain more alert and focused for longer periods of time. The movement breaks don't have to be long; they just have to be timely, occurring at least every 20 to 40 minutes. Teachers who notice that attention is fading need to ask themselves how long it has been since students last moved.

Teachers, who notice that attention is fading, need to ask themselves how long it has been since students last moved.

Building in Learning Downtime

> Humans are natural meaning-seeking organisms, but excessive input can conflict with that process. . . . You can either have your learner's attention or they can be making meaning, but never both at the same time. The brain needs time to "go inside" and link the present with the past and future. Without this, learning drops dramatically. We absorb so much information unconsciously that downtime is absolutely necessary to process it all. The brain has an automatic mechanism for shifting (internal and external) and for shutting down input when it needs to. (Jensen, 2000, p. 123)

When students are taking in information from any external source—for example, by listening, reading, seeing, or doing—pauses must be built in systematically to give the learner time to absorb and organize, reflect and process the information, make connections, and construct personal meaning. If teachers don't consciously attend to this, the learner will do it anyway out of necessity and will appear to have stopped paying attention. In Chapter 11, "Clarity," we discuss guidelines for how often and how long the pauses for processing should occur.

MOVES TO FACILITATE STUDENT ATTENTION

Skillful teachers lay the groundwork for focusing student attention by systematically incorporating the "Attention" principles and guidelines into the everyday fabric of classroom life. There are a wide range of in-the-moment moves that a teacher might use to capture, maintain, and recapture or refocus student attention. Teachers tend to need these most when a learning experience is whole-group oriented and teacher directed.

Within this general class of "Attention" moves, there are five categories: (1) desisting, (2) alerting, (3) enlisting, (4) acknowledging, and (5) winning. These moves can be thought of as having affective characteristics (negative to positive) and power-sharing dynamics (authority to attraction). The skillful teacher's repertoire for getting and keeping students on task should include at least a few moves from each of these categories. This is critical to being able to match the choice of move to what the situation warrants.

Keep in mind as we describe each of these that this list is meant to be an objective list of moves teachers make that get students' attention. In other words, we are describing every type of move we have seen or heard a teacher do that was for this purpose, but without judging the appropriateness, effectiveness, or relative merit of any individual move on the list. In order to determine the appropriateness of each of these moves, each teacher has to examine the context within which it is being used and its impact on the student.

Desisting Moves

Videos: "I" Messages (1 & 2), Signals, Private Desist, Gestures, and Private Desists

Desisting moves carry the message, "Stop what you are doing and shift your attention elsewhere," or "Get with it." They are most applicable when students are drifting off course. All the moves in this category are ways of telling students that they are doing something we want them to stop doing. Some are subtle, even silent. Others are more up front, out loud, and forceful. Some imply or state specifically what the students should be doing instead. Each can be a constructive way to signal we mean business and to get a student to shift focus or re-engage.

Table 5.1 identifies a range of desisting moves, ordered from most to least forceful (or authoritative) and gives an example of each. To use these moves most constructively, it is essential that our selection and delivery is aligned with our motive to ensure that students' attention is focused on what's important while maintaining a positive feeling tone in the classroom. Hence, we need to apply two guidelines in this category: (1) start small (use the least authoritative or forceful move that will get the job done) and (2) escalate only as necessary, especially with any of the more direct and forceful moves toward the top, to signal that we mean business and deliver the message in a calm but firm tone and ideally privately to save face for the student while constructively re-engaging him.

Table 5.1 Twenty-Four Desisting Moves

Move	Sounds or Looks Like
1. Punish, or deliver a consequence	"That will cost you half of recess." "You will be making up this time and the work this afternoon on your own time."
2. Exclude, or remove, the student	"Leave the group, Michaela, and come back when you feel you are ready to focus."
3. ~~Sarcasm~~	Should not be used. See page 50 for more detail.
4. Threaten with a consequence	"Stop it now or leave the group."
5. Judgmental reprimand	"Stop that annoying tapping."
6. Order	"Get back to work now." "Sit on your hands until you're absolutely sure you're not going to touch anyone."
7. Specific verbal desist	Naming the behavior to stop and giving the student the appropriate replacement behavior: "Stop dancing, Jim, and get back to your lab report."
8. General verbal desist	Vaguer language to stop a behavior: "Amanda, cut it out."
9. Private desist	General or specific but spoken to the student privately.
10. Group pressure	"Rafael, none of us can leave for gym until you're with us." The classmates chime in, "Yeah, Rafael, come on!"
11. Peer competition	"John's ready. Are you, Beth?"
12. Move seat	"Jimmy, move over to table four, please." "You two are such good friends that you will be continuously distracted if I let you sit together."
13. "I" message	(1) a nonjudgmental description of the behavior, (2) the way it makes you feel, and (3) the tangible effect: "When you are talking in your table groups while I am giving directions, it frustrates me. There are some real challenges to doing this task, and some of you won't be aware of what to look out for."
14. Remove distraction	Without speaking to her, Mr. Glade walks by Antonia and picks up the object she is playing with. He puts it in his pocket and continues the discussion with the class.
15. Offer choice	Observing Antonia playing with the eraser, Mr. Glade says quietly, "Antonia, you can put it away or give it to me."
16. Urge	"C'mon, Jill, let's get in gear!" or "Okay, let's settle down and be really good listeners."
17. Remind	"What are you supposed to be doing, Shelly?"
18. Flattery	"You're too conscientious to waste your time this way." "That kind of behavior is beneath your dignity. You are better than that."

Table 5.1 Twenty-Four Desisting Moves (continued)

Move	Sounds or Looks Like
19. Signals	Timer goes off, raised hand and countdown 5-4-3-2-1, music begins to play, or something similar established with the students in advance and used routinely without verbal comment to call all activity and noise to a halt (momentarily or to make a transition). Or, without breaking the flow of talk with one student, the teacher holds up a hand in a "stop" gesture to a third student, signaling him to cease interrupting (or whatever else he's doing) and perhaps implying by facial expression and body language, "Wait a minute. I'll be right with you." Note: bright or flashing lights and buzzing, humming sounds have been associated with triggering epileptic seizures and should therefore not be used as signals.
20. Pause and look	Teacher pauses and looks at the child or group until the behavior ceases.
21. Name dropping	Dropping a student's name into the flow of conversation (not to call on the student but for purposes of attention): "Now the next problem—Jess—that we're going to tackle has some of the same elements—Jess—but the exponents are simpler."
22. Offer help	"How can I help you get started with this, Hilda?"
23. Touch	Teacher places a hand gently on the student's shoulder or some other neutral place—or points to a specific part of the text in front of the student. This may or may not be accompanied by the teacher's stopping the activity and making eye contact.
24. Proximity	Being or moving physically near the student whose attention is wandering or likely to wander.

Desisting Moves to Avoid

We believe the use of sarcasm is too costly to the overall psychological and emotional climate of the classroom.

A move that can sometimes be seen and heard in today's classrooms that we believe should not be used is sarcasm. It can be damaging.

Regrettably, some teachers use sarcasm to redirect student attention and it usually does get students' attention: not only the student to whom it is aimed but to many others in class who may dive for emotional cover when it is delivered, hoping they won't be the next target. Sarcastic remarks, like these, are intended to mock or deride a student:

▲ "Did you leave your head at home again, Grant?"

▲ "Imagine that! Grant is so busy watching what is going on outside that he doesn't know where we are in the book."

▲ "Mackenzie (who is combing her hair and looking in the mirror), your hair is ready for the cover of *Seventeen*, but I'd rather you were looking at the test tube and what is going on in it."

Because sarcasm always involves some degree of personal derision—and because teachers are such powerful role models for students during these impressionable years—we have taken the philosophical position that it shouldn't be used in any context. We believe the use of sarcasm is too costly to the overall psychological and emotional climate of the classroom and is at least a small killer of relationships.

Alerting Moves

Alerting moves are aimed at keeping students on their toes. Most of them, listed in Table 5.2, function as moves intended to minimize distraction and attention dropout and maximize participation and engagement. As with desisting moves, the various alerting moves differ in the degree of force expressed in the move.

Video: Random Order

Table 5.2 Thirteen Alerting Moves

Move	Sounds or Looks Like
1. Startle	Doing something out of the ordinary or surprising to capture attention. Noticing that attention is wandering as a group listens to a recording, the teacher abruptly hits the Stop button and pops a question: "Why do you suppose Jefferson felt that way about Hamilton?"
2. Using student's name in instructional example	"President Kiesha Royston sits impeached and convicted. Who then would become president? And we thought life was tough under Kiesha! Now Vice President Christiane Baker becomes president. It's time to pack our bags and move to Canada!"
3. Redirecting partial answer	Wendy has begun to answer, and you say: "Take it from there, Andrew. How would you finish what Wendy is saying?"
4. Prealert	"That's right. Take the next one, Dwayne. Check him, Holly, and be ready to step in if he calls for assistance." (This is aimed at keeping Holly on her toes.)
5. Unison	"6 times 6 is—Jane? That's right. 8 times 8 is—everybody?" The goal is to get all students to respond at once; other versions include students responding to questions or problems on individual whiteboards that they hold up all at once (see dipsticking in Chapter 11, "Clarity" for more ways to do this).
6. Looking at one, talking to another	Looking at Royce, who is distracted and inattentive in the moment, the teacher says, "Antonia, give us an example of—" (This lasts but a moment.)
7. Incomplete sentences	". . . and so, as we all know, the thing that we put at the end of a sentence is a—" This might be accompanied by open hands and raised eyebrows at the group or hand gestures encouraging someone to respond.
8. Equal opportunity	The teacher establishes some sort of system (calling sticks or name cards, for example) so that students know they will each be called on sooner or later, and perhaps at any time. Students also know that they're not off the hook once they are called on and could be called on again at any time.
9. Random order	Students are called on out of sequence of their seating pattern so they can't predict when it will be their turn and therefore have to be alert.

Table 5.2 Thirteen Alerting Moves (continued)

Move	Sounds or Looks Like
10. Circulation	The teacher physically moves around the room while facilitating large-group learning experiences.
11. Wait time	Explaining to students in advance that "think time" will always follow a question that is posed and consistently inserting three to five seconds or more of silence after posing a question to the whole group, allowing thinking time for all to process before any one responds. Or once a student has been called on, the teacher stays out of the way for at least five seconds so the student has the opportunity to construct a response. During the silence, the other students are induced to focus on that question silently in anticipation that it might be referred to them next.
12. Eye contact	The teacher makes frequent eye-to-eye contact with all students in a group.
13. Freedom from visual and auditory distraction	Arranging the room so that small-group work takes place facing a corner or away from the main visual field in the room, or so that instructional or quiet work areas are separated from active and noisy areas. Alternatively, you direct the class, "Close your eyes and just listen."

Video: Piquing Students' Interest

Enlisting Moves

We call the third category enlisting moves because their purpose is to enlist, or sign up, an individual student's, or an entire group's voluntary engagement in curriculum activities. These moves (listed in Table 5.3) are intended to captivate students and sweep them away in the interest or excitement of the activity. They capture attention by emphasizing the appeal or attractiveness of the activity.

Acknowledging Moves

Sometimes students are inattentive for reasons that have nothing to do with what's going on in class or how skillful the teacher is. Some outside event is weighing on them (or exciting them)—for example, their best friend refused to sit next to them on the bus this morning, their parents have just separated, they are playing in a championship game that afternoon, or hail the size of golf balls starts falling outside the classroom window.

Merely acknowledging out loud to students your understanding of the distraction—or what's on their mind—can enable them to pay more attention in class. It is validating (and rare) to have one's feelings really heard, and simply acknowledging those feelings can facilitate attention. Here are a few examples:

▲ **Example 1:** There is a big game scheduled tonight. The teacher says, "I know you're excited about the hockey game tonight, especially with three

Table 5.3 Nine Enlisting Moves

Move	Sounds or Looks Like
1. Voice variety	The teacher varies his speaking tone, pitch, volume, or inflection to emphasize points and add interest.
2. Gesture	Using hand or body movements to emphasize points or add interest.
3. Piquing student's curiosity	"What do you suppose could possibly have caused Alexander to behave in such a bizarre way?"
4. Suspense	With her back to the students, the teacher puts on a costume, a face, a wig, or something else; ten to fifteen seconds elapse while the students wait to see what the costume represents.
5. Challenge	"This next one will fool all of you!"
6. Making student a helper	"Jim, will you hold up those two test tubes for the group to see, please?" (Jim's attention has been wandering.)
7. Props	Using physical objects related to the content (for example, the take-apart human torso or hats to represent different vocations).
8. Personification, or attributing human characteristics to inanimate objects	"So, Sodium says to Chloride, 'How'd ya like to hook up?'" or "Now, if Mr. W were to walk through the door right now and look for things that started with his sound, what would he find to make him feel at home?"
9. Connecting with student's fantasies	"So the NFL drafts Ben and signs him for three years at $28 million a year. Which tax bracket is that likely to place him in?"

star players right here in our midst. But I'm asking you all to put that on the shelf for a while because today's review is very important."

▲ **Example 2:** Seven-year-old Sadé is distracted during reading group. Her glance shifts repeatedly to the place she left to come to group (a display of dolls from foreign lands that she was arranging). In a flash, the teacher sizes this up and, knowing that Sadé realizes that lunch will immediately follow reading, figures out that the child is feeling that she'll never be able to finish arranging the dolls. After lunch can seem like forever to a seven-year-old, so the teacher makes an acknowledging move: "Sadé, I know it's important to you to get all the dolls neatly arranged. You can devote yourself to that right before we go to lunch, I promise. Only now you need to work with us on this reading because we won't be doing this later. I'll make sure you get back there." Getting the dolls arranged may not seem important from an adult point of view, but such seemingly trivial matters can be consuming to children and block their involvement unless teachers perceive and respond.

Acknowledging out loud to students your understanding of the distraction—or what's on their mind—can enable them to pay more attention in class.

▲ **Example 3:** Perceiving that Marvin is concerned about something, the teacher makes this acknowledging move: "Are you afraid you'll miss your turn at the listening station, Marvin?" Marvin nods. "Look, take your time, and do this paper well. I'll see to it that you get your turn as soon as you're done, even if we've passed you on the sign-up sheet."

▲ **Example 4:** Sometimes the teacher just needs to ask, "Brenda, what's on your mind? You don't seem with us this morning." Further probing and active listening may or may not release this attention block. However, sometimes just talking about what's on the student's mind, without any solution from the teacher, will be unburdening enough to permit the student to re-enter here-and-now tasks.

Winning Moves

Winning moves, listed in Table 5.4, are similar to enlisting moves in that they are positive and tend to attract rather than force students' attention to the learning experience. However, we have distinguished winning moves from enlisting moves because winning moves focus students on the teacher, whereas enlisting moves focus students' attention more on the activity or the content. This is where teachers use their personality to mediate attention.

Table 5.4 Five Winning Moves

Move	Sounds or Looks Like
1. Encouragement	Prompting students' ongoing work, usually by means of voice quality and facial expression: "Keep going, you're getting it." A student says, "I don't know . . ." and the teacher responds, "Sure you do. What's one?"
2. Enthusiasm	"That's a fascinating topic for a paper, Nikki! Wait 'til you see what's in this Web site!"
3. Praise	Specific comments that acknowledge effort a student has invested and the concrete impact it is having: "You really worked hard on that, Priya, and it shows everywhere!"
4. Humor	Joking in a positive, supportive manner, without sarcasm, that is mutually enjoyed by the students.
5. Dramatizing	Acting out or performing material related to the lesson, or directing students to dramatize experiences. Here the teacher switches into role and speaks a line of dialogue through the persona of a character whose identity he has assumed, even if just for a single sentence: "Well, here I go into the den of smiling vipers." (The teacher has become newly elected President Abraham Lincoln entering his first cabinet meeting where all the officers think they'd be a better president than he and are in fact plotting to get rid of him.)

ANALYZING ATTENTION BEHAVIOR

All of the moves from all five categories could be arranged along a single continuum whose rule is authority to attraction (see Figure 5.1). Moves and categories at the upper end of the continuum employ the most teacher authority most directly and firmly applied. As one travels down the continuum, the authority component becomes less and less dominant. Thus Attention is an area of performance of teaching that involves a more-or-less continuous scale of values along a functional attribute, the functional attribute being moves whose end is to engage, maintain, or re-engage students' attention in the learning experience.

One way of thinking about the items in the figure is as a set of tools. We might consider those in the desist category to be different types of hammers, those in the alerting category to be different types of wrenches, those in the enlisting category to be screwdrivers of various lengths, sizes, and tips, and so on. Just as a craftsperson would recognize the various categories of tools and the subtle differences among items within a category, so too can teachers study each of the categories and items on this list as discrete and distinct tools available for use. And any craftsperson would know that hammers are designed for certain types of jobs, wrenches for other jobs, and so on. They select the tool that is best suited (or matched) to a particular situation or job. So too it is with this toolkit for teachers: being familiar with and knowing how to use each of the tools is a goal to aim for over time. Acquiring a few of the tools in each of the categories—that is, building a repertoire from which you can pick and choose depending on the nature of the job—is essential to becoming a master of your trade.

PDF

Check Your Attention Moves

One way to use this continuum is to profile one's own teaching performance. Which attention moves do I use? How many and which of the five categories do I use? What does my profile reveal about my attention repertoire? Some teachers have had colleagues or supervisors observe them to gather concrete examples of attention moves in their notes. Then later, using the notes as evidence, they check off on the continuum the moves the teacher made. A self-profile or the pattern of attention moves shown from such an analysis can be used to examine your existing repertoire and the appropriateness and effectiveness of your choices, which leads to the issue of matching. (Visit *The Skillful Teacher* website to complete a self-assessment.)

Matching Attention Moves

The Attention Continuum is intended to be an objective list; that is, no judgments are implied about moves at the bottom being inherently better than moves at the top, or vice versa. We are arguing, in fact, that all the moves have a place, and each may be appropriate in a given context. This array of attention

Figure 5.1 A Repertoire of Attention Moves

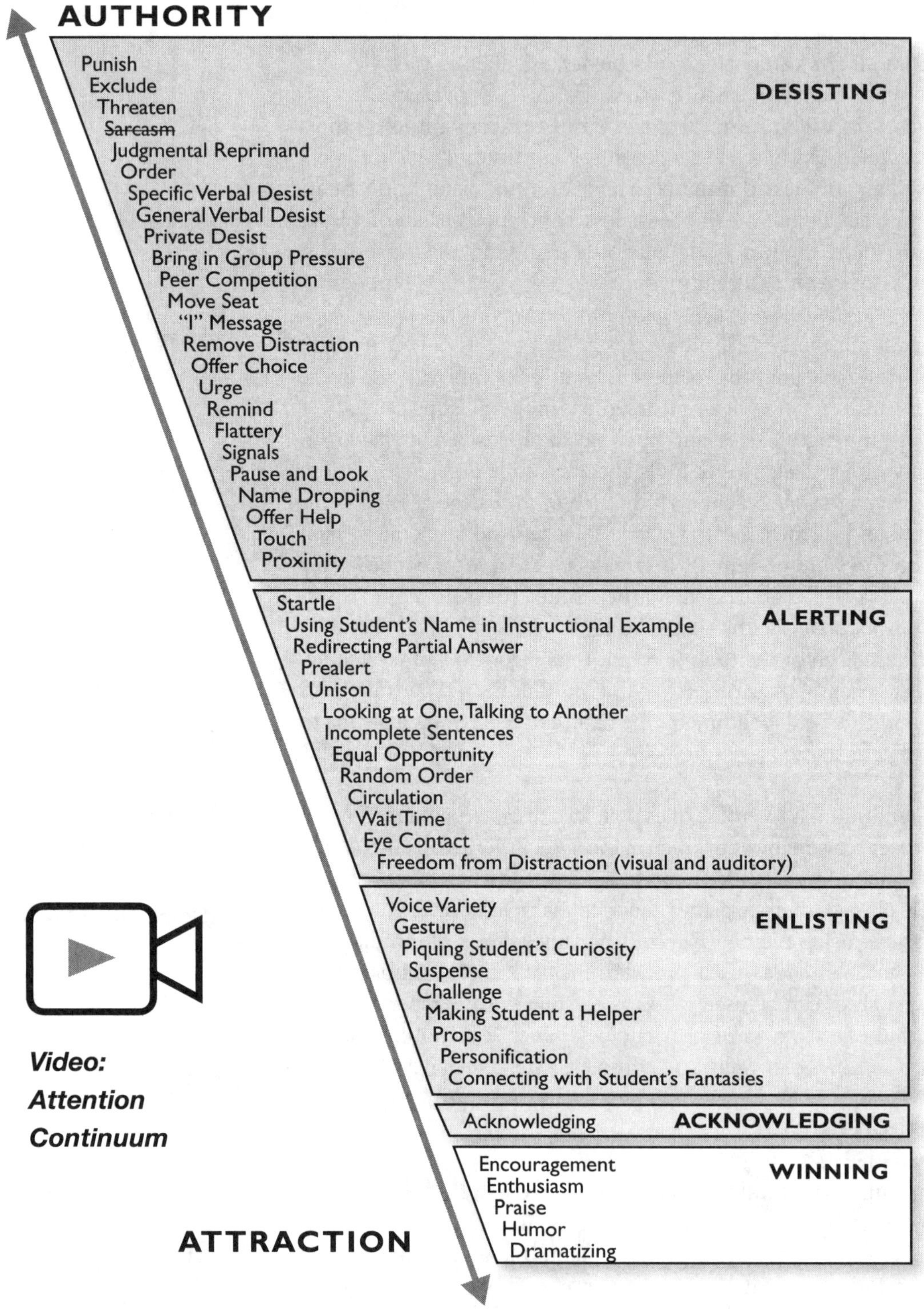

Video: Attention Continuum

moves offers a wealth of possibilities to classroom teachers. Teachers with well-developed repertoires in this area of teaching respond to different students in consistent but different ways. The following examples illustrate how Mrs. T skillfully matches her attention moves to individual students:

- ▲ **Example 1:** Mrs. T knows that Daryl looks for power conflicts; he invites tests of will with her or any other authority figure. When she uses almost any of the desisting moves with him, he gets worse. For instance, he takes a specific verbal desist as a challenge to tap his pencil even louder and see what he can goad Mrs. T into doing, so she has learned to use alerting and enlisting moves with him. If he really gets out of hand, she will move firmly and remove him, but she often avoids the necessity for doing that and does get Daryl to pay attention by challenging him with a question, pre-alerting him, or by using the move of making a student a helper. She uses this last move when she sees him tapping the pencil and says, "So there really were four pyramids for the kings. Daryl, will you advance the PowerPoint to the next frame so I can point to things from the front?"

- ▲ **Example 2:** Monica is a different sort of child. Although she also engages in frequent off-task behavior, enlisting moves seem to overstimulate her. Mrs. T explains, "It's as if she interprets enlisting and winning moves as 'I want to be your friend' or 'I want to play' messages from me. She gets carried away with the interaction and focuses too much on me." While she looks for other ways and other opportunities to meet this need for closeness that Monica seems to have during work times, Mrs. T uses midrange desisting and alerting moves (reminding, the look, pre-alerts) consistently, and successfully, with Monica when she's off task.

Individual students with different needs require different moves, and skillful teachers deliberately match their moves to students.

Individual students, with different needs, require different moves, and skillful teachers deliberately match their moves to students. Some experienced teachers are intuitive about the way they differentiate these moves across their students, and they are known as effective classroom managers. They may not be able to explain why they choose what they do. They just seem to know that they have it right. Perhaps, it is a subconscious acuteness they have at matching attention moves to various students.

Whether or not they have this intuitive flair, all teachers can benefit from reflecting on the patterns of inattention among their students and examining them in relation to the patterns of moves they seem to be making in response. They may discover that they are overlooking part of their available repertoire because they get so irritated with Adam, or that the repertoire could be enlarged, or that they could do better matching if they looked for the reason behind the inattention. Talking about a student (or a group) with a colleague using the Attention Continuum can be a highly engaging and productive activity.

CHAPTER QUICK GUIDE

Preconditions for Student Attention:

- ▲ Frame each learning experience for students.
- ▲ Use a range of auditory, visual, and kinesthetic explanatory devices when presenting information.
- ▲ Pay attention to the feeling tone of the learning experience and mood of the students, and adjust where necessary.
- ▲ Consider pre-assessment to determine where students are currently in relation to where you want them to be by the end of the lesson, and design for differences in student readiness.
- ▲ Pause regularly and periodically to have students process what they are taking in before adding more information.
- ▲ Plan for at least two minutes of physical movement of some kind within every 20 to 40 minutes of sitting time.
- ▲ Laugh with your students, and pay attention to the emotional climate in the room.

The Attention Repertoire:

1. Desisting
2. Alerting
3. Enlisting
4. Acknowledging
5. Winning

To check your knowledge about Attention, see the exercises on *The Skillful Teacher* website at www.RBTeach.com/TST7.

CHAPTER

6

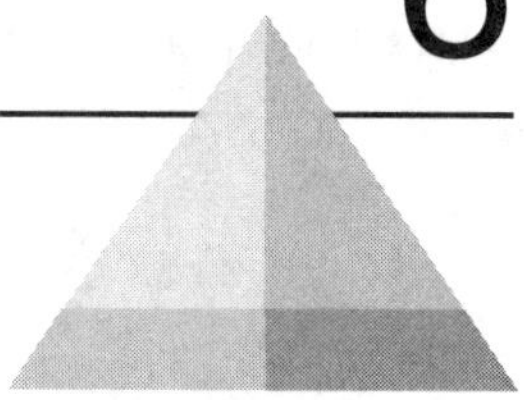

Management: Momentum

The concept of "Momentum" pertains to the smooth, ongoing flow of events in the classroom (Kounin, 1970). Teaching is full of interruptions to momentum. When these interruptions occur, students' concentration is broken, and they are distracted or prevented from becoming involved in learning activities. They experience downtime—time spent waiting for things to get ready, get started, or get organized. When Momentum is not maintained, students become bored or look for things to do, potentially filling their time by daydreaming or engaging in disruptive behavior. When Momentum is effectively maintained, students experience smooth and rapid transitions from one event to another. Movement of students and equipment happens without bottlenecks, traffic jams, conflicts, arguments, or pushing and shoving. In this chapter, we examine the behaviors teachers perform to manage Momentum and keep things moving along in the classroom.

When momentum is effectively maintained, students experience smooth and rapid transitions from one event to another.

CONNECTIONS TO OTHER AREAS OF PERFORMANCE

In a general sense, many areas of performance relate to the concept of Momentum. In Management: Attention does, insofar as students are kept interested or at least focused on learning experiences; Routines do, in that efficient design of routines for recurrent procedures expedites organizing and setting up, and speeds transitions; Space does, in that effective arrangement of space facilitates students' finding things and getting involved and minimizes distractions; and Time does, in that appropriate schedules provide for the ebb and flow of pupils' available energy and attention span, avoiding unreasonable demands.

In Motivation: Expectations for work do, in that teacher persistence and clarity about how things are to be done enable students to work more automatically and make students individually efficient at moving from one thing to another; Personal Relationship Building does, in that students' regard for the teacher makes them less likely to resist or disrupt.

Several of the Curriculum Planning areas of performance (Objectives, Assessment, and Differentiated Instruction) can also have an impact on Momentum. Mismatched material that is too hard, too easy, or inappropriately presented can lead to bored or frustrated students who will certainly break the momentum of classroom flow. In a broad sense, any mismatch of curriculum or instruction to students tends to break momentum.

But to cast Momentum so broadly is to subsume all of teaching under its umbrella. Indeed, any area of teaching performance, whatever the primary purpose of the behaviors it considers, does have a secondary effect on momentum. However, we believe that it is valuable to focus on aspects of teaching that relate primarily to maintaining momentum in the classroom. Therefore, we narrow our definition of Momentum to eight key subareas (or kinds of teacher behavior) whose primary purpose is to keep things moving along. Otherwise, if ignored or improperly done, they break the orderly flow of events.

The eight categories of Momentum behaviors are an eclectic group, comprising items that pertain to maintaining or at least enabling student involvement in learning experiences, as all other management areas of performance do. But unlike the behaviors in other management areas of performance, which can be associated with other missions, these eight do not fit any other area of performance and are primarily aimed at Momentum. They are (1) provisioning, (2) overlapping, (3) fillers, (4) intrusions, (5) lesson flexibility, (6) advance notice, (7) subdividing, and (8) anticipation.

PROVISIONING MOVES

Provisioning means having things ready to go—the space and the materials. With adequate provisioning, the teacher does not call a group of students together and then leave them for a minute to fetch something needed for the lesson from the closet. Students do not run out of needed materials during learning experiences so that they have to stop what they are doing and solicit new stocks from the teacher. This does not preclude pupils' restocking themselves from known and easily accessible storehouses or supply points. It is when the supply point is out of paper, for example, that momentum suffers. Materials are out and organized before the start of lessons, and the space is arranged as necessary before instruction begins. The room is equipped with things the students will need or are likely to need for the activities that may predictably occur over the day. Provisioning, like much of the rest of good management, becomes conspicuous by its absence. Nevertheless, there are many observable signs of good provisioning.

> **Example:** Audio visuals, technology, and demonstration equipment are set up in advance. The teacher writes information on the board behind

a pulled-down map, so that the information is readily available when the map is raised, and handouts are stacked near the site of a planned lesson. For the room itself, activities, kits, games, listening stations, books, manipulatives, and problem cards are laid out in an orderly and visible fashion for pupils to find and engage; supply points are adequately stocked; and a computer is ready. Next to it is a pad of paper with a note giving location codes for three different areas students are assigned to research that day. When provisioning is skillfully done, the small amount of teacher time spent provisioning the environment during the school day results in a maximum amount of time available for focus on students.

OVERLAPPING MOVES

We borrow the term "overlapping" from Kounin (1970) and expand on his definition: overlapping is the ability to manage two or more parallel events simultaneously with evidence of attention to both. "Manage" here includes two aspects of teaching performance. First is keeping in touch with what is going on in several groups, areas, or activities at once (the teacher may be involved in one, more than one, or circulating among several sites). It implies knowing the nature of the activity, the appropriate pupil behavior within the activity, and the current quality of the pupil's performance. Second is making moves to help pupils over blockages. Blockages may come from pupils' not understanding directions or not knowing what to do next, their inability to resolve interpersonal disagreements (for example, about sharing materials or about how to proceed next as a group), their encounter of material above their frustration level, attention wandering, or finishing an activity and needing help making or planning transitions to the next activity.

Overlapping requires something Kounin (1970) calls "Withitness," meaning that a teacher always knows what is going on in the room and shows it. It is a prerequisite for overlapping. This withitness—a form of radar or "eyes in the back of the head"—is necessary for noticing and responding to misbehavior in its early stages. But in contrast to its disciplinary application, it is also the basis for overlapping several simultaneous instructional events, as it enables teachers to keep in touch with the flow of all of the events.

Building on withitness, teachers make moves to keep momentum going when they notice a blockage or potential blockage. Here are a few examples of moves that maintain momentum by helping students avoid or work through blockages:

Example 1: The teacher, seeing a student nearing the end of an art project, says, "Where are you going to put it to dry, Jimmy?" Jimmy replies, "Under the woodworking table." The teacher responds, "Okay, fine. After that, you can finish the book you started this morning." The teacher has provided a focus for the closure of the activity and the transition to the next activity.

Example 2: As a pupil across the room appears stuck on his lab experiment, the teacher says, "Mark, ask Jane for some help if you're stuck."

Example 3: As the teacher sees a child using the last of the paint, he gestures for her to come over and reminds her to refill the paint jars when she's finished.

Example 4: When the teacher sees a group arguing over the position of a senator on a bill, she says to them, "Where could you find out for sure?" This is a way of directing the students back into constructive involvement.

The point of overlapping is that all of these moves to maintain the momentum of groups and individuals are made while the teacher may be instructing a punctuation-skill group, listening to students in a group explain their thinking behind the math problem they are solving, holding a reading conference with an individual student, inspecting a pupil's lab report, or engaging in some other primary focus. The teacher makes the management move without leaving, interrupting, or seeming to remove attention from the primary focus but for an instant. It is an accomplishment to perform overlapping effectively at any time, and especially so when the teacher has a primary active role in a particular learning experience.

FILLER MOVES

It happens regularly during the course of a day that teachers are caught with groups of students for short periods (from 1 to 10 or 15 minutes) where nothing is planned. Sometimes this happens in awkward places where standard classroom resources are not available, for example, outside waiting for a late bus, in the hallway waiting for a late class to come out of a specialist's room (gym, music), in an instructional group just ended where students have had it with work, yet when there isn't enough time to assign them anything else or even to let them choose and start some other activity around the room before it will be time to dismiss for lunch.

In such situations, what does the teacher do to prevent the disruption of momentum? Some may be inclined to comment, "Why does the teacher have to do anything? The students will just have to sit and wait, that's all. Students should know how to wait: it's an occasional and unavoidable occurrence in life. It's not up to the teacher to entertain them at these times." We would answer, "Yes," a consummation devoutly to be wished. But it doesn't always work that way.

For some groups, not so in command of themselves, and for some situations, relying on students to patiently sit and wait can be an unreasonable expectation and may result in disruptions. In such instances, teachers may pull out a filler to hold the class together for those few minutes, as these teachers did:

> **Example 1:** Because the clock in her room is wrong, Ms. M arrives with her first-grade class 5 minutes early for gym. There's no use trekking all the way back to the room; they'd just have to turn right around and return. So she asks the children to sit against the wall and move close together so they can all see and hear her. "While we wait for the other class to finish up, raise your hand if you can think of a word that rhymes with fish." She calls on three students who give different rhyming words. "You're clicking this morning. . . . Now . . . one that rhymes with . . . lamp." She calls on two more students.
>
> **Example 2:** Surprisingly, lab teams 1 and 4 have finished their earth science experiments and write-ups early and put their equipment safely away. Ten minutes still remain in the period. Mr. L knows the remaining lab teams will be asking questions, and he'll need to be available for them. But to prevent downtime and fooling around for teams 1 and 4 (a distinct possibility with this class), he quickly writes eight science vocabulary words on the board and calls up those students. He gets them seated and started on a 20 questions review game and is then back circulating among the experimenters in a scant 45 seconds.

Sometimes fillers are not as directly curriculum relevant as in these examples. Primary teachers may just play Simon Says. A fifth-grade teacher may say, "Okay, without anyone looking at their watches, raise your hand when you think one and a half minutes are up. Go!" This game is a good way to quiet a noisy bus for a few minutes. Secondary teachers may begin chatting with a class about current events or school teams. None of these is necessarily a waste of time, but it is worth distinguishing between fillers that pass the time and fillers that bring in something of the current curriculum.

MOVES FOR INTRUSIONS

Sometimes a teacher's day can seem like a series of intrusions punctuated by moments of instruction. These intrusions take many forms: pupils wanting work corrected, wanting help, wanting directions clarified, or wanting disputes arbitrated; adult visitors; incoming messengers; and public address announcements. Every intrusion has the potential to disrupt momentum, but teachers can handle intrusions in a way that minimizes their distracting influence on student's involvement with learning experiences.

Every intrusion has the potential to disrupt momentum, but teachers can handle intrusions in a way that minimizes their distracting influence on students' involvement with learning experiences.

Four basic levels of performance describe a teacher's ability to deal with intrusions:

> **Level 1:** Allows intrusions to fracture momentum.
>
> **Level 2:** Deals with intrusions in a uniform way. For instance, the teacher never allows students from outside an instructional group to ask questions (that is, doesn't tolerate intrusions of any kind), or always refers intruders to peers for help, or always has intruders wait nearby until an appropriate moment to help them arises.
>
> **Level 3:** Deals with intrusions in a variety of ways using different ways at different times.
>
> **Level 4:** Matches the response to the intrusion to the characteristics of the students involved or to the particular situation. For example, this may mean that the teacher knows that Andrea (the child she's working with) has fragile concentration and that even a delayed response to an intruder will lose Andrea for good. At other times, it is the intruder's characteristics to which the teacher adjusts, sending off Charlie to get help from a peer because she knows that Charlie can handle that, but holding John in close while signaling him to be silent until she can briefly and quietly help him because she knows John doesn't have the confidence to approach a peer. In summary, while the situation is similar the responses are different and the matching may be to the student or to students in the group (those intruded on or to the intruder).

Video: Intrusions

Sometimes the teacher matches the response to the situation rather than to the student. For example, the case of a fast-paced verbal game involving a large group may prompt the teacher to brook no intrusions at all, even from a student the teacher would normally accommodate, in order to preserve the momentum of the game. Like all of the areas of teaching in this book, intrusions remind us that the better we can match our responses to students or situations, the more effective we will be.

LESSON FLEXIBILITY

What do teachers do when lessons or planned activities are bombing? How do they control momentum? We can distinguish four levels of teacher performance:

Level 1: Presses on with the lesson anyway.

Level 2: Drops the lesson and switches to something else.

Level 3: Keeps the lesson objective and tries to teach it another way or vary the format of the lesson.

Level 4: Matches a new format to the needs of the group, or adjusts it for characteristics of individuals.

Here is an example of the last and most sophisticated level of lesson flexibility:

Example: A group of students is full of energy, charged up after physical education class. They are having trouble settling down for paper and pencil exercises on contractions. The teacher, sensing this, draws a grid on the board, puts contractions in it, and calls the students up to play a modified "Concentration" game in which they can actively participate. The teacher has simultaneously maintained focus on the instructional objective and the momentum of the lesson by matching the format to the on-the-spot needs of the students.

"Momentum can be broken if students are not prepared for transitions."

(Arlin, 1979)

ADVANCE NOTICE

Momentum can be broken if students are not prepared for transitions (Arlin, 1979). For example, if they are abruptly directed to cease one activity and begin another without time to come to some satisfactory closure in what they are doing. This is especially true when pupils are heavily invested in their activity, as is often the case with creative expressive endeavors. They resent having to stop what they are immersed in as much as a sound sleeper resents being rudely awakened.

Teachers anticipate and soften these transitions by giving students advance notice of when a transition is coming so they can get ready for it. For example, the teacher turns on the song "Time Is Tight" and students know that by the time the song ends they need to have ended what they are doing and be ready for the next activity, or there is a digital timer projected on the SMART Board counting down the three minutes left for students to wrap up. Perhaps it is just a verbal warning, "two more minutes." To continue the earlier analogy, advance notice serves as the snooze button on the alarm clock.

SUBDIVIDING MOVES

When groups of students travel through the room during transitions between activities or between phases of an activity (to line up, get their coats, go to the library, get microscopes, hand in papers), they sometimes get clogged in physical bottlenecks. These jam-ups result in crowding and general unpleasantness, and they cause downtime while students wait for the crowd to thin. Subdividing (or fragmentation, as Kounin [1970] calls it) means anticipating these times and acting to prevent the jam-ups by dividing the groups into smaller units (individuals, pairs, tables, teams, children wearing sneakers) that move one at a time under the teacher's direction. Meanwhile, students not in the unit currently moving are occupied with finishing tasks, putting away materials, or other aspects of the transition (perhaps a filler).

Some teachers use their subdividing moves to reinforce items of recent curriculum. For instance, they dismiss students for the bus by asking multiplication facts or spelling words, or they call on individuals and allow them to exit if they get the answer—"their ticket," some teachers call it.

The kinds of subdividing described above are most appropriate for primary-age children. Older students who can manage themselves in situations involving potential jam-ups may simply be allowed to proceed. In this case, efficient teacher moves might include detailing several students to pass out materials to the rest; storing materials at access points that accommodate several students getting them at once; or sequencing or pacing activities so that small units of students naturally come up for materials (or pass the potential jam-up or downtime point) at different times.

ANTICIPATION

Anticipation is a quality of mind inherent in all seven situations described previously. But teachers possessing this quality exercise it in many subtle moments outside the boundaries of those seven. So we need a general grab-bag category to hold and describe such situations, and this is it.

> **Example 1:** Consider this incident: The teacher has given the class advance notice to get ready to go to the auditorium where a brass quintet

will play for a middle school audience. "I hate concerts!" says Georgette. One minute passes; some students are putting things away. Two minutes pass; a few students are gathering by the door. Georgette is looking nobody in the eye and appears sullen. "Georgette, will you go down to the auditorium and see if the seats are set up for us?" says the teacher. Georgette goes. The class quickly lines up at the door, and the teacher sets off with them. They meet Georgette halfway there; she reports that the seats are set up and joins the class without protest as they proceed to the auditorium.

Skilled teachers perform this way every day. They anticipate trouble spots—incidents that will break momentum—and make moves to sidestep them. They move students out of the way of temptation, give resistant individuals face saving ways to get out of self-made corners, and anticipate situations or combinations of personalities that will break momentum and alter them—always before the trouble starts. Here are a few more examples of situations that benefit from a teacher's use of anticipation:

Skilled teachers anticipate trouble spots—incidents that will break momentum—and make moves to sidestep them.

Example 2: When children are called to the rug or to a class meeting after cleanup, the teacher may anticipate that some will finish before others and that an ever larger group will slowly be assembling in the meeting area and waiting without focus (the meeting won't start until they're all there). The same may happen with a middle school class that filters into the room in dribs and drabs before the bell and at the bell is dispersed all over the room. In both cases, by anticipating what is likely to happen, the teacher can arrange to be present at the meeting area doing some thing of interest to absorb the children as they arrive (riddles, general chatter, a game, a brainteaser, writing something of interest on the board, holding a novel object). Some groups left without a focus at a time like this will provide one of their own—wrestling, arguing, or other momentum breakers. A teacher who can recognize the potential of the group will anticipate these times and be there to greet them with some engaging activity as they arrive.

Example 3: Realizing that a small group will require much help and teacher time as they do follow-up work on a new geometry skill, the teacher will be sure the rest of the students are doing things they can handle comfortably, both in terms of procedures, directions, and content. Otherwise, the teacher may feel "nibbled to death by ducks," overloaded with demands for attention and help. As a result, the students will experience downtime, and momentum will falter. So on the spot, the teacher assigns a "challenge problem" that involves cumulative review and application of previously learned concepts from the previous section of the text (ones they can handle independently) to the bulk of the class and calls together four individual students for a 10-minute review of the new concepts taught.

Both of the previous examples involve anticipation and addressing the concern with a filler activity. Fillers and anticipation are related. Anticipation is the quality of mind that warns a teacher that without a filler at this moment, for this group, there may be trouble. But fillers are only one response showing anticipation. Anticipation is a bigger category than fillers. It is a kind of thinking, usually spontaneous, and often tacit, that says, "If I don't do X, momentum will break down here." X may be many things besides a filler.

Anticipation warns a teacher that without a filler at this moment, for this group, there may be trouble.

Example 4: Mrs. R, in ending a class meeting of first graders, picks children for the clay area first, then assigns other children to other areas. She does this because clay is the most popular activity and everyone wants to go there. She anticipates that if she doesn't deal with clay first and get it off everyone's mind, as well as reassure all children that they'll eventually get a chance there, it will be on everyone's mind while she tries to get the children to choose from among the other activity areas. Thus the sequence in which she fills activity stations reflects her anticipation of what would happen if she didn't deal with clay first.

Anticipation is a difficult skill to observe, and for teachers to notice themselves applying, because those who excel at it typically perform anticipation moves spontaneously and intuitively rather than pre-planning them. But teachers who experience difficulty in this area can often benefit from running advance mental movies of the day they have planned, especially if they do so out loud in the company of a colleague who's helping them problem-solve momentum issues. In this way, potential stumbling blocks to momentum may surface, and steps can be taken to avoid them.

The Momentum area of performance is clearly concerned with teacher behaviors whose primary purpose is to minimize downtime, delays, and distractions and to keep things moving smoothly in the classroom in order to protect maximum time for learning within each of the subareas. Teachers perform a variety of moves specifically aimed at maintaining momentum. The more skillfully teachers select from their Momentum repertoire to match their moves to the needs and characteristics of the students or situations involved, the more smoothly and efficiently transitions are made and the more successfully momentum is maintained.

CHAPTER QUICK GUIDE

The Eight Categories of Momentum Behaviors:

1. **Provisioning**: have the space and the materials ready to go.
2. **Overlapping**: the ability to manage two or more parallel events simultaneously.
3. **Fillers**: unplanned activities to fill short periods (1 to 15 minutes) of time.
4. **Intrusions**: the response to the intrusion should match the characteristics of the student or particular situation.
5. **Lesson Flexibility**: match a new lesson format to the needs of the group, or adjust it for characteristics of individual students.
6. **Advance Notice**: give students advance notice of when a transition is coming so they can get ready for it.
7. **Subdividing**: divide groups into smaller units.
8. **Anticipation**: anticipate trouble spots that will break momentum and make moves to sidestep them.

To check your knowledge about Momentum, see the exercises on *The Skillful Teacher* website at www.RBTeach.com/TST7.

NOTES

CHAPTER
7

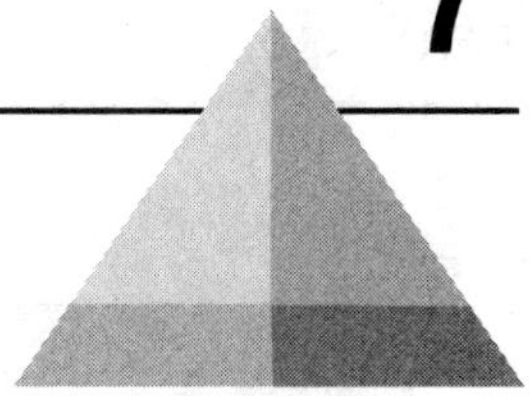

Management:
Space

Architects, interior decorators, and environmental engineers believe that the way things are arranged in space (including the space itself) makes a difference in how people function. These professionals make their living helping people to be happier and to function more efficiently through better use of the physical environment. Schools need to apply their insights to education for similar payoffs: increased satisfaction and productivity. This chapter explores ways in which teachers can make the most advantageous use of classroom and school space. There are two equally important but different ways of looking at teachers' use of Space.

One is to look at the way arrangements of furniture, materials, and space support the kind of instruction going on. What are the goals of the lesson? What kind of learning environment does it ask for? How does the use of space support the lesson? Since lesson goals and lesson forms change, space arrangements can be expected to change also. Teachers can use a variety of space arrangements, and those arrangements can be rationally matched to the active form of instruction.

The second way of looking at Space focuses not on its varying uses but on how certain constant space-related issues of student life are handled: ownership and privacy. Different students have different needs in these areas, and there are ways that teachers can meet those individual needs. We look at Space in both of these ways.

MATCHING SPACE TO INSTRUCTION

Teachers experience a wide variety of office arrangements when they confer with school principals. Some principals speak to teachers across a desk; some have the teacher's chair next to the desk so that the conversation takes place across the corner of the desk. Other principals have their desk in a corner facing a wall and turn their chair around to confer. Still others leave their desk and confer with teachers around a coffee table where two or three chairs are set. Each of those arrangements sends a different message about authority and uses physical setting to set the climate for the kind of interaction the principal

Teachers' arrangements of classroom space send messages about their image of the learner and the kind of learning they intend.

desires. In the same way, teachers' arrangements of classroom space send messages about their image of the learner and the kind of learning they intend. Jacob Getzels (as cited in Lewis, 1979) has associated four such images with four different patterns of classroom space.

First, he ties the "empty learner" image to the rectangular room arrangement: "In these classroom designs, which were the standard in the early 1900s and continue to be the most prevalent today, the teacher's function is to fill the learners with knowledge. Hence all desks face front in evenly spaced rows toward the front of the class and the source of knowledge, the teacher and his or her desk" (Getzels as cited in Lewis, 1979, pp. 155–156). Getzels next connects the image of the "active learner" to the square room arrangement: "In these rooms furniture is movable, arrangements are changed, the teacher's desk joins those of the children and the learner becomes the center" (as cited in Lewis, 1979, p. 156).

Getzels's third model is the "social learner" and the circular classroom: "Learning was perceived as occurring through interpersonal actions and reactions" (as cited in Lewis, 1979, p. 156). It is the shape that many affective education programs use today. One commercial affective education curriculum guide even calls its program "The Magic Circle." The final model is the "stimulus seeking learner" and the open classroom: "Where learning centers, communally owned furniture, private study spaces, and public areas replace classrooms, halls, and traditional school furniture. The learner is seen as a problem finding and stimulus seeking organism" (Getzels as cited in Lewis, 1979, p. 156).

Learners are, of course, all of these things. It is appropriate that students should sometimes be good receivers of information, sometimes active learners within teacher-planned tasks, sometimes heavily involved with each other in discussion, and sometimes shapers of their own activities. No one of these physical environments is the best; they are simply different and support different forms of learning appropriate to a particular lesson's goal.

Teachers can change space arrangements quite quickly for different purposes. One high school teacher we know sometimes has four different arrangements for four successive periods. The changes are made easily and quickly because the students know the basic formats and do all the moving of desks in one or two minutes, usually between classes. The teacher spends time at the beginning of the year explaining these formats to the students and doing a bit of practice arranging them, so the students can set up quickly from then on.

On one day we observed, the first class (seniors) started with desks in rows for a recitation and presentation lesson on Russian short stories. The second class (juniors) quickly rearranged the desks into clusters of six and began "committee work," cooperative teamwork on planning and preparing analyses of various American playwrights' works. The teacher signaled the format as students were entering the room, asking the first few students to set up for committees as they came in. Others then joined in. The third class (sophomores), again on signal, quickly put the desks in a large circle around the perimeter of the room for a discussion of a class book-writing project involving elementary school children in a neighboring school. As a class, they were going to make some decisions and lay out a schedule for the project. The next period, a new class (also sophomores) had a drill and practice lesson analyzing themes for variety in sentence pattern. Their desks were arranged, as you may have guessed, facing the teacher. Some basic arrangements lend themselves more easily to this kind of flexibility. For example, "Mr. Orr's grade five class sat at individual desks placed around the perimeter of the room [perhaps facing the wall]. The open area at the center of the room was used for more of the formal instruction and for small group activities" (Winne & Marx, 1982, p. 496). This type of arrangement gives students some privacy and insulation from visual distraction when they are doing individual work. For a class meeting or total group instruction, all they have to do is turn their chairs around and they're in a circle. They can go to tables in the middle for small-group work, either with a teacher or in cooperative groups.

CONFIGURING CLASSROOM SPACE

Twos

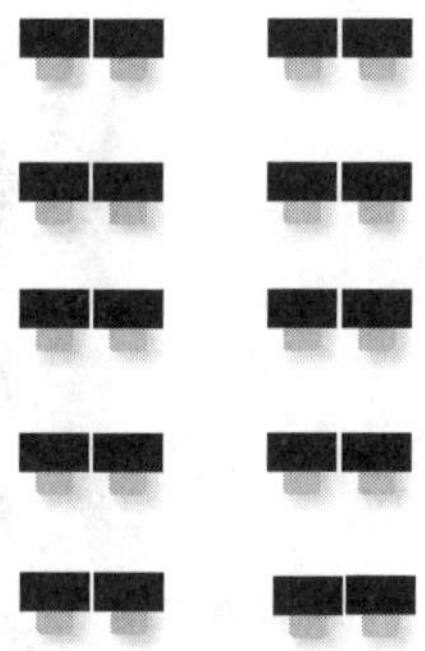

This configuration enables partner work for any number of teacher directions: "Compare your answers with a partner and reconcile any differences" or "Turn to a partner and discuss how this character's action compares with other books we've read by Judy Blume." The pairs of desks can be arranged in such a way as to give the teacher maximum visibility and also to create aisles of movement for the teacher to get proximity to each student quickly, either for one-on-one help or for regaining wandering attention.

Circle

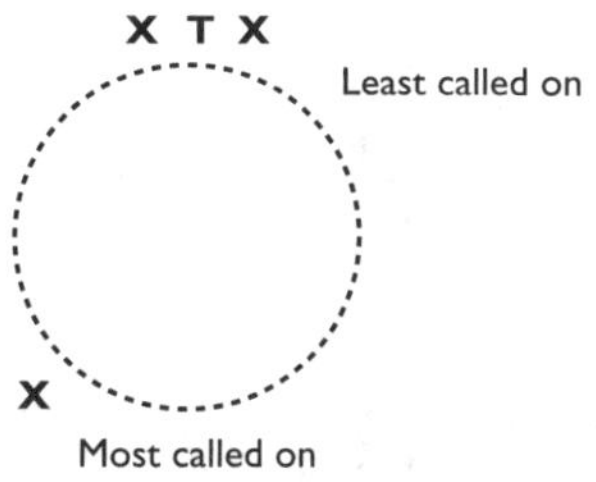

Either a circle or a "U" of chairs or desks enables eye contact among all the students and supports true discussion better than other arrangements. Many teachers report that the participation and interaction they want to induce among students in reform-oriented math classes simply don't happen as well with traditional seating arrangements. So for teachers who work to "make students' thinking visible" as we describe in Chapter 11, "Clarity," this arrangement is highly desirable.

Clusters

Students seated at clusters of desks or large tables support group work or committee work where students need to talk with teammates. This arrangement also supports tasks for which materials need to be spread out for sorting, arranging, comparing, or making displays.

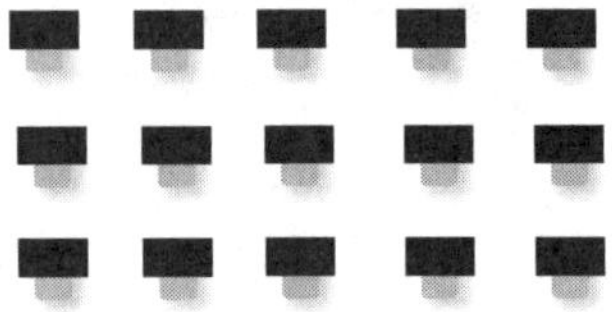

Rows

This traditional arrangement supports solo student work, listening, viewing, and test taking. It minimizes social distraction but does not prevent teachers from pairing students up for periodic summarizing during instruction.

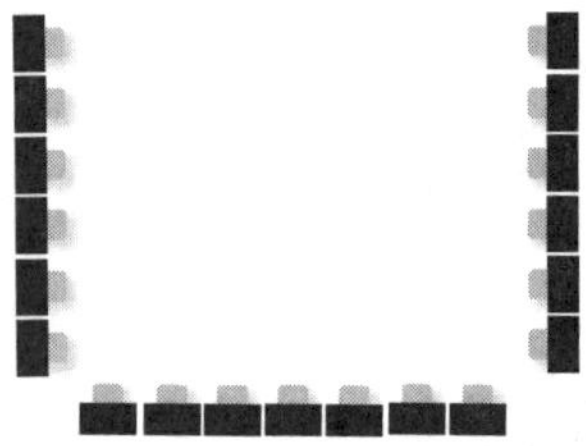

Perimeter

In this arrangement, desks are placed around the perimeter of the room with the student chairs facing the wall. This arrangement reduces visual distraction, yet allows students sitting next to one another to consult each other and do partner work. The wall space in front of each student can be personalized with a corkboard and other displays pertaining to that student's classwork or personal artifacts. If students simply turn their chairs around, a "U" is instantly formed for class discussion or for participating in a teacher-led lesson. This flexible arrangement also gives the teacher a clear field and open path for reaching any student quickly for help or management purposes. The room has to be big enough so that all the students fit in the three-sided layout. The fourth side is usually the blackboard or whiteboard and presentation section of the room.

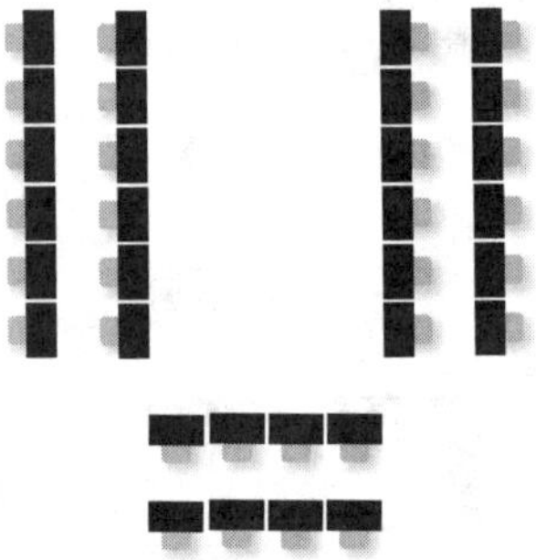

"U"s

This arrangement packs in many students in large classes efficiently, yet it supports discussion, partner work, and proximity to the teacher. Teachers have a harder time getting close to students in the back row, but this is a good compromise for large class sizes.

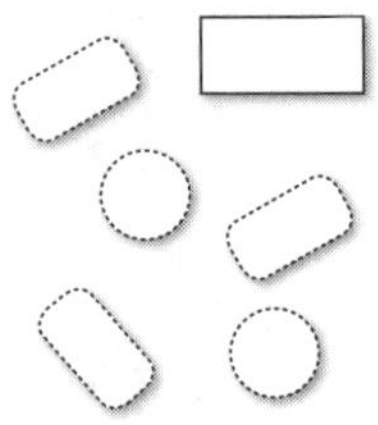

Centers

This arrangement is intended for academic periods when students are expected to move around to different stations or centers. Each center has a display or a task with materials the students are supposed to engage in. Traffic aisles between centers have to be clear and wide enough to facilitate easy student movement. This arrangement requires clear and accessible directions at each station and feedback mechanisms so students get information on how well they have done with the task.

CHOOSING THE BEST ARRANGEMENT

A key consideration in examining use of space is to note whether it is a rational use. That is, are things arranged deliberately to best support the kind of instruction under way? If so, a second consideration is whether the arrangement varies when the instructional format or objectives change. Hence, use of classroom space can be classified according to one of the following levels:

Level 1: The teacher takes the space the way it comes (from the custodian, the previous period's teacher, tradition, or something else).

Level 2: Space is arranged according to a conventional design and used conventionally and consistently, without variation.

Level 3: The space is rearranged periodically but experimentally, without a clear rationale, mostly just for change itself.

Level 4: The space arrangement is constant but appropriate for instruction.

Level 5: The space is used flexibly for different instructional purposes at different times, matched to curricular goals.

Within a given arrangement of space, the placement of materials can further support instructional goals. Primary-grade teachers are often particularly thoughtful about the placement of various items in relation to each other. For example, art materials may be placed near a creative writing area to encourage painting as a follow-up to creative writing. This kind of attention to location and activity flow, though, applies equally well to high school. A display of nineteenth century American art may be placed over the supply table where students periodically go for assignment sheets and to turn in papers in an English class. The display might serve as a stimulus for a unit on American authors of the period. References and connections to the pictures can be made when the instruction starts.

OWNERSHIP AND PRIVACY

Getzels (as cited in Lewis, 1979) raises the issue of what spaces belong to the students in a classroom or a school. She provides the following list:

- **Desk:** This is probably the most valued and protected space. In traditional classrooms, it may be the child's only source of personal space.

In more open classes, it may be shared with others or no longer be a part of the school furniture.

- **Locker:** This is considered a convenience space, and also private if solely for the student's use.

- **Special class seat:** In music, art, and library, if seats are assigned, a certain degree of ownership will be attached to them.

- **Chair:** Often individuals and the group recognize individual ownership of chairs. Robert Sommer (1969) notes, "People who remain in public areas for long periods—whether at a habitual chair at a weekly conference or on a commuter train—can establish a form of tenure. Their rights to this space will be supported by their neighbors even when they are not physically present."

- **Boys' or girls' room:** This is definitely a child's space. The bathroom can be a private retreat for tears, anger, fights, secrets, mischief, and daydreams. In some schools, it becomes the communal news center for the underground student communication network. In some secondary schools, it may become the property of a group of students, or it may be locked by the administration.

- **Playground:** This space is child-owned and shared with other children. It is powerfully real and memorable, considering the relatively limited time spent in recess.

- **Hall:** These are no-man's-land in most schools, a public avenue. Nobody owns them, but they're very familiar territory. Perhaps the sense of ownership would be similar to that felt for one's lane or street at home. In secondary school, it is the hub of socializing.

- **Classroom:** In some rooms, children feel a sense of ownership for the whole room or sections of it. In other rooms, the desk may be the only owned space.

- **School building:** Feelings of ownership increase with the years spent in the building. Variations in intensity also depend on school philosophies, building dimensions, and the degree to which children participate in school activities.

(Getzels as cited in Lewis, 1979, p. 130)

Many students have a strongly felt need for a place of their own—not just a cubby or a mailbox—but a workplace to occupy that is regularly theirs. Adult readers may identify with this need. One of the authors consulted on a weekly basis with a school for several years without such a space, and it drove him crazy!

Left on their own, middle and high school students regularly take the same desk in a class. It becomes "their" seat. College students and adults do the same thing. As teachers plan classroom space, they should consider whether they have adequately met students' needs for ownership of space. That need varies considerably with individuals, as does their need for privacy.

Private spaces like carrels or individual practice rooms restrict visual distraction and noise. There are students who benefit greatly from having such places created for them or put at their disposal. Skillful teachers respond to these students and match them with spatial arrangements that suit their needs. As they look at their classrooms and other school facilities (libraries, media centers), they ask themselves if enough private spaces have been provided to accommodate such students, because there are always a few of them.

TEN RECOMMENDATIONS FOR USING SPACE

The literature on the use of school space is sparse, and the research is even thinner. A series of interviews we conducted with teachers showed support for the following ten recommendations:

1. Materials students use should be visibly stored and accessible to facilitate efficient getting out and putting away.

2. Avoid dead space—open, purposeless space which lends itself to random or unproductive student activity.

3. In some settings, for reasons of safety or control, it may be appropriate for space to be arranged so the teacher can see all of it, with no blind spots. In other settings, this guideline may be inconsistent with goals relating to trust, privacy, and independence.

4. Vertical space (walls, dividers, closets, and movable cabinet doors) should be employed productively—for example, for display, learning stations, or storage of materials—effectively increasing usable space in the classroom. Hanging artifacts or displays from the ceiling or mul-

tilevel use of space in addition to the floor (lofts, for example, or other erected structures) can increase effective usable space within a room.

5. Dividers placed on a diagonal with respect to the ninety-degree orientation of the walls can channel student movement and visual fields in interesting and deliberate directions.

6. Have a display area where students' work, art, and other kinds of products can easily be seen and examined.

7. Keep active areas distant from quiet areas in a room to minimize distraction and interference.

8. Keep adjacent activity areas far enough apart, or clearly bounded from their immediate neighbor, so as to prevent distraction and interference.

9. Have clear traffic paths connecting functional areas of the room that do not necessitate students' walking through one area (and disturbing things there) to get to another.

Video: Choreograph the Flow

10. Empty furniture absorbs energy. Therefore, if you have fewer students than chairs in a secondary class, don't let the students spread out around the periphery of the room with empty chairs between them and you. Either eliminate the empty chairs, or move the students forward where they can be in contact with you and with each other.

Overall, the message we get from reviewing the literature on space and classrooms is to be deliberate about its use. Teachers can make instructional spaces more attractive, efficient, and flexible; in short, they can control and change these spaces to best support instruction in moving from lesson to lesson.

CHAPTER QUICK GUIDE

Seven Classroom Configuration Options:

(1) Twos, (2) Circle, (3) Clusters, (4) Rows, (5) Perimeter, (6) "U"s, and (7) Center.

Ten Classroom Space Recommendations:

1. Materials students use should be visibly stored and accessible.
2. Avoid dead space.
3. If needed, for reasons of safety or control, arrange space so the teacher can see all of it.
4. Vertical space (walls, dividers, closets, and movable cabinet doors) should be employed productively.
5. Use dividers placed on a diagonal to channel student movement and visual fields.
6. Have a display area for students' work and other kinds of products.
7. Keep active areas distant from quiet areas.
8. Keep adjacent activity areas apart, or clearly bounded to prevent distraction.
9. Have clear traffic paths connecting functional areas of the room.
10. Either eliminate empty chairs, or move the students forward where they can be in contact with you and with each other.

To check your knowledge about Space, see the exercises on *The Skillful Teacher* website at www.RBTeach.com/TST7.

NOTES

CHAPTER 8

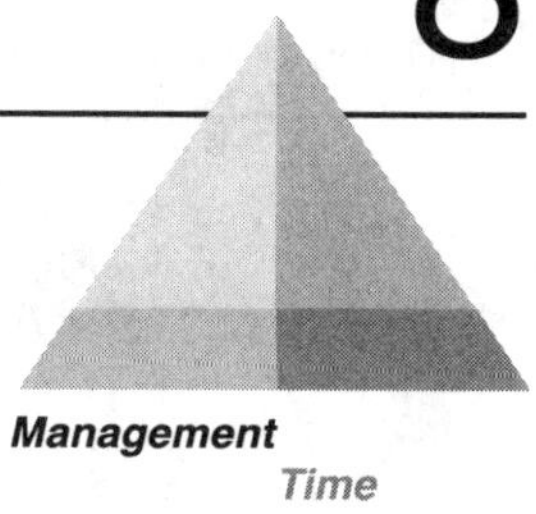

Management: Time

Time is the currency of life, and teachers run the bank for their students about six hours a day, an enormously powerful position. They run the bank even for "free choice" times, where the options available are those offered or allowed by the teacher. When students do what, in what order, and for how long is largely under the teacher's control, and we know from recent research that controlling how time is used has a big impact on student learning. This includes time spent in places other than the classroom, like the cafeteria. How long students spend in each of the environments the school offers and the quality of that time is something faculty members control.

Controlling how time is used well has a big impact on student learning.

This chapter is about being as deliberate as possible in managing student time use for maximum learning. It draws on the growing knowledge base of the field to help us be better time managers for our students. The issues of time management for students center on allocation, efficiency, and pacing. Investigating how we and our students are spending class time, and getting concrete and accurate data about that, is likely to yield some surprises and some interesting and useful insights.

TIME AS A CONSTRUCT

School effectiveness researchers over the past three decades have ranked time—and time-related instructional variables—either number one or number two on a list of eight to ten factors that are important to student achievement (Scheerens & Bosker, 1997; Berliner, 1990; Good & Brophy, 2000; Greenwood, 1991; Tindal & Parker, 1987; Marzano, 2000).

A superficial look at that research may prompt one to say, "So what else is new? Obviously, if students spend more time on math and less time fooling around, they will learn more math." But researchers are consistently in agreement that it's not that simple. Within reasonable limits, the issue is not about adding more time but rather about how time is used (Aaronson, Zimmerman, & Carlos, 1999; Evans & Bechtel, 1996). Embedded in the research—and in the claims associated with it—is a delineation and hierarchical classification of various categories of time (see Figure 8.1). Starting with time in school, each of the

Figure 8.1 Time Allocations in School

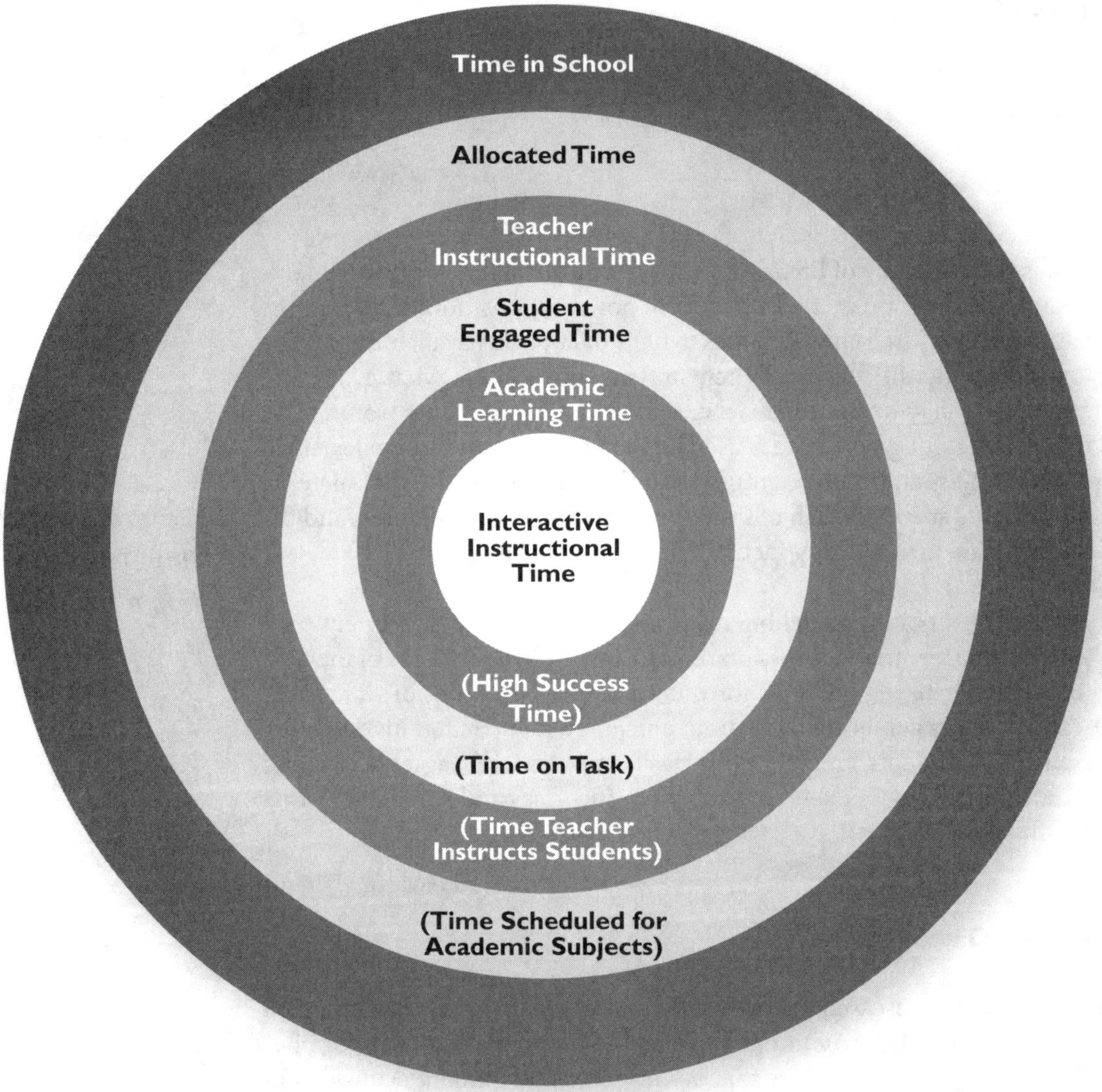

categories in Figure 8.1 includes and subsumes those below and inside its circle. The closer the category is to the core of the nested circles, the stronger the correlation is between time and student achievement. In this figure, time in school is the number of hours or days that a student should be, or is, in attendance. There are five categories of school time:

1. Allocated time is the amount of time in school formally scheduled for instruction (versus non-instructional activities such as lunch, recess, and changing classes).

2. Teacher instructional time is the amount of allocated time the teacher is actually engaged with students delivering instruction or actively monitoring learning experiences (versus doing management tasks such as taking attendance and setting up equipment).

3. Student engaged time, often referred to as time on task, is the number of minutes that students are observably paying attention to and focusing on instructional material (versus waiting, daydreaming, fooling around, getting organized, and listening to announcements).

Teachers who study their time use make significant changes and get better student learning.

4. Academic learning time is the portion of time students spend engaged in relevant academic tasks and performing those tasks with a high rate of success. Relevant academic tasks and a high success rate distinguish it from, and make it a subset of, student engaged time. For clarity, we will call it high success time here.

5. Interactive instructional time is time spent directly with a student getting instruction (one-to-one, small group, or large group), as opposed to time spent alone doing seatwork or projects or working with a group that's not interacting directly with an instructor.

These categorical distinctions are very useful as a framework for studying this area of performance and becoming ever more purposeful in maximizing its impact on achievement. Data show that teachers who study their time use make significant changes (Stallings, 1980) and get better student learning. Let's look at each one in more detail.

1. Allocated Time

Allocated time, or time set aside for instruction, reveals something about the values of a district, a school, or a teacher. Time set aside for instruction and time set aside for instruction in specific subject areas are related but separate considerations in this category. An examination of each should yield data that reflect some consensus across a school about what is important and what the priorities are within those things that are important.

It is likely that the current standards movement will press schools to pay more attention to and reach more common agreements about aligning time allocation with values and priorities and will result in providing some greater consistency or uniformity for students. Historically, however, while researchers have found little difference between time in school across schools, they have found some very big differences in allocated time for academic subjects, especially across elementary schools, and classes within a school where individual teachers tend to have more direct control over the daily and weekly class schedule. For example, Caldwell, Huitt, and Graeber (1982) found that:

> Time actually allocated for fifth-grade math ranged from 18 minutes to 80 minutes; allocated fifth-grade reading time ranged from 51 minutes to 195 minutes. Allocated time may also vary enormously within a class; for example, in one study (Dishaw, 1977) one fifth-grade student spent 39 minutes each day on math while another student spent 75 minutes. These differences in actual allocated time suggest that some students may have two to four times as much opportunity to learn specific academic content as other students. (p. 474)

Is it fair that because of a particular teacher's talents and inclinations, his or her class gets a great reading and writing program but practically nothing else? At the schoolwide level, it is imperative that we examine how time is apportioned throughout the day, the week, and the school year and ask questions like these:

- ▲ What percentage of time in school is allocated and protected for instruction?
- ▲ How else is student time expended?
- ▲ Do the percentages match our priorities?
- ▲ How might we decrease the amount of allocated time not devoted to instruction?
- ▲ Over the years, what amount of a student's time is spent learning what subjects?
- ▲ Is there some consistency and rationale to this expenditure of time? If not, then we are not really in control of the education we are delivering.

2. Instructional Time: A Matter of Efficiency

Instructional time—the percentage of allocated time a teacher is engaged with students delivering instruction and actively monitoring learning experiences—might be referred to as time on task for the teacher. Estimates of how much class time is devoted to instruction vary widely, from a low of 21% to a high of 69% (Conant, 1973; Marzano & Riley, 1984; Park, 1956; U.S. National Education Commission on Time and Learning, 1994). If we take the highest estimate of 69% as the upper boundary, we can conclude that of the 13,104 classroom hours theoretically available, only 9,042 hours are used for instruction. This comes to about 695.5 hours per year or about 3.9 hours per day (Marzano, 2003).

The research generally supports the positive impact of increasing the amount of instructional time. Walberg (1997) found a positive relationship between increased instructional time and learning in 97% of 130 studies (Marzano, 2003). One major study of 87 secondary classrooms (Stallings, 1980) found the average engaged rate of teacher to students to be 73%. Some teachers used 40 minutes of a 45-minute period to develop concepts; others used only 20 to 25 minutes (Good & Brophy, 2000). Teachers who had lower rates of interaction with students had classes with significantly smaller achievement gains (or no gain at all), especially for low-performing students. This is true even if students were on task most of the time. As Stallings (1980) explains, "The students are on-task, but the teacher is not teaching. In those classrooms where no gain was being made, the students were doing written assignments 28 percent of the time and reading silently 22 percent of the time, and teachers were doing classroom management tasks more than 27 percent of the time" (p. 14).

Research generally supports the positive impact of increasing the amount of instructional time.

Maximizing instructional time requires organizing instructional activities and expediting non-instructional ones (preparing materials, taking attendance, managing transitions, dealing with discipline, and so forth) so there is a minimum of downtime and unsupervised learning time. Hence, how much of the allocated time we preserve for instruction is directly tied to classroom organization and management skills.

There is also a need to look at instructional time from a schoolwide perspective. Marzano (2003) proposes that "schools should make every effort to convey the message that class time is sacred time and should be interrupted for important events only, a message that is commonly conveyed in other countries" (p. 31). He cites Stigler and Hiebert (1999) who found that instructional interruptions (such as PA announcements) were far more typical in American classrooms than in Japan and suggests that we take measures to eliminate these by decreasing or eliminating announcements during instructional time. Posting "Do Not Interrupt" signs on our doors and referring to specific parts of class as academic learning time helps students understand the need to put forth greater effort to attend during those times.

3. Student Engaged Time and Time on Task

Engaged time, a subset of allocated time, is the time that students appear to be paying attention to materials or presentations that have instructional goals. Although often used synonymously with the concept of time on task, Berliner (1990) distinguishes time on task as a subset—time a student is engaged in an appropriate learning task (for example, a student may be deeply engaged in mathematics work at a time that has been allocated for science). Early studies (Fisher et al., 1978) reported that, on average, students are engaged or attending for only a portion of allocated time—about 75% of it. But the range of student engaged time was large—between 50% and 90%. Some studies (Stanley & Greenwood, 1983) have shown significant differences in academic engagement of high versus low socioeconomic status (SES) student groups. They write,

> On a daily basis high SES students spent as much as 11 minutes (or 5 percent) more time per day engaged in writing, reading, and talking about academic matters than did their low SES counterparts. . . . At this daily rate, low SES students need to attend as much as one and a half months during summer vacation to obtain an equivalent amount of engaged time in one year. . . . Otherwise low SES students are at risk of academic delay. . . . because of their lower daily engagement rates. (p. 11)

While more recent reviews of the research can establish only a moderate correlation between engaged time on task and student achievement (Cotton, 1989), it is critical that we seize every opportunity to maximize engaged time for all students since it is the precursor to academic learning (high success) time. Recent studies of student engagement (Hunter & Csikszentmihalyi, 2003; Shernoff, Csikszentmihalyi, Schneider, & Shernoff, 2003), in which large numbers of secondary students used wristwatch devices to record their activity and feeling states eight times daily, found that students spend a majority of class time in non-interactive activities such as listening to lectures and doing individual seatwork assignments. Interactive activities such as participating in discussions (9%) and group or lab work (6%) accounted for only a small percentage of the total time. Engagement, measured as a composite of interest, concentration, and enjoyment, was higher in group and individual work compared to lectures, exams, or TV/video viewing. Students also reported being more engaged during "flow tasks"—those that students felt competent to complete and were high in challenge—compared to tasks that were low in challenge or that students felt were beyond their capabilities.

Differences in engagement rates were substantial. For example, 42% of students reported being attentive during low-challenge activities, whereas 73% reported paying attention during activities that were more challenging and required more skill (Emmer & Gerwels, 2006). Emmer and Gerwels cite other studies related to eliciting student interest. Mitchell (1993), studying secondary math classes, found that involvement in classroom materials was a strong predictor of student interest. Identifying two kinds of situational interest characteristics as "catch" and "hold" (elicitors and maintainers of interest), he found that group

Table 8.1 Areas of Performance Related to Increasing Engaged Time

Management	• Attention moves, especially those in the alerting, enlisting, and winning categories (Chapter 5). • Space arrangements that minimize distractions and facilitate learning objectives (Chapter 7).
Instruction	• Clarity concepts: framing the big picture by communicating objectives, itinerary, reason for activities, and activating student knowledge to create context and establish relevance; choosing explanatory devices that engage auditory, visual, and kinesthetic learning modalities; and making cognitive connections and checking understanding broadly and frequently to ensure students understand (Chapter 11). • Principles of Learning: embedded in lesson design, including active participation, vividness, meaning, feeling tone, degree of guidance, say-do, knowledge of results and feedback, reinforcement, goal setting, and keeping students open and thinking (Chapter 13).
Motivation	• Classroom Climate: addressing elements from all three strands—building community, creating an environment where it is safe to take intellectual risks, and cultivating personal efficacy (Chapter 16). • Expectations: employing the critical attributes of communicating expectations regarding four kinds of standards and expectations and ensuring that all actions and interactions with students communicate three key messages: "This is important; you can do it; I won't give up on you" (Chapter 14).
Curriculum	• Lesson Objectives: setting objectives that are challenging but attainable for students (Chapter 18). • Differentiated Instruction: learning experiences that are differentiated in input, process, and output to address differences in student readiness, interests, and learning styles (Chapter 20). • Assessment: ongoing in a learning experience to get and keep students on track (Chapter 21).

work, computers, and puzzles were three types of "catchers," and meaningfulness and involvement served to "hold." One of the best predictors of situational interest was involvement, measured by perceived enjoyment in the activity and "learning the material ourselves" and "doing something" versus listening to the teacher talk or "come in, take notes, go home, do homework and it's the same thing every day" (Mitchell, 1993, p. 436).

Other studies soliciting teachers' views (35 of 65 teachers were secondary level) of how they engage students found the most common method reported by all teachers was the use of hands-on activities (Zahorik, 1996). At least a third of the teachers also mentioned three other strategies: (1) personalizing the content (linking it to prior student knowledge or experiences), (2) building student trust (by using activities that permit students to share ideas and experiences, make decisions, and be involved in planning and making choices), and (3) group work. This research serves as an intriguing support for the kind of student discussions described in Chapter 11, "Clarity," on making students' thinking visible and the 24 verbal behaviors.

Many of the areas of performance discussed in other chapters can serve as direct resources for positively influencing student engaged time and time on task. Table 8.1 is a list of other areas of performance related to increasing engaged time and specific subcategories that are most relevant to this topic.

All of these areas of performance afford us resources and ideas to increase our capacity to influence student engagement. Most of them also serve as resources to maximize academic learning time—the most significant time of all regarding student achievement.

4. Academic Learning or High Success Time

In the research literature, the portion of engaged time that students are working on relevant academic tasks and performing those tasks with a high rate of success is referred to as Academic Learning Time (ALT). We will simply call it "high success time doing important work." This is the category of time found to have the most significant correlation with student achievement.

Similar to findings regarding student engaged time, the amount of high success time students experience across classrooms varies hugely. In basic skill-work, for example, it was found to be anywhere from 16 minutes per day in a group of low-average classes to 111 minutes per day in a group of high-average classes. High and low average does not refer to the ability level of the students; it refers to the teacher's ability to get more academic learning time for students (Caldwell, Huitt, & Graeber, 1982).

Academic learning time says something about what kind of match exists between the current state of the learner, the material to be learned, and the design of the learning experience itself (Anderson, 1983). High-average teachers provide "more than twice as much academic learning time as in the average case and more than six times as much as in the low average case" (Caldwell, Huitt, & Graeber, 1982, p. 477). These startling figures prompt a careful look at how our students experience school time, since high success time correlates strongly with achievement.

In order to increase high success time, we need to use time efficiently and structure learning experiences that enable students to be successful. Variance in high success time must be traced to the appropriateness of assignments, the diagnostic acumen of the teacher, and the adequacy of instruction and direction given before students are turned loose on individual tasks—in other words, our skill at clarity, structuring learning experiences, and matching objectives to individuals and groups. Many of the suggestions listed for engaged time can also serve as resources for attaining more ALT. Since scheduled time and allocated time set the upper limits for academic learning or high success time, it is worth considering things one can do in each of these categories to channel more available minutes toward this end.

When teachers are teaching, students are more likely to be learning; workbooks and other solo assignments that occupy students' class time don't teach.

5. Interactive Instructional Time

High success time can be positively affected by the degree to which students are engaged and interacting with the teacher, a category that researchers label interactive instructional time. Instructional time is that portion of allocated time when the teacher is actively focusing in some way on instruction and facilitating learning as opposed to attending to management issues. Engaged time is the portion of time the student is focused and attending to academic learning. Students may be on task but working independently (for example, doing seatwork, written assignments, or silent reading) while the teacher is working with other learners. Hence, interactive instructional time is yet a smaller portion of both of those—the amount of engaged time in which an individual student actually experiences direct interaction with a teacher, whether it is in whole-group, small-group, or individual situations. When it comes to interactive instructional time, research findings have indicated the more, the better. The point is that when teachers are teaching, students are more likely to be learning. Workbooks and other solo assignments that occupy students' class time don't teach. This is not a surprising finding when one considers the importance of teacher feedback, knowledge of results, degree of guidance, and other principles of learning.

In the past, this finding led some to advocate for the direct instruction pattern of teaching for whole-class groups as the most efficient form of instruction (Rosenshine, 1981). This recommendation really misses the point. In the direct instruction model, an individual student is not necessarily engaged and interacting with the teacher. For this model to maximize interactive instructional time, the teacher needs to draw extensively on strategies from outside the model. This means checking for understanding and building in processing and summarizing time for students in pairs and small groups so that the teacher can circulate and engage with individuals.

Furthermore, the direct instruction pattern (the "sage on the stage" model) is only one way to get teacher-student interactive time, and suitable to only one kind of teaching. There are learnings for which this pattern is clearly not the only or the best way—like teaching students to provide evidence for positions or teaching the scientific method. All the models of teaching in Chapter 13 can provide interactive teaching time, as can peer tutoring. Therefore, it is important to put direct instruction in perspective. Direct instruction is effective for teaching skills, and it works to the degree that it provides high proportions of interactive instruction time. But there are other learnings besides skills and two dozen other models of teaching that can provide interactive instruction.

Most students can learn anything if they have the prerequisite pieces of knowledge and skills in place and are given adequate time.

Another way to maximize interactive instructional time is by engineering lessons so that students are actively engaged in all phases of the learning experience (input, processing, and output). The teacher's role then is cast as the guide on the side: mediating, monitoring, and facilitating the learning process by providing guidance as needed, clarifying directions, responding to questions, posing questions to check for understanding and to stretch and extend students' thinking, and providing prompt and continuous feedback. For example, this would be what we would see in the most effectively designed and implemented cooperative learning experiences. What this actually sounds like is recorded in the Bodner scripts reproduced in Chapter 11, "Clarity."

Individualized programs are at high risk here. If they are poorly managed, students, though active and involved, may get only a few minutes a day with the teacher, and that is not enough. Teachers in this situation either need to do more group work or manage individualization so students get more feedback and guidance. It is the attributes of interactive instruction that are important any way you can get them. It seems to us those attributes are clear explanations, prompt feedback, knowledge of results, and appropriate degree of guidance. Good computer-based learning systems can provide these features.

DIFFERENTIATING TIME TO LEARN

Benjamin Bloom's work on mastery learning has added another important concept to the knowledge base about time to learn or time a student needs under optimal learning conditions to reach some criterion of learning (Berliner, 1990). The idea is that most students can learn anything if they have the prerequisite pieces of knowledge and skills in place and are given adequate time to learn it. Giving students adequate time to learn doesn't mean giving them material and just waiting until they've gone over it long enough to absorb it. It means task analysis of new learnings, careful ongoing assessment, and reteaching loops for students who need it—and for only those who do. The view of time from mastery learning puts teachers on the spot along with students. Mastery learning brings with it a requisite set of assumptions: that all students are capable of achieving mastery of appropriate learning goals; that when learning isn't taking place, something isn't yet right about how it is being presented to the student or the time given for the student to master it; that mastery is essential in order for the student to progress; and that modifications, adaptations, adjustments, and reteaching are all options available to support that happening. In other words, one doesn't blame the students if learning isn't taking place. Instead, there is a search for how to adjust, adapt, modify, and reteach until the student is on board and "getting it."

Mastery learning is a form of individualizing instruction. But individualizing means more than self-paced here, more than marching through programmed material. It means clear and comprehensive sequences of instruction laid out in advance, broken down into pieces, and with options for how to deliver instruction of those pieces to students. Above all, it means monitoring what students know and not giving up until they have met mastery criteria.

Finally, it means planning reteaching loops and simultaneous extension activities for students who got it the first time around. Such a two-ringed circus presents management and planning challenges that are a stretch for teachers who are unused to managing multiple events in a classroom. In other words, mastery learning requires differentiating learning experiences (one size doesn't fit all) and is once again an example of how the areas of performance of teaching are interdependent and ever present. A sincere and focused effort to address and afford students time to learn requires an exploration of concepts addressed in the chapters on Momentum, Lesson Objectives, Differentiated Instruction, and Classroom Climate.

CONDUCTING TIME AUDITS

At the beginning of this chapter, we suggested that collecting concrete data about how time is spent in the classroom is likely to yield some interesting and useful insights, as well as surprises. All of which can serve as a productive foundation for creative problem-solving around getting more currency for students to spend toward learning. Marzano (2003) refers to this as conducting time audits: gathering data that will reveal how much time in the day or a class period is devoted to actual instruction, how much time in class is generally taken up by non-instructional activities or management tasks, how much time individual students are focused and engaged, what they are doing or what is going on that distracts them, and so forth.

We once studied the time use of students in five classrooms of a K–5 school using a technique adapted from Engel (1977). The class was scanned every five minutes, and a notation was made for each student on a class roster. The notation recorded what the student was doing and with what level of attention or involvement. From these data, a color-bar graph was constructed for each student, color coded to study activities showing student time use over a whole morning. Coded cross marks in black were overlaid on the color bar to indicate degrees of inattention or non-involvement. Putting all the bars together on one graph for the class gave the teachers an enormous amount of information on individual students and patterns across the class.

For example, one teacher was losing a great deal of time in classroom management: passing out papers, setting up in the morning, and getting ready for transitions. Another teacher had students with low levels of involvement due to social chatter at table groups—quiet and unobtrusive but nevertheless persistent and interfering with their work. Another teacher found her students were involved with individual tasks and projects, but sometimes received only five minutes of direct teacher instruction in the course of the day. All of these teachers made changes to increase their effectiveness after they saw their class data. The changes involved more attention to momentum, rearranging space, rescheduling their own instructional time, and clarifying their expectations for student behavior. The point is that the obvious was not so obvious to them until they directly faced objective data about their own students and their own classes. When they had the data, they were able to improve their effectiveness. Academic engaged time and student time spent in interactive instruction may sound obvious enough, but teachers who get the numbers on their own classes may well find some new priorities emerging.

Although there are structured formal models to use to conduct this type of audit (Marzano, Kendall, & Gaddy, 1999), teachers could do much of this as action research in their own classrooms independently or with the support of a colleague present in the room. There are many kinds of data one might gather: noting starting and ending times of activities, transitions, and length of time spent on direction giving, for example. Comparing data gathered to what you might have predicted or anticipated the data would look like can lead to fine-tuning time estimates, problem identification, and pinpointing the means for using time more effectively. Or a colleague could collect data for you about how individuals or groups of students are spending their time: How much are they engaged and on task? When they aren't, what is going on? How much is interactive instructional time versus independent work? What kind of success are they having? The resulting data can be used to make adjustments and modifications that might increase student productivity and level of performance.

Leinhardt, Zigmond, and Corley (1981) found that:

> Teachers must be vigilant in their search for children who are losing out. While the average off-task rate was 15 percent, some students were off-task more than 30 percent of the time. While the average amount of teacher instruction (in reading) was 16 minutes a day, the range was from 1.4 minutes per day to 35 minutes per day (within the same class). While the average time spent in silent reading was 14 minutes per day, some students spent no time at all reading silently. Fortunately, teachers can dramatically change the experience and performance of those students who seem to be losing out without changing things for those who are not. (p. 358)

But first, the teacher must become aware of who the students are and how their time is being lost. Good time management comes from handling a number of other areas of performance well. When students are on task, productive, and experiencing success, it is more than good time management; it is successful education. Good use of student time is a criterion for good teaching, an outcome of all the things that go into good education. But there are some skills that are distinctly part of efficient time management itself.

PACING AND RHYTHM

Matching has been an important theme with each area of performance. We have advanced the notion that an area of performance contains a repertoire and that skillfulness comes in matching choices from it to individuals, groups, and curricula. So it is with pacing and scheduling. The same pace will not work equally well for all classes. Carolyn Evertson (1982) found that the way teachers paced activities varied greatly and corresponded to their success with high and low performing classes, but they made quite a difference in low-performing groups. Students in low-performing classes have a clear tendency to drop in and out of participation, especially during seatwork. Some students refuse to participate at all. Evertson (1982) provides descriptions and commentary on two junior high teachers' classrooms to show how differences in pacing affect low-performing students.

Example 1: Teacher B and the disrupted classroom

> [The teacher has just put the seatwork assignment on the board.] Marie says, "I don't have a book." The teacher says, "Look on those shelves," pointing. Marie says, "Those aren't ours." The teacher says, "Some of

> them are." Marie gets herself a book. Chico raises his hand and says, "I need help." About five students start the assignment right away. [There are twelve students present.] The others are talking, have their hands raised, or are going to the teacher's desk. The teacher says, "Come on up, Randy," when she calls on him. When he gets there, "Larry, leave him alone." Larry stands and visits by the teacher's desk. Chico puts his hand up again. The teacher says, "Chico, what do you need?" He says, "Help." The teacher says, "Okay, wait a second." Larry sits down by the teacher's desk and looks on as she tells him something. Chico calls out, "Miss, are you going to help me?" She says, "Yes, Chico, but come up here." He says, "Aw, Miss, it's too far." The teacher ignores him, and he goes to the teacher's desk. [At this point, five students are at the teacher's desk.] (Evertson, 1982, p. 182)

This classroom description shows rather dramatically the difficulty students in a lower-performing class can have in getting started and participating successfully in an activity. At one point, five students were at the teacher's desk, and most of them were waiting for help. The teacher eventually helped nine students at her desk during this seatwork activity. Having so many students in such close proximity to each other frequently created problems and led to misbehavior which the teacher was forced to respond to.

The dialogue also illustrates the poor task orientation that generally characterizes the lower-performing classroom. Chico's behavior here is typical of many other students who are behind. He did not take academic activities seriously, he was not willing to begin work on learning tasks, and he was not interested in participating. Poor task orientation on the part of one student can lead to disruptive behavior from others, as we find when we continue this activity:

> While the teacher is trying to work with Marie, Marie follows Chico's lead in teasing the teacher. She grabs the stapler. The teacher says loudly, "Uh uh, come on, Marie." Later, Marie grabs her paper away from the teacher, wads it up, saying, "You wrote on my paper. You're not supposed to write on my paper." Marie sits down. Billy, meanwhile, has continued to play around and talk to Larry. The teacher says sharply, "Billy, you come up here!" Larry says loudly, "That's exactly what Miss ____ says, and it works for her, too." As Billy scoots his desk up, Larry sings, "Row, row, row your desk." (Evertson, 1982, p. 182)

When the teacher had to give individual attention to so many students, she could not monitor the class efficiently, and it was more difficult for the students to get the teacher's attention according to the prescribed procedure:

> Chico, who has his hand up, calls out, "Miss, I can't wait forever." The teacher says, "Just a minute." Mark yells loudly, "Miss!" The teacher ignores him and continues helping Marie. Then she goes to Pam, who has had her hand up for a long time. A girl calls out from the front of the room, "I need help." She has her hand up, but she calls out. The teacher looks at her and says, "Okay, I'll be there in a second." (Evertson, 1982, p. 182)

It should be noted that two of these students do not simply call out; they have their hands raised. However, they know that simply raising their hands is not as effective a signal as calling out. The teacher did not consistently enforce (in fact, hardly enforced at all) the rule against calling out under these circumstances:

> Chico calls out, "What time is it?" Billy tells him what time it is. The teacher ignores them both. Billy and Chico are trading epithets like, "Dumb head." The teacher, helping the girls near the front, ignores them. Then, she looks up and says, "Chico, do you need something else to do?" Chico says, "No." The teacher says, "Then be quiet." (Evertson, 1982, p. 182)

A basic conflict existed in lower-performing classes between two demands of the teacher: (1) the need to help students, and (2) the need to control disruptive behavior. In this example, the teacher did not want to interrupt her interchange with the girls near the front, but she was finally forced to respond when the off-task behavior threatened to become disruptive.

Example 2: Teacher F and the productive classroom

The comparatively high achievement gain of Teacher F's lower-performing class recommends it for closer examination. Teacher F allocated considerably more time for checking and discussion of work (13.7 minutes) and the presentation of material—lecture or introduction to seatwork (14.4 minutes)—and considerably less time for the final seatwork activity (22.5 minutes) than was characteristic of the lower-performing classes in general. In addition, the lecture or introductory phase of seatwork was structured differently, frequently punctuated by two or more very brief, highly focused seatwork activities. In this class, the lecture or introduction to the final seatwork activity usually exhibited the following pattern:

> Teacher F goes to the board, where there are 25 numbers written, and begins rounding off the first one. He has the students do this on paper. He says, "I want you to do the first five." They are in columns of five. He continues, "Then put your pencils down." They are writing these numbers down and he moves around the room. He stops the class (after about

> 6 minutes) and asks David what his answers were. David frowns and says that he didn't get anything. "Who can help him out?" asks the teacher. Robert says, "I got it." The teacher moves on to the rest of the column and then goes on to the A column which should be rounded to the nearest hundredth. The students then do this column. Kermit calls out, "Are we going to have homework, too?" The teacher says, "I'll assign that in a minute." Kermit says, "Well, we don't have time to work on it if we're going to do all of these." Teacher F says, "Oh, we are not going to do all of these." The teacher goes to the board and asks for the students' attention and begins to go through the second column. He asks Jackie to help him round off the first, and she says she didn't get it. He says, "I just asked you to help." She looks at it and begins to try it. He walks her through the problem. [At this point, when there are approximately 10 minutes left, the teacher gives the seatwork assignment.] (Evertson, 1982, p. 182)

This is another instance of interruption by brief seatwork periods:

> [The teacher] says that they will be talking about addition of decimals. He says that this is not really much different than adding whole numbers. The teacher has Johnny write the first problem out for him. He says to him, "Tell me what to put down." Johnny adds three and two and says that it's five. Then he adds six and nine and says that it's 15; put down the five and carry the one. The teacher then asks him, "Where do I put the one? Down here?" Johnny says, "No, you put the one over the eight." Then he adds the eight and gets nine. He tells him to put the decimal between the nine and the five. When he's through, the teacher says, "Very good." The teacher then starts asking them review questions on decimals. As he asks questions, he reminds students to "Raise your hands and tell me what place the decimal is in." The teacher calls on Gracie to do the second example on the board. She declines, and then the teacher goes on to call on Edward. Edward works through the problem and then says, "Tell me what's wrong." The teacher says to him, "Well, let's find out. How can we tell?" The students call out that they can subtract to check. At 9:28 the teacher puts up a third example. He tells the class that they'll be doing the assignment on their papers, and that they should go ahead and do number three to see if they can get it right. The teacher starts walking around checking to see if students are getting the problem right. There's some quiet talking in the room and the teacher is still walking around. At 9:41 the teacher says, "Let's look up here." (He works the problem on the board. After that, he assigns them another problem to do at their seats and walks around checking them.) (Evertson, 1982, p. 182)

Teacher F copes with the problem of sustaining seatwork in his lower-performing classes by incorporating some of the seatwork into the lecture (or introduction to seatwork) in very brief segments, placing the responsibility for maintaining lesson continuity with the students for only a very brief period of time. The advantages of this format appear clear. First, a brief seatwork activity is more likely to have a high task orientation than an extended activity. Surrounding seatwork periods with lecture allows the more easily maintained lesson continuity of the lecture to help support seatwork. Second, these brief seatwork activities incorporated into the lecture enable the teacher to provide more immediate feedback than extended seatwork activities. The teacher can thus modify explanations during the lecture if necessary rather than interrupt a long seatwork activity, as frequently happens in lower-performing classes.

In summary, the lower-performing class of Teacher F presents an important contrast with Teacher B's lower-performing class. Teacher B had a significantly longer seatwork period and shorter checking and lecture activities, possibly adding to her difficulties, inasmuch as seatwork is often a problematic activity in lower-performing classes. In contrast, Teacher F minimized this problem in his lower-performing class by reducing the length of independent seatwork activity, which contributed significantly to the higher task orientation of his class, as determined by observer ratings. The comparison suggests that long, extended seatwork activities are counterproductive, adding to management problems and minimizing good task orientation in low-performing classes.

Many middle and high school teachers have both high- and low-performing classes in their schedule. Are they able to make adjustments, as Teacher F above did, and pace classes differently for different groups? That is what we mean by pacing and rhythm. One can look to see if time is structured for certain individuals, as Teacher F did for a whole class. And the reasons for varying it certainly go beyond the global word ability. In the Evertson (1982) study, "ability" really meant achievement on California Achievement Tests. There was a distinction between high- and low-performing classes. There are many reasons for high and low performance besides native ability, with its implication about intelligence. Very capable, but easily distracted, students may learn best when their pacing is regulated for short bursts of highly focused activities. Skillful teachers look to create such arrangements for those who need it, while the rest of the class may be paced quite differently.

Most secondary teachers who make the shift from the traditional seven-period day to block scheduling find themselves needing to re-examine how they pace and chunk the period to maintain student engagement. It is not a question of whether students can stay focused for 75 to 80 minutes but rather how the activities in the overall period are structured and balanced that counts. This might be length of time; balance of information input, processing, and output; opportunities for physical movement at least every half hour or so; and variety in interaction complexity (working alone, working interactively, participating in large group).

SUPPORTING STUDENTS WITH ADD/ADHD

Another area of exploration regarding time and pacing has to do with students who are diagnosed with attention deficit disorder (ADD) or attention deficit hyperactivity disorder (ADHD). Educators and medical professionals have expressed serious concern over the rapidly increasing percentage of students diagnosed with and medicated for ADHD. Data from CDC (2017) validates those concerns:

- ▲ Approximately 11% of children 4–17 years of age (6.4 million) have ever been diagnosed with ADHD as of 2011. The average age of ADHD diagnosis was 7 years of age. Boys (13.2%) were more likely than girls (5.6%) to have ever been diagnosed with ADHD.

- ▲ The percentage of children with an ADHD diagnosis increased from 7.8% in 2003 to 9.5% in 2007 and to 11.0% in 2011. Less than 1 in 3 children with ADHD received both medication treatment and behavior therapy, the preferred treatment approach for children ages 6 and older.

- ▲ Prevalence of ADHD diagnosis varied substantially by state, from a low of 5.6% in Nevada to a high of 18.7% in Kentucky.

In *Ritalin Nation: Rapid Fire Culture and the Transformation of Human Consciousness* (DeGrandpre, 1999), psychologist Richard DeGrandpre argues that ADHD has more to do with changes in time expectations in our society than better diagnosis of a physiological problem. Chip Wood (1999) wrote:

> I see children who exhibit ADHD behaviors as suffering from temporal trauma. Sadly, they are serving as "canaries" in the cage of time, especially in our schools, where their failure to thrive should tell us something about their environment.
>
> School schedules speed up year after year, putting more and more pressure on children to manage a world filled with more transitions, extended curricula, less predictability, and less time to accomplish more. It's tough on all children, but for these "canaries" who have a heightened sensitivity to time pressures, it's impossible. Our society and schools are faced with

two possibilities. One is medicating more and more children in an effort to decrease their sensitivity to our ever faster, less regulated pace of life and education. Another is making changes in the structure and pace of school life to reduce temporal trauma for all of our children. (p. 23)

WAYS TO REALIZE TIME RELATED GOALS IN THE CLASSROOM

Clearly there is a lot to consider when it comes to this area of performance. At various points throughout this chapter, we have mentioned ways in which time issues are intertwined with other areas of performance in teaching. Tables 8.2, 8.3, and 8.4 summarize areas of performance that relate specifically to managing time efficiently and in service of supporting student learning and achievement.

Table 8.2 Goal 1: Minimize Non-Instructional Time and Develop Efficient Management Systems

Establish routines and procedures	Develop a plan for dealing with housekeeping issues (lunch count, attendance, permission slips, cleanup, announcements) so these don't compete with instructional time. (Routines)
Delegate jobs	Teach students how to do some of the management tasks you would ordinarily do (wheeling the overhead projector into place, distributing and collecting materials, changing desk arrangements, or moving furniture to match the planned activity for the day) to reduce setup time and maximize the amount of time guiding their learning.
Reward efficiency	Recognize and reward students who are using time wisely and managing it well.
Have instructional materials ready and supplies conveniently available	Students can access and return them independently and efficiently. (Momentum: Provisioning, Space)
Allow sufficient time for transitions	Avoid a harried pace, but challenge students to be efficient, and teach them how to implement routines that save time. (Routines, Space, Momentum)
Minimize time spent on discipline issues	Deal with disruptions and off-task behavior quickly, directly, privately when possible, and with the minimum it takes to get the students back on track. (Attention, Discipline)

Table 8.3 Goal 2: Manage Pacing and Rhythm During Instructional Time

Give notice before transitions	Provide students with advance notice when they have been cognitively or physically engaged in a task or activity so they have time to shift gears. (Momentum)
Start and end lessons on time with meaningful activities	The opening and closing minutes of lessons are the moments that are most naturally remembered. (Principle of Learning: Sequence)
Plan for active engagement during the opening and closing minutes of the class	During opening minutes activate knowledge for an upcoming lesson, recall or practice something previously taught, or record objectives for the class in their notes and during closing minutes by summarizing and reflecting on what they have learned in class that day, answering a question related to the day's objective. Or use the closing minutes to give assignments slowly and carefully, to pose challenging dilemmas for students to ponder (end without closure), or to get personal involvement or commitments from students on controversial issues or on contracts. The main point is to use them, not lose them, by giving sharp focus and purpose to the beginning and ending minutes.
Have short independent opening assignments	Establish a routine where students anticipate coming into class and starting immediately and independently on a 3- to 5-minute opening assignment. (Principle of Learning: Similarity of Environment)
Calibrate time thoughtfully, and help students monitor it	When there is an activity students are expected to complete within a time frame, make sure it is a reasonable time frame, let them know what it is at the outset, and provide them with a way to monitor their pace accordingly (for example, a transparent timer on a whiteboard, intermittent pacing reminders, or student timekeepers within groups).
Pause for students to process and make meaning	Pause every 8 to 10 minutes of direct instruction, and require students to process what they have been hearing, seeing, or doing so they have an opportunity to absorb it, register it in memory, and connect existing knowledge with incoming information. (Principle of Learning)
Pulse the learning	Balance or chunk periods of direct instruction and information input with independent or small group opportunities for students to practice, apply, and get feedback and support with new learning tasks. Consider the length of chunks that are best suited to the performance level of the learners and the complexity of the material, and volley between input and guided practice accordingly.
Allow time for thinking	After posing instructional questions to all students, pause and protect at least 3 to 5 seconds of silence so all have the opportunity to process what the question is asking and to construct a thoughtful response (Wait Time I). Pause again after a student answers to allow the response to be heard and absorbed by all and to give the student time to extend, modify, or elaborate on the thoughts she has expressed. (Wait Time II)
Plan for physical movement	If a learning experience requires students to sit still for long stretches, plan ways for them to get intermittent physical movement (for example, stand and share, find a learning partner or other processing activities that require movement) at least every thirty to forty minutes to keep their brains functioning at their highest capacity. (Brain research on cognition)

Table 8.4 Goal 3: Maximize Engaged and Academic Learning Time

Balance the interaction complexity	Strike a balance between whole-class, small-group, paired, and individual learning time. Different learners have natural preferences, and too much of any one format can be a hindrance to learning. (Differentiated Instruction)
Prepare students for independent work	Be clear in your explanation of what is expected, and have students summarize directions and expectations with partners to avoid confusion and helplessness when they are expected to begin the work. When appropriate, have students attempt an example while you circulate, and check understanding before assigning a longer period of independent work to ensure that engaged time becomes academic learning time.
Involve students in modeling and demonstrating work (being the teacher)	Do this prior to or after independent practice while you act as a guide on the side. It enables you to check understanding and keep students more actively participating.
Monitor independent work	When students are working independently (alone or in small groups), consider it an opportunity to gather assessment data to inform instruction. Monitor the learning by walking around to find out how they are doing and to provide guidance and feedback, which will keep them on track and increase the amount of high success time for all of them.
Accommodate different rates of task completion	Plan learning experiences so there can be some flexibility with the length of time individual students have to master skills or concepts and the degree of guidance they receive while doing so.
Have relevant and meaningful supplemental work ready for students who finish tasks early	Often this requires planning for and managing more than one concurrent activity that students work on during an instructional period. (See Momentum: Fillers and Overlapping, Differentiated Instruction.)
Collect data on how time is actually being used	This allows you to make informed adjustments to allocate time to maximize learning time.

WAYS TO REALIZE TIME-RELATED GOALS AT THE SCHOOL LEVEL

If you are a school administrator, you have a role to play in prioritizing and protecting learning time in your school's classrooms. Here are a few suggestions for how you might do that:

- ▲ **Prioritize allocated time.** Develop agreements about how much time should be allocated in the schedule for various subjects and curricular areas. Encourage teachers to collect data about how time is spent in their classrooms.

- ▲ **Protect instructional time.** Minimize or eliminate disruptions and intrusions into classrooms during instructional time; develop alternative ways to relay messages, make announcements, and touch base with teachers.

There are probably no teachers anywhere who feel satisfied that they have had sufficient contact time with students to be able to accomplish all that they hope to, or all that they are expected to, in a given class period, day, or year. What we have tried to do in this chapter is (1) show how multifaceted this area of performance is, (2) suggest some ways in which one might thoughtfully and intentionally examine how students are spending this valuable resource, and (3) encourage the collection of concrete data in order to discover ways in which we can take increasing control of time in school to get the highest rate of return on student achievement. To quote a respected colleague, "The quality of our teaching is what changes time in the classroom. As teachers we have the power to control the clock even if we often feel like the clock is controlling us" (Wood, 1999, p. 217).

CHAPTER QUICK GUIDE

Five Categories of School Time:

1. Allocated time
2. Teacher instructional time
3. Student engaged time
4. Academic learning time
5. Interactive instruction

Three Time-Related Classroom Goals:

1. Minimize non-instructional time and develop efficient management systems.
2. Manage pacing and rhythm during instructional time.
3. Maximize engaged and academic learning time.

To check your knowledge about Time, see the exercises on *The Skillful Teacher* website at www.RBTeach.com/TST7.

NOTES

CHAPTER 9

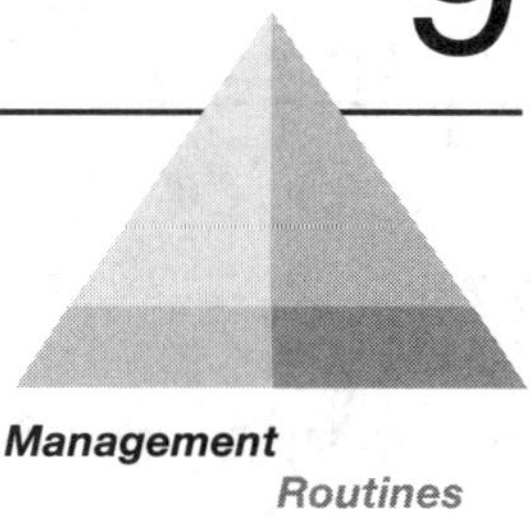

Management:
Routines

Where would we be without routines in our daily lives? We have routines for getting up and ready for the day, routines for finding and storing important items at home and at work, and so on. We all have hundreds of them that we practice unconsciously when dealing with everyday recurring events or situations. Clearly, routines are essential to our daily lives. They become layered one on another, operate automatically, and free us to maximize the time and energy we have to spend on more thoughtful and interesting endeavors. For these and many other reasons, well-thought-out procedures and established routines are vital to successful classrooms. Or as high school art teacher and author Michael Linsin (2014) puts it, "Routines are the lifeblood of a well-run classroom."

Classroom routines reflect well-rehearsed procedures thoughtfully designed to nurture a positive learning environment where students experience both cognitive and affective payoffs.

Classroom routines reflect well-rehearsed procedures thoughtfully designed to nurture a positive learning environment where students experience both cognitive and affective payoffs. The routines we establish include ones related to housekeeping, safety and operational procedures, work habits and procedures, developing social skills and behaviors, and academic processes. Procedures become routines when students do them automatically without prompting or supervision (Wong & Wong, 2009). Thus procedures need to be clear, efficient, and directly taught. They must be modeled for students and practiced by them to ensure that they fully understand them.

Embedded in the routines we establish, and in how we support students in mastering them, are expectation messages about what we think is important and our belief in students' capacity to achieve the standards of performance we set for them. Do our routines represent respectful and challenging standards of performance from students? A very important overall question to consider also is how our procedures and routines reflect an understanding of and respect for the cultures of our students and the values they bring with them to school. These are the dimensions of routines we explore in this chapter.

WHY ARE ROUTINES IMPORTANT?

Routines provide security because they provide a sense of order and predictability.

"All students have some characteristics in common; one of the most significant is the need for structured time. From energetic kindergartners to sophisticated seniors, students need routines in their school day to keep them on track" (Thompson, 2007, p. 88). Whether it is how to enter class and be ready for the day (whether or not the teacher is visibly present), or how to secure materials without the aid of the teacher, routines provide students with a sense of order, predictability, and efficacy that they can manage and control things.

On the first day of school, Danielle Conway greets her first graders one by one while assigning a number that coincides with their alphabetic position in the class roster. Their first task, as they enter the room, is to use their number to find the desk with the matching number along with their name plate. During that first morning, students will learn that their number will also guide them to their designated space in the coat closet, and to know their line-up position when the class is going somewhere together. They will learn where and how to store their snacks in one basket and their lunches on the shelf. They will practice how to unpack, empty, and store their backpacks, in an orderly way, in the coat closet ("sitting up tall and all going this way") and how to line up in numerical order. Before the end of the day, they will practice where to get mail and where to insert it in their green "take home" folder (left is the "keep it home" side and right is "return to school"). As the days progress, they will practice what it means to "get started" in the morning, how to sit during partner reading, how to do their weekly job assignment, the morning work routine, how to lead their classmates in the daily calendar activities, and many more procedures that recur daily. The closing to this chapter captures in one substitute's note the overall impact of all of this on the students. Routines provide security because they provide a sense of order and predictability. When they don't have it otherwise in their lives, this sense of order and predictability is a cornerstone of what makes some of our students want to come to school.

Procedures communicate and clarify our expectations for students. The extent to which we practice them with students until they are learned, communicates our conviction that they are important and we believe students can do them.

> Knowing what to expect makes you comfortable; not knowing what to expect is when you have anxiety. It is such a simple thing to be consistent; students know what they need to do (to get started for class). If they get started without me, then I know I have done my job. (Meghan Conley, HS Chemistry teacher)

Procedures and routines minimize downtime and delays and maximize time for learning. In Ms. Conley's chemistry class, students enter the room, pick up their name cards on a side table (this serves as attendance taking) and place them on their desks (which enables the teacher and classmates to learn names quickly at the beginning of a semester, thus contributing to a more personal classroom climate and sense of community); work to be submitted goes in the "in-tray" on the windowsill; extra handouts from earlier in the week are in colored and labeled folders on the supplies table for students to access; completed homework is on the right side of students' desks; planners or notebooks are open to today's date; the focus question or learning target of the day and the assignments due for next class are posted on the board and students are copying them into their notebooks while those who finish first are copying their solution to a homework problem on the board. If it is a lab day, students are reading over the lab with a focus question that they will be answering at the end of class as their "ticket to leave" and gathering the materials they will need for the lab. In either case, three minutes into the class period we haven't heard anything from the teacher, yet all students are settled and either reading, writing, or comparing their solutions to those put on the board by classmates. This whole procedure is aimed at saving both student and teacher time, eliminating the "what do I do with . . ." or "where can I get . . ." time-killer questions at the beginning of class, maximizing engagement from the minute the bell rings, and freeing the teacher to circulate, gather data about homework (Has it been attempted? Is it complete? Where are the struggles? What needs to be reviewed or retaught?), and touch base with individual students.

Routines can be used to teach and help students develop skills such as self-management, self-control, and self-direction.

Routines can be used to teach and help students develop self-regulation skills such as self-management, self-control, and self-direction. These skills "help students engage in behaviors such as attending, participating, following directions, organizing, managing materials and time, and completing assignments—behaviors associated with increased academic and social performance across a variety of subjects and school levels" (Korinek, 2016, p. 232). For example, when students are taught how to routinely use organizational tools (schedules, planners, notebooks, checklists) where they regularly record and monitor assignments or keep track of books read, steps they have completed in a project, time spent on tasks or assignments, and so on, they are learning transferrable organization skills. We can help students develop time management skills by teaching them to use a visual timer to pace themselves in completing a task or to monitor when it is time to transition from one center (or one activity) to another.

Some teachers use a piece of music to signal the beginning and end of transition time or the time within which a task has to be completed with the expectation that students will learn to pace themselves accordingly. High school art teacher and author Michael Linsin (2014) makes the case for using music when implementing routines as a way to "add energy and bounce . . . a productive whirl of movement, of intent and purpose . . . and promote a spirit of cooperation and liveliness among (our) students." In his blog post *How to Use Music to Make Routines More Fun and Effective* (Linsin, 2014), he elaborates on the importance of choosing the music to fit the particular routine:

> What's so cool about this strategy is that the music both cues the start of the routine and sees to its conclusion . . . It acts as a timing device, moving students along as they hustle to complete their responsibilities before the song ends.

While there are many sources of free downloadable music available on the web, Linsin mentions three sites he uses as resources for this purpose: *Sound Project 2014*, *freeplay*, and *Televisiontunes.com.*

Routines can be curriculum by virtue of their particular purposes and the learning embedded in them. Designed thoughtfully and deliberately, they can support what many would call the hidden curriculum: the indirect personal and social learning students receive just from being present in a particular classroom where the teacher has what we like to call "Overarching Objectives" (see Chapter 22). Personal learning refers to students learning something about themselves or some ability that might be described in terms of character development rather than skill. Social learning refers to students' learning something about others, groups, or people together (e.g., cooperation, sharing). Programs such as Responsive Classroom (www.responsiveclassroom.org) and Open Circle (Wellesley College Stone Center at www.open-circle.org) are full of routines where students learn and practice personal and social skills such as how to greet each other, how to compliment and receive compliments, how to apologize, and so on. See Chapter 16, "Classroom Climate," for more about these programs and how we make this type of hidden curriculum an explicit agenda in our classrooms.

Videos: Entering Class & First 5 Minutes

ROUTINES AND PROCEDURES FOR WHAT?

The Routines area of performance encompasses a variety of kinds of classroom procedures.

Housekeeping:

- ▲ How to enter the classroom, empty and store backpacks, organize coats and boots, and get ready for class.
- ▲ The first 5 minutes.

- ▲ How attendance (lunch count, etc.) will be taken.
- ▲ How and where to access supplies and replenish them when necessary.
- ▲ How to clean up after working in an area (lab station, center, project area, etc.).
- ▲ How to do various housekeeping jobs that will be assigned throughout the term.
- ▲ How to clean and organize your desk or cubby.

Safety and Operational Features of Class Business:

- ▲ Attention signals for making announcements.
- ▲ Noise level control.
- ▲ Leaving the room.
- ▲ Turn-taking.
- ▲ Lining up.
- ▲ Population limits at centers, work area, lab stations, etc.
- ▲ How to carry chairs, scissors, pencils.
- ▲ When and how pencils are sharpened.
- ▲ How to get supplies you are missing/forgot to bring.
- ▲ How to sit in a desk or where to sit in a meeting area.
- ▲ How to set up, use, and care for lab equipment.
- ▲ Emergency procedures (fire drills, lockdowns, etc.).

Work Habits and Work Procedures:

- ▲ How to enter the room and get ready for class.
- ▲ What to do when you finish work early.

- What to do when you have a question, are confused, or need help with something.
- Procedures for using an easel, computers, and other equipment.
- Where to submit assignments.
- How to use a timetable and milestone chart of events to track your progress and be checked by the teacher when you are preparing for oral presentations or a term paper.
- How class ends or what to do when the bell rings.
- How to get into and work in pairs or small groups.
- How to set up and manage your notebook or planner.
- What to do when you have missed class.
- Where to find handouts or missed assignments due to absence.
- How you can participate in and contribute to a class discussion.

Developing Social or Personal Skills:

Video: Learning Positions

- How to give and receive compliments.
- How to ensure that everyone is included and participating in small groups.
- How to greet one another or refer to a classmate.
- How to show you are really listening when a classmate is talking.

Academics:

- Weekly goal setting and self-assessment of progress toward the goal.
- How to lead calendar time, and what we do and in what sequence.
- How to present your work to the class.
- What form to use when preparing for discussions.

- ▲ Where and how to sign up for extra help before requesting a retake on an assignment or quiz.

- ▲ How to share your work with peers and get and give feedback to improve it.

When skillfully performed, all of these routines are valuable ways of organizing and managing a class while developing student skills, self-discipline, and self-management.

COMMUNICATING AND DIRECTLY TEACHING PROCEDURES

A first set of questions to ask about the use of routines is, Do the students know clearly *what's expected* of them in the way of procedures and routines? Do they know what they're supposed to do?

"Since a procedure explains how you (teacher) want something done it is the responsibility of the teacher to have procedures clearly stated" (Wong & Wong, 2009, p. 170). Effective communication requires behaviors similar to those for communicating expectations for work, including:

It is the responsibility of the teacher to have procedures clearly stated.

- ▲ Being direct: procedures are explicitly brought to students' attention.

- ▲ Being specific: all important details are explained.

- ▲ Communicating with positive expectancy: a "you can do it" flavor.

The next set of questions is, Do students know *how* to do what is expected? One of the most common misconceptions about routines is that procedures can simply be announced and that students should know how to behave by now. "Procedures become routines when students do them automatically without prompting or supervision" (Wong & Wong, 2009, p. 170). A routine is a well-rehearsed procedure designed by us. Therefore, it must be taught (Exhibit 9.1).

Direct teaching of a procedure includes the following:

- ▲ Modeling for students to see exactly what it looks like in action.

- ▲ Practicing until the procedure is mastered.

- ▲ Tenaciously adhering to it until integrated.

- Reinforcement to make sure students absorb it and know that we consider it important.

In short, to establish routines we need to communicate procedures clearly, teach them directly, ensure that students understand and can practice them effectively, and revisit or have students practice them again when we notice they are slipping. Here are some additional thoughts to consider about procedures and routines:

- Along with teaching a procedure, provide the rationale for why it is important and how it will be beneficial to students.
- Plan strategically which procedures to introduce when and how many to introduce at once. Korinek (2016) states:

  > Rather than simultaneously opening all specialty areas, centers, or equipment in the classroom for independent student use . . . strategically focus on a limited number of areas, model their use, and practice with feedback to ensure most students are using spaces and materials appropriately prior to introducing new options (Brown, 2013; Kenworthy et al., 2014). (p. 234)

- Post procedures for students to reference when they are still not sure what to do.
- To support students with limited reading skills due to age, disability, or language differences, add pictures along with words to allow students to be increasingly independent in following a procedure.
- Notice and acknowledge when students are practicing routines effectively. Catch them doing well rather than focusing on what they aren't doing.
- Periodically, evaluate how well routines are working and whether you are getting the most mileage out of them. Take action when they need to be revisited, reviewed, or practiced again with feedback.
- Include students in assessing the effectiveness of the routine and in deciding what needs to happen to improve or modify it.

Exhibit 9.1 Teaching a Routine

1. **Explain:**
   a. Define the procedure in concrete terms and give a reason for it.
   b. Demonstrate the procedure; don't just tell.
   c. Demonstrate a complex procedure step by step.
2. **Rehearse:**
   a. Have students practice the procedure, step by step, under your supervision. After each step, make sure that the students have performed the step correctly.
   b. Have the students repeat the procedure until it becomes a routine. The students should be able to perform the procedure automatically without teacher supervision.
3. **Reinforce:**
   a. Determine whether students have learned the procedure or whether they need further explanation, demonstration, or practice.
   b. Reteach the correct procedure if rehearsal is unacceptable and give corrective feedback.
   c. Praise the students when the rehearsal is acceptable.

The routines we establish and reinforce with students communicate to them what we think is important and believe they are capable of doing.

ARE OUR STANDARDS APPROPRIATE?

The routines we establish and reinforce with students communicate to them what we think is important and what we believe they are capable of doing. We use the word "standard" to represent the level of challenge or rigor embedded in a procedure. We use the word "expectation" to represent the level of conviction we have—and communicate to our students—about their ability to meet the standard we set. Hence, another critical set of questions to consider is about the appropriateness of the standards inherent in the routines we establish. Are the standards challenging yet attainable for students? When a standard is challenging (but attainable) students will have to rise to a new level and develop their capacity in order to meet the challenge. Thus when students demonstrate mastery of a routine they have reason to take pride in their accomplishment. If students aren't successfully implementing a routine might it be because the standards we set are unreasonably high? Or conversely, are the standards we set so low that students aren't taking them seriously? Are they clear? And finally, what support structures are in place for the few students who will need initial scaffolding in order to perform a routine successfully? In Danielle Berwick's first grade class, students enter class, immediately take out their planners, and copy in the homework for that night that is posted on the board (e.g., "Study your spelling words," or "Read for 10 minutes," etc.). One student in her class had very challenging attention issues. He couldn't focus long enough to look at the board and look back at his planner and get the message copied. After a couple of weeks of both teacher and students struggling for up to 30 minutes to hold him accountable to do this, Ms. Berwick consulted with her instructional support team. Together, they developed a plan: create labels that match the homework assignments for the week, place them on the ledge under the message from the board, and have him go and find the label that matched the posted homework message instead of having him copy the message. Once he did so, he could bring it back to his seat and post it in his planner. Not only did this result in his getting the homework into his planner as was required of all students, but it did away with the frustration for both teacher and student, and sometimes he actually began to ask to try again to copy the message into his planner. Sometimes students just need a little support to be able to successfully execute a routine that is otherwise appropriate for the majority.

ARE THE STANDARDS EMBEDDED IN OUR PROCEDURES?

As with standards for the quality and quantity of academic work we set for students, standards for work habits, procedures, and routines can be analyzed using the following scale:

- High but reasonable: demanding but attainable by all students?
- Matched: appropriate for most students and scaffolded for others where necessary?
- Too high: Are we demanding too much of students?
- Too low: Are we demanding less of students than they are capable of?
- Confusing: inconsistent or unclear to students?
- Non-existent?

See Chapter 14, "Expectations," for expanded definitions of each of these standards and a discussion of various levels of matching.

Table 9.1 Self-Assessment of Classroom Routines

	True?
1. No routines are established for relevant events; I react on an ad hoc basis.	
2. A few routines are erratically followed.	
3. Stable routines exist for most relevant events, with evidence of student training.	
4. Stable and highly efficient routines are in place for all relevant events.	
5. Routines are varied. I modify, experiment with, and use alternative forms to achieve the purpose.	
6. Routines are matched to the group; they vary from class to class.	
7. Routines are varied or scaffolded to match characteristics of individuals and mapped to goals for them.	

ANALYZING WHERE WE ARE WITH ROUTINES

The scale shown in Table 9.1 is a basis with which we can analyze and assess our current level of performance when it comes to classroom routines. This scale spans a range of answers to the question, Why are my routines the way they are? They may serve efficiency, a valid and common orientation. They may serve a general goal, such as giving students security through the predictability of certain recurring events. They may map to more specific goals for groups or for the class as a whole, such as having students routinely record books they have read in a register so that they take some responsibility for a form of record-keeping and get to see and participate in building a cumulative index of their books read; or assigning teams to areas of the room for cleanup so that the children have to come to grips with group responsibility, handling the division of labor, and dealing with individuals who won't carry their weight. Exhibit 9.2 lists the elements of an effective routine.We may create or adjust routines in the service of objectives for specific individuals. For example, in a primary-grade class, Gabriella may start each day by taking down a few chairs and then moving into woodworking or clay (something with a motor emphasis), whereas Diego's starting routine may be worked out to reflect academics and time in a private space. In an older class in which students are routinely expected to check the board for morning assignments or for feedback from previous work, Annelyse may need a personal "greet and escort" over to the board or a folder of her own in which this information is placed. Tenth-grader Nico may be asked to end each study hall with a log entry on what he has accomplished as a way of focusing him. Braden may be asked to arrange the furniture for committee work at the beginning of each social studies period, as a way of settling him down (and getting him to class on time).

Exhibit 9.2 Elements of an Effective Routine

An effective routine is

- efficient,
- clear,
- communicated with positive expectancy ("You CAN do it. You WILL do it."),
- taught to mastery (i.e., modeled, repeated, and practiced until it is internalized and no longer a "nag"),
- matched to a purpose and group, and
- sometimes matched to individuals where appropriate and necessary.

HOW IS CULTURE REFLECTED IN OUR ROUTINES?

In *Managing Diverse Classrooms: How to Build on Students' Cultural Strengths,* Rothstein-Fisch and Trumbull (2008) share an in-depth account of the Bridging Cultures Project, a project that was created to support teachers to use cultural knowledge to increase the educational success of their students. Working in collaboration with a group of seven teachers (who became researchers in their own classrooms and schools) where immigrant Latino students from Mexico and Central America constituted the majority, they report that:

> The result of the teacher's efforts is a mountain of innovation: a collection of strategies and ideas for classroom organization that are completely field-tested by teachers who have come to understand the central role of culture in learning and teaching. The teachers did not set out to explore classroom management, yet it became the first thing that they changed as a result of their new understanding of the cultural values of their students. (p. xiv)

It is not possible to do justice to summarizing all that Rothstein-Fisch and Trumbull's findings offer us in the short space of this chapter; for anyone who is interested in developing capacity in this area, the entire book is worth a good read. Instead, here we will share some highlights that might be useful in bringing a cultural lens to examining the appropriateness of our routines and how we teach them to students, with an eye to ensuring that none of our students is put in a compromised position where they have to act in opposition to what they have come to believe is the appropriate way to be.

One framework for understanding culture (that served as the foundation of the Bridging Cultures study) focuses on some very fundamental differences

Exhibit 9.3 The Individualism/Collectivism Framework

Individualism	Collectivism
Representative or mainstream: United States, Western Europe, Australia, and Canada	Representative of 70% of world cultures (Triandis, 1989), including those of many U.S. immigrants
Well-being of individual; responsibility for self	Well-being of group; Responsibility for group
Independence/self-reliance	Interdependence/cooperation
Individual achievement	Family/group success
Self-expression	Respect
Self-esteem	Modesty
Talk orientation	Social orientation
Cognitive intelligence	Social intelligence

Adapted from Rothstein-Fisch & Trumbull (2008, p. 9)

between two types of cultural orientations: individualistic and collectivistic. Rothstein-Fisch and Trumbull (2008) explain the differences:

> The fundamental distinction between these two systems is the relative emphasis placed on individual versus group well-being . . . it is not a matter of valuing one or the other—individual or group—but rather the degree of emphasis accorded to each. (p. 9)

Exhibit 9.3 summarizes some of the most important contrasts between the systems. Acknowledging that although this framework has limitations (as is true of any framework), Rothstein-Fisch and Trumbull (2008) found it to be "a good place to start in order to grasp major differences among cultures" (p. 19). They report that "using this streamlined framework . . . teachers were able to generate an almost endless array of strategies for working with the students and families they served" (p. 8).

Because these particular teachers were working with students who more typically come from a collectivistic cultural orientation, many of the shifts they made in management strategies were guided by that filter: "an approach to students as a group that takes advantage of its sense of community and desire for group harmony" (Rothstein-Fisch & Trumbull, 2008, p. 101). They prefer to use the term "classroom orchestration" versus "management." Some examples include routines established that involve students carrying on a group activity (versus working independently) if or when the teacher is temporarily absent from the classroom, or transitioning between activities by having all students gather in the meeting area and sing a song together or do a movement exercise. One teacher, who had previously withheld recess as punishment for failure to turn in homework, replaced this with a system in which volunteer students helped their classmates successfully complete missing homework (p. 107).

Another interesting exploration of the ways in which cultural values intersect or conflict with classroom procedures and expectations comes from Weinstein, Curran, and Thompson-Clarke (2003). Here are a few of their examples:

> Because Ms. Frank values collaborative learning, she places her students' desks in clusters and encourages them to help one another. But she spends a lot of time at the beginning of the year explaining to her second graders exactly what that means. She takes pains to distinguish between *helping* and *doing the work* for the other person. She and her students role-play different situations; for example, Ms. Frank pretends she doesn't know how to do a math problem and asks a student for help. Then she asks the class, "Was that good help? Was that *explaining* or was that *doing the work for me*?" Ms. Frank and her students also talk about when it's *not* permissible to help one another. She explains that sometimes work has to be done *independently* so that she can see what people know how to do on their own. Ms. Frank realizes that it's important to be absolutely explicit about the norms for helping in her very diverse classroom. Some of her children have cultural roots in individualistic cultures; it is likely that the values of individual effort and self-sufficiency have been deeply engrained, so these children may resist her efforts to encourage peer assistance. In contrast, the children from more collectivist cultures (e.g., African, Asian, Hispanic, and Native American) have probably been taught the value of providing assistance to others; they may find it difficult to *resist* helping their peers, even when they are directed to work independently. (pp. 271–272)

When we establish norms of behavior, we have to ensure that students understand what the norms mean in terms of specific behavior.

> This is especially critical in culturally diverse classrooms, since different cultures hold different views about appropriate behavior. In some cultures, for example, making eye contact is a sign of respect, while in others respect is communicated by maintaining an averted gaze. Teachers may

> expect children to sit quietly and "listen when someone is talking," but some African American students may be accustomed to a more active, participatory pattern of behavior ("call-response"). (Weinstein, Curran, & Thompson-Clarke, 2003, p. 271)

These are but a few examples of how we might use our understanding of cultural values to guide the design of routines. Clearly, there is far more to culture than this contrast of individualistic versus collectivistic presented here. This is but one example of the relationship between cultural orientation and respectful and effective classroom management. What this underscores is the need for us to continuously develop our awareness of our own cultural orientation (internalized values, assumptions, and beliefs) while simultaneously seeking to better know those of our students, and to use that information collectively to guide the design and implementation of classroom procedures and routines. Cultural proficiency is an essential belief in The Skillful Teacher Framework (see Chapter 2 and Chapter 4).

Rothstein-Fisch and Trumbull (2008) sum it up in this way:

> As teachers we need to know how to examine our own cultural values; develop understanding of the values of others and regard them in a non-judgmental way; and apply what we learn about cultural differences to the improvement of classroom practices. (p. xiv)

ORGANIZED CLASSROOMS ARE EASY TO RECOGNIZE

Routines and procedures are established so that the classroom seems to run automatically. Students know exactly what to do and when to do it (Stronge, 2002, p. 28). When classroom procedures are poorly thought out—or not thought out at all—the results are seen in disorganization, poor momentum, and often discipline problems.

Most important of all, valuable instructional and learning time is lost. At the end of one day in Ms. Conway's first grade classroom, a substitute teacher wrote the following note: "Anytime you need a sub for Ms. Conway's room, call me. I didn't have to do anything. The kids ran the whole day: they knew what to do, how to do it, when to do it. I just followed their lead." On a scale of 1–10, that's a 10 in this area of performance!

CHAPTER QUICK GUIDE

Routines Encompass a Variety of Classroom Procedures:

- ▲ Housekeeping
- ▲ Safety and operational features of class business
- ▲ Work habits and work procedures
- ▲ Developing social or personal skills
- ▲ Academics

How Procedures Become Routines:

- ▲ Modeling procedures for students to see exactly what it looks like in action.
- ▲ Practicing until the procedure is mastered.
- ▲ Tenaciously adhering to it until integrated.
- ▲ Reinforcing to make sure students absorb it and know that it is important.

Cultural Differences Need to Be Reflected:

- ▲ We need to be aware of our own cultural orientation (internalized values, assumptions, and beliefs).
- ▲ We need to better know the cultural orientation of our students and use that information to guide the design and implementation of classroom procedures and routines.

To check your knowledge about Routines, see the exercises on *The Skillful Teacher* website at www.RBTeach.com/TST7.

CHAPTER
10

Management
Discipline

Management:
Discipline

Good student behavior in a classroom derives from many sources. This chapter provides a comprehensive accounting of those sources and how to put them together. It is also a diagnostic map of what could account for off-task students and misbehavior when that occurs, and how to start at root causes to remedy the situation. Think of this topic as having two strands, both contributing to good student behavior:

There is no question that good discipline is a prerequisite for good education.

Strand 1: a set of tools to prevent, diagnose, and treat problem behavior.

Strand 2: a set of tools for building student cooperation and self-discipline.

We also bring in material from other chapters that influences student behavior—Personal Relationship Building, Clarity, and the Management areas of Space, Time, Routines, and Momentum—each of which can cause behavior problems if poorly handled. The sequential map of the two strands is shown in Figure 10.1. It synthesizes the diagnostic sequence we describe in more detail later.

This chapter is also very useful to any teacher implementing PBIS (Positive Behavior Intervention and Supports) because of its concrete detail and examples. The PBIS literature is useful for any school or district that wants to plan carefully and effectively for schoolwide consistency and implementation with fidelity and correct pacing. However, this chapter enables a teacher who wants to carry out PBIS in an individual classroom to go deeply into successful implementation.

"What do I have to do to get students to apply themselves to their work and stop fooling around and being disruptive?" That is the bottom-line question of Discipline. Many teachers spend a disproportionate amount of energy dealing with it. Some then leave teaching because they find they rarely deal with anything else. There is no question that good discipline is a prerequisite for good education. We must bring all of our best knowledge to bear on it to stop the needless dissipation of both teacher and student energy that it causes. We have the knowledge and capability to retire this issue and move on to the question most teachers are more interested in: "How do I build self-discipline and responsibility in my students?" In this chapter, we address both questions. We urge staff developers, principals, and instructional coaches to pay particular attention to this section.

Our approach is organized around the following assumptions:

- ▲ All behavior has an origin or cause.
- ▲ There are at least 12 different causes of inattentive or disruptive behavior.
- ▲ Effective responses to disruptive behavior are chosen from a repertoire to match the cause or causes.
- ▲ Effective discipline is built on a comprehensive approach that includes four levels:

  1. Laying a foundation of sound classroom management, solid instructional design and delivery, and building relationships with students;
  2. Establishing authority by communicating expectations, setting limits, and eliminating disruptions;
  3. Building a strong classroom climate that nurtures cooperation, responsibility, and self-discipline; and
  4. Being familiar with more complex models of discipline that may be necessary to implement with a very small percentage of especially troubled or recalcitrant students.

TWELVE CAUSES OF DISRUPTIVE OR INATTENTIVE BEHAVIOR

All behavior has an origin or cause.

All behavior has an origin or cause, and there are at least 12 causes of disruptive or inattentive behavior in classrooms (Table 10.1). We'll take a quick look at these causes and then examine a few of them in depth. The reason for doing this analysis is that prevention and response to off-task or disruptive behavior must be done in relation to the cause of the behavior to begin with. Some of the causes of these behaviors have their origins in our choices, not the student's faults. As we walk through each of the causes of disruptive or inattentive behavior, we point to the many tools available to address specific issues of student behavior addressed in detail in relevant chapters of this book.

Table 10.1 Twelve Causes of Disruptive or Inattentive Behavior

Cause 1: Poor General Management
Cause 2: Inadequate Personal Relationship
Cause 3: Inappropriately Matched or Boring Work
Cause 4: Confusing Instruction
Cause 5: Unclear Standards, Expectations, and Consequences
Cause 6: Student Not Knowing How to Do the Expected Behaviors
Cause 7: A Need for Fun and Stimulation
Cause 8: Value and Culture Clashes
Cause 9: Internal Physical Causes
Cause 10: External Physical Causes
Cause 11: Extraordinary Emotional Issues
Cause 12: Student Sense of Powerlessness

- Causes 1 to 4 all have to do with laying the foundations of management, relationship building, and solid instruction. All are related to aspects of teaching over which teachers have nearly complete control and, when well executed, can serve as preventive measures to discipline issues.

- Causes 5 and 6 are directly related to establishing authority and safety by ensuring that students know what is expected and how to do it.

- Causes 7, 8, 9, and 10 highlight characteristics that might be part of a student's makeup or natural or learned behaviors that collide with their otherwise instinctive tendency to cooperate and participate in school.

- Cause 11 suggests the need to become familiar with seven sophisticated models of discipline for the small minority of recalcitrant or troubled students.

- Cause 12, student sense of powerlessness and alienation, is dealt with extensively in Chapter 16, "Classroom Climate."

Cause 1: Poor General Management

Competent handling of Attention, Momentum, Space, Time, and Routines forms a foundation for good student behavior. Conversely, absence of their

Inattention to or mismanagement of Attention, Momentum, Space, Time, and Routines can leave students with downtime on their hands and distracted, frustrated, bored, and/or tuned out.

skillful handling creates distraction and fragmentation. Here are some important questions to consider in your classrooms:

▲ Have you anticipated potential downtime, delays, and distractions, and planned in advance for them? Are you periodically monitoring what and how students are doing when they are working independently? (See Chapter 6, "Momentum.")

▲ Before you begin instruction, do you ensure that students are focused and attending? Do you use strategies that will keep students alert and on their toes throughout a learning experience? When students resist or are unfocused, do you draw on a wide range of moves to bring them back, or does your repertoire collapse into repeated authoritarian moves that result in power struggles? (See Chapter 5, "Attention.")

▲ Are the space and furniture arrangements conducive to all students seeing the board and having adequate private or quiet time for working independently? Are all students within your visual range most of the time? (See Chapter 7, "Space.")

▲ Are time allocations reasonably matched (not too long or too short) to what students will need to complete tasks, participate productively in group activities, and sit still? (See Chapter 8, "Time.")

▲ Have you established routines for what to do when a student enters the classroom, needs help, is finished with work, and a myriad of other aspects of daily classroom functioning so that you minimize downtime and unnecessary nagging and reminders? Do students know how to carry out the routines you have set? (See Chapter 9, "Routines.")

The bottom line here is that inattention to—or mismanagement of—Attention, Momentum, Space, Time, and Routines can leave students with downtime on their hands and distracted, frustrated, bored, and/or tuned out. When this is the case, it is likely that they will find an outlet somewhere for their energy and creativity, and that outlet may well be disruptive to the class. One might argue that with prolonged boredom, disruptions are probably a sign of good mental health and physical vitality in normal children. So when there are discipline problems, especially if the problems are endemic to the whole class, these management areas are the first places to look for causes and solutions. What this points to are the measures teachers can take to minimize discipline problems by applying the best of what they know in each of these areas of performance.

Cause 2: Inadequate Personal Relationship

The same holds true for personal relationship building with students. When teachers invest time in getting to know their students, show them respect as individuals, and treat them fairly, most students tend to reciprocate in kind. Gordon and Burch's *Teacher Effectiveness Training* (2003) devotes entire chapters to communication skills that contribute to positive and productive relationships with students. In the absence of a good relationship, it is far easier for students to act out, ignore expectations set for their behavior, and be resentful (see Chapter 15, "Personal Relationship Building").

Teachers who know their students well know what other challenges their students may be dealing with outside the classroom. They may be able to refer the student for additional resources to better support that student academically or emotionally. A significant part of personal relationship building is showing interest in and respect for students. There is strong message here for schools where most of the children are of color and from poverty.

Students of color are disproportionately disciplined and suspended far in excess of their proportionality in the population. This is often explained as an inevitable consequence of violent neighborhoods, broken families, and poverty. It is not, however, inevitable at all when students of color receive culturally responsive teaching and a deliberate focus on community building by teachers who are also "warm demanders" (Gregory & Weinstein, 2008).

Ullucci's (2009) ethnographic study of six very successful teachers in an inner city shows that structured, consequence-laden environments are not the automatic default necessity:

> While their classrooms were clearly in control, there was little actual attention paid to management throughout the day. The positive behaviors that were evident were not the result of punitive discipline policies. Instead, teachers relied on community building first, and management tactics second. Teachers focused on relationships, communication, and instilling a sense of belonging in their classes.
>
> Management was less about rewards and punishments and more about norms. From the classroom space itself, we can see teachers interested in showing children that they belong. Their heritages and languages found places in their classrooms, both through the materials available and the conversations pursued. I believe students felt more a part of these classrooms because teachers talked openly about students' lives and

> experiences, and incorporated discussions around race and difference rather than ignoring them. "Race does matter," shared Peter during one interview. And having conversations about things that mattered seemed paramount to these teachers.
>
> Students were expected to talk to each other, solve community problems and tap into the role of emotion and feeling, both in their own lives and in academic work. When students did misbehave, the actions were taken in stride. Teachers often used humor to redirect students instead of reading misbehavior as a personal attack on them. When needed, teachers definitely redirected children who were off-task, but in a style of warm demanders: teachers who have great commitment and respect for their students while being disciplinarians. This distinction is key. Teachers in this study were direct and sharp with their discipline. However, this style did not tear at the dignity and self-concept of the children. (pp. 24–25)

Cause 3: Inappropriately Matched or Boring Work

Teachers need to make sure the work is appropriate for the students: challenging but attainable. If it is too hard, too easy, or a consistent glaring mismatch to a student's learning style, the risk is frustration or boredom, either of which may induce disruptive behavior. Considering how to scaffold and differentiate learning experiences so that all students can productively work toward achieving an objective is an essential aspect of effective planning. But even if basic management is handled well and instruction is of reasonable difficulty, there may still be problems (see Chapter 18, "Lesson Objectives" and Chapter 20, "Differentiated Instruction").

Using the same format or activity structures day after day (too much lecturing, too many worksheets, low-level questioning, or something else) may also induce boredom and acting-out behavior in some classes. Consult Chapter 20, "Differentiated Instruction," which highlights variables that can be manipulated to provide balance and variety in lessons.

Cause 4: Confusing Instruction

Confusing instruction induces frustration and boredom. Are concepts presented to students in ways they can absorb and understand? Do they have time to process and make sense of them? Does instruction align with what we know about different modality preferences (auditory, visual, and kinesthetic), multiple intelligences, and variety in learning styles? Are we checking for understanding frequently across all students to ensure they are "getting it" as instruction proceeds? Do students know what they are expected to get out of a learning experience and why they are doing particular activities? All of these concerns are related to clarity of instruction. Consult Chapter 11, "Clarity," and Chapter 12, "Principles of Learning," which both serve as resources for minimizing confusion during learning experiences.

For a self-assessment of where one stands on handling these first four causes, go to *The Skillful Teacher* website (www.RBTeach.com/TST7) and try out the protocol "Discipline/Learning Environment Self-Assessment."

Discipline/ Learning Environment Self-Assessment

Cause 5: Unclear Standards, Expectations, and Consequences

A more serious and more common cause of inattentive or disruptive behavior is unclear expectations and consequences. The intricate web of mutual understandings that goes with them may not be clearly established between the teacher and students. We have yet to find a teacher with widespread discipline problems (rather than just one resistant child) who did not need help here.

Cause 6: Students Not Knowing How to Do Expected Behaviors

Students bring to school both the manners and the cognitive habits they have learned elsewhere. Failure to meet teacher expectations for lining up without running, listening to directions, lining up their work neatly on paper, or for putting materials away in an orderly way may simply come from the fact that they don't know how to do so. It is a fact that some kindergartners don't know how to walk rather than run in certain situations (which is to say they don't know how to predict consequences, control impulses, or plan physical movements). For some children, it is important to directly teach some of the hidden rules of school and formal behavior: classroom survival skills such as how to stay in their seat, how to participate appropriately, and where to put their things.

Some older students don't know how to categorize objects to expedite a cleanup, much less plan their time and movements during it. In these cases, teaching the behaviors step by step, not clever consequences or contracts, is the antidote to the disruptive behavior. There's no use trying to motivate students to do something for which they lack the tools. Assumptions can cause teachers to overlook these possibilities. It may simply never occur to them that the deepening cycle of threats and punishments has its origin in simple ignorance. We urge teachers facing disruptive behavior to examine their students carefully. More often than is realized, teachers assume capacities that are not there in students' behavioral repertoires. In these cases, putting the behaviors into their repertoires is needed. A question not to overlook when trying to figure out a resistant class or individual is, "Do they know how to do what I am asking them to do?"

In *Lost at School* (2008), Ross Greene goes into depth about teaching particularly resistant students the skills they are lacking. He combines positioning the behavior as a problem to be solved, being empathetic with the student, and making a plan with the student that teaches the skills. His findings from research and writings in this decade elevate this cause as one we should seriously consider when analyzing student behavior.

Cause 7: A Need for Fun and Stimulation

Fooling around with friends is natural and healthy. Children would almost invariably rather fool around than do their work, so teachers should expect that and not resent it. (Truth be told, we were probably like that too. And it never completely goes away for some of us; watch adults at faculty meetings.) This doesn't change in any way the teacher's responsibility to make instruction interesting and relevant or to make the rules clear and enforce student engagement. But it does perhaps temper irritation to remember that social urges and youthful energy underlie some disruptive behavior.

Cause 8: Value and Culture Clashes

Cultural clashes between teachers and students may underlie resistant behavior. This cause should be considered in classes where students' home life has strong ethnic roots in a culture different from the teacher's. In addition to ethnicity, another cultural dimension to be aware of is tacit rules—unspoken cues and habits—of different socioeconomic groups:

> For example, being able to fight or have someone who is willing to fight for you [may be] important to survival in poverty. Yet in the middle class, being able to use words as tools to negotiate conflict is crucial. (Payne, 2005, p. 60)

Other examples Payne cites include laughing when disciplined as a way to save face in matriarchal cultures; inappropriate or vulgar comments that may be the only language a child has learned for dealing with conflict; not following directions, which may be due to the absence of practice or procedural memory training; and incessant talking, which may be a manifestation of the participatory nature of the family dinner table. Some of these examples border on stereotyping. But other cultural differences, like avoiding eye contact and not participating in class discussion, may be rooted in cultural norms and need acknowledgement rather than criticism.

The bottom line here is that a student may be behaving in ways that are consistent with their own culture (racial, ethnic, or socioeconomic) but may be considered inappropriate in the school culture. It is imperative to examine inappropriate behavior with that in mind as a prerequisite to teaching replacement behaviors for students.

A student may be behaving in ways that are consistent with their own culture (racial, ethnic, or socioeconomic) but considered inappropriate in the school culture.

Cause 9: Internal Physical Causes

Sometimes seemingly inattentive students in fact don't hear well. They fail to carry out directions not because they're daydreaming or willful; they simply mishear key words. We have known inattentive students to be diagnosed with hearing loss after several years in primary school and after much energy went into behavior modification and other focusing strategies for the children. Be sure to rule out physical causes when working with children who appear resistant or inattentive. These include vision, organic hyperactivity, thyroid irregularities, fetal alcohol syndrome, drug dependency, ADD/ADHD, and a host of other possible physical problems.

Cause 10: External Physical Causes

The environment of the class itself may be a mismatch for certain students, and a simple change of the environment can reduce or eliminate problems for them. The most obvious variable is the degree of structure in the class (Colarusso & Green, 1973). High-structure environments leave students less choice in what activities to do when, with whom, and where in the room. Low-structure environments (which may nevertheless be highly planned and highly organized) have more student movement and more flexibility in who does what and when, since students are making more choices and are more in charge of their personal schedules.

For some students, the predictability and organization of a highly structured classroom environment represents a haven of comfort and security from an otherwise outside world (or home life) of uncertainty or chaos. A classroom in which daily schedules are published and adhered to, reasonable rules and routines are established and followed, supplies are orderly and accessible, and personal space (desk, locker, cubby, and so on) is assigned and controlled by them can render school a welcome environment for some students, fulfilling the basic human need to feel in control in ways they don't experience elsewhere.

In addition to structure, other environmental variables that might influence behavior include the amount and kind of auditory and visual stimulation in a classroom. Some people can completely tune out ambient noise, and others are highly sensitive to and distracted by it. This is also the case regarding the visual environment. The type or amount of lighting in the room can be a factor interfering with or supporting concentration for some students. Learning style experts (Dunn et al., 1995) highlight temperature and seating arrangements as additional variables that can affect learners. A room too hot or cold leads to physical discomfort that interferes with concentration. Thus there are a number of environmental factors that might affect student behavior.

In *Teacher Effectiveness Training* (2003), Gordon and Burch have some useful checklists for other ways to modify the environment. When considering how to improve students' behavior, teachers should also look at the appropriateness of the environments. They need to weigh how much these environments may be contributing to (rather than reducing) problems. The goal is to arrange them so that they do not play to students' weaknesses and trigger disruptive behaviors.

Cause 11: Extraordinary Emotional Issues

Some strong emotional reactions may be short term and the impact short lived, such as a feud with a friend, anxiety over a test, or a fight at home. Or they may represent long-term, cumulative, and more significant psychosocial issues, such as being convinced one is a failure, homelessness, abuse, or mental illness. Some adolescents and even middle elementary students bring a sense of alienation and hopelessness to school that manifests alternately as withdrawal and disengagement or defiance and hostility. Consult Chapters 15 and 16, "Personal Relationship Building" and "Classroom Climate," which contain more guidance for working with these students. The issue for these students is not discipline; it is motivation and meaning. Whereas the foundations for orderly classroom life that are presented in this chapter are necessary for alienated students, they are insufficient; those foundations will not be enough to get them engaged. Students who do not believe school has anything for them in life or who have given up on their own capacity to improve their lives through education require reaching beyond this chapter. The "Arenas" section in Chapter 14, "Expectations," and the teacher behaviors laid out there aim directly at students who do not believe in themselves or in the value of school.

Despite all the best efforts in responding to these issues, there may still be a few students who resist learning and do not function well in school. They may be passive and withdrawn or act out severely and consistently. The final section of this chapter addresses these students—the few, not the many; the troubled, not the norm. There are at least seven major systematic approaches for dealing with resistant students, each cohesive and each different, and they are all effective if used with the right students.

Cause 12: Student Sense of Powerlessness

Schools as institutions can resemble the army, prisons, and hospitals in the way they may systematically make students feel powerless. They can frustrate the basic human need for control by leaving little or no room for initiative, decision-making, and leadership. This environment makes a significant percentage of children want to push back, and they do. If we use unilateral power, we can control these students—but we will probably also make them hate school and learn less. This is not a pitch for free-for-all schools. Learning is often hard work and requires doing assignments given by teachers, and that is okay. But without compromising high academic standards, teachers can structure their classes so that students feel some ownership and control over their learning experiences. Every increment of progress in this direction takes pressure off behavior management because students' energy starts to push *with* instead of *against*. Later in this chapter and also in Chapter 16, "Classroom Climate," we elaborate on how teachers can do this "power sharing."

A COMPREHENSIVE APPROACH TO DISCIPLINE

Figure 10.1 summarizes the elements of a comprehensive approach to discipline and represents the necessary sequence to be accomplished for building a powerful learning environment for students. The diagram can serve as a resource for diagnosis and problem-solving when discipline issues are interfering with classroom learning.

The levels in this figure are sequential and should be handled in priority order. Experienced teachers may be working on climate and expectations at once from day one, but they are sequential in the sense that each requires the one before it to be successfully in hand before accomplishing the next level of tasks. For example, if the environment is poorly structured (e.g., Momentum, Space, Time, Routines), then the class operates chaotically and the teacher has a tough time catching all the disruptions and becoming a person of significance to the students.

If the rules are unclear (communicating Expectations), the teacher won't be able to deliver consequences for student behavior without being resisted and

Figure 10.1 Discipline Tasks and Toolboxes

POWERFUL LEARNING ENVIRONMENTS

LEVEL 1
ESTABLISHING FOUNDATIONS

MANAGEMENT
- Attention
- Momentum
- Space
- Time
- Routines

MOTIVATION
- Personal Relationship Building

INSTRUCTION
- Clarity
- Lesson Objectives
- Differentiated Instruction

↓

LEVEL 2

ELIMINATING DISRUPTIONS

COMMUNICATING EXPECTATIONS
- Am I clear?
- Do I have conviction?
- Do Students Know?

LIMIT SETTING
- Body Language of Meaning Business

BACKUP CONSEQUENCES
- Logical
- Varied
- Escalating

BUILDING A CLIMATE OF COMMUNITY AND COOPERATION

COMMUNITY

RISK-TAKING

INFLUENCE AND CONTROL

↓

LEVEL 3
DEALING WITH VERY RESISTANT STUDENTS

MODELS OF DISCIPLINE
- Teacher Effectiveness Training
- Reality Therapy
- Logical Consequences
- Personal Influence
- Self-Awareness
- Behavior Modification

seen as unfair. If the consequences are not clear, certain, and fair from the students' point of view, not only will the worst disrupters start to get the upper hand, but the class as a whole won't invest in building a responsible, inclusive classroom community (Climate).

No teacher can focus on climate building if the earlier jobs are not solidly handled. This sequence from bottom up is also a progression teachers can use to diagnose potential causes of discipline issues as well as to uncover a myriad of variables to adjust or fine tune.

Now, here in more detail are the four levels for establishing an orderly, safe, and cooperative classroom environment.

Level 1: Establishing the Foundation

Begin by establishing a welcoming environment conducive to smooth management. This means do the following:

- ▲ Make sure the environment in which the students learn is set up properly with routines, time schedule, procedures, and physical space to facilitate smooth operation and minimize downtime and distractions.
- ▲ Build relationships of regard and respect with students to signal that this is a place where they are valued as individuals.
- ▲ Design and deliver instruction in a way that all students can experience both challenge and success.

In examining causes one through four of disruptive or inattentive behavior we proposed ways in which several of the Management areas of performance (Attention, Momentum, Space, Time, and Routines) lay a solid discipline foundation. We also discussed the importance and benefits of investing in Personal Relationship Building with students. Finally, we highlighted instructional areas of performance (Lesson Objectives, Clarity, and Differentiated Instruction) that can serve as toolboxes for making the foundation structurally sound.

Collectively, these areas of performance afford us a solid foundation for establishing preventive measures and for diagnosing and responding to discipline issues that arise. The above-mentioned chapters of this book and the subtasks associated with them are the place to begin when dealing with discipline. Are they all in good shape?

Level 2: Eliminating Disruptions

Communicate through your actions that students can rely on you to maintain a safe and orderly environment. Even if you are totally committed to having a democratic classroom where students are responsible for their own behavior, this is necessary in order to garner the respect and significance you will need to create any classroom climate you care about.

Establishing Authority and Safety Has Three Major Subtasks

- ▲ **Subtask 1:** Establish expectations for behavior with confidence and clarity and build a crystal-clear understanding of the rules and the social contract that will be the reference point for behavior. Involve the students to the degree possible in creating a social contract, and act out the boundaries of the rules so there is no ambiguity of what they mean. Later in this chapter, we describe strategies for involving students in developing these rules.

- ▲ **Subtask 2:** Set limits by reacting with speed and decisiveness when behavior is inappropriate or disruptive. One does this by noticing when student behavior needs a response and responding quickly with the body language of meaning business (Jones, 2013) and any other steps that are necessary to preserve order and safety, both physical and psychological. Linda Lantieri (2001) describes the relationship of classroom order and psychological safety as follows:

  > "Children do not always know what is safe for them or for others," said Dorothy. "Discipline and limits are a way we create a circle of safety for those not yet ready to do this for themselves. Picture these limits as a big hug—our strong arms encircling the child with comfort and safety."
  >
  > Once we see discipline as an act of love and containment, we can be creative and responsive to the style and degree of discipline needed with a particular child or group. . . .When we distinguish respect from fear and provide limits to prevent children from harming each other, we are not defending our power as teachers; we are helping group members create the safety to be vulnerable and authentic with one another. (p. 121)

- ▲ **Subtask 3:** The final subtask is responding to student behavior when necessary with consequences that are clear, swift, fair, and certain. This means having an escalating scale of consequences in mind and the backup systems in place.

Establishing Expectations at the Beginning of the Year

The opening weeks of a term or year are the prime time to ensure solid understanding of expectations, establish routines, and begin to build class cohesion. It is useful to think of this period as one of teaching or training for the students. Training requires practice; thus, if students are noisy and disruptive in the hallway, the teacher can say, "I can see we need more practice in hall walking from the way we just came back from gym," and take the class out for some practice right then. This is not punitive; it is logical as a consequence.

The opening weeks of a term or year are the prime time to ensure solid understanding of expectations, establish routines, and begin to build class cohesion.

> **Example:** Nick Aversa, an eighth-grade teacher we worked with, spent the first part of every period in the first weeks of school rehearsing his students in how to enter class and get right to work. The routine included crossing the threshold to class and stopping all talking, finding a seat, getting out their notebook, and working on the opening activity for class. Initially, he taught them why this is important and then walked them through a series of practices from hall to classroom. From then on, anytime someone forgot the procedure, the consequence was to go back out into the hall and reenter correctly. Nick would signal this by simply establishing eye contact with the offending student and then looking at the door. The student would know what he had to do.

We have seen classes where the teacher's expectations for student behavior are lowered by the students; their behavior is so poor that the teacher concludes they can't behave any better. Watch out, though; the minute a person starts justifying behavior (or academic achievement for that matter) by saying, "What can you expect, given their environment," the students are in trouble. We are convinced that what you expect is what you get—not right away, of course, but eventually. The students may have to be taught how to meet higher behavioral standards, but they are not constitutionally, genetically, or environmentally unable to.

There are examples all over the country that demonstrate that children from the most chaotic and disadvantaged families and neighborhoods can behave perfectly well in school if the adults demand it, teach them how to do it, and believe in them. This last factor, "believe in them," is the subject of Part Three on "Motivation" (Chapters 14, 15, and 16). Students who don't believe school has any value for their future, especially in secondary grades, are much more likely to be discipline problems; they feel they have little to lose. Maybe they are frustrated and angry. So building their motivation to succeed in school has a strong bearing on their willingness to respond to the environment of responsibility and self-discipline that this chapter is about. Our point here is simply to alert readers to our responsibility, both in our individual classes and collectively for the school, to maintain the highest standard for civil and respectful behavior for our students.

In Chapter 14, "Expectations," we describe four areas of classroom life where teachers set standards of performance: (1) the quantity and quality of work, (2) work habits and procedures, (3) business and housekeeping routines, and (4) interpersonal behavior. When it comes to discipline, we are primarily focusing on setting and communicating expectations in the last three areas.

Clarity and Conviction About Expected Behavior

The starting point here is the teacher. Do we (teachers) have clarity about what we want from our students? Do we have conviction about what we can reasonably expect from our students? The distinction here is an important one. Clarity about what we want a student to do or measure up to sets standards of behavior; what we think a student will do—or is capable of doing—is about our beliefs and expectations. Each plays a critical role in the results we get from students. If we aren't clear about standards of performance, students won't know what we are asking of them. If we don't have conviction that students are capable of achieving a standard of performance, we aren't likely to inspire them to do so.

Is it reasonable to expect first graders to sit and listen at a classroom meeting for more than 10 minutes? Are they capable of doing so? If you believe that your first graders will never be able to sit for more than 10 minutes, they won't. Are your inner-city high school students too conditioned by street culture to give respectful silence to peers doing a mock debate? If we believe that, then disrespect is what we will observe.

Every year, we work with at least one or two excellent teachers who are talented and caring people but whose effectiveness is reduced by their ambivalence about expectations. They are unsure how reasonable it is for them to expect and to push students toward more responsible and attentive behavior in class. They see the irresponsible behavior of students who appear out of control but have family and other problems and feel they must make allowances. Thus they undersell the students and undershoot with their goals for student behavior. Who says first graders can't sit still in a circle and listen to each other for a 15-minute meeting? Who says ninth graders can't learn to function in self-organized task groups to plan and organize a project?

Again and again, we have seen it demonstrated that teachers can get what behavior they want if they work hard enough at it, are tenacious and determined enough, are committed to the idea that it is right and attainable behavior for their students, and are willing to teach the skills their students may need to function at that level. This is true even for some disturbed students, though they are more taxing, the setting may need adjustment, and this work will take considerably longer. Expecting anything less is ultimately a disservice to students. What you decide to "want," of course, can be unreasonable and age inappropriate, in which case what you get is what you deserve.

If you have a clear notion of what you want, and you keep expecting, expecting, expecting, and say so out loud to students, with consequences when they don't measure up, with explanations of "why" over and over again, and with as much kindness and rationality as you can muster, you will get there. But first you must make some decisions about what is acceptable and unacceptable behavior and decide in order of priority what you want and that you will commit to getting it.

The Taboo Exercise is a useful first exercise for faculties to do together to get clarity, consensus, and conviction about behavioral expectations. A version of this is a built-in feature of PBIS. Through the exercise, and the discussion it necessitates, people get clearer about distinctions between the most serious and unacceptable student behaviors that warrant uniform, immediate, and consistent responses and consequences from the whole staff, and about behaviors that are important to address or extinguish but far less serious and therefore not worthy of community time and investment. In the latter case, individuals decide how to address them. (See the Taboo Exercise on *The Skillful Teacher* website at www.RBTeach.com/TST7.)

Taboo Exercise

Do Students Know What Is Expected of Them?

The prerequisite for strength in this area is that students have a clear and unambiguous picture of the expectations for their behavior. Something must happen to get that information across. There are numerous ways this may be done: tell them directly, make up a chart, brainstorm, or negotiate the class rules at a class meeting. Expectations are sometimes not codified as formal rules or laid out all at once, but they become known to students through what a teacher reacts to consistently. Students must be clear about what we want from them. We save a lot of time and energy if we communicate expectations directly rather than leaving it to chance that students will figure them out.

Furthermore, expectations must be specific so there is no misunderstanding or room for argument. It may not be enough to call for silent reading time; the class may need clarification on what silence means. Does it mean absolute silence, or whispering, or quiet talking? Can the students see the difference and modulate in a controlled way between those levels? If "silence" really means "quiet," then perhaps it really should not be called "silence" and vice versa. If students are supposed to arrive on time for class, does that mean being no more than two minutes late, being in the room when the bell rings, being in their

Exhibit 10.1 Sample Bill of Rights

You Have the Right:

- ▲ To be called only by your given or chosen name.
- ▲ To do your work without being disturbed by others.
- ▲ To be treated with the same respect that all people should have.
- ▲ To have your personal property rights respected.
- ▲ To ask questions when you don't know until you understand.
- ▲ To get a good education and do your best work.
- ▲ To have and express your own opinion, even when you disagree with others, including the teacher.
- ▲ To know how you are doing in your schoolwork.
- ▲ To be safe from someone hitting or harming you.
- ▲ To have fun and play safely on the playground without being bothered by others.
- ▲ Not to be criticized for things beyond your control or for things that you didn't know about.
- ▲ To be by yourself.
- ▲ To speak and listen to language that is appropriate for school.
- ▲ Not to be teased for being different.

Adapted courtesy of David Crump, former principal, Harrington Elementary School, Lexington, MA.

seats, or being in their seats with notebooks open and ready to go? Where these boundaries are drawn is less important than that they are established clearly. There must be no doubt as to when a rule has been broken.

A Social Contract

Mendler and Curwin (1999) describe a comprehensive strategy for involving students in rule making—called the social contract—to promote responsibility and respect and ensure there are clarity and buy-in regarding the rules of classroom interaction. (See "Creating a Social Contract" on *The Skillful Teacher* website at www.RBTeach.com/TST7.)

Creating a Social Contract

Some teachers call this beginning-of-the-year rules exercise "constructing a classroom constitution" or "bill of rights and responsibilities." A colleague of ours and a former classroom teacher, Dave Crump, used to start each school year by having his students develop a list of what they wanted to be able to count on as rights to be respected in their classroom that year (see Exhibit 10.1). Once they had generated a good list, they would discuss what each idea meant and why it was important. Finally, they would vote on their top priorities and construct a manageable list of 10 to 15 rights that everyone promised to abide by. The final document was prepared, and each student signed it.

When infractions occurred or conflicts arose around behavior, Crump would send students straight to the "Bill of Rights" to determine which of their rights had been violated—or which right they had violated—and to decide what a fair consequence might be. Frequently, this deliberation and discussion diffused tension between peers, and by the time they were reporting back to Crump they had pretty well resolved their issue.

Expectations need to be repeated often.

Expectations need to be repeated often. That means, especially in the beginning of the year, restating and reminding students about expectations and eliciting expectations from students just prior to events that may strain the behavior. It might sound like this: "We're going to the auditorium now. What might it be like there as we walk in? What will we need to do? What should we keep in mind for our behavior as a good audience?"

Home Contact

Another useful strategy to clarify and reinforce expectations and build relationships with families is early home contact to establish a positive connection long before problems arise, and to enlist their support and cooperation throughout the year in reinforcing the class contract. See *The Skillful Teacher* website at www.RBTeach.com/TST7 for "Guidelines for Home Contact" provided by Fred Jones (2013).

Guidelines for Home Contact

Attitude of Positive Expectancy

Teachers should have an attitude of positive expectancy embedded whenever they state and restate expectations. Positive expectancy has two aspects. The first has the sense, "Why of course you're going to do it!" This is not something the teacher says outright, but it is the assumption conveyed by body language and attitude. The other aspect of positive expectancy is encouragement and confidence—the "I know you can do it" attitude. It is often associated with positive statements of specific behaviors or questions ("Remember you want to raise your hand") rather than direct desists ("Stop calling out!").

Explicit verbal "positive attribution" conveys expectations as well. Consider the following scenario:

> The little boy, Albert, was standing near the teacher's desk and when he saw the drawings he promptly remarked, "They stink."
>
> Brigit's smile vanished. The teacher took Albert aside, bent down to him and said, "You may not know it, but that hurt Brigit's feelings because she really worked hard on those pictures. Now, I'm sure if you knew that you were going to hurt her feelings, you wouldn't have said that about them. I don't think you'd ever want to be that kind of boy, would you?"
>
> Albert swallowed, and with his face down, he muttered, "No." His teacher then took his hand and said, "Come, let's take a good look at her pictures together, and we'll tell her which one we like best."
>
> The teacher did not simply scold and disapprove, although her approval was certainly at stake for Albert. What she did was remind him of a standard he already understood, but that had not yet become a guiding principle for his actions. Even though she didn't state the standard formally, her reminder that "It's bad to hurt people intentionally" came through very clearly.
>
> Albert was induced to apply this standard to his actions because of two things his teacher did:
>
> - She attributed underlying good intentions to him ("I'm sure if you knew that you were going to hurt her, you wouldn't have said that"). By doing this, she was granting him membership in the good persons "club"—a membership she assumed he desired. If he continued to ignore the standard, he'd lose his "membership"—not just because his teacher disapproved of him, but because the categories "person who intentionally hurts others" and "good person" are mutually exclusive. Research on children's understanding of logic shows that even five-year-olds can understand the idea of mutually exclusive categories.

- She asked him to define the kind of boy he didn't want to be (one who intentionally hurts others). By doing this, she was forcing him to choose whether or not he wanted to keep his status as a good person. If he did, he'd have to use the standard as a guide for his behavior toward Brigit, as well as his future behavior toward others. (Shulmand & Meckler, 1994, pp. 113–114)

Another way to convey positive expectancy is to be assertive in requesting appropriate behavior. Lee Canter (Canter & Canter, 2001) calls for using one of four attention moves—eye contact, proximity, mentioning the student's name while teaching, and proximity praise—to redirect students back on task. Here's an example he gives for mentioning the student's name:

> While at the board, the teacher notices that Tanya and Michael are off task and not paying attention. The teacher, in a matter-of-fact manner, continues the lesson saying, "I want all of you, including Tanya and Michael, to come up with the answer to this problem." As soon as their names are mentioned, Tanya and Michael immediately begin paying attention. (p. 135)

If students counter with excuses or other diverting moves, Canter recommends the broken record technique:

> **Teacher:** "Sue, I want you to raise your hand and wait to be called on before you speak." (Statement of want)
>
> **Sue:** "None of the other kids do."
>
> **Teacher:** "That's not the point. I want you to raise your hand." (Broken record)
>
> **Sue:** "You never call on me."
>
> **Teacher:** "That's not the point. I want you to raise your hand." (Broken record)
>
> **Sue:** "Okay, I will."
>
> In this interchange, the teacher kept repeating (broken record) what she wanted from the child and would not become sidetracked by Sue's responses. The teacher maintained control of the interaction with the child.

> In using this technique, you first need to determine what you want from the interaction with the student (for example, "I want Sue to raise her hand"). This becomes your statement of want and the gist of your interactions. You can preface your statement of want with, "That's not the point, but I want you to raise your hand" or "I understand, but I want you to raise your hand." No matter what manipulative response the student presents, if you respond with your statement of want—"that's not the point, I want you to . . ." the statement will be more effective. (Canter & Canter, 2001, pp. 79–80)

This technique can be surprisingly effective, especially with students who are verbal. When you use it, you must know what consequences (or range of consequences) you are prepared to deliver if the behavior persists. Without that clear image, your assertiveness will be hollow. Furthermore, after reasserting the expectation three times, you must be ready to implement a consequence.

Recognizing and Rewarding Responsible Behavior

No discussion of consequences would be complete without examining positive consequences: how to respond to students—individual students or a whole class—who are meeting expectations. Canter and Canter (2001) recommend three guidelines for positive consequences: they should be things teachers are comfortable with, that students like, and that comply with school and district policies. Rewards might run the gamut from specific verbal praise ("Very nice job of managing your participation in the small group discussion and including everyone in the conversation"), a chance to be the line leader or the messenger for the day, a "good news" note, a postcard or call home, a positive note sent home addressed to the student, or a ticket that entitles the student to "purchase" items in the class store.

There is a case to be made that good behavior should not be rewarded; it is expected and should be the norm, so there should be no reward system. Nevertheless, with certain classes where discipline problems are an issue, explicit reward systems can play a useful role.

Mendler and Curwin (1999) note that some rules can have only positive consequences when followed. They cite an example of a middle school teacher who had a rule that paper airplanes could not be thrown in class during instructional time. The consequence for every week of no airplane throwing was that the class would have a paper airplane throwing contest. They report that "this creative contract stopped paper airplane throwing for the year" (p. 82). They believe there should be at least one positive consequence for each rule. In their earlier work, Mendler and Curwin (1983) suggested an approach to positive consequences that relies more on social praise delivered in private. They like to catch students being good and deliver both positive and negative consequences quietly, so only the receiving student can hear. Thus when the teacher is bending over a student to say something privately, the rest of the class doesn't know whether it's something like, "You have continued talking to neighbors despite two warnings. The consequence is you'll have to stay after class with me and work out a plan to avoid this behavior" or "You've been focusing on your work and written two balanced sonnets this afternoon. That's what I call being productive!"

In *Tools for Teaching: Discipline • Instruction • Motivation* (2013), Fred Jones concisely describes a successful system he calls Preferred Activity Time (PAT) for recognizing cooperation and efficiency in student behavior. PAT is not free time. It is structured time for an activity the students really like to do; it is commonly a lively game put to use as a review of academic material, but many other choices are possible as well. With appropriate modifications, it works equally well with secondary classes. With students, Jones calls this system "Responsibility Training" because they are learning to be responsible with time in everything they do (not dawdling, off-task, or fooling around).

PAT is free. The generous teacher gives the class 30 minutes for use on Friday each week (or 10 minutes each day); the rhythm of this choice depends on the particular class and their capacity to defer gratification. The real hook of the system is students' ability to increase PAT with bonus PAT.

> Class, before you get out of your seats, let me tell you what I want you to do during this lesson transition. First, hand in your papers by laying them on the corner of my desk. Then if you need to sharpen your pencils, this is the time to do it. If you need a drink of water, this is the time to get it.
>
> I want my cleanup committee to erase my boards and straighten up the books on the shelf. I want everybody to pick up any paper you see laying around the room and get your desks back on their marks.
>
> I will give you two minutes to get this done. But you know from past experience you can get it done in half-a-minute. So, let's see how much time you can save. All of the time you save will be added to PAT. Let's check the clock. [Pause until the second hand passes 12.] Okay, let's begin. (Jones, 2013, p. 266)

Skillful teachers work the room to prevent any "bootleg reinforcement" for fooling around that peers might deliver. In these pages, Jones gives a number of subtle tips about how to make the class successful and concludes the scenario by adding 1:17 to the classes starting total of 30 minutes.

Despite generous allotments of time for transitions, student don't always "win" a bonus, and 5 seconds over the set time will become a minus on the tally for PAT that is always on display. However, time loss of PAT should not be used as a consequence when a teacher can apply body language instead. The only time that doesn't apply is for high-rate disruptions (out of seat, talking) when the teacher is seated and working with a small group.

All the pluses and minuses of PAT are noted by the teacher with the same neutral affect we will see in the "Body Language of Meaning Business" section (see p. 149). The implied message is, "This is just the way it is. You, the class, are in charge of whether PAT is going up or down. You're in control."

Jones has sections in his book and on his website for desirable activities for PAT at all grade levels and a section on how to deal with students who are willfully sabotaging the class. We recommend this section and, in fact, his whole book. Jones' PAT is a well-scripted version of the Good Behavior Game, a time-tested form of recognition with 40 years of research supporting its power (Flower et al., 2014).

Appropriate Consequences

Punishment breeds resentment, whereas logical consequences teach students.

Logical, Not Punitive

Rudolph Dreikurs (Dreikurs & Cassel, 1972) understood that punishment breeds resentment, whereas logical consequences begin to teach students the reality of the social order. Every act has a consequence, and to avoid unpleasant results, students must behave in a way that will help guarantee favorable results. Punishment is any aversive stimulus (like writing, "I will not throw paper on the floor," one hundred times) intended to discourage the recurrence of the behavior. The student will be less likely to do the behavior next time because this unpleasant thing may happen again. Logical consequences, however, are connected to the behavior in such a way as to feel like fair retribution for the violation. If a student has broken a rule against copying another's homework, a logical consequence is to have to do it all over again under supervision (rather than stay after school as punishment). The point is always to search for logical consequences if consequences are deemed necessary.

A Range of Consequences

If each rule has an automatic consequence tied to it, you can get boxed into a corner. Having only one consequence for each rule is a mistake. Mendler and Curwin (1999) cite the case of a teacher whose consequence for undone homework was staying after school to finish it. One day one of her best students said, "I'm sorry, Miss Martin, but my father was very sick last night. I had to babysit while he was taken to the hospital, and in the confusion, I didn't have time to get my homework done." The teacher is now in the dilemma of either being unfeeling and rigid ("I'm sorry, but you have to stay after school anyway") or letting the child off and teaching the rest of the class that good excuses can pardon undone work. This could have been avoided if the teacher could pick from an appropriate range of consequences for each rule. Mendler and Curwin (1999) devote two chapters to developing and implementing consequences and recommend four generic consequences that might be applied to most rules: reminder, warning, practice following the rule, and a written plan. Hence, for undone homework, the range of consequences might be: reminder; warning; hand in work before the close of school that day; stay after school to finish it; and conference with the teacher, student, and parent to develop a plan.

With this range of alternatives, Miss Martin could gently remind the student that homework is due on time and then ask how her father is doing. In this way, she is implementing one of the prescribed consequences yet is not being overly rigid. With another student, who had been late six times that month, she might make him stay after school and finish it. Fair need not always be equal.

Delivering Consequences

Every time an expectation is not met, we must consistently react (meaning "react every time" though not necessarily the same way every time). The reaction may be anything from a reminder to a consequence, but something has to happen. Otherwise, the students—especially resistant students—come to disregard the expectation or become confused over where it applies. The transgression usually cannot be ignored. Sometimes we may choose to ignore certain behaviors when they are minor and calling attention to them would just reinforce them, or we may recognize them briefly. The general mission here is to communicate to students that your expectations are really your expectations. You mean them. They get this message when they find we reliably call them on certain behaviors and usually there is a consequence (Canter & Canter, 2001; Jones, 2013; Mendler & Curwin, 1999; Rogers, 1987). Mere admonishing and reprimanding without action that goes beyond words usually sends the message that expectations are weak.

Every time an expectation is not met, we must consistently react.

We must be tenacious about restating expectations and consistently reacting. Individuals and sometimes whole classes will test teachers to the limits on this. The thing is not to give up, even though misbehavior continues in the face of specific expectations consistently upheld. Some very difficult students will push to see if we really care (meaning care about them). If the reactions to the misbehavior are reasonable, appropriate, and fair, tenacity will carry the day.

Lee Canter (Canter & Canter, 2001) tells the story of an aggressive third grader who consistently abused other children verbally and physically. On several occasions, he extorted money from his classmates. At a meeting with the child's family, the principal, and the teacher, a contract was signed that Carl would be excluded from school if he did any of the following things: threaten children, cuss them, extort money, or physically assault them. The family agreed to follow through with the exclusion at home.

Inconsistency and lack of follow through, early in the school year, are a common cause of school discipline problems.

The next day, on the way into the classroom, Carl got into an argument with another student and roughly shoved him. Ms. S immediately went up to Carl and simply told him, "You pushed Sol. You've chosen to go home for the rest of the day!" Ms. S contacted the office, and the principal called Carl's mother, who came to get him. Carl went home and spent the rest of the school day in his room doing the work he would have done had he stayed in school.

The following day during a spelling assignment, another student refused to let Carl copy his work. Carl became angry and threatened to beat the student up. Ms. S, hearing this, told Carl what he had done and that he would be going home again. His mother picked him up, and he spent the rest of the day at home in his room. Carl behaved appropriately for the next two days. On the third day, during free choice, Ms. S observed him cursing and screaming at a girl who would not give him the puzzle that she was playing with. Ms. S repeated the same procedure of informing him of what he had done and that by behaving inappropriately, he had chosen to go home. For the first time, Carl became upset. He began to cry and say that he did not want to go home. Ms. S simply told him that "he made a choice" and would be going home.

As was typical, the third time was the charm. Ms. S's ability to deal assertively with Carl's behaviors let him know that his disruptions would not be tolerated. Carl thus chose to control his temper and behave in an appropriate manner with his fellow students.

It takes determination and tenacity to keep delivering consequences when the behavior persists. But without that tenacity, students will not believe teachers are serious about their expectations. Follow-through at the beginning of the year on plans, such as the one Canter describes, will be keenly observed by the rest of the class and lets them know you mean what you say. Inconsistency and lack of follow-through, early in the school year, are a common cause of school discipline problems. One teacher we worked with developed the protocol in Exhibit 10.2 to keep herself neutral and clear because she knew Billy could thwart her resolve if she were not absolutely clear and consistent.

Exhibit 10.2 Sample Protocol for Dealing with a Challenging Child

Memorandum

TO: Staff
FROM: Ms. X
DATE: May 15, 2016
RE: Strategy to Help B

Here is the summary of our strategy for helping B improve his behavior:

Prevention: Before an activity begins, tell B.
If there is a change, alert him beforehand.

Intervention: Rationale:
To help B be aware of his behavior and its effect on others.
To provide him strategies to cope.

Strategy Steps:

1. Nonjudgmental, nonhumiliating, private warning combined with statement of expectation and choice for B. For example: "B, you are______________.
I expect you to sing the song. You have a choice: You can stop _____________ and start singing, or if I need to speak to you again, you'll need to take some time out."

2. If B persists, call Mrs. L on the intercom phone and ask her to connect you to Mrs. Q.

3. If Mrs. Q is not there, Mrs. L will contact another person and tell you where to take B. The code words are, "I need to send you a message."

4, Say to B: "You've made a choice by continuing to ____________.
You need to take some time out.

5. If B balks, say "B, you have made a choice. You can either go on your own, or if not, I will call Mr. S."

6. If B still doesn't go, say, "You've made a choice by not going on your own. I will call Mr. S."

7. Call Mrs. L to reach Mr. S.; Mrs. L will cancel with Mrs. Q.

PRAY

I've provided words to use should you find that helpful. The key idea is *a choice* and conveying to B that by acting in certain ways he is making the choice.

Canter elaborates on the virtue of persistence and consistency:

> Children may not care if you keep them after school once, suspend them every now and then, or send them to the corner infrequently. But there are few children who would not care if they knew that they would have to stay after school every day they chose to, even if it meant five days straight. There are few children who would not care if they knew they would be suspended every time they acted out, even if it meant three straight days of suspension. There are few children who would not care if they knew you would send them to a corner for their inappropriate behavior every time they chose to go, even if it meant five times a day.
>
> What we are trying to say is this: if you really care, the children will really care. If you are prepared to use any means necessary and appropriate to influence the children to eliminate their inappropriate behavior they will sense your determination and quickly care about the consequences which they will have to face consistently if they choose to act inappropriately. (Canter & Canter, 2001, pp. 109–110)

Almost any behavior we really want to get, we can get if we have the determination because we do have the power. Does this mean that if one keeps delivering consequences persistently, the behavior is sure to change? First, it is possible to deliver a consequence over and over again consistently and have no effect. That can happen if the consequence is not strong enough, or if it somehow turns out to be a reward for the child. It can also happen if the behavior comes from a physical cause, ignorance, or a value clash. Second, the way in which the consequence was delivered in Canter's scenario had a lot to do with its success. The teacher did not blame, criticize, or humiliate the student; she simply, but promptly, went up to him, noted the behavior ("You pushed Sol"), and delivered the consequence ("You have chosen to go home for the rest of the day"). She pointed out that going home was the child's choice, in this case, since he knew that pushing Sol would lead to that. Thus the teacher reacts with matter-of-fact emotion rather than anger. It is, in fact, easier to react that way when you know precisely what you are going to do. That knowledge (versus the helpless feeling when dealing with a child who seems outside your control) gives a teacher both confidence and calm, which allows for better judgments. So being persistent with consequences can also fail if the consequence is not delivered in the right way.

The specific technique described in Canter's scenario is a strong one: systematic exclusion of a student to eliminate particularly disruptive and persistent behavior. But it can be very effective. Seymour Sarason (1996) describes another powerful exclusion technique (a time-out in a colleague's classroom) that works without families or contracts. It relies on the cooperation of another teacher into whose room the child is sent for exclusion. The host teacher has a special place the student goes to that is not fun and where the student does work (see Consequence 11 on pages 167–170).

Limit Setting with Escalating Consequences

A consequence should be logical and fit the infraction in terms of magnitude and severity. Hence, it is important to develop a range of responses, from small to large. The general rule of thumb in limit setting is to apply the law of least resistance. Start small and escalate only as necessary to extinguish the behavior. Knowing that we have a series of escalating consequences available enables us to remain calm, yet firm and convincing, when addressing inappropriate behavior. Remaining calm is essential to setting limits and establishing credibility and authority while preserving relationships of regard and respect. Table 10.2 lists a hierarchy of escalating consequences, which we explain in detail in the following sections.

A consequence should be logical and fit the infraction in terms of magnitude and severity.

Small Consequences

The consequences in this section take a low amount of time and effort from the teacher and usually no follow-up.

Consequence 1: The Body Language of Meaning Business

We owe a lot to Fred Jones, who studied people with the "aura," the teachers with whom nobody seemed to fool around, and discovered that it was not magic that caused students to respond to them. It was the subtle but specific, observable, and learnable body language they manifested. This body language communicated that they were serious about their expectations and would do whatever it took to get them met. They rarely had to do more than send body language signals, and they rarely had to implement backup consequences.

We recommend Jones's *Tools for Teaching: Discipline • Instruction • Motivation* (2013) to all beginning teachers and any teacher struggling with discipline issues. The details of learning and implementing effective body language are spelled out at length there. To give readers an idea of the nature of this body language, Table 10.3 summarizes the steps from Jones (2013) for addressing off-task behavior. It begins with understanding never to go any further with the following limit-setting sequence than is required to produce the desired result as described in Table 10.3.

Table 10.2 A Hierarchy of Escalating Consequences

Small Consequences
1. Body language of meaning business/poker
2. Acknowledging a change in behavior and offering help
3. Quiet time
4. Verbal warning, privately delivered
Medium Consequences
5. Re-education (cafeteria school)
6. Hold up a mirror
7. Pulling the card
8. Letter home taped to desk
9. Account for behavior in writing
10. Time-out in classroom
11. Time-out in a colleague's room
High Impact Consequences
12. Phone call home with student reporting in teacher's presence what happened
13. Parent conference with home reporting and consequences; contract signed by teacher, student, and parent
14. Parent accompanies student to classes for a day as a condition for readmission (with parent supervision finishing work in isolation)
15. In-school suspension
16. Saturday school
17. Deliver a student to parent at work
Last Resort Consequences
18. Suspension
19. Police
20. Expulsion

Table 10.3 Steps for Addressing Off-Task Behavior

Notice	**Notice the disruptive behavior . . .**
Excuse and square off	Terminate whatever you're doing, and say to the students you are working with, "Excuse me. I'll be right with you."
	Turn completely.
	Face the student squarely and look the student in the eye.
	Make your face expressionless, arms hanging comfortably.
	Take two relaxing breaths.
Name	Say the child's first name only, in a bland tone.
	Take two more relaxing breaths.
	The student may fold, but if not . . .
Move in (say nothing)	
	Walk slowly to the edge of the student's desk until your legs touch it.
	Stand upright.
	Take two relaxing breaths.
The student probably folds, in which case you:	
Thank and move out	Thank the student, genuinely and warmly.
	Wait fifteen seconds more.
	Go to the second student who was involved (if relevant).
	Thank him or her.
	Wait fifteen more seconds.
	Return slowly to the student you were previously working with.
	Wait for two relaxing breaths.
	Resume instruction.
But if student doesn't fold . . .	
Lean and prompt	Lean over at the waist, resting your weight on one palm. (You're back at the student's desk.)
	Deliver a prompt on exactly what you want him or her to do next. ("Carrie, you have two more problems to do. Let's finish them up.")
	If the student starts working, wait for two relaxing breaths.
	Then do the "thank and move out" sequence.

Table 10.3 Steps for Addressing Off-Task Behavior (continued)

Notice	**Notice the Disruptive Behavior**
But in the unlikely event student still doesn't fold:	
Palms (say nothing)	Lean slowly across the child's desk, and place both palms flat on the far side of the desk from you (ooze, don't swoop).
	Look at the student for two relaxing breaths.
	When he or she resumes work, wait two more relaxing breaths.
	Then do Moving Out.
Backtalk	If the child displays helplessness, crying, denial, compliments, blaming, tangents, or accusing you of incompetence, say nothing and take two relaxing breaths.
But if there's more backtalk . . .	
Elbow and prompt	Bend your elbow, and place it on the child's desk.
	Repeat the prompt.
If a second student chimes in . . .	
Camp out behind	Stand slowly and walk around until you're between the two students.
	Lean your elbow on the table.
	Reestablish eye contact with the first student (blocking student 2).
	Take two relaxing breaths . . .
	Slowly move out.

Adapted from Tools for Teaching: Discipline • Instruction • Motivation (Jones, 2013)

Jones's premise is that limit-setting in classrooms is like a poker game: students play a card (test limits by trying out behaviors) and wait to see what card we will play. If we "see them"—that is, respond in some believable way—the student generally "folds" (gives in). Sometimes we need to "raise them" again—escalate the consequence. The bottom line is not to play any higher a card than is necessary to get the child to fold. We must play the game with confidence and conviction, signaling that we are in control without needing to get emotionally rattled. This premise is embedded in the sequence of steps illustrated in Table 10.3.

Reading this list of steps does not enable one to learn and carry out body language poker successfully. One must practice it repeatedly and get feedback to do it well, as Jones arranges in his courses and we do in ours. We urge readers to take this information seriously (though the study and practice of this behavior is fun and does provoke lots of laughs) because it is so potent. If there was ever a good example of acting one's way into a belief, this is it. Practicing these behaviors is practicing an attitude as well—the attitude of teacher resolve and persistence—and developing confidence.

Here are accounts from three teachers who have been in our courses—one each from high school, middle school, and elementary—of their experience applying the body language of meaning business. All three were experienced teachers, well regarded, and successful. They did not have significant discipline problems, but they still found learning these techniques well worth the effort.

Example 1: Charlotte Thompson—High School

I have been working on discipline this week. Luckily, I have not gotten to the "palms and ooze" stage! In fact, I have noticed that by waiting for the students to turn squarely and completely around facing me, all problems were cut off at the pass. [She means a long pause after a desist move until the student has completely re-engaged attention.] This week I stopped the class with, "Excuse me, class," and went over to two girls and quietly explained why it was necessary for them to stop talking. I assume because the entire class was watching me speak to them very quietly while leaning over their desk that they were a bit embarrassed. It did correct the problem.

I did have one student this week who was rather persistent in not settling down. I went over to his desk and just stared. Unfortunately, he seemed to enjoy that and did not cease his showing off. I got to step 6 with him, although I must admit I skipped step 5. I was not at all confident that he knew what to do, so I was somewhat anxious to get to the prompt. He spends a good deal of time spacing out. But it did get him back to work and he stayed settled afterward for a pretty good length of time.

Example 2: Jeanne O'Reilly—Middle School

Using the sequence sheet on body language, I decided to try it in class. The first day I used it, I was amazed at how easily and well it worked. In my first class, I never went beyond saying the name and taking the two breaths. For the purpose of this experiment, I want to focus on what happened with Phil. Phil is a good student, though easily swayed. He is very capable, and therefore though he disrupts the learning of others, his behavior rarely damages his own grade. He tends to infuriate his teachers.

On that fateful day, body language was really more in the back of my mind. I had been rereading the steps and finally decided to use it. I was at the front of the class leading a discussion when Phil started up with little comments to everyone within range. Normally, I would walk over to a student like Phil not saying anything but just standing near him or behind him while continuing the discussion.

I almost surprised myself (as well as Phil) when I excused myself to the class, squared off, waited, and said his name as blandly as I could. He folded immediately. It occurred twice more, and that was it.

Well, I immediately began using it. My favorite thing about body language is how much it minimizes my own anger. I simply don't become as irritated, and the breaths really do keep me calm. My problem is remembering to use it. I find that when I'm tired or stressed, I lapse back. I do feel that this is one of the most valuable techniques I've learned anywhere.

Example 3: Lisa Farmer—Elementary School

There are times when children's behavior is inappropriate. In my kindergarten classroom, inappropriate behavior surfaces during our morning calendar meetings. The children usually talk and move about, switching places with their classmates. What I find most difficult is disciplining the behavior while keeping the momentum of the meeting. I decided to try the science of body language to see if more body language and less speaking would help at the meeting.

While I was beginning our morning meeting, Michael had his back to the circle and faced the blackboard talking to a friend. I called his name and made my face expressionless. He turned around and looked at me.

When he saw my face, he looked at his classmates and quickly and dramatically sat down. He then gave me what I believe is a "smiley face." Because I kept looking straight at him, he looked down. I waited. He did look up again and found me still looking at him. What was most interesting was the reaction of the rest of the class. Michael's friend Adam turned around and followed Michael's lead in settling down. The others sat quietly watching. This first episode ended with my saying thank you and moving on to the calendar without interruption from Michael.

The first lesson I learned was that you can make a child aware of and stop inappropriate behavior with the bare minimum discussion. Without discussing it, the behavior stopped, and neither of us felt put down, angry,

> or uncomfortable. Though I have used a look or eye contact previously, what made this effective was the waiting through two breaths. Since that first episode I have used this technique with other children and other situations effectively. During recent attempts, I have had to move close to the child, but I have never had to do more. One more important component is squaring off. The student seems to know you mean business because you are not moving.

"Body language poker," as Jones calls it, is a form of consequence for students who fool around. It is the lowest stakes and most common form of response successful teachers make to disruptive or inattentive behavior, and it eliminates most of it. But teachers must have a clear series of escalating moves to reach for in order to have the confidence to implement good body language. "What if it doesn't work?" runs through every teacher's mind, especially beginning teachers. If the body language doesn't work (it will almost all the time, if done well), one can move up the hierarchy of responses and consequences slowly, always escalating only the minimal amount necessary to eliminate the disruptive behavior, confident in what you can do if you have to.

Consequence 2: Acknowledging a Change in Behavior and Offering Help

This is a gentle and positive way of reprimanding and is similar to the desist move in the Attention Continuum (see Figure 5.1 in Chapter 5) called "offer help." The teacher talks privately to a student and says something like, "Jim, I notice you've had a hard time staying focused today. Is there some way I could help you get back on track?" or, "What would help you refocus and get back on track?" Sometimes this will lead to help in the form of moving the student's seat.

Consequence 3: Quiet Time

This consequence is really an opportunity offered for a student to regain composure and self-control when behavior, such as excessive talking, is getting out of control. "Juan, I think you need a little quiet time to regain your focus. What part of the room would be good for you to use?" Quiet time can be replaced with a walk around the classroom or a one-minute stroll in the hallway that the student takes to regain control and focus.

It is different from time-out (Consequence 10) because time-out is teacher enforced and the beginning and ending times are usually teacher determined. Teachers can work out a cuing system with individual students who do not read their own signals and indicate when it would be advisable for them to take such a quiet time. The agreement is that the reason for taking the quiet time is for the student to take the initiative to refocus.

Consequence 4: Warning

Warnings inform individual students that they are getting near the threshold of receiving an aversive consequence. The warning can be delivered privately in the student's ear. "That's 1, Kiesha." Maybe when she gets to 3, the consequence becomes automatic. Students have to know what the consequence is, and everything we said in the previous section about consistent and certain implementation of the consequence must be carried out.

Warnings may also be delivered publicly by writing a student's name on the board and putting a stroke next to it for stage 2. These warnings are objective, low-affect moves that can be delivered without even mentioning the student's name or interrupting the flow of instruction in any way. Calm, neutrally delivered warnings avoid confrontation and blame, and they convey the message that this is just the way of the social order, as Dreikurs (Dreikurs & Cassel, 1972) would say.

It is not absolutely necessary that students know exactly what will happen to them when they cross the threshold. In fact, it can be even more effective if they don't, as long as they know something will happen, and they won't like it. And even if they don't know what will happen, you (the teacher) need to know the range of options you may actually carry out.

Medium Consequences

These consequences require some teacher time and effort, and they are somewhat risky and inconvenient for the student.

Consequence 5: Re-education

Cafeteria school is a favorite example of this consequence. Students, who misbehave in the cafeteria, are required to attend cafeteria school following afternoon dismissal or during recess. They receive a real "class" in cafeteria manners and appropriate behavior with modeling, practice, and testing. The unstated assumption is that if they knew how to behave properly, they would. This positive attribution of intent is slightly tongue in cheek, but not entirely.

Many students in early grades do need practice in the impulse control and expected norms to wait quietly in audiences or contain their urge to run in hallways. The older the students are, the more aversive cafeteria school is. And the bonus is that students don't want to repeat being sent to it and don't form the usual resentment that detention or other punishments generate.

Consequence 6: Hold Up a Mirror: Simple Counting or Anecdotal Record-Keeping

This consequence is about holding up a mirror to the student about his or her behavior. Here's an example of the first version: simple counting.

> **Example 1:** Latoya is always calling out and interrupting in class.
>
> It is impulsive on her part, and the teacher decides to use simple counting to highlight the behavior and call Latoya's attention to it. After a group one day, the conversation goes something like this.
>
> **Teacher:** "Latoya, do you know that you call out a lot without raising your hand? It's really distracting to me and unfair to the rest of the kids who want to speak."
>
> **Student:** "I'm sorry. I'll stop. I promise." (They have had these conversations before.)
>
> **Teacher:** "Are you really willing to work on it? Well, I'd like to help you. How many times do you think you call out in a lesson?"
>
> **Student:** "I don't know—maybe five?" (It's more like 25.)
>
> **Teacher:** "Well, let's see tomorrow. I'll put a piece of masking tape on my wrist, and every time you call out, I'll put a mark on it without saying anything or stopping the lesson, but you'll be able to see me doing it and you'll know what it means. Okay?"
>
> **Student:** "Okay."
>
> This technique can be highly effective in reducing habitual or impulsive behaviors when no more serious issues are involved than attention getting and impulsivity. Simply seeing the teacher make a stroke on the tape reminds the student of the goal: to reduce calling out.
>
> "Oops," says Latoya, as she sees another stroke going down. Soon she learns to anticipate a stroke before a call-out and starts inhibiting the call-outs herself. Afterward, the teacher and Latoya can add up the total call-outs and set a goal to reduce the total tomorrow. A week of this may be sufficient to teach the inhibition Latoya needs to control calling out.

This technique, and other forms of specific counting or record-keeping about behaviors, make students more aware of what they're doing and make the reduction of unwanted behavior a mutual teacher-student goal. The counting is the feedback to students about their progress and needs to be prompt, complete, and frequent (Van Houton, 1980). Students have to be willing to try for the technique to work. Sometimes a teacher count of a behavior before discussing it with students produces data with which to confront them. They may be so surprised by how often they behave inappropriately that the shock value will motivate them. Teachers can use the technique on a whole class as well as on individuals. Here the goal becomes lowering the class total of call-outs or whatever is the inappropriate behavior being brought to awareness.

Another version of this strategy is anecdotal record-keeping: pausing to write verbatims of incidents when children have outbursts or interruptions, and then sharing the data with the student. The simple power of data without judgment is illustrated by the story of Simone.

Example 2:

Simone Was Out of Control

I thought I'd tried everything—until the day I stumbled onto a solution that completely changed my teaching style.

Watching Simone, my tallest, lankiest, loudest third grader clunk around the classroom in my wedge heeled shoes was enough to make anyone chuckle. (Teachers who've chosen comfort over style will understand my shoes weren't on my feet.) But Simone's frequent, disruptive outbursts were no laughing matter.

"Simone," I demanded stridently, "take off my shoes!"

"I was just trying them out," she replied, not at all abashed, continuing her jaunt around the room. Michael had the audacity to smile as she sallied past.

"What are you laughing at, stupid face?" Simone snarled.

"Sit down, Simone," I intervened wearily, "and please try to remember that we don't call each other names here. You owe Michael an apology."

"I do not!" she exploded. "He laughed at me, and I don't like his ugly face."

Losing all remaining composure, I yelled, "Sit down and be quiet."

I Was at a Loss

This was just one of many times Simone's inappropriate behavior upset me and unsettled the whole class. Sometimes her explosions were angry; sometimes they were rambunctious. But they were always frightening. Simone simply had no idea how overwhelming she was to me or to her classmates.

Despite all our troubles, I couldn't help liking Simone for her generosity and enthusiasm. And I know she liked me, too. She frequently brought me an apple in the morning. "For you, because you're the best teacher I've ever had," she'd announce as she put the apple on my desk. But our up-and-down relationship was underscored by the fact that I rarely got to eat my apples. Simone was usually angry at me long before noon, and when she got mad, she'd reclaim the apple or hurl it into the wastebasket. Many times, she'd jab her pencil into it with harsh, angry thrusts.

The pattern was set by mid September. Several times a day, Simone would explode, and I would reason, cajole, placate, issue ultimatums—and too often yell—in vain attempts to control her outbursts. I'd already tried sending her to the principal's office, but she liked going there. I'd called her mother several times, but our conversations led nowhere.

Nothing was working, and I was exhausted at the end of every day. Correctly or not, I blamed Simone for how out of control I was feeling in the classroom. In truth, I was an emotional wreck—too caught up in the daily drama to think of a way out of my predicament.

When Out of the Blue . . .

Though it was only September, I was beginning to look longingly to summer vacation as my only out. Then suddenly, and unexpectedly, I stumbled on an amazingly simple solution.

I was with a reading group—not Simone's—and the other groups were working independently. Suddenly, the relative calm was shattered by a spate of Simone's angry, hurtful words. I simply couldn't summon up the energy to play my usual role—rush over to her, reprimand her sternly, and try to make amends to whichever of the children was her victim. Instead, I thought to myself, *I'm going to write down what happened, and by the end of the day I'll at least be able to remember what she did that was so horrible.* So I leaned over to my desk, picked up a yellow tablet and pen and began writing. When I had a verbatim record of her words, I looked over toward Simone to find her and most of her classmates staring at me. Sensing that the fireworks were over for the moment, I laid down my pen and returned to my reading group.

The next explosion occurred as we were about to begin a science lesson. Simone couldn't find her textbook, so she snatched Kara's book, screaming angrily: "Kara keeps stealing my stuff." Again, I reached for my tablet and began to write.

This time, Simone hurried over and demanded to know what I was writing. Showing her the tablet, I said, "I'm just writing down what you say and do." Seeing her words appear in front of her seemed to shock Simone: she returned to her seat, and we had science without a single interruption.

By 3 o'clock, I noticed that whenever I saw Simone starting trouble or gearing up for an outburst, all I had to do was pick up my pen and she'd stop instantly. I kept up this new strategy. Within a week, Simone's tirades no longer controlled my classroom.

It Was Magic

I was thrilled. Now that I could finally think straight, not only did I continue to wield my mighty pen but I had the time and energy to notice what Simone and her classmates were doing right. I began taking care to praise them for their good behavior. Consequently, there was more of it.

By now, I was completely enamored of my pen, and I began to experiment with extending its power. Whenever I felt overwhelmed or bewildered, I found I could clarify things by jotting down notes. It was a way of taking a step back and surveying what was going on.

If this writing strategy works so well for me, I thought, why wouldn't it work for 8-year-olds, too? I issued a new classroom rule. Henceforth, all complaints had to be in writing. I designed and duplicated complaint forms that provided space for the signature of the complainant, the name of the accused, and a description of the crime including date, time, conditions, corroborating witnesses, and details of any physical evidence. I stored the forms next to a "Complaint Box."

Initially, I checked the box each afternoon and rendered judgments and punishments. Soon, however, I hit upon the idea of rotating the judgeship. Committees were formed to review the complaints, eliminate frivolous claims, and decide valid ones. The students also suggested punishments, although I retained veto power.

Apogee and Apples

The new system made the children responsible for their own behavior. That made them feel powerful and more confident. They even began to come up with their own rules—such as the rule that no one involved in a dispute could sit on a committee that week.

Just when our classroom was beginning to look more and more like *The People's Court*, the number of disputes started declining. By spring, we were holding court only once a week, and the committee that reviewed the complaints rarely had more than one or two they considered valid.

Looking back over that year, I find myself saying a silent thank you to Simone. I've been reaping the benefits of what she taught me ever since that stormy September morning when I picked up a pen and started writing. Just as my pen and yellow tablet had come to signal serious intent to her and the class, the complaint form and a pencil reminded the children to stop and reason. As for me, besides enjoying the taste of success, I got to eat a lot of apples. (Arnold, 1987, pp. 44–45)

Consequence 7: Pulling the Card

This behavior from Fred Jones (2013) is a more developed form of the warning. To implement, you must have a card file on your desk with the name and home phone number of each student, including the work number of a family member. When misbehavior reaches a certain level, having already issued a warning to a student, you (1) catch the student's eye; (2) take a relaxing breath; (3) walk slowly to your desk without calling attention to yourself; (4) casually pick up the card file; (5) leaf through it; (6) pull the student's card while looking at him and lay it on the corner of your desk face up; (7) look again at the student without expression (Jones calls it "your best Queen Victoria face") as you place the card file back on your desk; and (8) resume instruction, giving the student one final look.

Consequence 8: Letter Home Taped to Desk

No discipline management technique comes with a guarantee, so what if the disruption continues even after you have pulled the card? How can you still stop the disruption without taking on the cost and risks of medium backup responses? The final response in your hierarchy of small backup responses is one more that comes from Fred Jones (2013): write a letter home to the student's family and tape it to the student's desk with an appropriate warning.

The procedure goes something like this:

> 1. Following at least two other warnings (small consequences), catch the student's eye, go to your desk, and sit down and begin to write a brief letter (five sentences or less) home:
>
> "Dear [parent's name]:
>
> Today in class I have had to deal with [briefly describe the behavior].
>
> I need your help.
>
> If we work together now, we can prevent this from becoming a real problem. I will call you tomorrow, at which time we can make a plan.
>
> Thank you for your help."
>
> 2. Sign the letter, and put it in an envelope.
>
> 3. Address the envelope, but don't stamp it yet.
>
> 4. Take the letter and tape it to the student's desk while privately letting him know it is a letter to his parents or guardians about his behavior in class:
>
> "If I see no more of this behavior before the end of [the day or week] then, with my permission and in front of my eyes, you may tear up this letter and throw it away. If, however, I see any more of this behavior, I will send the letter home or hand deliver it. Do I make myself clear? For now, all I care about is getting some of this work done. Let's see if we can keep life simple." (pp. 316–317)

Consequence 9: Student Has to Account for the Behavior in Writing

Many schools require students who have been sent to the administrator's office to write an account of why they have been removed from class and sent there. The writing is not much of a nuisance for the student since he or she has nothing to do in the office anyway, and it gives the student a chance to make his or her side of the case. The writing is not such an aversive behavior. But when the writing has to take place in the student's own classroom and be given to the teacher who saw the behavior and called it, that is a different matter. Some years ago, Viv Swoboda, then an eighth-grade teacher, used the writing accountability technique to quell a rising tide of off-task behaviors. Here it is in her own words:

Because the class I have this year is particularly challenging and continually testing the established limits, I have done a lot of thinking about logical consequences for inappropriate activities in school. I am very conscious of how much school time gets wasted dealing with inappropriate behaviors, and how some students continually draw the class and me away from the day's lesson. I struggled with what would be appropriate logical consequences for the various class disruptions that I could consistently implement without giving myself a lot of extra work in the process.

I decided that I would develop a form that a student would have to fill out each time they did something inappropriate in school. I asked the students to respond to five questions:

1. What was your inappropriate activity in school?

2. Why was your activity inappropriate for school?

3. What are the negative effects that your inappropriate actions have on others?

4. What consequences would keep you from doing this inappropriate activity in the future?

5. Why is it necessary to have rules in order for a school to function smoothly?

I would give the student the form after asking them to stop the inappropriate activity. The form needs to be returned to me by 8:00 the following morning. Students knew I recorded the inappropriate activity in a notebook, but I usually didn't record it until after class because I try not to break the momentum any more than necessary.

In the beginning, there was a lot of complaining from the students every time I gave them a form to fill out. I had spent a lot of time talking about what I was doing and why and had asked for their suggestions for ways to eliminate the many inappropriate activities that happened during classes. I made a slide of the form, went over the form with each one of my classes, and explained why I had included each of the questions. When it came time to use the form, I wasn't going to discuss it and continue taking time away from the lesson. In the beginning, some of the students tried to engage me in a debate, but I simply gave them the form, reminded them I needed it back by 8:00 the following morning, and quickly tried to refocus the class on the lesson.

After two days, the students realized that they weren't going to draw me into a debate and that I was consistently going to ask any student who was doing something inappropriate to complete one of these forms. Ninety-nine percent of the students brought back the forms by the next morning. I had the one percent of students who didn't return the form complete it during their ten-minute break that occurs during the middle of the morning. It was torture for those students to have to sit at their desks and complete this form rather than be able to socialize with their friends. They decided they would rather complete the form for homework than give up precious time with their peers.

The number of inappropriate activities in my class has diminished tremendously. Before I started using these forms, there may have been twelve times a day that I might have spoken to students about doing something that was inappropriate in class. When I first started using the form, I would give out about six forms a day. Now I may pass out one form in three days.

I learned that my students really could control their inappropriate actions in school. This form really isn't a terrible punishment, but it is enough of an annoyance that it encourages most of my students to think before they do inappropriate things in class. This system has worked for me because it doesn't require a lot of my time. I keep the forms in a folder on my desk that I can reach easily, so I keep the break in the class's momentum to a minimum. Students asked what I was going to do with these forms. I told them it depended on whether the inappropriate actions stopped.

Some students didn't want their parents or school administrators to become involved, and these forms were a clear record of who was disrupting the class. After the students all saw the form, they felt there should be a question asking why they did what they did. They felt it was important for me to have that information. I will include that question on a revised form.

Consequence 10: Time-Out in the Classroom

Time-out is an elementary technique not usually suitable in secondary school. It is often a feature in behavior modification programs and thus is unpopular with educators who prefer more child-centered approaches. However, Ruth Charney (2002), one of the most humanistic and child-centered educators in the United States, devotes an entire chapter in *Teaching Children to Care* to implementing time-out. We recommend her version.

> Marty is jostling Kintara for the second time in the back row of the rug area where classroom meeting has just started. "Marty, time-out."
>
> Marty gets up from her seat and goes to the time-out chair, located in a visible (not central) area of the classroom. She sits for five minutes or until she receives a gesture from her teacher to return to her group. Signaled by her teacher's nod, Marty quietly returns to her place. There has been no explanation, no discussion. The unstated message is: "You know the rules. You know you are disturbing the meeting. You will be able to recover your controls and return as a member of the group." Later, the teacher will check in to make sure that Marty does understand why she was sent to time-out. (p. 168)

Charney (2002) makes a point of introducing the procedure of time-out to the children carefully and completely. "It's a way that grownups help children get back in control. Children can also teach themselves to get back their controls and remember their rules. I stress that time-out is a job; it is work to recover your controls." Note the careful way Charney (2002) frames time-out:

> Everyone forgets their controls sometimes and everyone forgets the rules sometimes. Children forget the rules, so do teachers and parents. Our rules make it safe and good for everyone in school: not just me, not just one or two other people—everyone. So it's very important that we respect the rules and use them. When we do forget or choose not to use a rule, we need to remember. We need a time-out. *Time-out is a chance to recover the rules* so we can keep our classroom safe and good and to gather our own controls. Then we are ready to come back and join the group.
>
> The key to using a time-out effectively is to pay attention to the small disruptions [see the echo of this principle in Fred Jones], the minor infractions and misbehaviors. We take action before the lesson is in ruins, before self-controls—the student's and our own—deteriorate. When we wait for things to get worse, we are rarely disappointed.
>
> We don't allow the minor drumming on the desk to reach a crescendo. The nagging and nuisance behavior does not go on until finally all our "buttons" are pushed. The background whispers and snide teasing are not ignored until fists fly and tears pour. (p. 173)
>
> A pattern of casual "shut-ups" is not allowed to grow into one of constant insults. Noah may not call Mark "Fatty," even if he claims he's joking. Kevin may not use his superior size to push others aside, take a pencil

> or reserve first place in line. The group lesson might be stalled if I say, "Martin, the blackboard is this way!" for the fiftieth time between clenched teeth instead of saying, "Martin, time-out." The small sideshows will not devastate the lesson or the temper of the teacher. But, unless they are confronted, these "small disturbances" add up to constant noise and interruptions which drain and divert the best intentions. Often they are the very things we pretend not to notice.
>
> Alex regularly careens around the room—his idea of walking is full speed ahead. He's a large boy, and he frequently bumps into the furniture, other children, and even largish teachers. He's quick to say "sorry" and express genuine regret, but if he slowed down he would hardly crash at all and no one would get hurt. Why make a fuss? He's only ten—he can't help it. But the fact is he *can* help it. He can move slowly and with planning—or not move at all.
>
> It is important that children understand that they can help it. Minor disturbances are within their control. (p. 175)
>
> In the immediate enforcement of time-out, lengthy verbal explanations and negotiations are strictly avoided. Imagine if instead of the directive, "Time-out," the teacher had said, "Donny you need to go to time-out, because you are rolling a ball and not listening to Christie." Would Donny, now the center of attention, be more apt to agree or argue, "I *was* so listening . . ." An argument might lead next to a confrontation, and Christie's sharing would quickly take second place to the duel between teacher and student.
>
> If the teacher had just reached over and taken the ball from Donny, called his name or nudged him gently back into the activity, with no mention of time-out, wouldn't that be as effective and easier? Not likely. Too many reminders (more than one) allow small disturbances to keep erupting like popcorn—one after another—and keep taking the attention of the teacher and group. Time-out sends the message that you are *truly* expected to follow the rules. (p. 178)
>
> At the right moment—after a time-out—explanation and discussion help students construct meaning and take responsibility. At the wrong time—while a rule is being enforced—discussion stimulates evasion. (p. 180)

We recommend readers read Charney's (2002) entire chapter (and book, for that matter) to get the full flavor of this decisive yet humanistic version of time-out.

Exhibit 10.3 How Time-Out in a Colleague's Classroom Works

1. Introduction
   a. Introduce exclusion move to the whole class with its causes and consequences. It is a way of helping students remember and follow rules that allow them to enjoy learning.
2. Implementation
   a. Give one private warning with specification of behavior.
   b. Give a public explanation of why the child is being removed.
   c. Remove the child, voluntarily or physically if necessary, or call the parent.
   d. Time-out is maintained for a half-hour.
   e. The child is excluded from participation or interaction with the second class.
   f. Review the situation with the class:
      -Alternative ways the excluded child might have acted
      -Reasons for the rule
      -How to help the child follow the rules
3. After-School Interview
   a. To help, not to embarrass, is the motive.
   b. The teacher hopes a warning will be sufficient in the future.
   c. The teacher explains that it was the child who decided, by his or her behavior, when to be excluded.
   d. Show the child affection and respect.

Adapted from Sarason (1996) pp.165-167.

Consequence 11: Time-Out in a Colleague's Room

Time-out in a colleague's room was first written about, to our knowledge, by Seymour Sarason in 1971. It was intended for elementary grades. With modifications, we have used it successfully in high schools as well, including inner-city high schools. Here is Sarason (1996) describing the version for young children (see Exhibit 10.3 for a summary):

> Relationship building techniques for influencing the unmanageable child are indispensable to involving him constructively in the classroom, but they are usually insufficient to produce the dramatic suppression of hostile defiance that is necessary if he is to be allowed by the principal to remain in school. For the child's own welfare, therefore, it is necessary to work out with the teacher influence techniques that effectively suppress the child's defiant outbursts almost at once, unless teacher and psychologist feel that he would profit from a brief exclusion from school. The use of exclusion from school as an initial influence technique, however, is usually not nearly so effective with the defiant child as other measures. One of three techniques for suppressing defiant outbursts is implemented along with the relationship building techniques in the case of each unmanageable child.

The most commonly recommended technique for suppressing defiant behavior is that of excluding the disobedient child from his classroom and placing him for half an hour in a classroom nearby. The success of exclusion depends on the preparation given by the psychologist or counsellor to the teachers and school personnel involved, the support or toleration of the principal, and *the precise manner in which the teacher prepares her class and implements the technique* [italics added]. Any such dramatic recommendation, of course, requires the approval and comprehension of the principal, whose begrudging acceptance of the plan could undermine teachers' use of it. The principal must also participate in selecting the relatively experienced teacher with whom the unmanageable child's teacher pairs. Teachers have an antipathy to imposing on each other: the excluding teacher usually feels embarrassed about depending on another teacher, and the receiving teacher is concerned about her class being unsettled by the visitor. These understandable concerns must be recognized and assurance given that the plan may be stopped if it creates more problems than it solves. The participating pair of teachers must be fully briefed on the rationale and dangers in the plan so that they experience as few surprises as possible in implementing it. From our experience with the exclusion plan we now routinely brief participating teachers on several points. When a child is received in another room, he is to be given a seat at the back and excluded from any form of participation or interaction in the class. Before making this clear to teachers we occasionally found the excluded child excitedly participating in the receiving teacher's classroom activities. We also now prepare the excluding teacher for the problem of a child refusing to leave the room. He is to be carried out by the pair of teachers if he is in kindergarten through second grade. Older children refusing to leave their rooms are to be informed that unless they do so their parents will be phoned immediately. Never has a child refused to respond to either pressure. Never has an excluded child posed the slightest problem in the receiving classroom. Never has a child greeted the exclusion with anything but distasteful embarrassment.

So far the exclusion has the ingredients of an effective technique for suppressing defiant outbursts: it immediately terminates the disobedient behavior without introducing complications in either the receiving or excluding classrooms. Its unpleasant quality for the child renders it an effective influence technique in shaping more compliant subsequent behavior. The most significant source of power adhering to the plan, however, is probably not its unpleasantness per se but its decisive ability to force on the consciousness of the child the limits beyond which he may no longer go; in short, to underline by dramatic action those rules that other children remember and obey through verbal injunctions alone. It also gives the teacher a measure of authority she had been lacking in verbal injunctions. If the plan is to maximize the child's chances of remembering and following classroom rules it must be introduced to the whole class not as an angry punitive retaliation by a distraught teacher but as a way of helping children to remember to follow rules that allow them to enjoy learning. It should be explained to the children repeatedly that a child will be excluded not because he is unwanted or disliked but because he needs the brief opportunity in another classroom to reflect on the rules he has been disobeying. By introducing the procedure to the entire class in a group discussion it does not appear as though the defiant child is being singled out; the shock of implementing the technique is reduced to more manageable proportion; and its rationale is communicated during a period of relative calm in the classroom. In their actual implementation of the plan teachers are cautioned against excluding children when they are furious with them, waiting instead until they have regained their composure. At that point the child is to be given one private, unembarrassing warning that clearly states that if a specific behavior does not cease he will be excluded. If several children are acting up defiantly they are to be warned publicly, but in no case is a child excluded unless he had one and only one private warning from the teacher to remind him clearly of the rule he is breaking and of impending exclusion if he does not stop disrupting the class. Contained in such private warnings must be the teacher's attempt to explain to the child how he is disrupting the class, together with whatever relationship building techniques she feels appropriate and feasible. Should the child subsequently defy the warning intentionally, he is to be led out of the classroom by the teacher who explains to the entire class in the presence of the child why he is being excluded.

On returning to the classroom after delivering the child to the receiving teacher, the excluding teacher reviews the situation with her class, emphasizing the reasons behind the relevant rules and alternative ways in which the excluded child might have acted. Whenever possible her remarks are channeled into a group discussion that can be used to marshal the support of the class in helping the excluded child. Once children have expressed their expected bitterness toward the defiant child in such discussions, the teacher can elicit more sympathetic interest from them in helping him, especially when she points out that she needs help from the class in teaching the excluded child to follow class rules. Such discussion can be used to marshal the support of the class on a meaningful basis for the teacher to develop with her children a causal and change oriented view of surface misbehavior. If the excluded child is to derive from his exclusion the maximum incentive and minimum discouragement to changing his ways, the teacher must schedule a short after-school

> interview with the child on the day of his exclusion. Like the class discussion, the follow-up interview is an essential ingredient in effecting a rapid suppression of his defiant outbursts. During the interview the teacher can explain how she excluded the child to help him remember class rules rather than to embarrass him, how she hopes that in the future a warning will be sufficient to induce the child to control his behavior, how it is the child himself and not the teacher who decides whether he is to be excluded from the room. Finally, the teacher can use the interview to explore with the child whatever difficulties he is experiencing in the classroom, promising the child confidentiality if he wishes to reveal something personal. Throughout the interview the teacher makes clear her affection and respect for the child, indicating how his misbehavior is at least as discrepant with his own hopes for himself as it is with hers for him. The psychologist can be helpful in reducing the aversion some teachers express about "psychoanalyzing" their students. As long as they do not probe deeply and listen warmly and acceptingly to any problems the child discusses, their common sense and professional ethics, he tells them, are adequate guides. Most of the inner city children who require psychotherapy will never receive it; thus the teacher's may be the only interest ever expressed in their emotional lives. Of course, the psychologist is always available to review with a teacher any material that baffles or disturbs her. We have never regretted encouraging teachers to conduct such therapy like interviews, though we have played down the suggestion with some teachers more than others. One outcome of such interviews is that they establish an open line of communication between child and teacher by dramatizing the teacher's wish to help him by talking with him rather than by forcing him to change. (pp. 136–139)

For older students, physical removal is obviously inappropriate, but most of the other features of Sarason's original design still apply. A receiving teacher, preferably in a grade widely separated from the student's, has to be identified, and a routine for accepting the student nonjudgmentally but in a non-reinforcing setting must be prearranged. The wide separation of grade level results in young children going to older children's rooms and vice versa. This adds to the aversive nature of the strategy because of the embarrassment or intimidation of being sent to such a room.

A monitoring adult, dean, or security officer may be needed to escort the student to be removed to the receiving classroom. And some work for the student to do should be sent with him or her as well.

High Impact Consequences

These consequences are particularly aversive for the student and signal that serious improvement is needed.

Consequence 12: Phone Call Home with Student Reporting What Happened in Teacher's Presence

The teacher calls the parent: "Mr. Palmer, this is Justin Rivera, your son's teacher. There's been an incident in class with your son, Michael, and I've asked him to explain to you himself what happened. Would you hold a second while I pass the phone to Michael?" If the student leaves out any important details, the teacher can remind him to insert them.

It is sometimes surprising how tough adolescents will turn to jelly after lots of hostile bluffing when you actually pick up the phone. **If there is strong reason to expect physical abuse will follow at home, do not use this consequence.**

Consequence 13: Parent Conference with Home Reporting and Consequences; Contract Signed by Teacher, Family, and Student

In this fairly heavy-duty consequence, the family has been in for a conference with the teacher and perhaps the assistant principal as well. A behavioral contract has been written with certain behaviors and consequences at home as well as at school (Exhibits 10.4 and 10.5). Reports are sent home frequently about the student's behavior, and the consequences delivered at home are contingent on the reports from the student's teachers.

Consequence 14: In-School Suspension

In-school suspension is a vehicle for students to evaluate their behavior and make choices. It is important that the suspension be framed that way for the student and carried out with that effect authentically. Those supervising the suspension room must see their role as helping a student evaluate choices and making a plan for successful re-entry into mainstream classes. This counseling presence is important for a successful in-school suspension program.

Consequence 15: Saturday School

Students who have been disruptive repeatedly during the week in school and failed to respond to consequences have probably missed significant amounts of class time. As a consequence, they may be required to come to Saturday School (usually Saturday morning from 9 to 12) where they must make up missed work. Staffing must be available to implement this approach, and it must be clear that Saturday School is not a place to "serve time" in a punitive sense, but rather a requirement to make up work the student missed during

Exhibit 10.4 Student Agreement

Smith Middle School
STUDENT AGREEMENT

Smith Middle School (SMS) is a place of learning and growing through a variety of experiences. Each student has the rights and privileges of our program as well as the responsibilities. Each student owns his behavior and the consequences of the behavior, good and bad. Upon entry to SMS, Daniel will be expected to abide by the code of behavior as described in general in our school handbook (pages 25 and 26). More specifically, he will be expected to demonstrate the following appropriate behavior:

Arrive to school on time daily.
Arrive to each class on time and prepared with class materials, books, and writing utensils.
Complete all assignments (homework, classwork, and special projects) according to teacher directions and turn them in on time.
In class: Pay attention.
Focus attention on the class lesson.

Any behavior that interferes with his learning or the learning of other students will not be tolerated. This includes:

Speaking out
Moving out of his seat
Looking around
Making sounds

If he does act inappropriately, the teacher will simply state, "Daniel, this is inappropriate. If you do it again, you will report to the office."

Daniel will report to the housemaster, and the discipline referral form will be completed.
Mrs. Z will receive a copy of all discipline referral forms.
If two discipline referral forms are necessary in one day, Daniel's mother will be contacted, and he will have to go home for the day.

It is important to note that each referral involves the assignment of two demerits, and once the demerits add up to a suspension, it will be assigned.

Mature behavior is also expected in the corridors, cafeteria gym, and locker room.
There will be no pushing, shoving, swearing, or insulting. The same results as described earlier will apply.
Daniel will leave the school grounds at 2:05 unless he has been asked to stay by a teacher.

As is the case for all SMS students, Daniel is welcome to attend our roller skating parties, dances, and special events. However, again as is the case for all SMS students, if Daniel's behavior warrants it, he will be asked to leave, and attendance to future events will be subject to review.

A meeting will be scheduled after Daniel has been at SMS for four weeks to review his behavior. It is important that he understand this STUDENT AGREEMENT and sign it.

____________________(Principal) ____________________(Student)

____________________(Housemaster) ____________________(Parent)

____________________(Coordinator) ____________________ (Chairperson)

Exhibit 10.5 Educational Contract

EDUCATIONAL CONTRACT

Student's Name: Daniel
Effective: Nov. 15, 2017
Review: Dec. 15, 2017

Classroom Behavior Expectations

Daniel will arrive to class on time.
Daniel will come to class prepared (pencils, paper, book, etc.).
Daniel will speak out in class only after raising his hand and being recognized.
Daniel will conduct himself in a courteous and respectful manner.
Daniel will not interfere with other students' rights to learn, or the teacher's right to teach.

Consequences

First Offense: After a violation of the stated expectations, Daniel is required to leave the classroom and study in the Quiet Study for the remainder of the period.
Subsequent Offenses: On a subsequent offense within the day, Daniel is required to leave the classroom and will be sent home after the parents have been notified.

Teacher

After a violation of the expectations, the teacher will signal Daniel to leave the class and notify the office. The teacher will in no way influence Daniel to do or not to do anything. (No urging, reminding, coaxing, encouraging, or scolding.) The teacher agrees to respect Daniel's right to fail or succeed on his own.

Principal

On notification of a violation of the expectations, the principal agrees to see to it that Daniel leaves the class if the signal has been given by the teacher is not acted on by the student.

Student

Daniel agrees that he is fully responsible for himself and that everything he does and does not do is done or not done by his own choice. He agrees to take responsibility for his failure as well as his success.

Cc: Mrs. X
Mr. Y
Ms. G
Daniel's teachers

the week. Thus it is required as a logical consequence of disrupting learning time, not an alternative way to sit detention.

Consequence 16: Parent Accompanies Student to School

The embarrassment factor is at work in this consequence, which is both novel and effective from the middle grades on up. Here is an account of how one middle school implemented this consequence:

> Bob Browning spent a day at Wilson Junior High School in Hamilton, Ohio, some time ago. That in itself is unremarkable: Browning, after all, is president of the city's board of education. As he moved from class to class, taking his seat at student desks and quietly sitting through each period, some of the teachers got nervous. "They had no reason to," Browning says, "but it was understandable." Yet the most uncomfortable person in any of those classes was Browning's son, Sam, an eighth-grader, because Bob Browning wasn't in class in his official capacity. He was there in a more important role, as Sam's father, and he was taking part in a program that subjects kids who break school rules to an ingenious—and devilishly effective—deterrent: bringing Mom or Dad to school.
>
> "I got the idea accidentally," remembers John Lazares, Wilson's 37-year-old principal. "A kid came into my office whom I had seen a number of times for minor discipline problems—talking in class, being late, not bringing materials, driving the teachers crazy. I just got fed up and said, "The next time I see you, we're going to have your mother come in and see what we have to put up with all day." The reaction I got from him was, "Do anything you want, but don't have my mother come in." I'd never had this reaction from a kid before—and we've had kids arrested for drugs, suspended and expelled. He begged me not to have his mother come in. Something lit up in my head."
>
> Situated in an industrial city midway between Cincinnati and Dayton, Wilson has a student body that reflects the city's racial, economic and ethnic diversity—and divisions. Until nine years ago, when a controversial new school superintendent began a citywide disciplinary crackdown, Hamilton's schools were scarred by violence, tension and drug use. By the time Lazares became principal last January, the school had a functioning code of conduct and an improving reputation. But up to 60 of Wilson's 860 students were expelled every semester, and dozens more were being suspended for everything from tardiness to fighting in school.
>
> "One of the worst things that can happen to a child is to be suspended from school," says Lazares. "It's a waste. He spends three days at home for some little misdemeanor, and it makes him happy to be out of class.

> I decided to tell parents, "Okay, if you'll come in and spend one day in class with that kid, I'll take the suspension away."
>
> So far about 60 parents have put in their time at Wilson. "I thought it was great that I could come down and eliminate a little trouble for my son," Bob Browning says gamely. Sam was in trouble for missing detention. "I enjoyed it," says Ella Neal. "It helped me a lot to understand what the teachers had to go through and to understand my child much better." Her son, James, had been disrupting his seventh-grade class. Kids seem to improve dramatically when their parents come to Wilson. After-school detentions are down from 20 a day to zero on some days; expulsions have dropped to 11 since the program began. Only a handful of parents have refused to join what Lazares calls his Parent Involvement Program; many are eager to come. "For a lot of them, it's their first time in a school building since they graduated," he says.
>
> On a recent morning, a few "veterans" discussed the program. "I was embarrassed," said Sam Browning. "One kid cried all day," said Shane Isaacs. Shane cleaned up his act when his parents simply met with the principal and threatened to go to class with him. "This is a tool for preventive discipline," says Lazares. "Kids who have seen other kids' parents in school stop causing problems, because they don't want their own parents to sit with them all day."
>
> Punishment is only one aspect of the Wilson program. "In education, we're only as effective as the parents," says Lazares, "and now we have parents who call us once a week to check up on their kids' progress. If a child has been a discipline problem and goes for a while without causing trouble, I call them up and say, "You're doing something right." Each teacher now makes five phone calls—positive or negative—to students' homes every week. Lazares personally calls the parents of every child who makes the honor roll: 200 phone calls one week. "I want to notice those kids who do a good job" he says. (Ryan, 1987, p. 10)

Consequence 17: Deliver Student to Responsible Adult at Work

This consequence follows an escalating series of responses to a student's disruptive behavior. A responsible adult, who should be no stranger at this point to the problems in school, is notified that a car is on the way over with the student.

Last Resort Consequences

These consequences do nothing to improve behavior or reintegrate the student into school life and we should go to extreme lengths to avoid them. Suspension, especially for older students, can easily be a reward of free time to get in trouble out of school and has the huge opportunity cost of students missing instruction. In-school suspension is always better and at least preserves both time for learning and for reintegration of restitution.

Consequence 18: Suspension

We do not recommend suspension because it is usually a reward rather than a penalty, at least for older children. Students get unsupervised time away from school, lose academic time, and have more access to getting into trouble. It may become necessary, however, to separate a student from campus for a period of days where facilities are not available for in-house suspension. In this case, every effort should be made to arrange for the student to be in a supervised environment, perhaps some form of community service. Above all, when the suspension is over, a plan needs to be made with some accountability in it between the student, family or guardian, and the school for the conditions of readmission to school.

Consequences 19 and 20: Police Involvement; Expulsion

By the time we get to numbers 19 and 20, we have effectively given up. These extreme measures are obviously the end of the line and require hearings and due process. We include them to complete the loop on the hierarchy of consequences. Interestingly, Restorative Discipline, to be discussed at the end of this chapter, can sometimes get us out of this last resort situation.

Level 3: Building a Climate of Community Safety and Agency

We want to build responsibility and self-discipline into classroom life. This means moving away from teacher control to building internal controls in each student and community responsibility for the classroom climate and environment (see Chapter 16, "Classroom Climate").

Giving Students a Real and Legitimate Sense of Control, Influence, Responsibility, and Power

Teachers can structure classes so students feel some ownership and control of what goes on. Doing so can reduce discipline problems. However, this is no substitute for clear expectations and consequences. They should come first. One first-year teacher, who never did get expectations and consequences sorted out that first year, nevertheless salvaged the year from total disaster by starting an individualized contract learning system. This system gave students some ownership and control by setting academic goals and providing them with good feedback. The students invested in it, and energy that might have gone into fighting the teacher went into meeting their learning goals instead. But it was still a rocky year with less than optimal learning. If expectations had been established right from the beginning, her contract system would not just have salvaged this particular class, it would have put it into orbit. So though we are strong advocates of the ideas to follow, our caution for any beginning teachers reading this section is to invest in getting expectations and consequences clear first.

There are three excellent approaches for giving students ownership in classroom life:

1. Negotiating Mendler and Curwin's social contract (see page 139).

2. Using goal setting (see Chapter 12, "Principles of Learning").

3. Teaching through one of the five cooperative models of teaching (see Chapter 20, "Differentiated Instruction").

Sometimes teachers grant students ownership or a stake in classroom operations because they let the students in on something the teacher has noticed and invite them to work on addressing the problem. A high school English teacher in one of our courses shared the following example:

> **Example 1:** While studying the Clarity area of performance, the teacher had an insight that he might often be playing "guess what's on the teacher's mind" in his question asking. He shared this with his class the next day and asked if they concurred. They did. He then asked them what they could do about it, specifically what action class members might take if he victimized them with such a question or if they observed him doing it to someone else. After collecting ideas in a general class discussion, they settled on the following procedure: when students felt that they had been asked such a question, they could call the teacher on it and ask him to restate the question. Alternately, students who could not answer a question could redirect it to another student in the class by name. At other times, the teacher would go around the class in order, asking review questions about the text read for homework. If the student could not answer a question or answered incorrectly, the next student would get the same question. If three students in a row failed to get the answer, the teacher would acknowledge that it was a poor question and rephrase it. The net result for these students, previously a low-performing class, was higher class participation and higher achievement.

It is our belief, however, that there was a lot more going on here than simply eliminating "guess what's on the teacher's mind" questions. First, the teacher was showing fairness in admitting that he could be the cause of a problem for students and looking in an open way for a solution (see Chapter 15, "Personal Relationship Building"). Second, these techniques gave the students some voice in determining the rules of the classroom game and controlling the flow of events.

> **Example 2:** Another way to give students influence and control is through incentive and reward systems. One teacher we know tried to increase students' motivation for doing homework assignments well. It had been his practice to give students daily quizzes based on homework readings. One day he told them that if they got four 100s in a row, they could earn a free 100 points that they might then "spend" on future quizzes at any time and in any way they pleased. They could skip some future quiz and take 100 on it, they could take 30 points of it and elevate a 70 to 100 sometime in the future, or just save the points. He found that students' efforts on homework assignments and quizzes dramatically improved, even those students who had already been doing well. Our hypothesis is that what was powerful about this technique was the way in which it gave students something to control: a bank account of earned points. Whether they earned them and how they would spend them was entirely within their control. (For the students already scoring well, perhaps it was insurance against future mishaps.) Other teachers have replicated that technique but have eliminated the requirement that the four 100s be in a row: simply attaining four 100s earns the 100-point bonus.

These two ingenious experiments suggest to us that there are many places in classroom life to look for ways to give students more legitimate control.

Building Community in the Class

William Glasser's (1969) classroom meetings, Gene Stanford's (1977) cycle of activities for developing effective classroom groups, relationship building activities (Wilt & Watson, 1978), cooperative learning (Dishon & O'Leary, 1998), the social competency program (Krasnow, 1993), and the Responsive Classroom program (Charney, 2002) are all approaches for building the kind of affiliation and harmony in a class that can prevent discipline problems. When relationships among class members are stressful or fractious (or both), these strategies can lower the pressure and productively rechannel energy that is going into fighting with one another. The Collaborative for Academic, Social and Emotional Learning (CASEL) is the leader in advancing these curricula today (Durlak, Domitrovich, Weissberg, & Gullotta, 2015).

Classroom Meetings

Classroom meetings are a powerful practice for building a general sense of community in a class or handling problems such as scapegoating, bullying, and cliques. In *Schools Without Failure*, Glasser (1969) describes in detail how to conduct classroom meetings and reports: "I haven't met a child incapable of thinking and participating to some degree in school if we let him know we value what he can contribute" (p. 97). That belief is essential for a teacher who wants to make classroom meetings work, because being nonjudgmental and accepting of student contributions is a key skill in leading meetings. The meetings are the vehicle through which students experience participation, the sense of being valued, and a sense of being part of something real. Class meetings are held regularly (at least weekly and preferably several times a week), with students and teacher seated in a tight circle. Teachers lead the whole class in nonjudgmental discussions about topics that are important and relevant to them. There are three types of meetings:

1. Open-ended
2. Social problem-solving
3. Educational diagnostic

In open-ended meetings, either teacher or students introduce a topic for discussion. One of the teacher's roles is to build a focusing question for the students around the topic, which can be anything of current interest to the students. In citing a meeting where the students wanted to talk about Disneyland, the teacher asked, "Who would like to go to Disneyland?" Almost every child responded affirmatively. "Suppose someone gave me two tickets to Disneyland and said I should give these tickets to two children in my class. To whom should I give the tickets?" In addition to translating open topics into focused discussions, teachers use skills of active listening and summarizing. Open-ended meetings begin building a sense of involvement with each other and lay the foundations for using the meetings for generating significant investment in academic work and the more difficult area of social problem-solving.

Glasser's (1969) description of a social problem-solving meeting explains how classroom meetings can be used to improve some of the more intractable (and usually untreated) sources of disruptive behavior in classes:

> At another meeting, Mike was introduced as the topic. Physically overweight and not too clean-looking in appearance, with hair in his eyes and a very loud, offensive voice, and holes in all his tee shirts caused from biting and twisting and chewing on them, he was not pleasant to behold! Mike said he didn't like the class because they didn't like him. When asked why they didn't like him, he said it was because he was fat. The children eagerly disagreed.

> They said that had nothing to do with it. Mike wanted to know why, then. He was given the opportunity to call on those children he wanted to explain to him what they found offensive about him. Someone said it was because he wears funny hats to school, like the pilot's helmet he wore the day before. (Incidentally, he never wore it again.) Some said he dressed sloppily. Martin said it was because he said things that hurt people. For example, when Martin came home from Europe and showed the class several treasures that he brought to share, Mike said he didn't believe they were from Paris and that he bought the same things here. Martin said that hurt his feelings. David said that when he shared things with the class, Mike blurted out similar derogatory remarks. (Mike still has not cured himself of this, by the way.) John, who had become much more introspective and perceptive, said it was because Mike always made funny faces and looked up at the ceiling with a disgusted look on his face when people tried to talk to him. While he was saying this, Mike was doing just that. John said, "See, Mike, you're doing it right now, and you don't even know it." Mike was asked if anyone, in his opinion, went out of his way to be nice to him. He said, only Alice, whom he liked. Everyone giggled. Alice said she didn't care if everyone did laugh at her, she liked Mike and was not ashamed to be his friend. She liked being nice to him. We talked as a group about the importance of having one friend at least.
>
> The others found that no one really tried to go out of his way to be his friend, but each person would try to make some gesture to show they would try in the next week. They really rose to the occasion, but soon forgot about it and were their usual apathetic selves. However, no one seemed to go out of his way to be nasty, which was a change. Alice continued being nice to Mike, and the children stopped teasing her about it. Harriet, who was one of the girls who was teasing Alice, apologized in a class meeting for doing so and she said she had once been teased for befriending someone without other friends, and that it took more courage to be his friend and yet she wanted to. She told Alice that even though it had hurt her feelings when the others teased her, she had forgotten and teased Alice and that she was sorry, and she could really understand how Alice felt. There has been a tremendous change in Mike this semester. He is not lackadaisical about his work or appearance, speaks more quietly, uses more self control, plays a fairer game in the yard, gets along much better with others, and has more (or some) friends. (pp. 152–153)

We have had teachers read this account and get scared off by it. It seems to some like opening wounds or beginning a process that could get out of control. Yet two teachers with difficult classes with whom we have worked have brought up comparable issues in their own classes and view their own series of meetings as among the most significant accomplishments of their careers. We are glad they took time to work up their courage, because they were also working up their skills at leading meetings on safer topics.

These kinds of issues can fester and hurt and drain students' energy, and bringing them out into the open with skillful leadership can make dramatic differences in class climate. Neither the teacher in Glasser's (1969) account nor those with whom we have worked were trained in counseling techniques. They were regular classroom teachers who had the courage and the commitment to want to help students build strong community within their classes and knew that there were large dividends for the effort in academic learning as well.

The teacher in the excerpt above decided that Mike could benefit from specific examples of how his behavior put others off and called for them. Furthermore, the teacher decided that it would involve Mike more (and make it safer for him) if Mike did the calling on other children. When the teacher asked Mike if anyone went out of his way to be nice to him, the teacher sensed an appropriate moment to turn the discussion around and focus on the positive. When the group talked about the importance of having one friend at least, the teacher asked a few key questions to guide the discussion that way.

Regularly practiced classroom meetings are one of the most significant climate builders for successful learning.

Recognizing such key junctures and opportunities comes from the learning that occurs in undertaking social problem-solving classroom meetings. It is not the sort of thing one rushes into the first week of school, but these skills are within the grasp of most teachers. Overall, regularly practiced classroom meetings are one of the most significant climate builders for successful learning. While he was teaching high school English, Gene Stanford (1977) came to the same conclusion and developed a carefully sequenced series of activities to build class cohesion over a year. He organized activities according to the stage of growth a class was in as it moved toward mature functioning. Students have to know something about one another before they can appreciate or become involved with one another, so Stage I is orientation. In Stage II, activities explicitly develop norms of group responsibility (through teaching awareness of others), responsiveness to others (meaning good listening skills), cooperative skills, consensus decision-making skills, and social problem-solving skills. Stage III is coping with conflict; Stage IV is about productivity; and Stage V is about termination, that is, dealing with the end of the year, the end of the life of the group, and people's feelings about that. All this he integrated with an academic program and an emphasis on writing.

A number of models of cooperative learning structure academic tasks in such a way that students build affiliation, mutual understanding, and class cohesion. These models usually have students work in groups, with the activity structured so that either task completion or reward (or both) depends on everyone's participation. Yet groups are not penalized for having slow students or rewarded for having the best students in them. For an excellent summary of how to implement these techniques, see Dishon and O'Leary (1998). Cooperative models are also outlined in Chapter 20, "Differentiated Instruction."

This section of the Discipline area of performance has attempted to connect good discipline—meaning more narrowly an absence of disruptive and resistant behavior—with building a sense of community in the class. From our point of view, building community would be worthwhile in and of itself, but there is no denying it is also a powerful preventive force against discipline problems. Simultaneously, it is a wonderful source of strength for building environments that support the best kind of academic learning. Chapter 16, "Classroom Climate," has much additional material on these themes of ownership and community building.

Mr. Butler's Class

As a capstone to this section on developing student ownership and involvement in classroom life, we offer the amazing case of Mr. Butler, the only teacher in an entire high school with a functioning ninth grade class, and what Kitzmiller (2013) calls his invention of "Apprenticed Authority" for creating an engaged learning community among students. "This apprentice model clearly delineates the rules and norms, and once they demonstrate compliance with these rules and norms, they earn the right to positions of authority" (p. 25).

> As I looked around the room, I noticed that, in many ways, this classroom looked quite similar to others in the building. Even though it was a sunny day, the windows were so filthy that they only allowed the faintest of light to penetrate the glass panes. Many of the blinds in the room were ripped; the floor was warped and stained. And like the other classrooms, Mr. Butler's fluorescent lights emitted an unappealing pale yellow light and a slight humming noise that could distract anyone, especially ninth grade adolescents. The television that rested on the back table had a black streak across the screen from a permanent marker. It was a demonstration of the vandalism that plagued the entire building.
>
> Yet, at the same time, there were marked differences between this classroom and others that I had visited. There were several handmade posters displayed on the walls. One had an image of an infant with a barbell that said, "Baby, this is Mr. Butler's class. You have to pull your own weight." At the front of the room, the chalkboard contained a meticulously handwritten outline detailing the learning objectives for today's lessons. Directly next to each task on the outline, he had indicated how each activity

in the lesson plan corresponded to the state standards and the school district's mandated curriculum. Such clearly articulated learning directives and goals were rarely seen at Washington High School. At the front of the room, Mr. Butler had posted a list with each student's name and class standing. The list contained a tally of the student's completed and outstanding assignments for the semester. In other classes, Washington students complained that they never knew how they were progressing in the semester. They did not know what assignments were missing; grades, they argued, were arbitrary and calculated completely at the instructor's discretion (Fieldnotes, January 28). In Mr. Butler's classroom, each student could easily track the grades that he or she had earned over the course of the semester. Furthermore, missing assignments were clearly indicated. Again, this was a rare sight.

At 9:23, the bell rang for the beginning of fourth period and Mr. Butler told me that this class is a General English class (the chalkboard lists plans for both his General and Honors courses). As students entered, they exhibited behavior that one might observe at any high school. Some of the girls set their books on their desks and immediately moved to the hallway to sneak a few minutes of gossip before the final bell rings. Others walked in, took their seats, and discussed lunch options. At 9:27, the bell rang again to indicate the beginning of class. Suddenly, the tenor of the classroom changed. One of the students leaped out of his seat and locked the classroom door. (I later learned that this was a safety precaution so that other students do not barge into his classroom and it prevented late students from entering without being acknowledged). Then, the student read the journal question on the board, which is the first objective on the lesson plan. As the young man did this, Mr. Butler calmly walked around the room, clipboard in hand, and looked around to see who was present that morning. Once the young man finished reading the journal prompt, the students began writing their responses. At that moment, I realized I was witnessing an unfamiliar sight. There were no cell phones. There were no late arrivals. There were no shouting students. I was stunned. In the past seven months observing other classrooms at Washington High School, I had never seen a ninth grade classroom seated and ready to learn the instant the bell rang.

As soon as everyone was settled, Mr. Butler told me to sit next to Malika and asked her to explain how classroom expectations, seat rank, and mentor position operated. Malika told me that classroom expectations were a list of rules that students must follow in Mr. Butler's classroom. The expectations were a combination of school rules—students must arrive at class on time in their uniforms—as well as rules that were specific to Mr. Butler's classroom—students must respect the classroom mentor. In theory, everyone in the school should have abided by the school uniform rule (khaki pants and a white or green collared shirt) since it was a school policy. There are explicit rules that tell teachers to send students who have jeans or hooded sweatshirts to the main office immediately. However, I witnessed a variety of ways that students routinely violated this rule during my observations over the course of the academic year. For example, one morning, a young woman walked into her classroom, unzipped her khaki pants and revealed a pair of jeans that she had worn under the khaki pants. When I questioned her about it, she said, "I do this all the time. I wear the khaki pants to get through the metal detector in the morning and then I take them off. I like jeans better" (Student 5, interview; Fieldnotes, January 28). Other students hid hooded sweatshirts, which the administration called "hoodies," in various lockers around the building. They entered the school building and passed through the metal detectors in their uniforms and then went to their lockers to put their hoodies on over their uniforms (Fieldnotes, February 1). Students routinely ignored this rule since teachers and administrators did not consistently punish those who violated it.

Things operated differently in Mr. Butler's classroom. When students failed to uphold this or any other classroom rule on the list of expectations, he never raised his voice and he did not negotiate. Rather, he simply asked them to pull out their sheet, told them which expectation they broke, and deducted a set number of points from their class average. Malika told me that students did not like this because losing points for behavioral or academic problems on the class average affected the student's class seat or rank. This concept of seat rank mimics the methods professional orchestras use to determine where each musician sits. The points determined the student's rank, which in turn, determined the student's seat. Students earned points based on their academic progress as well as their adherence to classroom expectations. Thus, students who excelled academically, yet fail to meet other classroom expectations were ranked lower than those students who met expectations and did well academically. The points can fluctuate each day, depending on student performance on exams, journal entries, and behavior. When students entered the classroom each day, they checked the point sheet hanging on the wall in the front of the classroom to determine where they were supposed to sit. Since this information was public, each student knew the peers' performance.

To help students with their academic progress, Mr. Butler gave them a list outlining the assignments that they must complete each marking period. The list indicated each assignment's due date and point value. Malika remarked that this list is "very useful because it helps me remember what I have to do in his classroom." She continued, explaining that in other classrooms, teachers often did not explain assignments or return student work, and so, "it is difficult for me to know how I am doing in those classes." Even though "the work is much harder" in Mr. Butler's classroom, she explained, "at least I know what I need to do" (Student 6, interview; Fieldnotes, March 28). Mr. Butler required students to write the lesson plan and journal questions each day in their notebooks. According to Malika, there were two reasons for this. First, if the students had the lesson plans in their notebooks, they always knew what assignments and tasks they must complete. Second, since each lesson plan clearly indicated the learning objective for the day, the students had a clearer sense of what they were learning and why. Malika told me that this system helped her with her academic work since she knew exactly what Mr. Butler wanted her to do each day and how it related to the learning goals he set for them.

Malika explained the classroom mentor's role, saying that the classroom mentor does "whatever a teacher would normally do." During this visit, Jeremy served as the classroom mentor. Jeremy, not Mr. Butler, locked the door and read the lesson plan at the beginning of class. When the students completed their journal entries, Jeremy asked for volunteers to share what they have written. Jeremy selected two students. The students walked to the front of the room and read their journal entries to the entire class. As they did this, two students who were seated in the back of the room began talking. Eventually, the noise escalated to the point where everyone in the room could hear them. Mr. Butler deducted points because these students violated the expectation that students will be respectful while others are speaking. Then, he told Jeremy to sit next to these two disruptive students and remind them to be respectful and sit quietly during the presentation. Jeremy walked over to them, sat at their table, and calmly told them that they should not be talking during presentations. Suddenly, their chatter ceased (Fieldnotes, March 28).

The mentor position is one example of how Mr. Butler distributed authority in his classroom. During my observations, classroom mentors took attendance, passed out books, led class discussions, and disciplined students (Fieldnotes March 31, April 4, and April 18). When I asked Mr. Butler about the mentor position, he told me that the position is a privilege; it is not automatically given to students. Students must earn the right to be in this position of authority. To be a mentor, students must have completed all of their assignments and must have followed expectations. Furthermore, Mr. Butler reserved the right to revoke the position at any time if the mentor did not maintain good standing in the community (Fieldnotes, March 31). During my observations, this never happened.

For the most part, teachers at Washington High School constantly lamented about the unruly, unmanageable, disobedient ninth grade class. As a result, the roster chair divided ninth grade sections among teachers so that one teacher did not have to bear the burden of teaching too many ninth grade sections. Typically, teachers had one, maybe two sections of ninth grade students. Not Mr. Butler. He had five. Everyone knew that his sections lacked the characteristic disruption, chaos, and confusion that plagued the other ninth grade sections. As a result, other ninth grade teachers envied him and were eager to try his system in their classrooms. They argued that it seemed easy to replicate. It seemed simple. Mr. Butler gave students points for good behavior and academic work. He deducted points for inappropriate behavior and weak academic work. However, every time teachers tried to model Mr. Butler's practice, they failed. I saw this discussed over and over again, in whole-school faculty meetings, in department meetings, and in casual conversations. Everyone told Mr. Butler that his system simply did not work in his or her classroom. They would credit their failures with a multitude of excuses. He had "better students" than they did. He had "easier classes." His schedule was better. No one asked him why it might have failed (Fieldnotes, November 26 and March 1).

It seems that these teachers did not realize that Mr. Butler's point system was not simply a form of glorified behaviorism where students earn and lose points, which in fact, seems like Weber's notion of power (Weber, 2005). Rather, the points and expectations provide the structural support that enables him to distribute authority to his students. I must admit that I never realized the complexity of his practice until I questioned him about it one afternoon. In April, I told Mr. Butler that I had some reservations about his practice and asked if he would be willing to answer a few questions that I had. I was increasingly concerned that the point system, with its ranks and expectations, promoted a meritocracy that focused primarily on individual efforts among his students. Mr. Butler bluntly remarked that he thinks competition can be a useful tool for engaging students. Besides, he said, much of our success later in life is based on individual merit and competition, and so, he believed there was room for competition in any classroom. He explained that he tried to balance the meritocracy by giving students "booster points." These points, he argued, created a sense of community while simultaneously acknowledging individual achievement.

Mr. Butler explained that his idea of "booster points" stemmed from his own experiences as a runner in college. The coach wanted all of the athletes to run a mile in less than seven minutes; if they accomplished this goal, they could go home. If they did not accomplish it, they had to continue running. Of course there were some that could do this easily, while others struggled. Like any race, the fastest runners stayed in the front of the pack and the slower ones were relegated to the back. One day, however, the group decided to try something new: the fastest runners ran in the back to push the slower runners. They called this the "booster mile" because it boosted those who were not initially successful.

Mr. Butler took this idea and applied it to his own teaching practice. According to him, booster points served as a mechanism to help students understand that they are responsible for supporting their peers in the classroom. Students could earn "booster points" for a variety of things. For example, he assigned them to peer editing groups, and when students were ready to turn in their work, they turn in a final product as well as drafts with peer editing marks. Mr. Butler assessed the final product as well as the support that the student received from his or her group. If the peer group was supportive, the students receive booster points. Students also earn booster points for helping their peers with presentation skills or with exam preparation. While this process is difficult in the beginning, since it is so new for these ninth graders, by the end of the year, the students began to realize that they were more successful working together than they were working on their own.

As he continued, he told me that "my practice is like bamboo. There is a clear structure, but it has flexibility." He said that the classroom expectations and seat ranks provided him with the structure, but the booster points promoted flexibility and allowed him to distribute authority more widely for students as they are ready for it (Teacher 6, interview; Fieldnotes, April 18). For example, as I said, he encouraged students to study together for exams, and in a nontraditional twist, he allowed students to take exams whenever they are ready (Fieldnotes, March 31 and April 4). Thus, students did not always take exams on the same date. Every day, the mentor asked if anyone would like to take an exam that day, and those who were ready selected the exam that they wanted to take. They used their expectations sheets to gauge what needed to be done by the end of the marking period and adjusted their schedules accordingly. This

> flexible system gave students freedom and power, in other words, the authority to decide when they were ready to take an exam and prove what they have learned.
>
> Students did not challenge Mr. Butler's authority because they recognized it as legitimate (Weber, 2005). Furthermore, by giving students positions of authority that are typically reserved only for teachers, Mr. Butler not only asked his students to recognize his authority—he also challenged them to become active participants in cultivating and upholding the authority he deliberately distributed to the entire community. He wanted them to become his apprentices, and thus, instead of one teacher, there were 24 teachers in his classroom. He clearly articulated expectations that he believed they could reach; he provided flexibility to help each student succeed; and he distributed authority to encourage them to participate in upholding the structures he instituted. The approach works because, as John Dewey suggests, "the social control resides in the very nature of the work done as a social enterprise in which all individuals have an opportunity to contribute and to which all feel a responsibility" (Dewey, 1997, p. 163). This is the secret to his success. (Kitzmiller, 2013, pp. 25–31)

This is mighty testimony to the power of student ownership and empowerment, and an intriguing challenge to the urge to over control.

Level 4: Dealing with Very Challenging Students

Over the years, one can build a repertoire of advanced models of discipline to use for the most resistant students who have the most emotional issues. This is not a target for beginners. Successfully mastering the first three levels will take care of the vast majority of the discipline issues any teacher faces. But for the most intractable students, the sophisticated models of discipline will be useful from time to time.

For our most challenging students, approaches beyond what we have presented in this chapter may be necessary. For these students one of the seven therapeutic models of discipline developed in the 20th century may be called for. These are students who continue to resist and disrupt despite clear expectations and consequences and despite the teacher's best efforts at creating ownership and building community in the class. These children bring significant emotional issues through the door with them every morning and act out their needs in disruptive behavior that is resistant to standard measures of behavior management. Fortunately, there are not too many of them. Most of the students who initially appear to be in this category just need more clarity, conviction, and tenacity about expectations and consequences.

The Skillful Teacher website explores these seven models in some detail and presents an important matching framework for how to choose from among them to match the apparent psychological needs driving the student behavior:

1. Behavior Modification
2. Self-Awareness Training (Cognitive Behavior Modification)
3. Personal Influence
4. Logical Consequences
5. Reality Therapy
6. Teacher Effectiveness Training
7. Restorative Discipline

Seven Therapeutic Models of Discipline

Each model has an intellectual parent, a central figure who has pulled it together and written extensively about it. The exception is Behavior Modification, which has so many parents, aunts, uncles, and cousins it is hard to single one out. All seven models are good when used appropriately, and no one of the seven is inherently better than any other. It will be our position that anyone with the position of "Behavioral Interventionist" or "Adjustment Counselor" should be thoroughly trained in all seven, and know how to match them to student needs and how to coach teachers in supporting implementation of the best model choice for their most challenging students. You can learn more about the seven models on *The Skillful Teacher* website at www.RBTeach.com/TST7.

A NOTE ABOUT POSITIVE BEHAVIOR INTERVENTIONS AND SUPPORTS (PBIS)

The comprehensive approach to discipline laid out in this chapter integrates basic management, personal relationships, crystal-clear expectations, and appropriate consequences along with a developmental approach to building strong classroom climate among students. This is a climate of community, social learning, and student ownership. PBIS does the same. The difference is that PBIS, a nationally supported approach to discipline developed by George Sugai of the University of Connecticut and R. Horner of the University of Oregon (Sugai, & Horner, 2006) lays out a systematic plan for getting buy-in to the approach on a schoolwide and districtwide basis. In the PBIS literature, which we recommend, one can find a systematic model of phases and stages for explaining the comprehensive approach, getting parent buy-in, building faculty interest, and bringing teachers together to get agreement about expectations, consequences, and positive "gotchas" to systematically give positive acknowledgement for helpful student behavior. PBIS divides consequences into 3 Tiers which roughly correspond to the four levels of the Hierarchy of Consequences in Table 10.2.

CHAPTER QUICK GUIDE

Twelve Causes of Inattentive or Disruptive Behavior:

Cause 1: Poor General Management
Cause 2: Inadequate Personal Relationship
Cause 3: Inappropriately Matched or Boring Work
Cause 4: Confusing Instruction
Cause 5: Unclear Standards, Expectations, and Consequences
Cause 6: Student Ignorance of How to Do the Expected Behaviors
Cause 7: A Need for Fun and Stimulation
Cause 8: Value and Culture Clashes
Cause 9: Internal Physical Causes
Cause 10: External Physical Causes
Cause 11: Extraordinary Emotional Issues
Cause 12: Student Sense of Powerlessness

▲ Effective responses to disruptive behavior are chosen from a repertoire to match the cause or causes.

Effective Discipline Is Built on a Comprehensive Approach of Four Levels:

1. Laying a foundation of sound classroom management, and solid instructional design and delivery, as well as building relationships with students.

2. Establishing authority by communicating expectations, setting limits, and eliminating disruptions.

3. Building a strong classroom climate that nurtures cooperation, responsibility, and self-discipline.

4. Being familiar with more complex models of discipline that may be necessary to implement with a very small percentage of especially troubled or recalcitrant students.

To check your knowledge about Discipline, see the exercises on *The Skillful Teacher* website at www.RBTeach.com/TST7.

NOTES

Instruction
Introduction

Part 3
Introduction to Instruction

Instruction addresses the skills teachers use to deliver the goods: the cognitive knowledge and skills of their academic disciplines.

Chapter 11: "Clarity" summarizes over a century of research on cognitive science as it applies to successful teaching and learning. This is the material most people think of when they hear the word *teaching*. In this book, we have defined teaching as a much bigger construct: anything a person does that increases the probability of intended learning. Nevertheless, Clarity skills are vital for creating successful learning experiences for students. They scaffold learning, make it accessible in varied and powerful ways, check to see if it has been assimilated, and get inside students' heads to identify misconceptions and confusions. The repertoires within Chapter 11 form a bedrock of good pedagogy.

A supplementary document that analyzes the manifold purposes of questions is available on *The Skillful Teacher* website (www.RBTeach.com/TST7). The "Questioning Skills" document summarizes the research on higher- and lower-level questions and shows the need for all students to experience higher-level questions and higher-level thinking, regardless of their current skill level. We then make the case for planning questions in advance and model how to do so in a way that brings out the most important aspects of our content. It describes how to teach *students* to ask good questions, an important life skill.

PDF

Questioning Skills

Chapter 12: "Principles of Learning" summarizes over a century of laboratory research by cognitive psychologists. This domain of teaching skill, neglected in recent decades and substantially missing from teacher preparation, is a powerhouse of cognitive science for making learning efficient. Those interested in accelerating student learning and making it more durable will find a treasury of techniques here.

Experienced and already successful teachers often exclaim on meeting this body of information, "Why haven't I heard about these principles before?!"

Chapter 13: "Models of Teaching" will appeal especially to readers 5 to 15 years into their careers who are looking for intellectual stimulation for themselves and their students. This is the section of the knowledge base for designers who wish to craft lessons that develop thinking skills as well as academic knowledge.

The application of cognitive science in Part 3 is a rich resource for teachers when they are planning lessons. It is especially valuable for teachers working together in professional learning communities to come up with reteaching strategies.

CHAPTER 11

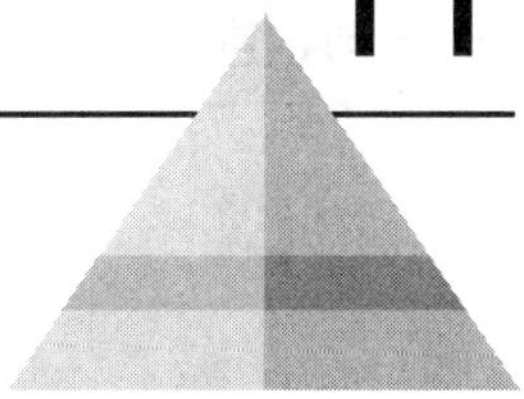

Instruction: Clarity

Why is it that some people are better than others at getting us to understand things? What do they do to be more clear? Clear teachers do far more than speak or lecture in an organized and easily comprehensible way, though that is not irrelevant to student understanding. These teachers guide student thinking in deliberate ways along a structured route engineered for thinking and learning. This is the scientific part of teaching. We can use what we know from a century of cognitive science to maximize the chances of students' assimilating, integrating, remembering, and being able to use concepts and skills. No content expert comes into teaching already equipped to accomplish this skill-intensive job.

"Clarity" is an area of performance that targets mental acts within students' heads that result in understanding or being able to do something. If they use the knowledge base of cognitive science well, what teachers do has a great deal to do with what goes on in students' heads. Unfortunately, as Graham Nuthall (2005) points out, it is possible to have a smoothly functioning, lively classroom where all the students appear happily occupied with worthwhile tasks and yet no mental acts conducive to learning are taking place. Consider this episode:

> $2^2 \times 2^3 = ?$ is the problem, and many in the class have gotten it wrong.
>
> "What many of you did," says the teacher, "was to multiply the 2's so you got $2^2 \times 2^3 = 4^5$. That's wrong. It's 2^5." He erases "4^5" and writes "2^5" in its place. "The 2 doesn't change." Then he moves on to the next problem.

The teacher has covered the problem, but he certainly hasn't explained it. The episode is notable for its omissions—for what didn't happen—more than for what did. The teacher didn't check to see if there was any understanding of the rule at work for doing this sort of problem ($N^a \times N^b = N^{a+b}$). He didn't ask students to explain the rule to see if there was any conceptual understanding of why the rule works. He didn't do any explaining of the process for doing the problem. Importantly, he didn't elicit any student participation to see how many students and which ones might still be confused. For instance, he didn't check to see if any students could now do a similar problem. All he did was indicate wrong and right answers. There is little about this episode that is clear—to either the teacher or his students.

Clarity is the heart of what people usually mean when they think of teaching: cognitive interaction. There are 10 categories of teacher behavior in Clarity, each with its independent, deep, and validated research base (see Figure 11.1). We have grouped them into these five functions:

1. Framing the learning
2. Presenting information
3. Supporting mental engagement
4. Getting inside students' heads (that is, cognitive empathy)
5. Consolidating and anchoring the learning

We examine each of these categories of behavior and discuss the choices or repertoires available to us within each category.

1. FRAMING THE LEARNING

Framing the learning is divided into two groups of teacher behavior: (1) *Communicating the Big Picture,* which includes information teachers share with their students to provide context for the lesson of the day, and (2) *Assessing Readiness to Receive,* which involves gathering data from students to determine what they already know or having them make preliminary connections to the upcoming learning experiences.

Communicating the Big Picture

This first group of behaviors consists of behaviors that help students place new information in a larger framework of meaning in the beginning of a lesson. They are the following:

▲ Communicating the lesson objective: what the students will know or be able to do at the end of the upcoming instruction.

▲ Giving students the itinerary: the list of activities or sequence of events they'll be doing.

Figure 11.1 Clarity Functions and Categories of Teacher Behavior

FIVE WAYS TO SUPPORT STUDENT UNDERSTANDING

1. Frame the Learning

- **Communicate the Big Picture:**
  - Objectives
  - Itineraries
  - Connect to a big idea
  - Preview academic vocabulary
  - Explain why the objective is worthwhile
  - State reasons for activities
  - Communicate criteria for success
- **Assess Readiness to Receive:**
  - Activate and build students' current knowledge
  - Pre-assess
  - Anticipate confusions and misconceptions

2. Present Information

- **Explanatory Devices:**
  - Analogies and metaphors
  - Gestures, demonstrations, and modeling
  - Modeling thinking aloud
  - Physical models, and visual representations
  - Graphic organizers
  - Interactive whiteboards
  - Mental imagery
  - Presentation software
  - Minimal and progressive cueing
  - Simulations, educational games, and role plays
  - Choose an explanatory device
- **Speech Patterns:**
  - Vagueness and mazes
  - Respecting formal and informal English

3. Support Mental Engagement

- **Explicitness:**
  - Intentions of cues
  - Focus of questions
  - Necessary steps in directions
  - Meaning of references
- **Make Cognitive Connections:**
  - Showing resemblance
  - Compare and contrast
  - Extend to implications and future actions
  - Make transitions between ideas
  - Signal activity, pace, level, or content shifts
  - Foreshadow

4. Get Inside Students' Heads

- **Check for Understanding**
  - Press on
  - Read body language
  - Ask questions
  - Dipsticking
- **Unscramble Confusion**
- **Making Students' Thinking Visible:**
  - 24 operating principles
  - Break unhelpful practice habits

5. Consolidate and Anchor Learning

- **Summarizing**

Video: Framing the Learning—Itineraries and Big Ideas.

- ▲ Reminding students of the big idea or essential question of this lesson.
- ▲ Previewing academic vocabulary embedded in the lesson.
- ▲ Explaining the reason for an activity and how it helps meet the objective.
- ▲ Explaining why the learning is worthwhile and why it might matter to learn this material.
- ▲ Identifying criteria for success when a student product or performance is involved.

Research shows consistent correlation between these behaviors and improved student learning. We do not yet know with numerical accuracy the proportional role each plays in the ocean of factors that bear on student learning, but we do know that each one matters and that there are a variety of ways to accomplish each of them. We know further that a repertoire of these ways has been developed by practitioners. That is where we have discovered the repertoires developed below and, indeed, throughout *The Skillful Teacher*.

Communicating the Objective

The main point in communicating objectives is to introduce lesson activities with something that casts them within a bigger frame, purpose, or objective so that the students know what they're going to learn, and what to focus on when they read, listen, watch, or perform during instruction. Communicating objectives lets students know, ideally, what they will know or be able to do as a result of the lesson.

This teacher is making a clear statement of an objective by letting students know what they'll be able to do when the instruction is over: "Today, we're going to learn how to write on paper what you've been telling me out loud in math groups—that you have one-half, one-fourth, or three-fourths of a whole something. There is a special way of writing numbers that stand for those things, and when we're done today you'll be able to use it." On the board, she writes: "SWBAT [students will be able to] use math language with accuracy and understanding to represent simple fractional parts."

Most of us have been taught how to say and write behavioral objectives. That language serves a purpose, but it need not be used all the time. The example above happens to *be* a behavioral objective stated in language to match eight-year-old children, but the objective may not be a detailed behavioral one at all.

Other language patterns can serve as well, for instance, "We're going to look at this film and see what we can learn about the personality characteristics of Hemingway the man." Once again, students are directed toward what they're supposed to focus on while viewing and what they're supposed to know at the end of the lesson. Such statements frame the big picture and should be worded in student-friendly language to give students an overall orientation to what is to follow so they can attend to what is important and make sense of subsequent activities.

We have found that many schools now require teachers to write a daily objective on the board for students. That can be a useful practice so that students have something to refer back to, but posting it is not sufficient. It has to be accompanied by making sure students know what it is and what it means. The point is that learning is empowered when students understand what they are aiming to learn (Beesley & Apthorp, 2010), and something has to happen beyond posting the objective on the board to assure that students understand it. In Chapter 18, "Lesson Objectives," we go more deeply into how one ensures the objective is appropriate for the students and that they understand it. Those are the main points to remember.

Certain forms of constructivist teaching do not need to start with a statement of the objective at the beginning of a lesson. Instead, the lesson might be framed by a question to be answered through inquiry. In this way, students can channel their efforts and curiosity, and focus their observations productively. For example, the objective for a math lesson in the elementary grades might be, "Students will be able to explain how a fractional part of an overall area can have different shapes within that area." Rather than state this at the outset of the lesson, the teacher might say, "How many different ways can you make quarters with rubber bands on this geoboard?" It is essential that we know in clear terms what the mathematical objective is and eventually cause the students to produce language that captures this understanding in their own words.

We don't really know if the students understand the lesson objective unless we ask them. A physics teacher we know regularly invites a visitor into his room, especially during lab periods. The students have a checklist where they get a bonus point if they explain the objective to the visitor; another, if they explain how the activity they're doing serves the objective; and yet another, if they can explain the relevance to life of what they're learning. Exhibit 11.1 presents the rubric used for this activity. Visitors are very popular with students in this classroom!

Exhibit 11.1 Teacher Spot-Check Rubric

<table>
<tr><td colspan="2">Physics I
Teacher Spot-Check Rubric</td><td colspan="2">Pre-Archimedes
Name:</td></tr>
<tr><td colspan="4">For the teacher spot-check, you will be graded by the following rubric.
You must have at least 2 rubrics completed that meet the standard.</td></tr>
<tr><td>Standard</td><td>Exceeds</td><td>Meets Standards</td><td>Comments</td></tr>
<tr><td>S7d: Student explains a scientific concept to others.</td><td>☐ Explains how the activity will help them to learn the content.
☐ Makes a connection between activity and the real world.</td><td>☐ Explains the activity to the visiting teacher. Knows the goal of the lesson.
☐ Explains what has been discovered so far in the activity.
☐ Explains what their role is in the activity.</td><td></td></tr>
<tr><td colspan="4">Teachers:
If students don't offer up information unsolicited, please ask them probing questions regarding the items in the "Meets Standards" column.
If a student is unable to explain any one of the items in the "Meets Standards" column, do not give them credit.
Please initial on the appropriate line below.
Exceeds Standards ____________
Meets Standards ____________
Does Not Meet Standards ____________
Teacher Signature: ____________________ Date: ____________</td></tr>
</table>

Adapted from Janece Docal and Jeff Schmitz

Giving Students an Itinerary

An itinerary is like an agenda or roadmap. It delineates the sequence of events that will occur over the course of a class period. It tells what activities will take place and in what order. For example, it is common to hear a teacher say, "This morning we'll be going over questions you have about last night's assignment, then beginning our study of cell structure with a video. The last 30 minutes of the period will be time to continue working together on your group projects." This useful information gives students a mental sequence to follow and lets them know what to expect. An itinerary also affords students the opportunity to keep track of what has happened, what is currently happening, and what's still to come. Learners with sequential learning styles are particularly responsive to the practice of posting itineraries in a visible place.

An itinerary serves as a complement to the objective but doesn't replace communicating the objective itself. The objective specifies the learning outcome for students (the destination); the itinerary tells them how they will get there. The true test of whether students have understood the objective of a lesson might be whether they can explain the connection between events on the itinerary and what they are expected to know or be able to do when they have reached the end of the journey (the objective). Giving clear directions and outlining what procedures students are going to follow also complements but does not replace communicating an objective or sharing the itinerary.

Connecting to a Big Idea

Another aspect of communicating the Big Picture and putting the immediate lesson in the larger context is connecting students with the big idea of the unit, and perhaps the essential question that embodies it. For example, "The water cycle is one of the natural processes the earth uses to keep itself alive; and us alive too. We're exploring whether that cycle is in any danger and if we can do anything about it."

At the beginning of a unit, the teacher may spend considerable time developing these big ideas. And during the unit, teachers often remind students of the big idea at the beginning of a given lesson and connect the objectives of the day with that idea: "After today's material on water shortages, we may have a new slant on private-public utility companies."

Another possibility is to return to an advance organizer or concept map that was used at the beginning of a course or unit of study to visually preview for students how all of the concepts in the unit are interrelated or connected, or to make connections between a new topic and what students have studied previously. The intention is to help students see where the daily focus of an objective is part of a larger overall picture. Hattie (2009) cites research showing that advance organizers, when used to introduce new material, have a facilitative effect on both learning and retention (Luiten, Ames, & Ackerman, 1980).

Previewing Academic Vocabulary

When the content of the lesson or the learning experience includes academic vocabulary that might be new to students, this means highlighting those words, expressions, or phrases in advance (posting them somewhere visually where they can be revisited during the lesson) and explaining what they mean. Sometimes it means simply posting them and mentioning that they will come up during the lesson and explaining them later when they appear in context. Sometimes it means adding them to a word wall or having students illustrate what they mean to ensure understanding. This anticipation of and attention to unfamiliar technical or academic vocabulary or expressions ("in comparison," "as a result") is especially critical for second language learners (Short & Echevarria, 2005).

Explaining Why the Objective Is Worthwhile

Communicating to students why the objective is worthwhile is the "Who cares?" question. Students may know exactly what it is about the Vietnam War that their teacher wants them to understand at the conclusion of the lesson, but they may not think it matters. For some students, understanding the usefulness or relevance of a learning objective makes a big difference in their investment in the lesson. Writing about "quadrant-one learners" in describing different learning styles, McCarthy and McCarthy (2005) make the point that all learners need reasons for why they are studying what their teachers are asking them to learn. But knowing the reason is more than nice; it's essential for imaginative learners. Many teachers erroneously assume that students buy into learning because they see their teachers as experts who know what should be learned (McCarthy, 1987a). McCarthy says, "Students need reasons of their own. Giving them a reason, a need of their own for proceeding, is so simple and fundamental that one can only marvel that it is not done" (p. 92). We think, parenthetically, that this same generalization applies to all adult learning as well, whether it be in college courses, staff seminars, or professional development offerings. For all learners, it will be useful to know why the topic is important to learn, and for a segment of each audience it will be essential.

It is particularly important for some learners (and useful to all) to know the reasons for understanding the principal causes of the Vietnam War and U.S. involvement: "The reason this is important to us is that the Vietnam War has causes in common with many other wars in history. If this country enters another war, it's likely that many of you will be urged to enter into the armed services and have friends who go to fight. Therefore, it will be important to you as citizens to be able to follow current events and the decisions of your leaders in government to see where we're headed. As citizens, you can make informed choices in voting for leaders who stand for policies you want. Our study here will help you decide in the future what you think we should fight for as a country —and at some point, that choice is sure to be yours."

Although not as dramatic, we might be equally clear about why it is worthwhile learning geometric proofs; studying myth as a literary genre; or learning to identify by their attributes igneous, sedimentary, and metamorphic rocks. Giving reasons for learning doesn't necessarily happen with every lesson. Many lessons are taking students one increment further or developing their skill one degree higher on a particular objective. At the beginning of new units or topics,

Figure 11.2 Reasons for Activities

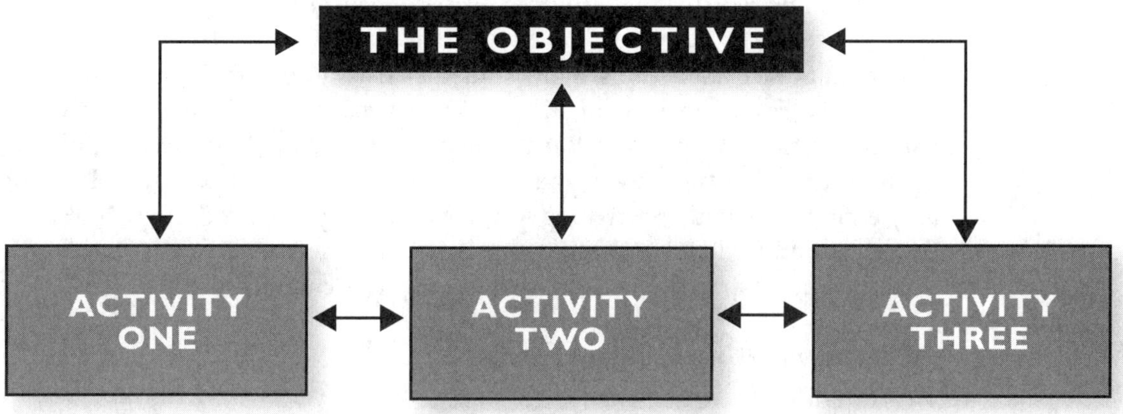

however, giving reasons for our objectives can be particularly appropriate. And it never hurts to remind students from time to time why something is important. Preparing to deliver these reasons to students can be a useful exercise for us as teachers too. If we can't formulate a good reason for learning something, maybe we shouldn't be teaching it.

Stating Reasons for Activities

Surprisingly, students often have no notion about the purpose of activities they are asked to do and make no link between activities, the lesson objective, and instruction they have just received (Tasker, 1981). "Reasons for activities" simply means telling students why they are asked to do a particular activity; why the activity will help them learn something or contribute to a larger learning or task performance. This is an example: "The reason we're doing this experiment is to show how hard it is to take data and record information simultaneously. You just can't do it. So like all scientists, we're going to have to extrapolate our readings. Remember that term—extrapolate—from the graphs we worked on in the chapter?" Here is another example: "The reason we're doing these sentence-combining worksheets is so you can use these same techniques to make your own writing more interesting in the adventure stories we're writing." These moves build a series of links back to objectives from individual activities and between activities themselves as seen in Figure 11.2.

Sometimes the explanation shows students how the current activity fits into patterns of other experiences they've been having or are about to have. This is an example: "The reason I'm asking you to locate these references in the online database is to ensure that you know how to use the software. Next month, when you start your research papers, you'll want to use this database a lot, and I won't be around to help much of the time. So you've got to be able to use it independently to find worthwhile resources related to your topic."

Without these explanations, many students do assignments mechanically, with minimal care and investment. They do them because they're "work" and you're supposed to do your work. But the work isn't leading, in a meaningful way, toward anything they understand. Teachers who have worked with learning styles and studied the intriguing work of McCarthy and McCarthy (2005) and Gregorc and Butler (1984) know that quadrant-one learners—that is, big picture people—especially need to understand these connections.

The criteria for success reveal in detail what we really want the students to know or be able to do.

Communicating Criteria for Success

The criteria for success in a student task, often a bulleted list, reveal in detail what we really want the students to know or be able to do. Coming up with criteria is a planning skill. Communicating them to students is a clarity behavior. Clear teachers don't keep criteria a secret; they make sure students understand them and can use them to self-assess their work.

Video: Criteria for Success

Chapter 18, "Lesson Objectives," addresses, in detail, developing criteria for success and the related topics of rubrics and providing students with exemplars of student work that meet criteria. We mention these here, however, because it is important to introduce and ensure that students understand the criteria for success at the beginning of instruction or prior to working on a product or performance in which they are expected to demonstrate achievement of the lesson objective. We want to do everything we can to ensure that the quality of their work meets the established criteria.

Assessing Readiness to Receive

The behaviors in this category also take place prior to instruction with new material—sometimes in an earlier lesson—and increase the likelihood that instruction will be effective for more students. Two of the three (activating prior knowledge and pre-assessment) provide data for the teacher to take into consideration when finalizing the instructional plan, and may, in fact, provide data to inform the third: anticipating confusion. Consider the importance of these moves when it comes to our second language learners.

> Many English language learners struggle with curriculum content because they lack background knowledge of the topic or have gaps in the information they have learned. Teachers must either activate what prior knowledge exists and apply it to lessons or explicitly build background knowledge for these students. For example, immigrant students may not have studied the

> US Civil War in their native countries, but they may have studied another war or even experienced a military conflict firsthand. By tapping into what students know about such conflict, the teacher can set the context for a lesson on the US Civil War. (Short & Echevarria, 2005, p. 11)

Coming up with examples of concepts in ways that connect to students' cultural history (for example, immigrants from El Salvador and that country's civil war) does two things. First, it validates their culture and history; culturally sensitive teachers go out of their way to do this. Second, it enables cognitive connections to something the students understand.

Activating and Building Students' Current Knowledge

Video: Activators

An activator is an activity designed to get students' minds active and in gear about a topic before they learn anything new about it. Activators can serve many different purposes. They can be used to accomplish the following:

- ▲ Have students preview upcoming information.
- ▲ Pique student interest and support mental engagement.
- ▲ Gather data about what students already know.
- ▲ Surface misconceptions.
- ▲ Build confidence: "I already know something about . . ."
- ▲ Adapt lesson plans to match students' background knowledge.

Research shows a cognitive payoff for student learning when teachers do this. Techniques that activate students' current knowledge about a topic not only get students' minds into a state of interest and heightened awareness but can prevent the dreaded "Charlie Brown syndrome":

> Recall what Charlie Brown does when he gets a new book. Before he even looks at the book, he counts pages—625 pages—"I'll never learn all that!" He is defeated before he starts, before he has had a chance to realize that he does not have to learn all that. It is not all new. He already knows something about it. He has not given himself the chance to learn what he already knows about what he is supposed to know. (McNeill, 1984, p. 34)

There are many different ways one might activate and build students' knowledge. A teacher might ask students, "What do you already know about X (the upcom-

Exhibit 11.2 Sample KWL Chart

Global Warming		
Know	Think I Know	Want to Know

ing topic)?" And as students brainstorm, the teacher records (or has students individually record) their connections. As the concept or topic is studied, students can go back to these initial lists to compare what they have learned with their original ideas. Sometimes students find themselves fitting new learning into old charts, and sometimes they find parts of their old conceptions contradicted. In any event, having created an image of what they already know about a topic places a map before them against which they bounce (and into which they put) new information. It is in this way that activating serves the big picture.

Several variations of this idea (having students start with a blank piece of paper and fill it with what they already know or at least think they know to be true) are widely used in classrooms. "Know, Want to Know, and Learned" (sometimes referred to as "KWL" or the "three-column activator") is one such example used to preview and then summarize learning. As ideas are generated, they are recorded in one of two columns: "What I Think Know" and "What I Want to Know." As students pursue the topic, they review the initial chart and complete the third column, "What I Learned." We use an alternate version in which the three columns are "Know," "Think I Know," and "Want to Know" (see Exhibit 11.2). We introduce a topic or show students a stimulus on a topic they haven't yet studied (headlines from a newspaper article, a picture on a book cover with the title) and ask them to share aloud what they know, think they know, or would like to know about this. As they share ideas, they assign them to one of the three columns. No discussion or question answering occurs during the building of the chart. This activity produces active participation, reveals student preconceptions, and generates student-owned agendas for reading, viewing, listening, and investigating.

The charts are worth saving for a return visit after reading the piece or studying the topic. Some "knows" may turn out to be untrue; some "think I knows" are validated and others overturned; and all the "want to knows" should have been answered or might lead to follow-up research.

Figure 11.3 Wordsplash

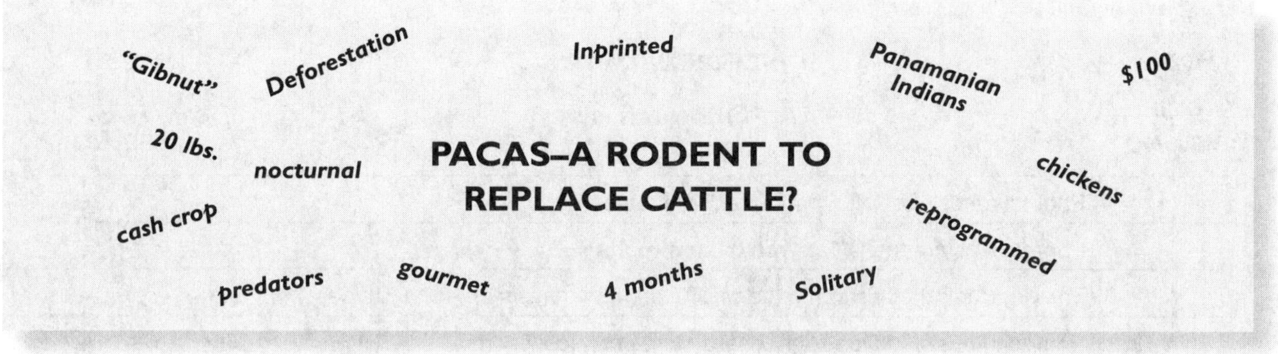

Sometimes students need more than a blank sheet of paper (figuratively speaking) to surface prior knowledge and begin to make connections to a topic. There are other forms of activating that give students data to think about in relation to the topic. A wordsplash (Hammond, 1985) takes 10 to 15 key words or terms from an article, story, or text chapter and "splashes" them at random angles and positions on a chart or whiteboard with the topic or focus of the article in the center. In the sample (Figure 11.3), the words are about an animal, the paca, found in Central America. Prior to reading, students are asked to follow the rules of brainstorming in groups with a recorder as they respond to the following direction: "Generate sentences for each of these terms to show how you think they might be related to pacas, which are rodents found in South and Central America." This technique promotes wide student participation, higher-level thinking, focused reading, and better comprehension. Because the responses they generate should be considered tentative or speculative—and subject to verification later—only one student in each group should record the ideas generated, and the recording can be done directly on a copy of the wordsplash. Once students have studied the topic, they can each have copies of the wordsplash and create a final reference copy for themselves with correct connections for each term.

Sometimes students need to be given even more information about a topic in order to preview it and activate their current knowledge. An Anticipation Guide (Exhibit 11.3) invites students to react to statements about a topic with either an agree-disagree or true-false response. In true-false, the statements all reflect something a student should know with certainty when the lesson or unit is complete. Some of the information contained in the statements might be more familiar, affording all students an opportunity to feel confident that they know something. Some of the statements might be ones that raise curiosity, but most they wouldn't be sure about; others might actually contain a common misconception with the intent of finding out how many of the students

Exhibit 11.3 Sample Anticipation Guide

Preview		**Anticipation Guide**	*Review*	
I think . . .		**Photosynthesis**	*Now I know . . .*	
YES	**NO**		**YES**	**NO**
		Photosynthesis is ONLY performed by plants.		
		Phototrophs are the ONLY type of autotrophs.		
		The organism that performs the MOST photosynthesis on earth is algae.		
		Photosynthesis converts light energy into chemical energy.		
		Photosynthesis can only occur during the day.		
		Photosynthesis converts organic compounds into inorganic compounds.		
		Leaves are a special organ adapted for absorbing and catching sunlight.		
		Phototropic cells contain special organelles called chloroplasts.		
		Chloroplasts contain a special green pigment call chlorophyll.		
		Chlorophyll absorbs mostly green light.		
		Chlorophyll is the only pigment in chloroplasts that absorbs sunlight.		
		Plants and other phototrophs absorb carbon dioxide and release oxygen.		
		Plants never need oxygen.		
		Glucose is the only end product of photosynthesis.		
		Oxygen released from phototrophs comes from the oxygen originally found in carbon dioxide.		

Shared with permission by Paul J. Frisch, Science Department, Fox Lane High School, Bedford, NY

have already bought into inaccurate information that will need to be addressed head-on during the lesson/s. The advantage to this format is that regardless of background knowledge all students can participate, take a stand on each item, and hopefully get invested in finding out whether or not they are correct as they learn about the topic. Once again, the ideal would be to return to this activator during the course of instruction—or at the conclusion—and have students identify the correct responses to the statements. They might be asked to turn the incorrect or false statements into true statements. With an agree-disagree format, students can return to their original opinions as they study and decide if they have changed their position. The important thing is that they are previewing and reviewing ideas and concepts that are at the heart of the learning objectives.

A whole repertoire of activating techniques has been developed by practitioners and researchers in the reading and language fields and are well worth studying by teachers in all academic disciplines. They vary in terms of how much information is given to students and how much students are asked to generate themselves. Some take more time than others; some are verbal; some are visual; some require advance preparation of materials; others don't. What they all have in common is that students actively seek to make connections to an upcoming topic prior to beginning the study of it. Thus all have the effect of getting students cognitively engaged and ready to receive.

To choose an activator that best matches a particular lesson or unit of study, consider the following:

- ▲ What is my purpose?
- ▲ What is most important for students to know about this content, skill, or strategy?
- ▲ What data do I already have about student understanding of this content and what level of student interest in this content do I anticipate?
- ▲ What additional data do I need?
- ▲ Which of the activators will best suit these needs?

For a repertoire of activating strategies, visit the www.RBTeach.com website and see our publication, *Activators* (Saphier & Haley, 1993), which gives detailed directions for implementing 24 techniques.

Pre-Assessing Students' Knowledge

> Although it is true that the extent to which students will learn new content is dependent on factors such as the skill of the teacher, the interest of the student, and the complexity of the content, the research literature supports one compelling fact: what students *already know* about the content is one of the strongest indicators of how well they will learn new information relative to the content. (Marzano, 2004, p. 1)

Ausubel (1968) writes, "The most important single factor influencing learning is what the learner already knows. Ascertain this, and teach him accordingly" (p. 36). Gathering this information matters. If adequate prior knowledge is absent, even a great lesson on new material will go for naught. If students know more than we thought, we can go faster. If they lack some necessary prior knowledge, then we need to alter the lesson plan and fill those gaps.

Pre-assessment and the data we collect as a result serve as the foundation for critical planning decisions. This includes how we might want to differentiate instruction; what we will address with whole-group instruction; how we can form flexible small groups to match teaching and learning experiences to student levels of readiness or need with particular skills and objectives; and how to identify confusion, misconceptions and other problems that might cause students difficulty with mastering an objective.

The activators we described earlier, have the purpose of getting students' minds engaged with a new topic. In addition to creating a desire to know and a sense of competence in students, some activators can also serve as assessments of students' prior knowledge if completed individually by students, thus getting us two for the price of one.

An Anticipation Guide is one example; a Sort Card activity is another. In a math Sort Card pre-assessment, every student is given a set of cards each containing a fraction. Students are asked to sort them into categories based on their value. That can tell us quickly how well (and which) students understand and can identify equivalent fractions. Here is another example: give students a set of cards containing science vocabulary words, definitions, or sentences missing key vocabulary words. Ask them to create triads of cards that go together. This will give us a quick sense of what terminology is familiar and what needs to be explained or studied prior to introducing a new science topic.

The main purpose of a pre-assessment is to find out what students know and to ensure that students' prior knowledge gives them the readiness they need for the upcoming instruction. Thus an important distinction between an activator and a pre-assessment is that an activator can be done with large or small groups of students working together, whereas a pre-assessment must be done as an individual activity in order to gather data from every student and to use the data to guide instructional plans. This enables us to give all students the additional instruction they need to prepare for the new learning. This is particularly important with background knowledge that is going to show up in a text and is assumed by the author to be available to readers. Lemov (2017) emphasizes this point. In *Building Background Knowledge for Academic Achievement* (2004), Marzano discusses six principles we can apply to building background knowledge and delineates thousands of academic vocabulary terms that are foundational to understanding concepts in 11 different content areas.

There are many other direct ways besides activators to find out what students know. A brief quiz the day before a lesson, a scan of the previous night's homework, a 3-2-1 self-assessment of students' degree of familiarity or confidence with terminology or processes relevant to a topic, a quick-write: all these might serve as a tool for pre-assessments.

Anticipating Confusions

There are three forms of anticipating confusions. One of them means finding out what the misconceptions are and addressing them directly. Otherwise, they will linger and distort students' assimilation of instruction (Eaton, Anderson, & Smith, 1984). Strategically designed pre-assessments or activating activities can serve as terrific resources for uncovering misinformation students have internalized. The Photosynthesis Anticipation Guide (Exhibit 11.3) is a good example of that. Can you find the untrue statements that are based on misconceptions?

Two other forms of anticipating confusions are predicting in advance the material that will be hard to learn and noticing or perceiving on the fly that students might not understand.

1. Misconceptions

A cartoon shows a little boy standing on his head on a bathroom scale. His friend reads the weight and says, "Your head weighs 43 pounds—same as your feet." As in the cartoon, students bring many misconceptions to instruction, misconceptions that can be resistant to change and interfere with instruction if they are not recognized and contradicted.

A series of investigations by science educators (Eaton, Anderson, & Smith, 1984; Eylon & Linn, 1988) revealed many misconceptions students have about how the world works: for example, "air is empty space", "my eyes see by direct perception" (rather than receiving reflected light), and "we have summer when the earth is closer to the sun." They bring these misconceptions to instruction, and unless we discover them, surface them, and explicitly contradict them, students hold onto them and reconcile them with the instructional information. The resulting maps they create in their heads may seem logically consistent, but they're wrong and present serious obstacles to learning. This can happen even when the instruction is ostensibly clear as a bell—because of the failure to account for the misconceptions students bring with them to the instruction. And though the research is best developed for science concepts, there is no reason to believe the same thing does not happen with concepts from any discipline. We must be aware that students do not come to class as blank slates.

2. Predicting in Advance

In a second form of anticipating confusion, teachers use what they know about their students and their content to anticipate confusion and probable points of misunderstanding because the material is difficult to understand or easy to misinterpret. The teacher anticipates, for example, that when explaining free fall in physics, students might think *free fall* refers only to an object falling toward earth, straight down from a height. *Free fall,* however, means any situation in which an object is moving only because of the force of gravity. That includes the motion of an object in orbit around a central body, like the moon around the earth. It is accurate to say the moon is in free fall around the earth or that space shuttles are in free fall around the moon when they are in stable orbit. *Free fall* in these situations means "falling around," that is, with circular motion of objects in orbit in space.

By anticipating confusions, teachers become aware of places where students are likely to have difficulty understanding and can spend time clarifying the material before students become confused. Science curriculum supervisor Jaunine Fouché (2015) describes a protocol she uses that includes "predictive questioning" and "strategic discourse" to effectively uncover and clarify students' misconceptions. The protocol has four phases where students predict (the outcome of a potentially discrepant event), explain (their reasoning), observe (the actual phenomenon or data), and revise (by engaging in small-group discourse that leads to them revising their explanations based on new evidence).

3. Noticing "On the Fly"

Sometimes a teacher becomes aware of a possible confusion on the fly while teaching and makes a preventive move right then. A student is correctly solving an algebra equation but is manipulating terms in his head at a rate the other students might not be able to follow. So with an on-the-fly move to prevent confusing the other students, the teacher interrupts the student and says to the class, "Wait! See what he's doing here. He's doing two steps at once in his head; he's cross-multiplying and taking the square root. Okay, go ahead, Todd." This teacher has slowed the action for the benefit of the others and unpacked the two steps that Todd was doing simultaneously in his head, which the teacher anticipates the other students might not be able to understand.

Anticipating confusion on the fly is one of the most subtle and difficult performances to observe because when one does this effectively, students do not, in fact, become confused. We "head it off at the pass," taking care of the potential lack of understanding before it develops. For this reason, it represents a high level of sophistication in clarity. It requires both the disposition and ability to get inside students' heads. This is, in fact, the foundation of this entire set of clarity

Table 11.1 Explanatory Devices

• Analogies and Metaphors	• Minimal and Progressive Cueing
• Gestures, Demonstrations, and Modeling	• Simulations, Educational Games, and Role Plays
• Modeling Thinking Aloud	• Computer or Tablet Applications
• Physical Models and Visual Representations	• Charts and Diagrams
• Graphic Organizers	• Audio and Video Recordings Including Singing
• Interactive Whiteboards	• Highlighting Important Information
• Mental Imagery	• Pictures and Photographs
• Presentation Software	• Translation into Simpler Language

skills. Teachers who are skillful at clarity want to know how learning is going for their students, and they have a repertoire of ways for finding out. They have a degree of cognitive empathy for the workings of the learners' minds—an ability to put themselves in the learners' shoes—and that guides everything they do.

2. PRESENTING INFORMATION

This section is about that part of teaching and learning in which we are directly teaching (or reviewing) new content, concepts, and skills. Two major considerations here are the devices we use to introduce or explain a skill or concept and the characteristics of our verbal presentation that accompanies them.

Explanatory Devices

Explanatory devices are tools that can be used to present information and explain concepts within any content and any approach to teaching. The repertoire includes the explanatory devices listed in Table 11.1.

When a concept or a process is being presented and explained, we know that some learners will rely heavily for understanding on visual representations (diagrams, models, demonstrations); some on auditory representation (verbal analogies, modeling thinking aloud); and others on tangible, concrete representations (physical models or materials they can manipulate, simulations they become a part of). Most of us rely to varying degrees on all three modalities for taking in and absorbing information most effectively. Known for his extensive research on second language learning and bilingualism, Jim Cummins (2001) uses the terms "context embedded" and "context reduced" to describe the difference between information communicated with and without accompanying contextual clues (intonation, gestures, visuals, etc.) that support meaning making. He underscores the critical importance of accompanying verbal or linguistic presentations with visuals and other contextual cues to ensure that cognitively demanding concepts are made accessible to second language learners.

Thus when we think about how to best serve all of our students with these tools, we must ask ourselves, "Am I explaining in ways that enable all students to see, hear, and experience the content or concept?" If not, we are missing some learners. An advantage to planning with this in mind is that we are more likely to maximize the benefits of even a singular explanatory device by enhancing how we use it. For example, we might want to use fraction rods (a physical model) to demonstrate the concept of equivalent fractions. Students will see the model and hear us talk through the explanation as we demonstrate. But if we give each of them a set of fraction rods to construct the model along with us, we incorporate the third (kinesthetic) modality.

Any one of the explanatory devices—or a combination—can be powerful vehicles for supporting student understanding. Because many of the explanatory devices are self-explanatory, we discuss these in more detail: (1) analogies and metaphors; (2) gestures, demonstrations, and modeling; (3) modeling thinking aloud; (4) physical models and visual representations; (5) graphic organizers; (6) interactive whiteboards; (7) mental imagery; (8) presentation software; (9) minimal and progressive cueing; (10) simulations, educational games, and role plays.

Analogies and Metaphors

Analogies support student understanding when they connect the new learning to something the students already know. In some cases, they create visual images, for example: "The growth of a glacier is like pancake batter being poured in a frying pan. As more and more substance is added to the middle, the edges spread farther and farther out" (Ormrod, 2004, p. 245). When appropriately chosen, analogies are effective devices for augmenting student learning (Bulgren, Deshler, Schumaker, & Lenz, 2000). However, Ormrod cautions that teachers must "point out ways in which the two things being compared are different, otherwise students may take an analogy too far and draw incorrect conclusions" (p. 224).

"A metaphor basically reimagines or re-expresses something in one category (domain) in terms of another category (domain) to clarify or further thinking" (Wormeli, 2009, p. 6). For example, English teacher Karen Molter describes an epic as a baseball game: "the hero starts at home, needs to leave for a quest, encounters trials along the way that prevent him from his ultimate goal: returning home"

(Wormeli, 2009, p. 151). These can be especially effective to support understanding for second language learners when we can create a metaphor that re-expresses a concept in a domain that is familiar to the students. Wormeli offers a "metaphor quality scale" as a guide to ensure that our metaphors serve our intended purpose of supporting understanding of a concept. He includes the following attributes:

- Items being compared are identifiable to the student.
- The metaphor doesn't distort the truth or leave to chance students focusing on an attribute of the compared item that is misleading.
- Taken literally, the metaphor can't be true.
- The items being compared exist in different domains.
- The metaphor engages the recipient personally (has personal meaning, is clever or witty). (Adapted from Wormeli, 2009, p. 12)

Gestures, Demonstrations, and Modeling

Video: Gestures

The best, most charismatic speakers and influencers know the importance of using hand gestures (Van Edwards, 2015). While it may seem a small or inconsequential part of our presentations and explanations, there is a considerable body of research that highlights how beneficial the intentional use of physical gestures can be for reinforcing and highlighting the content we are presenting. In a 7-minute YouTube video, Vanessa Van Edwards (author and founder of the website The Science of People) highlights several ways in which we can use hand gestures to "underline or bold" our words and create anchors or hooks for our students. For example, anytime we mention a number ("there are 4 reasons why . . ." or "3 critical attributes of . . .") we can punctuate by holding up a matching number of fingers. If we are talking about growth, "really BIG growth" or a "really BIG problem" can be represented by stretching our arms wide; "just a tiny bit of growth" or "just a little problem, no big deal" can be expressed with a slight separation of two fingers. To support students in tracking and keeping separate our explanations of two ideas, groups, characters, etc., we gesture by holding one in the left hand and one in the right ("in this election, we have the leading Republican candidate"—left hand—"and the leading Democratic candidate"—right hand). Then, anytime we reference one group or the other, we hold them in the hand as originally referenced. For more examples of this kind of gesturing visit www.scienceofpeople.com.

Teachers of world languages capitalize on the intentional use of gestures and modeling when speaking in a language that students are learning. Students learn vocabulary and structure of the language by simultaneously hearing it modeled and seeing gestures that cue the meaning. Total Physical Response (TPR) is a popular scheme for embedding gesture in language learning (Asher, 2003).

Demonstrations and modeling are more self-evident as devices for explaining a process or a concept. They might include a physical education teacher demonstrating the proper way to hold or swing a bat, a first-grade teacher modeling for students how to space letters when printing a word, an art teacher demonstrating how to throw clay on a wheel, or a math teacher demonstrating the use of a graphing calculator. The teacher serves as an example when both visual and auditory demonstration of the steps in a process are needed. Note how this form of modeling is different from the one that follows, Modeling Thinking Aloud.

Modeling Thinking Aloud

Modeling Thinking Aloud is another one of the least seen and most powerful of the explanatory devices. It is especially useful in teaching any kind of problem-solving or multi-step complex operation or procedure. Yet it is noticeably absent especially in middle and high school classrooms (Lapp, Fisher, & Grant, 2008). It is done in front of the class as a dialogue with oneself thinking through a process step by step as a student would, and role-playing just what to do. This includes being puzzled, making mistakes, self-correcting, and checking oneself along the way. By doing the thinking aloud, we show students where the pitfalls are and how to get through common hang-up points, as well as model the appropriate steps.

A partial example of modeling thinking aloud for organizing notes to write an essay on the Civil War might sound like this:

> Let's see. I've got all these note cards I wrote while I was reading the different books. Let me lay them out in front of me. [Lays cards out on table.] Hmmmm. Now, how can I use them to figure out what to say? Maybe I can group them. Let's see . . . these three are notes about how different battles went, the mistakes, and the good strategy moves. Okay, I'll put them together. . . . And these ones are about Lincoln hiring and firing the various generals. [Puts those together.] And these are about the stuff and money each army had behind it, and how they raised money in the North versus the South to pay for the army. [Puts those together.] . . . No, wait. This one with "value of land" isn't really about financing the war. It's about farming and getting supplies. [Goes on grouping the note cards and saying out loud what she's thinking.]

> . . . Okay, now I've got the groups. What's the point I want to make about each group? The topic sentence? . . . So this group, the generals. Well, Lincoln went through a lot of them before he found Grant. That could be the point. . . . Anything else? Well, actually he gave them each a long time and a lot of leeway before he fired them. They had to really mess up before he would relieve them of command. And they all did! Okay, that's my point then, two points really: that Lincoln gave them a lot of leeway to prove themselves, but he replaced them when they messed up. Now let's see, how will I frame that topic sentence?

Subsequent modeling thinking aloud in this scenario might be used to show how one chooses supporting details for the topic sentence from the note cards.

Think-alouds can be used with all age levels to explicitly teach reading comprehension strategies (making connections, visualizing, asking questions). It is applicable in any content area for showing how good readers do certain things before, during, and after reading. Think-alouds can be used to model thought processes a tennis player goes through in planning and executing a serve, or how to factor a quadratic equation, or how to apply criteria for success to self-evaluate a piece of work.

Modeling Thinking Aloud is different from explaining the steps in a process through direct teaching. Figure 11.4 illustrates the planning steps for effective Modeling Thinking Aloud. While we are doing it, we become actors on stage, intentionally not interacting with our audience, and instead putting on a kind of "cognitive show" for them. We need to alert students in advance that they will be our audience, should watch closely what is going on, and be prepared to describe afterwards what they saw and heard. As we make our internal dialogue external, students should hear us:

Video: Modeling Thinking Aloud—Elementary

- ▲ Asking ourselves questions.
- ▲ Weighing alternatives and using criteria to choose.
- ▲ Self-correcting after false starts.
- ▲ Persisting when an initial approach doesn't yield progress.

The last step in modeling thinking aloud is to collect from the students what strategies they saw us use, what questions we asked, etc. This summarizing on their part enables us to assess what they did and didn't notice, and to highlight anything essential that they missed. If we record the essentials as they sum-

Figure 11.4 Four Planning Steps for an Effective Modeling Thinking Aloud

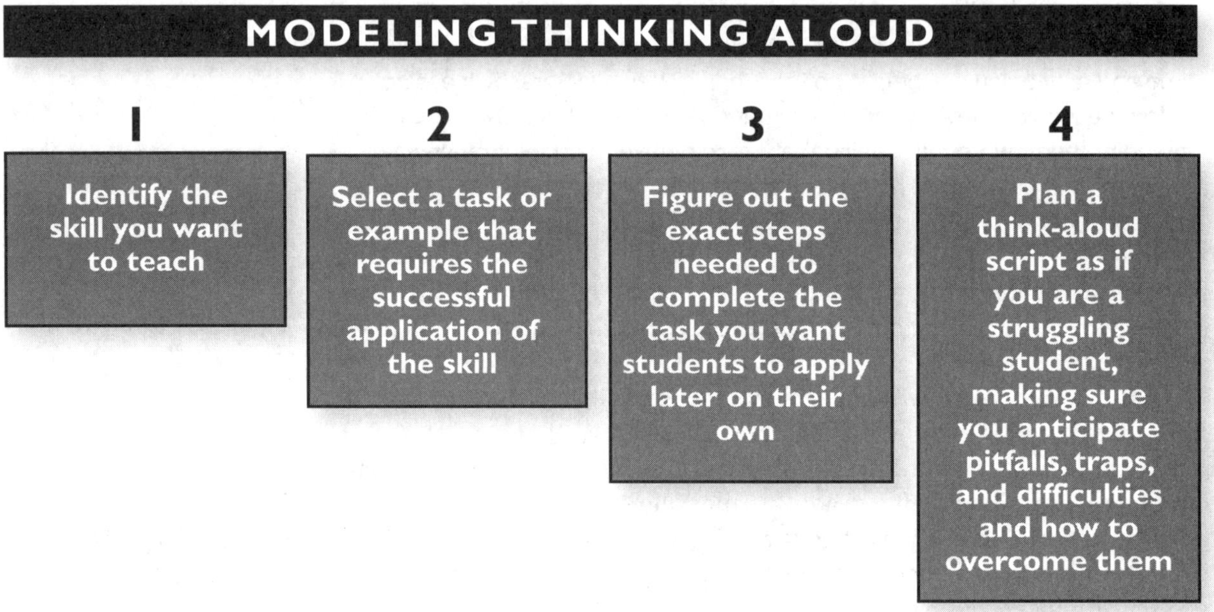

marize, we also create a visual artifact (a poster) that can serve as a reference of the process for students when they are working independently.

Video: Modeling Thinking Aloud—Secondary

Lapp and colleagues (2008) describe a process of interactive think-alouds that embeds the gradual release of responsibility (Pearson & Gallagher, 1983) in three stages: modeling, scaffolding, and practicing independently. Following the initial teacher modeling, the think-aloud becomes interactive, guided by the teacher with pauses that prompt students to use the strategy on their own or with a partner. Lapp illustrates the interactive nature of this phase in a detailed script of a high school chemistry teacher modeling for students how a proficient reader grapples with the problems of unfamiliar vocabulary, new concepts, text features, and text structures and how to apply what they already know to comprehend complex text. As the teacher moves into the interactive phase, she continues to read the text aloud, pausing intermittently, and prompting students to apply a strategy: "Make a prediction . . . now read with a partner and check your prediction . . . turn to your partner and share an experience you have had like this . . . what does this make you think about? . . ." Thus students have a guided opportunity to try on relevant and specific strategies that will support them in making meaning. The final phase has students summarize what they have learned and practice independently.

Exhibit 11.4 Ten Steps for Modeling Thinking Aloud (MTA)

Guidelines for Planning the MTA

1. **Identify the skill** you want to teach.

2. **Select a task** or example that requires the successful application of the skill.

3. **Figure out the exact steps needed** to complete the task you want students to apply later on their own.

4. **Plan a think-aloud script** as if you are a struggling student, making sure you anticipate pitfalls, traps, and difficulties and how to overcome them.

Guidelines During the MTA Lesson

5. **Explain Why.** The students have to know why the teacher is doing the modeling. Tell them what you want them to learn from it.

6. **Model.** Model the skill using the following guidelines:
   - **a.** Put yourself in the role of the learner
   - **b.** Have an audience
   - **c.** Do not let the audience interact with you
   - **d.** Think aloud through the task, operation, or problem. Be sure to include asking yourself questions, weighing alternatives and encountering difficulties, false starts and self-corrections, persistence.

7. **Debrief.** After completing the think-aloud, ask the students what strategies or procedures they saw you utilize as you performed the task.

8. **Record and Display.** Record the steps of the task and post the visual where students will be able to refer to it for future use.

9. **Practice the Steps.** Have students practice the steps out loud so that they can get feedback on whether they covered all the steps. Think-Aloud Paired Problem-Solving (TAPP) is a powerful way for students to practice the think-aloud steps in groups.

10. **Extend.** Encourage student to think about using the Think-Aloud process for other applications.

To be most effective, think-alouds should be planned in advance, outlining for ourselves exactly what needs to be modeled: the thought processes and structures that are most salient, the traps, and pitfalls that students are likely to encounter, and the strategies students need to navigate difficulties. See Exhibit 11.4 for a summary of the steps for effective Modeling Thinking Aloud.

Physical Models and Visual Representations

Video: Physical Models

A model is something students can see and sometimes touch that is used to explain an idea, or the nature or meaning of a concept to be learned. Models might be actual concrete objects (tools or artifacts from another time period to understand aspects of a culture), physical replicas (a torso of the human body containing removable organs and components of each system, a scale relief map showing various geologic formations), manipulative objects that represent the value or nature of the concept (Cuisenaire rods for demonstrating math operations and place value concepts, multi-colored cubes that can be linked together to show DNA structure), or visual representations (showing how multiplication works using arrays of cut-out graph paper).

Figure 11.5 A Model of Three Ways to Multiply

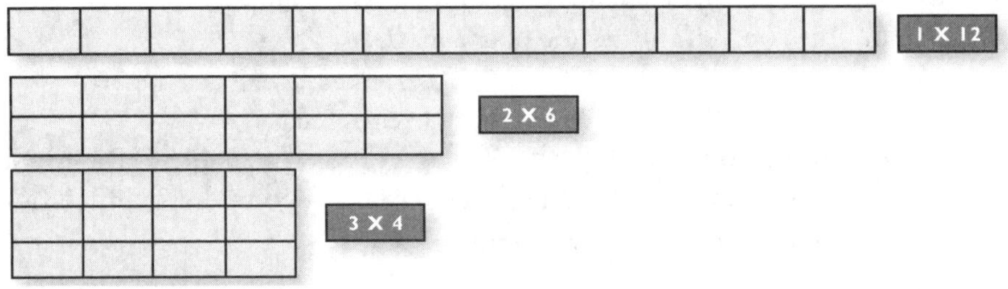

An example of a visual representation 1 x 12 is shown in Figure 11.5. One long column of 12 squares cut out from chart paper where the squares are one square inch represents 1 x 12; 2 x 6 is represented by two columns of six squares, also cut out from the same chart paper and taped on the board next to the 1 x 12 column; and another array of three columns with four squares in each column (3 x 4 = 12) is taped right next to the other two. This presents a model of three different ways to multiply numbers and get the same product. Thus it serves as a sense anchor in memory for the concept that teachers and students can use as common references for the idea, "Remember when we had the arrays of graph paper taped to the board? Well, that's the kind of relationship that's going on in this word problem." Figure 11.6 shows additional models representing multiplication in different real-world situations.

Figure 11.6 Multiplication Models

Equal Groups
Three bags of candy with 4 in each bag.
How many candies?

3 x 4 = 12

Allocation/Rate
She walked 3 miles each hour. She walked for 4 hours. How many miles did she walk altogether?

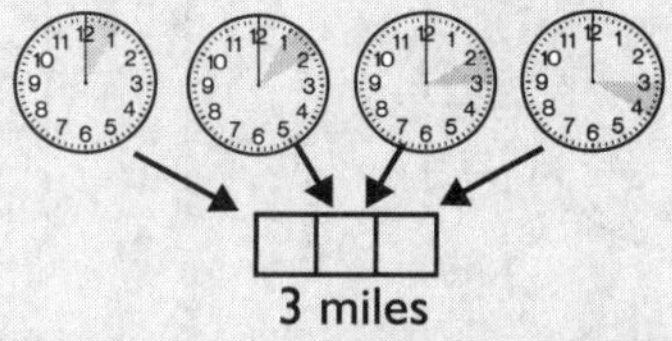

3 x 4 = 12

Array Models
Sue has a cupcake tray. It holds 4 cupcakes in each of the 3 rows. How many cupcakes does she have?

3 x 4 = 12

Area Models
The room is 3 feet by 4 feet. How many square feet of carpet are needed?

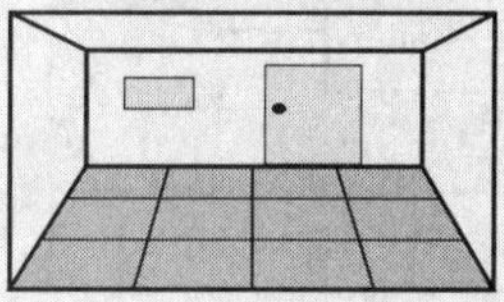

3 x 4 = 12

Scaler Models
Sue has $4. Tom has three times as much.
How much money does Tom have?

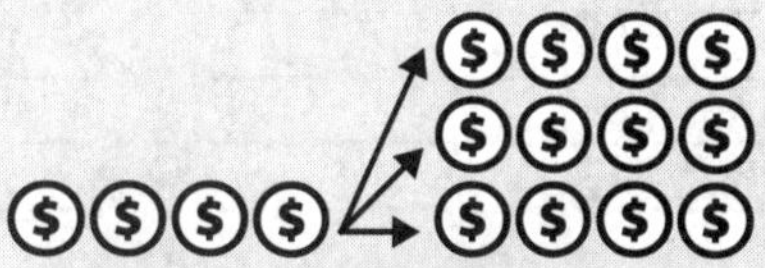

3 x 4 = 12

3 times as many

Cartesian Models
She has 3 pairs of pants and 4 shirts.
How many different outfits can she put together?

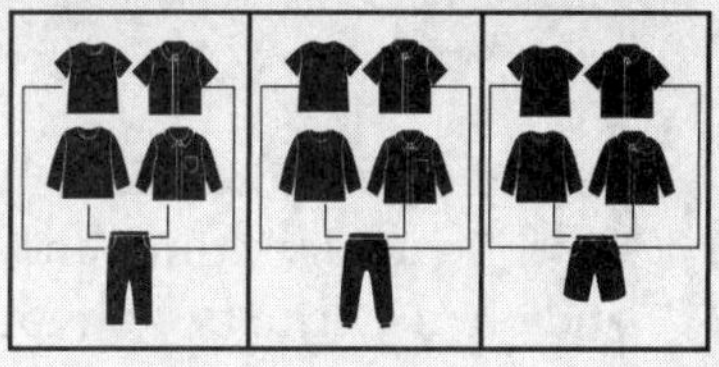

3 x 4 = 12

Linear/Measurement Models
She measured 3 groups of 4 inches.
How many inches?

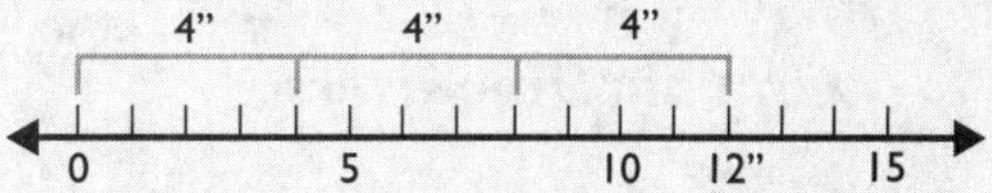

3 x 4 = 12

Figure 11.7 Graphic Organizers

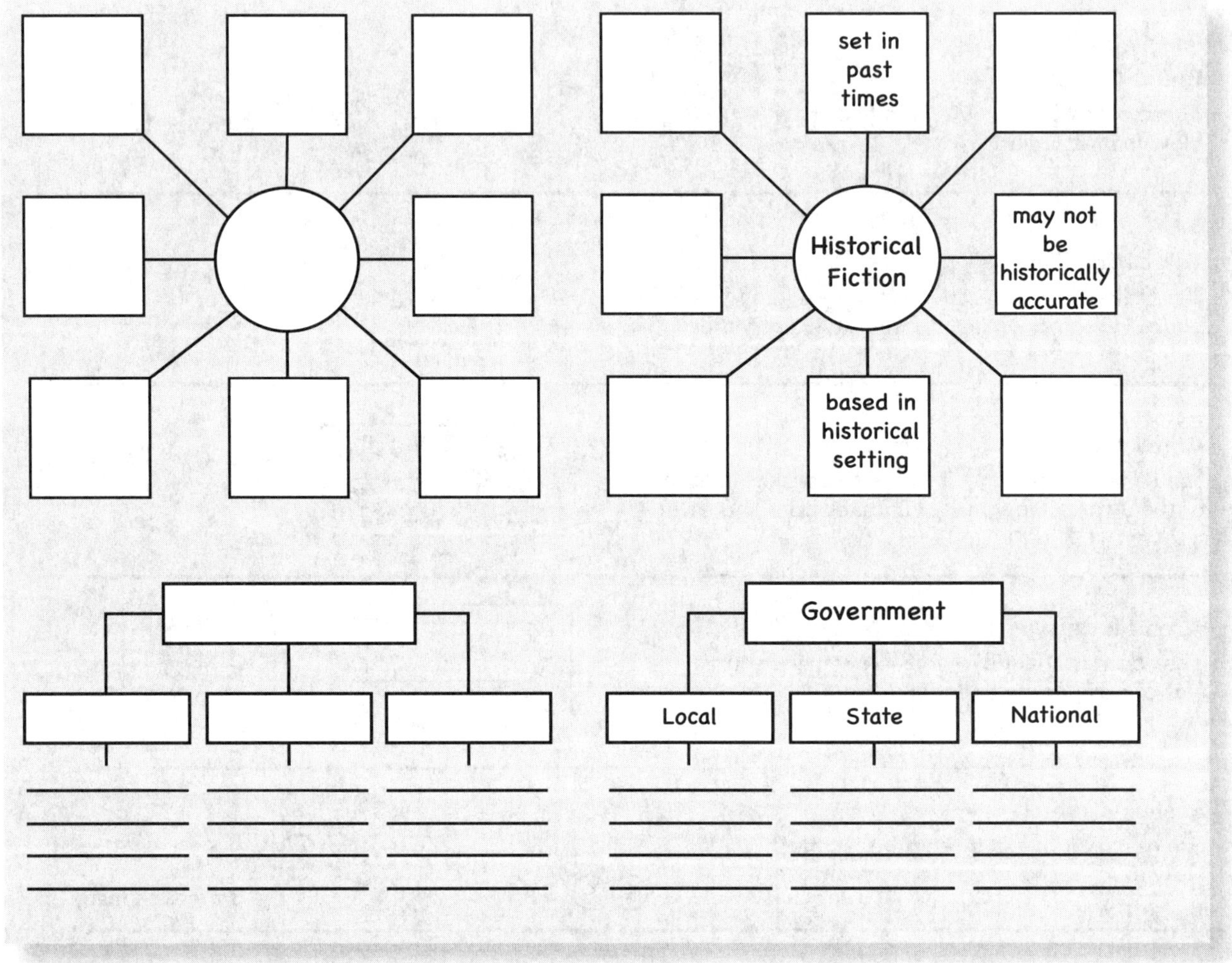

Technology affords us an unbounded variety of opportunities to explain concepts, structures, time, and place using visual models that are colorful, animated, and often able to be manipulated by students and viewed from a 3-D perspective to support understanding.

Graphic Organizers

Graphic organizers (Figure 11.7) are "words on paper, arranged to represent an individual's understanding of the relationship between the words" (Clarke, 1991, p. 30). Concept maps (Novak, 1991) and thinking maps (Hyerle & Alper, 2011) are a specialized subset of graphic organizers where the form of thinking (cause-effect, part-whole, comparison and contrast, description, or problem

Figure 11.8 Compare and Contrast Double Bubble

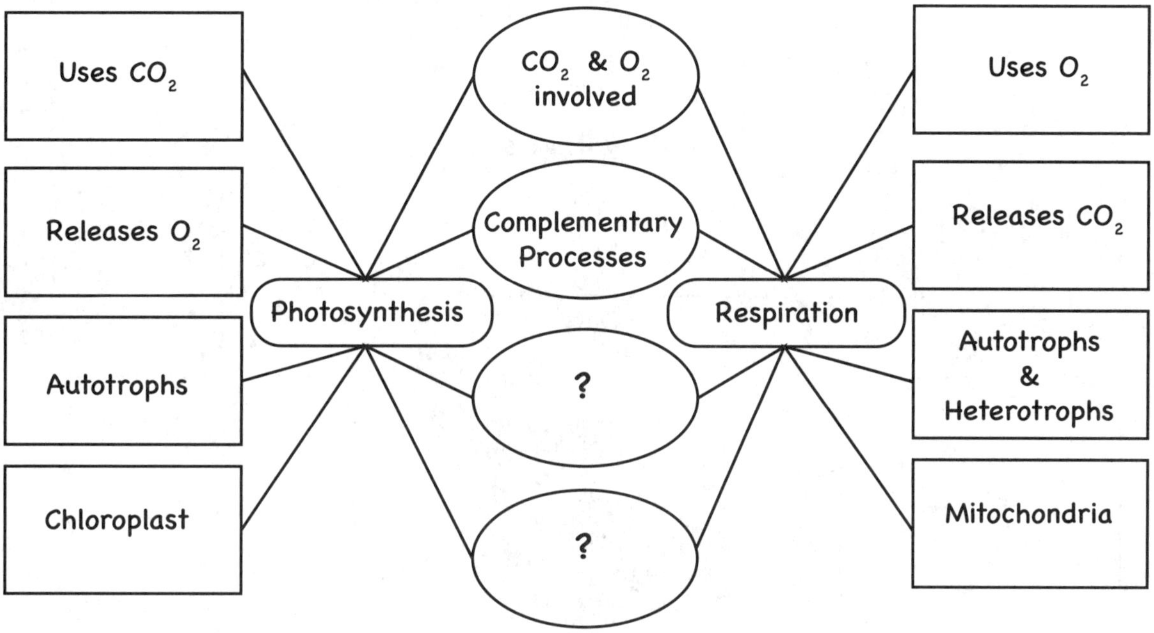

and solution) embedded in printed or spoken text indicates the use of a particular format for the diagram. In other words, the visual form of each organizer is matched to the kind of thinking it is intended to represent.

When used as an explanatory device in a presentation, students witness a teacher recording key ideas or terms and their relationships on an enlarged version of an organizer to make the verbal presentation more visual. See Figures 11.8 and 11.9 for an example of how science teacher, Nancy Sanger, uses two organizers (compare-contrast and cycle) to explain the processes of photosynthesis and respiration, how they are similar and different, and the interplay between the two processes in the production and absorption of carbon dioxide and oxygen. As she walks through her presentation, she records key words in their respective places. Thus students are able to track visually what she is explaining verbally. At the same time, students are recording along with her (taking notes) on their own copy of the organizer. Finally, students are asked to use the organizer to explain the processes to a partner and to sketch or explain these processes in their own words in their interactive notebooks where they have inserted the organizers. Note the interplay and progression Nancy has embedded here between teacher narrative and visual representation followed by student-generated narrative in an effort to support true assimilation of the content and concepts. What do you think this accomplishes?

Figure 11.9 Carbon/Oxygen Cycle

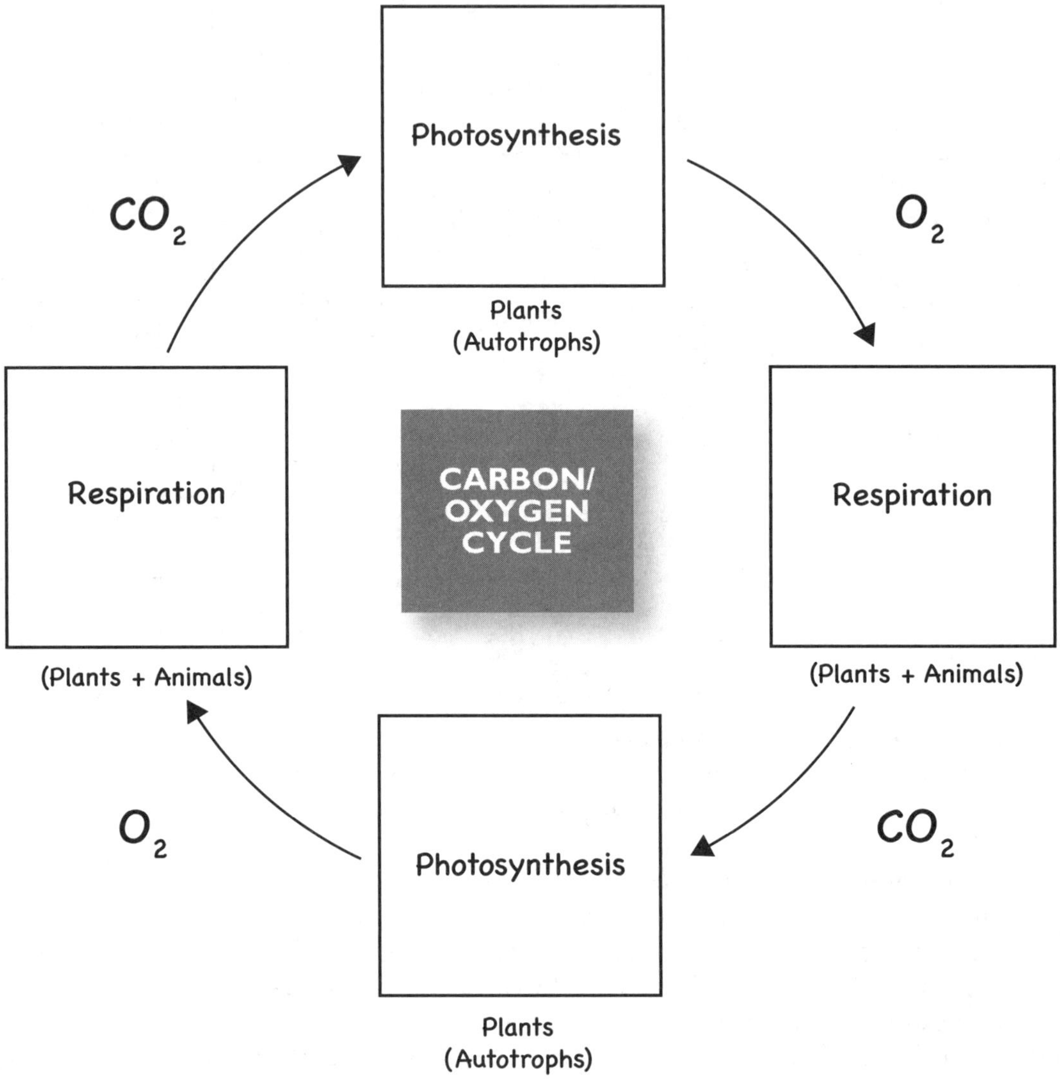

There are a great many terms used for special-purpose graphic organizers: *mind maps, story maps, semantic maps, webs, concept maps, thinking maps,* and *clusters.* Some of them (mind maps, clusters, semantic maps) are used for recording a rapid flow of ideas, and are taught to students for their own use in recording and organizing their thoughts prior to writing or research. Others (story maps) are used when students are reading literature to record plot line and character development in visual form. Still others (concept maps, a term commonly used in science and social studies) are used to record the relationships between concepts and facts in visual form and profile the essential attributes and non-attributes of the concepts themselves (Bulgren, 1991). A research tradition in the reading field (Armbruster, Anderson, & Ostertag, 1989; Heimlich & Pittelman, 1986; McGee & Richgels, 1986) has demonstrated that graphic organizers improve comprehension when used as adjuncts to good instruction. Even students in the primary grades can understand ideas more clearly when they are represented through graphic organizers.

Graphic organizers help students accomplish the following:

- See relationships between concepts and elements.
- Organize information into a coherent structure.
- Pay attention to important items.
- Capitalize on visual learning and activate the right brain.

Beyond their use as explanatory devices, graphic organizers are very worthwhile tools for students to learn to use for planning (a piece of writing or presentation), organizing their note-taking when reading text, and summarizing their understanding of content or concepts and their relationships to one another. For some students, using a graphic organizer to represent their understanding can be preferable to writing a narrative. In order for students to use organizers in these ways, they have to learn that all text is written according to some structure of thinking. Then they need to develop a mindset for analyzing what type of thinking or relationships are embedded in text and be able to identify a corresponding graphic form that could be used to represent it. Thus the different forms of organizers need to be introduced systematically and practiced over time. Then one might hear a teacher give this assignment: "Take notes on your reading tonight and choose the form of graphic organizer you think most appropriate." This is asking students not only to be active readers, but also to be analysts of the form of thinking used to organize the information.

Teachers can move students toward independence with graphic organizers, and toward being active thinkers and readers by phasing in these devices slowly, as in the following sequence over several weeks or a semester.

- **Phase 1:** The teacher makes a presentation or leads a discussion and records information using a graphic organizer as class discussion develops.
- **Phase 2:** The teacher chooses the form and fills in the main entries and subordinate entries as discussion proceeds. The teacher identifies the form of organizer being used and names the kind of thinking it represents.

- **Phase 3:** The teacher chooses the form, fills in the main elements of the form for the students, and has the students fill in the rest.
- **Phase 4:** The teacher chooses the form of the organizer, and students make all the entries.
- **Phase 5:** Students choose the form and make all the entries.

Graphic organizers are very useful tools for directly teaching thinking skills because identifying and naming the form of thinking behind the organization of the material under study automatically happens at mature stages with this device.

Interactive Whiteboards

> In a study that involved 85 teachers and 170 classrooms, teachers used interactive whiteboards to teach a set of lessons, which they then taught to a different group of students without using the technology (see Marzano & Haystead, 2009). . . . The results indicated that, in general, using interactive whiteboards was associated with a 16 percentile point gain in student achievement. This means we can expect a student at the 50th percentile in a classroom without the technology to increase to the 66th percentile in a classroom using whiteboards. (Marzano, 2009, p. 80)

Marzano (2009) identifies three features of interactive whiteboards that have a statistically significant relationship with student achievement: using the *learner response devices* (26-percentile point gain in student achievement); the *use of graphics, and other visuals* (pictures, video clips, sites such as Google Earth, graphs and charts) to represent information; and the interactive whiteboard *reinforcer* in which teachers signal that an answer is correct. This may include dragging and dropping correct answers into specific locations, acknowledging correct answers with virtual applause, and uncovering information hidden under objects. Interactive reinforcers were associated with a 31-percentile point gain in student achievement.

But the point is, it is not just using whiteboards, it is using them well. Because the study also showed that in 23% of the cases teachers had better results without the interactive whiteboards, video was used to study teachers using the boards and found several potential pitfalls in the use of the technology:

- Using the voting devices but doing little with the data.
- Not organizing or pacing the content well (running through important information quickly without allocating time for students to analyze or interact with one another).

- ▲ Using too many visuals (making it difficult to identify the important content).
- ▲ Paying too much attention to reinforcing features (where the emphasis seemed to be on eliciting applause rather than clarifying content).

He makes the following recommendations for using whiteboards more effectively:

- ▲ Group information into small meaningful segments before developing digital flip charts, then develop the flip charts to complement the organization.
- ▲ Plan places to stop the presentation so students have an opportunity to process and analyze new information.
- ▲ Ensure that visuals clearly focus on the important information.
- ▲ Limit the number of visuals and amount of written information on a flip chart.
- ▲ After collecting student responses using voting devices, pause to discuss the correct answer along with the incorrect answers and elicit opinions from as many students as possible as to why they chose a particular answer.
- ▲ When using reinforcing features (like virtual applause), make sure students focus on why an answer is correct or incorrect to keep the focus on essential content.

When used effectively, additional advantages of whiteboards cited in other research include the positive effect they have on student engagement and motivation to participate, the ability to support a variety of learning modalities (auditory, visual, and kinesthetic), and the opportunity to enhance student retention and review processes (SMART Technologies White Paper, 2004).

Mental Imagery

One of the most powerful and least used explanatory devices is mental imagery. When used for explaining and supporting student understanding, it means guiding students through a well-structured comprehensible narrative that enables them to form images in their heads of a concept; an analogy for a concept; or a setting, a mood, a period in time that is unfamiliar to them, or is difficult to explain or represent through other means. The narrative is used to guide the details of the images we want them to form. The uses of guided imagery are legion and cross all curriculum areas. A guided imagery trip of a seedpod traveling from the mother plant to germination miles away can illustrate the steps and mechanisms of seed migration memorably. A trip inside an imaginary atom can illustrate properties of nuclei and electron orbits in ways that would not be feasible or accurate using a physical model. An imagery trip around a familiar playing field can firmly anchor the concept of perimeter. Using guided imagery to reconstruct conditions inside the *Mayflower* prior to landing on the New England coast can make the study of the colony's founding vivid and real for students. Using imagery to have primary children see themselves re-entering the room after recess, checking the assignment board for tasks, and walking slowly and quietly to their places can dramatically improve behavior at transitions.

The following guidelines are useful for planning imagery exercises with students:

▲ Clarify for students the purpose of the imagery experience: "*I want you to be able to understand the vast relative distance that exists between the nucleus of the atom and the electrons orbiting around that nucleus.*"

▲ Set the scene: "*We are going to take a trip inside an atom.*"

▲ Provide background knowledge and/or vocabulary to support mental images. Sometimes a simple teacher-drawn sketch or picture will enable students to understand the imagery: "*So in an atom we have three critical components: the nucleus that contains the protons and the neutrons and the electrons orbiting outside of the nucleus. This imagery is designed to help you see what I can't sketch accurately here: how far away from the nucleus an electron can be at a given point in time.*"

▲ Direct participants to get in a comfortable position, preferably without crossed limbs. "*Relax, check that your feet are on the floor, head is up to support you in forming images, eyes closed.*"

▲ Prepare and deliver a script with sufficient detail to evoke images.

▲ Plan pauses at appropriate points to allow images to form.

▲ Use music if it fits. "New age" or baroque pieces are often recommended. Note: While music can be really useful in blocking out a myriad of distracting sounds in the environment and anchoring the images students form, there might be some learners who find the music itself a distraction because they get focused on the music rather than the narrative. It is a good thing to find out after using it a first time whether students found the music helpful or distracting to guide your planning in the future.

- ▲ Check for understanding. We need to conclude any imagery experience by checking for understanding, asking students to describe or draw what they saw to ensure that they absorbed the most important points the imagery is trying to represent.

As effective as mental imagery can be for supporting student understanding, we need to be aware that in any class there may be some students who are weak visual learners and cannot image easily. This is no reason to avoid using imagery; strengths can be built through practice. But it is a strong reason to acknowledge the possibility beforehand to prevent such a student blaming himself or herself (or you) for inadequacy. Bailey White (2009) has written a humorous piece titled "The Dance of the Chicken Feet" that could be used to address this issue with middle to upper grade students. Finally, as is the case with any one of the explanatory devices, this is also a reason not to rely exclusively on imagery to teach a particular piece of content.

We need to prompt students who have imagery skills to use them as tools for comprehending and teach those who don't how to use it. A natural extension of using imagery to explain a concept is to teach students how to form images in their minds to support comprehension and retention of what they read. Conyers and Wilson (2014) refer to them as "brain movies" that help students make sense of complex nonfiction subject matter. Citing research by Allan Paivio on dual coding theory (the notion that human "cognition consists of both a verbal system for language and a non-verbal visual spatial one for images"), Conyers and Wilson (2014) advocate the need to explicitly teach students how to form images as they read in order to "tap into both the verbal and visual-spatial representational systems, making abstract concepts more concrete and thus more meaningful and memorable." They outline a process for doing the direct teaching of imagery.

Algozzine and Douville (2004) describe a strategy called the Sensory Activation Model (SAM) which is designed to assist students in constructing their own multi-sensory images (see it, hear it, taste it, smell it, feel it). With SAM, teachers model and then explicitly teach students how to use SAM as an aid in the construction of their own images to enhance both reading and writing processes.

Imagery has long been used in sports to improve physical performance (Whisler & Marzano, 1988). Athletes use mental rehearsal to focus their minds, concentrate, and practice and, in the process, improve their performance. In school, these same powers can be brought to bear to focus attention on academic material, elucidate meaning more clearly, and activate visual and right-brain channels for stronger learning.

Presentation Software

Presentation software includes any program (PowerPoint, Prezi, Keynote, Haiku Deck, etc.) we might use to create a sequence of text and graphics, and sometimes audio and video to accompany our direct teaching. To use it effectively, many of the same guidelines mentioned earlier for interactive whiteboards apply (Boesenecker, 2011):

- ▲ Plan your presentation first, then design your slides to support and complement it.
- ▲ Less is more: limit the number of slides (approximately 5 substantive slides for every 15 minutes of presentation) and limit the number of words per slide (some experts recommend a "6 x 6" guideline: maximum 6 bullet points per slide and 6 words per bullet point).
- ▲ Keep the focus on the content—avoid complex or brightly colored backgrounds; stick to black on white or something equally simple.
- ▲ Stick with simple animation—"appear on click" vs. slide, twist, or warp text as it is introduced.
- ▲ Use the slides as a complement to your verbal presentation—design bullet points that present key words, phrases, or ideas; use your slides as visual cues for your presentation.
- ▲ Avoid reading from your slides and face the audience, not the screen, as you present.
- ▲ Use slides to show material you can't present verbally: to integrate graphics, images, tables/charts, or video.
- ▲ Include a summary slide that captures your main points or leaves students with an important thought.

Minimal and Progressive Cueing

Sometimes all a student needs by way of explanation is a simple cue. In small-group or one-to-one tutoring, a teacher might use silent finger pointing as a minimal cue to call a student's attention to an attribute of a word or a part of a problem he needs to look at again. For example, if a student reads "cot" as "cat," the teacher silently points to the "o" in "cot" as a minimal cue. The minimal part of the cue-giving is important here. It is just enough to get students to look at what they need to but not so much as to deny them an opportunity to think through the error. If necessary, the teacher progresses up the scale of cues, making successive cues less and less minimal, until the student gets it. In the example above the next cue might be to spell the word aloud, stressing the "o" in "cot" but not telling the word. If that doesn't do it, a next cue might be to supply a more familiar word with the same pattern and vowel sound, like "not." Once again, the minimal aspect of the cueing is the intent—just enough to support student success without doing the thinking for them.

Simulations, Educational Games, and Role Plays

The terms "role play" and "simulation" are often used interchangeably, and both can have qualities that are game-like (entertaining and fun). All three are closely related forms of attempts to represent reality through experiential learning activities where learners interact with one another or virtually in a context related to a learning objective.

Role play can take on a variety of forms, but all require learners to put themselves in someone else's shoes or themselves to be in an imaginary situation. Each participating learner has a specified part to play. It is typically an unrehearsed dramatization in which individuals improvise behaviors (dialogue and actions) that illustrate acts expected of persons involved in defined situations. In successful role plays, learners assimilate information that is provided about their role and then act out the assigned roles in accordance with their interpretation of how their character would behave in the situation (Killen, 2006). Examples of this might include debating an issue as representative members of political parties running for office, or dramatizing a contemporary scene as characters from a Shakespearean play. Role plays can involve students playing the part of inanimate objects such as becoming molecules and acting out their behaviors in a chemical reaction. Role plays can also be used to help students develop specific skills. For example, how to ask for assistance in a foreign country, how to answer the telephone courteously, how to respond to a racist remark or sexist comment, or how to respond with growth mindset talk when someone speaks from a fixed mindset.

Simulations are about things (or systems) and how they behave, and they may or may not incorporate role play. A simulation might involve students learning about how infectious diseases spread and become an epidemic; emergency management when dealing with a disaster in which they assume the roles of emergency management personnel, prepare for, and then deal with a disaster; the separation of powers in the federal government by designing a new school lunch menu with specialized roles (lead chefs, menu writers, nutrition inspectors). Simulations can be live, face-to-face interactions among students, or they can be computer-based.

Referring to computer simulation technology as "interactive pretending," Prensky (2007) highlights several advantages it offers as a tool for explaining:

> Computer simulation technology is a way of looking at objects or systems that encourage a learner not only to wonder "What would happen if . . . ?" but also to try out those alternatives virtually and see the consequences. It is a way for learners to acquire experience about how things and systems in the world behave, without actually touching them. Because so many of the things we need to understand these days are either too complex, too vast, too small, too far, or too dangerous to be experienced directly, we can no longer rely exclusively, as we did for so long, on hands-on learning. Simulation provides us a solution and is in fact the only way to experience, try and learn many of the things we want our students to know about. (p. 2)

As is the case with several of the other explanatory devices (mental imagery, modeling thinking aloud), it is critical that learners not only have the experience, but that we also build in the follow-up step of getting the learners to process and summarize what they have learned. Otherwise, we can't be sure the activity was successful in promoting understanding and connecting to the intended objective. Killen (2006) cites Brookfield (1990) and Davis (1993) in offering the following menu of sample questions for debriefing a role play:

- ▲ How did it feel to play this role?
- ▲ How do you feel now?
- ▲ What do you think you learned from this role play?
- ▲ Do you think that your actions and reactions, and those of the other players were realistic?
- ▲ What issues do you think remain unresolved?
- ▲ Could other approaches to resolve the issues have been more effective, realistic, or satisfying to you?

Questions for observers when a role play is done by a few students with others observing:

- What do you think were the key points or actions in this role play?
- How realistic was the situation portrayed in this role play?
- Did the role play highlight any general principles related to the issues we are studying?
- Which actor behaviors do you think were appropriate or inappropriate?
- Did any of the role players behave in stereotypical ways?
- What would you have liked to see in the role play that did not occur?

Choosing an Explanatory Device

To analyze your own use of explanatory devices, you can make a simple count of how many and which you use in explaining and clarifying information. There is no evidence we know of that any one of these devices is better than another, but there is considerable support for variety in teacher presentation as correlated with effectiveness. Using several devices in lessons is one form of variety certainly. Common sense argues that by using a repertoire of these devices, a teacher can increase the likelihood of retaining students' attention and engaging their learning style. Given that these are explanatory tools, it is important to consider variety from the perspective of learning modalities. Do the explanatory devices you use afford students the opportunity to receive information through auditory, visual, and kinesthetic modalities? If not, how might you bring your teaching more into balance along those lines so that all learners, regardless of modality strengths, will have equal opportunity for learning?

By using a repertoire of explanatory devices, a teacher can increase the likelihood of retaining students' attention and engaging their learning style.

Speech Patterns

Another critical factor in presenting information to students is the clarity of our speech and the many aspects that encompasses. It must meet certain minimum criteria for diction, pronunciation, articulation or enunciation, grammar, syntax, choice of words (appropriate vocabulary) in order for students to absorb and understand what is being explained or presented. We also need to monitor our rate of speech coupled with intentional pauses in our delivery to allow time for students to digest what we have said. Even the pitch and tone in our voices can support a comfortable atmosphere for learners, or can induce a stressful climate. All of these characteristics of our speech become paramount when we have second language learners in our audience.

Vagueness and Mazes

Smith and Land (1981) have analyzed the speech patterns of effective and ineffective teachers. Their studies and others consistently show negative effects on students' achievement when teachers use "vagueness terms" and "mazes" in their speech. They give this example of vagueness terms (italicized in the following passage):

> This mathematics lesson *might* enable you to understand a *little* more *about some things* we *usually* call number patterns. *Maybe* before we get to *probably* the main idea of the lesson, you should review *a few* prerequisite concepts. *Actually,* the first concept you need to review is positive integers. *As you know,* a positive integer is any number greater than zero. (Smith & Land, 1981, p. 38)

This example illustrates mazes (with the mazes in italics):

> This mathematics lesson *will enab . . .* will get you to understand *number, uh,* number patterns. Before we get to *the main idea* of the lesson, you need to review *four conc . . .* four prerequisite concepts. The first *idea, I mean, uh,* concept you need to review is positive integers. A positive *number . . .* integer is any whole integer, *uh,* number greater than zero. (Smith & Land, 1981, p. 38)

As evident from the examples, mazes are false starts or halts in speech, redundant words, and tangles of words. Vagueness terms take many forms (see Table 11.2). Hiller, Fisher, and Kaess (1969) and Smith and Land (1981) presented evidence that vagueness occurs as a speaker commits himself or herself to deliver information that he or she can't remember or never really knew. It can also occur when a teacher does not wish to appear authoritative about information and allows a confused sense of personal relationship building to obscure clarity. Such confusion can occur when a teacher endeavors to be seen as open to student ideas and as a facilitator rather than an information giver. What results is a tentative teacher who uses many vagueness terms. Delpit (2006), in her work with linguistically diverse students and her writing about second language acquisition, underscores the importance of the clarity of our speech and what we model for students:

Table 11.2 Vagueness Terms

Category	Examples
Ambiguous designation	Conditions, other, somehow, somewhere, someplace, thing
Approximation	About, almost, approximately, fairly, just about, kind of, most, mostly, nearly, pretty (much), somewhat, sort of
Bluffing and recovery	Actually, and so forth, and so on, anyway, as anyone can see, as you know, basically, clearly, in a nutshell, in essence, in fact, in other words, obviously, of course, so to speak, to make a long story short, to tell the truth, you know, you see
Error admission	Excuse me, I'm sorry, I guess, I'm not sure
Indeterminate quantification	A bunch, a couple, a few, a lot, several, some various
Multiplicity	Aspect(s), kind(s) of, sort(s) of, type(s) of
Negated intensifiers	Not at all, not many, not very
Possibility	Chances are, could be, maybe, might, perhaps, possibility, seem(s)
Probability	Frequently, generally, in general, normally, often, ordinarily, probably, sometimes, usually

> The acquisition and development of one's native language is a wondrous process, drawing on all the cognitive and affective capacities that make us human. . . . Learning to produce an alternate form (second language with alternate vocabulary, register, style etc.) is not principally a function of cognitive analysis, thereby not ideally learned from protracted rule-based instruction and correction. Rather it comes with exposure, comfort level, motivation, familiarity and practice in real communicative contexts. (p. 49)

Respecting Formal and Informal English

Beyond acceptable speech in general, there are some things that are not so obvious. A teacher might match aspects of speech—choice of vocabulary, level of formality or informality, cadence, rate—to their students, thus making concepts, directions, and examples more readily comprehensible to all. This would include making connections and translations with students whose neighborhood and family language is not standard English.

There are ways of speaking and using language different from standard English that derive from children's family and ethnic culture. There are four points we'd like to make about these language patterns. It is important that we do the following:

1. Notice them and understand how they work.

2. Value them as the sophisticated and complex systems of syntax and grammar that they are, and not hold them as "less than."

3. Observe how they affect communication in such ways as story structure, cadence, and speech pattern.

4. Use all of this in a respectful and pedagogically planful way to teach standard English.

In her groundbreaking book, *Ways with Words* (1983), Shirley Brice Heath studied the language of communities of poverty in Appalachia. Her analysis included normal discourse and storytelling structure. Heath goes into depth analyzing both discourse and storytelling in the town of Tracton, where the population is black. Heath's analysis shows how it is subtle and sophisticated, but quite different from neighboring Roadville. The story syntax of the whites in Roadville is also idiosyncratic, often containing proverbs or witty sayings, but different from the blacks. Heath concludes: "Both Tracton and Roadville are literate communities and each has its own traditions of structuring, using, and assessing reading and writing" (p. 230).

When we have children from cultures that have nourished alternate speech and story forms, it can be a strong tool to use that knowledge as a base from which to develop student proficiency with standard English. In *A Framework for Understanding Poverty* (2005), Payne gives a number of suggestions for how to use this base:

- ▲ Formal register [standard English] needs to be taught.

- ▲ Casual register [culturally specific variations on standard English] needs to be recognized as the primary discourse for some students.

- ▲ Have students write in casual register and then translate into formal register. To get examples of casual register down on paper, ask them to write the way they talk.

- ▲ In the classroom, tell stories both ways. Tell the story using the formal story structure, and then tell the story with the casual register structure. Talk about stories: how they stay the same and how they're different.

- ▲ Encourage participation in the writing and telling of stories.

- ▲ Show students how much the formal register affects [life chances, including] their ability to get a well-paying job. (pp. 34–35)

A problem with Payne's book is that she associates these alternate forms of language use with poverty. These variations are culture and race specific rather than generically characteristic of poor families. And furthermore, many families—white, black, or Latino—who find themselves living below the poverty line have good standard, or as Payne would say, formal register English in their repertoires.

Payne uses Martin Joos' terms "formal" and "casual register" to distinguish colloquial language with a cultural base from standard English. By calling formal register middle-class English and associating casual register with poverty, Payne puts language patterns into economic categories, thus glossing over differences that are race and culture specific. She has been criticized for generalizing about children of generational poverty so as to create a negative stereotype about behavior and language that is associated with income and class (Bomer et al., 2008; Gorski, 2006).

The larger point we should take away, however, is that whatever the cultural roots for speaking and writing children bring, they must learn standard English to maximize their employment opportunities in 21st-century United States. Teachers need to recognize the validity of the cultural forms of speaking with which their children arrive and use this understanding in instruction. Even more important would be to understand the values, norms, and history of their original family culture so as to include connections within the curriculum (Culturally Relevant Instruction). This duality—insuring that all students become literate and skillful with standard English while continuing to integrate the rich cultural identities they bring with them to school—is aligned with Django Paris' (2012) notion of culturally sustaining pedagogy. For more on this see Chapter 15, "Personal Relationship Building."

3. SUPPORTING MENTAL ENGAGEMENT

If we were to liken clear instruction to a solidly constructed brick building, then framing the learning would be similar to framing the building itself. Our presentation and use of explanatory devices would be the bricks in the structure, and this next category would be like the mortar that connects the bricks and holds them together. Being explicit and making cognitive connections for students are tools we can use to strengthen the learning experience and preempt obstacles to student engagement and understanding.

Explicitness

Explicitness is a category of behaviors—four different kinds—that stitch together instructional episodes. Explicitness means expressly communicating and not leaving to implication these four events:

- ▲ Intention of cues
- ▲ Focus of questions
- ▲ Necessary steps in directions
- ▲ Meaning of references

When any one of these is missing, instruction falls apart, and so does learning. These behaviors are often more visible when absent because of the confusions and cognitive gaps that occur when they are omitted.

Intentions of Cues

Effective explainers cue students explicitly to make the connections and use the kinds of thinking that will lead to learning the material. They leave no logical gaps. Instead they build little bridges for students between cues they give and how the students are supposed to use them. For example, while studying the onset of World War I, a teacher says, "Be sure to read the generals' speeches on both sides that are in the Appendix. They will give you ideas about where they stood on the importance of glory vs. suffering." Thus there is an explicit heads-up about what to read for.

Teachers who are not explicit make assumptions (unfortunately, often faulty) about students' ability to read their cues or their intentions. These teachers are often guilty of playing "guess what's on the teacher's mind" or "guess why we're doing this" games that intimidate and confuse students. Here is an example of inexplicit cuing behavior. The teacher is attempting to build an image that will help students learn the word *concave:*

> Before defining "concave," Orr [the teacher] asked, "Where do bears sleep?" He thought students would create an image of a cave that would help them remember the definition. Both students [we interviewed] noticed this odd question and understood that it was supposed to provide a device for learning the definition. However, neither perceived that this device was an image. (Winne & Marx, 1982, p. 510)

Orr didn't have a bad idea here. He was just so inexplicit with his cue that the students couldn't use it. He intended the image of the cave to be a visual mnemonic: "When you stand in front of a cave, the space seems to belly away from you. Likewise, a concave surface curves away from you." If he had said that, the students might have understood his cue and been able to use it to remember what *concave* means.

Focus of Questions

Sometimes the focus of questions isn't explicit, and the result is another version of "guess what's on the teacher's mind." In the previous example, there are several good answers to Orr's question, "Where do bears sleep?" (in the zoo, in the woods, all over North America, etc.). But he wants only one from the possible universe of correct answers.

Video: Explicitness

Here is another example. A Latin teacher has a student read a question from an exercise in a text. "What type of question is that?" the teacher asks. The student does not respond. No other students volunteer or appear to know either. What the teacher really means is, Which of the six types of questions on yesterday's handout—questions with *quid, cur, quis, quem, ubi,* or *quo*—is this? He assumes the student realizes this, but the student doesn't. The teacher doesn't realize that "what type" is not a cue to the student to scan the six types on yesterday's worksheet and pick one. The universe of possible answers the student is scanning is not six choices; it is infinite, and so he is at a loss.

The teacher then directs the student to turn to yesterday's handout and read the first item. The student obliges. In a tired voice, the teacher says, "Okay, please read the next item." Again, the student obliges. This second item is an example of the type of question from the exercise that confounded the student. The student finishes reading it. There is a pause. The teacher gives the student a wide-eyed look: "Well?" "Oh," says the student and goes on to identify the text line as a *quid* question.

This confusion would have been avoided if the teacher had been explicit about the mental operation he wanted the student to do: "By 'what type,' Luis, I mean which of the six types we discussed yesterday. Check your handout compared to the text line you just read. Everybody else check, too, to see if you'll agree." Teachers who are explicit show students directly how what they're doing (now or next) is connected to something familiar, something they know or have done previously that will help them get to the learning goal.

Being explicit means anticipating and intentionally inserting links, references, or phrases that enable learners to know why questions are asked and how directions or examples relate to learning tasks. "He always asks us questions we can't answer," is a common report that students make about unclear teachers. They can't answer questions because the teacher fails to define or at least reference the domain the question is tapping. Consider this episode: "What is good writing?" asks Ms. Arroyo, and she has a specified list of attributes in mind that she proposes to get up on the board. But the question is a "sucker" question; students are going to volunteer all sorts of plausible answers that don't fit in with her lesson plan. That would be okay if she were to collect them all, discuss them, and then perhaps compare them to the text list she has in mind. If instead, she's going to say "no," and "that's not quite what I'm looking for," and invalidate much good student thinking as she "develops" (that's how her lesson plan puts it) her list, then she doesn't really mean, "What do you think good writing is?" She means, "What do *I* think good writing is?" In other words, "Read my mind."

Another easy trap for teachers to fall into regarding explicitness is asking questions in series. Good and Brophy (2000) describe a teacher, who in discussing the War of 1812, asks the following in one continuous statement:

> "Why did we go to war? As a merchant how would you feel? How was our trade hurt by the Napoleonic War?" The teacher is trying to clarify the first question and focus thinking on an economic cause of the war. In his attempt, he confuses. If instead he were to say, "Our focus question is, What economic conditions existed in the United States that might have precipitated our decision to go to war? Let's start with what you know about the merchants." (p. 390)

Questions in series are a temptation when we ask a question and get silence from the whole class. We want to give a clue, so we ask another question that is intended to lead the students toward our focus. What we may accidentally do is jerk students' train of thought around, and leave them confused as to what we are really after.

Necessary Steps in Directions

We may direct students to begin tasks but inadvertently leave out necessary steps in the directions. This can happen when we make unwarranted assumptions that students understand the conventions for how certain tasks are done. A teacher says, "Get together in groups of four or five and brainstorm as many endings as you can for this short story." He has not instructed groups to choose a recorder, to aim for a target number of possibilities, and to generate many different possibilities but *not* develop those possibilities in detail until later. So they all start brainstorming without recording, some groups stop after their first one or two ideas, and some take their first idea and get lost in the details of an idea that turns out not to be very logical or interesting. Just a few more explicit steps in the directions could have made a huge difference in groups' productivity. Another example of giving inexplicit directions is, "Fix these sentences and then move on to the next assignment." Some students have interpreted "fix" as "cross out and write over the words that are wrong" (which the teacher, in fact, intends). Others are recopying the entire sentences with the corrections, which is taking four times as long. As a result, they won't have time to finish the second assignment. A simple insertion like, "Fix these sentences by crossing out and writing over words that don't belong or need to be revised" would get everyone on track.

A still deeper way to get students to understand the focus of directions is to give a partial model of how to frame their thinking to carry out a task given to them. This can be a sentence starter. For example, we have asked students to contrast the reasons different politicians in the South gave for secession in 1860 and said, "So when you're answering, you might say: Jones argued for the preservation of the rights of states to make their own decisions, *whereas* Smith thought preservation of the Southern economy based on slavery was the main argument. He called this the Southern way of life."

Including specific language forms in sample answers ("Jones said X, *whereas Smith* said Y" or "Jones said X, *in contrast to Smith,* who said Y") and asking students to model their answers cues them to what their teacher meant by the direction. Language and thought are intertwined, so sharing sample language forms of exemplary answers when giving directions guides students with more precision into productive work. Overall, the goal of this area of performance is to spell out completely what we mean in our directions and not assume the steps are obvious to our students.

Meaning of References

Sometimes we make references to famous people, ideas, events, or works that are intended to elucidate current instruction, but the students may not know the references, and so they confuse rather than clarify. In fact, they may detract from instructional effectiveness because as students try to puzzle about the reference by asking themselves what it means, they may miss the next one or two points that are made. For example, a teacher who says, "Reading James Michener's *Hawaii* can make one feel like Sisyphus, which becomes apparent by about Chapter 25." That sentence won't mean anything to students who don't know that Sisyphus was a cruel Greek king who was condemned to forever roll a huge stone up a hill in Hades, only to have it roll down again every time he neared the top. Therefore, to feel like Sisyphus means to feel hopeless about ever finishing. An art teacher walking by a student who is doing detailed beautiful work on his piece comments: "You are going to be the Michelangelo of the 21st century." While the teacher means Michelangelo, who painted the Sistine Chapel, the student is envisioning a ninja warrior named Michelangelo, a comical crime fighter living in the sewers of New York City. Being explicit at times like these would not foreclose our using arcane references, but would cue us to explain them on the spot so students could understand.

Making Cognitive Connections

The behaviors identified in this section are a complement to moves described in the explicitness section because each represents a way of building bridges for students. The bridges may be related to time: between what is happening in the present, previous, or future learning. Or they may signal shifts and transitions between ideas, activities, pace, or level of difficulty. All of them are intended to positively affect student engagement and understanding.

Showing Resemblance to Something Students Already Know

It is useful to show how new learning resembles students' previous work or knowledge, demonstrating to students how things we are talking about resemble what they already know (Book & Galvin, 1976). It is appropriate to make this move within many styles of teaching simply as a good clarifier. Here is an example of this move:

Teacher: "When we first worked on multiplying, you learned that it was related to addition. . . . how?"

Student: "Repeated addition."

Teacher: "Right! Meaning what?"

Student: "Multiplying is like adding the same number over and over again . . . as many times as you're multiplying it by."

Teacher: "Okay, very good. Now this division operation we've been working on today is really a lot like multiplication, except what it's doing in short-cut fashion isn't adding a number over and over again, it's . . . what?"

Student: "Subtracting it."

Teacher: "Right! Everybody see that? Matt? Can you explain in your own words how division is like multiplication?"

> **Student:** "It's the backwards of multiplying."
>
> **Teacher:** "An interesting way to put it; Lily, what do you think Matt means by *backward?"*

Here's another example from a beginning chemistry course:

> **Teacher:** "So we've proven this welding torch burns hotter than the straight propane burner. Do you remember what we did at the beginning of the year, heating sodium chlorate in the test tube? What happened when we held a glowing ember over the tube?"
>
> **Student:** "It burst into flame."
>
> **Teacher:** "How did we explain that?"
>
> **Student:** "Heating the sodium chlorate drove off oxygen and the oxygen made the ember burn faster and hotter."
>
> **Teacher:** "Right! And a welding torch is like that. We've got these two tanks . . . [and goes on to show how a welding rig mixes two gases, acetylene and oxygen and that the presence of the extra oxygen vastly increases combustion temperatures]."

The integrating of the old with the new takes place here and builds intellectual links between items of information in such a way as to keep the picture of the whole emerging chain visible too. As students learn the new item, they simultaneously see the whole chain that is now one link longer. The link and chain analogy may break down for bodies of information that relate in other ways—like a web, for example. But the Clarity move serves the same purpose of linking the new item with the larger picture of established knowns (Ausubel, 1968; Gagné, 1992).

Bulgren (1991) and others, from the Institute for Research on Learning Disabilities at the University of Kansas, use anchoring tables to show in a visual and precise way exactly what the similarities and differences there are between new and old concepts.

An anchoring table (Figure 11.10) is a graphic organizer—in this case, a special-purpose one—to compare and contrast new information to previously learned information. The steps for phasing in the use of an anchoring table with students are the same as those described for other graphic organizers.

Figure 11.10 Anchoring Table

FAMILIAR INFORMATION		NEW INFORMATION
FACTORY CHARACTERISTICS	Similar Concepts	CELL CHARACTERISTICS
Management	Controls activities	Nucleus
Fence/ Security System	Regulates what enters or leaves	Membrane Cell
Power Plant	Produces energy	Mitochondria

SUMMARY: A cell is a structure in which the nucleus controls activities, the membrane regulates, and the mitochondria produces energy.

The purpose of showing resemblance to something students already know is to look backward. We make the connections for the students because we want them to see that the new learning coming up really isn't so new or different (or so hard), and that it fits in with something they already know—there already exists a structure or a continuum in their heads to accommodate it.

The difference between this kind of integrating and "activating students' current knowledge" is that activating looks forward. It gets up on screen, as it were, students' existing conceptions. The associations or connections come from them as they see it at that moment. Thus their minds are warmed up, and they have something to compare and contrast with the new learning when it comes along. What they already have may or may not be accurate, may be complete or incomplete. The purpose of eliciting the information from them is to get them thinking and give them a reference point against which to test the new learning. They may ask themselves, "Is what we learn about chemistry indeed what we thought chemistry to be?"

Asking Students to Compare and Contrast

Another way of getting students to see connections between past and present concepts or topics is to structure an activity that prompts them to generate connections. "Compare and contrast the Hemingway short story we just read with the O. Henry story we read last week." This task calls for students to review each story, go into it, analyze it, and extract attributes of each author's writing to see how it is like or unlike attributes of the second author.

Skillful teachers use graphic organizers as powerful tools to empower learning.

Compare and contrast tasks implicitly call for higher-order thinking in which one actively uses one's knowledge of the two items. You have to retrieve what you know and then manipulate it mentally. This is one of nine instructional practices included in Marzano's list of instructional strategies that have a high probability of enhancing achievement for all students in all subject areas at all grade levels. The effect size for this teaching practice is very high (1.61) for an average percentile gain of 45 (Marzano, Pickering, & Pollock, 2001).

Marzano and Pickering (2010) offer several guidelines for structuring the compare-contrast task in order to increase its effectiveness. These include having students relate new content to something familiar, or topics of personal interest or relevance, and identifying the characteristics upon which the comparison will be based. In other words, when we ask students to generate these connections, we explicitly identify the basis for the comparison: physical characteristics ("How is the structure of an atom similar to/different from the parts of a bicycle?"); a process ("How is the process of photosynthesis like playing a game of soccer?"); a sequence of events ("How is the sequence of a bill becoming a law like . . . now name a sequence of events familiar to the student"). Comparing and contrasting lends itself beautifully to graphic organizers; skillful teachers draw on that powerful visual tool to empower the learning.

Extending to Implications and Future Actions

Anything we do that causes students to think actively about academic material is an aid to learning. That is why questions that propel students to apply knowledge to a real situation (or to think about how they would apply it) augments learning. These are examples: "How might this court ruling affect criminal investigations?"; "What effect do you think this genetic finding will have on the way people live their lives?"; or "How could you use this knowledge about area and perimeter if you were redoing your kitchen?"

Discussions that develop from initial application questions like these can strengthen student understanding significantly. The 24 operating principles described in the upcoming section on Making Students' Thinking Visible serve as a rich repertoire of tools for facilitating these kinds of discussions.

Making Transitions Between Ideas

These are brief, within-lesson transitions like segues made by an announcer and mostly applicable where direct instruction is taking place. We don't have the opportunity to guide transitions between items of information unless we are leading the instructional activity. In terms of clarity, these moves are verbal markers that help students follow the roadmap as the teacher makes a left turn here, a right turn there, or circles back to the point of origin. It might sound like this: "Okay, that word problem required us to multiply. Now let's move on to the next one and see if it is the same." Notice the difference between that remark and a teacher who simply says, "Okay, let's move on to the next problem." Telling the students to move on gets them from one place to the next but does not provide a transition.

A transition move takes something about what has just been done and relates it to what's coming up immediately. It provides intellectual links like integrating moves do, but instead of linking to the learner's past experience, or learning from other disciplines or other times, this link is between what has come immediately before and what's coming right now—in the lesson itself (Murray, 1991). Here's a good example: "So that's how the commercial banking system multiplies money deposited in checking accounts and creates new money. Now another way new money gets created is through consumer credit. Let's look at how all those plastic credit cards add to the banking system to create even more money."

Signaling Activity, Pace, Level, or Content Shifts

These moves are simple statements at transition points to prepare students for a change in the nature of cognitive work:

- ▲ Shift in activity: "Okay, that's all we're going to do with the lab reports today. Now let's take a look at the next chapter so we can preview the new material."
- ▲ Shift in pace: "We're going to pick up the pace now, so get ready for a little more action!"
- ▲ Shift in level of difficulty: "Now we're moving on to three-step problems instead of two-step, but still with the same operations."

- ▲ Shift in content: "Ladies and gentlemen, we're going to be using these vocabulary words today in our essays, so keep them handy and in a safe place." This kind of shift makes direct links between what has just been completed and what's immediately to come in the flow of instruction—even if "immediately" is interrupted by overnight.

Foreshadowing

Foreshadowing puts intellectual markers or hooks in place for items that are down the road and will not be dealt with the very next time students work on this subject. Consider these two teacher statements:

1. "Well, you couldn't *have* two hydrochloric acid molecules on that side of the equation because it wouldn't balance. You don't have to worry about that now, but soon we will get to this notion that chemical equations must balance. When we talk about balancing equations, we'll be experimenting with the proportions of different chemicals that get used up in a chemical reaction."

2. "And if you think Laura worked hard helping Ma around the house, wait 'til you see what she did with Pa Ingalls around haymaking time." "What's that mean?" a student asks. "Well, that's harvesting the hay and that was a very important part of farm life then . . . now too. Anyway, haymaking is coming up in a couple of chapters. I think you'll enjoy that section."

These examples of foreshadowing take a term or an idea that crops up and create brief images of what it will be like or what it will be about. This is done so that when the students get to that point, it's not totally strange territory. "Oh, I remember we talked about that last week," a student may say to himself and start assimilating the ideas into his cognitive framework. Foreshadowing moves may crop up as moments of opportunity during instruction and are often unplanned. For instance, in the case of the second example above, the students commented on how hard Laura works around the house, and their remarks made the teacher think of the days of hard labor Laura spent with her father making hay, so she brought it up for comparative purposes, knowing it was coming up in a few chapters.

4: GETTING INSIDE STUDENTS' HEADS: COGNITIVE EMPATHY

Cognitive empathy means the teacher is viewing and actively assessing the learning experience from the student's perspective in order to find out what is going on in their heads and to make strategic decisions from that frame of reference. This dimension of clarity is directly aligned with formative assessment practices and is central to good teaching because it enables teachers to know when and what students aren't understanding and to zero in on and clarify what they don't understand.

To accomplish this, there are three categories of moves a teacher might make: (1) checking for understanding frequently and in a variety of ways to monitor for student confusion, (2) unscrambling confusion to identify specific points of confusion or misconceptions and address them, and (3) getting students to make their thinking visible thus revealing how and how well they are understanding the material at hand. Each of these categories contains a repertoire of options, and there is increasing depth of access to student thinking among the three. Making Students' Thinking Visible, a new level of sophistication in teaching skill, is a constellation of 24 principles of teacher action that does give diagnostic information of where student misunderstanding lies. But Making Students' Thinking Visible combines and goes far beyond simple checking and unscrambling; it also creates a robust talk environment where all students participate and high-level thinking skills are called for.

Checking for Understanding

Video: Checking for Understanding

We use the word *checking* to describe what teachers do to determine whether students are understanding or confused. When teachers are checking, they are attending to—and proactively reaching out to gather—data from students, or responding to indicators that students are struggling, in an effort to determine "yes . . . no . . . who?" is getting what. There are five ways we can describe what we might see:

1. Pressing on
2. Reading body language
3. Asking recall-level questions
4. Asking comprehension-level questions
5. "Dipsticking"

These five are not mutually exclusive. We might be employing several of them at different points or simultaneously during the same lesson. Each provides us with a different kind of data about who is or is not understanding, what is unclear or confusing, and what we need to do to clarify. As you move from the first to the last option, notice that we get increasingly specific and deeper information from students. In the last instance (dipsticking), we are also ensuring that we get the data from *all* students. What is important about checking is that we are doing it frequently, getting the kind of data we need to assess the depth and breadth of understanding across all students, and using the data to guide our instruction.

Pressing On

Pressing on is essentially the absence of checking. It means presenting information or assigning tasks without any active or apparent check for understanding. In some limited instances, pressing on might be intentional and appropriate (i.e. in fast-paced reviews of material previously taught when it is more of a summary to highlight or review key information that has already been learned). But it is a liability if it is happening regularly, or if we fail to check because we are unaware that a concept or task might require more or different explanation than we planned. Thus pressing on should happen sparingly in most lessons.

Reading Body Language

Reading body language means attending to students' posture, gestures, facial expressions, and using them as indicators about whether students are "getting it" or not. While students' overt body language might cue us when there is confusion, it is risky to rely solely on body language as evidence of understanding. Students might look totally attentive and absorbed in what is being presented but be totally confused, and either unaware that they are or good at giving us the look that implies they are engaged when they are totally lost or tuned out.

In one study of student thought processes during instruction, Peterson and Swing (1982) describe how students fooled observers who judged them to be attending to the lesson:

> Melissa's responses to the stimulated-recall interview suggested that she was not attending [although observers judged from her behavior that she was] and instead seemed to be spending much of the time worrying about her performance and the possibility of failure. For example, when asked what she was thinking after viewing the first videotape segment, Melissa replied: ". . . since I was just beginning, I was nervous and I thought maybe I wouldn't know how to do things." After viewing the second segment, Melissa said the following: "I was thinking that Chris would probably have the easiest time because she was in the top math group." After viewing the third segment Melissa responded: "Well, I was mostly thinking about what we talked about before—I was making a fool of myself." Finally, after the fourth segment, Melissa stated: "Well, this might be off the subject. I was thinking about my crocheting meeting `cause I wanted to have it done." (p. 485)

Bloom's Taxonomy

Asking Questions

To check more overtly and directly for general student understanding, we typically ask questions. Putting Bloom's taxonomy (Bloom & Krathwohl, 1956) to the side for a minute, the types of questions we ask can be considered as two categories: (1) questions that require students to recall information, and (2) questions that require students to demonstrate comprehension or higher-level thinking.

Asking Recall Questions

Recall questions call for factual answers that come directly from the material presented, and they actually dominate most classroom discourse. They are about who, what, when, where; usually have a right answer; and are often referred to as closed questions. Two examples are, "What is the formula for finding the area of a triangle?" and "What are the three events that contributed to our involvement in Panama?" This type of checking enables us to ensure that students have the foundation information or can recall the facts or basics necessary to think and reason at higher levels.

Questioning Skills

Asking Comprehension Questions

Comprehension questions require students to use information they recall and apply it in some way. Frequently, these are "How? Why? What if?" types of questions that invite students to demonstrate deeper levels of understanding of a lesson's concepts or operations. The question, "What would you multiply to get the area of this triangle (one that has measurements marked, but no terms labeled)?" requires both the recall of the formula and an understanding of how to apply the formula to a specific triangle. Comprehension questions can be answered only if students truly understand the concept being checked. Another example is, "Why couldn't 'gobble' be on the page (where the guide words on the dictionary page are *hunt* and *mound*)?" Students can only answer this question if they understand how guide words bound the range of entries on a dictionary page.

Note that during checking, we sometimes think we are getting a reading on comprehension, but in reality, we are only checking recall of key words: "So the key elements of photosynthesis are . . . ? . . . (chlorophyll) right and (sunlight) right, and one more . . . (carbon dioxide). Right. OK, you really do understand photosynthesis." Compare this to a question like, "In which of these environments (enumerate a-b-c) do you predict the plants would grow stronger and healthier? Why?" For a more in-depth exploration of questioning, see the document "Questioning Skills" on *The Skillful Teacher* website at www.RBTeach.com/TST7.

Figure 11.11 Forms of Dipsticking

FORMS OF DIPSTICKING

WITH SIGNALS		WITHOUT SIGNALS
Self-Assessment	**Content Check**	
• Thumbs up • Hands on head if ... • Sign turned over • Red, yellow, green cards	• Fingers make math operation sign • Correct punctuation marks in air • Hold up cards: A for area P for perimeter B for both	• One-question quiz • Unison response • Lots of questions • Verbal fill-in-the-blank sentences • Short writing assignment

Dipsticking

We refer to the fifth way of checking as *dipsticking,* a term popularized by Madeline Hunter in the 1970s. It means taking a reading on the learning and deciding whether to move on or to add some more teaching, just as the oil dipstick in an auto engine gives you a reading on whether the oil level in the reservoir is sufficient to drive on or if it needs refilling. Dipsticking involves quick and frequent checks for understanding and data gathering throughout the lesson and getting responses from most or all students simultaneously. Figure 11.11 highlights three different forms of dipsticking one might use.

Dipsticking for Self-Assessment Using Signals

Hunter and her colleagues taught students to use signals—thumbs up, thumbs down, thumbs to one side—to self-assess and to send periodic messages to teachers about how well they understand something. There are any number of other ways to gather similar data. For example, asking students, "Nod your head if you're with me so far" or "Show me your green card if you are really with me, a yellow if I am starting to lose you, a red if I've completely confused you . . . I'm checking my teaching." We have found that when teachers make it clear that this is an assessment of their teaching—not an evaluation of the students' learning—they get more honest and accurate data from students. Enlisting students in giving us this kind of feedback throughout a lesson leaves us less reliant on body language for detecting confusion and can be very useful for determining the need to pause and clarify. Getting students to take responsibility for honestly assessing how well they are understanding and thereby helping us regulate the pace and clarity of our teaching is one way of building a classroom culture where students become agents of their own learning. The obvious limitation of this kind of self-assessment is when students don't know what they don't know, or think they do understand when actually they don't.

Dipsticking with Content Check Using Signals

A more developed form of dipsticking gets an actual content answer from each student, often in the form of multiple choice where all students choose and signal a response. In trigonometry, a teacher says: "When I call for the signal, hold up one, two, three, or four fingers to show in which quadrant the angle will terminate." In an English class, each student has cards that say S (for sentence), F (for fragment of a sentence), and RO (for run-on). The teacher says, "Hold up the appropriate card after I read each of the following . . . "

Dipsticking Without Signals

Videos: Dipsticking 1 & 2

Both of the earlier forms of dipsticking involve students' sending signals with their hands, cards, or another device. Dipsticking can also be accomplished by getting all students to respond in ways other than signaling. Some teachers pause in the middle of classes and give one-question quizzes or short writing assignments and then circulate and look over shoulders as students are writing to see how everyone is doing.

A teacher might ask a high volume of questions across a broad range of students in a short period of time. Many classrooms are now equipped with electronic response systems (clickers) where students enter responses to multiple choice or short answer questions simultaneously and the overall class results are posted anonymously to a large screen for all to see. Thus in an instant, a teacher and students can get feedback about areas of confusion or concern. Dyer (2016) provides a useful list of such devices and apps on the Northwest Evaluation Association website at http://www.nwea.org/blog/2016/take-three-55-digital-tools-and-apps-for-formative-assessment-success.

We can use dipsticking to assess recall, or comprehension to a degree, or both. Recall or comprehension questions enable us to assess the depth or degree of student understanding. Dipsticking is used to simultaneously assess the breadth of understanding—how many students respond successfully or appropriately to a given prompt or question. Finally, the intent is that this type of assessing is happening frequently across all students during instruction.

Dipsticking does not have to be a constant feature of every lesson. It could be out of place in true discussion where a line of argument is being developed or in a conceptual change lesson when students are encountering events in conflict with their native theories, constructing new theories to account for what they've observed, and testing the new theories. But even here there will be benchmarks when we will want to check students' understanding of something everyone should know. At those times, taking a true dipstick reading will provide much needed information about who does and who doesn't understand.

Unscrambling Confusion

When we detect that students are confused, the next clarity task is to find out what the students are confused about and tailor re-explanations accordingly. We call this *unscrambling confusions,* and it has a number of options from which to draw:

- ▲ Do nothing at the moment.
- ▲ Acknowledge the confusion and move on.
- ▲ Re-explain.
- ▲ Isolate the point of confusion with pinpoint questions.
- ▲ Have a student explain his or her own current thinking.
- ▲ Persevere and return.

The first option, doing nothing in the moment, means making no response to the perceived confusion and continuing with the lesson.

The second option, acknowledging the confusion, means making it known to students that we are aware of it but want them to stay with us a little longer before dealing with it. "I know this is a little difficult to see just yet, but hang in there, and I think it will make sense with a few more examples."

A third option is to launch into a re-explanation of the item. It may be slower or more detailed than the first explanation, or it may be a re-explanation using a different explanatory device. In either case, we are presenting the same thing over again without any venture into the students' thinking, relying heavily on what we perceive to be the source or the nature of their confusion, and re-explaining from that perspective.

A fourth option is to pose pinpoint questions to discover precisely where in the sequence of learning the student became confused. When that point is isolated, we swing in, economically omitting re-explanation of anything the students have already assimilated, and move on with the re-explanation from there.

A fifth option is to ask students to describe or explain their thinking, probing for how a student thinks about the concept or operation. This means truly listening to students and trying to understand their frame of reference or way of conceptualizing the item.

Questions or prompts like these can draw out the understanding:

- "How did you get that answer?"
- "How do you approach this kind of problem?
- Tell me what you did or thought about?"
- "What did you try first? Why?"
- "Tell me what you do understand. Let's start there."

You will notice that as we move through this continuum of choices, we gather more evidence about the source of confusion from the student, and thus we are more informed about what we need to do to clarify or reteach effectively. When we choose to get students to explain their own thinking we sometimes discover that apparently "wrong" answers aren't really wrong at all if we understand the student's assumptions and logic. As well, using the student's frame of reference with its meaning orientation enables us to re-explain the concept (or ask a series of questions that will bring the student closer to self-discovering the concept) from a vantage point that will have more meaning for the student. We might also discover that the concept turns out to be outside the boundaries of the student's thinking system, in which case, it's an inappropriate objective altogether. That is quite an important thing to find out. For example, if we are working on clarifying the different powers municipal governments have from county governments, we may discover some students don't really know what a municipal government is!

The final option, persevering and returning, might be an integral part of the previous three but with an additional element: the return. We persevere when we find a student confused. We stick with the student, perhaps have several exchanges with him. Other students may then contribute missing elements of the explanation. Then, most importantly, we come back to the first student to have him summarize or fully state the explanation. This "return" visit is not only a check for understanding of that first student but is also an important signal of confidence in the student. It gives him an opportunity to emerge in triumph as the final synthesizer.

Sometimes there isn't time in the period for us to unscramble all the confusions of all the students—a reality we all live with. In that case, what a perseverant teacher does is note or record who specifically is still foggy on the new concept, and make some provision for a return engagement with those students (e.g., arranging for a short small-group session right then and there perhaps, or asking Rafael and Olivia to stop by after classes for a few minutes to ensure that they will receive the support they need). Notice how this option ties in with sending high expectations messages. In Chapter 14, "Expectations," we include returning to students who don't get it yet as one of the 10 arenas for sending the three key messages: "This is important; you can do it with effective effort; I won't give up on you."

Making Students' Thinking Visible

The context thus far for having students explain their thinking has been to unscramble confusions. The notion of making a student's thinking visible, however, has far greater reach. It is about creating a robust talk environment for all students where they are both challenged and enabled to think deeply, frequently, and critically, and to interact with one another while developing deep understanding of the concepts we are teaching.

Videos: Making Thinking Visible—Explain Your Thinking 1 & 2

Over a five-year period, District 2 in New York City went from sixteenth to first place in achievement by investing in the development of these skills broadly in all their teachers (Alvarado, Elmore, & Resnick, 2000). Making Students' Thinking Visible (MSTV) was not the only focus of their improvement efforts, but it was a major factor in the improvement of teaching and student cognitive engagement.

We take the phrase "Making Students' Thinking Visible" from an article published by David Perkins (2003) and a title repeated in recent years in a book by Ritchhart, Church, and Morrison (2011). The design of this complex teaching skill has origins going back to 1975 (Easley & Zwoyer) and a rich history in the '80s with clear examples in the work of Deborah Loewenberg Ball, Magdeline Lampert, and Deborah Schifter. Lauren Resnick advanced "Accountable Talk" in the '90s as another version of these powerful ideas. During that decade, Lucy West and others in New York's District 2 developed these skills further as a key element of their groundbreaking instructional coaching model.

Making Students Thinking Visible brings together six strands of successful teaching and learning (Figure 11.12). It's the *combination* of these strands that produce the results. Consider the following:

Videos: Agree/Disagree, Teachers Getting Students to Talk

- ▲ If you can both listen to children and accept their answers not as things to be judged right or wrong but as pieces of information which may reveal what the child is thinking, you will have taken a giant step toward becoming a master teacher (Easley & Zwoyer, 1975, p. 25).

- ▲ It was listening to their own students solve problems that made the greatest difference in [teachers'] instructional practice (Borko & Putnam, 1995).

Figure 11.12 Diagram of MSTV Six Strands

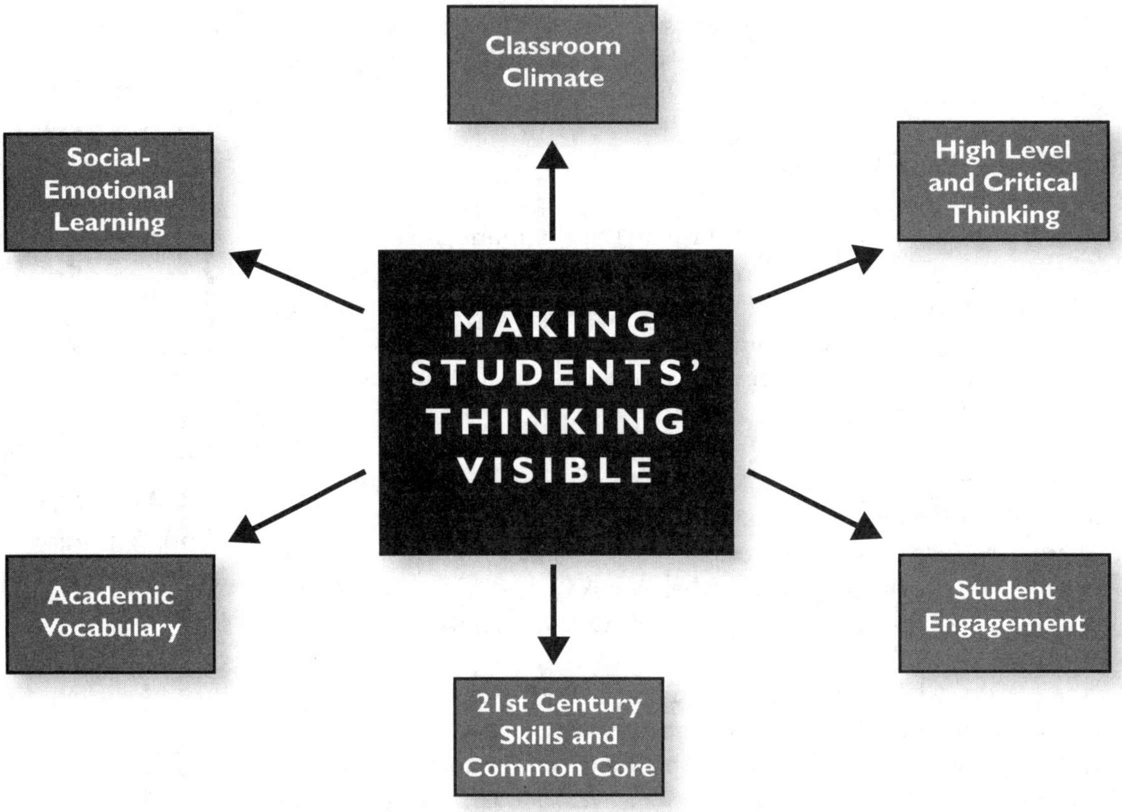

- ▲ My definition of a good teacher has changed from "one who explains things so well that students understand" to "one who gets students to explain things so well that they can be understood" (Reinhart, 2000, p. 478).

These authors argue for the special importance of knowing what is going on inside students' heads. The behavior they are urging, however, goes beyond the checking and unscrambling behaviors we have profiled previously in this chapter. They are part of a tradition of educational research that advises teachers to:

- ▲ Structure your interaction with students so you have frequent access to what and how they are thinking about the topics you are teaching. This means asking them to frequently express, verbally or in writing, what their thinking is.

- ▲ Get students engaged in explaining the rationale for their thinking and supporting it out loud.

- ▲ Cause interaction and discussion among students about the thinking that surfaces.

- ▲ Build a climate of safety and mutual inquiry among students so they are not afraid of being wrong and will actively speak their minds (see Chapter 16, "Classroom Climate").

Videos: Struggle—Normalizing Mistakes, MSTV Demo

Making Students' Thinking Visible means creating a classroom environment where students:

- ▲ Do the majority of the talking.

- ▲ Are expected to explain their thinking.

- ▲ Show they are listening to one another.

- ▲ Are willing to admit confusion or not knowing.

- ▲ Challenge each other's thinking nonjudgmentally.

- ▲ Take initiative to explain another's thinking (including how s/he might have made an error).

- ▲ Take responsibility for helping others who don't get something as quickly as they have.

In the long run, these behaviors become a way of being and interacting for the teacher and students, thus permeating the environment. So what does it take to make all of this happen? Figure 11.13 represents the multiple dimensions that it takes to create this learning environment, beginning with the constellation of teaching skills involved.

24 Operating Principles

24 Operating Principles

"Constellation of Teaching Skills" on the concept map includes the use of 24 operating principles, the ability to dig into content and identify the most important concepts that should be the focus of instruction, and designing substantive questions that will guide classroom exploration and lead to student understanding of those concepts. **A repertoire of 24 operating principles one can use to facilitate student talk and check how one's practice is develop-**

Figure 11.13 MSTV Concept Map

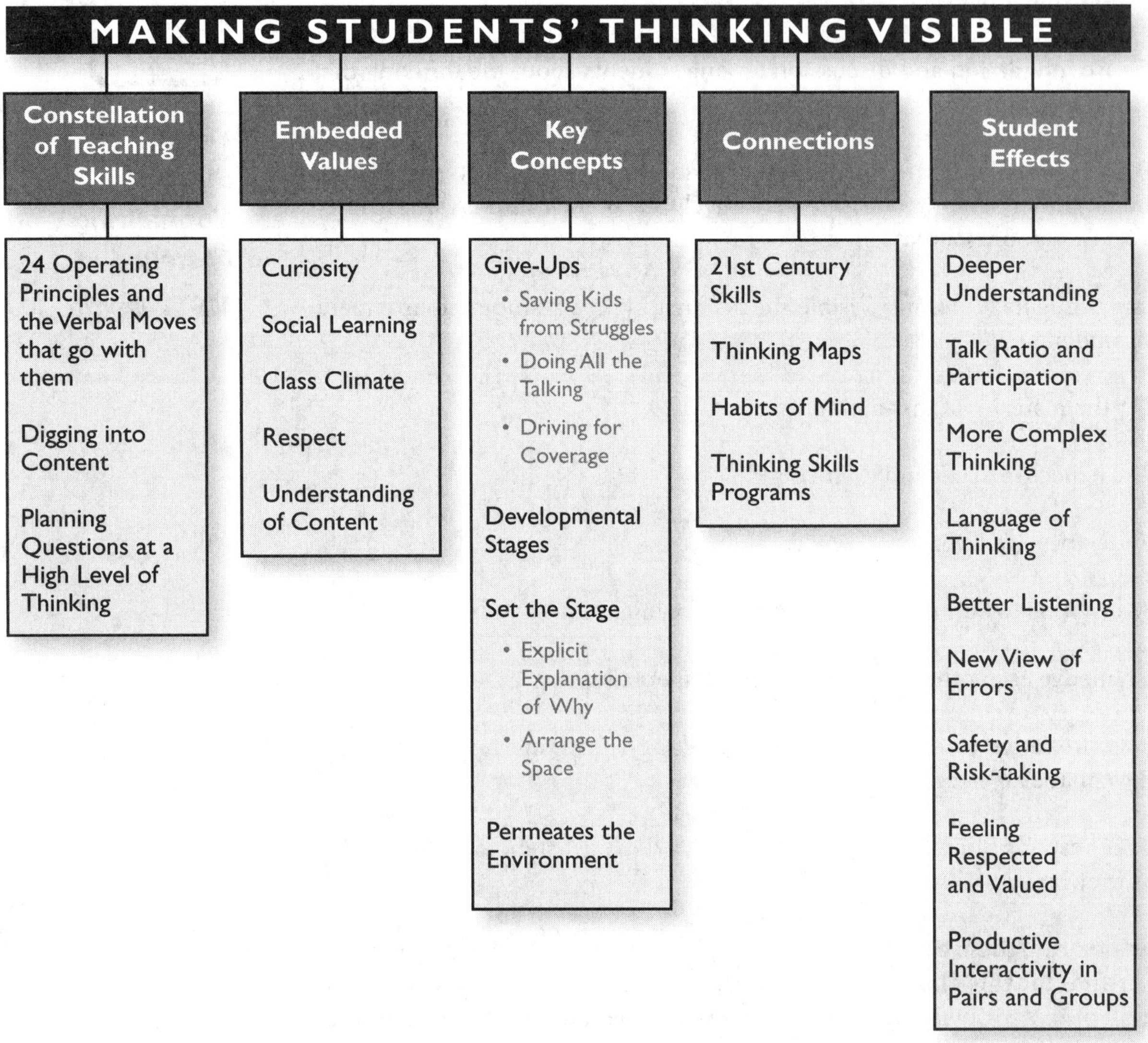

ing is available on *The Skillful Teacher* website at www.RBTeach.com/TST7. These operating principles name and explain choices a teacher makes during a discussion to engage more students in the conversation, to facilitate student-to-student dialogue, and to get students to reveal and evaluate their reasoning in support of developing genuine understanding. Many of the operating principles can and should be taught to students so they can adopt and apply them when working independently in peer-group learning experiences. They can be used as a checklist for how one's practice is developing. Our online course (www.RBTeach.com) is a carefully designed three-credit experience to learn how to implement these 24 principles in the classroom. The course contains dozens of video examples of K–12 teachers who are proficient with these skills.

As is true in so many aspects of instructional practice, the operating principles represent only one component of a larger constellation of teaching skills necessary for successful implementation. Knowing how to unpack content to identify the "must knows," the most important knowledge and skills (or big ideas) for all children to understand is essential (see Chapter 18, "Lesson Objectives"), because there will always be more potential material than time allows. Finally, we have to design substantive questions. Therefore, in planning we should come up with interesting, meaty questions that will get at these most important ideas, and challenge students to explore their understanding of a topic or concept.

In addition to teaching skills, there are the following embedded values (see Figure 11.13, MSTV Concept Map) that drive building skill at Making Students' Thinking Visible:

Videos: Accountable Talk, MSTV in Small Groups, Classroom Climate

- Curiosity about what really is going on in students' heads and commitment to making instructional adjustments as needed.
- Valuing student-to-student social interaction as a powerful facilitator of learning.
- Desire to create a climate where students will risk being wrong and know it is safe to do so.
- Respecting all learners as capable thinkers.
- Determining that every student should understand the content; thus illustrating and engaging students in exploring concepts, ideas, and skills in multiple ways until they do.

Breaking Unhelpful Practice Habits

Creating this kind of student-centered talk environment often forces us to give up some of these common competing habits of our practice.

Doing Most of the Talking

If we are accustomed to doing the majority of the talking during learning experiences, we have to give over time for students to do more of it, keeping in mind that learning takes place when the teacher stops talking and students start processing.

Coverage

If we yield to the constant pressure for speed to cover a lot of material in exchange for ensuring students' understanding, it winds up being a lose-lose. We may have to re-evaluate and prioritize what's most important to cover and how we can teach it most effectively so students have the opportunity to learn it.

Saving Students

Video: Allow Struggle

If we are uncomfortable when students struggle and feel the need to "save them from embarrassment," we need to consider the messages it sends when we bail them out rather than support them in working through their struggle. Letting a student struggle, and hanging in with them while they do sends two critical expectation messages to the student: "I believe you can do this and I won't give up on you." The other side of restraining our urge to save students and re-explain ourselves is that we enable the thinking that brings students to new insight and ownership of solving problems or overcoming confusions.

As we have worked with teachers who are committed to fully implementing Making Students' Thinking Visible, we have discovered a few other things worth mentioning here. Implementation is a developmental process for both teachers and students. For the students, an initial introduction can be really worthwhile. Share with students some things you will be doing that are different from what they might be accustomed to (asking them to explain their answers, to agree or disagree with one another's thinking, to add on when someone else speaks, etc.) and explain your reason for doing so (e.g., not because their answers are necessarily incorrect but because you are interested in hearing the thinking behind them). You might need to address the fact that you will be shifting from students raising hands to calling on anyone and all because everyone has something to contribute, and you and they should hear many ways people are thinking about an idea to truly ensure their understanding.

There are also some room arrangements and behavioral norms to consider. Is seating arranged so students can see each other's faces when someone is speaking, and look at one another when they are responding? Are students accustomed to speaking loudly enough so everyone can hear? What norms of behavior do you want to establish with them about how to do things like disagree respectfully, use one another's names when they are commenting on what someone said, etc.? The operating principles are also sequenced to a degree to reflect an evolutionary process: calling on all students, pausing after posing a question or after a student answers (wait time), responding nonjudgmentally, and validating confusion are foundational to creating a safe and inclusive learning environment. Asking students to explain their thinking, restate what someone else has said, or turn and talk to a partner before sharing with the whole group are a next set of moves that are less challenging for both teacher and students to implement initially. From there on, the progression is a bit less linear and is intended to offer many options for building a rich talk environment over time.

Thinking developmentally from a teacher's perspective, the initial stages are likely to be first—identifying which of the operating principles (or moves) we want to add to our practice and experimenting with them until they become more automatic. Over time other stages include the following:

- Expanding the variety of moves we use to get more students participating and interacting with each other.
- Using these moves with individuals and groups that tend to be less confident and participatory in class discussions.
- Teaching our students how to use these principles when they are working together in groups so that this kind of talk environment permeates all that we and they do.

Some teachers we have worked with actually provide students with a printed list of the operating principles and identify a few they want them to practice in their small-group learning activities. Another shift comes from focusing on what *we* are doing to focus on the impact of our choices on *students*—on their dialogue in the classroom, things like which and how many students have participated and how frequently, whether students entered the conversation voluntarily or at our request, and the degree to which students' contributions build on and are connected to other's ideas. In other words, we shift from reflecting on our own practice to examining at a deeper level the impact all of this is having on our students.

PDF

The History of Making Students' Thinking Visible

For an interesting history of the development of this constellation of skills, see "The History of Making Students' Thinking Visible" for this chapter on *The Skillful Teacher* website at www.RBTeach.com/TST7. A powerful constellation of skills like this has many intellectual parents and skilled masters of application. It is well worth reading because it establishes the durability of the effects and also honors those who have done so much to build a potent element of our professional knowledge base. Included in this history is an excellent view of how the skills develop in children over a one-year period in Jill Bodner Lester's class. Please check out this resource.

5. CONSOLIDATING AND ANCHORING LEARNING BY SUMMARIZING

Video: Summarizing—Exit Tickets

Summarizing is the final item in the list of instructional strategies for clarity. It means explicitly pulling everything together for all to see or hear. It can be done at strategic points during a lesson after a cohesive chunk of content has been dealt with: "OK everybody, before we go on to the Legislative branch of government, draw a diagram that represents what you know about the Executive's powers." It should be done at the conclusion of every lesson to maximize the likelihood that students' final focus is about processing and internalizing the most important takeaways from the lesson. Summarizing can be accomplished by the teacher or the students, but getting the students cognitively active in doing it is of primary importance.

Video: Summarizing—The Stoplight Method

There are two principles of learning (see Chapter 12) that underscore the importance of summarizing at the conclusion of a learning experience: sequence and say-do. The sequence principle says that what happens in the beginning and end of events or experiences is what people tend to retain longest. We increase the likelihood that the important ideas will stick when we begin a lesson by sharing the objective with students and protect the last few minutes of a learning experience to revisit the objective and summarize essential ideas or understandings related to it. The say-do principle tells us that whether learners take in information by reading it, hearing it, seeing it, or some combination, retention is limited until the learner reconstructs it for himself. It is when the learner has to shift from receptive into active mode with new information (putting it in his or her own words and images, talking about it, writing about it, explaining it to others, applying it) that retention improves significantly. In other words, when students get cognitively active with the material, they have to personally reorganize the information and concepts they have received so that they can represent them in their own words.

Asking students to do the summarizing means asking them to represent what they have learned in their own words. It is the "in your own words" feature that is critical because it forces learners to sift, reorder, and organize information themselves. They can't just let the new learning lie on the library shelf of their minds as a memory trace. They have to pick up the pieces and put them together, and the very act of doing so strengthens the learning. When we ask students to do the summarizing themselves, we increase the likelihood that more of the learning will stick, and that they will deepen their understanding of concepts. When the summarizing task or prompt is clearly aligned with the objective of the lesson, the responses students produce enable us to assess the accuracy, depth, and breadth of student understanding, and to use the data we collect to make instructional decisions for the next lesson. Finally, when all students are involved in summarizing simultaneously (a short individual writing or drawing activity), another powerful factor is added, the principle of learning called "Active Participation" (see Chapter 12, "Principles of Learning").

There are many ways to accomplish this summarizing so that all students are involved. Having students keep a learning log where they enter the lesson objective as a question ("How are fractions and decimals related?") at the beginning of class and respond to the question at the end of the lesson is one option. Similarly, students might summarize with an exit ticket that requires them to solve a sample problem representative of the lesson objective. Each of these puts students in the "reconstruct and process" mode while also providing us with formative assessment data to determine how well and which students have mastered the objective so we can make reteaching plans for those who aren't there yet.

Robert Marzano makes a strong case for getting students to represent new information in nonlinguistic formats that don't rely on language. Citing a 2009 study (Haystead & Marzano, 2009) he notes "across 129 studies in which teachers used non-linguistic strategies—such as graphic organizers, sketches, and pictographs—with one class but not with another class studying the same content, the average effect was a 17-percentile point gain in student achievement" (Marzano, 2010, p. 84). He goes on to discuss five key characteristics of nonlinguistic representations to take into consideration in maximizing the benefits:

- ▲ Nonlinguistic representations come in many forms, and the selection should match the type of content addressed and the amount of time available.
- ▲ The representation chosen and completed by the student must focus on the crucial information to be learned and represented.
- ▲ Students should explain their nonlinguistic representations to communicate their intentions and reveal their confusions of misunderstandings.
- ▲ Nonlinguistic representations take time, and to get the full effect the time has to be allocated.
- ▲ Students should revise their representations for accuracy when necessary.

While each of the above examples gets students to summarize on paper, we can also ask students to do it verbally, in pairs at the end of class, or at appropriate stopping points within class. Doing this addresses the say-do and sequence principles, and affords students the opportunity to hear other's thinking and to talk ideas through, thereby increasing the likelihood that students will clarify their thinking and remember and retain important ideas. What we lose when it is not an individual written response is the opportunity to gather formative data from each student. Thus it is important to decide when and how it is critical to have that information and to structure the summary format accordingly.

How frequently should summarizing occur within a lesson? Rowe (1983) has demonstrated that students' performance increases when we pause after approximately 10 minutes of teacher-led instruction and provide about 2 minutes for students to process what has been presented. Prompting students to sketch an important concept, or to respond to a focus question with a partner or small group, to explain a concept, to fill in a graphic organizer, to read their notes to one another—any of these might be the focus of the two-minute processing time. Thus when a lesson is going to include input to students (teacher presentation, textbook reading, video viewing, group discussion) for periods longer than 10–15 minutes, we need to chunk the input by inserting pauses and processing prompts. These prompts should require students to reconstruct for themselves what has been presented in each chunk. That will maximize the likelihood that they internalize and retain what is being presented.

Summarizing questions can be made specific and tailored to any content: "Based on our discussion so far, tell your partner the principal causes of the Civil War. Then have your partner tell them back to you." If the class has reached consensus on the causes, this is a summarizing of the information. If the class has not resolved the question, having pairs work like this is more than summarizing, especially if they are asked to back up their respective arguments. In addition, a teacher may ask students to summarize in writing (perhaps in notebooks) the main idea of each section in textbook chapters. Having to stop and summarize periodically as they read forces active cognitive processing. Learners have to put what they have learned in their own words to write a summary. *Voila,* better learning. Studies have shown improved comprehension of text (not just stories) with convincing consistency (D'Angelo, 1983) when students do this kind of summarizing. A number of writers offer useful models for teaching students how to do this summarizing in writing as they read (Hahn & Gardner, 1985). Visit www.RBTeach.com to find a repertoire of formats for getting students to summarize. Our publication, *Summarizers* (Saphier & Haley, 1993), describes them in detail. Some are short, some longer; some call for verbal responses, while others call for written or sketched; some can be done individually, while others call for student-to-student interaction; some require advance preparation, others can be done on the spot. These are questions that help to decide the focus and the format of a summarizer:

- ▲ What is my purpose for using a summarizer? To check understanding? To surface confusion or misconceptions? To deepen understanding? To support retention? To gather formative assessment data?
- ▲ What is most important about the content, skill, or strategy we studied today?
- ▲ What data do I need about students' understanding of this concept?
- ▲ What level of thinking do I want students to do in processing this learning?

QUESTIONING SKILLS

Questions are the dominant mode of communication in most classrooms (Bellon, Bellon, & Blank, 1992) and the second most dominant teaching method after teacher talk (Cotton, 1988). Teachers spend between 35% to 50% of teaching time posing questions (Long & Sato, 1983 as cited in Hattie, 2009). Because questioning is done for many purposes, we could say that it occurs during nearly all the areas of performance described in *The Skillful Teacher*. Consequently, one of a teacher's most important skills is designing and posing worthwhile questions. The significance of this topic is reflected in the plethora of books written about questioning. We synthesize what we believe is the most practical and important information on this topic over the last 30 years. There are five main points about questioning that we want to highlight. Each has large implications for practice:

PDF

Questioning Skills

1. Be deliberate about the purpose of your questions.
2. Engage all students in higher-level thinking questions.
3. Use questioning strategies that maximize student engagement.
4. Plan questions carefully.
5. Develop students' capacity to ask questions.

We expand this section in the "Questioning Skills" document on *The Skillful Teacher* website at www.RBTeach.com/TST7 and invite particular attention to the pages on planning questions and developing students' capacity to ask good questions, which we see as an important life skill.

CHAPTER QUICK GUIDE

Five Ways to Support Student Understanding:

1. **Framing the Learning:**
   - ▲ Communicating the Big Picture
   - ▲ Assessing readiness to receive
2. **Presenting Information:**
   - ▲ Explanatory devices
   - ▲ Speech patterns
3. **Supporting Mental Engagement:**
   - ▲ Explicitness
   - ▲ Making cognitive connections
4. **Getting Inside Students' Heads:**
   - ▲ Checking for understanding
   - ▲ Unscrambling confusion
   - ▲ Making Students' Thinking Visible
5. **Consolidating and Anchoring Learning:**
   - ▲ Summarizing

To check your knowledge about Clarity, see the exercises on *The Skillful Teacher* website at www.RBTeach.com/TST7.

CHAPTER 12

Instruction
Principles of Learning

Instruction: *Principles of Learning*

This chapter describes 24 packages of power, each one self-contained and ready for use by itself, each a possible addition to any teacher's repertoire, and each certain to increase the rate and durability of students' learning. A strong claim? Perhaps. But for once in education, a certain one.

What do these names mean to you: Ivan Pavlov, Edward Thorndike, Clark Hull, John B. Watson, Edwin R. Guthrie, Hobart Mowrer, Kenneth Spence, Edward C. Tolman, and B. F. Skinner? We don't hear much about them these days, yet these are people who approached learning as a phenomenon about which universal laws might be deduced and operating principles discovered, and they discovered quite a few of them. The tradition of their research goes back to 1885 (with Hermann Ebbinghaus) and is the strongest, longest, and soundest base we have in education for how-to recommendations. Taken together, their principles do not add up to a cohesive theory or approach to teaching that we get from some of their more contemporary counterparts (Jerome Bruner, David Ausubel, Jean Piaget). Instead, each of these principles was shown in its own way to make a contribution to learning effectiveness, and they lie scattered about the literature like so many precious stones waiting to be picked up. Many of them were collected in the 1970s and put into accessible form for teachers by Madeline Hunter and her associates. *Teach More, Faster* is the title of one of her classic books. However, these principles have not become part of the currency of in-service teacher training or college teacher education.

Knowing the Principles of Learning enables us to design excellent learning experiences.

As you read this chapter, you will recognize some of these principles from your own teaching. We find that most teachers routinely use six or seven of them intuitively, without knowing the labels you will learn for them here. Some teachers use more, some fewer. We have yet to find a teacher who uses them all, however, and so we believe that there is something new in this chapter for everyone.

We have identified 24 of these principles in the literature (see Figure 12.1). What they all share in common is that each offers some sort of guideline for designing learning experiences. One might think of principles of learning like the spices used in food preparation: some seasonings are used regularly in most every dish a chef prepares (salt, pepper, sugar, parsley, to name a few), while

Figure 12.1 Principles of Learning

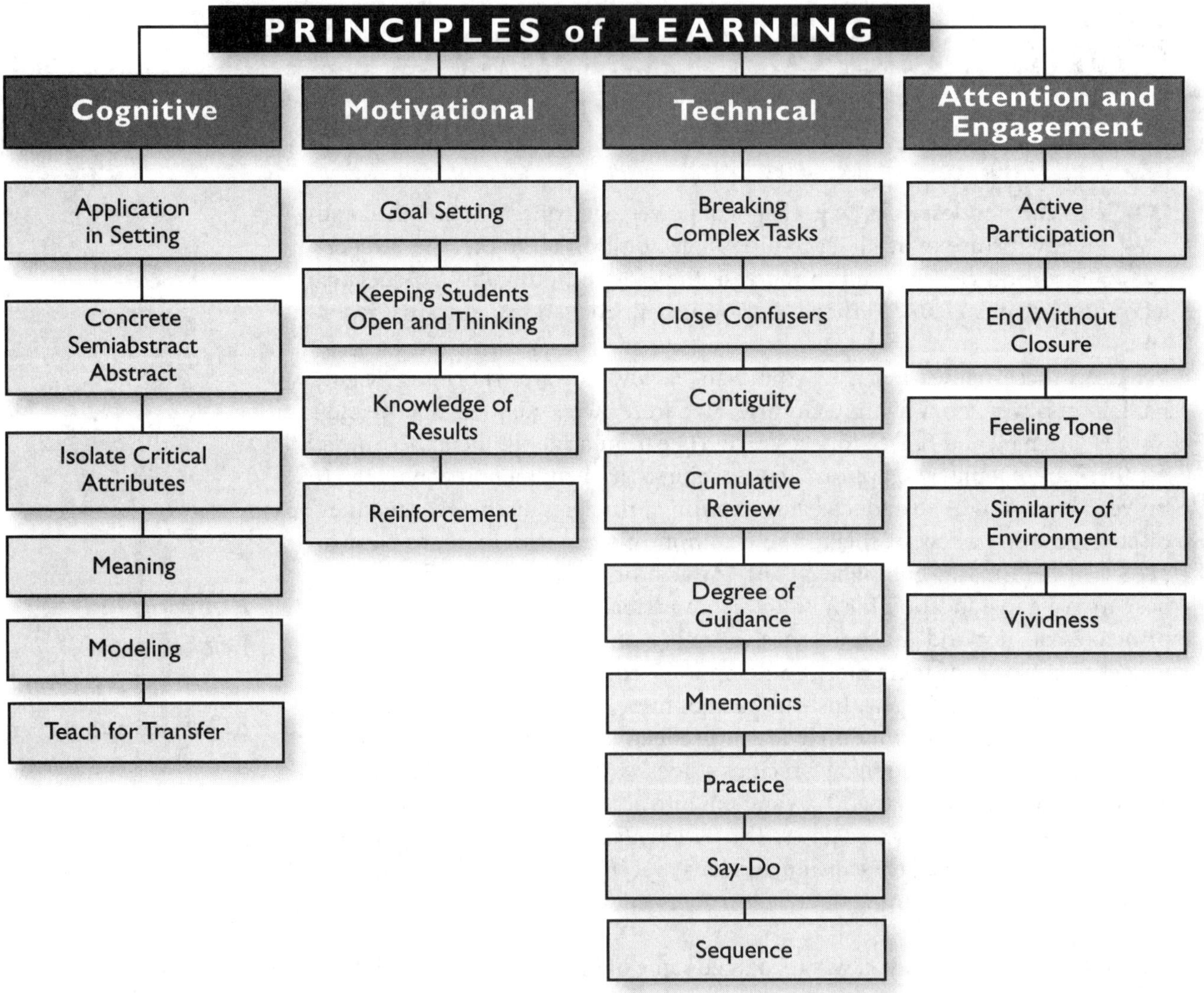

others are used more selectively (cumin, tarragon, coriander). To a chef it is not a matter of the more spices the better but rather knowing the spices and applying them strategically where they will enhance the flavor. This is also the case with principles of learning: some apply broadly to most learning experiences (meaning, active participation, say-do), while others apply more selectively (isolating critical attributes, contiguity, mnemonics). Knowing the principles of learning enables us to apply them strategically to design excellent learning experiences.

We have divided the principles of learning into four categories, those that (1) offer guidance for enhancing cognitive impact, (2) influence motivation, (3) address technical aspects of design, and (4) impact student attention and engagement. For additional summaries and extensions of the principles, see Hilgard & Bower (1966), Bugelski (1971), and Hudgins (1977).

DESIGNING FOR COGNITIVE IMPACT

Application in Setting (from Skill to Setting)

Students should practice new behaviors or skills in the settings and in the way those learnings will be used in life. Thus spelling will more likely transfer to composition if spelling tests embed new words in sentences (perhaps from dictation). The ability to listen to others will transfer to real discussions and to conflict resolutions if practiced in class meetings and real or simulated disagreements. Notice that we used the word *transfer* in both of these examples. Application in setting is a principle that, when applied, makes it more likely that transfer will occur. As part of teaching for transfer, one is likely to see several instances of application in setting. Application in setting is something we see and give as a label to single-instance activities that are having students use a skill in some real-life context, such as identifying and labeling logical fallacies (the straw man fallacy) in arguments of current political candidates. But to claim teaching for transfer itself, there would have to be a series of such activities deliberately orchestrated so as to progressively distance the skill from abstract academic contexts. Each of them singly may have been by itself an example of application in setting.

Concrete-Semiabstract-Abstract Progression

Teachers using this principle begin with tangible or manipulative materials at one stage of instruction, move to pictorial representation of the same material and, at still later stages of instruction, deal with the same materials with the students in purely abstract ways. This progression is effective not only with young children who are at Piaget's stage of concrete operation but also with adult learners. Dealing with concrete materials anchors images and experiences that later connect with and are summoned by the abstractions that refer to them. No one has to learn everything by experience (you don't have to be bitten by a rabid dog to learn they're dangerous), but experience anchors learning in a powerful way. Herron's 1975 study using models in chemistry instruction showed that using concrete materials was startlingly effective for developing concepts in college chemistry courses.

Isolation of Critical Attributes

Teachers who practice this principle identify the critical unvarying attributes or elements of the item under study and label them. Particularly with regard to definitions of new concepts, they isolate the qualities or attributes essential to the concept, attributes "without which it is not" (without which the object is not the object but something else).

Example 1: "What are the critical attributes that define an estuary?" The answer is "delta or fan shaped, at the bottom of a river, brackish water (part salt, part fresh), and sedimentary deposits at the bottom. Without any one of these four elements, we don't have an estuary."

Example 2: When preparing students to write myths in their study of literary genres, it is very useful to develop the following list at the start: (1) Heroic figures, (2) Magic, and (3) Explains the origin of a natural phenomenon. These are the essential attributes—the defining attributes of myth. If any one of them is missing in a story, it's not a myth. Teachers can develop the list of attributes in a number of ways—for example, by having students read a variety of myths and extract what they have in common, consult reference books for definitions of myth, or tell students the attributes in direct instruction with examples. However it happens, that it happens can make a positive difference to learning.

A second way to use the principle has to do with concepts that are similar but different—perhaps concepts that are close relatives. For example, in comparing tattling and reporting, the teacher could develop two parallel lists of attributes and compare them. For tattling and reporting, the lists would be identical except for one item: intent. Intent (to get someone in trouble as opposed to giving needed information) is the critical attribute that discriminates tattling from reporting. Here is a thought experiment: what is the critical attribute *that* discriminates prejudice from discrimination?

So far, we have discussed two slightly different ways to use the principle: (1) listing the definitional attributes that make something what it is ("myth" for example) and (2) comparing two parallel lists of similar concepts to distinguish the critical attributes that separate the target concept (tattling) from its close relative (reporting). A third use helps us see which from among the many attributes that may characterize an entity are the critical ones—the ones it must have to separate it from the pack. For example, many mammals have hair and bear their young alive (rather than in eggs), but some mammals do not have those characteristics. However, all mammals nurse their young. That is the critical attribute without which a mammal is not a mammal. Through any of these three variations—isolation of definitional, essential, and critical attributes—this principle can strengthen learning.

When teachers highlight items as important, that is not isolation of critical attributes. Things can be important without being critical attributes—for example, "These four formulas may be the most important things to know in the chapter" or "These three events may be the most important things to know about the month preceding the Civil War." Neither set of important things, however, is the critical attribute of anything. Highlighting important items is something teachers do deliberately, and usefully, to focus students' attention on more important items, but that is quite different from identifying the definitional attributes of a concept.

In exploring the difference between a developed and a developing country, the teacher may highlight certain critical attributes that define *developed*, such as mechanized planting and harvesting, an efficient national market distribution system, and an infrastructure of highways and transportation networks. It is not enough, however, for this list of attributes simply to be presented in the text or on the board. The teacher must see to it that the critical attributes are generated, call the students' attention to them (or elicit them from the students), and then have students apply the attributes in deciding which cases (here, what countries) do or do not contain those critical attributes. When students can discriminate developed from developing countries through analysis of critical attributes in new settings or in studies of countries where they're not specifically asked to look at them as developed versus developing, then learning has transferred.

Meaning

The more meaningful and relevant the task or application of information is to the students' world, the easier it is to learn. Teachers using this principle may make explicit references to students' personal experiences as a tie or a hook for connecting content with students' lives, or they may simulate the experiences in the learning activity or in some other way embed the new content in the students' meaning framework. One teacher using this principle gave us the following example: "The goal is to understand the difference between chronology and history. I do a two-part assignment. For one day, students are asked to keep a time line of their activities. The next day, they are to write a narrative history of the one day for which they kept the time line, showing, where possible, a cause and effect relationship." This assignment makes a nice distinction between chronology and history around a context that has intimate personal meaning for the students (i.e., their own day's activities).

The more meaningful and relevant the task or application of information is to the students' world, the easier it is to learn.

Modeling

Learning can be enhanced by modeling new skills or operations and preserving these models for student reference during early stages of learning. After explaining and demonstrating the algorithm for two-digit multiplication (or the format for writing a book report, or anything else with procedures and steps), the teacher leaves a model showing the separate steps on the board as students go to work practicing examples.

Conceptual models that have visual representations of what concepts mean and how they work improve student recall of the concept and performance on problems that ask them to extrapolate from what they have learned (Mayer, 1989). For example, a lesson on radar included a five-step diagram that showed a sequence in which a radar pulse moves out from the source, strikes an object, and bounces back, with the distance determined as a function of the total travel time (Van Merriënboer, 1997). Perkins and Unger (1989) posit that powerful conceptual models have four characteristics:

1. **Analogues:** provide some kind of analogy for the real phenomenon of interest.

2. **Constructed:** fabricated for the purpose at hand.

3. **Stripped:** extraneous clutter is eliminated to highlight critical features.

4. **Concrete:** phenomenon is reduced to concrete examples and visual images.

Transfer (from Setting to Setting)

Video: Transfer

This principle is at work when teachers create a series of assignments or tasks in which the call for using a skill is progressively distanced from direct instructional settings.

Example 1: After differentiating fact (that which is immediately verifiable by the senses or that on which most experts in the field would agree) from opinion (a belief; evidence exists to support differing beliefs), the teacher has students label examples as fact or opinion: for example, "Mary is wearing a sweater" and "Mary is the prettiest girl in the class." Examples are made progressively more difficult ("Some people believe in reincarnation"). Eventually, students are asked to generate the examples themselves. Then, they are asked to bring in newspaper articles (a new setting) to analyze for fact and opinion. Finally, students are given cues to transfer their skill to settings where it isn't an assignment to distinguish fact from opinion, as in text readings.

Sometimes there is no need to do anything extra for transfer to occur because it happens by itself. If students have learned to borrow in subtraction, they will probably transfer the skill to the supermarket that very afternoon when buying supplies for a class party. But for many skills, transfer does not happen spontaneously, so we need to engineer a series of events that will induce it. The final event in the chain, the actual transfer of the skill to a new context, is one that students take by themselves. That is what makes understanding this principle a bit tricky. We take students along a planned series of steps up to the edge of the water, but they have to jump in themselves for there to be evidence that transfer has actually occurred.

Example 2: Ms. Crane is teaching her middle school students about characterization. They look at pieces of dialogue and physical actions of characters in stories to see what these pieces of behavior reveal about the characters. The objective is to learn to recognize how authors develop readers' images and understandings of characters through dialogue and physical actions. In the long term, Ms. Crane wants her students to be able to use characterization in everyday life: to "read" people they encounter, making inferences about what they are feeling and thinking from bits of dialogue and physical actions the students observe. In other words, she wants them to transfer their ability to recognize characterization as a literary device to their own ability to use it to understand people they meet. After analyzing the text in novels for characterization, she assigns students to watch one of their favorite TV programs. They are to take down bits of dialogue, or describe physical actions they see that are in some way indicative of the character's personality. Later in the week, her students are asked to bring in examples of characterization from their observations of people in their neighborhood or their family. Thus she is progressively distancing their use of characterization from the academic context of novels they are reading, and pressing them to use the skill in ever closer approximations of real life.

If students have learned to read novels and plays for authors' biases, transfer has occurred if they then read nonfiction and magazine articles in the same way. Teachers encourage this kind of transfer by proper sequencing of assignments and pressing students to be aware of the multiple applications of their learning (Brown, 1989; Fogarty, Perkins, & Barell, 1991). This principle is easily confused with (but different from) application in setting, where a skill taught in an abstract setting is put to use right away in a realistic setting.

DESIGNING FOR MOTIVATIONAL IMPACT

Goal Setting

When students get involved in goal setting for their own learning, they learn more.

The point here is goal setting by students. When students get involved in goal setting for their own learning, they learn more. In addition to being common sense, this conclusion is strongly supported by a line of research (Schunk & Gaa, 1981). When students take ownership for goals (either self-set, teacher-set, or jointly negotiated), their motivation to accomplish them and their ability to self-evaluate (and self-regulate) increase.

Student goal setting will not happen by itself except for very motivated students. Teachers have to do something to facilitate the process—for example, take a few minutes of class time for students to write their goal for the period (or the unit) on a piece of paper or hold periodic goal-setting conferences with individual students at timely intervals (like the beginning of new units or projects). These conferences can be quite short, but the goals chosen should be recorded, and students should be asked later to evaluate how they did.

Student goal setting does not automatically lead to increased student performance. Certain properties of effective goals need to be present. They need to be specific, challenging but attainable, and able to be accomplished soon. Specific goals contain items that can be measured, counted, or perceived directly as criteria for accomplishment. "Try my best" doesn't fit this mold, "Master the twenty spelling demons" does.

The more difficult the goal is, the more effort the student will expend, provided the goal is viewed as attainable. In guiding students to set goals, teachers have to help them walk the tightrope between what is "duck soup" and what is unrealistically difficult.

Finally, goals that can be accomplished in the short-term work better than long-term goals. This does not mean long-term goals should not be set, only that long-term goals need to be broken down into short-term goals or subgoals with their own plans of action, if one is to be maximally effective in reaching them. Learning or work accomplishment goals for students seem to work best around specified skills and products, and for time spans of one period to several days rather than over several weeks or months.

A common misinterpretation of this principle is that it means students are picking what they will study (that is, the content). This is not the case. Much more often (and usually, more productively), they are setting goals about speed, quantity, or quality.

Example 1: Speed Goal

> **Teacher:** "Glen, how many of these do you think you'll get done in the next half-hour?"
>
> **Glen:** "I think this whole page."
>
> **Teacher:** "Really? Do you really think that's a reasonable amount?"
>
> **Glen:** "Yes, I'll do it."
>
> **Teacher:** "Okay. Show them to me when you're done."

Example 2: Quantity Goal

> **Teacher:** "How many references will you use in researching that, Brenda?"
>
> **Brenda:** "About six."
>
> **Teacher:** "Okay. If you think that's enough, put it down in your outline sheet."

There is no particular rate at which the researching must be done (except ultimately, the deadline of the paper). It is a commitment Brenda makes to do a specified amount. The same kind of goal might apply to how many books students will read for free reading or how many extra credit or supplementary exercises they'll do.

Example 3: Quality Goal

With these goals, students make a commitment to how well they'll do something. This can take the form of targeting what aspect of their work they'll focus on improving. Teachers can give them the assignment to explain what they're working to improve and perhaps ask for it in writing.

> **Teacher:** "So, Jamie, what's your quality goal going to be on this paper?"
>
> **Jamie:** "I'm going to work on improving spelling and punctuation."
>
> **Teacher:** "How about you, Tara?"
>
> **Tara:** "My goal's going to be to use fewer tired words."

The goal setting principle of learning is one of the least practiced in education.

By getting students to set goals, teachers do not relinquish their ability to make assignments. They enlist the students in making personal commitments to speed, quantity, or quality. It is possible to have students choose content in some cases—"I want to learn everything I can about frogs," says Freddy. There are places where it will fit in with curriculum requirements and time available to help Freddy do so (especially if one of the teacher's goals is to stimulate and support an inquiring attitude). But it may be equally powerful to get students to set quality goals, thus involving them inevitably in self-evaluation to come up with a target for improvement. In our experience, this principle of learning is one of the least practiced in education. If we devoted just a little time and energy to it, we might see big payoffs in student performance and in students' learning directly about self-regulation and self-evaluation.

Teacher Responses to Student Answers

Art Costa (1985) pointed out that the way teachers respond to student answers is probably more important than the questions themselves. Every time a student answers a question, a teacher does something. Similarly, if a student responds with silence because he or she can't answer the question or is slow to think it through, teachers can still do something: give a cue, refer it to another student, or offer to help. It is through these acts—repeated hundreds of times a day—that teachers set a climate about whether it's safe to open one's mouth in this class. It is through teachers' patterns of actions at these moments that they exert a force either to keep students open and thinking or to become a force to restrict thinking and risk-taking.

This arena of classroom life—responses to student answers—is also an arena through which teachers send the three critical expectation messages: (1) "This is important," (2) "You can do it," and (3) "I won't give up on you."

Knowledge of Results (Feedback)

This teacher skill is more often called "feedback" than "knowledge of results." Knowledge of results should be specific and timely. Practitioners of this principle give explicit feedback to students on their work as rapidly as possible after completion. The rationale is that this feedback has optimum corrective impact when most proximal to the student's engaging the materials and maximum communicative effect when it is both full and specific. Full and complete feedback is a form of respect by which teachers show students they value students' work enough to look at it closely. In Chapter 14, "Expectations," we go into considerable detail about how to give feedback to students in effective ways. Here are two examples of knowledge of results:

Example 1: On completing a worksheet on social changes resulting from the Industrial Revolution, students see answers displayed on an overhead (or revealed from behind a rolled-up map). They correct their own papers and then ask the teacher clarifying questions.

Example 2: Students correct their own workbook and worksheet pages from answer books, fixing all individual mistakes and explaining their errors.

What empowers learning is feedback that is rapid, specific, and complete.

Feedback from a teacher to students does not mean this principle is in operation, and finding out how they did on a test is not the principle. Students find out how they did at some point in every class, so there's nothing special about that. What is special and what empowers learning is feedback that is rapid, specific, and complete. Computer games give instantaneous knowledge of results, though not always with specific information about how to improve.

Teachers can claim they're using knowledge of results if they're giving students feedback about how they did very soon after they perform, along with an opportunity to self-correct or at least see what would have to be done to improve (Butler & Winne, 1995).

Reinforcement

A reinforcer is anything that strengthens a behavior and can range all the way from edibles and tokens to teacher statements of recognition like, "You stuck with that hard one until you got it and you didn't give up!" Verbal reinforcement is the focus here because although it is so overworked in the literature and is such a common part of teacher vocabulary, it is astonishing how seldom it is used skillfully. Many opportunities for applying this powerful stimulus to learning are missed. The knowledge base tells us that verbal reinforcement should be precise, appropriate, and scheduled from regular to intermittent.

Precise means that the statement should specify exactly what it is that the learner has done that is good: "You didn't rush today, and you got them almost all right" is better than "Good work." The student is much more likely to reproduce the high accuracy rate, which is due to not rushing, if not rushing is explicitly reinforced. When a teacher says, "You finished those problems and then you put your stuff away without my giving you any reminders, and you started on your writing. That's great," the student knows what is great.

Appropriate reinforcement is important. If a student doesn't want it, it's not reinforcing. Being praised in front of someone else may be embarrassing. Being told his handwriting is "nice" may turn off a sixth-grade athlete and get him kidded by his pals. More appropriate feedback for him might be, "John, you're one of our best ball players and I see your fine motor coordination is just as good as your coordination on the ball field" (Hunter, 1977). It is easy to see why studies of praise and reinforcement that count frequency of the behavior and look for correlations to student achievement never get anywhere. Only appropriate use of reinforcement works.

Scheduling is the third important feature of reinforcement. B. F. Skinner discovered that behaviors established through operant conditioning become more stable and more durable if reinforcement is delivered with every occurrence of the behavior at first. But then, reinforcement should skip occasional occurrences at random, and the span of unreinforced occurrences between reinforcers should gradually be lengthened. Use of intermittent scheduling to establish behaviors is more in line with a systematic plan for behavior modification a teacher might use to develop hand raising versus calling out or promptness versus tardiness to class.

Although researchers universally agree on the positive effects of intrinsic reinforcement, a debate has raged for years over whether extrinsic reinforcers ought to be used. Chance (1992) has put the matter in perspective by pointing out the conditions under which extrinsic reinforcers are not only okay (meaning they do not damage students' motivation to do the activity when there are no reinforcers around) but are helpful to learning. Chance points out that extrinsic reinforcers include teachers' smiles, praise, congratulations, saying "thank you" or "right," shaking hands, a pat on the back, applauding, providing a certificate of achievement, or other behaviors that "in any way provide a positive consequence (a reward) for student behavior" (p. 203). Extrinsic rewards can decrease motivation to engage in a behavior (say, reading) if it is given as a task contingency—for merely participating in an activity, without regard to how well one does at it. But when rewards are success contingent, that is, delivered when students perform well or meet goals, there is no negative effect on engagement with the activity later when rewards are no longer given. Indeed, success-contingent rewards tend to increase interest in the activity.

Intrinsic rewards are available to students only if they can perform sufficiently well in an area to get the reward, for example, if they can read well enough to get the pleasure of a good story. "While intrinsic rewards are important, they are insufficient for effective learning for all students" (Chance, 1992, p. 206) if one has to rely on them exclusively.

TECHNICAL PRINCIPLES OF DESIGN

Breaking Complex Tasks into Simpler Parts

One often sees evidence of this principle when teachers are attempting to explain or clarify operations students have failed to grasp. The task is broken down into smaller parts, and one part, now isolated, is focused on for learning. For example, if students are having trouble with word problems, the teacher may have the students identify the central question and the operation called for without doing any computing. Or students may be asked to draw a picture of what happens in the problem as a way of conceptualizing it, again without any computing. This principle manifests as task analysis and ensures that sequential prerequisites for present learning tasks are established.

Close Confusers

Ensure an adequate degree of original learning before "close confusers" are introduced. Teachers following this principle are careful not to confuse or weaken recently learned items—say, the letter "d"—by introducing too soon new items easily confused with it—the letter "b." In this example, the primary teacher will go on to "t," then maybe "f," then some other letters, all the while reviewing "d" in the expanding set of letters recognized, and then finally introduce "b" as a new letter when "d" has been thoroughly learned and practiced.

Video: Close Confusers

To generalize the statement of this principle in other terms, teachers should not sequence new material so as to require fine discriminations between two contiguous terms when grosser discriminations can be used first. The making of fine discriminations can be demanded when at least one item of the content pair has had an adequate opportunity to be thoroughly learned. This is something to monitor in using textbooks where close confusers like rotation and revolution, weathering and erosion are introduced at the same time. Similarly, exceptions to rules are not to be introduced until original rules are practiced and established sufficiently. Mindful of this principle, a secondary teacher writes:

> Constitutional law is a central part of any middle school social studies curricula. Instruction frequently involves explanations of the Bill of Rights, including illustrations of case law. For example, "freedom of speech" is usually tackled by considering yelling "fire" in a crowded theater. Before a teacher can realistically ask students to distinguish between acceptable and unacceptable forms of "free speech," he must be sure that they have a grounding in the basic concepts, including the important case law. Once they have this, they can examine a more complex situation.

Contiguity

"First impressions stick" is one way of thinking about this principle. Events, objects, operations, and emotions close to each other in time and space tend to become associated in the mind of the learner. A first association, once learned, is hard to unlearn—whether it's calling Mary Ann "Mary Lou" the first time you meet her and finding yourself doing so every time thereafter, or adding the tens column first, then the ones, and finding that a hard habit to break.

Learners should not be allowed to practice errors and build an incorrect association. Students who practice footnotes in the wrong format the first time find that the wrong model interferes with the right one when they finally learn it. This principle pertains mainly to paired associate memory and procedural learning like vocabulary words and math algorithms, not higher-level thought questions. For memory learning, the implication for teachers is to anticipate errors where they are likely to occur and prevent these errors, even by giving the right answer where appropriate (for example, a new sight word) before a student has a chance to make a wrong guess (and thus learn a wrong association that must later be unlearned). Teachers should never allow a student to leave a paired associate learning situation with a wrong answer; the last response that occurs should be correct.

Teachers should also be on the watch for potential negative emotional associations students may form. For example, students coming into class after a recess full of fighting and negative emotions who are then introduced to a new topic may form negative associations with the topic that will interfere with their future learning. This is not the time to introduce poetry for the first time, for example. The teacher might preface the introduction to the topic with a brief activity that raises positive feelings in students.

Cumulative Review

Any information or skill one doesn't actively use tends to be forgotten. Therefore, old learnings should be included in practice and drills of new material so that these old learnings are periodically exercised. As students move on in a skill sequence, the range and number of skills demanded in the practice exercises grow cumulatively to include all the old skills. To prevent practice tasks from becoming unwieldy when the range of skills is big, only a representative sample of them is included in exercises focusing on new material.

Certain skill sequences automatically cumulate old skills in new products without any design steps required by the teacher—for example, report writing. As students learn new punctuation and grammar skills, these are automatically practiced each time writing takes place and are expected to be done correctly. And as students use more elaborate language forms and learn to organize ideas better, these are also automatically expected to be continued in future writing. But other skill sequences require more deliberate design for cumulative review to take place effectively.

In drilling on flash cards to learn times tables, each new pack should contain a representative sample of all previously learned facts, and occasional packs should be reviewed entirely to solidify old learnings. In learning geographical features of a country in South America, the features should come up again and again in the context of the questions about the country's elections, political system, and economy. A violation of this principle would see students studying the geographical features of all the South American countries in sequence, then going back and studying all their political systems, then all their cultural highlights, and so on.

Degree of Guidance

How much guidance will students need to get the most out of or just to get through the task? Guidance should be high with new tasks and withdrawn gradually with demonstrated student proficiency.

Evidence for this principle cannot be simply to observe teachers delivering different degrees of guidance to different students. Evidence must cite different degrees of guidance offered to the same student or group of students over time as they progressively show increased proficiency with the new material. "Gradual release of responsibility" is another phrase for this idea. This is sometimes difficult to see in short observations. Nevertheless, a teacher may introduce a new skill to a class, and immediately provide adequate guidance in practicing it. This may mean working with just one group after introducing haiku to the whole class, while giving the rest of the class something else they still need to practice but without so much teacher guidance. And then rotating through the class with groups that focus on the new skill. Or it may mean the teacher puts on track shoes and gets around to everybody, giving guidance and help where needed. The latter is more time efficient if the teacher can pull it off. Pulling it off is not so much a function of teacher skill as good judgment—what new material will or will not require more intensive individual guidance for students to be able to use it proficiently.

Mnemonics

Teachers using this principle help students use mediational devices for remembering new learning—devices such as imagery, anagrams, or jingles ("30 days hath September"). Here is a familiar one:

- Desert: one "s" all alone in the desert.
- Dessert: you get bigger in the middle if you eat too much of it.

There are many mnemonic devices, and a growing body of research comparing their effectiveness. For example, one particularly effective technique, the keyword technique, is used for learning new vocabulary words and new terms. Students are asked to learn a keyword (word clue) for the new term that sounds acoustically similar to it (for example, "purse" for "persuade"; "he's a date" for "hesitate"). Then, students are asked to remember the content of a cartoon that contains the keyword interacting in some way with the definition of the new term. Levin and others (1982) show a cartoon for the new vocabulary word "persuade." One woman points to a purse in a store and says, "Oh, Martha, you should buy that PURSE!" Martha replies, "I think you can PERSUADE me to buy it." At the bottom of the cartoon is written, "Persuade (Purse): When you talk someone into doing something." In these cartoons, one character's utterance contains the keyword, and the other contains the new term to be learned. Studies have been highly positive and uniform in demonstrating the effectiveness of this technique for learning new words (Levin, 1993).

Long practice sessions with academic skills quickly reach a point of diminishing returns.

Here are the steps in using mnemonic keywords:

1. Think of a sound-alike or rhyming word you know that resembles the new word you're trying to learn. This word is the keyword.
2. Make up a visual cartoon in which both the keyword and the word to be learned are represented in the action or the objects.
3. Have dialogue between two characters in the cartoon, one using the keyword and the other the word to be learned.
4. Make the dialogue meaningful, and arrange it so that the context of the dialogue and the cartoon illustrates the meaning of the word to be learned.

Practice

Practice should be massed (frequent practice sessions, close together in time) at the beginning of learning a new skill or operation, then distributed over increasing intervals of time. The smallest unit of new information that retains meaning should be practiced at any one session, and worked on for the shortest unit of time to allow the students to feel they have accomplished something. After students have achieved proficiency, they should practice learned items two or three more times to make the learning more permanent (over learning). Unlike athletics and motor skills, where practice makes perfect and the more the better (up to a point), long practice sessions with academic skills quickly reach a point of diminishing returns.

Example 1: For areas like the times tables, each fact is a unit of meaning on its own, separate from the others, and only one or two of them should be introduced at a time, embedded in groups of already known facts for drill. Certain tables and groups of facts, however, such as the 10 times table, group all at once as a single unit of meaning. In teaching students to analyze a story, which is a complex task, only one part would be assigned at first, say, identifying the setting; describing the plot would come later. In practicing a difficult piece of music, the student would practice not a page or a bar (which might be too small a unit to have meaning) but a measure.

Practice sessions should be short (2 to 5 minutes) and frequent (twice a day).

Practice sessions should be short (two to five minutes) and frequent (twice a day rather than twice a week). This is quite at odds with the schedules we often see when students labor over workbooks in classrooms.

Example 2: If a teacher wants students to practice writing news stories in a journalism course, the lead (that is, the opening sentence or paragraph that contains all the critical information of who, when, where, why, and what) is a meaningful unit. Students may be asked to practice writing just leads for frequent short practice periods before being asked to write entire stories.

Say-Do

The more perceptual modes one engages for students—seeing, hearing, moving, touching—the better the learning will be. But in striving to increase the range of perceptual channels made active during learning, be particularly aware of the power of having learners say their learning out loud and get involved in using it to do something. The title of this principle, say-do, is meant to highlight the powerful effects achieved when these two channels for expressing learning are engaged.

The more perceptual modes one engages for students—seeing, hearing, moving, touching—the better the learning.

What do we know about the relative power of various perceptual channels for acquiring information? How much do students retain over time if the only way they acquire information is to read it versus hearing it versus seeing it? What if they both see and hear the information? What if students were to read the information and then summarize their learning out loud to someone (read, say)? What would be the learning retention effects if students read information to acquire it, then had to summarize it out loud to someone, and finally put the

Figure 12.2 Relative Effectiveness of Different Perceptual Modes

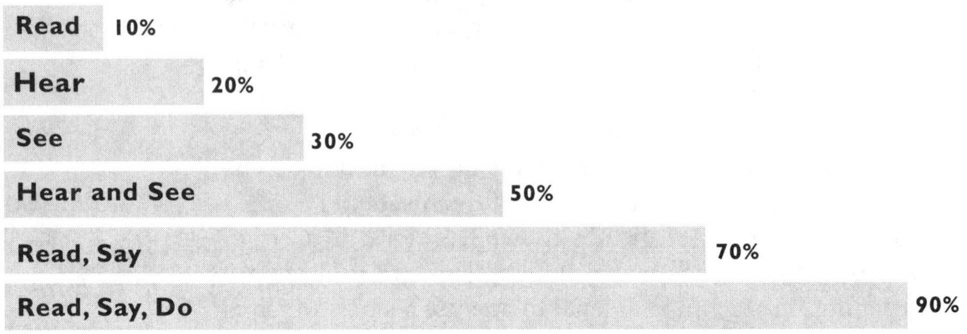

Adapted from many studies.

information to work by actually using it to do something? The graph in Figure 12.2 summarizes the relative effectiveness of different perceptual modes. At first glance, the most surprising assertion in the chart is the magnitude of the boost in learning retention when "say" is added to the simple input channel of reading. The effect would probably be similar for see-say and hear-say, though there are no studies found to verify this claim. Studies of the effect of learning logs and dialogue journals confirm positive learning effects for hear-write and read-write (Connolly & Vilardi, 1989; Fulwiler, 1987; Pradl & Mayher, 1985).

To summarize in your own words, either verbally or in writing, what you have learned in a given experience is a complex cognitive act. It causes search and retrieval of memory, organization of ideas, and summoning of language to recast the meaning in your own terms. It is logical that this complex set of cognitive acts would create neural networks and deepen memory traces. The implications for teaching and learning are large. Foremost is the call to have students stop and summarize, either singly in journals or together out loud in pairs, what is important in a recent episode of learning. The need to create such pauses means that a teacher will build periodic summarizing into teaching as a regular practice. The "do" part of this principle means getting students active, as soon as possible, using the materials in some realistic way.

Despite the popularity and frequent citation of the bar chart, it is an oversimplification of the research findings on complex material (Fadel & Lempke, 2008). There is a considerable literature, however, on the effects of student verbalizations of their learning (King, 1990; Morrow, 1985; Pauk, 1974; Webb, 1982). One particularly well-designed study by Mackenzie and White (1982) comes close to including all the conditions in Figure 12.2. In their study of eighth and ninth graders' learning and retention of geographical facts, they involved learners in three different conditions to learn facts and skills in the geography of coasts, including information about landforms and plants. All three treatment groups studied a carefully designed programmed learning package of materials containing 35 pages and 37 questions to encourage processing (Read). The program was supported by 60 photographs on 35mm slides (See).

> Other characteristics of the program were statements of expected performance, worked examples and test items, practice at working new data, prompts to stimulate recall of relevant information and subordinate skills, indications of relevance of information to subsequent application, and transfer of verbal propositions to maps, diagrams and slides. (Mackenzie & White, 1982, p. 626)

Treatment group 1 received the package described. Treatment group 2 also went through the programmed package and in addition went on a field trip to a beach, two sets of cliffs, and two mangrove flats where the pictures in the program had been taken. The students were given an explanatory field guide designed to reinforce the information in the program they had done at school. A teacher guided them around the five sites, pointing out items in the guide. In the middle of the trip, students had to complete one set of questions. So in addition to the classroom-based instruction of treatment group 1, this group had a great deal more of seeing and hearing built in to their experience, as well as more calls to answer questions about the information. Treatment group 3 also went on the field trip, but with some powerful additions:

> At each site students received a worksheet, a map of the area, and a tide table. The teacher supervised while the students, individually and in groups, completed the tasks on the worksheets. Group discussions (Say) were held frequently. Students were continually required to do things (Do): observe, sketch, record, answer questions. Several unusual events were arranged, such as walking through the mud of the mangrove shore, tasting foliage for salinity, scrambling over cliff platforms, wading in the sea. It is emphasized that the students in [treatment group 2] saw the same things . . . and spent the same time at each site. They had information repeated to them more often, but did far less. (Mackenzie & White, 1982, p. 627)

The achievement results in this experiment were striking. In the initial achievement tests, both field-trip groups outperformed the classroom-only group by a wide margin, but the two field-trip groups were about equal to each other in student achievement means. After 12 weeks, however, the retention with respect to initial mean scores was 51% for the classroom-only group, 58% for the treatment 2 field trip-group, and 90% for the treatment 3 field-trip group. The addition of say and do together in this condition had a huge impact on long-term retention.

Sequence and Backward Chaining

Video: Sequence

The first and last items in a series are the easiest to remember; the one just past the middle is the hardest. Learning can be accelerated by chaining a sequence backward from the last item, and sequences can be broken into small parts to avoid interference. This set of principles is applicable to rote learning and is easily observed when practiced in math fact and spelling drills or any other body of items in some sequence that students are expected to memorize (such as poems). Teachers can use this knowledge to improve the learning of items in the difficult positions. The sequence (or list) can be shortened or split in half so the difficult item becomes first on the shortened list. The order of items can be changed; the hard parts can be given extra practice; the hard items can be made more vivid (darker print, use of colors). A high school Latin teacher writes:

> Students are expected to learn ten new Latin vocabulary words each week. (1) They quiz each other from the list at the beginning of each class period for five minutes. (2) Then they drill alone on the ones they missed in the partner quiz. (3) They write the list in their notebooks along with the meanings, putting the ones they missed first and last in the reordered list (and second and ninth if need be). Words they know best are put in the just past the middle position. They cover the answers with their hand and go down the list several times quizzing themselves. This procedure is repeated each day, with missed words in first and last positions. The whole thing takes about ten minutes, which I use to circulate and talk to individual students.

This principle of sequence and the importance of the first and last positions is also applicable to the use of time. What happens at the beginning and end of a class period (or day or term) is most easily remembered. Thus these spots should be milked to maximum advantage for learning (for more see Chapter 8, "Time").

PRINCIPLES FOR ATTENTION AND ENGAGEMENT

Active Participation

In classes where teachers use this principle, students are operating, responding, moving, and talking during the course of the learning experiences. Sitting passively and listening is not characteristic of learning experiences embodying this principle. Active participation of all students might not require small or large muscle movement or manipulation. It could conceivably involve written participation, with each student responding to each question, or it could be all verbal participation, with the setting structured in such a way that many students can talk at once, divided into pairs or small groups to reach consensus on something or debate some issue.

There are many techniques for structuring this kind of participation from students. For example, after finishing a presentation of the structure of an atomic nucleus and the meaning of atomic number versus atomic mass, the teacher says, "Okay, now explain to your neighbor the difference between atomic number and atomic mass." Teachers aware of this principle look for opportunities to make that kind of move.

End Without Closure

Consider the impact of this teacher statement: "Think about three ways you might get out of this dilemma and be ready to share them with us tomorrow when you come in" (Russell, 1980). Leaving students without an answer and with something percolating overnight may be more effective, in some cases, than coming to a neat ending of each class with all issues resolved.

Feeling Tone

Feeling tone propels learning in proportion to degree. This principle posits that students learn more, and faster, in proportion to the level of feeling—positive or negative—provoked during the learning. The rule is held to apply only up to a point. On one side, the more pleasurable the learning experience is, the more the learning will take place—up to the point where the pleasure takes over and begins crowding out the learning. In other words, there is a point of diminishing returns for efforts to make learning pleasurable. When teachers raise the level of students' concern ("I'm going to check you all individually on this material this period"), learning is potentiated, but only up to a point. Too much concern turns into anxiety, quickly interferes with learning, and blocks it. Again, a point of diminishing returns is quickly reached.

Application of this principle sees teachers either making moves to make learning experiences enjoyable (without becoming hedonistic) or raising levels of concern ("We'll be having a quiz on this material sometime this week"), but neither to the extreme. Judging the extreme, or the point of diminishing returns, is not a judgment for which rules can be cited. To credit this principle as operative, however, an observer would have to cite evidence of teacher moves to raise positive or negative feeling tone and be subjectively convinced (by watching student reactions) that extremes had not been violated.

Similarity of Environment

Similarity of environment (actions, feelings, formats, routines) elicits the learner's mindset to perform.

Similarity of environment (actions, feelings, formats, routines) elicits the learner's mindset to perform. This principle holds that certain features of the environment, when regularly associated with a particular type of learning or a period in which a type of attention or work is expected, trigger a mindset in learners that "plugs them in" and turns on their operators for that particular kind of lesson or activity.

For certain kinds of learning, teachers can regularly use repetitive formats of the environment—certain space, time, and routine features—to create expectational mindsets in their students for that kind of work. For example, a science teacher we know has 30 lab coats hung on a row of pegs inside his classroom door. When students enter, they are expected to put on a lab coat and proceed to their seats. The lab coats signal a change of mindset into being scientists.

In addition, teachers may warm up students for a lesson by doing an activity that starts them thinking the way they'll be asked to think in the lesson. For instance, suppose a teacher is going to do a lesson on outlining that requires students to categorize their ideas into topical groups. The teacher may warm up the class by playing "Guess My Category" (Table 12.1). The teacher slowly develops the lists below on the board, writing the terms one at a time in the order indicated, under "yes" for positive examples of the category and "no" for negative examples. The students must guess the category to which the "yes" examples belong (in this example, "southern states").

Table 12.1 Guess My Category

Yes	No
Mississippi	New York
Virginia	Wyoming
Georgia	California
Kentucky	Iowa
Florida	Arizona

When the game is over, the teacher says, "Now, the kind of thinking we were doing here is similar to what our minds have to do with facts in this outlining activity for today. Take out your note cards and . . ."

Russell (1980) points out that this activity is also an excellent sponge for students arriving in class (see Chapter 6, "Momentum"). It gets them involved immediately with a meaningful activity, yet does not penalize those who haven't arrived yet. Thus it eliminates downtime and waiting.

Vividness

Video: Vividness

The vividness, liveliness, energy, novelty, or striking imagery of a learning experience is thought to impress new learning on students more deeply through mediation of the attentional mechanisms. One can claim this principle to be in operation by virtue of observed student reaction to learning experiences. An example would be the "oohaah" reactions, the high level of arousal or emotion (surprise, fascination) attributed to observed student behaviors (wide eyes, open mouths, rapt gazes, unusual stillness). In trying to practice what he preaches, one of us once introduced a group of teachers to the principles of learning by pulling a series of small giftwrapped packages out of a case labeled "idea bag" to highlight that each principle is discrete and valuable, self-contained and important.

In the next chapter on "Models of Teaching," we look at teaching as a playwright looks at a script. We look at the design and sequence of the whole lesson and what discrete teacher moves have to do with the overall design of a particular kind of learning; the principles of learning are always there and always relevant.

CHAPTER QUICK GUIDE

Designing for Cognitive Impact:

1. Application in Setting	Practicing new behaviors in settings where they'll be used.
2. Concrete-Semiabstract-Abstract Progression	Following as a progression with the introduction of new material.
3. Isolation of Attributes	Highlighting and labeling the attributes.
4. Meaning	Connecting to students' personal experience.
5. Modeling	Stepwise products, procedures, and processes preserved for student reference.
6. Transfer	Engineering a planned sequence of activities that progressively distances the skill from abstract academic contexts.

Designing for Motivational Impact:

7. Goal Setting	Student ownership, specific, challenging; able to be accomplished soon, then over the longer term.
8. Teacher Responses to Student Answers	Supply questions for which answers are right, deliver promptly, and hold accountable.
9. Knowledge of Results	Promptly through monitoring (feedback).
10. Reinforcement	Precise, regular, and intermittent.

Technical Principles of Design:

11. Breaking Complex Tasks into Simpler Parts	Simpler, smaller pieces; isolating trouble spots for focused work and practice; higher frequency practice and repetition of new items.
12. Close Confusers	Ensuring an adequate degree of original learning before introducing close confusers.
13. Contiguity	Don't allow practice of errors.
14. Cumulative Review	In practice, periodically including representative sample of previously learned material.
15. Degree of Guidance	High with new tasks; withdrawn gradually with familiarity.
16. Mnemonics	Devices to aid in memory (keywords, images in sequence, jingles).
17. Practice	Massed at beginning, then distributed; smallest meaningful units; short practices; overlearning.
18. Say-Do	Using all perceptual channels but emphasizing particularly saying and doing.
19. Sequence and Backward Chaining	First and last are easiest; just past the middle is hardest.

Principles for Attention and Engagement:

20. Active Participation	Encouraging through unison, checking with a partner, signals, and so on.
21. End Without Closure	Follow-up at a later time, to invite percolation.
22. Feeling Tone	Fun, but not too much; worry, but not too much.
23. Similarity of Environment	An activity that gets minds in gear for upcoming events.
24. Vividness	Varying of practice formats.

To check your knowledge about Principles of Learning, see the exercises on *The Skillful Teacher* website at www.RBTeach.com/TST7.

CHAPTER 13

Instruction
Models of Teaching

Instruction: *Models of Teaching*

For students of teaching, few other efforts are as rewarding and as challenging as learning new models of teaching. Even the most mature and sophisticated of professionals can add to their repertoires and their power to reach a broader range of students. It is an ideal area of study for advanced professionals between their fifth and fifteenth year of teaching.

A model of teaching is a pattern of instruction that is recognizable and consistent. It has particular values, goals, a rationale, as well as an orientation to how learning shall take place. This could be by induction, discovery, wrestling with puzzling data, organizing information hierarchically, or through heightened personal awareness. That orientation is developed into a specific set of phases teachers and students go through in order, with specific kinds of events in each phase. Each model of teaching is a particular entity with specific components, well worked out, and with markedly different appearances and effects.

A model of teaching is a pattern of instruction that is recognizable and consistent.

Each of the dozens of models (Figure 13.1) is a design for planning lessons to achieve two outcomes: (1) the teaching of content and (2) the teaching of a particular kind of thinking. Almost any model can be used to teach a given piece of content. Although the information learned may be the same, the intellectual experience for students will be different.

For example, if Mr. Jones uses Taba's inductive model for a lesson on Hemingway, he wants students to learn not only about Hemingway but also to learn to think inductively. The model is carefully sequenced to get students into that kind of thinking. If he teaches through the Jurisprudential Model, he may want the same learnings about Hemingway, but he also wants his students to think like lawyers, taking positions and arguing them with evidence. If he uses the Group Investigation Model, he may still want students to learn the same core information about Hemingway, but he also wants them to learn about group process, leadership, and coordinated plans of inquiry. If he uses the Advance Organizer Model, he wants them to learn about hierarchical thinking and subordination of ideas. Models of teaching provide a way for teachers to be more articulate and precise about implicit learnings students take from instruction. They enable us to broaden the ways we instruct and thus broaden the range of students' intellectual experience in school.

Figure 13.1 Families of Models of Teaching

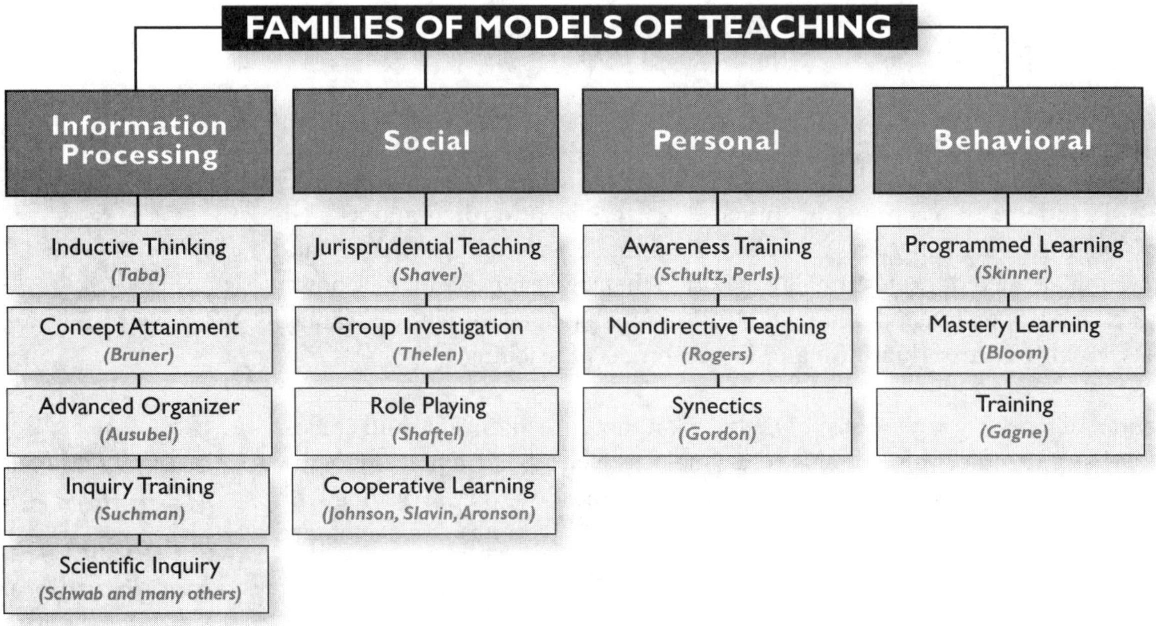

Research over many decades has shown that no one model is superior to the others for achieving learning as measured by test scores. That only stands to reason, since that was not their intention. Models of teaching were not created to be more efficient hypodermics to inject knowledge into students' heads. They were intended to teach students how to learn and think in different ways. Educators can use a variety of models to match students' preferred learning styles and broaden students' capacity as thinkers and learners beyond their favored style.

Teachers who have multiple models in their repertoires may use several different ones in a day or even within a class period. Teachers who master additional models find themselves able to modulate across them like connoisseurs, thus giving professionalism a new dimension. Let us examine the models themselves, first with a more detailed description of what a model is and then with a look at a number of specific models.

An Example: The Inductive Thinking Model

The Inductive Thinking Model has nine logical steps:

1. Enumerating or gathering data
2. Grouping
3. Labeling
4. Discriminating
5. Comparing
6. Inferring
7. Hypothesizing
8. Evidencing
9. Generalizing

This model, introduced by Hilda Taba, prizes developing students' ability to make inferences from data. Like all other models, it has a series of phases that unfold over time like acts in a play. Each phase looks and sounds different from the previous one, but like scenes in a play each is carefully articulated with the previous and the succeeding phases to achieve a cumulative effect.

A teacher who wished to use the model to present a lesson on Ernest Hemingway might start by showing a video biography of Hemingway's life. This is phase 1: gathering data. After the video, the teacher would ask students to relate items of information they remembered and would record the information on the board or on charts. The items might appear disconnected and random: "Had a fishing boat named the Pilar." "He went to Spain three times during the Spanish Civil War." "He had a house in Key West." "He liked to write early in the morning while sitting on a balcony overlooking the streets of Paris." Perhaps, the class might collect two dozen such items that students would remember and contribute to the list. Phase 1 of the model always collects a database of some sort.

In phase 2, students would group the items from the database that belong together. They would look at the sentences on the board and put certain items together because they bear some relationship with one another.

In phase 3, students would give a title or a label to the groupings they were creating. Examples might be, "Hemingway's work habits as a writer" or "Hemingway the outdoorsman," in which information about hunting on the Serengeti and fishing in Michigan would appear. Students around the class might group items in similar clusters, but there would also be some differences in the categories students created.

In phase 4, the students' groupings of the items about Hemingway would be displayed in some fashion for all to see (charts, overheads). In this phase, discriminating, students explain the thinking behind their categories. "What really made this grouping hang together?" The categories and the thinking behind them are compared and contrasted as the teacher guides the students through a discussion of the different ways the information could be grouped and why.

In phase 5, the students make inferences, for example: Are any ideas occurring to them about Hemingway as a result of what they have done so far? Are there any inferences they would be willing to make about Ernest Hemingway as a man? In a recent demonstration lesson we did with adults, one person said at this point, "I think Hemingway was really a very lonely man." At no point in the video does Hemingway's biographer ever make that point explicitly, so no single item of information in it would ever lead a viewer to that conclusion. Yet as a result of having been through these phases and manipulating the data intellectually in the way those phases require, inferences such as this and others become available to students.

There are several other phases to this model, but we will not develop them in any detail. Our objective is only to show that the steps or phases in a model of teaching unfold in a planful way so as to lead students toward developing a particular way of thinking. We could summarize the first five phases of Taba's model by listing the key question of each phase:

Phase 1: What are the data?

Phase 2: How would you group the data?

Phase 3: What name would you give to your categories or groups?

Phase 4: What makes your groups hold together?

Phase 5: What inferences would you be willing to make about the topic?

EIGHT MODELS OF TEACHING

The notion of models of teaching was introduced by Bruce R. Joyce in 1968 through *Teacher Innovator: A Program to Prepare Teachers*, funded by the U.S. Department of Health, Education, and Welfare. In 1972, Joyce and Marsha Weil published *Models of Teaching*, which described a large number of models in detail. These descriptions have been updated in eight subsequent editions (1980, 1986, 1992, 1996, 2000, 2003, 2008, 2014), which have added models and elaborated prior descriptions until we now have over two dozen models of teaching well described with anecdotes, examples, and outlines of steps. These books have been an important contribution to the literature on teaching because they made operational the theoretical approaches to learning developed by such luminaries as Jerome Bruner, David Ausubel, B. F. Skinner, William Glasser, Richard Suchman, Jean Piaget, and others.

To analyze each model of teaching, Joyce and Weil asked and answered the following questions for each theorist:

▲ What is the orientation to knowing and learning to know in this model? Does the teaching appear to be aimed at specific kinds of thinking and means for achieving it?

▲ What sequence of events occurs during the process of instruction? What do teachers and students do first, second, third?

▲ How does the teacher regard the student and respond to what he or she does?

▲ What teacher and student roles, relationships, and norms are encouraged?

▲ What additional provisions, materials and support systems are needed to make the model work?

▲ What is the purpose of the teaching? What are the likely instructional and nurturant effects of this approach to teaching?

The descriptions of these models display the range of teaching alternatives and allow comparison of their unique features. The language of models enables us to visualize clear patterns of action in teaching and learning. Thus we can talk more precisely about what we might do if we taught a lesson through a different model. We can also talk more precisely about why we might do so and what the expected effects of using a particular model might be.

Figure 13.2 Progressive Differentiation in Geometry Concepts

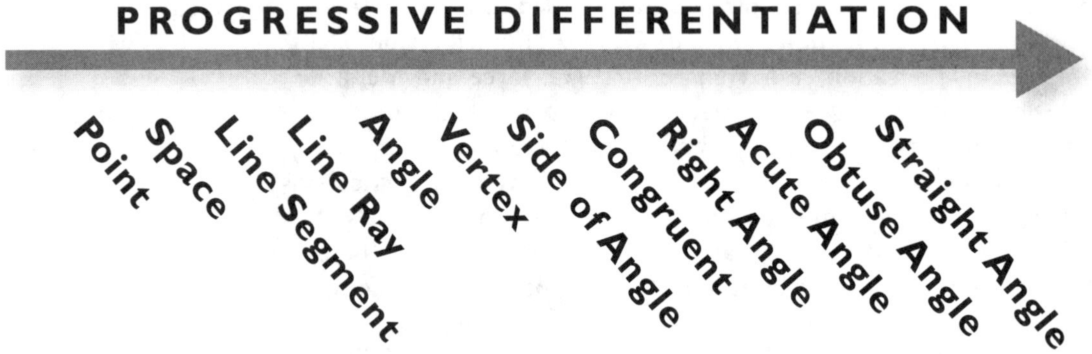

This chapter provides an introduction to eight models of teaching. Each is described in only the briefest details; in-depth study is required for gaining skill in them. We illustrate the range of models that have been developed and the wonderful menu for learning that lies before us. Most teachers already use one or two of these models, but few of us have been exposed to the full range, much less trained in the subtleties of implementing them and matching them to different students and curricula.

Models of Teaching Bibliography

Our intention is to give a flavor for the different qualities of mind that models of teaching develop in students. Readers can focus further reading and learning on models that best meet their current priorities. On *The Skillful Teacher* website (www.RBTteach.com/TST7), we provide a bibliography of original sources on the models for readers interested in going beyond this chapter on a given model provided by Joyce and Weil. To make the models more vivid, we use a specific content area, beginning geometry, in our survey.

Advanced Organizer Model

Advanced organizers are concepts derived from well-defined bodies of knowledge: mathematics, grammar, sociology, and so forth. The set of geometry concepts in Figure 13.2 illustrates a well-defined, integrated, and progressively differentiated set of organizing concepts.

In the Advanced Organizer Model, these concepts are introduced by the teacher progressively, one by one, through lectures, films, demonstrations, or readings. The student then applies the organizer and demonstrates mastery of the geometry concept. For example, the teacher might define an acute angle as any angle that is less than a right angle (less than 90 degrees), and then might clarify specifics through examples. In phase 2, the student might be asked to make a drawing

Figure 13.3 Exemplars of Concept Attainment

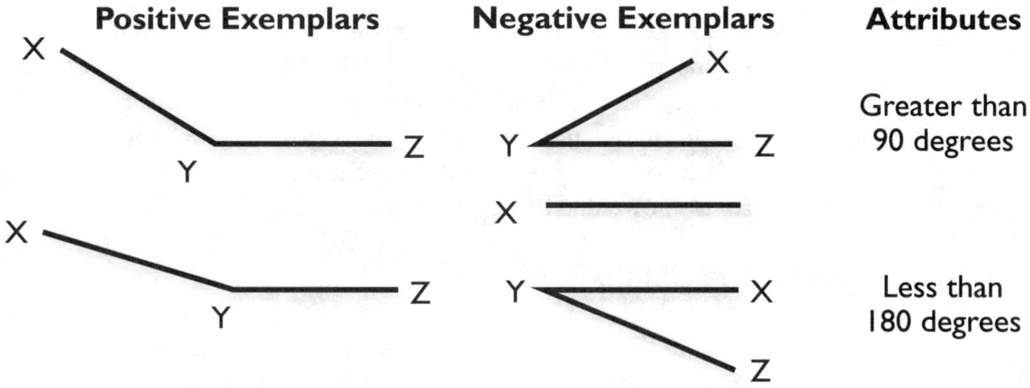

that represents an acute angle and to label it ABC. From exercises, such as this one, the teacher can determine student mastery, step by step, and integrate new ideas with previously learned content, which Bruner calls "integrative reconciliation" (Bruner, 1979). Then, the teacher moves on to subsequent organizers.

A teacher using this model primarily seeks to advance the conceptual organizers of a body of knowledge and promote a meaningful assimilation of information. "Meaningful" means within the context of a hierarchical arrangement of knowledge. Students are expected to learn these organizers because they are basic and fundamental to academic knowledge. Some consider these conceptual organizers the bread and butter of school learning.

Concept Attainment Model

Closely related to the Advanced Organizer Model is the Concept Attainment Model—learning by logic, analysis, comparison, and contrast. Instead of advancing the concept, the teacher presents the concept in the form of positive exemplars, and the students search for attributes to identify the concept (Figure 13.3). The teacher also uses nonexemplars that do not contain attributes of the concept to assist students in determining relevant attributes.

The student is expected to arrive at the concept inductively—to learn by identifying the salient features and formulating an abstract statement. The concept illustrated in Figure 13.3 is, "any angle that is greater than a right angle and less than a straight angle." The mathematical label is less important than the student's awareness of these defining attributes. Later, the students can learn the name for this concept: obtuse angle. In the model of teaching, students learn the attributes of the concept first by deriving them.

The value of using the Concept Attainment Model is that students learn not only the concepts themselves but the awareness of how concepts are formed from attributes. They acquire sensitivity to logical reasoning and a deepening regard for alternative points of view. These instructional and nurturant effects are learned through practice with concept attainment. The student, in effect, reconstructs knowledge through guided learning.

Inductive Thinking Model

The Inductive Thinking Model enables students to generate knowledge as if they themselves were scholars responsible for producing insights into factual reality. Consider the array of data in Figure 13.4. Then, ask a series of questions to lead students through a systematic sorting of the basic angles:

- ▲ What do you see?
- ▲ Which ones belong together? Why?
- ▲ What would you call them? Why?
- ▲ What do you notice about one of the groups?
- ▲ What similarities and differences do you see?
- ▲ What do these tell you about geometry?
- ▲ What do you think would happen if . . . ?
- ▲ What evidence would you use to support your guess?
- ▲ What can we say is generally true?

The likely concepts from such a logical process might more or less approximate formal knowledge of geometry, but there is no guarantee, nor does it matter to the teacher that a student doesn't know the concepts in advance. In this model, the teacher values student thinking: attention to logic, sensitivity to language, awareness of building knowledge, and concept formation. The students work cooperatively toward building ideas about the shapes.

Figure 13.4 Using the Inductive Thinking Model to Generate Knowledge

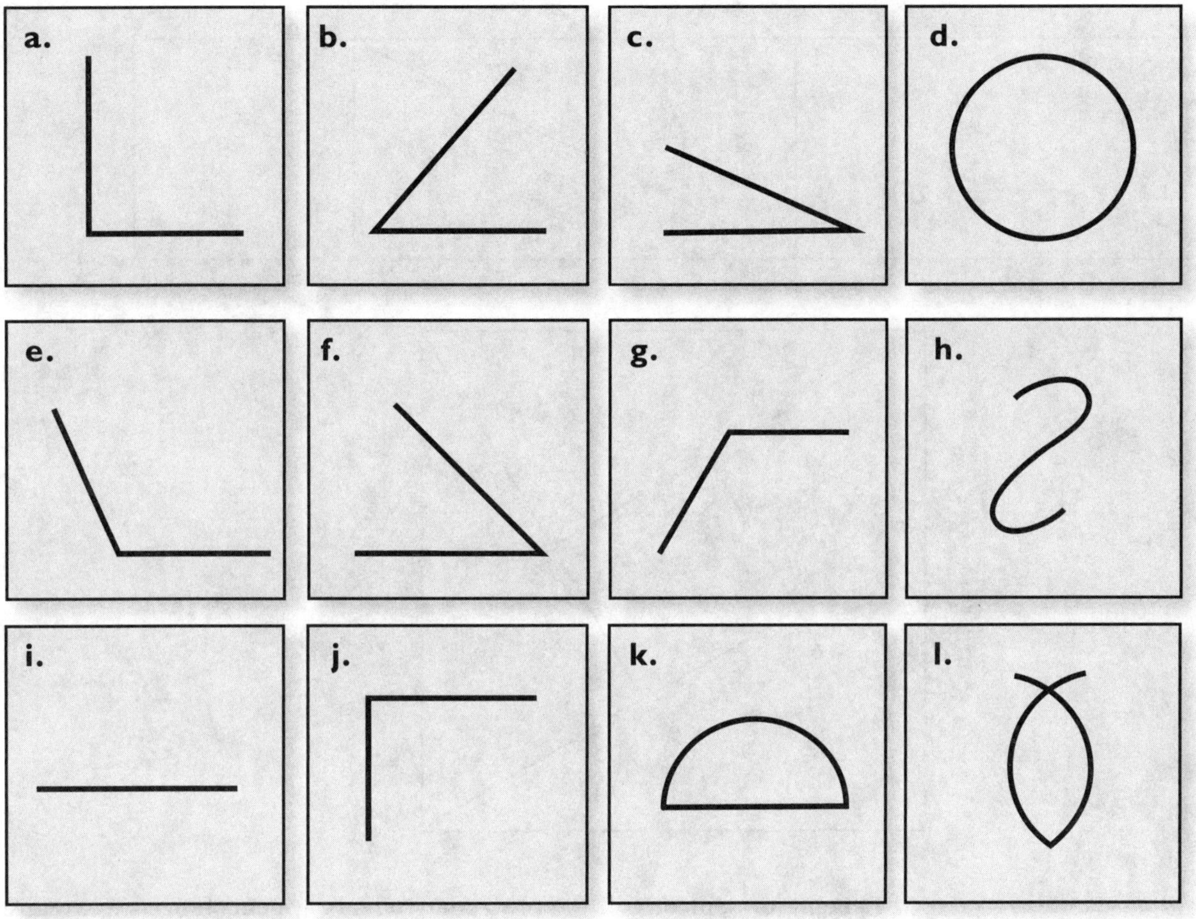

Inquiry Training Model

In inquiry training, the student is expected to put his or her knowledge to work to solve a problem. In the process, there is more knowledge to be gained in both substance (mathematical knowledge) and process (inquiry training).

Let us say that the problem is to make two squares and four equal triangles out of a rectangle measuring 5 inches by 1 inch. To solve the problem, the student needs to construct a solution consisting of geometry concepts—a process of verifying relevant facts about objects, properties, conditions, and events—and simultaneously hypothesize possible configurations of space, shape, and size. For example, the student might think through the solution shown in Figure 13.5.

Figure 13.5 Inquiry Training Solutions

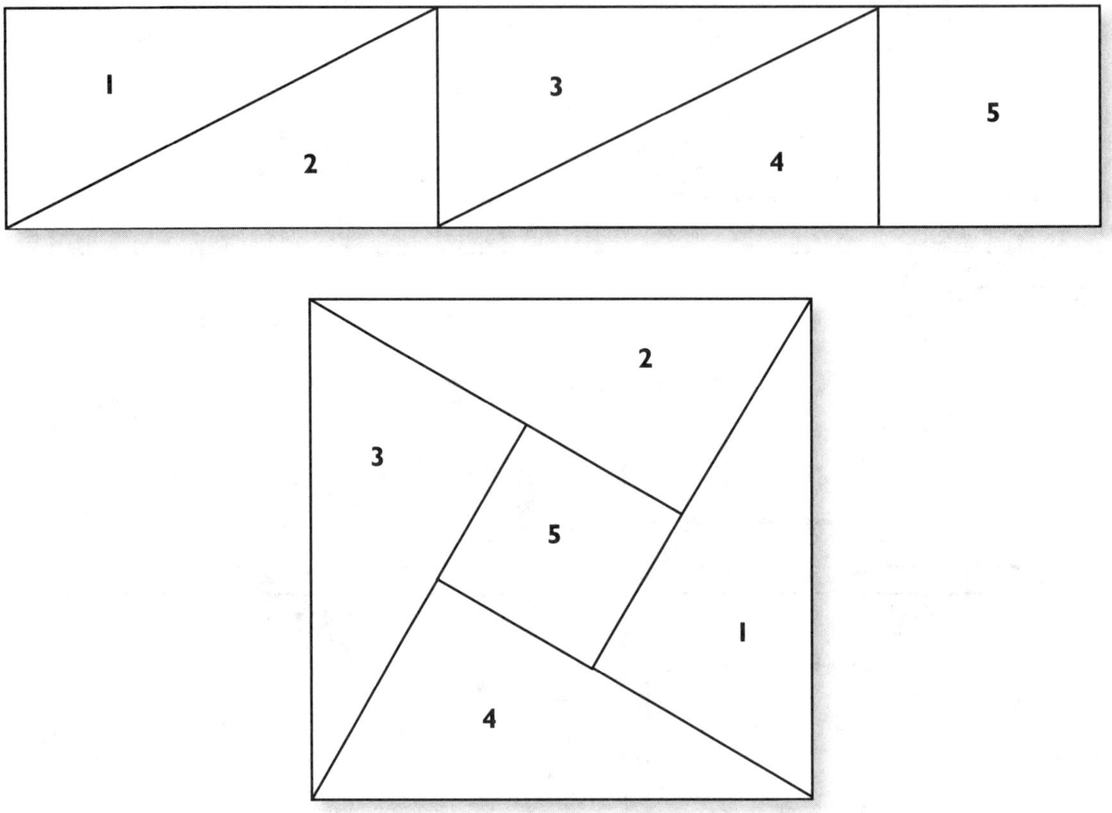

After being presented with the problem, students are encouraged to inquire together as a group while the teacher answers yes-no questions, seeks clarification, encourages student verifying, hypothesizing, and explaining behavior, and guides the group dynamics.

This model introduces a more tentative knowledge in which organized knowledge from the disciplines is synthesized and employed in the formulation of a solution. Mastery of knowledge is not the goal of instruction. Rather, the student is expected to test out his or her own knowledge. In addition, students learn strategies for inquiry by witnessing their own inquiry behavior and learning to ask questions about objects, events, properties, and conditions. This happens when teachers and students go over their problem-solving behavior following the total class exercise. There is an interdependence in inquiry learning too. Students learn to listen well and use the insights of others for solving a problem. It also provides learners with experiences that prepare them for the uses of knowledge in actual situations.

Figure 13.6 Awareness Training Model

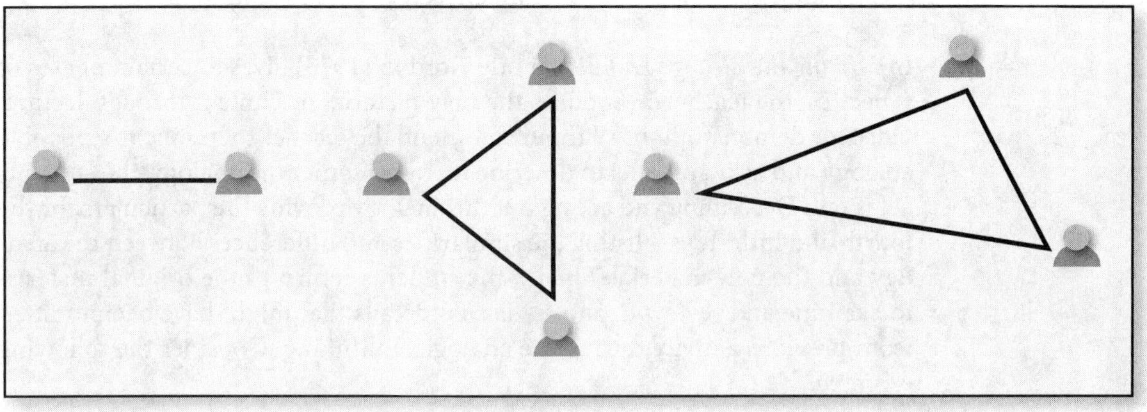

Awareness Training Model

The preceding models were developed from information processing theory and represent traditional approaches to teaching. However, knowledge of geometric space and points in space can be a personal experience as well. Awareness training seeks to bridge the individual's own experiences with experiences of other people—in this case, those of a mathematician. Imagine students with a rope who are able to experience geometric configurations equivalent to line segments and triangles (see Figure 13.6). After experiencing geometry in this way, students would be encouraged to discuss their feelings and thoughts—that is, to give form to them in language within the social context of the classroom.

These experiences may appear elementary, but they are in fact extremely rich in personal relevance and serve to integrate knowledge and self. The teacher values the students' world and the students' ability to express themselves. In this model, personal awareness is held as a first type of knowing that can undergird subsequent learning. It takes advantage of the insight that we all like to be around people who can express their personal realities as well as those more commonly held by communities of scholars.

Synectics Model

The synectics model has been derived from a set of assumptions about creativity and analogies. Creativity means seeing connections between the familiar and the strange, and exploring new solutions to old problems. It means creating and attending to psychological states such as detachment, involvement, autonomy, speculation, and deferment. We attain these psychological states through analogies, which lead to the attainment and mastery of new and difficult material and novel vantage points for reconsidering problems. Both the means and ends of teaching are influenced by these assumptions.

In *Making the Strange Familiar,* a title Gordon (1973) gives to certain phases of synectics, the teacher introduces the new material or content through lecture, video, or demonstration. Without comment, the teacher then solicits a possible analogy and asks students to describe it. To personify the analogy, the students act it out. Describing and acting out the analogy provide the particulars for the fourth and fifth steps—listing the similarities and differences between the analogy and the new material. Finally, the students return to the original material to examine and review it, and to discuss details that might have been omitted from previous activity during the analogical thinking. Consider the following example:

Step 1: The teacher presents material on geometry.

Step 2: The students select an analogy—in this case, a tree.

Step 3: The students describe the tree in detail.

Step 4: The students act out being parts of a tree.

Step 5: The students point out similarities between the tree and geometry—for example, the "angle of the branches to the tree trunk" or "the points from where the branch begins to end."

Step 6: The students point out differences—for example, that the crooked branches are not straight lines.

Step 7: Teacher and students consider what aspects of geometry were not covered in the discussion of similarities and differences.

The synectics process induces creative thinking and mastery learning of content. It is both a personal experience that integrates geometry and personal knowledge and an analogical one that capitalizes on students' ability to make connections. In addition, it is a wonderful group experience. Those who diversify their efforts to learn through the Synectics Model achieve several goals: mastery of subject matter, analogical thinking, personal integration, fun, and group productivity.

Nondirective Teaching Model

Learning is a personal experience. In this model, the student experiences planning, responsibility, and a teacher who values the individual's perspective. Acquiring responsibility for one's own learning and the skill to plan and develop those plans is no small matter. A teacher who wants students to become independent learners can use nondirective teaching to establish the interpersonal relationships that can facilitate personal productivity. The following conversation shows how this works:

Learning is a personal experience.

> **Mr. Rogers:** "John, we're going to study geometry for the next three weeks, and I'm hoping each person will plan a personal project."
>
> **John:** "What do you mean, Mr. Rogers?"
>
> **Mr. Rogers:** "Well, what would you like to learn about geometry?"
>
> **John:** "I'll be honest: I never thought about geometry. To me it's just another school subject."
>
> **Mr. Rogers:** "I understand. We plan so much of your activity in school that it just doesn't seem right to have to think about it for yourself. However, it is important to me that you have this opportunity to set your own goals, to develop the project, and to share with me in assessing your progress."
>
> **John:** "I wouldn't know where to begin."
>
> **Mr. Rogers:** "I'd like to help you. As a teacher, I've learned a great many planning skills. I guess that's what makes this project so important to me."
>
> **John:** "What do you mean?"
>
> **Mr. Rogers:** "Well, I want you to learn to organize your own learning, to feel a sense of responsibility for where you're going and how you get there—more important, that you feel progress. I know you can do it, and I want to help you."

This type of experience for the student is not casual or mindless teaching. In its own way, it is a rigorous experience for both the teacher and the student. The teacher who normally plans and organizes instruction uses that knowledge and skill to facilitate the student's own efforts. It is necessary to share the student's anxiety and anger, yet remain firm in efforts to support him or her. The student lacks the know-how to move along, but with courage, experience, and a sense of making progress, structuring learning becomes easier and more productive.

There are some persuasive reasons for using the Nondirective Teaching Model. Students learn to take charge of their own school lives, not in the sense of excluding teachers and other students but in the sense that some part of what goes on is from the individual; it belongs to the student. Personal development is a goal. Students also become aware of their feelings and thoughts about themselves and others, and they are required to deal with them. Finally, students learn to plan and organize, carry out, and evaluate their own learning.

Group Investigation Model

When a teacher thinks about teaching geometry, he or she is not often likely to consider social-oriented models of teaching because the traditions of mathematics education have been centered on the individual and mathematics content. Nevertheless, there are many opportunities for group activities that promote affiliation and interpersonal skills, and also provide opportunities for collective inquiry and other problem-solving experiences. In this model, the individual gains mutual support during the time spent learning problem-solving behaviors. These are relevant to students not only during schooling but after graduation, when the application of mathematics is done in the workplace as members of teams.

Group Investigation, a problem-solving model for groups of students, consists of the following events:

1. Students experience a puzzling situation.
2. Students discuss their reactions.
3. Students identify the problem.
4. Students make a plan and discuss roles.
5. Students carry out the plan.
6. Students reflect on their experiences.

In these events, the teacher guides the group dynamics and acts as a resource person. The social climate is cooperative.

An example of the application of group investigation to teaching geometry is how to measure heights. Such objects as flag poles, buildings, and trees are difficult to measure with devices, and getting students to plan and carry out original strategies for problem-solving has both the effect of practical problem-solving plus enhancing the more mathematical solution to the problem. The students need to explore aspects of the problem in practical ways, and their efforts to resolve these practical problems provide varied experiences, which help them appreciate a more generalizable solution.

In order to teach geometry through the Group Investigation Model, a teacher has to appreciate both the instructional and nurturant effects of instruction. The experience involves respect for different people's points of view and knowledge construction, learner independence from the teacher, effective group process, a commitment to group inquiry and social dynamics, and disciplined inquiry. Group investigation synthesizes these value orientations. From an observer's vantage point, we need a multifocal perspective to appreciate the richness of this model of teaching.

PATTERNS OF INSTRUCTION

Besides the models of teaching, there are three other common patterns of instruction in classrooms today: lecturing, recitation, and direct instruction, which probably between them account for the majority of what goes on in classrooms.

Lecture

A good lecture is systematic and sequential and conveys information in an orderly and interesting way. Effective lecturers draw skills from the Attention, Clarity, and Differentiated Instruction areas of performance, as well as from the Lesson Objectives and Curriculum Design areas of performance. The pattern of teacher behavior in lecturing, however, draws nothing from any internal theory of good lecturing or cohesive theory of learning. A lecture is a composite, with no secondary goal about learning how to learn. When the lecture is a step in the Advanced Organizer Model, then the story is different. Nevertheless, a good lecture is a worthwhile educational experience and certainly has a place in schooling.

A lecture is poor when the performance on one or more of the five areas of performance listed earlier is poor, not because of poor performance of a model called lecturing. A poor lecture may qualify as no teaching at all. If the content is not organized around the course objectives and is not designed with the principles of organization in mind, even an interesting speaker, who holds students' attention or keeps them amused with clever anecdotes, may be doing no teaching. Students can look forward to class and be entertained but leave without having learned a thing.

Recitation

A recitation is an oral test. The teacher asks questions, students respond, and the teacher makes value judgments on the responses. Its goal is to cover the material, go over it, ask questions, and see who knows what. By the time it's over, all the important material should be out (or have been said by someone and heard by all). Reviews for tests are often recitations. A recitation doesn't have a series of steps, but we could construct this list of events and qualities that might determine a good recitation:

▲ Covered all the material.

▲ Highlighted important items.

▲ Identified student confusions.

▲ Got maximum student participation.

▲ Took opportunities to stimulate higher-level thinking.

If we wanted to judge the quality of a recitation lesson, we would have to go back to the management areas of performance of "Attention," "Momentum," and "Clarity." Recitations have a place in school, but not as large a one as they seem to occupy. When a recitation is over, students and teachers are aware of who knows what, who has read the assignment, and who gets A's. As an educational experience used for more than an occasional review, it has no guiding principles or point of view behind it and little chance that the students will get better at learning in some particular way.

Direct Instruction

Direct instruction is usually used for skill work and does have a series of phases, which Joyce calls a syntax:

1. The teacher states the aims of the lesson.
2. The teacher presents concepts or an operation.
3. The teacher gives examples or demonstrates.

4. The teacher asks questions to check student understanding.

5. Students practice with direct monitoring, feedback, help, and hints from the teacher, usually in the group.

6. Students practice alone (seatwork or homework).

7. The teacher corrects and decides whether to reteach, regroup, or move on.

8. The teacher gives frequent assessments.

Direct instruction lacks model status because it has no theoretical basis. It has no teacher-student response pattern or deliberate environmental conditions tailored to optimize a specified learning behavior among students. But we know that good direct instruction in groups with high time on task produces mastery of skills. Direct instruction reflects the current trends toward training, task analysis, and biofeedback. These preferences for instruction, which have evolved from the business community, reflect values of efficiency and effectiveness.

MODELS VERSUS PATTERNS OF INSTRUCTION

Lecturing, recitation, and direct instruction are prominent patterns of classroom instruction, and most teachers view them as models of teaching. But in theory and practice, they are not models at all. Models of teaching have elaborate theoretical statements, and descriptions of patterns of behavior that teachers can be trained to perform. There are discrete teacher-student interactions that characterize one model and distinguish it from another. Models are similar to theatrical plays, though not so closely scripted.

If teachers know the model, they can visualize the classroom activity before it occurs, and use that image to monitor and regulate the flow of activity. The content and goals of models are equally distinctive. In one model, the content is derived from an academic discipline, such as mathematics; in another it may draw from recent student experiences for the content. A model will be chosen not only to convey content but to stretch the way students think and learn about learning.

Models of teaching allow teachers to ask of good teaching, "Good for what?" and to answer out of the things (e.g. logical thinking, inductive reasoning, personal self-organization, cooperation, and group skill) a particular model is designed to be good for.

UPDATE ON THE MODELS OF TEACHING

Some readers will notice that the reference dates for these models of teaching range from the 1950s to the early 1970s. This indeed was a time of innovation in teaching, and many of the models of teaching were researched by scholars and elaborated on by educators interested in classroom instruction. Some educators embedded specific models of teaching in curriculum materials made available during that period. It was a productive time in American education, a time during which instructional innovations flourished under the leadership of government sponsored research and university scholarship.

What has happened between then and now? In many ways, the models of teaching are fully developed approaches to help students develop their thinking skills, and there are teaching guides with planning materials available to aid teachers and curriculum developers. Joyce, Calhoun, and Hopkins's *Models of Learning* (2002) recasts or refocuses these same strategies as models of learning. The authors describe their intent to teach thinking skills through curriculum implementation: "As we study the four families of *Models of Teaching*, we try to build a mental picture of what each model is designed to accomplish. As we consider when and how to use various combinations of models and, therefore, which learning strategies will get priority for particular units and lessons and groups of students, we take into account the types and pace of learning that are likely to be promoted" (p. 36). When teachers apply the models of learning to classroom lesson planning and planning units of study, the models often become fragmented. For example, the Inductive Thinking Model has nine logical steps, but in a lesson a teacher might find only two or three of them. This is important. The original models of teaching or learning are complete packages, but in classrooms today, only part of the full model may be in use.

Consider a U.S. history teacher who asks her students to enumerate the possible causes of colonists' discontent prior to the Revolutionary War. Though she might be implementing the Inductive Thinking Model of teaching, which has nine steps, she might be able to implement only enumerating the causes and getting her students to explain them. In a specific lesson, it may not be not possible to implement all the steps in the model, but the fragment nevertheless can contribute to the larger process of inductive thinking and learning.

In the 9th edition of *Models of Teaching* (2014), Joyce, Weil, and Calhoun included descriptions to approaches to learning that are potent but not fully developed models. They are, nevertheless, additions to our teaching repertoires valuable for any professional. For example, Joel Levin's Mnemonic Keyword approach to learning the meaning of words is a powerful strategy for blending visuals, meaning, and memory for new words in any language. The "cross cutting concepts" within the National Academy of Sciences Next Generation Science Standards and the integration of academic disciplines within these standards pushes the boundaries of teaching and learning in healthy and ground-breaking directions.

Few educational researchers understand teaching and learning better than Joyce and his colleagues. In the third edition of *Models of Teaching* (1986), they write about the different models, the effects on learners of the different approaches to teaching, and the need to adapt teaching to different learners' styles.

What makes these models attractive to teachers is that teachers can help students build a repertoire of thinking skills—inductive reasoning, deductive reasoning, analogical thinking, inquiry training, concept building, and others. Joyce and colleagues (2002) write, "Debates about educational method have seemed to imply that schools and teachers should choose one approach over another. However, it is far more likely that for optimum opportunity to learn, students need a range of instructional approaches drawn from the information processing, social, personal and behavioral families" (p. 70). Teachers can get excited about students having control over a repertoire of thinking skills as they work their way through elementary and secondary schools.

A second line of inquiry that Joyce and his colleagues pursued became a significant influence on the school culture literature of the era. This was the evolution of peer coaching, the collegial school, and their work on professional development. From the very beginning, they used peer coaching to learn specific models of teaching. Learning the teaching models required an understanding of theory and practice, strategies and specific teaching skills, and savvy attention to adult learning. Teachers worked together to study the theory of the teaching models, identified the mini skills that make the models work in the classroom, practiced the models by simulating them in small groups (pairings and triads), and discussed the place of models in the classroom. They worked with thousands of teachers over a 25-year period and evolved a peer coaching model that went from informal gatherings to a formal process called peer coaching.

Their model of peer coaching consisted of theory, demonstration, practice, feedback, and application by teaching in the classroom with their students. Joyce and his associates began work on peer coaching in the early 1970s as an effort to help teachers learn different models of teaching and implement them in their classrooms. In the 1980s, their research on peer coaching focused more on small groups of teachers and on student learning and how teachers can create better learning environments. Joyce and Showers (1986) wrote, "There is no evidence that simply organizing peer coaching or peer study teams will affect students' learning environments. The study of teaching and curriculum must be the focus" (p. 12).

It wasn't long before the importance of a collegial school environment surfaced as a key condition for in-service professional development. Improving schooling requires promoting the evolution of the school organization and the relationships between the adults to find a model of schooling that fits the 21st century. Current trends include greater accountability, shared power and governance, and higher expectations for student achievement. All of this activity to rejuvenate the schools requires cooperation among teachers, school leaders, and public officials. Teachers must ask themselves: "Am I prepared to work with formal knowledge of teaching and learning? Am I prepared to work with others to develop a collegial school and to create a professional environment for lifelong learning? Am I prepared to work toward more democratic schools for the 21st century?"

Like a good case study, models of teaching have evolved from an innovation in teaching and learning to a full-blown theory of schooling and professional development. The current conventional wisdom about the importance of collaboration, professional learning communities, and deprivatizing teaching owes a debt, that should not be forgotten, to the 40-year history of those who developed models of teaching and peer coaching.

So, as we go forward now, the models of teaching are there for our use in improving student thinking skills. Peer coaching is there to facilitate the process by which teachers learn new models and transfer that learning to their classroom teaching. We are still educating children by teaching them to read and write, but the school has a much larger purpose. Everyone in the school building has to grow stronger and better, and for that we need a different culture, a more collegial environment, and a school more accountable to itself and the public. The development of models of teaching play a significant role in the history of these growing perceptions.

CHAPTER QUICK GUIDE

Eight Models of Teaching:

1. **Advanced Organizer:** Designed to increase the efficiency of information processing capacities to absorb and relate bodies of knowledge.

2. **Concept Attainment:** Designed primarily to develop concepts and how they are formed from attributes.

3. **Inductive Thinking:** Designed primarily for the development of inductive mental processes and academic reasoning or theory building, but these capacities are useful for personal and social goals as well.

4. **Inquiry Training:** Designed primarily for the development of problem-solving, data gathering, and hypothesis testing.

5. **Awareness Training:** Awareness training seeks to bridge the individual's own experiences with experiences of other people.

6. **Synectics:** Personal development of creativity and creative problem-solving by connecting the familiar with the strange.

7. **Nondirective Teaching:** Emphasis on building capacity for self-instruction and through this, personal development in terms of self-understanding, self-discovery, and self-concept.

8. **Group Investigation:** Development of skills for participation in democratic social processes through combined emphasis on interpersonal and social (group) skills and academic inquiry.

To check your knowledge about Models of Teaching, see the exercises on *The Skillful Teacher* website at www.RBTeach.com/TST7.

NOTES

Part 4
Introduction to Motivation

Emotions are everywhere. There is never an instant of waking life when they are not present and influencing the energy level we bring to tasks, the level of focus, the amount of investment. Part Four addresses the things teachers do that influence the emotional state of students, either positively or negatively, and thus their capacity to invest in academic learning. Students' attention and investment in academic tasks is affected by their relationship with their teachers ("Personal Relationship Building"); it is influenced by their interpersonal relationships with peers, the feelings of support and community on the one hand, or on the other hand feelings of fear and defensiveness against ridicule ("Classroom Climate"). And finally, it is influenced by their own confidence that they can grow their ability to perform academic tasks versus self-doubt or belief in innate low ability ("Expectations"). For those who have wondered where the domain of feeling and the whole child enters into the picture of skillful teaching, this section is for you. Another way to cast these three chapters is that they circumscribe our influence on student motivation. Why are students motivated to work hard and learn? This question is important because motivation is the linchpin of student learning. Therefore, nurturing motivation where it doesn't seem to exist becomes part of our responsibility as teachers.

Motivation is the linchpin of student learning.

Do you accept that nurturing motivation is part of your job? Consider that the level of motivation any of us has is powerfully conditioned by people who are significant in our lives; people who are in relationships with us and who we admire, respect, like, or love. The adults who are the most influential figures in children's lives outside their families are their teachers. Teachers often spend more time with children than any other adult in their lives. Therefore, deliberately influencing student motivation is not a job we can dodge. As teachers, we are significant figures in our students' lives and in the motivation they form to be learners. Because we are so powerfully positioned to influence it, we are throwing away legions of children if we choose not to engage this task. Influencing students' motivation to learn happens in complicated ways, but in ways that we can see in behavior that is understandable. Part Four takes up the specific how-tos of this aspect of teaching by laying out the repertoires for building relationships, communicating belief, building confidence in students, and constructing classroom climates of community, psychological safety, and ownership.

Chapter 14: "Expectations" describes the Myth of the Bell Curve and shows what high-expectations teachers do to get low-performing, low-confidence students to believe in themselves. The six elements of "Effective Effort" are laid out as well as how to teach students to exert it.

Chapter 15: "Personal Relationship Building" goes into detail about how teachers make student feel known and valued.

Chapter 16: "Classroom Climate" describes how skillful teachers build a climate of community, risk-taking, and influence where students feel safe to make mistakes and that their peers are on their side.

"Long after leaving school, students remember fondly and in graphic detail those teachers who cared and painfully those who did not. They may not recall the content these teachers taught, but their human impact is indelibly imprinted in their minds."
(Gay, 2000, p. 49)

Here's an example of how the three fit together. Suppose one day I check for understanding and find you don't understand exponents. I then work with you after class to unscramble your confusions; I am using clarity skills, to be sure. But the fact that I take the time to do this and it's with you, that I pursue you to make the appointment and go out of my way to really help you get it—that's something I wouldn't do if I didn't value you. In fact, the whole episode conveys a Personal Relationship Building message: you are a valued person to me. I care about you. Now in addition, while I am explaining common denominators to you, I may use phrases that are encouraging ("Yes, yes, keep it up") and I may express confidence in your ability to get it ("You're almost there. I know you're going to get this!"). So within this event is also the positive "I believe in you" expectation message. When your friends hear you are staying late with me for twenty minutes and won't be going home on the bus with them, they are quite accepting of you putting out that extra effort; they don't make fun of you because you're staying with the teacher. The climate among the students in the class is supportive of one another putting out effort to learn and get help, either from each other or from the teacher. The range of these behaviors in this vignette prompts us to ask, how do we conceptualize our role in nurturing motivation and inspiring it where it doesn't exist?

The Anatomy of Caring: The expressions "caring" and "make students feel known and valued" are prominent in recent literature. Whether one surveys the current literature on what's needed most to improve our schools or on what parents and students say when asked what matters, the resounding theme that emerges is relationships and the sense that people care. How does caring present itself in the classroom setting? "My teacher is really caring." "How do you know?" "I know he cares about me because he: (1) won't let me get away with not doing my work. There's no escape! (2) encourages me and makes me feel smart; (3) goes out of his way to help me when I'm stuck and makes sure I get it; and (4) wants to know what I'm interested in and how things are going in my life." In Chapter 14, "Expectations," we deal extensively with the first two student responses. Chapter 11, "Clarity," presents the tools for the third response. The fourth response is directly connected to Chapter 15, "Personal Relationship Building."

CHAPTER 14

Motivation
Expectations

Motivation: Expectations

In 1968, Robert Rosenthal and Lenore Jacobson published a landmark book: *Pygmalion in the Classroom.* It caused such a public stir that they were interviewed on the *Today Show*. What they had proven was that if you created expectations in teachers, even false expectations, about children's potential to perform at high levels, the teachers acted as if they could. And the children's performance actually rose to higher levels. The thing was, the researchers had given the teachers false information about the children's potential—random IQ scores.

So, here we had a situation that birthed the line in the film *Stand and Deliver* in which the Jaime Escalante character says, "Students will rise to the level of expectations, Señora Molina."

Video: Pygmalion in the Classroom

What a profound finding! Acting toward students as if you believed in them and their capacity caused the students to act as if they believed it too! And therefore, they exceeded predictions and prior performance. Later in this chapter, we will go into the details of how teachers behaved toward these students and how different this behavior was from how they acted toward students for whom they held lower expectations. What should be noted is that Rosenthal and Jacobson's findings triggered a staff development program (Kerman, 1979) and a research tradition still active today (Hattie, 2012). And they brought to the fore a deep interest in how we convey our expectations to students in our daily behavior.

In this chapter, we unite three strands of this work. Strand 1 is how we convey to students the standards for good work that we want them to produce. Strand 2 is the theories that underpin a potential revolution in education: Attribution Theory, the Growth Mindset, and the countervailing evidence about the bell curve of ability. Strand 3 is the behaviors through which we convey our expectations and our beliefs in their capacity to each student personally. This strand also goes deeply into the behaviors through which we can do attribution re-training, that is, get low-confidence, underperforming students to believe in themselves and act effectively from that belief. In service of these strands, we distinguish by definition between standards and expectations.

Within Strand 2, we challenge explicitly the belief in the bell curve of academic ability and make the case that all our students, unless they suffer from organic

Figure 14.1 Standards and Expectations

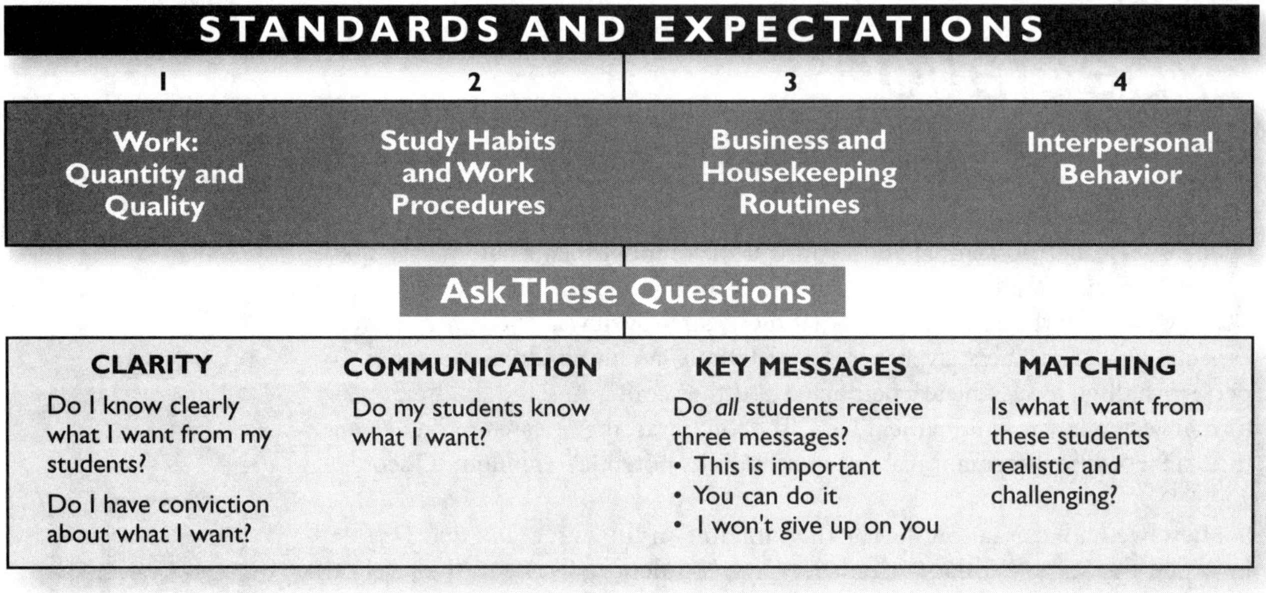

brain defects, have the capacity to achieve proficiency even if they are several grade levels behind. We advance this claim in the face of the many disadvantages we know children of color and children of poverty face. And we make the case that we can, and, in fact, that it is our job to give them the belief, confidence, tools, and desire to achieve proficiency. Our students can grow their ability, and we can teach them how.

STRAND 1: WHAT YOU EXPECT IS WHAT YOU GET

What are the meaning and significance of the terms "standards" and "expectations," and how does each have an impact on the learning environment we create? The word *expectations* can have two different meanings: (1) a standard of performance we are hoping for and (2) our anticipation (or prediction) about what one will be able to accomplish. Both are important constructs, and it is critical to separate and conceptualize each clearly, for each plays a significant role in creating an atmosphere conducive to student achievement at high levels. Throughout this chapter, we use the term *standard* to describe the level or type of performance a teacher wants from students and *expectation* to mean what a teacher thinks (believes or predicts) students will do. We illustrate the nature and critical importance of each and how they intersect with one another to influence the messages students receive that impact their performance and achievement. Figure 14.1 outlines the key issues for teachers to consider in addressing "Expectations."

Standards: Four Kinds

Standards signal to students what is important, what it is we want them to accomplish, and how we want them to behave. In a classroom setting, there are four general categories for which teachers set standards of performance:

1. Quality and quantity of work
2. Work habits and work procedures
3. Business and housekeeping routines
4. Interpersonal behavior

Videos: Hallway Conversations, Entering Class

Standards for the quality and quantity of students' work specify the characteristics of work that make it acceptable. These might include things like:

▲ Explaining how the student solved a problem in both pictures and words (quality).

▲ Supporting the hypothesis in a lab report with measured data (quality).

▲ Demonstrating proper form in four foul shots (quantity and quality).

▲ Responding to questions in complete sentences (quality).

Standards for work habits and work procedures pertain to how students go about their work, not the products of their work. These are ongoing habits and procedures that students are routinely expected to use in their work, not directions on how to do individual assignments. These might include things like:

▲ Responsibility and procedures for getting and submitting assignments when a student has been absent from class.

▲ The process for previewing directions before beginning a task.

▲ The procedure for entering class and getting started immediately on the "bell work" for the day.

▲ What, when, and how often to update an independent reading log.

At the beginning of the year, there may be repeated and direct attention to teaching these procedures to students, and the teacher will remind students of these ongoing procedures, from time to time, until they are established and working well. Eventually, they won't be talked about at all. They just function, underlying the academic work students are doing.

Standards for business and housekeeping routines pertain to nonacademic work-related procedures such as:

- ▲ How attendance and lunch count are done.
- ▲ Responsibility and procedures for cleanup in the lab or a work area.

There should be no secret about what is expected and what it will look like when students are meeting expectations.

Standards for interpersonal behavior pertain to how students should treat each other, interact with one another, and cooperate with the teacher, for example:

- ▲ Treat every classmate with respect; listen attentively when they speak; ask questions when you don't agree with someone or understand them; and be patient and quiet if someone needs time to think after you finish speaking.
- ▲ When asked to work together, make every effort to work in a way that is helpful to everyone.

Each of these four categories of standards is considered separately because it is possible for a teacher to be very clear about what's important and to have conviction that students will be able to achieve the standards set in one category but not necessarily to be as clear in all four. As a result, teachers might find that they get great results, for example, on students following work procedures but inconsistencies or low performance when it comes to their treatment of one another or the quality of work they are producing. This signals an opportunity for teachers to step back and ask anew, "So what is it that I think is important? What is it that I want from my students?"

How We Communicate Standards

How do students come to know what is expected of them? How do teachers ensure that students know and understand what is important? There should be no secret about what is expected and what it will look like when students are meeting expectations. Let's begin by examining 10 behaviors that are common among teachers who create atmospheres of high expectations and get great results with their students:

1. **Direct Communication:** The standard of performance is explicitly brought to students' attention, verbally, in writing, or through a visual model.

2. **Specific Communication:** The details of the standard for students' performance are clearly stated or otherwise spelled out. Criteria for success are delineated, and exemplars of student products or performances are shared and carefully examined with students. When the task or assignment is sufficiently complex or multifaceted, rubrics might be presented and explained—or developed with students (see Chapter 21, "Assessment").

3. **Repeated Communication:** The standard is repeated often to make sure students absorb it.

4. **Positive Expectancy:** The standards are explained with an accompanying expression of teacher confidence (sometimes challenge) signaling "You can do this." Another version of positive expectancy that has a more imperative quality is, "Of course, you'll meet this expectation!" The implication conveyed by tone and body language is, "It's what's done!"

5. **Modeled:** This has two meanings. The first is to show or demonstrate. A teacher may clarify for students what is desired by performing the behavior or providing models. The purpose of this form of modeling is clear communication. The second meaning of modeling is to "practice what you preach." In regular practice and behavior, the teacher is a model of thoroughness, self-evaluation, courtesy, or whatever else is expected of students. Whether it's standards for procedures, interpersonal behaviors, work habits, or application of skills, students take powerful messages from observing how faithfully teachers follow their own dicta.

6. **Personal Contact:** There are frequent occasions of face-to-face interactions with students—before, during, and after class, even in the hallway. Perhaps, they'll be jocular: "Hey, Noah! Before you get locked up in your shoulder pads this afternoon, you're going to see me with those corrections, right?"

7. **No Excuses:** Teachers hold students accountable, putting them on the spot when work is not turned in, is late, or is inadequately done, and do not let them off the hook by accepting inadequate explanations. Teachers give the work to students to correct or do over, set deadlines, offer help when necessary, or make provisions for students to get what they need to do the work (materials, peer tutoring, reteaching, or something else). "No excuses" means giving consequences without rancor or anger that are intended to improve performance when performance is poor.

8. **Recognizing Superior Performance or Significant Gains Over Past Performance:** When students do well, there is special recognition that

highlights their accomplishment such as posting especially good papers on a bulletin board, displaying a product in a public place, complimenting in front of the class, or giving a "Greatest Gains" award.

9. **Logical Consequences for Poor Performance:** Something happens as a result of not doing homework or classwork, or doing shoddy work, being late, sloppy cleanup, or the many other areas of student performance for which teachers have expectations. As a result, students become convinced the teacher means it. Effective consequences are made clear in advance to students, are varied so there is a range of consequences rather than just one rigid one for each expectation, are logical rather than punitive, are delivered with appropriate affect, and teachers make it clear that the students have made a choice. (These attributes are developed in more detail in Chapter 10, "Discipline.") For example, a student who chronically fails to do homework becomes a member of the "homework club" that meets two days after school. The student can choose which day to attend but is required to attend for a minimum number of weeks until homework is caught up and starts coming in on a regular basis. A student who does poorly on a test is required to attend two after-school help sessions before taking the test again to earn a better grade and will be granted the higher grade achieved in the retake.

10. **Tenacity:** Teacher persistence in pursuit of getting students to meet an expectation is convincing testimony that the teacher means it! But *how* the teacher displays tenacity and with whom can also be powerful messages, either pro or con, to low-confidence underperforming students. We will return to this topic later in this chapter when we tackle how teachers convince discouraged students that "smart is something you can get."

11. **Feedback:** Feedback about student performance is a final way students find out what our expectations are. Practicing good feedback is a critical element of successful teaching. It is part and parcel of a complex array of interactive and interdependent practices that successful teachers do. Our colleague, Caroline Tripp, shows in Figure 14.2 that the development of effective feedback systems is the product of and dependent on strength in three areas: objectives, assessment, and standards of performance.

    First, clear objectives must be communicated to the students in advance. No one can give (or use) specific and detailed feedback without a clear image of what students are supposed to be aiming for. Second, teachers must have appropriate assessment tasks or devices for observing and measuring student performance. Third, teachers must have precision about the specific

Figure 14.2 Areas of Effective Feedback

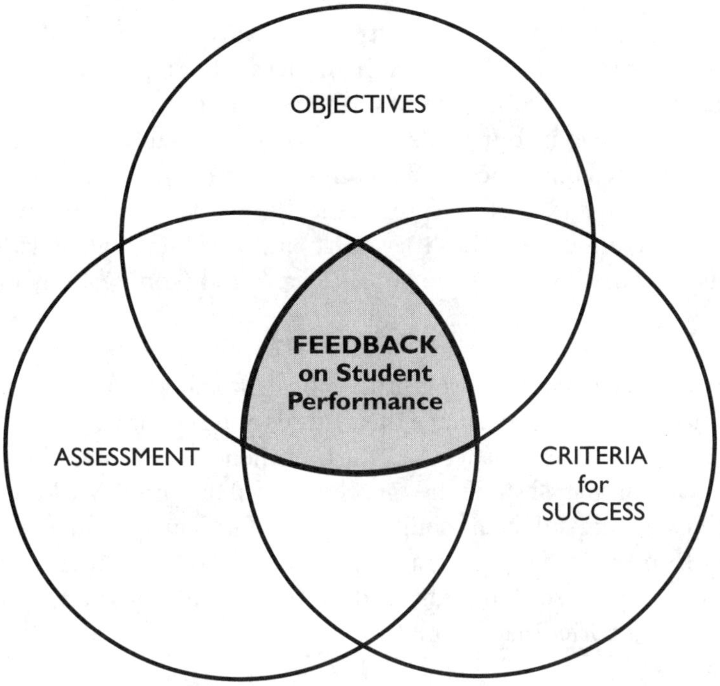

standards of performance (or criteria for success) to indicate proficiency and ensure that students know and understand these criteria so as to use the feedback given to improve their performance. In order to expend the energy it takes to create good feedback systems and implement them assiduously with all students, teachers must have expectations that all students have the capacity to succeed.

We need to make feedback a regular and ongoing event.

We need to make feedback a regular and ongoing event for students because it keeps them focused on what's important and supports them in investing their effort in incremental improvement and achievement. The effort we invest in providing specific, detailed, timely, and personal feedback to our students signals that we think the work is important, that they can do it, and that we are there to support them in investing their effort effectively. For feedback to have maximum effect, students have to be expected to use it to improve their work and, in many cases, taught how to do so. This is where student self-assessment and goal setting become part of the package. (See pages 350-355 for more on feedback.)

STRAND 2: GROWTH MINDSET (EFFORT-BASED ABILITY OR INCREMENTALIST THEORY)

We have stated that teacher tenacity and quality feedback are skill sets that move students toward believing in themselves. The implication is we wouldn't take the trouble to act in these ways (be tenacious and give useful feedback) if we didn't believe in our students and want them to succeed. But for low-performing, low-confidence students much more is needed. They don't think they "have it." That is, they don't think they're smart enough or have ability in a particular academic area. Thus they don't put forth sufficient effort for mastery. You may hear them say, "It's too hard," "I can't do it," or "Nobody in my family can either."

This section takes on the all-important constellation of teaching skills that enables us to get students to change their minds about their ability and to be willing to learn how to exert effective effort on their own behalf. This implies our own conviction that all students can achieve well in school. We have to perceive them all as having sufficient ability to do so and have confidence in our own capacity to meet students where they are now and move them incrementally toward meeting those standards. Both of these conditions can be seriously affected by the theories that we hold about people and their capacity to grow and develop.

How do our beliefs about "ability" influence our behavior, the messages we send to students about their intellectual capacity, and our effectiveness in communicating high expectations to all students? How do students' beliefs about ability influence their motivation to work hard and their confidence that they can achieve at high levels? We explore two theories about innate ability and its relationship to performance and achievement. As you read, consider which of these theories dominated the environment in which you spent your formative years and how each of these theories plays out in your teaching.

The Bell Curve of Innate Ability

The innate ability theory about achievement and development is best represented by the bell curve as an uneven distribution of intellectual ability in human beings (Figure 14.3). Carol Dweck (2008) has popularized the term "fixed mindset" to represent this view of ability. Embedded in this theory are the following assumptions:

- Intellectual ability is a "thing," a unitary entity that is real.
- Intellectual ability is innate; that is, it comes with us as a package at birth.

Figure 14.3 The Bell Curve

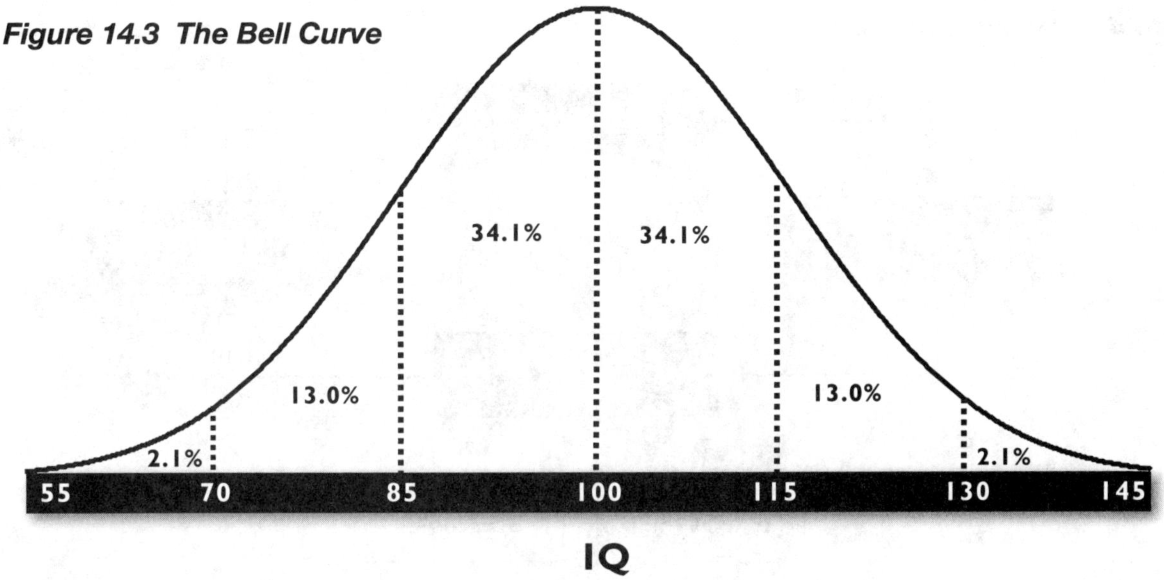

- ▲ The amount of intellectual ability we are given at birth remains relatively fixed or stable throughout our lifetime. It doesn't vary much as we proceed through our lives, and we can't change or affect it much.

- ▲ Innate ability is unequally distributed; some of us are born with more of it than others.

- ▲ Intellectual ability determines how far a person can go and how well he or she can do, especially at academic material.

- ▲ Intellectual ability is measurable. We can test to tell how much of it a student has and arrange for each student to be in the right kind of educational environment for his or her abilities.

Most of us were raised in an environment that reinforced this theory and set of assumptions, and we bought into those assumptions as if they were fact. This is not a statement of blame. It's a statement about the air we breathe in a society where this belief is played out more strongly than anywhere else in the world. These are undiscussed assumptions that dominated our country and our schools throughout the 20th century and still have pervasive influence. Our contention is that these assumptions are wrong. For a history of the concept of "intelligence" as it developed in the United States and evidence that it is malleable, see "Debunking the Myth of the Bell Curve" in *High Expectations Teaching* (Saphier, 2017). An abbreviated version of this history of the idea of

Videos: Debunking the Myth of the Bell Curve (1 & 2)

Figure 14.4 Effective Effort

Adapted from Jeff Howard, Efficacy Institute, Waltham, Massachusetts.

History of the Idea of "Intelligence" in the United States

"intelligence" and how it got so deeply embedded in American culture and school design is available on *The Skillful Teacher* website (www.RBTeach.com/TST7).

The effort-based theory (see Figure 14.4) posits that all children are born with sufficient innate ability to achieve anything asked of them in school, and that this ability (in fact, intelligence itself) is malleable through effective effort. Whether a student does achieve and develop (get smarter) is not a matter of having the raw material or ability, but rather believing he or she has what it takes (confidence) and investing effort effectively (working hard and acquiring knowledge and strategies for working smart). Another way of summarizing this theory is that "Smart is not something you are; smart is something you get (incrementally) by working hard and working smart" (Jeff Howard, The Efficacy Institute).

Indeed, all teachers see differences in children every day in their classrooms, sometimes big differences in readiness to learn, in speed of learning, in motivation, and current academic performance. Some students are way behind the others. But unlike a fixed mindset or entity theorist, where the differences would be explained away as how much intelligence or innate ability one is endowed with, a person with a growth mindset or an incrementalist believes that all children have the intellectual capacity to eventually meet proficiency standards. It is not a limited brain that is holding them back, but any number of other variables, all of which can potentially be modified, accommodated, or influenced in some way.

When confronted with differences in children's development or performance, those who hold to this theory interpret the disparity as a function of disadvantages (or lack of opportunities) that have created obstacles to their development and learning. This might include limited experiences, absence of mediation or intervention, conflict of values related to school achievement, low self-esteem, mismatch in learning-teaching style, and a myriad of other possible causes, none of which is internally hard-wired in a person, and all of which may be subject to change under the right circumstances. Students clearly have different aptitudes (a natural talent or ability for something), but they all have enough to attain proficiency in literacy and numeracy at rigorous standards. Two assumptions are embedded in this theory:

1. There is no way of telling from children's attitudes, speech, cleanliness, clothing, record of past performance, and current performance what they are capable of learning and achieving if given time, motivation, and instruction that reaches out to meet their needs.

2. Differences of color and culture have nothing to do with the capacities of children's brains.

Whereas the innate theory is deterministic, the incrementalist theory—or effort-based ability—is optimistic. Incrementalists engage in an ongoing quest to discover what will enable students to turn on and take off.

Attribution Theory

Both explanations for achievement and development have been explored historically as part of a body of research referred to as "attribution theory" (Dweck, 1999, 2002; Nicholls, 1978; Weiner, 1996). Attribution theory is concerned with the explanations we give ourselves when we succeed for why we succeeded, and when we fail for why we have failed. The research suggests that the explanations we give ourselves about the causes of our successes and failures (attributions) are based on our perceptions, and those perceptions and explanations ultimately influence our self-concept about our ability. They also influence our expectations for future situations, feelings of power and efficacy, and subsequent motivation to put forth effort. Weiner found four basic reasons to which individuals might attribute their success or lack thereof: ability, task difficulty, luck, and effort. Weiner arranges them in the grid shown in Figure 14.5. According to Weiner, successful, confident people attribute their success to internal factors (having the ability and exerting effort) and lack of success to the internal factor they control and can most readily influence (effort). Unsuccessful, low-confidence people tend to attribute success to external factors (task difficulty: "Must have been an easy test," and luck: "I guess I just luckily

Figure 14.5 Attribution Theory

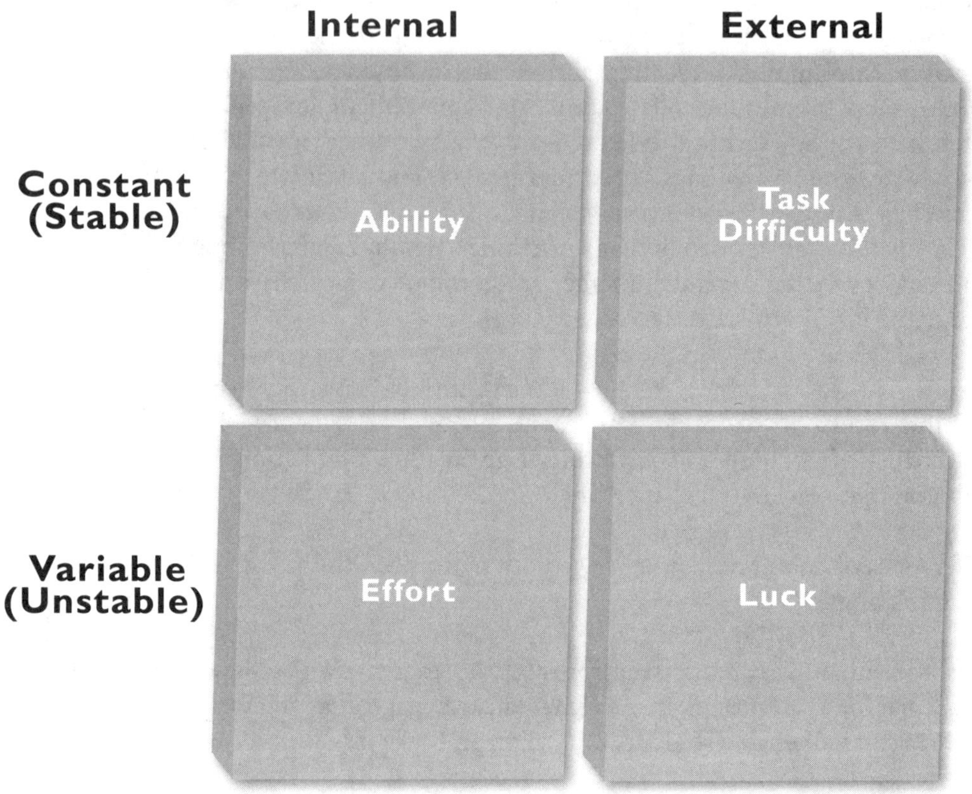

Adapted from Weiner, 1974.

studied the right chapters!") and lack of success to external factors (again, luck or task difficulty, those over which they have no control) with a secret inner fear that they really just don't have enough ability.

Young children believe success comes from effort; in fact, effort and ability are synonymous to them (Nicholls & Burton, 1982). But as they get older, some children start attributing academic success more and more to innate ability rather than effort. This creates a bind, because for such children the only possible conclusion if they are not doing well is that they must be dumb. Thus many low-performing students opt out of school and quit trying by middle school because it's better to be considered lazy (or not care) than dumb.

Dweck (1999) found that children (and adults) tend to be either entity theorists about intelligence and achievement or incrementalists. Entity theorists believe that intelligence is a thing—an entity that is fixed and responsible for any success. Conversely, having low intelligence results in poor academic performance.

Entity theorists take every assignment, every test, every task as an evaluation of their innate ability in a direct, causative way. These students form what Dweck calls a "performance goal orientation" toward academic work. Low performance (errors) indicates low ability. High performance indicates high ability. "I only like to do the things I already do well," says a girl who is an entity theorist. Incrementalists believe that ability is built incrementally through effort and use of feedback from the environment. They form a "learning goal orientation," according to Dweck, where their goal is to learn something new rather than to prove themselves able, as is the goal of an entity theorist.

The consequences of these two internal theories of intelligence and the goal orientations that go with them are huge. Imagine the pressure a student feels who is constantly on trial, who experiences every academic challenge as a measure of self on a dimension so highly prized in our society: intelligence. Not all students (or adults) are at the poles of the entity versus incrementalist continuum, but large numbers are. The closer students are to the entity pole, the harder it is to mobilize energy and strategies when experiencing difficulty. Instead, they tend to interpret difficulty as a measure of limited ability and frequently give up. The closer a student is to the incrementalist pole, the more likely he or she is to treat difficulty and errors as data saying that working harder or working smarter (different strategies) is what is needed in order to overcome the difficulty.

Videos: Attribution Theory (1, 2, & 3)

This is why an examination of standards and expectations is so central to the work of teachers. The standards of performance teachers set, and the beliefs they hold about a child's capacity to meet those standards play a vital role in the messages sent to students and ultimately in what students are likely to achieve. So just how do these come together and play out in our classrooms? Let's now examine how we might be influenced by our own attributions about students.

Are the standards (or level of proficiency) targeted for students appropriately rigorous (challenging but attainable)? How strong is your conviction that all students have the capacity to achieve them? We could place each of these constructs (standards and expectations) along intersecting continua (see Figure 14.6) with the x-axis representing a continuum of low to high standards and the y-axis representing a continuum of low to high expectations. The standards a teacher sets and the expectations a teacher holds about each student's capacity to meet or achieve those standards could be anywhere along those continua.

Figuring out where standards of performance should be set requires some knowledge of age-appropriate norms for students, clear proficiency targets in state frameworks, and some specialized knowledge of the class composition order to make valid judgments. Using these as guidelines, we need to strive to make the standards appropriately challenging but attainable for all students.

Figure 14.6 Standards and Expectations

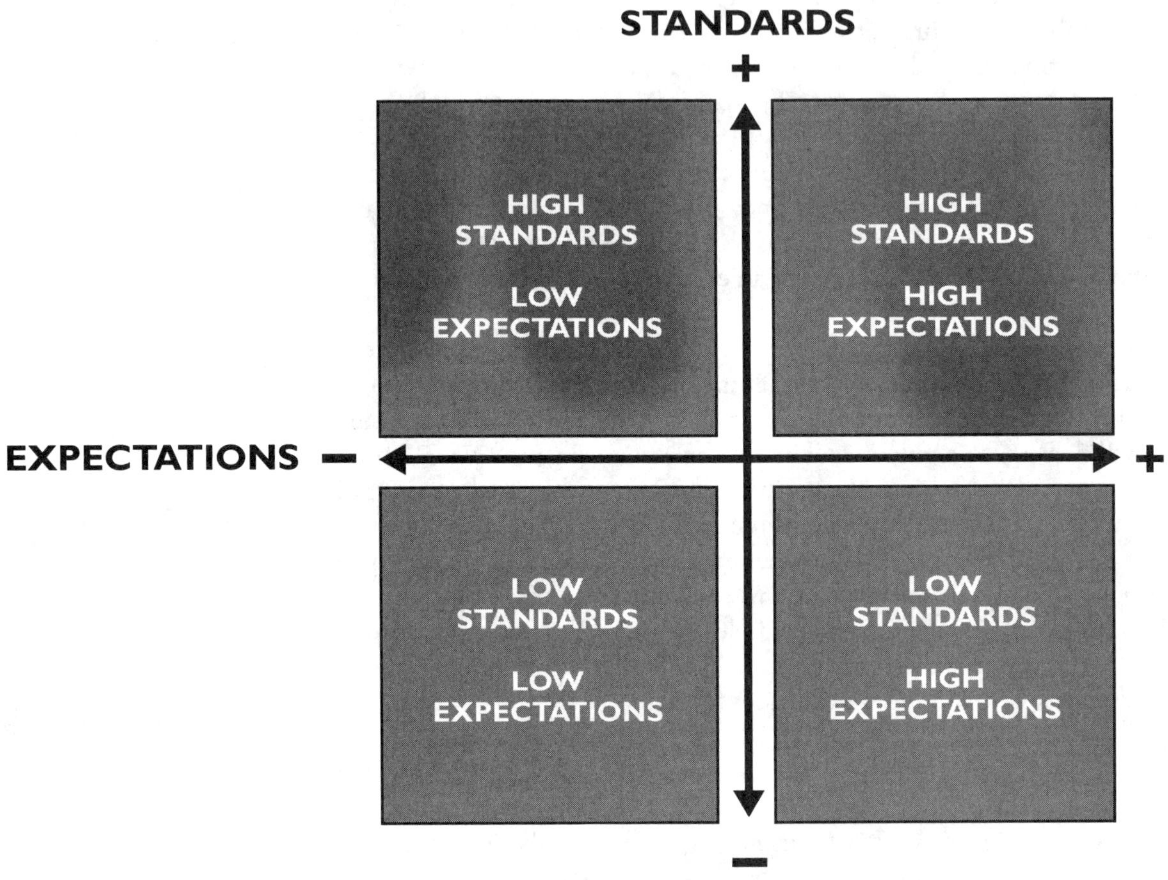

The relative rigor of the standards and the degree of conviction we have about the capacity of our students to achieve them will have an impact on how we behave and the messages we send to our students. It is possible, then, to create several different kinds of scenarios that might be played out in a classroom:

- ▲ **High standards, low expectations:** The teacher sets high standards of performance but does not believe or expect that all children can or will achieve them. A teacher with this mindset might say: "I set tough standards in this course. There's a certain amount of work to be done, and I expect everyone to do it. No excuses. Some will cut it; some won't. Some just don't have it—or have the drive—and will fall by the wayside. That's just the way it is."

- ▲ **Low standards, low expectations:** This plays out when a teacher has little conviction that students have the ability to achieve much and consequently sets low standards of performance. A teacher who holds this mindset might say: "I don't ask much of these kids. School just isn't the place for them. They are borderline dropouts. They are going to end up in hourly wage jobs. They don't see the relevance of this course to anything they will do one day. I just want to get through the semester with them without a hassle. At least they are coming to class. I'll do some things to make it fun, and if they behave reasonably, they'll pass the course."

- ▲ **Low standards, high expectations:** This describes a teacher whose actions are based on little conviction that students are capable of meeting high standards but wants students to feel good about themselves. So, he sets low standards of performance and celebrates students' meeting them. A teacher who has this mindset might inflate student grades based on the amount of effort the student has invested rather than on what he or she has achieved. This can create a negative enabling situation: giving A's for mediocre performance with the delusion that the good grade will build student confidence.

- ▲ **High standards, high expectations:** This teacher sets high standards of performance, believes all students have the innate ability to achieve them, behaves in kind, and is determined to do everything in her power to help students get there. "I understand that kids in here have different degrees and kinds of developed abilities and speeds of learning. I know some of them have more background for getting this material, and maybe they're just quicker. But I also know what a quality performance is like from a student, and I know what it means to really know this subject. I press them all toward that standard of excellence. I make special provisions for the students who are behind to try to bring them along as far and as fast as they can go. I provide extra boosts and help those who need it, and I know they'll still move along at different rates and with different degrees of success. But the standard is there, and I differentiate instruction to match their needs, scaffold learning experiences to support incremental progress, and push them all toward ever closer approximations of success. If they don't get there yet, at least they learn about excellence and get rewarded mightily for their incremental steps toward it."

Many states have frameworks that provide overall proficiency targets that students should reach at end-of-grade level or end-of-course. In this sense, the standards are externally set. The goal is to get all students to proficiency with these standards. But what about students who are way behind? We have to strike the correct balance of push and pace, accelerate the learning of students who are behind, and set standards of performance for them to reach each quarter or each year that put them on pace for proficiency at a targeted time in the future. The standard of performance we are talking about is one that represents an appropriate stretch, so that all the students who are behind can catch up to age-appropriate proficiency, and all the students already on pace can be stretched or deepened in appropriate ways.

Beliefs influence our perceptions of individual students and how we behave—and what students achieve.

The bottom line is that our beliefs influence our perceptions of individual students, and those perceptions influence how we behave—and ultimately what students achieve. We must consider how our perceptions about each student's capacity to achieve are influencing the standards of performance we set and the ways in which we behave daily. We communicate our impressions to students about their academic ability and capacity to achieve by subtle and indirect messages that students read and that influence their academic performance. Therefore, it is incumbent on all of us to take a step back and examine the mindset we hold about innate ability and the limits or liberties we bring to students' learning as a result. We explore the importance of beliefs in Chapter 3, "Essential Beliefs: Schooling," and in Chapter 4, "Essential Beliefs: Cultural Proficiency and Anti-Racism."

What else might we see in classrooms where all students are perceived as capable of achieving high standards of performance? What would we be doing if we believed the effort-based incrementalist theory, the Growth Mindset, and acted out of that orientation?

High Standards—High Expectations

Commitment to the incrementalist belief can show up in teachers' behavior, classroom practices, school structures, and even conversations with one another. Teachers set standards of performance they believe to be rigorous, important, and appropriate. They know where each student is in relation to those standards and adapt instruction to accommodate student differences in readiness levels (current knowledge or skills), learning and processing styles, and motivation. They don't pull back, give up, or dilute expectations and academic press for any of them. In other words, they differentiate their instruction (see Chapter 20, "Differentiated Instruction").

These teachers send positive expectation messages to all children regardless of their race, wealth, learning, or language differences. They seize every opportunity in regularly recurring classroom situations to reinforce the messages children get that their teacher believes they can do it and won't give up on them. Teaching policies and practices are conscientiously geared toward instilling in children life-liberating beliefs about themselves. These teachers teach students and families about attribution theory and make effective effort an explicit agenda to combat fixed mindsets. They don't expect all students to learn at the same rate or meet standards at the same time, especially when there are wide differences in their prior preparation. But these teachers take it as their responsibility to constantly examine and manage their own potential biases of seeing current student performance through the lens of innate ability. They teach children to believe in themselves and explicitly teach them how to work not just harder but smarter with appropriate strategies. Every teacher can create the conditions where children want to put forth the necessary effort, and this should be an integral part of all our work. Some of what this commitment looks like at the school or district level is the focus of the excellent book *Whatever It Takes* (DuFour, Eaker, Karhanek, & DuFour, 2004).

Three Critical Messages

Getting Students to Believe: "This Is Important, You Can Do It, and I'm Not Going to Give Up on You."

Video: You Can Do It

It will help to share current research with your students and teach them about brain plasticity, as Carol Dweck (2007) recommends, but that will not be enough for many students. This is because most of them have accepted the message of the bell curve that "ability" is fixed for math, ELA, sports, public speaking, and the list goes on. Sending high expectation messages like: "This is important, every single one of you can do it with effective effort by working hard and acquiring strategies, and I won't give up on you" and convincing students that they have the capacity to achieve at high levels (attribution retraining) is a moment-by-moment, everyday mission for a teacher. The messages can (and must) be woven into the fabric of everything that transpires in class.

Videos: Growth Mindset Explained, Growth Mindset MoJo 1–5

We acknowledge the influence of the many social factors (beyond our immediate control) on far too many children. But the one area we can do the most about is the messaging and positive support, both emotionally and through instruction, in the environments we do control—the classroom and the school. The power of these environments has been demonstrated again and again.

The point we want to make here is that students who are on the low end of the achievement gap—usually children of color and often also of poverty—have been getting messages about their "ability" all their lives and have experienced being behind academically so long that many have bought that story. How could they not? So if we are to eliminate the achievement gap, we have to change these students' minds about their ability and persuade them about the possibility of becoming good students.

Strand 3 develops that premise by examining 10 arenas of classroom life that are vital in our efforts to build student confidence and convince them we believe in them. Without focused attention to these arenas of everyday interaction, there is little chance of getting discouraged, uninvested students to invest their effort in school.

STRAND 3: THE BEHAVIORS

High Expectations Teaching: Ten Arenas of Classroom Life

What opportunities can we seize daily to convince students that "Smart is something you can get" and build their confidence and conviction that they can achieve proficiency? An arena is a place, structure, setting, or interaction in which regularly recurring events happen and can be observed. The arenas listed below in Table 14.1 represent opportunities for a teacher to communicate behaviorally to students what is important, and that he or she believes they have the capacity to achieve it. Reflecting on these arenas and our practices within each one affords us the opportunity to consciously align some of the most subtle behaviors and practices with sending powerful and positive high-expectation messages to all students.

Table 14.1 Ten Arenas for Communicating High Expectations

1. Calling on Students
2. Responding to Student Answers (including when students don't answer)
3. Giving Help
4. Changing Attitudes Toward Errors
5. Giving and Negotiating Tasks and Assignments
6. Feedback According to Criteria for Success: • Unmet expectations • Students doing well • Significant change in performance
7. Framing Reteaching
8. Tenacity When Students Don't Meet Expectations
9. Grading
10. Grouping

Arena 1: Calling on Students

The notion that teachers communicate their impressions to students about their academic ability by subtle and indirect messages is not new. In a landmark study, Rosenthal and Jacobson (1968) called attention to ways in which teacher perceptions of student ability result in differential treatment of students and have a positive or negative impact on their inclusion in classroom discourse and ultimately their performance in the classroom. Teachers were given falsified records of students' IQ scores: high-performing students might be represented as having high, average, or low IQs and low performers as having high, average, or low IQs. And that information, rather than the students' actual IQs, influenced how teachers dealt with their students and, most importantly, how the students achieved. Cooper (1979) later organized these differential teacher communication behaviors into five categories:

1. **Climate:** "It was found that teachers who believed they were interacting with bright students smiled and nodded their heads more often than teachers interacting with slow students. Teachers also leaned towards bright students and looked brights in the eyes more frequently" (p. 393).

2. **Demands:** "Students labeled as slow have been found to have fewer opportunities to learn new material than students labeled as bright" (p. 393).

3. **Persistence:** "Teachers tend to stay with the highs longer after they have failed to answer a question. This persistence following failure takes the form of more clue giving, more repetition, and/or more rephrasing. Teachers have been found to pay closer attention to responses of students described as gifted. Teachers allowed bright students longer to respond before redirecting unanswered questions" (p. 394).

4. **Frequency of interaction:** "Teachers more often engage in academic contact with the high- than low-expectation students" (p. 394).

5. **Feedback:** "Teachers tend to praise high-expectation students more and proportionately more per correct response, while lows are criticized more and proportionately more per incorrect response" (p. 395).

Video: Praise the Process

There are 12 distinct behavioral items in these five categories, and they provide empirical evidence that teacher perceptions of a student's ability can lead to classifying students as "brights" and "slows" and to acting differently toward them, thus creating self-fulfilling prophecies. Table 14.2 is a list of related questions you might investigate as you examine and reflect on your own practice.

Table 14.2 Pygmalion in the Classroom

How often do I do the following?	Never	Rarely	Sometimes	Very Often	Always
Smile and nod more toward "highs"?					
Lean more toward "brights"?					
Look "brights" more in the eyes?					
Give "slows" fewer opportunities to learn new material?					
Stay with "highs" longer after they have failed to answer a question?					
Give "highs" more clues when they fail to get an answer—more repetition or more rephrasing?					
Pay closer attention to the responses of "the gifted"?					
Allow "brights" longer to respond?					
Have more frequent academic contact with "highs"?					
Give "highs" more praise per correct response?					
Give "lows" more criticism per incorrect response?					
Do any of the above more with girls than with boys, or vice versa?					

Calling on students is a way of inviting them to participate in classroom discourse and to signal that their voice, thoughts, opinions, concerns, and questions are important. So in this arena we ask ourselves these important nine questions:

1. Who gets called on?
2. How do they get called on? By whom? Randomly? Systematically? Hand raising?
3. How do I ensure that everyone is included?
4. How frequently do individual students get called on?

5. What do I do if students don't volunteer to participate?

6. What are students called on to do?

7. What level of thinking is called for in the question?

8. Do I insert sufficient wait time (minimum of 3 to 5 seconds) after posing a question or a prompt before calling on anyone, so all students have an opportunity to process the question and construct an answer?

9. What do I do to ensure that all students can participate effectively?

Video: Pygmalion Effects

In addition, we might arrange for peer observation and feedback, as did Sam Kerman's program "TESA: Teacher Expectation, Student Achievement" (Kerman, Kimball, & Martin, 1980) for the behaviors we have listed under "Pygmalion in the Classroom" in Table 14.2. The bottom line here is to examine the extent to which there is some sort of equal opportunity for all students. Whether it is answering questions, participating in a discussion, surfacing prior knowledge, or some other purpose for student participation, all students must get the message that their input is important, that they are capable of higher-level thinking, and that their teacher believes they have important things to offer and will ensure that their voice is represented and heard.

Given that perceptions can have a powerful influence on behavior, we ask you to consider the possibility that all children have the capacity to do rigorous work to high standards and to act as if that were so to suspend disbelief and invest energy in searching for ways to create the conditions in which this would become a reality for all students. It is our contention that if we behave as if we can reach every child and we continue to strive to create the conditions that are optimal for their learning, we will see more miracles than we could have imagined and see more students reach proficiency than ever before.

Arena 2: Responding to Students' Answers

Another arena through which expectations are communicated is what teachers do right after a student has responded or spoken in class. This is a powerful arena, where the teacher's actions have embedded messages about what's important and about his or her belief in the student's capacity. Art Costa, professor emeritus at California State University, Sacramento, has pointed out that the way teachers respond to student answers may be more important than the questions themselves. These are moments that happen hundreds of times a day, and what we say and do at these moments can influence the way students participate in lessons from that point on. Our responses to student com-

Table 14.3 Responding to Students' Answers

Response	Sounds like
Criticize	"That's not even close. Come on, wake up!"
Give the correct answer	"No, it's pi r^2."
Redirect to another student after the first student's answer	"Judy, can you tell us?"
Redirect to get more, build, and extend	"Okay. You're on the right track. Judy, would you add anything to that?"
"Wrong" with the reason	"Not quite, because you left out the exponent." Then the teacher waits while the student tries again.
Supply the question for which the answer is right, cue, or hold accountable	"That would be right if I asked for the formula for the circumference. Now do you remember anything about the use of exponents in that formula? [Now the student gets it right.] Right! And I bet you'll remember that after lunch if I check you too. I'll ask you then, and I bet you'll get it!"
Wait time	Silence.
Follow up question to double check or extend	"Can you tell me how you were thinking about that?"
Acknowledge	"Umhmmm."
Restate in fuller language	"Okay. So, you get the area by multiplying pi times the radius of the circle squared."
Ask the student to elaborate	"Can you tell me more about what you meant by that?"
Praise	"Way to go!"

ments or answers signal to individuals—and cumulatively to the whole class—whether it is safe to speak out, whether a student can risk trying something that's hard, and whether the climate is supportive of thinking and effort or punitive for not having the right answer. Consider how a teacher might respond to students answering the question, "How do you find the area of a circle?" Let's look at the examples in Table 14.3.

Depending on how the teacher responds, a student may internalize one or more of the following messages:

▲ "I'm dumb."

▲ "Well, I muffed that one!"

- "My job is to guess the answer in the teacher's head, and say it in precisely the way he's thinking it."
- "I muffed that one, and I should get back in gear. I know this stuff."
- "The teacher thinks I can think this one through and get it."
- "What I said was worthwhile, but there's more."
- "My teacher really listens to what I say."
- "My teacher really wants to know what I mean. There must be something worthwhile in what I said."
- "My idea wasn't as good as that one. Boy, I'm glad I didn't get called on."
- "Wow, I guess I did pretty well on that one."
- "It's not safe to risk an answer here unless you're really sure."
- "It is safe to risk an answer in here. If I don't get it, I won't be put down."
- "I can say what I think and be respected and accepted for that."
- "If I can't get it, I'll be helped to remember or figure it out."

It is likely all of us have received these messages at one time or another in our experience as students. Clearly, the effects can be powerful. What the teacher does or says after a student responds in class can engage students and open their thinking or close them down; can make them feel more confident, curious, encouraged to participate, or afraid, timid, protective, quiet, and defensive. Simultaneously, the effect is either to stimulate students to search, scan, wonder about, reflect, think, try to get it right, shine, impress, and win (or protect themselves from getting wounded).

These responses form a repertoire (see Table 14.4). No one of them is inherently best, most appropriate, or most effective. Readers could create the context in which each of them, even criticizing (but not put-downs), could be appropriate. Matching is the name of the game. Several of them, however, are particularly effective for specific purposes and should be considered for inclusion into any teacher's repertoire. *Wait Time* (or silence) is one such behavior.

Table 14.4 Teacher Responses to Student Answers

Ways of moving on to another student	• Criticizes: "Come on. That answer shows no thought at all." • "No" and redirects to another student. • "No" then gives the correct answer. • "No" with the reason, which may serve as a cue. • Moves to another student if the first student doesn't answer. • Redirect to another student to add, build, or extend. "Would you add anything to that, Zach?" • Student authorized to call on another student to answer in his or her place.
Ways of sticking with a student	• Supplying the question for which the answer is right, cuing, and holding the student accountable. • "No, but it's good you brought it up because others probably thought that too." • "Try again." • Validate what is right or good about an answer and then cue, sticking with the student. • Ignore the answer and cue the student. • Wait time II. • Follow up with an expression of confidence or encouragement: "I think you know." • Ask the student to elaborate. • Call for a self-evaluation of the answer. • Follow up with an expression of confidence or extend. • Ask the student to elaborate. • Call for a self-evaluation of the answer. • Follow-up question to clarify: "Are you saying that . . . ?"
Ways of acknowledging, affirming	• "Um-hmmm." • Repeat the student's answer. • Restate the answer in fuller or more precise language. • "Right." • "Right" with the reason. • Praise or praise and extend.

In the late 1960s, Mary Budd Rowe (1987) discovered that if teachers purposefully paused and waited a minimum of 3 seconds or more after asking a question, many students who ordinarily did not answer did so, answers tended to be full sentences rather than single words or phrases, and the answers were at a higher level of thinking. Rowe also discovered most teachers wait on average less than a half-second after asking a question before jumping in with cuing, redirecting, telling the answer, or restating the question. Her research continued for almost 20 years with similar findings. Waiting 3 to 5 seconds after posing a question is referred to as *Wait Time I.*

Figure 14.7 Wait Time

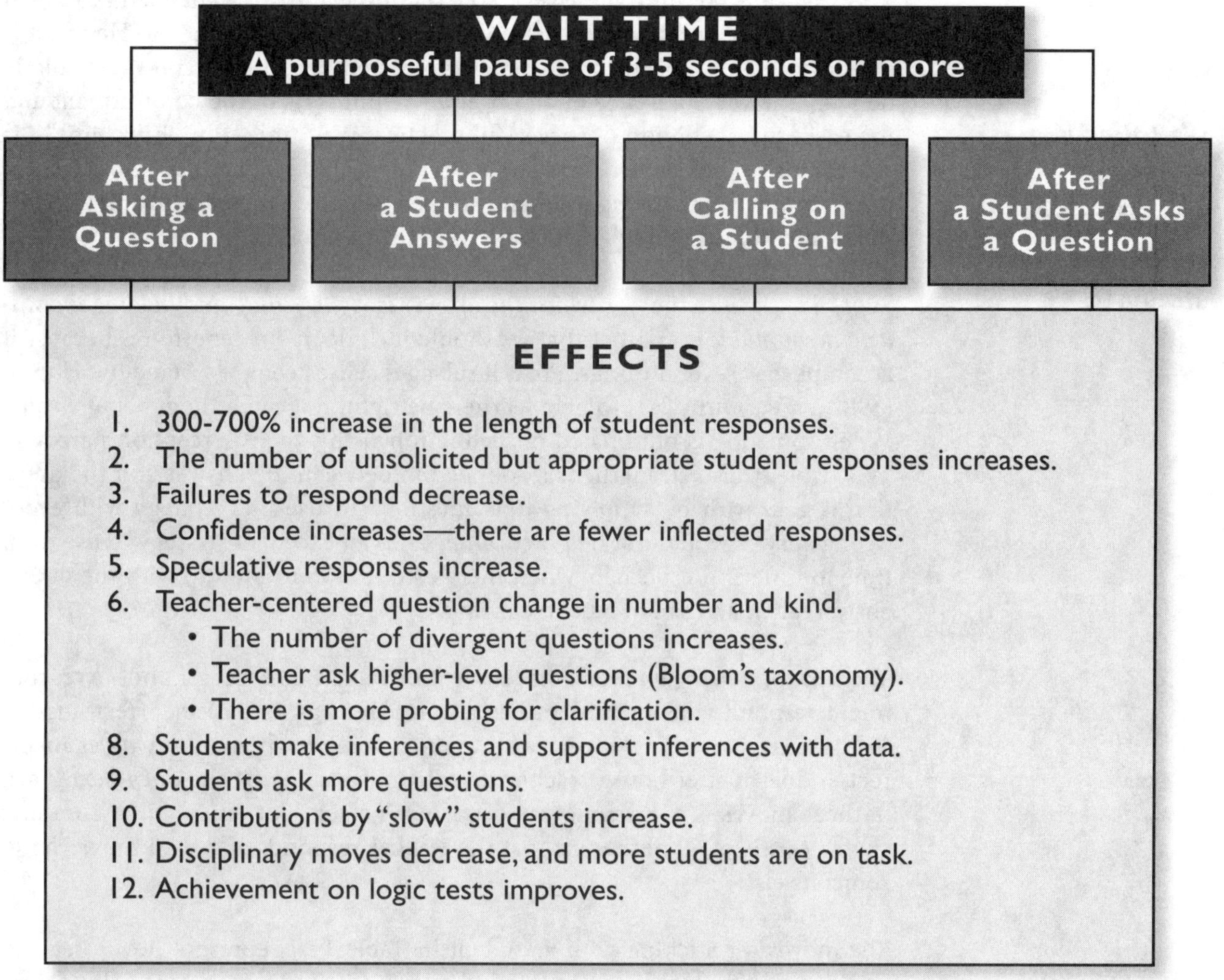

Waiting after a student has responded is called *Wait Time II*. This response behavior achieves similar desirable outcomes to Wait Time I. Teachers tend to increase the cognitive level of their questions, and students increase the cognitive level of their answers, speak in more complete and more elaborate sentences, exhibit less tentativeness in their responses, and are more likely to start responding to each other and to comment on each other's answers (Figure 14.7).

While the idea of pausing for at least 3 to 5 seconds after posing a question or responding to a student answer appears to be simple and straightforward, most who have experimented with it will agree that it is initially uncomfortable

Wait time is a behavior we believe teachers should teach to students.

and easy to forget to do. We are so used to filling silences with talk that unless we specifically commit ourselves to try wait time and get someone in to watch us trying it, we will likely fail to internalize this valuable behavior. Hence, it is a behavior where coaching or some form of peer feedback can be particularly helpful. The very presence of an observer reminds us of the commitment and increases the likelihood of successful practice. Wait time—or "think time"—is a behavior we believe teachers should teach to students so they know what it means and why it is being used and so they can be comfortable using it themselves and honoring it when it happens in the classroom.

Supplying the question for which the answer is right, cuing, and holding the student accountable is another that we should include in our repertoires because it accomplishes several things. First, it salvages self-esteem. As Madeline Hunter (1982) says, "Our job is to help learners be right, not catch them being wrong. When someone is humiliated or feeling unworthy, their perception narrows." This strategy also strengthens a connection between the answer and the question it goes with by supplying that question. To use this strategy with every wrong answer would not be practical, but it is an excellent strategy to use from time to time and especially when there's a question to link up with the wrong answer, often an item of recent learning.

The *ways of moving on to another student* in Table 14.4 represent how a teacher might respond when a student has an (apparent or actual) incorrect answer. While there is nothing wrong with making it clear when an answer is incorrect, it does matter how a teacher says it, and what he or she does next. Each of those moves is a different way of saying "no" or "not quite," but a common characteristic of all of them is that the teacher responds and then moves on to someone else.

The moves for sticking with a student in Table 14.4 represent how a teacher might stay with a student. Teachers who stick with students—especially if their initial response is seemingly incorrect—send messages that they have confidence in their students' ability to think through to an appropriate response. Giving a student a cue and lingering sends quite a different message from saying no and immediately calling on another student. Cuing the student but then calling immediately on another says the teacher doesn't really think the student has the capacity to use the cue. Whereas any response from this continuum might be effective in a given situation, the main point is that teachers who convey positive expectations and build confidence and risk-taking in students practice many moves from the middle of the continuum.

Sometimes teachers in our workshops ask how an instructor has enough time to do such sticking and cuing with students and still get through all the material they wish to. The fact is that it takes hardly any more time at all to do so —seconds more at most. Sticking with a student does not need to slow the rate of coverage (though for other reasons, such slowing down might be a very good idea). But consider the cost of not sticking with students who don't answer or answer incorrectly the first time. The individual student can easily feel inept at a moment like this and shut down cognitively. Also, by not sticking with the student, the teacher forfeits the chance to support a student's thinking and explicitly build confidence in his or her capacity to perform with academic material. Every long wait or period of silence when a student feels intimidated or unsure about a question is an opportunity to build confidence and capacity. Finally, it is not only the single response to an individual student that matters, but also the pattern of responses over time that signals what the teacher thinks is important.

There are other responses as well to student answers.

- ▲ ***Asking a follow-up question*** to double-check or extend (called a probe in research literature) is a way of checking to see if the student really understands the meaning of an answer or is just parroting. For example, a student might be able to recite "pi r^2" without knowing that *r* stands for the radius of the circle. So a follow-up question might be, "And the *r* stands for . . . ?"

- ▲ ***Asking students to elaborate*** on their responses helps the teacher know what they really meant: "Could you explain that further?" "I'm not sure what you meant by that, Jerry. Can you say a little more?" "You need to be more specific, Jane. How far exactly are you saying the fulcrum has to be from this end?"

- ▲ ***Acknowledging a student's answer nonjudgmentally*** leaves the door open for further comment from other students or for adding to the original answer by the same student. ("So one possible explanation is . . . Thank you. What might be some others?")

- ▲ ***Restating in fuller language*** is a move a teacher might do for the benefit of the other students—to make sure they understood what the answer meant. Teacher asks, "Why do you suppose we celebrate Lincoln's birthday but not all presidents' birthdays?" Student says, "He freed the slaves." Teacher says, "So you are thinking that he did something really important and that's how we decide whose birthdays to celebrate?"

- ▲ ***Giving Praise*** can be an effective response to a student answer, but only if used well (Dweck, 2002; Henderlong & Lepper, 2002). Brophy's (1981) definitive review of the research on praise summarized how to praise well.

To be effective, teacher praise must be:

- ***Specific.*** It specifies exactly what is praiseworthy about the student's performance: "John, I'm impressed with the variety of verbs and sentence patterns you used in this composition. This is your best work so far."

- ***Contingent.*** The praise is dependent on successful student performance and not given randomly or for encouragement. Noncontingent praise (given randomly and sometimes for incorrect answers) is frequent and found most often among teachers who have low expectations for student learning.

  > Within any given class, it is most likely to be directed toward the lowest achievers. No doubt such praise is given in an attempt to encourage the student. However, it seems likely that to the extent that the students recognize what the teacher is doing, the result will be embarrassment, discouragement, and other undesirable outcomes. (Brophy, 1981, p. 13)

- ***Genuine.*** The teacher means it. The praise is not manipulative, or given to reinforce (that is, engineer) a specific behavior, but it reflects real appreciation on the teacher's part.

- ***Congruent.*** Gesture, tone of voice, stance, and posture send the same message as the words. If the teacher leans back, looks away, and says in a bored tone of voice, "I can see you really worked hard on these problems, Freddy," Freddy is not likely to be convinced.

- ***Appropriate.*** The choice of words, setting, and style is matched to the particular student. Public praise to individual middle school students can embarrass them. Public praise for certain behaviors can make them want to crawl under the table: "Oh, John, your handwriting is so tidy and neat" (said to a macho eighth grader).

Brophy (1981) also points out that effective praise:

▲ Uses students' own prior accomplishments as the context for describing present accomplishments.

▲ Is given in recognition of noteworthy effort or success at difficult (for this student) tasks.

- ▲ Attributes success to effort and ability, implying that similar successes can be expected in the future.

- ▲ Fosters endogenous attributions (students believe that they expend effort on the task because they enjoy the task and/or want to develop task-relevant skills).

Each of the behaviors just described—wait time, supplying the question for which the answer is right, cuing, holding the student accountable, follow-up questions, asking students to elaborate, acknowledgment, restating in fuller language, and praise—has research to support it as an effective teacher behavior (Costa, 1985; Dunkin & Biddle, 1974). There is similar support for "redirecting" in the literature, and even a case for the appropriateness of criticism with certain students as long as the criticism is not a put-down (Graham, 1985). These findings have been reinforced by subsequent research (Dweck, 2002; Henderlong & Lepper, 2002).

Since many of these response techniques are inherently worthwhile in and of themselves for stimulating thinking and attaining clarity, they are worth adding to all teachers' repertoires. And it is a good bet that among the list cited, there are several new ones for any teacher. (Least frequently seen, in our observations, are wait time, asking students to elaborate, and effective praise.) But beyond incorporating them into one's repertoire is the issue of matching. Are the response techniques being used appropriately in the right situation and with the right students? Wait time, for example, is less appropriate when asking low-level questions or doing drills. Giving students time to think and process is most effective when higher-level thinking is called for. Redirecting prematurely can deny a student the opportunity to think through an answer or refine one already given. Restating in fuller language can aid the understanding of the rest of the class, but if done unnecessarily or to excess can teach students not to listen to one another. The bottom line here, as elsewhere in the quest to develop skillful teaching, is to work first to expand repertoires to respond more appropriately to more students in different situations, then improve the effectiveness of matching, and finally, skew responses to the middle part of the repertoire so as to take every opportunity to build confidence and capacity in students.

When Students Don't Answer

Sometimes students are called on and don't answer or don't have a ready answer, and there is that loaded second or two in which we must make a decision: Do we get embarrassed for the student and want to get the spotlight off that child? Do we stick with the student, giving cues? Do we ask the question over again? Do we redirect the question to another student?

Table 14.5 Responses to Use When Students Don't Answer

1. Wait time I
2. Repeat the question
3. Cue
4. Ask a simpler question
5. Ask a fact-only question
6. Give choices for the answer
7. Ask for a yes-or-no response
8. Ask the student to repeat or imitate an answer
9. Ask for a nonverbal response (shaking the head or pointing)
10. Instruct the student to say, "I need more time to think," or "I don't know yet. Please come back to me."

Adapted from Good & Brophy (2000)

There is a progressive continuum of responses (Table 14.5) we might employ to keep students open and thinking when they don't answer. The benefits of wait time have been described earlier. Simply enduring a little silence while Caitlin grimaces may give her the time she needs to come up with the answer. Modeling this behavior—taking time to think after a student has posed a question—can have a powerful influence too.

Once, we attended a session where David Perkins, co-director of Project Zero at Harvard University, was asked a question. He turned his head, looked sideways, then up at the ceiling, and continued in silence for a full 10 seconds. By this time, I was getting nervous for David as a presenter and looking for something to say, some way to jump in and rescue him from what seemed like a paralytic attack. But just at that moment, David looked the questioner calmly in the eye and delivered a brilliant reply, paragraphs long, with no wasted words. He didn't appear in the least ruffled. He had simply been comfortably thinking out his answer. It was I who had been uncomfortable with the pause, not Perkins! Several other times in that session, similar pauses for reflection followed complicated questions from the audience. After the first time, I was not worried about David anymore and spent the time thinking about the question too. In fact, Perkins's modeling of wait time for himself to think through an answer had an immediate effect on the class. The whole discussion became more reflective and thoughtful. And by having our instructor model his willingness to think before he spoke, we became more comfortable doing so. The result was to elevate the level of the entire discussion.

Turning to the other behaviors on the continuum, we see a progression where less and less is required of the student, until finally only imitation or head shaking is requested. This continuum was adapted from Good and Brophy (2000) for nonresponsive students. Their point is that students should not be allowed to practice nonresponsiveness, instead they should be expected to participate.

> As long as they appear to be trying to answer the question, the teacher should wait them out. If they begin to look anxious, as if worrying about being in the spotlight instead of thinking about the question, the teacher should intervene by repeating the question or giving a clue. He or she should not call on another student or allow others to call out the answer. (Good & Brophy, 2000, pp. 192–193)

Arena 3: Giving Help

Another arena of significance occurs when teachers give students help. This occurs in two ways: (1) students ask for help, or (2) students don't ask for help but the teacher gives it anyway (unsolicited help).

Student Asks for Help

Giving help happens dozens of times a day. Read the following two scripts. In one, the teacher conveys positive expectations for the student. In the other, the teacher conveys negative expectations (Good & Brophy, 2000, pp. 229–230).

Example 1: Positive Expectations

Student: "I can't do number 4."

Teacher: "What part don't you understand?"

Student: "I just can't do it."

Teacher: "Well, I know you can do part of it, because you've done the first three problems correctly. The fourth problem is similar but just a little harder. You start out the same, but then you have to do one extra step. Review the first three problems, and then start number 4 again and see if you can figure it out. I'll come by your desk in a few minutes to see how you're doing."

Example 2: Negative Expectations

Student: "I can't do number 4."

Teacher: "You can't? Why not?"

Student: "I just can't do it."

Teacher: "Don't say you can't do it. We never say we can't do it. Did you try hard?"

Student: "Yes, but I can't do it."

Teacher: "Well, you did the first three problems. Maybe if you went back and worked a little longer you could do the fourth problem too. Why don't you work at it a little more and see what happens?"

An analysis of word choice and phrases in each of these dialogues illustrates how powerful a brief exchange between teacher and student can be in sending positive or negative expectations messages. In the first script, the teacher's first question—"What part don't you understand?"—credits the student with understanding most parts and asks him or her to zero in on the stumbling block. When the student stalls, the teacher explicitly expresses confidence in the student's capacity: "Well, I know you can do part of it, because you've done the first three problems correctly." Then, the teacher goes on to give explicit coaching help and promises to return in a few minutes "to see how you're doing." The teacher will help but believes the student can do it. Nevertheless, the student won't be left hanging. The teacher will return as a safety net if there is still difficulty.

In the second script, the teacher asks, "Why not?" when the student says, "I can't do number 4." That's a "gotcha" question. If the student knows why she can't do it, she would be able to move forward and ask for more specific help. The teacher then responds to, "I just can't do it," with an injunction, "Don't say you can't do it," and a bit of moralizing: "We never say we can't do it." The teacher may mean that as an encouraging gesture, but whatever hope there is of being encouraging gets crushed by the no-win question: "Did you try hard?" If the student has already been trying hard, only one conclusion is possible: "I must be dumb." And if the student hasn't been trying hard, then she or he must admit sloth. The implication, though without much hope, is that maybe longer and harder will somehow put the student over the top. But the teacher gives no specific strategic help. "See what happens" is the parting shot, and the student is left feeling that not much more will happen.

The point of studying these two scripts is to increase awareness of word choice and approach when students ask for help. With only subtle changes in what we actually say, we can convey confidence, point out how students can use what they already know, give strategies or cues as help, and check back at appropriate intervals, or we can moralize, simplify or dumb down the task, suggest inadequacies, hint blame, and convey (sometimes masked behind polite words) that we really don't think the student is capable of doing the task. One outcome we desire for readers of this section is that you will find yourselves carrying a third eye and ear into your own classrooms. The third eye and ear are your own! And it is monitoring and giving you feedback as you speak when you are asked for help. What messages are you conveying as you interact with students to give help?

Videos: Confidence Building, Tenacity, Allow Struggle

Unsolicited Help

Graham and Barker (1990) and Zimmerman and Marinez-Pons (1990) found that when teachers give unsolicited help, students often conclude their teachers think the students are not able and need support. As a result, some will begin acting as if to confirm this belief. Another side effect of premature unsolicited help is that students learn not to struggle, that struggle is bad, that struggle means they are unable—which is exactly the way entity theorists plunge deeper into a subtractive belief system.

This is tricky, because teachers want to be available to the students who need the most support. In fact, we want to arrange our time and other resources to deploy them efficiently to support students who do need extra help. How do we do so without inadvertently sending debilitating expectation messages? We think the answer lies in the subtleties of word choice and body language, as in these examples illustrate:

▲ Instead of going right over to Brian on the first problem and saying, "Need help, Brian?" Mr. Flood works with another child near him and watches how Brian is doing.

▲ He is able to pick up early if Brian is struggling. "Trouble?" he says offhandedly while catching Brian's eye. "No," says the student. "Okay, a good scholar knows when to ask for help. So, struggle is good. But be strategic, and ask me or someone else if you hit a wall."

▲ "Trouble?" Mr. Flood says off-handedly as he catches Brian's eye. "Yeah," he says. "Okay. So, what part has you hung up?" "The whole thing." "Okay; now you can do this with a little coaching. What's the first step?"

Another recommendation is to make asking for help a rewarded behavior, used by "good students" or "scholars" in the culture of the classroom, when a student has used her own resources first. That way you won't have to give much unsolicited help. You can establish such a culture by teaching, practicing, and rewarding such behavior explicitly. It becomes part of the curriculum.

Videos: Persevere and Return, Mistakes Help Us Learn, My Favorite No

Arena 4: Changing Attitude Toward Errors—Persevere and Return

There are at least two ways in which any one of us can interpret errors or mistakes we make: as an indication of weakness or lack of ability or as an opportunity for learning and growth. If I believe errors are signs of weakness, I will avoid them at all costs. In fact, I will avoid topics and types of work where I think I may make errors so I don't have to face the "truth" about my low aptitude in that area. Also, I will get impatient with work that does not come easily or quickly because I will interpret the difficulty as a sign of my low ability. But if I interpret errors as feedback (data to be used to indicate gaps), I can fill or alternate approaches I must seek out; then I do not shy away from material I do not grasp quickly. This view requires an underlying belief in one's capacity to be able to understand the work ultimately by working at it and a belief that it's worth the effort.

Teachers have the opportunity every time they help students deal with error to help them interpret it as data to deal with rather than as a low-ability message—for example:

- ▲ "You can do this if you have the right strategy, Carl. So you must need a different strategy. Let's see, which ones have you tried, and which ones haven't you tried yet?"
- ▲ "You're able to understand stories when you have the right background knowledge, Julie. So there must be something the author is assuming about experiences you've had that isn't true. Let's see, what could it be? Show me one of the places you got confused."
- ▲ "Well, you do fine experiments when you understand what the task really is. So there must be something in the directions that didn't communicate. Take me through the lab setup, and show me where it's unclear."

Our intention here is to highlight the significance of students' attitude toward error and suggest how teachers might respond when errors occur so as to support the incrementalist view of intelligence and a learning-goal orientation. (In Chapter 16, "Classroom Climate," we examine how teachers build a climate for risk-taking and confidence so that students learn to treat errors as opportunities for learning.)

Arena 5: Giving and Negotiating Tasks and Assignments

In Chapter 11, "Clarity," we discuss many important aspects of giving assignments and tasks. These include ensuring that students know why they are doing the assignment (the purpose and objective), are clear about what to do (the directions), and know how their work will be evaluated (criteria for success). However, when we give students assignments we also convey messages about whether we think the task is hard or easy, whether we think students will struggle as individuals, whether we believe students will succeed, and whether we think success will depend on students' ability, effort, or luck. It is important to examine the messages we send students through the way we give assignments.

A teacher says to her sixth graders: "This weekend your assignment is to read the last three chapters of *Tituba* and be prepared to name the factors that you think contributed to a climate in Salem for the witch hysteria." So far that's pretty straightforward. The students may have some confusion about what "climate" or maybe even "factors" means in this context, but let's suppose the students know what's expected. No messages have been sent to individuals yet. How do they get communicated?

As the students go out the door, Ms. Hunt stops several of them for a private word:

- "Kaneisha, you should do really well on this. You've been reading carefully and taking good notes on each of the last two assignments. I think you're ready to put it all together."
- "John, how much time are you going to put in on this tonight?"
- "Marie, you're taking your book home, aren't you?" [Marie smiles and says, "Sure."] "Uh huh. Right!" [Ms. Hunt purses her lips.]
- "Do the best you can, George. At least read all three chapters."

Ms. Hunt has sent Kaneisha a high, positive-expectation message. She thinks Kaneisha is ready for a good performance that puts it all together. It's hard to tell what message she has sent to John. If John is a slacker and she has communicated before that she thinks he is, then John may interpret her question to mean, "I don't think you're going to really do this, John." And John may be inclined to conform with that preconception. But maybe she has had a series of conferences with John and done goal setting with him around planning his time use for homework. Perhaps, she is reminding him of the agreements he made and getting him to commit to a real number of minutes right now that she'll hold him accountable for the next day. Then the message is quite different from the slacker inference. It sounds as if

Ms. Hunt doubts Marie is going to take her book home. Her "Uh-huh. Right!" may give Marie license to skip the work—because her teacher expects her to. George is getting a low-expectation message. The teacher will be content if he at least plows his way through the words in the book, but she doesn't expect him to be able to think through the question. At best, George will plow but not likely think. The expectation is no higher than getting through the three chapters. The expectation is actually less, since the teacher has said, "At least try," which implies that he won't be able to do it but that "trying" a little is expected.

These examples illustrate how the choice of words combined with body language communicates inner beliefs (the confidence we have) about what students can do and about what they will do on a given assignment. In addition to individual comments at the door and elsewhere, teachers sometimes communicate to a whole class at once about an assignment. If Ms. Hunt says, "Now this will be hard; it requires thinking back to all the other chapters we read too. But I know you can do it if you take your time and use your notes from our previous discussions," she is sending a positive, high-expectation message to the whole class at once. Acknowledging the difficulty of the task validates students' exerting effort. It's not supposed to be easy. Calling a task easy is a no-win message. If it turns out to be easy, the student has no sense of accomplishment. Anyone could have done it. If children struggle and it was supposed to be easy, they may conclude they are stupid or not good enough at it, otherwise it would be easy.

In addition to verbal messages to individuals and whole-class groups, there are whole-class messages that may be embedded in written direction sheets to students about assignments: "This problem set is important and is a good chance to raise your grade. Use this opportunity well."

We hope readers will listen to themselves during these daily and repeated moments when they communicate assignments and tasks to students. And especially attend to the side comments they make to individuals right after giving the task and the directions. In addition, we urge readers to seize these opportunities to send deliberately positive and encouraging messages to individuals who may be low performing, have low motivation and low confidence: "Charlene, this is a good one for you to show your stuff on. Now come on, dig in tonight. You've got a great brain, and I want to see you use it as a leader in tomorrow's discussion!"

Arena 6: Giving Feedback According to Criteria for Success

Given the commitment we are focusing on here, namely to convince students that smart is something you can get, the manner, the precision, and the persistence with which we give feedback to low-confidence students is particularly important. We consider "capacity building responses" to be a refined and improved version of what is commonly called "feedback." Bellon and colleagues (1991) clearly state its critical importance: "Academic feedback is more strongly and consistently related to achievement than any other teaching behavior. This relationship is consistent regardless of grade, socioeconomic status, race, or school setting" (p. 277). Hattie concurs, "The most powerful single modification that enhances achievement is feedback. The simplest prescription for improving education must be dollops of feedback" (as cited in Ainsworth & Viegut, 2006, p. 89). These assertions are backed by a considerable body of research including a number of studies reporting the good effect-size that feedback systems can have on student performance. The ranges reported are between .5 and 1.8 (Black & Wiliam, 1998, 2004; Meisels, 2003; Rodriguez, 2005). An effect-size of 1 standard deviation translates into approximately 35 percentile points on a standardized test and 100 points on the SAT. So what exactly are teachers doing who get these effects? Skill at giving student feedback is a generic and foundational skill for successful teaching and deserves the intensive look that follows.

Video: Exemplars

Verbal Feedback to Students

Picture students working individually and in pairs, and their teacher walking around looking over their shoulders. There are many interactions that happen at times like this. A teacher may give a tip, ask a question, point out an error, stop and re-explain something a student appears not to know, give some praise. Usually, the starting point for the interaction is student work the teacher is looking at. Research on how to make these interactions have positive effects on student learning has been grouped into a category called "feedback." However, the term "feedback" is often defined quite differently.

Chappius (2014) says feedback occurs during learning and does not do the thinking for the student. She joins Hattie in saying it includes "guidance on how to proceed" (Hattie & Timperly, 2007) and suggestions where appropriate. Hattie (2012) further subdivides feedback into Task Feedback, Process Feedback, and Self-Regulation feedback. Black & Wiliam (1998) say feedback should be about particular qualities of a student's work, with advice on what the student can do to improve. Fisher and Frey (2012) recommend we use prompts and cues to guide students' thinking when we see shortcomings in their work. They also distinguish between responding to errors and to mistakes. A mistake is caused by failing to do or see something you could have done or seen. An error, on the other hand, is caused by lack of knowledge, a gap that needs to be filled. Wiggins (2012) defines feedback in a narrower way: it simply provides students with information about the gap between their current performance and one that meets the criteria for success. With all the good thinking by these authors about feedback, the multiple presumed definitions of the word without separation of functions gets confusing. We make the case here that feedback, guidance, advice, cuing, suggestions, challenges, prompts, and pointing out discrepancies are all different from one another and all useful when properly applied. What we are studying here is the skill of responding to student work or performance in the optimal way so that it builds student capacity. So let's use the phrase "capacity-building responses" as a category to reflect on all the different purposes of our responses to student work and how these responses can be productive. Here's why: looking at the significant amount of literature as far back as the 1950s there are two clear themes:

Use "capacity-building responses" to reflect the different purposes of our responses to student work and how these responses can be productive.

1. The response of a teacher to student work should include objective and nonjudgmental information.

2. The response should be helpful to the student in advancing his or her learning. It should prompt student self-evaluation and increase the student's capacity to improve or take the next needed step.

What kind of responses could do this? There are many, and they fall along a continuum of simple to more complex. At the simplest level is a cue. A cue is a minimal response that calls the student's attention to what's missing or wrong and is called a "progressive minimal cue" (see Chapter 11, "Clarity"). Here is another example. A student pronounces the word *hateful* as "hatful." The teacher covers the "ful" with a finger leaving "hate" exposed and asks the student what that word is. The student's attention is thus focused on seeing the "e" at the end and remembering what e's do at the end of a three-letter word to produce a long vowel sound. "Oh, hate!" says the student. Then, the teacher lifts the concealing finger and points to the whole word "hateful."

At the next level is a prompt. Fisher and Frey (2012) define it as a statement that causes the student to do some metacognitive work. For example:

Teacher: "I see page numbers in parentheses."

Student: "Oh, I gotta add quote marks or they'll think I stole the words."

Teacher: "I'm reading these words and they sound pretty academic, not like the rest of the paper."

Student: "I guess I better think about the sources a little more and make sure they're really my words."

At a more complex level, the interaction with the student may also give objective information comparing what the student has done with the criteria for success.

The late Grant Wiggins in 2012 wrote: "Feedback is not advice, praise or evaluation. Feedback is information about how we are doing in our effort to reach a goal" (p. 10). Wiggins was proposing a definition for the term "feedback" that was specific and contained four attributes. The characteristics of this kind of response to student work are that the responses are (1) specific, (2) detailed, (3) nonjudgmental, and (4) factually point out what aspects of proficient performance are present and which are absent (if any) from the current work the student has produced. "You have shown every step of your solution; your calculations are accurate. But your units are not labeled." In many situations, pointing out what's missing or which of the criteria for successful work have not yet been met, is enough to focus students on what they need to do next. If a teacher says, "But your units are not labeled," most students know they should go back and label the numbers with the appropriate units.

One might call it "pure" feedback. In everyday talk, "feedback" can mean anything said or written about a student's product or performance. Examples would be "Great job" (Praise), "You look terrible!" (Criticism), "That's pretty good, but it would be better if you included more details to support your case" (Judgment and Guidance). We want here to get away from the "anything goes" version of feedback to distinct and professionally defined terms.

Video: Guidance

Educational researchers, many of whom tacitly accept this broad "anything-you-say" concept of feedback, write about "good" feedback and "bad" feedback. We are working to create a profession with a common language and concept system and a professional vocabulary where important terms have clear definitions that are precise, broadly known, and used universally, like "tort" and "deposition" are in the legal profession. Therefore, we want to use an equally precise definition of *feedback*. It's a professional term with precise meaning, and we happen to know that when one gives feedback according to this definition, there are positive effects for students. Consequently, we adopt Wiggins's definition of feedback as a third level of capacity-building response after "cue" and "prompt" to student work.

In 2004, Wiggins separated the definition of feedback from guidance and evaluation, because sometimes pure "feedback" as defined above is enough to get a student to improve. But that isn't always so. If it's not, one should add advice or guidance to help the student take action to improve the product or performance. Feedback gives information about how current performance compares to mastery. Guidance tells one where to go or how to proceed to improve the product or performance. The findings about successful responses to student work are consistent around one aspect: what we say or write to students about a particular piece of work needs to help the students improve the work. So sometimes guidance is needed to enable students to address the missing attributes of good work that the feedback identified.

Video: Descriptive Feedback

For example, the teacher might say, "You identified the author's main points and showed evidence of why you chose each one, but you made no comments about the author's point of view about the generals" (Feedback). Or he might say, "Take a look again about what he said about the background of the WWI generals to see if you pick up anything about his point of view" (Guidance). Sometimes guidance needs to be more specific than "look at the background of WWI generals" and may take the form of a focusing question, such as, "What do you think was the generals' common experience studying the history of the British Empire and perhaps, also, the honor codes at their elite private schools . . . what might those two things have to do with their view of war?" (a more direct level of guidance). The research on responses to student work that increase student performance doesn't say that guidance must be present, it says the information must be useful to the students. Feedback without guidance can, indeed, be useful. But if it isn't enough, then plunge in with nonjudgmental guidance.

There is also a range of other responses to student work that have a positive place, such as encouragement, expressions of confidence in the student's capacity to reach proficiency or produce a quality product, excitement at the progress this current product represents (a form of encouragement), or request to show it to another student.

Video: Group Critique

Using Group Critique to Generate Feedback to Students

Ron Berger has a lovely video called "Austin's Butterfly" in which he shares with primary students progressive approximations, each one more sophisticated, of a drawing of a butterfly by a first grader. Austin received group critique of each of five drafts of the drawing that was "kind, specific, and useful" (Berger, Rugen, & Wooden, 2014, p. 151).

What this video illustrates is that useful guidance or advice as part of effective feedback can be delivered through group critique of student work samples guided by a teacher. Berger is careful to point out that the spirit of this critique must be continuous improvement, and the advice by peers guided by strong norms of support and helpfulness.

Thus far, we've constructed a continuum for "capacity-building responses" that is consistent with the research that points out that effective responses to student work must provoke active processing on the part of the student. We now have a continuum of "capacity-building responses to student work" that goes from the most simple to the most elaborate.

Separate from this continuum is the presence of affect in body language and/ or verbal language that is encouraging: "Oh, you're getting so close!" There is nothing in the research literature or the canon of common sense to suggest one should have flat, neutral affect, or in any way contain one's natural cheerfulness and enthusiasm. However, the literature does imply we must resist the urges to jump in, give the answer, re-explain, or do the work for the student. What we should do is (1) cue if that fits, (2) give pure feedback, (3) stop and see if the student can proceed, if not (4) give useful advice and suggestions for how the student can act to improve the work, and (5) include any encouragement or affect you think is appropriate. Be sure not to say, "This is easy" in an attempt to be encouraging.

There are a few important bullets to add to Grant Wiggins's list. We believe that pure feedback should also be:

- ▲ Timely (meaning in close proximity to the student producing the work)
- ▲ Frequent
- ▲ Clear

Written Feedback, Guidance, and Evaluation

Video: Feedback According to Criteria for Success

Everything we have said about verbal feedback pertains to written feedback on student work. What we would add is that on written feedback, there are choice points about how many areas to take on. The point is that guidance and evaluation make little difference unless the student is clear about goals, means, and feedback. When teachers respond to student writing, they have an opportunity to apply the attributes of feedback as we have defined it. However, responding to students' writing calls for us to do much more than give pure "feedback." Response in writing should often give students credible information about what they've done that is effective and why and give useful input about how to make it better. This is more than feedback. Teachers skilled at responding to student writing have a hierarchy of purposes in mind, and different ones may show up at a given time. For example, responding to students' mechanical and spelling errors for editing purposes may be reserved for a later draft and not occur at all in responding to an early draft. What thoughtful teachers do in responding to student writing is give help, specific suggestions, or some kind of guidance that students can use to improve their next draft.

Here are some different purposes skilled writing teachers have in mind in responding to students' writing:

1. To show what resonated for the teacher-reader as an audience.

2. To highlight, specifically, the things students are doing that are appropriate, skillful, or effective in their impact on a reader and explain why.

3. To lead the student to the next most appropriate stretch or improvement in their writing with suggestions or guidance, using the technical language of writers to do so ("show, don't tell," "use strong verbs"). This kind of response is not solely objective (that is, only comparing student products to exemplars), it also seeks to help the student improve by giving direct leads or asking focused questions that guide the student to improvement.

Let's examine the three different sets of comments on the same paper from professional development materials published by Writers' Express (www.amplify.com/curriculum/the-writers-express-curriculum) shown in Exhibit 14.1. Compare the first two examples to the third one. The first teacher catches every error. This could be appropriate for a piece of writing that was rich and complete, needing only technical repairs. But for this particular early draft the effect on the student might well be discouraging. Instead of asking for a thesis statement, the teacher supplies it for the student. There is the assumption that the student knows that "frag" means "sentence fragment" and can use that cue as sufficient to self-correct. There is little shown that the student can build on, nothing to motivate the student to improve the writing, only an implied injunction to fix a myriad of technical errors.

The second teacher tries to be encouraging in her comment, but winds up being wishy-washy and vague, offering no specific suggestions except "keep going." What reason would the student have to keep going? "Watch those fragments" may not be enough to help the student see where she's written one or know how to fix it. Because the comments don't respectfully engage with the student's work, they don't encourage him to continue writing. In addition, because they don't make clear what they want him to do next, they can't improve his skills.

The third teacher has crafted responses more likely to support good writing habits and lead to improvement. She does self-reports on the impact of specific words: "Yum. My mouth is watering." She underlines the words that produced that effect, thus identifying the specifics. She shows she is attending to the content by responding to an arguing point of the student ("I also feel like sleeping helps me to focus"). The teacher then challenges the student to improve her piece by focusing on a specific skill ("Show, don't tell") and gives her guidance for doing so ("Pretend you are in school after not getting enough sleep. Write 3 sentences to convince me . . ."). The exercise is constructed to highlight the right size bite for the student, which the teacher decides is writing the sentences to show, not tell—just that. So the exercise represents a diagnostically determined focus

Exhibit 14.1 Teacher Comments (Writers' Express)

The Impact of Teacher Comments

Approach 1: Catch Every Mistake

"Why School Should Start Later" (excerpt)

We need to stop feeling pressured everyday [two words] to be in school so early. I mean sure we get [colloquial] out early but what is the point of going if your [you] are not ready to learn all the time? We need to feel comfortable and willing to work. Focused [Frag.] and we need to take on challenges. We do not need to dream about how nice are [our] bed would be right now of [or] the yummy breakfast that we missed because we were too late. A few times I have dreamed about being asleep and walking up to a huge ham, cheese, and tomato omlet with a giant café colada to wash it down. If we are feeling this way, then who really wants to go? [colloquial] [to school] I know that school can be pretty boring to students anyway, but maybe we just don't want to go because we are to [too] tired. It is the perfect theory.

[No questions in persuasive writing.]

[You haven't stated your thesis/theory: "School should start later because students are too tired to concentrate when they wake up early."]

Exhibit 14.1 Teacher Comments (Writers' Express) (continued)

The Impact of Teacher Comments

Approach 2: Encourage and Nudge

"Why School Should Start Later" (excerpt)

We need to stop feeling pressured everyday to be in school so early, I mean sure we get out early but what is the point of going if your are not ready to learn all the time? We need to feel comfortable and willing to work. Focused and we need to take on challenges. We do not need to dream about how nice are bed would be right now of the yummy breakfast that we missed because we were too late. A few times I have dreamed about being asleep and walking up to a huge ham, cheese, and tomato omlet with a giant café colada to wash it down. If we are feeling this way, then who really wants to go? I know that school can be pretty boring to students anyway, but maybe we just don't want to go because we are to tired. It is the perfect theory!

✓ Good attitude

Watch those fragment

Funny.

You said it! Good start. I look forward to more. Keep going!

Exhibit 14.1 Teacher Comments (Writers' Express) (continued)

The Impact of Teacher Comments

Approach 3: Respond as a Reader; Instruct as a Teacher

"Why School Should Start Later" (excerpt)

We need to stop feeling pressured everyday to be in school so early, I mean sure we get out early but what is the point of going if your are not ready to learn all the time? We need to feel comfortable and willing to work. Focused and we need to take on challenges. We do not need to dream about how nice are bed would be right now of the yummy breakfast that we missed because we were too late. A few times I have dreamed about being asleep and walking up to a huge ham, cheese, and tomato omlet with a giant café colada to wash it down. If we are feeling this way, then who really wants to go? I know that school can be pretty boring to students anyway, but maybe we just don't want to go because we are to tired. It is the perfect theory!

I also feel like sleeping helps me to focus.

Yum. my mouth is watering.

Beatriz,
You're starting to convince me that a later start time would make us all more focused on school. I'm especially excited for the possibility of an Omlette and coolata! :) Carli

Showing Drill: Pretend you are in school after not getting enough sleep. Write 3 sentences to convince me that you're not focused. SHOW how you look and feel.

for this student, in this piece of writing, to improve the next most important skill as determined by the teacher. And what we hope is that the technical errors highlighted by the first teacher response are noted by this third teacher and that they will be targets for skill development in later feedback and remediation.

Responses to writing that show the teacher is thinking diagnostically, providing guidance for improvement, and matching response to students' particular needs is applicable in any academic discipline where writing is called for—social studies, science, music, art, and physical education. Guidance is also appropriate in response to student performance in any discipline even when writing is not called for! Let's look at a few examples:

▲ **Drama class:** "When you swung your arms while going stage-left (teacher starts with data), it strongly conveyed the character's cockiness (communicates effect of the behavior). Try it again at a slower pace so we can see what the effect is." (suggestion)

▲ **Art class:** "The sudden bright color here (data) draws the eye to the sun (effect) much as Van Gogh would do. Try muting the color down here so the competition for attention isn't too distracting to the viewer." (suggestion)

▲ **Science class:** "You adjusted the scale to highlight the similarities and differences in the treatments (data). That made your data collection and graphic display very clear and accessible (effect on reader). One can look at both your matrix and bar graphs and see your points (more on effect and why). But I cannot tell so clearly from your "conclusion" what you think the meaning of the data is for action in power plants." (feedback)

Exhibit 14.2 shows an example of a different kind of response in which the teacher focuses on asking good questions to push the writer, Christian, to expand both his plot and his character development. Note the progress of the student's writing between the first two drafts. Only on the third draft (not shown here) will the teacher focus on technical and grammatical elements.

Notice that there is an underlying belief in these transactions between teacher and student. The belief is that learning to write is a process of steady growth and has many different elements. Doing a piece of writing in this teacher's class is not an event that ends when an assignment is turned in. The message to the student is consistently invitational and encouraging. It is also respectful because it attends to helping the student develop characters and stories in which that student is interested. The intention of the response is to help the student develop some skills related to learning to write, not necessarily to produce a "correct" or finished product.

Exhibit 14.2 Teacher Comments (Writers' Express)

Mark is outside, walking around, he has to go to work, but he is thinking about going to the chess invitational. He is not worried about winning or losing. Mark can't cross the street because there are so many cars passing by. Mark starts yelling "Come on, Already!" waiting for the walk signal to show up, he pushed the walk signal 5 times. Mark starts to punch the pole just to hurt his right hand. Some people came by and started to make fun of him. They giggled silently and laughed hard when they got far away from him. It was even worse when he continuously punched the open box at the bottom. Still no walk signal.

Why would Mark punch the pole to hurt himself on purpose?

Christian – this is a good start for putting your character, Mark, in a situation. Mark is an interesting guy. He has a job and is a chess player, but I can also see by the way he "punches" the walk button that he is impatient, angry, and worried about what people think. Why is Mark so impatient. What might happen to him on the street that might CHANGE him or make him less angry. Think about CLIMAX. Let's talk!

Nice work.

Kate

Exhibit 14.2 Teacher Comments (Writers' Express) (continued)

Mark is outside his house, walking back and forth on his street, he has to go to work behind a hardware store's counter, but he is thinking about going to the chess invitational. He is not worried about winning or losing because he is not supposed to be at the invitational. He called in sick and had someone else substitute for him in his false absence. Mark cannot cross the street because there are so many cars passing by. Mark starts to yell, "Come on already, not wanting to wait patiently for the walk signal to show up. The walk signal does not show up on the screen so Mark presses the button five more times, it still doesn't show so he starts to kick the pole, releasing his anger. His face turns completely red as he continues to wait. Some people come by and start to make fun of Mark and his troubles. They whisper to each other as soon as they get far enough from him, they laugh hard because Mark is a man with problems, big problems. He finally gets across the street when thee is a green light, Mark walks slowly to the other side of the street. Suddenly, a Black Lincoln Continental with the windows all black and a black man wearing a black suit, not saying a word, stares Mark down as he waits for him to pass. Once he gets there, he sprints away fast to get away from him. There are no cars or people in sight, which scared Mark, and the light is red. The Driver drives away, before he did, he pulled out a pack of Virginia Slims Cigarettes and began smoking. The driver

the chess invitational is a great idea - it makes Mark an interesting character!

wow, chess is important to Mark! Does he really not care if he wins or loses?

Your strong verbs show me how angry Mark is. Why is he angry? Did something happen?

what problems?

good description!

Why does this man scare Mark?

Exhibit 14.2 Teacher Comments (Writers' Express) (continued)

was really angry, he drove when there was a red light, there was nobody to catch him drive on the red light. Mark still sprints.

Christian,

You've got a good start here for your polished piece. Mark is a very interesting character – he loves to play chess, but is very angry. I am interested in what happens to him! As you work on your second draft, let's talk about these questions:

(1) Why is Mark angry? Do we need to know why he is angry so we can understand the story?

(2) Why is Mark scared of the man in the Lincoln?

(3) What is the turning point in the story and how will Mark change?

Good work so far!

– Kate

(1) Because he is running late & his day's plan is to get there.

(2) ANGRY – detained at the light held back

(3) Man in black car scares him

(4) He gets there in the end

(5) Winning tournament changes his attitude.

Table 14.6 Implied Messages Embedded in Feedback

Feedback	Implied Message
"Jim, you listed your findings in the lab report but never addressed the next two questions about the conclusions you draw from the findings and new questions this has raised. This isn't up to your best work."	Jim, you are capable of good work.
"So these are the parts you have to improve to have a first-class essay."	You can, indeed, make this first class. There are some parts of it to address and then you'll be there.
"What help do you need in order to make this meet standard?"	If you identify the help you need, the resources are here and you can meet the standard.
"Now the only thing you have to do is get a really potent lead."	You've done a good job and have met most of the criteria. If you get a potent lead you will have a complete and high-quality product.

Threaded within teacher feedback are tacit expressions of confidence (or not) embedded in the language used. First, if feedback is specific, detailed, frequent, and useful, the implied message is that we want the students to master the material and are giving them every support to do so. Otherwise, we wouldn't take the trouble to create all the feedback. Second, while "pure" feedback is nonjudgmental and simply identifies what students have or haven't accomplished in light of a set of established criteria or standards, the responses we make to student work often do and should include more than pure feedback. They should also include encouragement, appropriate leads, and suggestions for how to improve it, and so on. This is especially true when responding to students' writing, both fiction and nonfiction (see more examples from Writers' Express at http://www.amplify.com/curriculum/the-writers-express-curriculum). So it is important not only to give students a high volume of specific, useful feedback, but also to pay attention to the embedded belief messages that surround the feedback (Table 14.6).

Reacting When Students Do Well

When students do well, it is important that the praise given to them attributes their success specifically to effort (and perhaps, secondarily, by implication to their having sufficient ability). It sounds like this: "You came in for extra help, studied before the test, and took your time checking your answers before handing it in. And it really paid off!" The *moment of responding,* the actual event in which it is delivered either verbally or in writing, is one of those moments when we need a heightened awareness of our choice of words, body language, and tone of voice so as to send a positive expectation message.

Two other regularly recurring situations call for teacher reaction: (1) when students don't meet the expectations we set and (2) when there is a significant change in performance. Each of these situations represents an opportunity to reinforce effort as the cause of the results a student has produced (attribution training). It is through these reactions that students get the message about how important something is, and whether we believe they are capable of achieving the performance targets.

The moment of responding is when we need awareness of our words, body language, and tone of voice to send a positive expectation message.

Reacting to Unmet Expectations

When students do poor work, it is important that they hear about it in a way that conveys our belief that they can do better, and that we are looking for investment of their effort because we believe it will pay off. Some students may display reluctance or resistance when we react in a direct (and sometimes high-energy) way. However, students can also easily interpret low affect, a neutral, or noncommittal response to low-quality work as an expression of our lack of interest or belief in them. And it often is.

In the absence of an appropriate reaction, many students will not believe sufficiently in themselves to work harder or do well. This danger is particularly present for students who believe it's their innate ability that either enables or disables them to perform (Dweck, 2002). When students who hold this belief find something to be challenging or do poorly at something they attempt, they interpret it as confirmation of not having enough ability. These same students, according to "attribution theory" (Weiner, 1996), believe that when they do poorly it is because of task difficulty—and underneath that belief, the damning suspicion that they are not bright enough. Therefore, when students do poorly, going after them with high-energy and positive affect becomes an implicit statement of belief in their ability and a call for more effort. It is an opportunity to retrain their attributions about what causes their success and failure.

Reacting to a Decline in Performance

A significant decline in performance is another opportunity to send expectation messages and do attribution retraining. It could sound like this: "This is nowhere near the standard you're capable of. We need to figure out what is happening and what you can do to get back on track." A remark like that from a respected teacher can be a powerful spur to a flagging student.

Reacting to Increase in Performance

Suppose a student with a D average gets an 83 on a test. The teacher stops the student on the way out the door and says, "You did really well on this test. Why do you think you did so well?" The student pauses, looks down, and mumbles, "Must have been an easy test." (Note the connection to external attribution—luck or task difficulty). The teacher replies, "Easy test! I don't give easy tests; everybody knows that. And you got number 14 right. That was the hardest one. Now come on, what do you think you did to accomplish that?"

This teacher is trying to get the student to consider that not only does he have the ability to do well, but that there is something he has done to bring about this result (effort attribution). But if the student doesn't see himself as having that ability, he will more than likely be silent at this point in the dialogue. The suggestion behind the teacher's question can be threatening in several ways: "What if I *am* capable of good work? Will she expect it of me all the time? What if I tried and couldn't do this well again?" Another student may want to keep expectations low just to avoid working hard.

Another possibility is that by challenging the student to think about why he succeeded, the teacher may be throwing him into social jeopardy. Some segments of school peer culture are built around not doing academic work well and not connecting to school. To embrace being a student and be seen as trying hard could be interpreted as a rejection of one's peer group norms. This dynamic may occur for some students of color where striving in school settings gets interpreted as "acting white" (Fordham & Ogbu, 1986). A teacher who seizes opportunities like the student doing unexpectedly well on a test needs to be ready to support the student through the thinking and the possible perceived risks: "Well, you think about it, and when you come in tomorrow, I'm going to ask you again why you think you did so well." Whether or not the student has a response tomorrow, the hope is that the student will start thinking about the possibility that he is capable of higher performance than he'd imagined and weighing the risks and rewards of trying hard. It is also a time for the teacher to devise strategies for how to work with him to provide support and scaffolds while he proves to himself that he has what it takes.

Arena 7: Positive Framing for Reteaching

It is a common event for a class to end with several students who don't yet fully understand the material. What, if anything, is going to happen so they have another chance? This is another of the regularly recurring situations where we can seize opportunities to build student confidence or miss opportunities and inadvertently signal to some students that there is no hope for them.

Figure 14.8 The Scholar's Loop

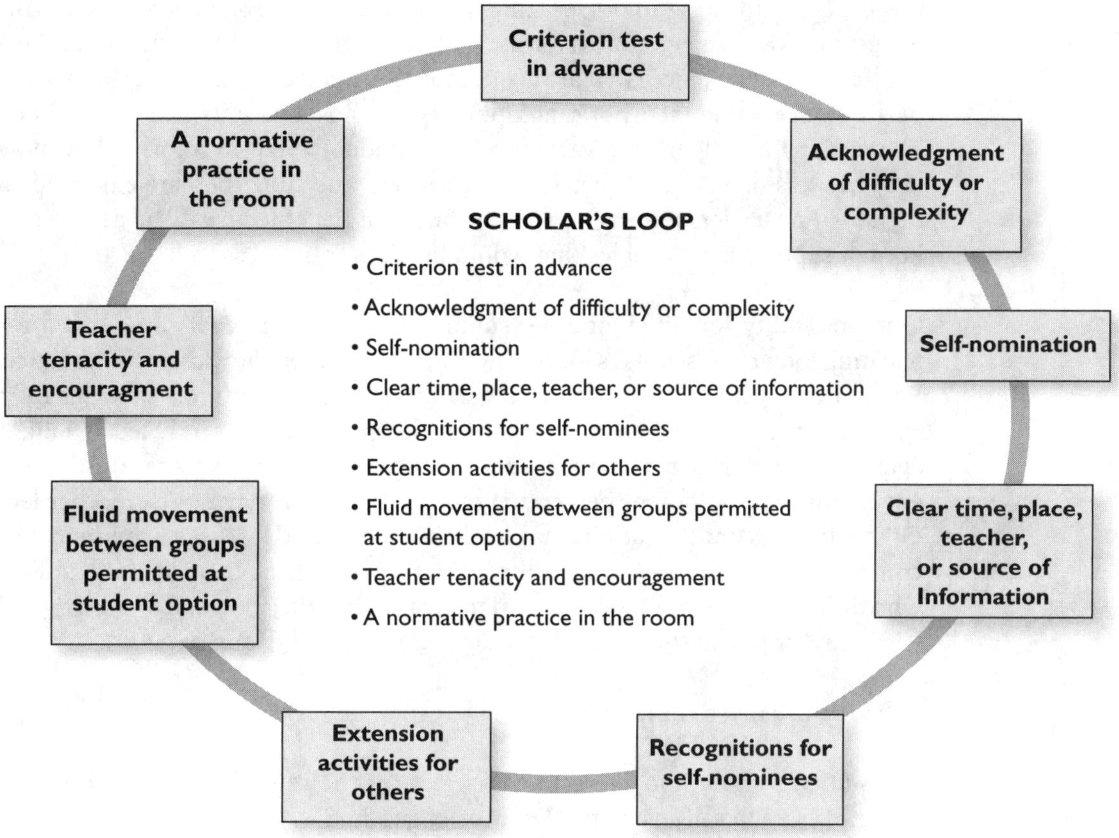

If we assume that some students won't or can't ever get it really, or get it only partially, we feel obligated to move on to new material and drop their gap in understanding by the wayside. "After all, they get what they can get. I can give them slightly different assignments (translation: less demanding) so they can feel success (what they really feel is shame). I have to move on with the curriculum. After all, I have to get these kids ready for the Regents/APs/finals! I can't hold the others back!" The belief behind this statement is that the slower students couldn't really ever get the material anyway, and that getting all students to pass requires slowing down the whole class and dumbing down the standards.

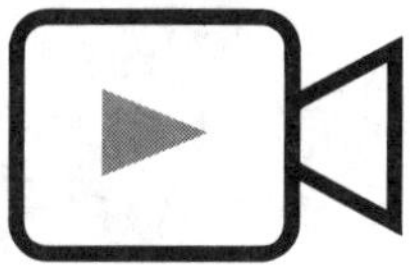

Video: Framing Reteaching

But what if we really believe that all students can reach a high standard given hard work, effective effort, and adequate prior knowledge? What instructional practices would we be considering? We would provide time and structure to reteach for students who don't "get it" the first time around. In addition, we would employ all of the best practices in differentiating instruction and take the initiative to design courses, units of study, and lessons accordingly. This means pre-assessing readiness levels, analyzing the data we collect, and designing learning experiences that are geared to a common objective and standard of performance while incorporating options as to how students will arrive there. The options might include variety in how students take in information, how they process or practice what is to be learned, and how they are expected to demonstrate understanding and achievement of the objectives. The degree and kind of support are variables that would be differentiated as well.

One possibility for differentiating support is setting up what some call a reteaching loop or a "scholar's loop" (Figure 14.8) as a regular classroom practice. For students who didn't get it quickly or the first time around, a scholar's loop is a time and place where a concept or idea previously introduced is taught again or made available again to students with additional explanations, different examples, or different perceptual modes. It may or may not be teacher led. Other students or other adults may lead it. Self-directed learning experiences or computer simulations may be in the loop. But something happens for students who didn't get it the first time around to ensure they do get it, and at the original level of rigor and at the original standard, not a watered-down one.

The loop has these components:

▲ Students should be asked to self-select for the reteaching loop. To do so, they have to self-evaluate: "Do I really get this?"

▲ Students need the clarity and aid of a criterion test or task given to them in advance so they can accurately self-assess. The learning target or the performance they are shooting for should be no secret.

▲ The teacher creates and continually reinforces a psychological climate of safety and esteem for students who nominate themselves for the scholar's loop by:

- Explaining to students when the process is introduced—and regularly reinforcing—that scholars are people who desire to understand something at a very deep level.

- Explicitly acknowledging the difficulty of the material: "This is really quite difficult, because you have to get used to thinking about two things at once: identifying the relevant information and the relevant operation."

- Praising the thoughtfulness of self-evaluation and the risk it takes to say one doesn't know something: "Good going, Kristina. You looked hard at your writing and decided to get a boost in this skill before moving on. You're going to know it very thoroughly when you're through, and probably incorporate this skill into your writing for life."

- The teacher encourages the students who have entered reteaching while they're there. "Keep struggling—you've almost got it. I know you're going to get there. Try to put it in your own words now."

- The teacher acknowledges difficulty and makes the reteaching loop a team effort: "I must not be saying it right. Manuel, can you take a crack at putting it in your own words and explaining it to Katrina?"

Carrying out the belief that all children can learn to a high level calls for more work from teachers.

The most important part of the reteaching loop is the tenacity and expressed confidence of the teacher to each student that sticking with it will bring success. That means frequent assessments and follow-up with the students until they succeed. Creating reteaching loops often requires breaking the class into groups and giving the other members of the class an enrichment or extension activity to apply their knowledge in new contexts. It takes extra time and effort to come up with those activities. There is no doubt that carrying out the belief that all children can learn to a high level calls for more work from teachers than if they allow those who don't get it first and fast to settle to the bottom of the tank. Sorting students has always been easier than teaching them. One way to make the workload more reasonable in managing reteaching loops is to team-teach. Two teachers with a double-size class can divide up the preparation chores when they decide they need to have reteaching and extension activities.

It is no small challenge to design differentiated learning experiences. To do so calls for a broad instructional repertoire, and implementation requires high levels of management skills. But we know it is what we have to do if we are to reach all of our students. Developing the capacity to offer this quality of learning experience for students must be the ongoing aim of any professional teacher. Then, we can convince low-performing, low-confidence students that they have what it takes to succeed in school and in life. (Chapter 14, "Models of Teaching," Chapter 19, "Planning," and Chapter 20, "Differentiated Instruction," present the keystones for differentiation.)

Arena 8: Tenacity

This quality surfaces in response to resistance, and it subsumes repetition and consistency. When students resist reasonable teacher expectations and getting them met seems hopeless, teachers who persevere display tenacity. For example, a teacher goes to study hall to get a student when he doesn't show up for an extra-help session or reminds a student she's expected at 1:15 to go over some work and hands the student a sticky note saying, "1:15 Room 310!" as she leaves class. The messages are, "This is important, you can do it, and I won't give up on you." After all, effective effort is the key to student achievement.

Effective effort is the key to student achievement.

Striking a Balance on the Tenacity Continuum

Tenacity is a quality or behavior that raises some interesting challenges and questions regarding the messages we send. On the one hand, the behaviors described have a quality of chasing a student in an effort to convince him that he can and must do it and that the teacher is there to ensure that he knows and sees that. Some amount of persisting is critical when dealing with students who don't necessarily believe in themselves and their capacity to do well yet. On the other hand, the responsibility for ensuring that learning takes place cannot rest solely with the teacher. Students must do their part in order to develop ownership and the self-efficacy that results from accomplishment. Decisions about how much to persist and when to back off—or get tough—and allow a student to experience the negative consequences of his inaction can be an ongoing balancing act (see Figure 14.9). How much persisting does a student need to internalize the message that a teacher really believes he can do it and cares enough to see him through it? How much support does a student need before he is ready to go it on his own? When is a student really prepared to assume more independent responsibility for his success? When is it time for the teacher to back off, hold the student accountable, and give him the reins to steer his own success? Persisting to the extreme can signal, "The only way you can succeed is if I do it for you." Getting tough too soon denies a student the opportunity to succeed.

For students with little confidence, the path we pursue along the tenacity continuum is rarely unidirectional. Instead, it is more like an ongoing, calibrated dance to the left and right of center, ever attempting through our actions to keep two messages in balance: "You can do this" and "I won't give up on you," and all the while signaling "this is important" (this being whatever we are being tenacious about). The message of tenacity is that the teacher cares. The choice about how to display that with individual students is a matching decision. When students (and adults) are asked to recall their best teacher and explain why, this quality is almost always high on the list: "I could run, but I couldn't hide." Tenacity isn't always appreciated at the time a student is experiencing it, but when all is said and done students know it means we care. They are grateful for it later.

Video: Frequent Quizzes and Self-Correction

Arena 9: Grades, Retakes, and Redos

Grading practices send strong implicit messages about what is important and the teacher's beliefs in students' capacity. Consider the practice of allowing students to retake tests. Many teachers allow students to retake a test if they do

Figure 14.9 The Tenacity Continuum

poorly. What is significant here is how we determine the grade the student receives. Does the student get the higher of the two grades, signaling that demonstrated learning—and persevering toward that end—is what matters? Or do we average the second (usually better) score with the first to compute the final grade? Consider the implications of this practice and the messages it sends.

Videos:
Errors and Retakes (1 & 2), Student Self-Correction (1 & 2), Peer Teaching

Students who manifest genuine effort and reach equal proficiency with others (who got it the first time around) get lower grades. Thus speed is rewarded over effort and all that may have gone with it (seeking appropriate help, consulting others, extra hours on the job, soliciting feedback and critique from others, goal setting). The implicit message this sends is that getting it the first time around—or faster—is more worthy or important than ultimately reaching high performance. We care more about speed than perseverance and demonstrating proficiency, for that is what we reward.

Some will argue that giving the higher score as the final score will encourage students to skip studying the first time, because they can always have another crack at it. We think, however, that very few students will be more inclined to put off study because they see retakes as a safety net. This has been borne out anecdotally with every teacher we know who has adopted the practice of allowing retakes. Students who adopt procrastination as a policy soon find themselves so far behind that the safety net doesn't help much. One teacher we worked with addressed this concern by requiring that students come for two after-school help sessions in order to be allowed to retake a test. This ensured that she and the student would have a chance to find out what kind of help and reteaching the student needed in order to be successful the second time. It also did away with the concern that students would abuse the retake system since a retake required extra investment of their time and effort.

Letter grading is another practice that sends strong implicit messages about what is important and our belief in student capacity. The A through F grading system is based on a belief that the purpose of schools is to sort students and identify those who get it and achieve proficiency and those who don't. But what if the purpose of schooling is to prepare all students to graduate with proficiencies that will equip them to be high-functioning, productive, competitive, and contributing members of society? What if we believed that society needs all students to meet the standards of the courses they take because the nature of the workplace and of the world requires all its citizens to be able to do problem-solving, work with others, and use language effectively? What if we believed that what we spend time teaching and what students spend their time trying to learn is important enough that all students need to attain proficiency? What if we believed that all students have the ability to meet standards we set given adequate prior knowledge, sufficient motivation, and good instruction? Then, the only grading system possible would be one based on mastery rather than sorting.

If that were the case, the only grades that would make sense are A, B, and "not yet," where "B" means "meets the standard" and "A" means "above and beyond the standard" or beyond the requirements of the course. Any student who has "not yet" met the standards of proficiency defined for the course or demonstrated mastery of the knowledge called for is not finished with the work of the course yet. The grade is an incomplete. To adopt this grading policy, we have to take seriously our efforts to get all students to meet a standard, which requires being clear about what the standards should be and what they look and sound like. In addition, opportunities must be available—after school, on weekends, in the evenings—wherever they can be found or created to offer students re-teaching and additional help. We know of several high schools that have adopted and attempted to implement this policy. In one, faculty members and community volunteers are in the school on Tuesday and Thursday evenings and on Saturday mornings to help students finish their "not yets."

To be sure, this is a dramatic shift from the way schools have done things up to now. As a result, it calls on us to be inventive, creative, and relentless in seeking ways to overcome the obvious obstacles to implementing such a practice. But until there is this kind of shift, schools will continue through current grading practices to contradict any mission that seeks to convince students that the whole purpose of schooling is to show them that they have the ability to achieve and to ensure that they have adequate opportunities to do so.

The belief that all students can achieve high standards with rigorous academic material transforms nearly everything about the way we approach schooling, and grading is only the tip of the iceberg. The practice of giving "A, B, not yet" grades opens a positive Pandora's box of implied changes in instructional practices, staff development for expansion of teacher repertoires, and community support for quality schooling for all children. Chapter 21, "Assessment," elaborates on what it takes to replace grading with more informative reporting systems.

Arena 10: Grouping

The grouping of students for instruction is an arena that can send powerful messages about a teacher's belief in students' capacity—not because of the practice itself but because of several important variables associated with grouping students:

- ▲ The standards students are pressed to reach once they are in a group
- ▲ The flexibility of entry and exit from the group
- ▲ The quality of instruction
- ▲ The tenacity of the teacher, and his or her expressed belief in the students' capacity to learn

- ▲ The understanding the students themselves have of why they are in a particular group

Many years ago, one of the instructors in our group at Research for Better Teaching was tracked with the lowest-performing eighth graders in his junior high school. This was true tracking. The students stayed together for all subjects and were put together on the criterion of prior academic performance—the classic low track. This placement might have condemned him to low performance and low expectations for the rest of his school career, but it didn't. The difference was that this teacher started the year saying to his whole group: "You've fooled people long enough. We know you have good brains and can do well in school. And we believe it's too important for your future to continue to allow you to do so poorly. So this year you're going to work as you never worked before, learn more, and do better than you ever have before." The students' pace was accelerated, and the assignments and demands escalated significantly, as did the intensity of the instruction they received. By the end of the year, most of them had mastered two years' worth of academic content!

Well-documented examinations of tracking in the United States (Oakes, 1985, 1995) show conclusively that low-track students are systematically disadvantaged by low expectations, less opportunity to learn, less interesting material, and less interesting teaching. The studies show further that children of color, especially in urban districts, are particularly disadvantaged. Yet recommendations to eliminate tracking and do heterogeneous grouping in secondary schools don't always appear to help. The reason is that changing the structure won't help without changing teaching, beliefs, and attitudes of adults and students. The one exception to this generalization may be the practice of summarily eliminating the lowest track in multi-track schools and applying the standards and expectations of the next higher track to the lower-track students who are incorporated into the next track up.

The research on heterogeneous grouping, synthesized from a number of original studies as well as two excellent research syntheses (Gamoran, 1992; Slavin, 1988), finds that the overall average achievement of students (referred to as "productivity" in the literature) in tracked and untracked schools is about the same. Tracked schools are not more "productive" than untracked schools—or vice versa. But tracked schools produce a bigger spread of student achievement than untracked schools. The highest-performing students do better in some tracked schools, probably because they are offered accelerated curricula (and boosted by the confidence of adults who expect them to do well). The low-track students do much worse in tracked schools than the lowest-performing students in untracked schools. On the surface, this seems to imply that untracking is good for low-performing students but cheats the most capable high-performing students of reaching their full potential.

Yet we know from individual studies that low-performing students in tracked schools can do well if grouped and given accelerated programs with high expectations for their success. And we also know that the most capable students in untracked settings can be suitably challenged if their teachers are equipped to differentiate instruction.

The inferences seem clear from studies of tracking in secondary schools:

- ▲ Eliminate the bottom tracks where multiple tracking is present.
- ▲ Help all teachers to internalize the beliefs and behaviors in this chapter for communicating high positive expectations to all students.
- ▲ Help teachers diversify their teaching repertoires and differentiate learning experiences so that top tracks can be collapsed and include a wider range of students without denying the highest-performing individuals their chance to be fully challenged.

Now, let's look at the data from the elementary studies. Tracking in elementary schools doesn't seem to affect the achievement of either the high-or low-performing students much. Slavin (1993) argues that the reason for this low effect is that elementary tracking probably does not reduce real heterogeneity very much. Thus the elementary tracks are still quite heterogeneous. However, many authors, such as Jeanne Oakes (1985, 1995), speculate that the damage to self-esteem and motivation inflicted on elementary children labeled as low track is deep and permanent and shows up later in secondary school performance. Consequently, tracking children in elementary schools seems to be all loss and no gain. The one exception is that certain studies show that gifted students may be advantaged by homogeneous grouping in the elementary school. Many of their needs, however, can be met by differentiated instruction in the regular classroom by teachers who have extensive repertoires.

Tracking and *between-class grouping* mean that groups of students are sorted by perceived ability or prior performance. Tracking tends to mean students are sorted by general ability and grouped together for all their courses in secondary schools. In less rigid school structures, students can take high-track courses in some subjects and lower-track courses in other subjects. *Between-class grouping* is the term most often used in reference to elementary schools and means forming grade-level classrooms that contain students of similar ability.

Within-class grouping—often referred to as "flexible grouping"—means students are grouped temporarily for instruction in some skill, concept, or operation where they all need exactly that instruction; they are homogeneous in their readiness for and need of what the group is going to work on. The research on this kind of temporary grouping is strongly positive when the following four conditions are present:

1. The students are heterogeneously grouped most of the day.

2. The grouping is for a specific skill being taught.

3. Grouping is flexible; it remains intact only as long as it takes for students to achieve the goal the group was formed to address.

4. Teachers adapt the pace and level of instruction to the readiness and learning rates of the students.

Another elementary grouping model, the Joplin plan, though rarely implemented, has particularly strong positive findings in numerous studies on reading achievement. This is an elementary grouping model where students are assigned to heterogeneous classes for most of the day but regrouped throughout the whole school for reading instruction with others who need similar instruction, regardless of class or grade. Since strong positive research findings often don't lead to wide adoption of proven practices, this story should not be a surprise. Why is this the case? It can be inferred that to implement a Joplin plan requires a high level of organization, leadership, and teacher communication, conditions for effective change absent in far too many schools.

What implications can we draw from the research on grouping?

1. Flexible within-class grouping should be used from time to time.

2. There is a risk that students will get remedial, dumbed-down instruction.

First, flexible within-class grouping should be used from time to time, even in high school classes, for focused instruction in specific areas where ad hoc groups need more input, guidance, or practice, as long as the four caveats cited above are followed. In order to do this within-class grouping, teachers need to have worthwhile activities prepared for the other students, be able to manage student engagement, and give feedback on progress to those not in the instructional group. Thus the teacher must bring to bear well-developed repertoires of Management skills in Space, Time, Routines, and Momentum, and Planning skills to include selection of Lesson Objectives, Differentiated Instruction, and

Assessment. Ninety-minute periods or some other configuration of extended class periods prove especially useful because they give the flexibility to do small-group instruction within classes and still have time for whole-group activities and discussions. The bottom line seems to be that good instruction for a wide range of students may require that teachers have the capacity to do small-group instruction, and good small-group instruction requires well-developed repertoires on a wide range of other areas of teaching performance.

Second, the greatest danger of tracking or grouping of any kind is that students get dull, skill-drill-oriented, remedial, dumbed-down instruction. The cost is not only their self-esteem but also their interest and motivation. Most likely, they don't believe they are very capable, and they don't need poor instruction and meaningless curriculum to reinforce that belief. Low-skill, low-performing students, whether grouped together for instruction or not, must be involved in learning experiences about interesting and relevant topics. Above all, these students must be involved with higher-level thinking and discussions rather than passive worksheet activities that call for little more than identification and recall.

Low-performing students, grouped together for instruction or not, must be involved in learning experiences about interesting and relevant topics.

For example, teaching approaches that make interesting discussions possible with low-skill, secondary-level readers involve explicitly teaching these students reading comprehension strategies, like reciprocal teaching (Palincsar & Brown, 1984); text-text, text-self, and text-world connection making (Keene & Zimmerman, 1997); study skills like note-taking, use of graphic organizers, and double-entry notebooks; and note studying within the regular curriculum. It also means teaching them discussion skills, discussion formats (e.g., literature circles, Socratic seminars), and social skills.

We need to systematically build with students the capacity to use the good brains they have to interact successfully with higher-level thinking. It is a reminder that we are not only content specialists and teachers of subjects but also teachers of learning. And that role includes teaching students how to use strategies and skills for more effective learning. This requires drawing on all the other material in this book on learning styles, variety in learning experiences, clarity devices, principles of learning, and so forth to identify strategies and skills to teach to students explicitly and magnify their school competence as effective learners.

Connections to Clarity

When a teacher wants students to believe in themselves and learn effective effort, certain of the "Clarity" behaviors presented in Chapter 11 become particularly important. Checking for understanding becomes a passion because the teacher intends to reteach skills or concepts to students who didn't get it the first time around. Thus the teacher is driven to collect formative assessment data in an ongoing way at the end of each chunk of instruction: "I've simply got to know where they all are to design the grouping for the next class."

Similarly, the commitment to reach the students who are behind or lack confidence makes these teachers extend themselves to those kids and make sure they understand the criteria for success and get feedback according to those criteria especially frequently.

"Making Students Thinking Visible" becomes a constellation of moves that surfaces students' misconceptions, gaps, and confusions—another key way for the committed teacher to gather data of who needs what (see Chapter 11, "Clarity").

Beyond the interactive behaviors and deliberate use of language described in this chapter are certain classroom structures, mechanisms, and routines whose very existence embeds the three critical messages of "This is important, you can do it, and I'm not going to give up on you." The how-tos of the mechanisms listed below are beyond the scope of this book but can be found in *High Expectations Teaching* (Saphier, 2017). They generate student agency and ownership in powerful ways.

Summarizing Arenas and Their Significance

The 10 arenas of classroom life highlighted in this chapter represent innumerable opportunities for us to positively influence students' confidence in their capacity. They serve as specific tools for building life-liberating beliefs (see Table 14.7). The tools are subtle, simultaneous, and ever present. We need to be aware of how we are using them, because the consequences on student motivation and achievement are enormous. Our patterns of behavior should be consistent with the belief that all students can learn rigorous academic material at high standards. What we say regarding "all students can learn" must be congruent with what we do. If we seek to overcome the constricting grip of bright-slow class prejudice, which researchers are saying is an unfair restriction on the equality of educational opportunity offered to students, then we will consciously monitor any tendency toward the unholy 12 behaviors Cooper (1979) identified.

We will seize the opportunities present in each of these arenas to send positive, high- expectations messages to all students, press all students toward excellence, and give students lots of opportunities to exceed our expectations. Using skills in these arenas, we can consistently send messages to students about what is important, that we believe they can do it through their effort (and ours), and that we won't give up on them.

Table 14.7 Life-Liberating Beliefs

Life-Limiting Beliefs	Life-Liberating Beliefs
• Mistakes are a sign of weakness.	• Mistakes help one learn.
• Speed is what counts. Faster is smarter.	• You are not supposed to understand everything the first time around. Care, perseverance, and craftsmanship are what count.
• Good students can do it by themselves. Competition is necessary to bring out the best in students.	• Good students work together with others and solicit help and lots of feedback on their work.
• Inborn intelligence is the main determinant of success.	• Consistent effort and effective strategies are the main determinants of success.
• Only the bright can achieve at a high level.	• Everyone, not just the fastest and most competent, is capable of high achievement

Adapted from Saphier & D'Auria (1993)

What about getting students to believe that their effort really can and does make a difference? Earlier in this chapter, we summarized attribution theory as the study of the explanations people give themselves to explain their successes or failures. We also summarized Dweck's research suggesting that children have a tendency to believe that it is either their innate ability or their effort that primarily accounts for their success or lack thereof. In the arenas section of this chapter, we suggested that we seize opportunities in these everyday interactions with students to convince them that they have more than enough mental capacity to do high-quality work. We have attempted to make a strong case that teachers must do everything possible to convince students that each one of them has the capacity to do rigorous work to high standards and that it is investment of their effective effort (working hard and acquiring strategies) that will enable them to see that for themselves. This brings us to attribution retraining.

EFFECTIVE EFFORT AND ATTRIBUTION RETRAINING

How can we teach students to exert their effort effectively? Attribution retraining means getting students to change their attributions of success and failure away from factors over which they have little immediate control (luck, task difficulty, and innate ability) to the factor over which they have the greatest control: effort. Teaching effective effort means making students aware that effective effort (effort that results in achievement of a goal) is a combination of working hard and applying effective strategies. Emphasizing the strategy com-

Table 14.8 Attributes of Effective Effort

1. Time	An understanding of how much time it takes to do the job well.
2. Focus	No TV or other distractions; concentrate only on the work.
3. Strategies	If one approach isn't working, keep trying different ways until you find one that works.
4. Resourcefulness	Knowing where to go and whom to ask for help when you're really stuck.
5. Use of Feedback	Looking carefully at responses to your work so you know exactly what to fix.
6. Commitment	Being determined to finish and do the very best work.

Adapted from a model developed by Jeff Howard.

ponent with students is essential to giving them an explanation other than lack of ability when they are working hard and aren't yet seeing progress.

Teachers need to make attributions and effective effort explicit topics of conversation with students so that they are aware of the variety of ways that people explain their successes and lack thereof. We need to find out what the students believe about what makes someone successful and help them to see connections between their accomplishments and the effort they have invested to achieve them. A number of teachers in our courses have taught attribution theory directly to their students as a way to get the conversation started. Students need to be taught what effective effort means and how to employ all six of its attributes (see Table 14.8).

Let's look at each attribute in more detail.

1. **Time: Do I put in sufficient time to get the job done?** Although time alone is far from sufficient to accomplish difficult academic tasks, it is absolutely required. And it is true that some students truly don't realize that several hours of outlining, drafting, and editing may be required to make an essay meet a high standard.

2. **Focus: Am I working efficiently and without distraction?** Work time should be efficient and low in distraction. There is plenty of latitude for individual style in defining focus. Some students don't find music, even loud music, distracting while they work. In fact, for some it is a way of blocking out other environmental distractions. But talking to friends about the upcoming weekend or watching TV while doing academic work is not compatible with the concept of focus.

3. **Resourcefulness: Do I reach out for help and know where to go for it?** Students need to know to reach beyond themselves for help, know how to

do so, and where to go. Sources of help may be other people (study buddies, homework help centers, relatives) or other sources (reference books, online services, reference librarians).

4. **Strategies: What strategies am I using or could I use?** Do I have alternatives when a strategy isn't working? Students need to know and use appropriate strategies to deal with academic tasks. A voluminous literature confirms that students do significantly better in academic work when their teachers explicitly teach them strategies for improving reading comprehension, organizing and revising writing, and reviewing, remembering, and summarizing (Paris, Wasik, & Turner, 1991; Pressley, Borkowski, & Schneider, 1987).

Video: Teaching Effective Effort

5. **Use of feedback: How or where can I get feedback on how I am doing? What does the feedback tell me about how to improve my performance?** Good students listen to and look carefully at the feedback they get from teachers and use it to improve their performance.

6. **Commitment: When something is difficult, do I stick with it? Do I really try hard?** Effective effort is grounded in will. You have to want to accomplish something to put out the effort and organize yourself to complete a tough learning task. You don't have to like it, but you do have to be committed to trying hard.

How to Support Effective Effort

Some version of Table 14.9 might be given to students periodically to reflect on a project they are submitting, or an exam they are preparing for, to keep in their minds what it means to invest effective effort.

Each of the attributes of effective effort has implications for things we can do to support students in investing their effort effectively:

- **Time:** It is worth discussing with students and coming to agreement about how much time they should expect to spend on an academic assignment to meet high standards.

- **Focus:** Students have to have a clear idea of what the focus is, that is, the precise instructional objective. We need to create clear images for students of the performances they should be shooting for. That means more than just telling the objective, it means showing them what meeting it would look like (communicating criteria for success and sharing exemplars where feasible). Focus also means eliminating distractions when studying.

Videos: The Power of Concentration, Teaching Strategies

Table 14.9 Student Effort Checklist

Student effort checklist	√
1. Did I put in sufficient time to get the job gone?	
2. Did I focus efficiently and without distraction?	
3. Did I reach out for help and know where to go for it?	
4. Did I use different strategies and alternatives?	
5. Did I get and use feedback during my work?	
6. Did I stick with it even when it was hard?	

▲ **Resourcefulness:** This means teaching students directly what the resources are and how to use them. In a fourth-grade class we visited, groups of children were giving reports on Native American tribes. It could have been any fourth grade in America—models of hogans, teepees, longhouses—except for one thing. Every group started its report with a child's recounting where he or she had gotten the information, what the obstacles were, and how the child had overcome them. This was a teacher who had taught the students how to use outside help to get information and who expected them to do so at every opportunity.

▲ **Strategies:** It is our responsibility to teach students how to use learning strategies, regardless of the content area and grade levels we teach. We all need to be teachers of reading, writing, thinking, and reasoning strategies as they are essential, transferable skills for learning in every discipline. Students need to learn how to use strategies like these to do academic work:

- Graphic organizers for planning, note-taking, and summarizing.
- Periodic summarizing to support retention and deepen understanding while reading, watching, or listening to information.
- Note-taking to bring meaning to and deepen understanding of what their notes say.
- SQ3R (Survey, Question, Read, Recite, Respond) to preview a reading to support comprehension.
- Mnemonic keyword technique for memorizing (see Chapter 12, "Principles of Learning").

Students should participate in constructing strategy lists ("Ways to Remember Something," "Effective Ways to Study for a Test," "Strategies for Getting Help") that hang on the classroom wall or go into their notebooks for future reference. Finally, students should have practice naming and evaluating the effectiveness of the strategies they have used, and identifying alternatives where necessary. David Perkins refers to this as developing reflective intelligence and proposes that it accounts for a significant dimension of a person's intelligent behavior (Perkins, 1995).

Teachers must also help students see how these strategies can be transferred to other academic tasks. Otherwise, students may not think to use the strategies beyond the specific context in which we teach them. (The how-tos of "teaching for transfer" are explained in more detail in Chapter 12, "Principles of Learning.")

Video: Students Use Feedback

▲ **Feedback and praise:** Earlier in this chapter, we discussed responding to student performance using feedback and praise. To use feedback and praise as a vehicle for attribution retraining, we need to intentionally embed specific effort and ability attributions in our responses:

- "You've proven in your work all week that you have the brainpower to do some very challenging problems. There must be some strategy you aren't using yet that would be the breakthrough on these. Let's look at how you are approaching them and do some brainstorming."
- "You really concentrated on organizing your ideas and taking time to plan before you wrote your final piece. Nice job!"
- "You stuck with the task—you never gave up—and now look at what you've accomplished."
- "When you saw that your first strategy wasn't working, you took another approach; and now look at the progress you've made on this."

Effective effort requires that we teach students to examine our feedback and use it. Behind students doing so to good effect is that they know the criteria for success and that our feedback tells them how they are doing on those criteria specifically. In the video referenced in the sidebar that supports this point, the teacher explicitly makes time and space for student to use the feedback, as Dylan Wiliam recommends in the video "Feedback According to Criteria for Success," referenced earlier on p. 355.

Videos: Perseverance, The Power of "Yet," The Power of Words

- **Commitment:** To help students understand the importance of commitment and to mobilize them to make it, we need to teach them how to set goals that are specific, challenging, attainable, written, and revisited (see Chapter 12, "Principles of Learning"). Goal setting and having students review their goals frequently gives students the tools for making commitments that go beyond hopes and empty promises. It also causes students to self-evaluate and brings them in frequent contact with their teachers to share the evaluation and the data on which the goal was based.

Attribution retraining requires us to monitor our language and replace statements like "Good luck" with effort-oriented statements such as, "Give it everything you've got," and replace comments like, "Don't worry; it's easy," with statements like, "This is really challenging work. It's hard stuff, so give it your undivided attention, stick with it, recall all of the strategies you have for [whatever is involved], and you will get it." And when students have done very well, instead of saying, "You are so smart!" we need to say something like, "You have obviously really applied yourself, and your effort paid off."

We need to talk with students about their life-limiting and life-liberating beliefs (listed in Table 14.7 on page 379) and consider how our classrooms and school can be designed to reinforce the life-liberating beliefs (see Chapter 16, "Classroom Climate").

Finally, we might give students a tool for self-assessing their effort (separate from their achievement) and ask them to score themselves at the end of certain assignments or projects. Marzano, Pickering, and Pollock (2001) offer the rubrics shown in Exhibit 14.3 that pair achievement with effort; the student scores both. Presumably, if one kept a running record of student achievement and effort using these rubrics, students themselves could draw conclusions about the connection between the two. This effort rubric focuses only on continuing to work or "pushing myself." An effort rubric could also include "using feedback" and "trying other strategies."

Some additional suggestions for teaching and reinforcing the value of effective effort, compiled by Ann Stern, a senior consultant at Research for Better Teaching are listed in Table 14.10.

Exhibit 14.3 Effective Effort Rubrics

Scale: 4 = excellent; 3 = good; 2 = needs improvement; 1 = unacceptable

A: EFFORT RUBRIC	B: ACHIEVEMENT RUBRIC
4. I worked on the task until it was completed. I pushed myself to continue working on the task even when difficulties arose or a solution was not immediately evident. I viewed difficulties that arose as opportunities to strengthen my understanding. 3. I worked on the task until it was completed. I pushed myself to continue working on the task even when difficulties arose or a solution was not immediately evident. 2. I put some effort into the task, but stopped working when difficulties arose. 1. I put very little effort into the task.	4. I exceeded the objectives of the task or lesson. 3. I met the objectives of the task or lesson. 2. I met a few of the objectives of the task or lesson, but did not meet others. 1. I did not meet the objectives of the task or lesson.

Student	Assignment	Effort Rubric	Achievement Rubric
Fri., Oct. 22	Homework— 5-paragraph essay re: *Animal Farm*	4	4
Wed., Oct. 27	In-class essay re: allegory	4	3
Thurs., Oct. 28	Pop quiz	3	3

Adapted from Marzano, Pickering, & Pollock (2001).

Table 14.10 Teaching and Reinforcing Effective Effort

How often do you?	Never	Rarely	Some-times	Most of the Time	Always
1. Tell personal stories of your effective effort.					
2. Ask students to recall times they succeeded because they didn't give up.					
3. Search for stories and examples of inspirational people students look up to who have achieved and excelled because of their persistence, determination, and hard work.					
4. Use literature; share books about effort and where the central characters don't give up.					
5. Make effective effort a theme in your team or school.					
6. Recognize and celebrate effort: "You have really developed your skill in creating vivid images in your writing. All of your revision efforts paid off. This piece should be published!"					
7. Praise effort, not intelligence, in your choice of language.					
8. Prior to doing a task, have students identify what strategies they will use to be successful. Collect them on charts. Post and add to these charts as time and tasks go on.					
9. When students succeed, ask them to identify what accounted for their success, and hold them accountable for figuring out how their effort played a role.					
10. Saturate your environment with efficacy messages.					
11. Have students use the effort and achievement rubric in Exhibit 14.3 to score themselves and track the relationship between their effort and achievement.					
12. When a student says, "This is easy," you reply, "It wasn't always easy. What did you do to get smart at it?"					
13. Have students visualize the actual physical moves (follow guidelines of mental imagery) for arranging time and place for effective practice or study.					

Coda

The Expectations area of performance is an example of the way in which teaching is more a calling than a job. If successful teaching involves getting students to be believers in themselves, then that is a way in which this business resembles the clergy more than a craft. The thrust of this whole chapter is that we need to behave as if we believe that all students can learn rigorous material at high standards.

Different though we each may be in our genetic endowment, if we could all do the incredibly complicated analytical task of learning to speak and communicate by age three, then we all have enough intelligence to do academic material well—that is, if we exert enough effective effort. The key word here is *effective.* Just exerting more effort—harder or longer—is no guarantee of success for a struggling student.

CHAPTER QUICK GUIDE

STRAND 1: What You Expect Is What You Get

Four Kinds of Standards:

1. Quality and quantity of work
2. Work habits and procedures
3. Business and housekeeping routines
4. Interpersonal behavior

Eleven Ways to Communicate Standards: (1) *Direct Communication, (2) Specific Communication, (3) Repeated Communication, (4) Positive Expectancy, (5) Modeled, (6) Personal Contact, (7) No Excuses, (8) Recognizing Superior Performance or Significant Gains Over Past Performance, (9) Logical Consequences for Poor Performance, (10) Tenacity, and (11) Feedback.*

STRAND 2: Growth Mindset—Effort-Based Ability or Incrementalist Theory

- "Smart is not something you are; smart is something you get (incrementally) by working hard and working smart" (Jeff Howard, The Efficacy Institute).
- The three critical messages: "This is important. You can do it. I'm not going to give up on you."
- Attribution Theory and Attribution Retraining

STRAND 3: The Behaviors of High Expectations Teaching

The 10 Arenas of Classroom Life:

1. Calling on Students
2. Responding to Students' Answers
3. Giving Help
4. Changing Attitude Toward Errors—Persevere and Return
5. Giving and Negotiating Tasks and Assignments
6. Giving Feedback According to Criteria for Success
7. Positive Framing for Reteaching
8. Tenacity
9. Grades, Retakes, and Redos
10. Grouping

To check your knowledge about Expectations, see the exercises on *The Skillful Teacher* website at www.RBTeach.com/TST7.

CHAPTER 15

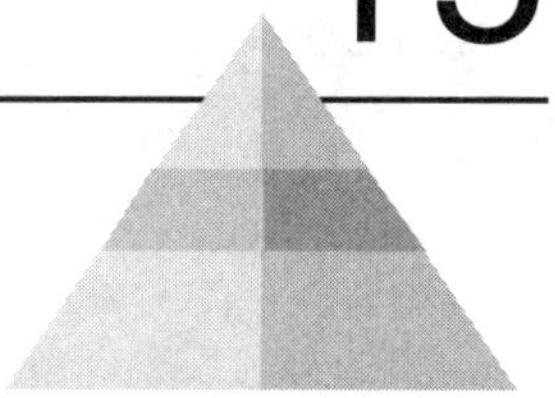

Motivation
Personal Relationship Building

Motivation:

Personal Relationship Building

> In his "Bearhug" poem, Ondaaje describes how his child from the bedroom has been calling him for a goodnight kiss. The father yells, "Okay, I'm coming." But he was finishing something and then does this and that before he finally responds to the child's calling. As Ondaatje slowly walks through the bedroom door he sees his little boy: "He is standing arms outstretched waiting for a bearhug. Grinning." Ondaatje gives a marvelous poetic description of the way a parent hugs a child. But then, almost as an after-thought, two short lines end the poem: "How long was he standing there like that, before I came?" (van Manen, 1991, p. 104)

All our children are standing there, not so obviously with their arms outstretched, waiting to be hugged. Do we see them? The long reach and powerful grasp of caring relationships in schools is well documented in close to seventy years of education research (Ancess, 2003). Consistent research suggests a strong association between student-adult relationships and student retention, achievement, graduation, and aspirations, especially in an urban context (Stanton-Salazar, 2001; Valenzuela, 1999). Emotional bonds with adults serve as a foundation for the development of intellectual and social competence in students (Newmann, 1993). This chapter addresses "caring relationships" in the classroom (Velasques, West, Graham, & Osguthorpe, 2013). One way students conclude teachers care about them is if the teachers are seen to be working hard to make sure they can learn.

Video: No Child Left Unknown

> You can tell the difference between a fake teacher and a real teacher. The real teachers want to get inside of how you're doing something, so maybe next year they can do it differently. A real teacher, he's someone who works the day shift teaching you, and taking the information he gets from you and going back on his lesson plan or the lesson plan he gets here from the school, he will take what they give him and change it up to what he thinks from what he got from his students will match how they learn. You're still getting what you need of all the elements in that class, but he's teaching it a whole different way. If the principal came in and said, "OK, what's this? We didn't give you that!" He'd say, "My kids will learn better if I did it this way." (Interview conducted by A. Platt, 2002)

So you show you care about my learning by going out of your way to reshape a lesson that didn't work the first time. You are also willing to take me aside and reteach materials and to make extra help readily available, and do so in a way that expresses belief in me (see Framing Reteaching in Chapter 14, "Expectations"). In Chapter 14, "Expectations," we provide an extensive view of tenacity: the persistence with which you will pursue me, do not accept poor work, express confidence in me, and push me to learn. Conflict and tension may arise between student and parent demands and what the teacher deems best for the student (Goldstein, 1998), but the teacher will not lower his or her expectations. About these teachers students often later say, "I could run, but I couldn't hide."

Personal relationship building complements hard work and insistence on quality production from students. As one Latina student stated about her teacher, "She [the teacher] tries to help me. Whenever I don't get something she tries to help me by reteaching the lesson." Another Latino student stated, "She asks if we need help" (Garza, 2009). Together, they result in what the literature calls "caring." But one also notes that "academic opportunities were balanced with relational experiences" (Velasques, West, Graham, & Osguthorpe, 2013).

HOW GOOD PERSONAL RELATIONS CONNECT TO STUDENT ACHIEVEMENT

Why is it that good personal relations are connected to student achievement? What do teachers do to create these relationships? What are the repertoires for developing and maintaining positive teacher-student relationships?

Geneva Gay (2000) writes:

> I think interpersonal relations have a tremendous impact on the quality of teaching and learning. Students perform much better in environments where they feel comfortable and valued. Therefore, I work hard at creating a classroom environment and ambiance of warmth, support, caring, dignity, and informality. Yet, these psycho-emotional factors do not distract from the fact that my classes are very demanding intellectually. Students are expected to work hard and at high levels of quality. (p. 197)

Judith Kleinfeld (1975) coined the term "warm-demander" to describe the person Gay pictures. "Warm" without the "demanding" is problematic. "Demanding" without the "warm" is as well (Rivera-McCutchen, 2012). A teacher who invests time and energy in building relationships with students signals to them that they are respected and valued as worthwhile individuals, which most often results in students' liking and respecting their teacher. In turn, students will participate and contribute positively to the classroom climate, and they will be less likely to buck the program or become discipline problems.

In the face of positive relationships, students more readily accept rules, procedures, and disciplinary actions that follow violations of the rules (Marzano, 2003). Students who have neutral or negative relationships with their teachers are less inhibited from misbehavior and more likely to disengage. In one study of how ethnically diverse high school students, who have experienced disciplinary problems, explain the causes of conflicts with their teachers, Sheets and Gay (1996) note that "the causes of many classroom behaviors labeled and punished as rule infractions are, in fact, problems of students and teachers relating to each other interpersonally" (pp. 86–87). Positive relationships contribute to a classroom climate where there is greater energy available for and devoted to learning.

> Adolescents are ready to work and achieve when they know that people care about them, that what they're learning matters, and that they possess the skills necessary to meet a given challenge. . . . Effective middle school teachers . . . recognize that if they do not meet their students' social and emotional needs, they will waste their content area expertise. Students simply will not achieve academically when their affective needs go unaddressed. (Daniels, 2005, p. 52)

Students simply will not achieve academically when their affective needs go unaddressed.

A strong positive relationship says to a student, "I value you and I want the best for you," which renders a teacher a significant adult in the student's life and affords the teacher opportunities to demand and support more academic rigor from their students. The relationship can serve as a vehicle for influencing academic identity, convincing students that they are capable of performing at high levels, and getting seemingly unmotivated students to come to school, stay in school, complete assignments, participate in class, and persist in the face of academic challenges. Teachers can use a relationship "as leverage to help students transcend difficult and troubling times, develop personal discipline, and reconnect when they are at risk of dropping out" (Ancess, 2003, p. 63).

As a result, we see strong connections between "Personal Relationship Building" and several other areas of performance, most notably "Classroom Climate" (affording students a sense of safety, belonging, and willingness to take risks), "Discipline" (and classroom management), "Clarity," "Differentiated Instruction," and "Expectations" (influencing students' willingness to work hard and see themselves as academically able to achieve high standards). Some suggest that Personal Relationship Building is the keystone to these other very significant areas of teaching performance. In addition, recognizing the importance of warm teacher-student relationships becomes an anchor for pursuing tailored instructional delivery and for the design of culturally relevant lessons.

EIGHT KEY TEACHER TRAITS AND BEHAVIORS

When students are interviewed about their relationships with teachers, there is a cluster of teacher characteristics or traits and certain classes of teacher behavior students repeatedly mention as important (Ancess, 2003; Cushman, 2003; Johnson, 1976). Following are these teacher traits (Figure 15.1):

1. Acknowledging students
2. Communicating value
3. Respecting students
4. Demonstrating fairness
5. Exhibiting realness
6. Being open to humor and having fun
7. Building students' interests into learning experiences
8. Culturally relevant instruction

1. Acknowledging Students

Students describe ways teachers make them feel noticed and acknowledged:

- ▲ Greeting students individually as they enter the room, pass in the halls, and so forth.
- ▲ Welcoming them back when they have been out due to illness.
- ▲ Making eye contact with them during whole-group instruction.
- ▲ Noticing when they aren't participating and encouraging them to do so.
- ▲ Noticing when a student has confusion on his or her face and doing something about it.
- ▲ Using procedures to ensure that all student voices are heard in class discussions.

Figure 15.1 Eight Key Teacher Traits for Personal Relationship Building

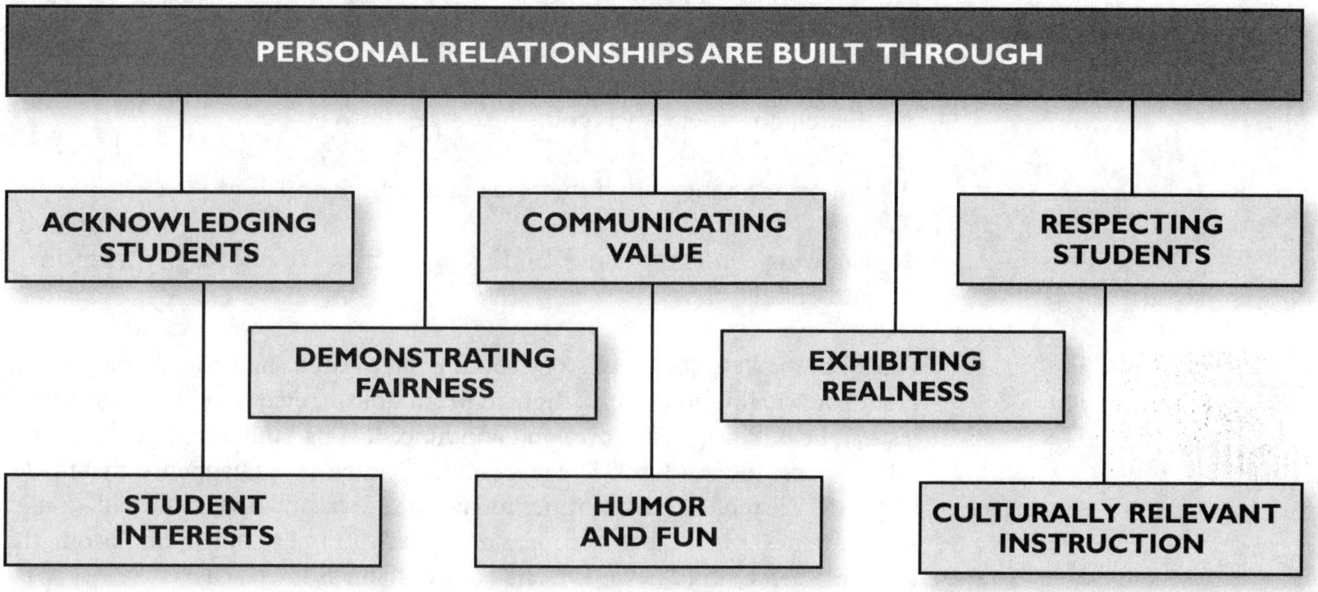

2. Communicating Value

We believe there are at least five subcategories of things students notice that give them a sense that the teacher values them: (1) showing interest in them, (2) being a good listener, (3) communicating high expectations to them as individuals, (4) re-establishing contact if there has been a reason to discipline a student, and (5) being accessible to them.

Video: Communicating Value

Showing Interest

Showing interest encompasses all the ways in which teachers show interest in students as individuals and as learners. This includes the following:

- ▲ Knowing where students live and what their neighborhood looks like.
- ▲ Listening carefully and actively learning about their concerns and fears.
- ▲ Asking about their strengths and interests.

- ▲ Finding out what their daily schedule looks like in and out of school.
- ▲ Knowing what their responsibilities are outside school.
- ▲ Getting to know these things early in the year.
- ▲ Asking how their day is going.
- ▲ Inquiring about them if they are out of school or ill.
- ▲ Knowing students' names, and using them when addressing them in and out of class.

One of our colleagues tells a story about a night when she was helping her fifth-grade son with his homework. Right in the middle of reviewing for his social studies test, he put his pencil down and announced, "I had the best day of my whole school career today, Mom!" She responded, "Really? What happened that made it so good?" He replied, "Three times today when I was walking in the hall, teachers who have never had me in their classes passed me and said, 'Hi, Jon.' Mom, they knew my name, and I never even had any of them as my teachers!"

Teachers can make students feel important by:

- Connecting academic work to their interests.
- Using their names in instructional examples.
- Having brief one-on-one conversations.
- Making time to see and be available to them outside class.
- Asking what's bothering them when their facial expression says something is wrong.
- Attending their extracurricular events to cheer them on

Showing interest in them as learners might include:

- Gathering data from them and teaching them about the types of learners they are.
- Finding out what their positive and negative experiences have been thus far in school or in a particular subject area.

- Finding out what they already know or have experienced in relation to a topic or skill to be taught.
- Interrupting a lesson to check their understanding (frequently and broadly across the class).
- Getting their input at the close of class about what supported their learning and what hindered it, and responding to what their responses reveal.
- Finding out why a student might not be participating.
- Finding out what they think is hard and what's not.
- Finding a way to discern if they aren't comfortable participating in a large group.
- Finding out how and with whom they are comfortable or uncomfortable working.
- Showing interest in the subject matter taught and presenting material to students with passion and enthusiasm.
- Making connections to their world so they see reasons why the material is worth learning.

Hammond (2015) extends this framework of interest to the compassionate level of being concerned when a student or student's family experiences illness, trauma, loss, or some other form of difficulty.

At a time when it is vitally important for adolescents to experience school as a stable, predictable, and hospitable place to be, Rodriguez (2005) underscores the importance of these efforts:

> Solid teacher student relationships give urban adolescents an anchor as they learn in an often unpredictable environment. To help students respond to our efforts, teachers must first acknowledge students as persons, legitimize their knowledge and experiences, and engage with them personally and intellectually. In doing so, educators recognize students as whole people and show them that they are valued, thereby relaying a message of hope. (p. 80)

Being a Good Listener

"She really listens to me" is a common statement students make about teachers they like and respect. "I know my teacher cares because he takes me seriously when I share my personal and academic problems." Students yearn for teachers who are willing to listen and really hear what they have to say (Daniels, 2005). We believe there are at least two dimensions of listening that matter to students: focus and empathy.

Listening with focus:

- ▲ Listening attentively and without interrupting.
- ▲ Acknowledging (verbally or non-verbally) what is being said.
- ▲ Inquiring for details rather than making assumptions when information is vague or unclear.
- ▲ Checking understanding by paraphrasing or summarizing to ensure that we have heard accurately.
- ▲ Posing reflective questions that invite further thinking or exploration of a topic of interest or concern to a student.

Many teachers practice these behaviors naturally and, at a less-than-conscious level, in situations that don't involve intense emotion. However, in times of high excitement (enthusiasm, stress, tension, anxiety, frustration, annoyance, distress) on the part of the listener or the speaker, we need to be more conscious of monitoring these behaviors.

Listening with empathy:

Listening with empathy means listening in a way that enables us to understand both the content of what the speaker is saying and the feelings that accompany the content. This is particularly important the more intense the emotional state of the speaker and/or the listener is, or in situations where one's perspective about something is quite different from another's.

Active listening, a core skill taught in communication and conflict management training, is a particular way of listening and responding to another person with the intent of coming to understand the other's point of view. Active listening involves paraphrasing or summarizing what the speaker has said, and the paraphrase is an acknowledgment, as well as a check for understanding, regarding the content of their remarks and the inferred feeling state of the speaker. It is an attempt to signal to the speaker that he or she has been heard on multiple levels (content and affect). For example, when a student says, "I just can't do this work! These problems are too hard. There is no way I will ever get this done. I don't have enough time. I give up!" An active listener might say, "So you're stuck on these problems [content] and getting really frustrated [feeling]."

A student who has come to class late, is without homework regularly, and has been falling asleep in class says in an after-school meeting with the teacher "I have to drop this class. I have too much work to do; I don't have time to do homework. My boyfriend says I never have time for him. I have to babysit my little sister and brother every day 'til my mother gets home at night, and I have a job three nights a week to help pay our rent." The teacher says, "So you have several very significant responsibilities in addition to everything you are expected to do to keep up in school, and you are overwhelmed with trying to balance it all."

In both instances, the teacher as listener is using the paraphrase of content and emotion to ensure that he has accurately understood what is going on for the student before offering suggestions, giving advice, or providing another perspective.

A teacher who actively listens communicates concern for the student's personal feeling states and her desire to understand. Although it can be used manipulatively and insincerely, on-target and genuine active listening is the verbal behavioral embodiment of empathy. When combined with accuracy and respect (Egan, 1975), active listening makes children feel understood and cared about (Aspy & Roebuck, 1977; Rosenberg, 1999).

High Expectations and Persistence

Students who have persistent teachers internalize a message something like this: "You wouldn't take the time or exert the energy to push me and persist with me if you didn't think I was a worthwhile person. Especially if you do it with humor, some nurturing, and encouragement. I know you value me. I warm to that, and feel respected by it."

Students interpret communicating high expectations, holding them accountable, and supporting them in meeting expectations as their teacher regarding them as a worthwhile person.

High expectations might be communicated about:

- ▲ Academic performance
- ▲ Work habits
- ▲ Interpersonal behavior
- ▲ Being an active participant in class
- ▲ Showing up and being on time for class
- ▲ Taking responsibility
- ▲ Assuming leadership roles

That a teacher communicates high expectations constitutes the basis for relationship building. How a teacher does this is the central focus of Chapter 14, "Expectations."

Persistence is what we do to "chase" when students aren't living up to our expectations or performing up to par; when they are resistant, passive, or practice avoidance behaviors in the face of challenge. In short, when students don't yet see themselves as capable of achieving or measuring up, persistence signals our conviction that they can do it, and we won't give up on them.

Persistence signals our conviction that students can do it, and we won't give up on them.

Persistence might show up as:

- ▲ Finding a student in the halls and reminding him he needs to see you.
- ▲ Making extra time to work or be with a student.
- ▲ Sticking with a student and explaining until he gets it.
- ▲ Finding three more ways to explain something when the first three didn't work.
- ▲ Wake-up calls to a student who is chronically late to school.

Persistence and support are the left and right hands of effectively communicating expectations.

Re-Establishing Contact

When a teacher strongly reprimands a student (for example, sends the student out of the room) or carries out some high-voltage disciplinary move ("You cannot destroy someone else's work. If you can't help him rebuild it, this area is closed to you for the day"), his or her relationship with that student may be under a cloud of tension (as it should be). After such incidents, the teacher who keeps good relationships looks to interact in a positive, personal way with the student around some other context. There is no apology in the teacher move or any implied backing down from the firmness of the previous move. It's simply a way of saying, "Okay, let's get in touch again. I still value you as a person." This is "re-establishing contact": conveying the message that, while the behavior was unacceptable, the teacher is not carrying a grudge, and the relationship remains intact. It removes the tension between the teacher and student, and gives the student an emotional entry back into the flow of activities.

Toshalis (2015) also makes the point not to react with anger when a child is displaying anger:

> We should consider ourselves lucky when students trust us with their anger. We often claim that when they share with us their despair, fears or excitement, it's a sign we have a good relationship with them, but it's rare when educators are also pleased when students trust us with their rage. And on those occasions when we choose to engage students' anger, we often squander a potential connection by attempting to tamp down their expression. We'll say "calm down," "take it easy," or "lower your voice." The message we're sending is that conditions that inspired their anger are far less important than the way the anger is articulated. This preserves inequity as much as it silences dissent. (pp. 19–20)

We want to point out that the anger Toshalis describes is not the impulsive outbursts of children who lack inner controls; that calls for a totally different way of thinking and responding (see Chapter 10, "Discipline").

Being Accessible

Being accessible means making time available for students outside class time. It might be to provide extra academic help to students or support with personal or social issues students want to talk about. Students notice when teachers are giving up their "own time" (lunch, before and after school, free periods) to be available to them, and they interpret this as a measure of the teacher's commitment to them (Ancess, 2003). It's not enough just to say to students,

"I'm available after class each day for help." Students have to believe we mean it and that coming to us will be a productive and confidence-building experience. Therefore, often we have to say it again and again, and sometimes be even a bit more tenacious by requiring some students to show up until they see it is really not a punishment but a service to and for them.

3. Respecting Students

"Respect and fairness (equity) are identified as the prerequisites of effective teaching in the eyes of students . . . at all levels of schooling—from elementary to high school" (Stronge, 2002, p. 16). Respect from the student point of view has several faces and has some overlap with acknowledging and valuing them. Table 15.1 lists some examples of how students define respect (Ancess, 2003; Cushman, 2003; Gay, 2000).

It is also interesting to note how often in interview studies students comment on the appearance and dress of teachers they like. Perhaps, students take good grooming and neat, clean clothes as a sign of respect and regard from us.

4. Demonstrating Fairness

> Students know that by coming to school they are making a bargain with teachers, and they want it to be a fair one. . . . Whether they are "hard" or "easy" teachers, the adults who win students' trust and respect are the ones perceived as scrupulously fair in carrying out this usually unspoken bargain. (Cushman, 2003, p. 24)

Fairness seems to be the absolute prerequisite for personal regard. Unless students perceive a teacher as being fair in making decisions that bear on them (making assignments, arbitrating disputes, giving help, choosing teams), they cannot begin to like him or her. So on what basis do students determine whether a teacher is fair? Table 15.2 lists examples of what students tell us about fairness (Cushman, 2003; Jackson, 2016; Kobrin, 2004; Wubbels as cited in Marzano, 2003).

Students are asking us to keep no secrets about what is expected of them academically and behaviorally, to inform them ahead of time exactly what we will use as a basis for assessing their performance, to give them feedback based on the established expectations, and to be treated as individuals capable of high performance. At the same time, they ask that we monitor and avoid anything that could be construed as preferential or discriminatory treatment.

Table 15.1 How Students Define Respect

Treat us as valued and capable human beings.	Give us chances to express our opinions and views without being put down.
Involve us in decisions that will directly affect us.	Speak to us with the same courtesy and respect you'd want from us.
Treat each of us as capable of challenging work.	Treat us as individuals and care about what's going on for us.
Appreciate our differences and individual styles.	Ask for our help or input when our peers are having problems.
Treat our work and products with care.	Don't compare us to other students.
Recognize why we might participate and why we might not. Afford us both options.	Respond to our inappropriate behavior or unacceptable academic performance without denigrating us.
Discipline us privately when the need arises.	Respond to misbehavior at the individual level rather than holding the whole class responsible for the actions of one student or a small group.
Be honest and matter-of-fact when rules are broken, and remind us why it matters.	Remember that we are often insecure, and when we act in unacceptable ways, please be kind and respond with that in mind.
Treat our mistakes as just that, and help us to learn from them.	Correct our errors without using put-downs, making us feel dumb, or shaming us.
Tell us what to do right.	Try to work out behavior issues with us before calling home.
Use our time well.	Be prepared for class or give us something meaningful to do while we wait.
Know your material, and present it enthusiastically.	Teach interesting and important material.
Use curriculum and activities that relate to our interests and strengths.	Present ideas and activities in ways that we can relate to.
Remember we need to stretch and talk periodically.	Show interest in our success, and help us to get what we need from school.
Display our hard work.	Give us feedback on our work that shows you really examined it.
Give us feedback that we can use to improve our performance.	Follow through on agreements and commitments, and don't betray our confidences.
Return our assignments in a timely manner.	Behave in ways you expect us to behave.
When we tell you things in private, keep them private.	When we take risks, support us, and protect our right to make mistakes and learn from them.
Inspire us as a role model of what you expect from us.	

Table 15.2 What Students Say About Fairness

Let us know what to expect from you so we don't get taken by surprise.
Let us know your plan: share the itinerary, objectives, expectations for work, and criteria by which you will assess our work.
Tell us how you will grade our work before we do it, and give it to us in writing (in a handout or on the walls).
Grade us fairly.
Create reasonable rules, apply them consistently and fairly, and be flexible.
Treat us consistently, but also as individuals.
Don't play favorites, alienating some of us while being friendly with others.
Don't favor the students you think will do best.
Don't make assumptions. Ask questions when there is something you don't understand.
When there is conflict between two of us [students], be sure you hear both sides of the situation before delivering consequences.
Let us know when you are displeased with our actions; don't just simmer until you blow up at someone.
Warn offenders two or three times at most; then impose the consequence.

5. Exhibiting Realness

Videos: Realness 1, 2

Students want teachers who "are willing to talk about their own personal lives and experiences" (Stronge, 2002, p. 15). Because a teacher is in a position of authority, this dimension of relationship building is important to consider. Authority can act as a screen that distances relationships and obscures the humanness of thinking, feeling people with personal histories of lived experience. When young children address their teacher figure as "teacher" rather than by name, we get a glimpse of the teacher as authority. Students begin to see their teacher as real, as a person, only if the teacher lets them. There are behaviors that reveal aspects of ourselves to allow this image of authority figure to be tempered by images of teacher as a real person. Sharing anecdotes with students from our own lives and integrating appropriate personal experiences into explanations and presentations enables students to get to know us as people.

One of the strategies, described in Chapter 5, "Attention," is an "I message"— a statement a teacher might make to a student or students in response to an inappropriate or off-task behavior. In an "I message" (Gordon, 1974), the teacher explicitly states her feelings and the behavior or circumstance that made her feel that way. When there exists a relationship of regard and respect, "I messages" can be another way to let students see their teacher as a person with feelings. Gordon reports numerous cases of children who, when confronted by "I messages," change their disruptive behavior; these children had no idea their behavior was affecting their teacher adversely.

Zaretta Hammond (2015) takes realness a little further by citing "selective vulnerability." "People respect and connect with others who share their own vulnerable moments. It means showing your human side that is not perfect. . . . Psychologists have long known that self-disclosure is one of the hallmarks of intimate, trusting relationships" (pp. 79–80). Examples include being willing to apologize and admit a mistake, as well as more revelatory acts like the following:

> Tell your story by weaving it into your lesson—what were you like as a student? What were your favorite subjects? What were some challenges for you? Bring in pictures of yourself as a child during your school days.
>
> Share a new skill or process you are learning—not the finished product but the less-than-perfect beginning and middle parts.
>
> Share your interests with the whole class and then find fellow fans . . . (Hammond, 2015, pp. 80–81)

6. Being Open to Humor and Fun

William Glasser (1998) says humor is a form of caring, and that the need to have fun is one of the five basic human needs. Teachers need not be comedians, but those who respond openly to humorous moments or who can kid with students seem to strike particularly responsive chords. Students talk about liking teachers who are happy and smile a lot, have a great sense of humor, tell funny stories, can laugh at themselves, can joke around and laugh when a student makes a joke that is funny or when something genuinely humorous happens in class. In other words, they want to know that we know how to have fun and can enjoy doing that with them.

7. Building Student Interests into Learning Experiences

The better we know our students as individuals, the more information we have with which to make instructional decisions like how to make the content relevant and personally meaningful, how to hook student interest, how to group students for academic tasks, and how and when to intervene or offer support. When these decisions reflect awareness of student interests, background knowledge and experience base, characteristic behaviors, and learning style orientation and preferences, we are most successful in matching the learning experiences to the unique needs of our students. Thus students have a greater chance of succeeding academically.

8. Culturally Relevant Instruction

A culturally relevant lesson design is particularly important for students of color and ESL students who may come from countries with different cultures than the dominant U.S. Eurocentric culture. Students will feel known and valued when their cultures, histories, and heroes show up in the references, connections, characters, and artifacts of lessons. Culturally proficient teaching allows students to process information (Hammond, 2015) because their minds are not fighting the energy to cope with a foreign environment. A classroom that has no recognition of a student's culture feels unfamiliar; it conveys the message "you are not included" to students. Zanger notes, "Interviews with Latino high school students found that they did not feel as if they were part of the school or the classroom; they spoke of feeling invisible and of being treated as if they were less worthy than other students" (as cited in Rolón, 2003, p. 41).

Elyse Hambacher and Elizabeth Bondy (2017) go so far as to call this kind of instruction "culturally relevant critical care," borrowing a term from Mary Roberts (2010):

> This way of thinking synthesizes the work of scholars, particularly scholars of color, who describe educators, care for marginalized students as an act of social justice (Bouboeuf-LaFontant, 2005). Such caring is "culturally relevant" because teachers learn about and respond to the values, knowledge, and histories of their students; it's "critical" because it shows insight into the sociopolitical realities of students' lives, particularly a history of injustice that shapes their educational experience and opportunities. (p. 50)

Two other ideas Bondy and Hambacher advance in this important article are "audacious hope" and "asset based thinking"—ideas that carry embedded caring for students of color. For more on this topic, see Chapter 4, "Essential Beliefs: Cultural Proficiency and Anti-Racism."

CHAPTER QUICK GUIDE

▲ The quality of relationships between teachers and students is a deep and constant backdrop to all that is transpiring in classrooms.

Eight Key Teacher Traits That Support Personal Relationship Building:

1. Acknowledging
2. Valuing
3. Respecting
4. Demonstrating fairness
5. Authenticity (realness)
6. Humor and having fun
7. Building students' interests into learning experiences
8. Culturally relevant instruction

To check your knowledge about Personal Relationship Building, see the exercises on *The Skillful Teacher* website at www.RBTeach.com/TST7.

NOTES

CHAPTER 16

Motivation
Classroom Climate

Motivation: *Classroom Climate*

The research on classroom climate is thin but clear. Thin because the volume of studies is much smaller than in the cognitive areas, clear because the findings are consistent across populations, ages of students, and subjects. Whenever students feel empowered, accepted, and safe to take risks and try things that are hard for them, they like school better and learn more (Fraser, 1986; Fraser & Fisher, 1983; Fraser, Malone, & Neale, 1989; Haertel, Walberg, & Haertel, 1981; Matsumura, Slater, & Crosson, 2008; Moos & Moos, 1978; Nunnery, Butler, & Bhaireddy, 1993; Reyes et al., 2012).

This sounds like common sense, and it is, but the research in this area is approximately where research on "Clarity" was 30 years ago. At that time, we knew that teachers who were rated as "clear" on a Likert scale got better results with students. We did not know, however, what they did in their practice to earn those ratings. We did not have a construct for the elements of clarity and how they were related to one another, an operational model for how they worked in interrelationship, or a sense of whether some of the elements were more important than others. We know a great deal more about clarity now. We can, at least, profile essential elements and use data to support their individual contributions to successful teaching and learning. The same is not true for classroom climate. We are still at the Likert scale stage.

Although the tradition of research on classroom climate has roots in the 1920s, Withall (1949) was the first to formulate a definition of the group phenomenon known as social-emotional climate. He noted a general emotional factor which appears to be present in interactions occurring between individuals in face-to-face groups. It seems to have some relationship to the degree of acceptance expressed by members of a group regarding each other's needs or goals. Operationally defined, it is considered to influence the following:

- Inner private world of each individual
- Esprit de corps of the group
- Sense of meaningfulness of group and individual goals and activities

Figure 16.1 Psychological Needs and Student Learning

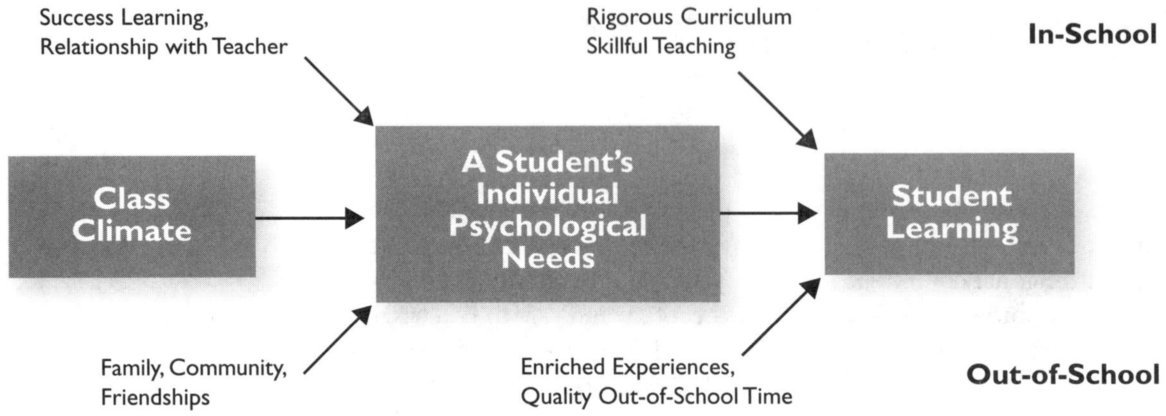

- ▲ Objectivity with which a problem is tackled
- ▲ Type and extent of interpersonal interaction in the group

Studies since then have examined high-inference variables and found better student achievement when the class is rated high on measures such as cohesiveness and satisfaction and low on measures such as friction, difficulty, and competitiveness (Fraser & O'Brien, 1985). Overall, these studies show that students' cognitive, affective, and behavioral outcomes are related to students' perceptions of psychosocial characteristics in classrooms (Battistich et al., 1995; Chavez, 1984).

Four propositions speak to the importance of classroom climate (Figure 16.1):

1. The basic psychological needs of all human beings make up an acknowledged and universal list: safety, self-control, affection, inclusion, self-esteem, recognition, self-actualization, freedom, and fun (Dreikurs & Grey, 1968; Glasser, 1965, 1998; Maslow, 1962; Schutz, 1967).

2. The degree to which one's psychological needs are met determines how much energy and attention is available for learning. If an individual is hurt and severely wanting in any of these needs, learning slows to a crawl or a halt. If these needs are adequately met, learning proceeds normally. If they are met at a high level and nourished, learning flourishes.

3. Classroom climate directly influences how students do in school. It influences individually how their thermometers read on each of the basic

psychological needs. It is a major variable shaping the degree to which each student's psychological needs are met during class time.

4. When the climate goes beyond meeting safety and security needs and develops strength on the important dimensions of climate—community, risk-taking, and influence—learning accelerates.

CLASSROOM CLIMATE: WHAT IS IT?

This is our operational definition of classroom climate: "the feelings and beliefs students have, and the cumulative patterns of behavior that result from those feelings and beliefs regarding community and mutual support, risk-taking and confidence, and influence and control." Community and mutual support are defined as an individual's feelings in relation to a group—feelings of acceptance, inclusion, membership, and maybe friendship and affection. Risk-taking and confidence represent an internal, personal dimension that is influenced significantly by the reactions of others to one's behaviors. Putdowns and sarcasm, however subtle they may be, reduce one's confidence that it is safe to risk thinking and trying. A classroom climate that rewards effort and persistence, de-emphasizes speed, and helps students learn that errors are merely opportunities for learning, not signs of personal deficiency. Influence and control represent the dimension of class climate that pertains to personal efficacy, defined as one's power to produce effects. It answers the following questions: To what degree do I, as an individual, get to make my presence felt legitimately in helping things function here? How am I empowered to be a player, an influencer, someone who matters, as opposed to a silent cipher whose existence makes no observable difference in the flow of life in the room, to say nothing of making choices about how I spend my own time? All three of these dimensions of class climate matter for student learning.

These three major strands of classroom climate are summarized in Figure 16.2, which treats each as a developmental aspect of climate. Developmental in that there are stages of sophistication and maturity for each of the three strands, so a teacher planning to strengthen any of them would do well to plan activities and new practices with the stages in mind. The stages for the first strand, community and mutual support, are well treated in the developmental literature (Aspy & Roebuck, 1977; Johnson & Johnson, 1995a; Wood, 1994a). The stages in the other two strands are more hypothetical, though their elements are supported individually by research. The sections that follow examine each strand separately and describe the meaning of each element in it. We also describe specific strategies and practices teachers can use to develop them.

Figure 16.2 Climate of High Achievement for All Students

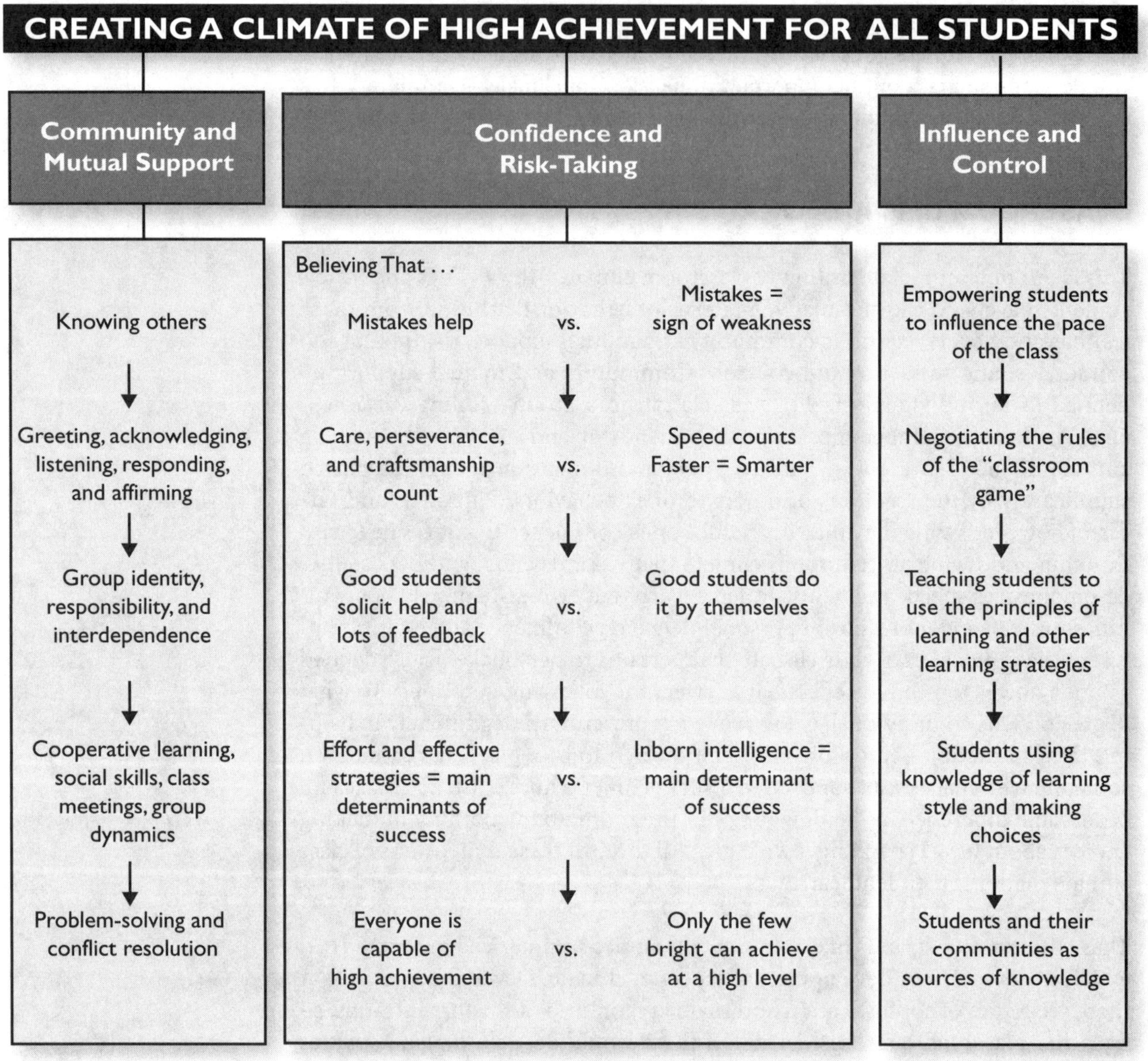

COMMUNITY AND MUTUAL SUPPORT

This dimension of climate describes the degree of inclusion, affiliation, and mutual support students feel with one another. When it is well developed, the student can say, "I feel accepted and included here. People are on my side. I can help others, and they will help me."

Within this dimension are five levels of development, each paired with a characteristic statement:

1. Knowing others: "I know these people and they know me."

2. Greeting, acknowledging, listening, responding, and affirming: "I feel accepted and included. People respect me, and I respect them."

3. Group identity, responsibility, and interdependence: "I'm a member of this group. We need each other and want each other to succeed."

4. Cooperative learning, social skills, group meetings, and group dynamics: "I can help others, and they will help me."

5. Problem-solving and conflict resolution: "We can solve problems that arise between us."

These relationships of warmth and inclusion don't get built by accident or by themselves. Teachers contribute through their behaviors to the strength and texture of the climate of inclusion and affiliation that students experience (Cabello & Terrell, 1993). This includes their verbal interaction patterns with individual students, their means of handling conflicts between students, the cooperative structures they introduce for interaction among students, and their explicit teaching of social skills.

Knowing Others

Gene Stanford, a high school English teacher, identified this strand of classroom climate as a developmental continuum in his 1977 book, *Developing Effective Classroom Groups*. He realized that the foundation of being a group member was knowing something about the others in the group. As a result, he regularly did brief "get acquainted" activities (21 are listed in his book) in the early months of the school year with students in his classes.

Teachers who periodically take a few minutes several times each week to do these activities do not report time problems keeping up with the curriculum or studying what is required. These modest frontend investments in building community increase efficiency and time on task in the long run. This is true for the other levels of community building in this strand.

Dozens of books are available with excellent "get acquainted" activities (Bennett & Smilanich, 1994; Seigle & Macklem, 1993; Shaw, 1992; Stanford, 1977) that are active and enjoyable. In "People Bingo" or the version called "Find a Person Who," students mingle and try to get signatures in boxes of a grid where facts are listed about others in the group, for example, "Spent a year outside the U.S." Each student has to find the person matched to that fact and get his or her signature in that box. Some activities are lengthier, like structured interviews of partners. After the interview, the partners introduce each other to the class or to a small group based on the interview.

One of our favorites has always been "Artifact Bags," which is just as popular among groups of adults as it is among fifth graders. Participants bring in unlabeled shopping bags containing five items that represent something about their lives or interests. At each session, one participant chooses a bag at random and displays the items in it one at a time to the other participants, who are sitting in a circle. Participants try to guess who the owner is. After the fifth item is shown and described by the person who has been picking from the bag (some items may be too small for all to see thoroughly when just held up), the group makes a collective guess. Then the real owner reveals himself or herself and explains the significance of each item. There may be time to do two or three people at each session. The popularity of this activity with adults signals how little opportunity there is in schools and school districts as workplaces to come to know one's colleagues. One doesn't have to take the whole faculty away on a retreat to pay attention to group and relationship building.

Community building strategies gain importance in the overall picture of classroom climate building for students as the forces of scheduling and course structures assume more importance starting in the sixth grade. These forces depersonalize and fracture the sense of community for students.

Greeting, Listening, Responding, Acknowledging, and Affirming

Have you ever noticed that in some settings (sometimes in whole towns) people look you in the eye, smile, and greet you when you walk by or enter their space? Beyond simply getting students information about each other, we should work on creating the conditions and teaching the skills of acknowledging and responding to one another. People who are greeted and acknowledged regularly feel affirmed and tend to be more available for learning. In the morning meeting structure at the Greenfield Center School in Greenfield, Massachusetts, the first activity uses one of the dozens of formats available for having the children greet one other around the circle. This is not a practice confined to the primary grades. Positive greeting is a form of acknowledgment worth fostering at any age. Wood (1994b) writes:

> It is important for students [of grades 4, 5, and 6] to not only greet each other in the morning, but to learn to greet any member of the class in a friendly and interested way. Issues of gender, cliques, and best friends are developmental milestones for 9–13-year-olds. Greetings help students to work on these issues in a safe structure every morning. It is the entry point for the teacher in her social curriculum each morning. (p. 162)

People who are greeted and acknowledged regularly feel affirmed and tend to be more available for learning.

A sample greeting activity appropriate for the elementary grades is a ball toss greeting, which can be varied so that it will be challenging and build cooperation for older children. It begins with the children standing in a circle and greeting each other one at a time by tossing a ball. For example, Leslie starts the greeting by saying, "Good morning, John!" and then tosses the ball to John. He returns Leslie's greeting, then chooses another child in the circle to greet and toss the ball to. When the ball has been tossed to everyone except Leslie, it finishes by returning to her with a greeting. In a variation, the ball goes around one more time silently (with no greeting or talking) repeating the pattern it just made. Children will enjoy doing it several times this way and competing against the clock (Stephenson & Watrous, 1993).

Acknowledging and affirming one another can be structured into group meeting times. The social competency curriculum (Seigle & Macklem, 1993) uses "Spotlight" as an activity to affirm positive attributes and behaviors. One child is picked by the teacher (a different one each time) to be in the spotlight. The others then take turns giving the selected child compliments with specific examples: "Tim, it's nice the way you are considerate of other kids, like when you made room for me to get into the circle." Each child may speak only once and must address the child selected, not the teacher. The child in the spotlight listens.

Good listening can be taught explicitly. Students can be warmed up to the qualities of good listening by doing a mirroring exercise. Two partners stand and decide who will be the leader (person A) and who the follower (person B). Partner A puts his or her hands up and moves them around, palms facing partner B, who has to make his or her hands exactly mirror A's hands. After about 45 seconds, the facilitator calls "time," and partners switch roles. A becomes the follower and B the leader. To do this activity well, both partners need to focus intently on each other; that sets the stage for direct teaching and practice of social skills, especially listening.

Direct teaching of children to listen involves role playing and practice. It can begin by asking students, "Think of someone who really listens to you. Why do you think that person does it?" Role play listening attentively with the class, and have them tell you what they saw and heard. Record their answers. Next, have students describe someone they know who doesn't listen. Do a role play with someone, and record what students say about the behaviors they heard and saw. Students are now ready to practice listening in trios: one listener, one speaker, and one observer.

Many teachers embed listening practice in classroom routines—for example, by asking a student who wants to speak to summarize what the previous students said in a discussion. This request is thrown out randomly so students can't predict when they'll have to summarize.

Group Identity, Responsibility, and Interdependence

Cooperative learning structures (Kagan, 2015) and cooperative models (Johnson & Johnson, 1987; Slavin, 1986) encourage team building because they form natural groups where individuals are allied with one another. Creating a team name, a logo, or a banner becomes a natural way for getting the students involved with one another. On a higher level, students start depending on one another and see how they need one another. Jigsaw structures (Aronson, 1978) force interdependence because students must rely on their peers to learn certain material so they can present it to the others on the team. In a Jigsaw, academic material is divided into parts and individual parts are assigned to team members. Team members study their parts and then meet in "expert groups" with other individuals from other teams who had the same part. In expert groups, the individuals compare notes and help each other prepare to go back to their home base teams and teach their parts to peers. Thus all members of a home base team are responsible for knowing all the information, but must rely on peers to get much of it.

"Broken Squares" is an activity often used to introduce students to interdependence. Five perfect squares, each 6 inches on a side, are cut into pieces, mixed up into five piles, and put in five envelopes (see Exhibit 16.1). Each team of five gets one envelope each. Their job, without talking or signaling, is to make five perfect squares. Individuals may not take pieces from anyone else; they can only give pieces away. When they give a piece to a team member, individuals may not put the piece in place in the person's puzzle; they can just give it to the person. Debriefing this activity with the questions listed in Exhibit 16.1 provides a fine entry point for discussing what happens if a person is ignored or withdraws or if someone tries to dominate the task. Regular academic tasks can be adapted to the "Broken Squares" structure. An oak tag sheet with spelling words (or techni-

Exhibit 16.1 Broken Squares Activity

Directions for Marking a Set of Broken Squares

A set consists of five envelopes containing pieces of cardboard cut into different patterns that when properly arranged will form five squares of equal size. One set should be provided for each group of five persons.
To prepare a set, cut out five cardboard squares, each exactly 6" x 6". Place the squares in a row and mark them as below, penciling the letters lightly so they can be erased.

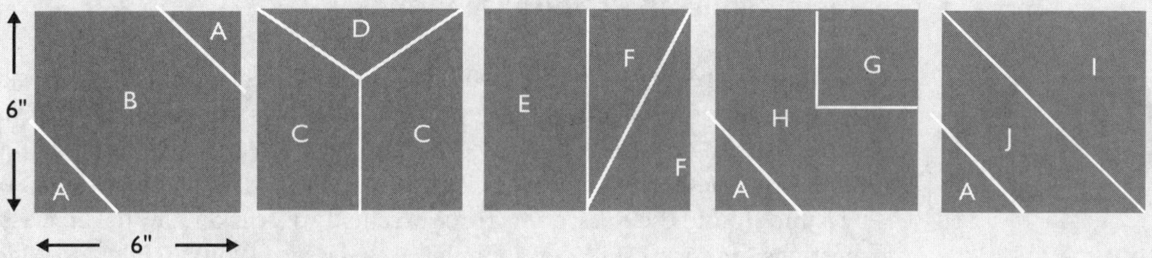

Lines should be drawn so that, when the pieces are cut out, those marked A will be exactly the same size, all pieces marked C the same size, etc. Several combinations are possible that will form one or two of the squares, but only one combination will form all five squares, each 6" x 6". After drawing the lines on the squares, and labeling the sections with letters, cut each square along the lines into smaller pieces to make the parts of the puzzle.

Label five envelopes 1, 2, 3, 4, and 5. Distribute the tag board piece into the five envelopes: envelope has pieces I, H; 2 has A, A, A, C; 3 has A, J; 4 has D, F; and 5 has G, B, F, C.

Erase the penciled letters from each piece, and write instead the number of the envelope it is in. This make it easy to return the pieces to the proper envelope, for subsequent use, after each group has completed the task.

Each set may be made from a different colored card-board.

Directions

Each of you has an envelope that contains pieces of oak for forming squares. When the signal is given, the task of your group is to form squares of equal size. Each square will measure 6" x 6". The task will not be completed until five perfect squares have been formed.

Rules

1. No members may speak.
2. No member may ask another member for a piece or in any way signal that another person is to give him or her a piece. (Members may voluntarily give pieces to other members.)

   (The letters on the pieces are irrelevant to the task; they are just for getting the pieces back into the right envelope at the end of the exercise.)

Processing "Broken Squares"

1. What happened first? What strategies were used in the beginning?
2. What were you (each individual) thinking about in the first few minutes?
3. What happened next? Did strategies shift? Were there different phases to how you functioned as a group?
4. Did someone make a move that shifted the group's approach or in some way broke up the log jam?
5. Did anyone feel left out or appear to be left out?
6. What roles did each individual play in the group?
7. What did you become aware of about yourself regarding cooperation and competition?
8. What insight/awareness did you get about the group's cooperative tasks?

Adapted from Pfeiffer & Jones (1974).

cal words or foreign language or English vocabulary words) can be cut up into a pile of individual letters. The letters are sorted randomly into five envelopes. Each of five team members gets one envelope. Their job as a group, without talking or taking pieces from another, is to build the words, spelled correctly. A poster of the words spelled correctly should be available for the group to consult while doing the task.

Social Skills and Group Dynamics

Video: Explicitly Teaching Social Skills

The fourth level of community building focuses more explicitly on developing the skills to work effectively in groups. Social skills are taught in the manner of the listening example described earlier. Class meetings become a common framework for teaching and exercising these social skills, which are often posted by name around the classroom. Three excellent sources on how to run classroom meetings for social skill development are Glasser (1969), Seigle and Macklem (1993), and Wood (1994b).

Consensus-seeking exercises with an analysis of behavior and results afterward are useful. Tasks such as "Lost in Space" and "Arctic Survival" (Lafferty, 1992) give problems to teams from fifth grade on up that require prioritizing a list of items; for example, which 10 of 20 potential items should be taken from a crashed plane if the group has to survive in subarctic conditions until rescued? Individuals do the task alone first, and then redo it with team members by sharing information and the rationales they used. The group choices almost always turn out to be closer to the expert's best answer than any individual's answer alone. Thus the point is made about the benefits of pooling expertise and using consensus. After the activity, groups follow directions to examine the roles various members of the group played when they were working together. Valuable learning emerges about what behaviors individuals can do to make groups effective. Information emerges about blocking behaviors, and what each individual could do to be a more potent group contributor next time.

"Mysteries" (Stanford, 1977) is another such structure. The clues necessary to solve a mystery are put on 3-by-5 inch index cards, and one clue is given to each student. The task is to identify the culprit with deductive logic by a process of elimination, if all the information from all the clues is available. The students who sit in a circle can read their card aloud but cannot give it to anyone else, and no student can read another student's card. This structure forces students to share information, organize it, and develop organization and leadership skills. As with all other such tasks, the analytical discussion afterward (called processing) is the most important part of the activity. It is here that students reflect on what helped and what obstructed the group's progress, and they make commitments about what they'll try to do better next time.

In "Mysteries," the class is asked to make an accusation only when they all agree. If they are wrong, the teacher doesn't give the right answer but sends them back into the group to re-examine the evidence. In any event, after 20 minutes, the activity ends if the guilty party hasn't been identified, and the class returns to the task on another day.

The things students learn about successful group processes and individual social and task skills from these activities do not necessarily transfer into their everyday behavior unless teachers specifically plan for that transfer. Successful teaching of social skills requires

1. naming the skill,
2. creating an understanding of the utility of the skill in life,
3. modeling it,
4. having students practice it, and
5. giving students direct feedback on how they're doing.

In addition to feedback from their teacher, having students process (that is, discuss and self-assess) their own level of functioning in a group consistently correlates with better skill development and better academic learning (Yager, Johnson, Johnson, & Snider, 1986). The explicit teaching of social skills and the frequent debriefing or processing by students of how they did build an expectation through repetition ensures that the skills will be used generally in the classroom. Transfer to settings outside school is more likely to happen by following the guidelines of the principle of learning called "teach for transfer" found in Chapter 12.

Problem Solving and Conflict Resolution

The final stage of development for a healthy classroom or school community is building the capacity of its members to solve their own conflicts. This work includes acknowledgment that conflicts are normal and that controversy, which is not the same as conflict, is actually good for learning.

Conflict is defined as a situation where the needs of two people are at odds, and the current course of behavior or action appears to make one the winner at the expense of the other. Conflict resolution means coming up with a solution that meets the needs of both parties or a compromise that both can live with. Most conflict resolution models have similar steps and teach similar skills. For example, Thomas Gordon's (1974) model includes the skills of active listening and I messages, which are vital communication skills to enable people to work through classic conflict resolution steps.

The following seven steps occur in most programs (see Johnson and Johnson [1995a] for details and elaboration of these steps):

1. **Recognize your anger.** Calm down and collect yourself. Some programs teach relaxation or self-imposed time-out techniques for this stage.

2. **Identify the real problem.** Break it down into these components:

    - Jointly define the problem as small and specific.
    - Determine what each person wants.
    - Determine how each person feels.
    - Exchange reasons and rationale for positions.
    - Reverse perspectives.

    This stage can take some time. Many models advocate teaching students to identify their needs, not to speak in terms of actions or the solutions they want. Probing questions, clarifying questions, and considerable active listening are often required here. That is why a neutral mediator is often introduced into the process.

3. **Decide on a positive goal.** State a desired outcome in positive terms—for example, "We will both get enough time at the computer to rewrite our drafts."

4. **Think of several solutions.** Brainstorming techniques are often taught to students in this stage.

5. **Evaluate the solutions.** Pick one to try.

6. **Make a plan.** Often just picking a solution (e.g., "Share the computer time after lunch fifty-fifty") isn't enough. A specific plan is needed des-

ignating who will do what, when, and where. The plan may need to be written and agreed to in writing.

7. **Evaluate the plan.** See if both parties are keeping their part of the bargain, if the plan is good, or if it needs to be revised.

We are convinced that Johnson and Johnson (1995a) are right; every student, not just some, should be trained as a mediator. It is in being a mediator that students learn and internalize the skills of conflict resolution. Only then will they have the skills available for their own autonomous use when they get into conflicts. The implication is that mediation training for all students is the most powerful model for teaching effective conflict resolution skills and getting students to transfer them into daily practice. Social problem-solving meetings, as described by Glasser (1969), are an ideal forum for developing these steps and the skills to go with them.

It is in being a mediator that students learn and internalize the skills of conflict resolution.

In the only classroom climate study to investigate differential effects of climate variables by gender and race, Deng (1992) found that the achievement gap between blacks, Hispanics, and whites in mathematics and between boys and girls in mathematics widened when community was weak and tension was high. This finding underlines the importance of community as a variable in academic achievement for girls in math and perhaps for students of color in all subjects when classes are integrated.

RISK-TAKING AND CONFIDENCE

As we move from community building to the domain of risk-taking, we examine what teachers can do to promote confidence and a safe atmosphere to "go for it." The five levels of this dimension of classroom climate are not as clearly developmental as they are in community because each level here is a belief rather than a set of steps. We believe that the foundation of intellectual risk-taking in classrooms is built on internal beliefs about errors and what they mean, about speed of learning and what it signifies, and about the need to get it on your own as opposed to working with others and getting help. Productive beliefs about errors, speed, and getting help may be derived from one's basic belief about intelligence (i.e., that intelligence can be developed and everyone can do well if they put in the time and use good strategies to learn). Whatever the relationships between these beliefs turn out to be, it is clear that we can identify a repertoire of teacher behaviors associated with strengthening each belief.

Table 16.1 Five Beliefs That Underlie Risk-Taking

Positive Beliefs	**Negative Beliefs**
On errors: Mistakes can help one learn.	*On errors:* Mistakes are a sign of weakness.
On speed: • You are not supposed to understand everything the first time around. • Care, quality, and perseverance count.	*On speed:* • Speed is what counts. • Faster is smarter.
On getting help: Good students solicit help and lots of feedback on their work.	*On getting help:* Good students can do it by themselves.
On effort and ability: • Consistent effort and effective strategies are the main determinants of success. • Everyone is capable of high achievement, not just the fastest.	*On effort and ability:* • Inborn intelligence is the main determinant of success. • Only the few who are bright can achieve at a high level.

Table 16.1 shows the five beliefs introduced in Chapter 14, "Expectations," that underlie risk-taking. The positive beliefs are life-liberating, the negative ones are life-limiting.

This risk-taking dimension of classroom climate concerns the amount of confidence a student has and the amount of social and academic risk the student will take. If it is well developed, a student might be able to say, "It's safe to take a risk here. If I try hard, learn from errors, and persist, I can succeed." There remains a need to collect specific strategies and approaches for nourishing student risk-taking. Some authors acknowledge the importance of risk-taking but seldom explain how to cultivate it. For example, Lampert (1990) writes, "A big piece of teaching for understanding is setting up social norms that promote respect for other people's ideas. You don't get that to happen by telling. You have to change the social norms—which takes time and consistency" (p. 26).

Here is another example. In a wonderful exposition on the practices of exemplary teachers who use cognitive strategies to move students from novice to expert in their problem-solving in various disciplines, Bruer (1993) writes:

> The benchmark lesson on gravity begins 6 weeks into the course. By this time Minstrell [the teacher] has established a rapport with his class.

> He has created an environment conducive to developing understanding, a climate where questioning and respect for diverse opinions prevail, a climate where the process of scientific reasoning can be made explicit and self-conscious. Even veteran teachers marvel at how uninhibited Minstrell's students are in expressing ideas, suggesting hypotheses, and arguing positions. (p. 42)

How does Mr. Minstrell get his students to be so uninhibited?

> A few days later, Minstrell and the class analyze their reasoning about the time it would take a 1-kilogram and a 5-kilogram object to fall the same distance. They run the crucial experiment—a miniature replay of Galileo's apocryphal experiment at Pisa. After both balls hit the floor simultaneously, Minstrell returns to the board where he had written the quiz answers. "Some of you were probably feeling pretty dumb with these kind of answers. Don't feel dumb," he counsels. "Let's see what's valuable about each of these answers, because each one's valuable. Why would you think heavier things fall faster?" (pp. 43–44)

Now we are beginning to get clues about creating this uninhibited atmosphere. Here is a final example acknowledging the importance of risk-taking:

> Inquiry teaching is difficult for teachers and requires skills that must be developed through intensive staff development. If a student whose answer is challenged does not trust the teacher, or the other students, the follow up question, intended to cause the student to think more deeply about the subject, may have the opposite effect. The student may interpret the follow up question as a clue that the initial response was wrong and that he or she is about to be made to feel foolish in front of the rest of the class. Threat seems to reduce our ability to think at higher levels, and what could be more threatening than public failure and ridicule?
>
> For this type of instruction to be effective, a teacher must create a classroom environment where students feel safe to express their thinking, where they trust their teacher and fellow students, and where they understand the difference between criticizing ideas and criticizing people. (Ellsworth & Sindt, 1994, p. 43)

This interpretation of the effect of removing threat—the threat of being laughed at, feeling foolish, or being wrong—is resoundingly confirmed by research on brain function (Sylwester, 1995). What then can we say about specific ways to strengthen the climate for risk-taking?

Normalizing Errors

Americans tend to believe in the fixed, innate, and unalterable nature of intelligence. Most children learn early in school that mistakes are signs of weakness instead of data to use and an opportunity for learning. Cultivating the latter belief about mistakes is the very foundation for confidence and risk-taking in the classroom. Thirty years ago, Jerome Bruner (1979) represented this idea when he said that a teacher's goal should be to help students "experience success and failure not as reward and punishment, but as information" (p. 90). People who succeed in building this element of climate do so explicitly. Beverly Hollis, a reading teacher in Sudbury, Massachusetts, writes:

> At the beginning of the year, when students are reticent to answer and wait time has been exhausted, I ask my class, "Is this a life or death situation? No, well, so what if you're wrong then? This is one answer out of the trillion you will give in your life, so what if it's wrong? If it is wrong, I guarantee I won't let you leave until you've heard the right answer, and you'll probably remember the information much longer for having missed it. But most importantly, you will have taken a risk by giving an answer. So many insightful answers and comments are never made and, therefore, never discussed and further explored because you, as students, are afraid to be wrong. I don't want that to be the case in this room."
>
> Having the ability to (1) risk being "wrong," (2) maintain a positive self image if you are "wrong," and (3) move on rather than dwelling on a "wrong" answer are essential attributes for success, not only in school but throughout life. I talk with my students about risks in my personal life—my month-long wilderness canoeing trip—and risks I'm taking by teaching a concept or a unit in a particular way. I'll say, "I want to try something new I've learned in a class I'm taking, and I need your feedback." I always ask for my students' feedback after every unit. I tell them they can say they disliked a particular approach I used on the material covered as long as they offer positive criticism in pointing out what they didn't like and why, and if they offer alternatives or suggestions of what I can do to make it better. [Notice that in letting students critique her units, Ms. Hollis is giving them power.] I also give them choices about how they want to learn a particular unit and ask them to tell me why this would be the best approach to take. They love having "the power"! They have been incredibly perceptive, and as a consequence, they have been very accepting of my high expectations and my criticism when they fall short of the mark. I have students earn extra credit points to improve their grades on tests by listing what they were mixed up about or how they "messed up" on a test answer and what they learned. And I openly and readily admit my own mistakes.

> Hopefully, this climate of honesty and risk-taking allows me to correct students and myself without any of us feeling guilty or stupid for having made a mistake. (Used with permission from Beverly Hollis.)

Anna Shine of The New England School of English in Boston says:

> One of the behaviors I encourage is making mistakes or guessing. I tell my students that I don't care if they are wrong, but I do care if they don't try, that there is no shame in trying and making a mistake or in falling short of their goals, but there is shame in not trying. And worse than shame, a learning opportunity is not maximized. Again and again, I say to them, "Mistakes are not important; understanding is."
>
> Obviously, students will not take risks unless it is safe to do so. So, in my classroom, I try to create this environment, to make it safe to make mistakes because students can learn from mistakes. In fact, I reward students with big (two inches in diameter) gold stars in two situations. One is if they produce great work, and the other is if they produce great mistakes.
>
> On the first day of class, when I show them my gold stars, they look at me as if I'm crazy. "A gold star for a mistake?" they think. "She doesn't know what she's doing." However, they soon learn that a gold star mistake is a mistake from which every student in the class can learn something. By making this great mistake, the student has provided everyone with a new learning opportunity, and the student himself has learned that it is safe to take a risk. By taking that risk, he grew (his knowledge and his confidence), the class learned, and he received one of the coveted gold stars. (Used with permission from Anna Shine, founder, The New England School of English.)

In a similar vein, Terry McCarthy of the North Pole Elementary School in Fairbanks, Alaska, gives "bravery points" to students who have the courage to try hard questions or problems even if they're not sure they can get them. In these and other ways, thoughtful teachers deliberately create and nurture climates of risk-taking and safety to make errors.

Care and Perseverance Versus Speed

A second belief about learning that children have is that faster is better instead of believing that care, quality, and perseverance are what matter. What do teachers do to disabuse students of the life-limiting belief in the virtue of speed versus care and perseverance? In Chapter 14, "Expectations," we described a policy on retakes of tests that would grant students as a final grade the higher score they got on a test or its retake no matter how many tries they took (assuming alternate forms of tests are available). This practice would replace averaging the test and its retake. Beyond that practice, giving only A, B, and "not yet" as grades signals that ultimate performance at high standards is what teachers are after, and nothing less will do. Getting there after suffering through a period of "not yet" does not make one's A any less valuable—just longer in coming.

Use of wait time, with an explanation of it to the class, is an everyday practice that reinforces thoughtfulness and perseverance rather than quickness. Mary Ann Pilat of the Wellesley Massachusetts Middle School uses a related practice, called the "Level Playing Field":

> I explain to students that linear thinkers can come up with prompt answers to class discussion questions, but that gestalt, divergent thinkers, an equally legitimate learning style, often are stimulated onto side connections and thoughts by questions in class. So while following those interesting thoughts, the speedster linear thinkers have answered the question and appear to be getting all the answers. Divergent thinkers tend to participate less in class. So to make the playing field level for them in getting ready for a class discussion, I put the major questions we're going to discuss on the board and give everyone five minutes to think about them first before starting the discussion. I've been getting much greater participation from lots more kids, including some who never spoke in class before.

A final strategy for valuing care and perseverance above speed is the routine practice of reteaching loops described in Expectations. To make reteaching loops do what they can for classroom climate, nominating oneself for inclusion in a loop must be a behavior of high esteem and status in the class.

Getting Feedback and Help

Another factor that obstructs learning and contaminates many classroom climates is the belief that "good students do it by themselves," instead of the belief that what makes good students is that they solicit help and lots of feedback on their work. Teachers support the development of this belief by explicitly modeling and encouraging it and creating structures that manifest it. For example, the peer editing process in place in many writing programs can be applied to reports in other subjects; students would be expected to have peers critique their drafts according to commonly understood criteria and to do final drafts with their input in mind. Other structures for mutual help can be made part of classroom routines:

- ▲ Students can take turns taking notes for the "absentee folder," which sits on a desk in the back of the room as a resource for absent students. When students come back after an absence, the notes help them catch up on what they missed, and the student who took the notes is available for personal help to the student who was absent.

- ▲ Teachers can organize students in groups or pairs of "study buddies" who are expected to help each other interpret assignments and prepare for tests.

- ▲ Various models of cooperative learning build in incentives for all team members so that each member does well. Improvement of any individual's score on a quiz over that person's previous average earns points for the whole team. Team study time is provided so the members can help each other out (Slavin, 1986).

Many other activity structures, such as Teammates Consult, Four Corners, Pairs Check, and Learning Buddies (Kagan, Kagan, & Kagan, 2015), are available to help students commit to asking for appropriate help.

Effort and Ability

To the degree that students believe intelligence is innate, fixed, measurable, and unevenly distributed, they will probably also believe that whatever quantity of intelligence they have is the main determinant of how they will do in school and elsewhere in life (Howard, 1995). It is difficult to be brought up in the United States believing anything else, for the concept of intelligence as an entity that regulates our possibilities is more developed and more influential here than in any other nation. In fact, the concept of intelligence as a fixed and measurable entity was created in the United States between approximately 1890 and 1920 (Gould, 1982; Oakes, 1985).

In this section, we move on to the consequence of this belief, to the fruits of its opposite, and how to transform students' belief into that opposite image. The opposite belief—the life-liberating one that fuels motivation and accelerates learning when it replaces the belief that innate intelligence is the main determinant of success—is that consistent effort and effective strategies are the main determinants of success (Howard, 1995). With these two things in place, everyone, not just the fastest and most confident, is capable of high achievement.

Attribution theory explains the dynamics at work in the two different belief systems (Weiner, 1972). The theory posits that the reasons we give to ourselves (the attributions we make) for our success when we succeed and for our failure when we fail have a dramatic impact on our future behavior. In fact, these internal explanations account for our future behavior. Teachers who want to help students change their beliefs about the value of effort and the importance of good strategies versus innate intelligence pursue positive behaviors in the 10 arenas of classroom life described in Chapter 14, "Expectations." For example, they stick with students who don't answer quickly, give cues, and use wait time. The arenas, through which the three messages—"This is important," "You can do it," "I won't give up on you"—are sent, are also the vehicles for convincing students they have enough intelligence to do rigorous material well. What students need to do is work long enough, be resourceful, and learn strategies that will help them. Their teacher's responsibility is to teach them those strategies explicitly.

STUDENT INFLUENCE

Successful teachers find ways for students to have some ownership and influence.

"Effective teachers know that to become engaged, students must have some feelings of ownership—of the class or the task—and personal power—a belief that what they do will make a difference" (Dodd, 1995, p. 65). This belief is echoed in two bodies of literature from the 1980s and 1990s. First, many frameworks for understanding thinking and personality style (Harrison & Bramson, 1982; Myers & McCaulley, 1985) find large percentages of people who have the need to be in charge or in control of at least certain aspects of their environment in order to function well. Second, the literature on constructivist learning and teaching posits that learning for true understanding requires students to construct their own meaning (Brooks & Brooks, 1993). This involves owning their own questions and pursuing their own lines of inquiry with teacher guidance. These two literatures support the same proposition: successful teachers find ways for students to have some ownership and influence over the flow of events and the intellectual life of the classroom.

There are many ways to offer students choice and influence over their lives in school. One pertains to the social system of the classroom—the rules of the classroom game—as opposed to the rules for interpersonal behavior one often sees posted on classroom walls. The rules of the classroom game pertain to social norms and procedures for conducting class discourse. They are often undiscussed and unwritten, though that is something we recommend changing. The teacher asks a question, the student responds, and the teacher evaluates is a typical cycle of discourse reflecting the "rule" that the teacher will control the talk in the room. Without losing control of the class or the curriculum, a teacher can permit students to participate in shaping and operating these procedural systems for discourse and class business.

Another route to ownership and influence goes through learning style and choices. Many authors (Mamchur, 1990) urge giving students choices whenever possible about how to work on learning new concepts or carrying out assignments. Student choice making can be improved and empowered by knowledge about their own learning styles. Finally, students can have some joint ownership of the intellectual life of the classroom through the way in which questions are posed and meaning is generated.

Five levels of depth and sophistication of strategic approaches give students authentic influence in classroom life. Whereas you could work on them in any order or even simultaneously, it is useful to understand which ones are more complex and why. Then you can choose them appropriately. You need not address the five issues sequentially and wait for a certain level of development before beginning practices aimed at another level. For example, there is no need to wait until students are stopping a class to ask for clarification before teaching students about their own learning style and how to use that knowledge to influence assignments. But it might be worth bearing in mind that the five approaches described do increase progressively in complexity. Therefore, if you are interested in developing student ownership and influence, you might start with the simpler and then move slowly to the more complex forms of student ownership.

1. Stop My Teaching

"Stop my teaching" refers to empowering the students to use signals to tell a teacher when the instruction is leaving them behind. Katz (1992) talks about giving her son, a beginning teacher, some basic principles of practice for successful teaching:

> One of the things you always want to do as a teacher . . . teaching children old or young, doesn't matter who, you always want to teach the children to say to you things like: "Hold it; I'm lost." "Can you go over this one more time?" "Is this what you mean?" "Can you show me again?" "Have I got it right?" . . . ways in which you empower the learner to keep you posted on where they need help. If the children are very young you just say, "Pull my sleeve," whatever, as long as the child has the strategy to say to you "I don't get it." "I'm lost." "You're going too fast." "Hold it" and so on.
>
> Teachers who take this injunction seriously develop signal systems that students can use to indicate on their own initiative that they are lost and want the teacher to stop and explain again. Hand signals like thumbs down held tight against one's chest could be such a signal. Or students could put red, yellow, or green cards on the corner of their desks like

traffic light signals. Thus teachers could get a quick visual read on how well students were understanding a discussion.

When the idea of stopping the teaching becomes part of classroom culture, other symbols or phrases come to represent the practice. One teacher told her class the story of a family vacation where she and her husband and six children stopped at McDonald's for lunch. Loading up hurriedly in the tightly packed van after their quick meal, they didn't do a head count and were four miles down the road before she said, "Where's Manuel?!?" Manuel was back at McDonald's.

The teacher now uses that phrase frequently in class as a coded signal: "Have I left you at McDonald's?" and the children also use the code to signal when they're getting lost. "Ms. Swift, I think I'm back at McDonald's!" The humorous shared code serves to authorize the practice of stopping the teacher's teaching, and the teacher's affirming reaction shows the practice to be a valued one that earns kudos for the child rather than a frown or a veiled accusation of inadequacy.

2. Negotiating the Rules of the Classroom Game

Negotiating the rules of the classroom game involves students in creating the routines and procedures of classroom discourse and class business. These rules are different from the rules of behavior that teachers and students commonly work out at the beginning of the year. The rules we are talking about here are usually tacit, underground, and unstated. They pertain to teacher-student and student-student interaction around such issues as questions and answers, class dialogue, and procedures and protocols for taking turns. Recitation lessons of teacher questions and student answers do indeed often turn out to be a game, where students try to win by getting the right answers and avoid losing by shrinking into invisibility when they don't know the answers. (For a good example of this, see Task 3: Building a Climate of High Achievement in Chapter 10, "Discipline.")

3. Teaching Students to Use Principles of Learning and Other Strategies

A third way to give students influence in classroom life is to share with them teaching and learning strategies we use ourselves. By including them in the secret knowledge of teaching and learning strategies, we give students choices, power, and license to control their learning.

Many of the principles of learning set out in Chapter 12 should be taught to students directly so they can use them to be more powerful learners. The same is true for a number of the explanatory devices in Chapter 11, "Clarity." This is a good moment to review those principles to decide which ones you think would be most beneficial to turn over to your students as tools for learning. The more we are interested in empowering students and giving them choices, the more we will explicitly put learning at their disposal and urge them to use it autonomously.

The more we empower students and give them choices, the more we explicitly put learning at their disposal and urge them to use it autonomously.

Here are some of our nominees for principles and tools to teach to students:

- **Sequence:** Students can use this principle to sequence their own lists when studying vocabulary words (or anything else that is sequential in nature) so that the items hardest for them are in the optimal first and last positions.

- **Practice:** Students can use knowledge of this principle to optimize their personal practice schedules.

- **Goal setting:** Students can use this principle to set realistic academic and behavioral targets for improvement and make effective plans of action to meet them.

- **Explanatory devices:** Visual imagery and especially graphic organizers can become regular tools for students. Imagery can be used to pause during study and construct meaning in a visual way. Graphic organizers can become a habit as a note-taking technology through which students assimilate information as they read, hear, or see it. Teachers can integrate the use of these devices into assignments and work toward having students choose when and how to use them.

While passing these strategies on to students, teachers who are aware of attribution theory and are committed to conveying the three expectations messages—"This is important," "You can do it," and "I won't give up on you"—will see they have a special opening. They will seize frequent opportunities to connect the use of these strategies with student success rather than let students attribute successful performance to intelligence. "Well, Kendra, did you use any graphic organizers when you reviewed that chapter? No? Well, look—you're a strong visual learner; you and I both know that. Let's go over how to use that strategy with material like this. I know you can make it work for you!"

4. Learning Style and Choices

"Students using knowledge of learning style" means teachers are not just using their knowledge of learning style to adapt lessons for the styles of their students. They are teaching the students about their own learning styles and the implications of those styles for what kinds of assignments will be difficult and which will be easier. Furthermore, they encourage students to use this knowledge to guide their study routines and even to ask for modifications in assignments that allow them to use their strengths. These steps set the stage for a more complex level of empowerment—giving students explicit choices over assignments, forms of tests, and forms of projects.

Helping students understand their own learning style sets the stage for some important forms of empowerment.

Hattie's (2009) meta-analysis shows that adjusting teaching for students' perceived learning style has a weak influence on student learning. But enabling student choice with learning style as one arena for exercising choice is different. The variable here is choice, and preferred learning style is one element in the repertoire of choices we can offer.

Many teachers have been to a workshop on learning style, and some may be trained in one or more of the learning style frameworks. These frameworks help us understand the similarities and differences in the ways humans take in, process, and express their learning. They also help to understand the features of the learning environment and the different kinds of activities that work best for individuals. For example, some people learn best when they can talk and interact with others as they deal with new concepts. Others like to read, listen, view, and assimilate alone before interacting with others. This body of knowledge about learning style preferences can be a powerful vehicle for giving students ownership in classroom life.

Helping students understand their own learning style sets the stage for some important forms of empowerment. First, students can predict (and teachers can help them predict and prepare for) the difficulty of certain assignments or tasks that do not match their preferred learning style. If teachers set the stage properly and teach about learning style, the value system associated with learning style frameworks enables students to see their difficulty in certain tasks as attributable to differences, not deficiencies. Second, the capacity to predict learning style match or mismatch to tasks enables students to mobilize extra effort and seek help when appropriate. When teachers encourage students to use knowledge of their own learning style to do either of these two things, they are empowering them in significant ways.

The simplest place to start teaching students about learning style is with modality preference: visual, auditory, kinesthetic, or combinations of them. Simple modality preference tests (Barbe & Milone, 1980) can be used to have students identify their preferences. Then teachers must look for and share out loud with students that they are looking for ways to vary their teaching to address different modalities.

Another framework for learning style differences that students can use in the same way is the left brain–right brain or global analytical framework. Dunn and Dunn (1978) provide another useful set for students to know about and use to empower their learning effectiveness. Gregorc's (1985) framework provides a fourth and more complicated but highly useful cut at style difference. McCarthy and McCarthy's (2005) 4MAT System is a fifth, and Gardner's (2006) multiple intelligences framework a sixth. Finally, the sophisticated Myers-Briggs provides a seventh.

All of these frameworks are worthy of study, and we believe they are a useful part of teachers' professional knowledge. But for the sake of classroom climate and this particular dimension of influence, the point is to choose one of them and work on giving the framework to students, that is, teaching them to use it not to label themselves but to modulate their effort, seek help when appropriate, and sometimes take the initiative to alter assignments based on their self-knowledge from a learning style perspective.

Giving students license and encouragement to speak up in this way to ask for modifications of assignments brings us to other ways to give students choices. What kinds of choices do students get to make about their academic work, and how do they do it? Carolyn Mamchur (1990) writes: "Giving students choices may seem like a complex issue. But actually, it is dead simple. The rule is this: whenever you can give a student a choice of any kind, do it" (p. 636).

A "nonreport," an idea we found some years ago in *Mindsight* magazine, is a good example of students' influencing assignments and the shape of products. There is nothing particularly unique about nonreports. They are simply outside assignments—but with several major differences.

> A nonreport is anything that does not fall into the category of straight written information. The task is to convince students accustomed to the way school is supposed to be that their teacher will accept and value their ideas. Their first question is usually, "What do you want?" since they know that pleasing the teacher is the quickest way to a good grade. Here is how a nonreport works:
>
> 1. Impress on students that a standard written report will receive no credit, since it does not meet the requirements of the assignment.

2. Make the assignment worth enough points so that not doing it will result in a substantial drop in grade. At first, there is a great risk in doing something not completely spelled out, so the risk of losing credit must be greater.

3. Create a grading scale that gives equal merit to content and to creativity (more loosely, to the effort the student has to make to personalize the knowledge he or she conveys).

4. Keep the topic very general, giving the students ample opportunity to select from among a wide variety of ideas. For example, if you are studying a unit on measurement, allow them to select anything at all dealing with measurement. Point out to them that there are few occupations (hobbies, sports, etc.) that do not contain measurement of some kind. Give them examples. Challenge them to name something that apparently has nothing to do with measurement—but be quick enough on your feet to find the measurement involved.

5. If they insist, and they may at first, give them a couple of examples of nonreport type formats (they are endless and limited only by imagination). For example, they could create a game, write a song, role play a game show, do a slide or tape presentation, make a scrapbook, or build a model. But warn them that they will receive more credit for doing something you haven't thought of than copying something you have. And stick by that statement!

6. Perhaps most important, don't do this assignment unless you are willing to truly value the students' ideas. If you can't suspend your own idea of what is right or good and try to see the product from their point of view, they will never believe you again. But neither should you give credit for hastily conceived and executed junk. I once received a shoebox with a hole punched in one end that was labeled "Working model of a black hole." Hah!

I have found that giving 10 points for the idea, 10 points for the execution, and 10 points for the content, plus 5 for effort, works out well—a total of 35 points. The effort points come in when a person has had three weeks to do a project that might be reasonably well done but obviously took only 15 minutes compared to someone else who spent several hours. You can tell by looking.

The first time you do this, you will probably receive the usual assortment of collages, collections, and posters copied from books. But when these

> students see the more adventurous, creative, and "fun" projects getting all the praise, they will be more willing to let go a little the next time.
>
> By the end of the first year that I had students do these projects, I turned them loose on a topic we had not covered in class: solar energy. They researched the topic, did their Nonreports—including a working parabolic solar cooker and a miniature solar greenhouse complete with Trombe walls made of plastic soft drink bottles—and presented them to the class, thus covering almost all the important aspects of solar energy—with no effort on the part of the teacher. One of the most rewarding aspects of these assignments is that, frequently, the students who usually get C's or D's in regular assignments really come into their own on Nonreports.
>
> Nonreports allow students to plan, research, and execute. It evokes their creative potential and forces interaction with the content. Many students sought "experts" to help them and learned the intricacies of carpentry, photography, sound and art—because they wanted to. And it is tremendously exciting to see projects come into the classroom that are far beyond anything the teacher would have assigned or expected. (*Mindsight*, New Lenox, IL, 1989)

We would add specific criteria for success that make it clear to students exactly what the attributes of quality work in the nonreport will be. For example, in the nonreport on solar energy, the criteria could be: (1) explains three different ways of converting solar energy, (2) discusses costs and efficiencies of various forms of solar energy, and (3) uses data to compare the efficiency of solar, fossil fuel, and nuclear energy. Students using these criteria could create dozens of different kinds of products to represent their learning, from radio shows to models to hypercard assemblies. Randolf and Evertson (1995) give a simple example of student choice that suggests how plentiful the opportunities are for giving them:

> Ms. Cooper often delegated tasks that would typically be assigned [by her] to students. We have already described students as providing the text for writing class through Sharing Models/Generating Characteristics. In this activity, students also took on the task of controlling the floor, which would traditionally be a teacher task. Areas of student control include deciding how to participate, getting the class's attention and leading the discussion by calling on peers. . . . Student readers usually stood in the front of the room, but Ms. Cooper gave students the option of reading from their desks. Students were given the same choice when they shared their rough drafts with the class. The fact that Ms. Cooper did not define this aspect of appropriate participation gave students choice in how to manage this aspect of controlling the floor. (p. 22)

The ability of students to make choices and control the activity flow and the discourse within the group is partially responsible for the success of cooperative learning. In all cooperative learning models, students work in groups in which they control the dialogue, who speaks, when, and for how long.

5. Using Students and Their Communities as Sources of Knowledge

This aspect of Classroom Climate building is about ways to reach out and respect the experience and questions students bring to class.

Constructivist Teaching

Constructivist pedagogy brings student influence to the intellectual life of the classroom and may be the most advanced level of student ownership. It is also the most complex and requires the largest paradigm shift for teachers. Most of us, after all, were educated in schools where other people's constructions of knowledge were handed to us for consumption and digestion. Brooks and Brooks (1993) provide five overarching principles of constructivist pedagogy:

1. Posing problems of emerging relevance to learners.
2. Structuring learning around "big ideas" or primary concepts.
3. Seeking and valuing students' points of view.
4. Adapting curriculum to address students' suppositions.
5. Assessing student learning in the context of teaching. (p. 33)

There is still a place in good education for "active reception learning," as Ausubel (1963) calls it. But there is also a large place for carefully designed teaching that allows students to construct meaning for themselves. Randolf and Evertson (1995) in their analysis of interactive discourse in a writing class describe this kind of pedagogy:

> The construction of knowledge, which takes place through negotiation, depends on the redistribution of power from teachers to students. The fact that knowledge is presumed to come from students defines students as knowledge holders, an identity usually retained by the teacher. (p. 24)

Constructivist teaching puts students in the legitimate role of knowledge generators and knowledge editors, whether in science, social studies, language arts, or any other academic discipline (Brooks & Brooks, 1993). The examples in the Randolf and Evertson study describe a series of lessons on literary genre. They show how teachers' conscious regulation of dialogue and interaction with students can make students genuinely empowered knowledge generators. For example, one teacher, Ms. Cooper, asked students to bring in examples of fables to share and discuss in class so they can extract the characteristics of fables by analyzing these examples. At one point, she asked the class to look for generalizations they could make about the morals of fables:

> **Teacher:** "What can we say about the characteristics of morals? [Students offer some suggestions.] Maybe we need to explain what a lesson or moral is—how to be a better person. I'm going to put that up, unless you have objections."
>
> **Laurie:** "They're trying to prevent you from making mistakes." [Teacher writes, "Stories are used to help you become a better person and not make mistakes."]
>
> **Tim:** "I disagree. Sometimes some of the things are wrong."
>
> **Hillary:** "Can be" [used to help you]. [Teacher changes "are" to "can be" in the sentence on the board: "Stories can be used to help you become a better person and not make mistakes."]
>
> **Onika:** "But everybody makes mistakes."
>
> **Teacher:** "You're right," [Adds to the sentence on the board: "or learn from characters' mistakes in the story."] "but the purpose of the fable is to help you not to make so many mistakes."

In analyzing this episode, Randolf and Evertson (1995) comment:

> The discussion begins with Ms. Cooper's question. The answers she receives do not give her the information she wants, so Ms. Cooper supplies her own answer: a moral teaches how to be a better person. In stating her answer, Ms. Cooper clarifies her question: she is asking about the purpose of a moral. With this new information, Laurie is able to supply a response that Ms. Cooper validates by incorporating it into the characteristic she is writing on the chalkboard. So far Ms. Cooper is in the position of authority in the classroom: she initiates the topic, students respond with possible answers, and she evaluates them, rejecting all responses until she hears one that fits her expectations.

> The nature of the interaction changes, however, as Tim questions the characteristic that is the joint construction of Ms. Cooper and Laurie. In effect, Tim takes on the role of evaluator of the response, moving Ms. Cooper into the role of co-collaborator with Laurie. Ms. Cooper's response is thus demonstrated to be as open to evaluation as any other participant's response.
>
> Onika and Susan then join the deliberation, questioning the need for morals as they have defined them in class more than they are questioning the definition itself. Why, they argue, should morals try to keep you from making mistakes, when you're going to make them anyway, and they help you learn? These contributions are initiations of a new topic, which Ms. Cooper responds to and evaluates by treating them as negotiations of meaning, signaling her acceptance by incorporating the new contribution into the statement on the board. Thus the characteristic as it is finally stated is the joint construction of Ms. Cooper, Laurie, Tim, Hillary, Onika, and Susan. (pp. 23–24)

Similar scenarios can be found in the literature for helping students construct knowledge in science and mathematics. This kind of teaching requires a role shift of significant proportions for some teachers away from being dispensers of knowledge to facilitating negotiation of meaning by students.

The role of the teacher in constructivist science teaching is often to involve students in predicting phenomena, then reacting to observed phenomena and constructing hypotheses, which they then test to account for their observations. For example, most students predict that heavy objects fall faster than lighter ones—which is incorrect. The hypothesis-making and dialogue about subsequent experiments and explanations that constructivist teachers facilitate have similar qualities to the dialogue in the Randolf and Evertson example.

The changes that take place when teachers move to include more constructivist teaching in their repertoire are subtle but significant. The classroom does not look any different, and the assignments and topics may not seem much different. Where the changes show up is in dialogue with students and in the roles teachers and students are playing in the conversations they have in class. Though surface changes may appear small, the role shift is large, and the evidence is strong that the effect is large in student motivation, effort, and understanding (Newmann & Wehlage, 1995).

Culturally Relevant Instruction

As fully half of all children in the United States are of color, it is especially important to be creating schools that acknowledge and value the culture of all students. Excluding these children's cultures from school artifacts, customs, arts, and curriculum not only demotivates but alienates significant numbers of students (Cummins, 1986). Ladson-Billings (1995) brings this argument into the more immediate domain of curriculum by pointing out that using the community as a source of curriculum experiences makes learning meaningful and active and also culturally relevant:

> Early in the school year, one teacher asked the students to identify one area in which they believed they had expertise. She then compiled a list of "classroom experts" for distribution to the class. Later, she developed a calendar and asked students to select a date that they would like to make a presentation in their area of expertise. When students made their presentations, their knowledge and expertise was a given. Their classmates were expected to be an attentive audience and to take seriously the knowledge that was being shared by taking notes and/or asking relevant questions. The variety of topics the students offered included rap music, basketball, gospel singing, cooking, hair braiding, and baby sitting. Other students listed more school-like areas of expertise such as reading, writing, and mathematics. However, all students were required to share their expertise. (p. 481)

Some may wonder how such open-ended assignments can be congruent with a school curriculum that contains specific skills the students are supposed to be mastering. By using practices described in Chapter 21, "Assessment," teachers can weave objectives for research, organization, reading, writing, and speaking skills (or any other skills that are in the curriculum) into the criteria for good presentations by student experts. The point that Ladson-Billings makes is that the students own the knowledge they present, and the knowledge is acknowledged to have value. The "classroom experts" assignment is a practice that is congruent with augmenting student ownership and influence because the knowledge of students and the culture from which that knowledge comes—the students' own culture—is explicitly validated by a school learning activity.

Culturally relevant instruction is the topic of the article from which the Ladson-Billings excerpt comes. Culturally relevant instruction does not mean teaching about other cultures, though that can have value. It means validating the culture of students by including in-school learning experiences, topics, scenes, and knowledge that derive from the culture of the students themselves. It looks not only to individual students but also to the community from which the students come as a source of curriculum experiences:

> One teacher used the community as a basis of her curriculum. Her students searched the county historical archives, interviewed long term residents, constructed and administered surveys and a questionnaire, and invited and listened to guest speakers to get a sense of the historical development of their community. Their ultimate goal was to develop a land use proposal for an abandoned shopping center that was a magnet for illegal drug use and other dangerous activities. The project ended with the students making a presentation before the City Council and Urban Planning Commission. One of the students remarked to me, "This [community] is not such a bad place. There are a lot of good things that happened here, and some of that is still going on." The teacher told me that she was concerned that too many of the students believed that the only option for success involved moving out of the community, rather than participating in its reclamation. (Ladson-Billings, 1995, p. 479)

CLASSROOM CLIMATE SURVEY

Classroom Climate Survey

This is a good point to assess where you are in your thinking and practices about classroom climate. We encourage you to respond to the survey questions in Table 16.2 and compare your answers with your colleagues'. (You can also download a survey from *The Skillful Teacher* website at www.RBTeach.com/TST7.)

Table 16.2 Classroom Climate Survey

1. Community and Mutual Support	**Your Answers**
How are students encouraged to get to know one another and to get to know other people?	
When are students listened to, acknowledged, and affirmed as worthwhile, important, and cared-for people?	
When do students learn group responsibility and interdependence?	
What opportunities are there for learning social skills and cooperative learning?	
How are conflict resolution strategies being learned and practiced in the classroom and around the school?	
2. Risk-Taking and Confidence	
What are the times when students are encouraged to take risks and find out it's okay to do so?	
What do I do to disabuse students of the life-limiting belief in the virtue of speed versus care and perseverance?	
When does the belief "good students solicit help and lots of feedback on their work" get communicated in the classroom?	
In what ways do students learn that effort makes the difference?	
3. Student Influence	
What are the times when students are in a controlling or influencing role?	
What principles of learning are students knowledgeable about and encouraged to use?	
What are the opportunities for giving control to students within the models of teaching being used?	
What opportunities are there to have students be authentic knowledgeable producers and structure classroom discourse from the constructivist perspective?	
What opportunities are there for students to be experts?	
What are the ways in which the local community culture is viewed as a source of authorized curriculum and as a worthwhile source of knowledge?	

CHAPTER QUICK GUIDE

▲ Whenever students feel empowered, accepted, and safe to take risks and try things that are hard for them, they like school better and learn more.

▲ Our operational definition of classroom climate: "*the feelings and beliefs students have and the cumulative patterns of behavior that result from those feelings and beliefs regarding community and mutual support, risk-taking and confidence, and influence and control.*"

Three Major Strands of Classroom Climate:

1. **Community and Mutual Support:**
   Knowing others; Greeting, listening, responding; Acknowledging, and affirming; Group identity, responsibility, and interdependence; Social skills and group dynamics; and Problem-solving and conflict resolution.

2. **Risk-Taking and Confidence:**
   Normalizing errors; Care and perseverance versus speed; Getting feedback and help; and Effort and ability.

3. **Five Ways Students Can Have Influence:**
   (1) Stop my teaching;
   (2) Negotiating the rules of the classroom game;
   (3) Teaching students to use principles of learning and other strategies;
   (4) Learning style and choices; and
   (5) Using students and their communities as sources of knowledge.

To check your knowledge about Classroom Climate, see the exercises on *The Skillful Teacher* website at www.RBTeach.com/TST7.

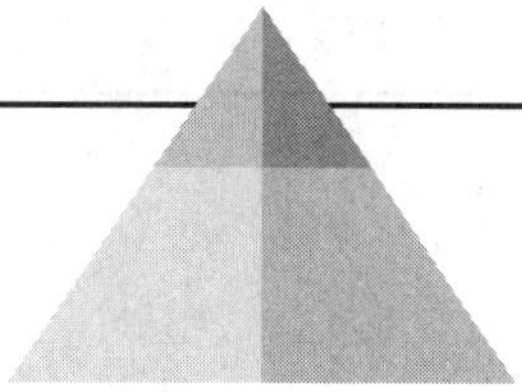

Part 5

Introduction to Curriculum

Part 5 addresses the thinking and design that go into planning successful instruction. The anchor and starting point of planning daily lessons is a good curriculum. The standards movement has caused a rethinking of what good curriculum is and how to create it. Since schools are making the commitment to have all students reach proficiency, just presenting material and covering topics is no longer acceptable. Curricula must be designed so there is great clarity about what schools want students to learn and how to know when they do.

> **Chapter 17:** "Curriculum Design" describes what teachers should have in hand from the district so their planning is solidly rooted in the commitments made to what children are supposed to be learning. A good curriculum provides the intellectual superstructure from which teachers take guidelines for the direction and content of their lessons.
>
> **Chapter 18:** "Lesson Objectives" that are clear and appropriate enable teachers to carry on with good lesson planning. Fuzzy thinking about objectives is at the root of an enormous number of teaching and learning shortfalls in our schools.
>
> **Chapter 19:** "Planning" is a detailed exposition of the cognitive scenarios good teachers go through in their heads prior to instruction. The planning never produces results if the objective is fuzzy or inappropriate.

Together these three chapters form a piece. They need each other. Good planning requires good objectives to be anchored and purposive. A good objective needs a good curriculum behind it to be important and clear. Successful teaching requires that professionals also be knowledgeable and skillful at all three.

> **Chapter 20:** "Differentiated Instruction" profiles the variables teachers control in designing learning experiences for their students. The thirteen variables described in this chapter are, in fact, a comprehensive layout of design features we can differentiate to address the individual learning needs of our students.

Chapter 21: "Assessment" provides the framework to make assessment a tool for student learning, not just a measuring device. It also emphasizes student ownership and the motivational opportunities inherent in good assessment practices.

Chapter 22: "Overarching Objectives" describes the way in which our core values and sense of personal mission can influence our instruction and have positive consequences for student learning.

CHAPTER
17

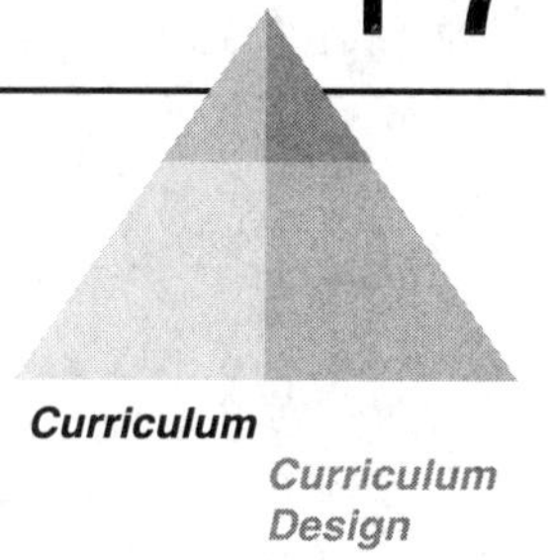

Curriculum: *Curriculum Design*

The curriculum for any subject or course at any grade level consists of a set of agreements between the district office (or academic department) and its teachers. This chapter describes those agreements. Teachers need to understand the status of these agreements thoroughly if they are to effectively choose instructional materials for daily use, participate in curriculum development groups, and, most importantly, be skilled at planning good lessons. After defining and describing these agreements, we highlight the ones we believe are essential for every district to have and for teachers to use as a foundation for their lesson planning. Whether a curriculum is tight or loose is determined by which of these agreements are firmly in place.

Whether a curriculum is tight or loose is determined by which agreements are firmly in place.

AGREEMENTS OF CURRICULUM

Records of the agreements that have been worked through can be found in curriculum guides in most schools and districts. The curriculum children actually receive depends on how faithfully these agreements are carried out. These agreements (the essential ones have an asterisk) address the following:

- ▲ Topics to be taught*
- ▲ Big ideas*
- ▲ Units of study organized around the big ideas*
- ▲ Learning expectations (or learning outcomes) for a grade or course*
- ▲ Uniform assessments (sometimes called benchmark assessments), especially final assessments, interim assessments, and unit assessments*
- ▲ Criteria for proficiency on assessment items*
- ▲ End-of-course samples of proficient student work (an exemplar everyone can look at to see exactly what the district really means by the learning expectation)*

- ▲ Pedagogical practices
- ▲ Pacing guides and curriculum maps
- ▲ Lesson plans
- ▲ Time allocations
- ▲ Instructional strategies
- ▲ Materials
- ▲ Resources

It is important to know the stance your district has taken toward curriculum so you know what you're accountable for. Otherwise, there's a lot that can go wrong.

Many districts are not sufficiently explicit about what their curriculum is. An additional problem may be insufficient control over how it is implemented, even when certain elements are clear. As a result, the experience of children going from grade to grade may depend on individual choices teachers make about what to teach. It is important to know the stance your district has taken toward curriculum so you know what you're accountable for. Otherwise, there's a lot that can go wrong. And what can go wrong with curriculum? Consider the following possibilities:

- ▲ There isn't one.
- ▲ There used to be one; it might be around here somewhere.
- ▲ There is one, but nobody teaches it.
- ▲ There is one, but people teach what they want out of it, which means the students' experience is inconsistent.
- ▲ There are no common assessments.
- ▲ The curriculum is the textbooks.
- ▲ The curriculum has neat activities, not a focus on student learning.
- ▲ There is a curriculum, but it does not match the standards teachers are responsible for.
- ▲ The curriculum office says what to teach, when, and for how long, with what materials, what methods, and exactly what to say as you teach it, making teachers feel as if they have no leeway.

Table 17.1 Matrix of Curriculum Agreements

Curriculum Element	Required	Recommended but Optional	Free Choice
Topics			
Big Ideas			
Units of Study • Big ideas • Guiding questions			
Learning Expectations			
Uniform Performance Assessments			
Criteria for Proficiency			
End-of-Course Exemplars			
Pedagogical Practices			
Pacing Guides			
Lesson Plans			
Time Allocations			
Instructional Strategies			
Activities, Materials, and Examples			
Resources for Teachers			

Districts can avoid these problems and give teachers a solid ground on which to stand that balances cohesiveness, accountability, and professional decision-making. The agreements that comprise a curriculum (or absence of agreements) are about what is required, what is recommended but optional, and what is free choice for each of the elements. Table 17.1 shows these same elements in a format that can be filled in with specifics to profile the status of agreements for any given curriculum.

It is certainly not necessary, or even desirable, to have districtwide requirements or uniformity on all the elements. However, we do advocate having the three key elements in place that together define learning outcomes: (1) end-of-course exemplars of proficient student work for a grade level or a course, understood, and used in common across the district for skills and academic content; (2) uniform final assessments; and (3) clear criteria for student success listed for interim benchmark assessment and the final assessment. The exemplars define for everyone what the standards are. When the interim or final assessment is a test (rather than a performance), the test items are quite important. This is because, when combined with criteria that define the desired level of performance, they also define the learning objectives. Without agreement on these three things, it is impossible to know what the district's standards are.

For consistency sake, we also recommend uniform unit assessments across grade levels and courses and at benchmark periods (e.g., quarterly). That's the most basic level to have a curriculum that is coherent. On that basis, the district can say to families, "We have consistency over the learning designed for your child."

Of course, districts should also come to agreement about what topics students should study in academic units, with big ideas specifically identified. This keeps teachers' daily planning focused on the big ideas (enduring understandings). For pedagogical practices, we recommend an emphasis on formative classroom assessment and frequent feedback to students. These items are required criteria in the "Standards for Accreditation" for K–12 schools issued by the New England Association of Schools and Colleges (2000). Finally, the foundation of any curriculum is a compact list of exactly what we want students to learn or be able to do (learning expectations or outcomes). The list should be one or two pages, suitable for handing to a newly hired teacher as a roadmap of the year. The items on this list should highlight the learning expectations that are essential versus those that are important or just nice to know.

For the other items listed, we take no value position. What is required and what is optional should be a local teacher and school decision based on context and needs. It's simply that what the local decision is should be clear to all concerned (and it often isn't).

DEFINING ELEMENTS OF CURRICULUM

In this section, we define each element of curriculum listed in Table 17.1.

Topics

A topic is a bounded content focus: for example, the Civil War, fractions, Henry David Thoreau, heat, or French Impressionism. Topics are usually divided into a list of subtopics. Wiggins and McTighe (2005) write about the overloaded curriculum and recommend choosing what is essential knowledge to teach as opposed to what is important and, finally, what is nice but not essential. Doug Reeves (2002) calls the essential items "power standards." He describes these as having durability and leverage because they are useful in a range of circumstances and academic disciplines. Graphing is an example. We apply our knowledge of graphs to reading newspapers, social studies and science textbooks, and directions for operating equipment we buy. The reason for making these discriminations is to enable teachers to prioritize the mass of material in their curricula. Agreement about which topics or skills are required is one way to take care of this need.

Themes are broad areas of inquiry thought to be of overarching significance, like social justice, understanding differences, how scientists think, and solving complex problems, that may run the duration of a course or a year. Not all curricula or school districts choose to embed themes in curricula. A theme by itself is an inadequate organizer for the topics in a curriculum or a unit, and excessive use of themes can lead to pure activity-based teaching ("Let's do friendship. I have some great books on friendship"). In contrast, an essential question for this topic might be, "What is friendship?" and the learning experiences might enable students to create a list of attributes for friendship. Properly chosen themes are really essential questions in disguise.

Properly chosen themes are really essential questions in disguise.

Big Ideas

Big ideas (or enduring understandings) are important ideas that students should carry away from the study of a topic. A big idea is an understanding that is intended to last a lifetime. Here are some examples:

- "The planet's resources are finite."
- "There is a conflict between acting in the long-term interest of the environment and the short-term interest of certain economic groups."
- "If you want to assess the effect of a change (mechanical, scientific, or even social), you have to hold the other variables constant while you experiment with changing one thing at a time."

An enduring understanding gets to the heart of the academic discipline. Table 17.2 provides some samples from elementary literacy and mathematics. Big ideas are interesting and applicable. They give students a reason and a focus for studying smaller elements in the curriculum. They provide a cognitive hook for the item currently under study in a unit. It is important for a teacher to show how an item under study connects to a big idea. When that happens, it serves both cognitive and motivational purposes.

Table 17.2 Enduring Understandings for Literacy and Math

Literacy
• Understanding is promoted by a reader's use of strategies and tools.
• Different forms of print have different functions.
• Knowledge about genre characteristics helps a reader construct meaning.
Math
• Estimation prior to performing a computation helps ensure reasonable answers.
• Any measurement other than counting produces an approximate rather than exact value.
• There is a one-to-one match between real numbers and points on a line.

Adapted from Weston, Massachusetts, public schools.

Curriculum is also empowered by well-chosen guiding questions (or essential questions) to frame and motivate the lessons. A guiding question is a fundamental query that directs the search for understanding. It is open ended and succinct, and it contains emotive force and intellectual bite. It raises other important questions and frames outcomes as culminating insights derived from inquiry. Everything in the unit is studied for the purpose of answering it. Examples would be, "What is worth fighting for?" "Where do waves come from?" "Who was a great person?" (Traver, 1998).

Units of Study

A unit is an organization of student experiences that are sequenced deliberately to create a cumulative effect. The unit package provides materials for students to study, materials for teachers to use for advancing ideas and skills, student tasks, directions for student activities, and a host of supplementary ideas and guidelines for teachers to use. Not all units contain big ideas, but they should.

Certain segments of elementary reading, writing, and mathematics instruction may not be organized into units, but rather be considered continuous strands of instruction. Primary reading curriculum is an example where a balanced literacy approach uses guided reading of sequenced texts to develop a wide range of skills arrayed on a continuum. Even without units of study, however, teachers can still teach for big ideas. Table 17.3 summarizes key terms from the Wiggins and McTighe model and shows their relationship to one another as well as to goals for units and the mastery objectives for lessons.

Good units are planned backwards from a clear image of what we want the students to be able to do at the end. The end-of-unit assessments are designed right after the identification of the big ideas. This is in marked contrast to the dominant 20th-century method, where the topics were picked first, then the activities were designed, and then the students were tested by assessments designed at the end. The two approaches are summarized in Figure 17.1.

Table 17.3 Examples for Examining Curriculum

Terminology	Example 1	Example 2	Where you might see it
Overarching theme of year	What is a just society?	What is a just society?	On a banner over the board
Enduring understanding (big idea)	There is a tension in foreign affairs between acting in one's national self-interest and respecting the national sovereignty of others.	The planet's resources are finite. There is a conflict between acting in the long-term interest of the environment and the short-term interest of certain economic groups.	This generalization may be brought out in class discussion, sought in student learning logs, or converted into a question for essays or debate, for example.
Essential question (guiding question)	Is the U.S. military justified in actively intervening in the internal affairs of another country? If so, when?	When is it appropriate to promulgate regulations for environmental safety that will cost jobs?	In a corner of the board or in materials framing the unit.
Broad content goal for a 2-week study (a unit objective)	The Panama Case: Using Defense Department and State Department documents from the period, as well as news reports from the *New York Times* archives, students will be prepared to compare and contrast the cases of the Falklands, Grenada, and Panama.	Using online national databases and reports from the EPA and the electric power industry, students will be able to take a position and defend their cases for raising or not raising pollution standards at electric power plants.	Assignment sheets.
Specific mastery objective (performance indicator) for the next 2 days (a lesson objective)	Students will be able to explain the mechanisms and sequence of steps in the drug trade through Panama in the 1980s.	Students will be able to use statistics about rising use of fossil fuel from multiple sources to graph the power industry's contribution to air pollution.	On the board as class begins and shared explicitly with students.

Figure 17.1 Design Sequence: Old Model, New Model

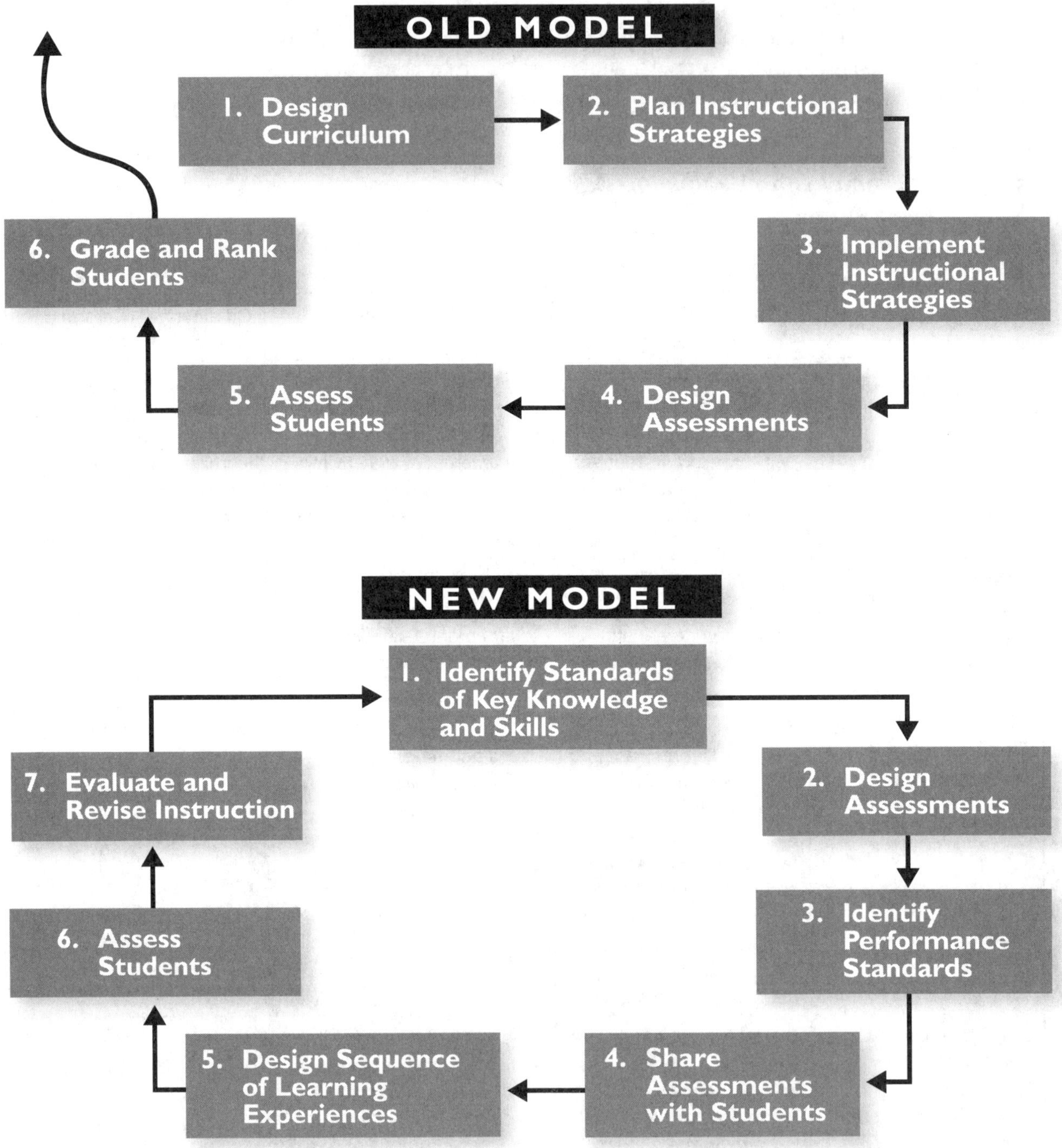

Learning Expectations

The following statements are taken from state standards documents and are examples of what might be given to a teacher to identify the knowledge or skills fourth graders are expected to master by the end of the year:

- Students will be able to identify the meaning of common idioms and figurative phrases (English Language Arts).
- Students will be able to express an opinion of a literary work or film in an organized way, with supporting detail (English Language Arts).
- Students will be able to use concrete objects and visual models to add and subtract common fractions and represent answers in lowest terms (Math).

These statements are typical of those found in standards documents across the 50 states. A more comprehensive list of such statements can serve as a simple map of what to teach. However, these statements do not specify the level of difficulty or complexity of the reading or the comparison that the students are expected to produce. These statements of learning expectations do tell us for what student performances we will need exemplars, but they don't spell out precisely the level of performance expected or the criteria for determining proficiency. So it is one useful resource in need of others.

Uniform Performance Assessments

Good curriculum contains specifications for evidence of student learning, specifically tasks, assignments, tests, and quizzes that would produce this evidence. This evidence may come from observations of student performance, interviews consisting of question and answer exchanges with students, and sample student products. Such assessments may also include performance tasks, products, and projects that are uniformly given to all students across a grade level in a given subject to evaluate student mastery of the material at the end of a unit. As curriculum gets more developed, uniform assessments come every quarter, not just at end of the course or year.

Criteria for Proficiency

The uniform performance task is not quite enough. We need explicit, public grading criteria as well. For example, consider this learning expectation: "Express an opinion of a literary work or film in an organized way, with supporting detail." Following are the criteria for success:

- An introduction that summarizes the work's genre, plot, or main point
- A statement of your opinion
- Three details to support your opinion
- One text-to-text connection
- Summary

These criteria direct us to scrutinize a student product for specific features that, if present, allow it to be evidence of proficiency. Criteria are sometimes represented in analytic rubrics, devices designed to show relative and specific degrees of completeness of student product in relation to specific criteria. It is the criteria behind the rubrics that are most important, however. Rubrics are not always needed, but criteria are.

End-of-Course or End-of-Year Samples of Proficient Student Work

An end-of-course or end-of-year sample of proficient student work (often referred to as an "exemplar") is a template against which to compare evidence that an important proficiency has been met by a student. It embodies in a finished product and makes concrete exactly what we expect students to be able to do in a particular academic area at the end of a semester or school year. These are, for example, sample student responses to data-based questions that meet criteria for proficiency, writing products that show the level of skill students are expected to display, projects, problems solved, lab reports written, and videos of verbal presentations, among others.

A benchmark is a specific performance to shoot for that marks progress toward, not final attainment of, a higher goal. Runners set themselves targets or benchmarks that gauge their progress toward a winning time. They feel good when they pass the benchmark, but their training isn't over yet. The benchmark signals that a significant increment of improvement has been passed. Thus there should be more benchmarks in a course or grade level than just one at the end of the course or semester. There can be as many or as few as are appropriate for the content or skills being learned. In guided reading in the primary grades, each alphabetical level of book is a benchmark of a sort. A child moving up from "M" to "N" books has passed a benchmark with specific observable performance associated with it. In many schools, quarterly assessments are developed to spell out intermediate levels of performance on the road to final proficiency.

Pedagogical Practices

A pedagogical practice is a commitment to a form of instruction that has a research base or perhaps a philosophical base. For example, a district or a curriculum department may have a commitment to writing across the curriculum, in which case all teachers may be asked to have students keep written learning logs of some kind in which they reflect on their learning each day. Or the school may have a commitment to cooperative learning, project-based learning, integration of technology, or a certain balance of formative and summative assessment that they expect, as well as student self-assessment and goal setting. Such commitments might show up in how curriculum is constructed and implemented. Above all, such practices, if expected, should be explicit to all and part of induction for new teachers.

Pacing Guides

A pacing guide is an approximate timetable that lays out how much time it usually takes to complete each set of lessons of each unit of study. This is particularly useful to teachers who haven't taught a curriculum before. A scope and sequence chart often lays out a sequence of topics or skills for a content area but does not give a sense of how long components take to learn under normal circumstances. A curriculum map (Jacobs, 1997) is a diagram that shows the development from year to year of content and skill knowledge. This allows a school and district to avoid repetition ("But we learned about latitude and longitude in fifth grade and seventh grade . . .") and make sequencing of content rational, reinforcing, and without gaps.

Lesson Plans

Lesson plans are detailed implementation scenarios that specify the learning objectives and experiences students will go through and tasks they will be asked to do. Many other components may be part of the scenario too, like motivators, activators, descriptions of equipment to use, pages in books, and assessment devices. We devote Chapter 19, "Planning," to this important topic.

Lesson plan samples are often part of good curriculum guides, but detailed plans for individual lessons should be made up by teachers who use the unit plan as the framework and district lesson plans and materials banks as resources to draw from. Why? Because good planning requires teachers to think deeply about the content, analyze what prerequisite skills and knowledge will be fundamental to understanding the new material, and consider that in light of what they know about their students. They need to plan pre-assessment, determine how to best present a concept to match the needs and their students' background knowledge, anticipate confusions students may have during a given lesson, and so on. Consequently, a detailed implementation scenario should stem from the teacher having dug into the content herself and determined how to support all students in achieving the lesson objective.

Time Allocations

Certain districts mandate how many minutes per day must be spent on certain subjects in elementary school. In some schools, this can go so far as how many minutes within the language arts block are spent on guided reading, interactive writing, free reading, and other topics. These time allocations may be recommended, mandatory, or nonexistent. It all depends on what is decided in the local context and what has been clearly agreed to.

Instructional Strategies

It is also possible that there are some schoolwide or grade-level commitments to particular instructional strategies, like the use of certain graphic organizers, selective manipulatives in math, and particular discussion formats or reading comprehension strategies. Sometimes they are integrated into curriculum designs. In contrast to pedagogical practices, which are big conceptually like constructivism and active learning, an instructional strategy is small such as modeling thinking aloud, "Carousel Brainstorming," and so on.

Activities, Materials, and Examples

At a very detailed level, it may be expected or perhaps only recommended that teachers use particular instructional materials, like fraction bars for math or the TCI History Alive Curriculum (www.teachtci.com) or a particular apparatus to illustrate acceleration as a principle of Newtonian physics. Required use of certain textbooks adopted districtwide falls in this category.

Resources for Teachers

Depending on the size and budget of the district, any of the resources listed in Table 17.4 may be available for teachers to draw on. A distinction must be made between materials and resources. Materials are tangible items used to implement lessons, to teach the curriculum. Resources are what teachers use to prepare themselves to teach it well.

Table 17.4 Resources for Teachers

1. Print Materials	• Curriculum guides • Lists of recommended books and materials • Unit guides • Recommended websites • Sample lessons • Curriculum libraries of great units
2. Physical Materials	• Math manipulatives • Science apparatus
3. Human Resources	• Building-based curriculum specialists • Staff development on planning skills • District curriculum specialists • Staff development on analysis of data • Staff development of teachers • Culture of sharing units and materials • Professional norms of joint planning
4. Other Resources	• Collections of instructional materials available for loan • Association memberships • Funds for attending content area conferences and professional development workshops

A LESSON FROM A CURRICULUM POINT OF VIEW

Lesson plans are guided by the curriculum but not necessarily spelled out in the curriculum. Let us define a lesson as a time span when a teacher takes a bounded chunk of material from a unit or a topic and creates an experience or a series of experiences for students. The idea is that when the lesson is over, most of the students have learned whatever was the target, whether a skill (for example, locating places by latitude and longitude) or a concept (for example, the separate powers of the three branches of the U.S. government and their checks and balances on each other).

This definition of a lesson is, therefore, tied to material to be learned rather than to time. A lesson can take more than one class period. If a lesson is good, it will have most of the following parts, although not all may be used in a single class period because some steps are coming later or have already happened:

- **Precision:** A clear statement of objective in mastery language (what students will know or be able to do) exists, plus other elements profiled in Chapter 19, "Planning."
- **Connections:** There are links with similar lessons being taught elsewhere in the district with regard to rigor, consistency, and alignment.
- **Rigor:** The standards for proficiency are high enough.
- **Consistency:** "Proficient student performance" has the same meaning throughout the school or the district.
- **Alignment:** What's supposed to be taught is actually taught and actually tested.

LESSON PLANNING AND INSTRUCTION

The implementation of a lesson is marked by unplanned behaviors that come from a teacher's instructional repertoire and decisions made on the fly that are not always premeditated. These include the following:

- Checking for understanding (frequently and broadly) to identify when to slow down, stop, or reteach, and for whom.
- Unscrambling confusions by getting students to make visible their thinking, assumptions, or processes.
- Being explicit.
- Making cognitive connections.

Teachers design lessons that are based on what is in the curriculum. Their lessons may or may not draw heavily on district support materials, unit guides, and other resources. But the lessons themselves, that is the sequence of activities and tasks students do daily, are formulated by the teacher as designer. They are not specified and required in the curriculum. This does not mean that the teacher has to make them up from scratch each day. It's just that in a district that values professionalism, the teacher makes choices about what the appropriate activities and tasks are for their students. The teacher is a designer of student work. To prescribe what teachers should do in lessons can be insulting to skilled professionals and deny students the benefit of skillful professional decisions about the how, when, and how fast of instruction.

In a district that values professionalism, the teacher makes choices about what the appropriate activities and tasks are for their students.

We acknowledge that for novice teachers and para-professionals, it may be appropriate to provide scripts of what good presentations or questioning would sound like and to prescribe in considerable detail how to set up materials and get students to engage. But such scripts should be used only as needed for inexperienced teachers and only until their diagnostic and planning skills reach professional levels of proficiency. Table 17.5 shows the relationship of lessons, units, and courses.

Table 17.5 Relationship of Lessons, Units, and Courses

	Lesson	Unit	Course
Duration	1 to 2 class periods	Weeks or months	Semester or year
Central Elements	Mastery Objectives	Big ideas/Enduring understandings Guiding/Essential questions Evidence of learning	Overarching theme Proficiency targets: • Exemplars • Criteria • Rubric
Measured by	Observation Inspection of student work Quizzes Products Q & A interviews	Projects Unit tests Performances	Benchmark performances or products Final examinations Comprehensive orals
Records	Checklists Gradebooks Anecdotal notes Running records	Grades tied to rubrics	Certification of proficiency (3 on a 4-point scale) Credits Final grade

INDICATORS OF A WELL-DEVELOPED AND COHERENT CURRICULUM

Besides the existence of good curriculum documents (blueprints, frameworks, and guides), one might find the following indicators of a school's well-developed curriculum:

- ▲ Book closets and audiovisual repositories where materials consistent with the curriculum are stored and accessible to teachers.
- ▲ A compilation of assessments that are uniform and used by all teachers of a given subject or topic.
- ▲ Talk at grade level or department meetings about curriculum implementation and improvement.
- ▲ State standards and framework documents readily available.
- ▲ Individual classrooms outfitted with a copy of relevant standards and curriculum guides.
- ▲ Banks of exemplars of student work at proficiency for various units and skills available for teachers.
- ▲ Lesson plan banks of exemplary lessons available.
- ▲ Time built into the professional development schedule for improving the teaching of specific units or topics in the curriculum.

The common understandings and agreements here about good curriculum not only enable us to achieve consistency in our teaching, but also to agree on common maps about what is important to teach. The elements can also be used as a template for design in a district that is in the process of creating curricula.

In addition, common understanding of exactly what student performance schools are shooting for and what good performance would look like is a prerequisite for effective team meetings when grade-level teachers or middle school and high school teachers who teach the same content meet together. Teachers can't collaborate to look at student work and problem-solve about how to teach certain items better if they're not teaching to the same standards and in agreement about the criteria for good performance.

Our hope is that teachers know what questions to ask about the agreements their schools and districts have made regarding what to teach and what good student performance should look like. In addition, this chapter should serve as a guide for what work needs to be done when teachers serve on curriculum development committees. And finally, we hope that it is apparent how important a clear and consistent set of curriculum agreements is for planning cohesive instruction that can move all students to proficiency.

The next two chapters profile the teacher skills required to move from curriculum to the planning and implementation of good lessons based on that curriculum.

CHAPTER QUICK GUIDE

▲ The common understandings and agreements between the district office (or academic department) and its teachers about good curriculum enable consistency in teaching and agreement about what is important to teach.

Curriculum Agreements Address:

- Topics to be taught
- Big ideas
- Units of study organized around the big ideas
- Learning expectations (or learning outcomes) for a grade or course
- Uniform assessments (sometimes called benchmark assessments), especially final assessments, interim assessments, and unit assessments
- Criteria for proficiency on assessment items
- End-of-course samples of proficient student work (an exemplar everyone can look at to see exactly what the district really means by the learning expectation)
- Pedagogical practices
- Pacing guides and curriculum maps
- Lesson plans
- Time allocations
- Instructional strategies
- Materials
- Resources

▲ A good lesson has precision, connections, rigor, consistency, and alignment.

Lesson Implementation Includes:

- Checking for understanding
- Unscrambling confusions
- Explicitness
- Cognitive connections

To check your knowledge about Curriculum Design, see the exercises on *The Skillful Teacher* website at www.RBTeach.com/TST7.

CHAPTER 18

Curriculum
Lesson Objectives

Curriculum: Lesson Objectives

The teacher skill described in this chapter is a thinking skill. It is employed before a lesson takes place, yet it is responsible for how the lesson looks and sounds. It is also a hinge for how much student learning takes place. The quality of teacher thinking about objectives accounts for much of what we see (or don't see) in classrooms.

A clear objective—we use the terms "objective," "learning outcome," "learning target," "learning intention," and "mastery objective" interchangeably—serves as a control tower for a lesson, always in touch with and carefully guiding the pilot and the passengers from the take-off through the flight path, the approach, and the landing. We show how that is so and provide guidelines for crafting good objectives and making them visible to students throughout lessons.

When students clearly know what they are supposed to learn or get better at, they learn more.

The objective of a lesson is what the students are supposed to learn or get better at when it is over. When we, as teachers, get crystal clear about what that objective is, we design a much better lesson. We also check more thoroughly for understanding because we're focused on what we want for the students and we want to know whether they have gotten there or not. In parallel, when students clearly know what they are supposed to learn or get better at, they learn more. Here research supports logic: if you know where you're headed, you're more likely to get there. There are two central tasks to lesson objectives. First, is the need, as a teacher, to get clear about it. This task will bring us to examining the language of the objective and the crucial determination of whether the objective is the most appropriate one for the students in front of us today despite what the curriculum manual or the pacing guide may say. The second task is getting students to understand what the objective is, which requires far more than writing it on the board (Brookhart & Moss, 2014).

For decades, we have been in classrooms where the objective is posted on the board in compliance with a directive (or a strong expectation) from administrators. However, this alone is not sufficient for the following reasons:

- ▲ The objective may be written in language the students don't understand.
- ▲ Students may understand the vocabulary, but not put it together for the meaning of the objective.

Try the exercise in Exhibit 18.1. What did you notice?

- ▲ The objective may be read aloud, but never touched again as the teacher plunges the students into activities, so any connection between what they do and the objective is lost.
- ▲ The students don't connect to the objective; it has no relevance or meaning for them.

There's nothing wrong with posting an objective on the board. It's just that it's a useless act unless we make sure the students understand it and connect what they are doing in class to accomplishing that objective. Posting the objective can become empowering if we then get the students involved in self-evaluating their progress toward the objective at the end of the lesson time.

Exhibit 18.1 Actions Related to Objectives-Driven Lessons

Rate the frequency with which you do (or observe) each of the following practices:	**Always**	**Sometimes**	**Never**
1. The objective is written on the board.			
2. Prior to the lesson, the teacher analyzes the content to identify the most important items in the objective that should be highlighted as the lesson(s) proceeds.			
3. Students have taken a pre-assessment.			
4. The objective describes what students will know or be able to do with a specific performance verb.			
5. The teacher expands the objective in student-friendly language.			
6. The itinerary (agenda) is posted and reviewed with the students.			
7. Students can tell a visitor what the objective is.			
8. The teacher provides an explanation of why the objective is worth learning.			
9. The criteria for success are apparent and visible.			
10. The objective is referred to during the lesson.			
11. Teacher and students spend several minutes unpacking the objective at the beginning to find out what they understand and don't understand about the vocabulary used and meaning of the objective.			
12. Students self-evaluate using the criteria for success.			

A CLEAR OBJECTIVE CREATES A CLEAR IMAGE OF STUDENT PERFORMANCE

A clear objective creates an image—a picture in your mind, a sentence of inner speech you say to yourself, or a written statement—of what a student will know or be able to do when the instruction is over. What's important is that the image is framed from the students' point of view. The objective is a clear picture that the teacher has of desired student performance, which then becomes a clear picture for the students too.

We would argue that all objectives can be framed as a clear image of student performance—even objectives pertaining to attitude or appreciation. For example, if the focus of a lesson is for students to be able to appreciate why disruption of the ozone layer should be of concern to us then we can ask ourselves, "What would we look or listen for to ensure that they had developed that appreciation?" Second, objectives that are not thought through in this way typically wind up with coverage, activity, or involvement thinking. All three are weaker than mastery thinking which we explain in Chapter 19, "Planning." Third, mastery thinking improves teaching by leading teachers to do more goal stating with students, more checking, more feedback according to criteria, better record-keeping, and more diagnosis of individual student needs.

Objectives that only say "students will be exposed to" are not acceptable. If you're going to "introduce" students to an idea or "expose" them to an experience, do you expect anything to stick? If you do, you can say what it is and go for it specifically. If you don't, why are you exposing them to the idea to begin with? In our work, we have found that the question, "Was there a clear objective?" can be answered by "yes," "no," or "yes, but fuzzy." The type of class most likely to look like a "fuzzy" on objectives is a rambling discussion that touches assigned material in an erratic way or covers course material without making relevant connections between items or linking to other course material. Another "fuzzy" class is one where there are weak connections between the activity students are doing and what they are supposed to be learning. A "no objectives" class has some students doing busywork, often on worksheets, about material they already know or have mastered. Calling this "reinforcement" won't wash. Practice has its place, of course, but the practice must be strengthening a learning that needs it.

Madeline Hunter, former director of the UCLA Lab elementary school, used to tell a story that illuminates how fuzzy thinking about objectives can dilute learning. She finds a kindergarten teacher holding her head amid a room that's a mess of paper and glue. There are paper turkeys all around on which children have been pasting squares of colored tissue paper to make Thanksgiving collages. Madeline asks what's been going on. "Well, it was an art experience for the kids," is the reply. The exchange then continued:

> **Madeline:** "Why did you go to the trouble of mimeographing the turkeys? Why not just give them a piece of paper and the tissue, and let them be creative, express themselves?"
>
> **Teacher:** "It really wasn't that. It was really a lesson in eye-hand coordination."
>
> **Madeline:** "Well, then why didn't you have them outline the turkey? You can't tell whether they stayed within the line or not when they've got them pasted all over the turkey."
>
> **Teacher:** "Well, it really wasn't that. It was a lesson in conservation."
>
> **Madeline:** "Conservation!"
>
> **Teacher:** "Yes. The kids have really been very wasteful of paste. So I was trying to teach them to put just a tiny piece of paste on."
>
> **Madeline:** "Then why didn't you give them a piece of paste, or a paper of paste, and see how much of their turkey they could finish before they ran out of paste? You can't tell if there's a cup of paste under some of these turkeys."
>
> **Teacher:** "Oh, for cryin' out loud, can't kids just have fun?"
>
> **Madeline:** "Sure they can have fun. What do your kids like to do?"
>
> **Teacher:** "The thing they like to do best is just chase out on the school grounds."
>
> **Madeline:** "Why didn't you take the last half-hour and go around, supervise them while they chased, and you wouldn't have this mess to clean up." (Hunter, 1977)

So again, the big question is, "Was there a clear objective?" When you reflect on the class period, can you infer a clear statement of what students were supposed to know or be able to do at the end? If you can't, the students probably can't either. And if they can't, that's trouble. It doesn't matter if the objective is on the board, it matters that the students can tell you what it is and with understanding. We encourage teachers to write lesson objectives on the board; but unless they do something to ensure that students understand it we might as well save the board space.

STEPS TO DEVELOP A CLEAR AND WORTHWHILE OBJECTIVE

We lay out the steps required for objectives to play a powerful role in student learning. "Improvement is not doing one thing exceedingly well; it's doing many aligned things well" (McAdams, 2006, p. 36). This is no simple matter because the objective (think "learning target" if that language has been adopted by your peers) must be appropriate for the students to begin with; certain students may be ready for it and others not.

> ***"Improvement is not doing one thing exceedingly well; it's doing many aligned things well."***
>
> *(McAdams, 2006)*

Here are the 12 steps we explain in some depth:

1. Identify the most worthwhile objective.
2. Determine whether students have adequate prior knowledge.
3. Compose the objective in mastery language so you get it clear in your own head.
4. Post the objective.
5. Communicate the objective in student-friendly language as a paragraph of talk.
6. Check for understanding of the objective and the vocabulary in it.
7. Tell students the steps we'll go through to meet the objective.
8. Get students to understand why the objective is worth learning.
9. Establish the criteria for success you would take as evidence of mastery.
10. Have students self-evaluate according to the criteria for success.
11. Return to what the objective is at least once during the lesson and again at the end.
12. Provide for thinking-skill objectives that students might have to learn.

Step 1. Identify the Most Worthwhile Objective

Identify the most worthwhile objective for these students, at this time, by analyzing the materials you've picked (or that the curriculum presents) for subconcepts, relationship of concepts, possible misconceptions, and points of difficulty. This requires several steps that analyze the content itself from different angles. Doing so often creates insights that have a substantial positive effect on the lesson design. Here are the steps:

- ▲ Analyze the content for the most important elements you want your students to learn–the "must have" takeaways.
- ▲ Look for the relationship (sometimes the hierarchy) of ideas and skills in the content.
- ▲ Identify the misconceptions or particularly difficult items that may be obstacles to the intended learning.
- ▲ Get a read on the prior knowledge and skills students need (perhaps secured by pre-assessment) to be successful in learning the content.

These are all aspects of *content analysis* that take place before designing the lesson. It need not take a great deal of time (typically 10 minutes), but it does mean doing a few of the problems yourself, doing a quick read of the chapter in the social studies book, or a quick read of the short story they will be discussing. Get out the lab manual, the science text, or the language exercise and look at it carefully yourself.

Matching Stated, Lived, and Worthy Objectives

Sometimes the objective that is stated (and written on the board) does not match the objective in action—that is, the stated objective and the objective-in-action (lived objective) are not aligned. It could be that neither one exploits the full potential of what could or should be the objective, meaning a worthy objective.

We recently visited a freshman world history class with the high school principal. Before class, the teacher explained that her objective was for students to see how Napoleon's invasions and conquests spawned nationalism as a strong force in European countries that had previously been socially and politically fragmented. This was because the people united against a common enemy (Napoleon) and saw themselves as having common cause. During the first

Table 18.1 Stated Objectives, Lived Objectives, and Worthy Objectives

Stated Objective	**Lived Objective**	**Worthy Objective**
What's posted on the board or written in the lesson plan. It might even be what the teacher tells the students the objective is.	Objectives that are actually being addressed through the activities the students are participating in.	Learning targets that would have benefitted the students the most.
Students will understand the impact of Napoleon's reign on Europe.	Students will listen to a presentation on Napoleon's three big mistakes and copy the teacher's board notes into their notebooks.	Students will be able to explain what nationalism is and how it shows up in the modern world. OR Students will be able to explain how Napoleon's foreign actions stimulated nationalism in every country he touched. OR Students will be able to explain how Napoleon's arrogance led to suffering and death for millions and also led to his downfall. OR Students will be able to organize main ideas and subordinate ideas they extract from text into Cornell note style. OR Students will be able to use three conventions in textbooks (sections titles, color cues, and sidebars) to guide their reading.

part of the class, the teacher gave a lively lecture about Napoleon's big military mistakes and students appeared highly engaged. At the teacher's direction, students were copying into their notebooks the main points she was putting on the board. At the conclusion of the lecture, students were assigned to triads to locate information in the text about Napoleon's big mistakes and make a poster illustrating those mistakes.

It's important to look at the materials the students are working with and the task they are working on.

Reflecting later on what actually took place in that class, it was difficult to determine how the activities of the day matched either the objective she had stated in our earlier conversation or what she had written on the board which was, "Students will understand the impact of Napoleon's reign on Europe." Because Napoleon's reign had many different effects on Europe, it was even unclear from the board what specific effect she wanted students to "understand."

Her presentation, the notes students took, and the small-group activity focused entirely on Napoleon's big military mistakes. There was no mention of nationalism in the lecture or the activities. Although the text addresses the whole issue of Napoleon's impact on nationalism in several of the countries he invaded, students were directed to research his mistakes, thus missing the bigger picture or more important objective. Later during the class, while students were working in triads, we questioned individual students about the meaning of nationalism. Three quarters of them couldn't explain it.

Given what was in the text and the other learning needs these students revealed, including not knowing what nationalism was to begin with, a number of other objectives could have been worthwhile choices (see Table 18.1). Because there was no checking for understanding going on, the only verifiable objective, if we are really honest about it, was to get the students to copy her notes off the board and then search text to make a poster.

Level of Difficulty

Even before J. McVicker Hunt (1961) named it the "challenge of the match," educators were striving to make the work given to students not too hard and not too easy but just hard enough to stretch them toward optimum rate of learning. The problem of the match makes teachers look at where students are now and ask, "How big a bite can I give them for the next increment of learning?"

For example, judging the size of the bite for six third graders may lead their teacher to teach fractional notation and adding of fractions with common denominators in the same lesson. They can grasp that. The students in an eleventh-grade German history class may not only assimilate the background and content of Bismarck's "blood and iron" speech but also, in the same class, explain it in terms of Bismarck's character.

If you think this sounds like individualizing, you're right. It is individualizing the number of learnings tackled at once and their pace—the size of the bites of learning—to individuals and groups. There are many other variables that the term *individualizing* may include. Most of those variables are about *how* the learning shall proceed. Here we are talking about what, and how much, shall be aimed at for learning, regardless of the how.

What evidence might there be that the size of the bite was a good match for a group of students? Perhaps there was some initial struggling but then grasping of new ideas; perhaps moments of silence followed by student questions and clarification of difficult concepts; perhaps episodes of puzzlement culminating in "aha!" reactions; perhaps there was diligent note-taking. Negative evidence is easier to spot: confusion, dismay, frustration, or mute silence for work that's too hard (or inadequately presented); boredom as pencil tapping, looking around, chatting, or sloppiness for work that is too easy. Easy work is far from the only cause of this litany, but it should be checked out when the behaviors occur.

It is possible, as well, that none of those overt behaviors may be present, yet the objectives might still be mismatched to the students. In that case, only knowledge of the students' prior work in relation to the demands the teacher is making could help us have a conversation about the appropriateness of the objectives. Classroom observers can only surmise the match between the worthy objective and the lived objective if they look at the materials the students are working with and the task the students are working on. For teachers who teach the same content, discussing these choices with one another at team meetings with prior student work on the table is a very productive use of time.

Video: Compose in Mastery Language

Step 2. Determine Whether Students Have Adequate Prior Knowledge

Pre-assessing the students enables you to find out if there are any prior knowledge gaps you need to fill in before beginning instruction. Reflecting on how the students did yesterday, however, including looking at the work they produced, will be better and usually suffice for daily planning. Formal pre-assessment is a good fit when starting a totally new topic like "ecology," "immigration," "memoir."

Step 3. Compose the Objective in Mastery Language

Make sure you know what student performance ("will be able to do") you would take as evidence of mastery. This means being sure the language you use with yourself (for this is not what you will say to the students) is not an activity, a task completion statement, or a set of directions. This will yield better planning for the activities and tasks you choose, the sequence of what the students do, and how you frame it all for them.

All mastery objectives start with the learner as the subject: "Students will be able to . . ." or other language to that effect. For example, "Participants will demonstrate that they can . . ." Then comes the all-important verb. It has to be an action verb that can be observed—for example, "explain in their own words," "make a model that displays . . . ," "list the evidence that supports. . . ," "describe the attributes of . . . ," or "compare and contrast the elements of . . ."

Verbs that are about unobservable processes cannot stand by themselves in a statement of a mastery objective. Examples of such verbs are *understand, appreciate, witness*, and *see*. You can, of course, use these verbs if you then go on to say how the students will show that they know or understand.

You know it's a good objective if you can answer these two questions:

1. What is each student going to walk away with inside his or her head that wasn't there before; in other words, something the student understands and can explain or something he or she can do as a skill?

2. How will I know the students can do this?

Our colleague, Mary Sterling, suggests the following sentence structure for framing objectives: "Students will demonstrate an understanding of . . . [know] by . . . [able to do]." Teachers in her courses practice framing their objectives in this form. Then they ask one another, "Is the 'able to do' deep enough and strong enough to convince you that they know?" In pairs, Sterling asks teachers to exchange their statements and single underline the "know" and double-underline the "able to do" parts.

The language of a good mastery objective:

▲ Is specific in terms of curricular knowledge, whether it be declarative or procedural.

▲ Names an active performance (observable behavior) that demonstrates mastery.

▲ Avoids using mental action words that do not inform students about what they will have to do to demonstrate mastery such as: understand, learn, be familiar with, know, recognize that, have a grasp of, see that, appreciate that, recognize significance of . . .

- ▲ Begins with "Students (or "you" or "I") will be able to . . . ," indicating development of capacity versus completion of an activity.
- ▲ Includes strong clues about assessment.
- ▲ May include a level of performance or be accompanied by criteria for success.

Language Objectives for ESL Students

For ESL students it is also an important practice to communicate a "language objective"—a process-oriented statement with action verbs—of how students will use English in the content (see *The Skillful Teacher* website at www.RBTeach.com/TST7 for a description of the *why* and *how* of these objectives).

It is easy to lose track of where you're going if you don't think or write objectives in terms of student mastery. A teacher can get tied to materials and activities, and have students involved and liking their classes, but be achieving uncertain, erratic, and unpredictable results. Student involvement and enjoyment of school are important goals, but they do not by themselves make for effective teaching and learning.

Video: Student-Friendly Language

Step 4. Post the Objective

Be sure the objective is posted somewhere in the room so that students can refer to it. The objective can be written on the board, on a poster, in a syllabus the students have received before, or on an electronic resource.

Step 5. Communicate the Objective in Student-Friendly Language

This means rehearsing what you will actually say, because for many of us preparing the extended "student-friendly" expositions of academic objectives is not a common practice. After a while, it will become natural and require no rehearsal.

Videos: Unpack the Objective 1 & 2

Student-friendly language often requires a paragraph of talk. For example, "Ladies and gentlemen, we've been studying the three branches of government and what they do—legislative, judicial, and executive. Now it turns out that each of them has a way of stopping the other from doing something if they want to. It's like they have brakes they can apply to the other branches in certain situations. Today, we'll learn how they do that. It's called "Checks and Balances" on each other. So here's the objective: I can give examples of how each of the three branches of government exerts checks and balances on the other two."

Some current writers call these "I can" statements "Learning Targets" (Berger et al., 2014). "Learning Targets" are formal objectives translated into language the students can understand and own.

Step 6. Check for Understanding of Objective

This means pausing for a minute or two to be sure the students understand the words in and the meaning of the objective. We've got to ask questions and get the students to say what they think the objective means. For example, "Someone tell me what you think the word "checks" means in the objective/learning target for today."

See the two videos from the Expeditionary Learning website referenced on *The Skillful Teacher* website (www.RBTeach.com/TST7) to see what it looks like when this kind of "unpacking" takes place. Notice how in both cases the "unpacking" moves of the teacher reveals terms the students don't yet understand.

Step 7. Tell Students the Steps to Meet the Learning Target

This usually means posting some sort of Itinerary or Agenda for the day (see Chapter 11, "Clarity").

Step 8. Get Students to Understand Why the Objective or Learning Target Is Worth Learning

This means connecting the objective or learning target to something real, meaningful, or useful in life that the students can understand. You may have done that previously (for example, when learning about punctuation) and not have to do it every time you begin work on a new element of correct punctuation. (See Chapter 11, "Clarity," for more on "the reason why.")

Step 9. Establish the Criteria for Success You Would Take as Evidence of Mastery

Video: Criteria for Success

Generate the criteria for success in performances or products you would take as evidence of mastery. This will be a bulleted list of attributes or elements that will be present in the students' products or performances. Exhibit 18.2 provides some examples.

Exhibit 18.2 Criteria for Success

Definition

Criteria for success are the qualities that must be present for performance and products to meet the standards and be deemed successful. "What are the criteria" means:

- "What should we look for in examining students' products or performances to know if they were successful?"
- "What attributes should we use to judge the effectiveness of the product or performance?"
- "What counts?"

A list of criteria (and exemplars) enable students to assess their current performances in light of the target performance. Criteria for success do not state what the teacher will do. They do not state what the student will do. Criteria for success name or describe the characteristics of the product or performance, so the subject of the criteria should be the product or performance.

Examples of some criteria for products:

1. The lab report:
   - Lists all the steps for the process of _____.
   - Explains your observations.
   - Explains your conclusions about the relationship between _____.
   - Uses technical terms correctly.
2. Your learning log:
   - Summarizes the major events in the chapter.
   - Identifies the central conflict and progress toward its resolution.
   - Includes your own reflections on the decision that the protagonist is making in her attempt to deal with and solve her problem.

Examples of some criteria for a performance:

1. Your oral presentation:
   - Clearly states your position on the topic.
   - Presents the arguments supporting your position.
   - Supports all arguments with reasons and evidence.
   - Responds to arguments opposing your position.
   - Is accompanied by visuals (e.g., charts, overheads, handouts).
   - Is loud enough for everyone in the room to hear easily.
   - May be spoken with notes but not read.
   - Is fluent in delivery and confident in tone (which means you practiced).
2. Your sharing of your independent reading tells:
   - The title and author of your book.
   - The most interesting part so far.
   - At least one vocabulary word that is new or interesting to you.
   - A prediction of what will happen next.

Step 10. Have Students Use Criteria for Success to Self-Evaluate

This means pausing to do things such as having the students self-evaluate where they are in their progress toward attaining the objective/learning target, or connecting how the next activity they're doing is aimed to move toward accomplishment of the objective/learning target.

Video: Return to Objective

Step 11. Return to What the Objective Is at Least Once During the Lesson and Again at the End

The discipline of returning to the learning target keeps us focused on the outcome we want. It acts as a deterrent to tangents. But more important, it keeps the students focused on what they are supposed to learn or get better at. Their attention is constantly drawn to the meaning of the activities they are doing.

Step 12. Distinguish Between Thinking Skill Objectives and Mastery Objectives

There is an important distinction between thinking skill objectives and mastery objectives. They are both, to be sure, a form of mastery. In the latter, the goal is for students to master knowledge (e.g., be able to explain the causes of the Civil War) and operational skills (e.g., write with good grammar, solve three-step word problems, locate points on the globe with latitude and longitude). In the case of thinking-skill objectives, the goal is for students to master a generic form of thinking skill, like comparison and contrast, or understanding one's assumptions, or defining the real problem before listing solutions. Put another way, the goal is for students to learn or get better at a particular mental process and be able to transfer it to material other than today's content.

Let's say that your geography lesson today includes being able to list the attributes of an estuary: (1) fan-shaped land formation, (2) at the mouth of a river, (3) containing sedimentary deposits, and (4) filled with brackish water. But more generally, aside from today's geography lesson, you want your students to know that many concepts have a set of attributes that define them, and all the attributes need to be present for the concept to be the concept. You want them to be able to analyze the attributes of an item. That's a generic thinking skill. An example would be to use the attributes of representative democracy to analyze which of two countries, both of which have elections, are really democracies.

Merely giving assignments whose fulfillment calls for certain thinking skills is not teaching the thinking skill, just as round robin reading, which calls for students to perform reading, is not necessarily teaching them anything about how to get better at reading (Duffy, Roehler, & Rockliffe, 1986). For example, asking students to compare and contrast the motives of the North and the South at the beginning of the Civil War does not teach students anything about the act of comparing and contrasting two things if they do not already know how to do that. Almost everything teachers ask students to do requires them to think in some way. But only when they are deliberately and explicitly teaching a particular kind of thinking skill that can be named can we say that there is a thinking skill objective.

If you want your students to learn thinking skill X, you may repeatedly give them tasks that call for it, that is, do a task that requires the thinking skill to complete correctly. But you are not teaching the thinking skill. When teaching a particular thinking skill is the real objective, we advise naming the thinking skill, teaching it, coaching it, and arranging for the students to get feedback on how they're doing with it—all this in addition to having them practice it. If a teacher has a thinking-skill objective for students (rather than just an assignment or a task that calls for thinking), the teacher should do the following:

1. Name the skill.

2. Deal explicitly with how to do it (for example, model aloud with the steps or have students share strategies for doing it).

3. Highlight steps.

4. Give tips and coaching pointers.

5. Have students practice with feedback.

6. Evaluate how the students are doing with the thinking skill.

Unfortunately, we usually see only step 6. That's not teaching a thinking skill; that's testing for it and hoping the students will learn the skill from the test or the task.

The explicit teaching of thinking skills has a marvelous literature of its own. Tishman, Perkins, and Jay (1995) describe school structures and practices that support the explicit teaching of thinking skills. In fact, they are interested in fostering schools where thinking dispositions such as open mindedness, strategic spirit, and inquisitiveness are core values of the institution. Similar positions are taken by Barell (2003) and Costa and Kallick in their excellent book,

Learning and Leading with Habits of Mind (2008). Teachers and leaders who want these things for their children have an overarching objective for what a school should be.

OBJECTIVES ABOUT SOCIAL SKILLS AND ATTITUDES

Objectives need not be solely about cognitive topics. Imagine pairs of students coaching individuals on a certain bookkeeping procedure, and we infer that there is an objective about cooperation and helping others in the room.

Deirdre is excluded from the class meeting (first grade) and sitting near (though facing away from) a pile of blocks. We hear a few remarks and see some body language from the teacher that leads us to conclude she has an objective in mind for Deirdre: take responsibility during clean up; you can't get out of your responsibilities to others by pouting and stalling.

Mr. Caswell wants students to develop a positive attitude toward classical music. How would he know if he'd accomplished that? What does he mean when he says, "I want my students to appreciate Beethoven"? He might mean that he expects knowledge of the intricacy and subtlety of the design of a Beethoven symphony to generate respect. Further, he may believe that for some people, having to listen in a focused way to the symphony as they analyze its parts will lead to aesthetic enjoyment. All of that may be his concept of "appreciation"; respect through knowledge and liking through repeated experience. If that is his concept, it will lead him to do certain activities in class aimed at generating specific student performances like being able to analyze parts of the symphony and label a score, describing in words the principles by which Beethoven developed and restated themes, or identifying the different symphonies.

All of these student performances he can picture because he has thought about what "appreciation" means. But if he doesn't translate "appreciation" into some sort of student performance in his head, then what Mr. Caswell does with students in class may be random in its effect. He will not be looking inside their heads to create anything in a planful way. He will be operating outside their heads with activities and presentations that may or may not contact anything inside students. Who can tell? Without that image of the student performance he's aiming for, Mr. Caswell may do activities that lead to no performance or to an opposite student performance.

DETAILED BEHAVIORAL MASTERY OBJECTIVES

Popham and Baker (1970) and Mager (1962) popularized the writing of detailed behavioral objectives in which criterion levels for performance were specified as well as the conditions under which students would perform them—for example, "Given 10 multistep word problems involving multiplication and division, students will complete them in a half-hour at 90 percent accuracy." This movement, which eventually became the butt of jokes and a target of scorn, had aimed to sharpen thinking about student outcomes and improve accountability for student results.

Particular kinds of content do lend themselves well to very detailed behavioral objectives, typically operational skills that can be observed at criterion levels of mastery (mathematical manipulations, decoding in reading, and technical writing skills, for example), but this same kind of objective may not serve instruction so well when one attempts to apply it to an area like cooperation. How can a teacher meaningfully specify a criterion level for mastery with respect to cooperation? He could have a student discriminate cooperative from non-cooperative behavior at a criterion level in stories read or video clips viewed, but how useful would that be?

Different levels of specificity in language serve best with different types of content. Thus teachers need to use different kinds of objectives and use the language most suited to the content at hand. The use of detailed behavioral objectives for an art curriculum or an oil painting course might well trivialize that content.

But what about the teacher who uses general language in objectives for material that would lend itself nicely to detailed behavioral objectives? Here's an example: "Children will add three-digit numbers with medial zeros competently." What is "competently?" Here Popham and Baker (1970) would argue that a criterion level for mastery is essential for sharpening the delivery of skills and the evaluation of who knows what.

OBJECTIVES AND STATE STANDARDS

The standards movement represents a commitment of educators all over the country to raising the academic rigor of school curriculum. The impetus for this movement was alarming national reports in the 1980s and international comparisons in the 1990s that were not flattering to U.S. student achievement.

Equally important, the standards movement also became an equity movement based on the realization that students need a 21st-century education if they are to succeed, and that can't mean something radically different in Des Moines than in Detroit. We need to standardize the skills and concepts we offer in schools to achieve consistency, and more particularly, equity, by teaching the same skills and concepts to children of poverty as to children in schools serving affluent children. If schools expect less and offer fewer higher-level skills to children of poverty, they will continue to offer them unequal educations and unequal chances in the race of life. This equity in educational rigor is especially needed now since the greatest 2014–24 job growth rates projected by the U.S. Bureau of Labor Statistics will come from jobs that require some postsecondary education (Figure 18.1). These jobs are expected to make up almost 50% of new jobs.

So how does the standards movement, especially the Common Core, translate into educational practice? The first level of response has been to create state standards documents that attempt to promulgate high and uniform learning expectations for all students in the state. The actual standards in documents published by the states are general statements about the kinds of competency students should have in the academic subjects. They are not very specific; they define the broad areas of knowledge and skill. In New York, for example, Standard 3: Mathematics—Elementary is, "Students use number sense and numeration to develop an understanding of the multiple uses of numbers in the real world, the use of numbers to communicate mathematically, and the use of numbers in the development of mathematical ideas."

The meaning of this general statement becomes slightly more focused when such documents give indicators of what meeting that objective might look like. For example, students:

- ▲ Use whole numbers and fractions to identify locations, quantify groups of objects, and measure distances.
- ▲ Use concrete materials to model numbers and number relationships for whole numbers and common fractions, including decimal fractions.
- ▲ Relate counting to grouping and to place-value.
- ▲ Recognize the order of whole numbers and commonly used fractions and decimals.
- ▲ Demonstrate the concept of percent through problems related to actual situations.

Figure 18.1 Percentage Projected Change in Employment by Typical Entry-Level Education (2014–24)

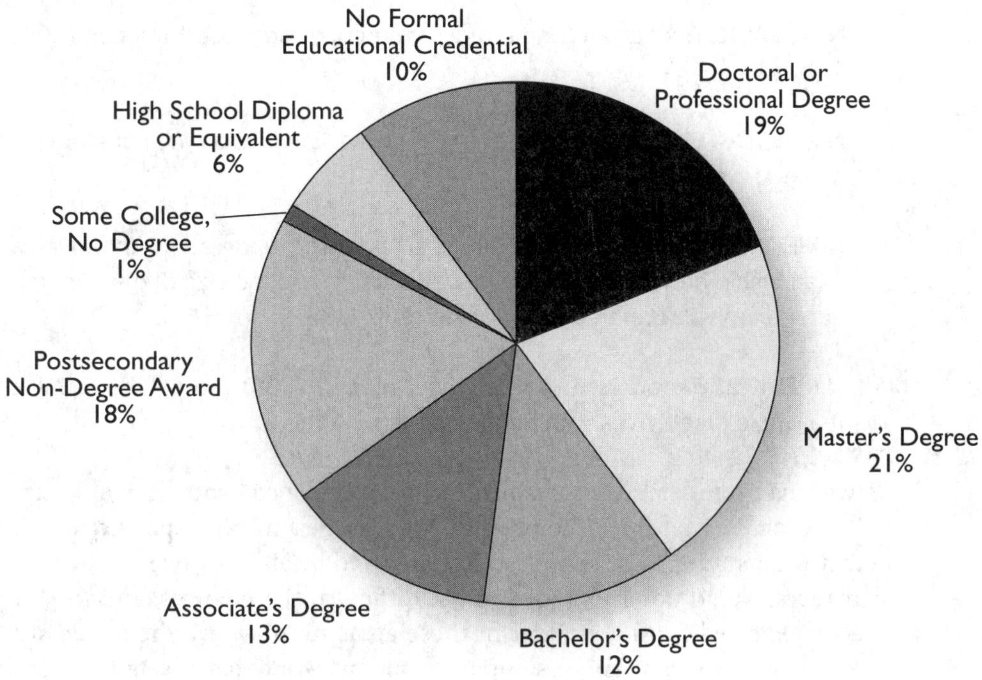

Adapted from Employment Projections Program, U.S. Bureau of Labor Statistics

Standards documents then sometimes give sample pieces of evidence to show that a student is meeting the standard. For example:

- ▲ Count out 15 small cubes and exchange 10 of the cubes for a rod 10 cubes long.
- ▲ Use the number line to show the position of 1/4.
- ▲ Figure the tax on $4.00 knowing that taxes are 7 cents per $1.00.

Some states move down to yet another level of specificity by listing within content topics exactly what the learning expectations (sometimes called "content expectations") are for a grade level. Within the second-grade content expectations document for the State of Michigan, we find these expectations for working with unit fractions:

> N.ME.02.18 Recognize, name, and represent commonly used unit fractions with denominators 12 or less; model 1/2, 1/3, and 1/4 by folding strips.
>
> N.ME.02.19 Recognize, name, and write commonly used fractions: 1/2, 1/3, 2/3, 1/4, 2/4, 3/4.
>
> N.ME.02.20 Place 0 and halves, e.g., 1/2, 1 1/2, 2 1/2, on the number line; relate to a ruler.
>
> N.ME.02.21 For unit fractions from 1/12 to 1/2, understand the inverse relationship between the size of a unit fraction and the size of the denominator; compare unit fractions from 1/12 to 1/2.
>
> N.ME.02.22 Recognize that fractions such as 2/2, 3/3 and 4/4 are equal to the whole (one). Work with unit fractions

So we have "standards," "indicators," "sample evidence," and "learning expectations," each derived from the previous one, and each more specific in telling a reader what students are supposed to know and be able to do (Figure 18.2). But as readers, we do not know the level of difficulty, the nuances, and the level of quality expected from a student in these areas until we see the actual student task that will assess it and a sample of student work that meets the standard. At this writing, state standards documents are still quite varied in the level of specificity they provide educators and families in their states. They also differ in their content. Generating more agreement across states is one of the reasons for the formation of Project Achieve in 1996.

The Common Core standards indicate shifts in the amount of time spent on certain types of content in math and literacy and puts a well justified emphasis on students' capacity to reason and justify verbally and in writing their explanations. The level of abstraction in the standards, however, is the same as the high-level statements described above.

> Math: 5th grade, standard 8a:
>
> "Understand that, just as with simple events, the probability of a compound event is the fraction of outcomes in the sample space for which the compound event occurs."
>
> ELA: 9th grade, standard 1a:
>
> "Introduce precise claim(s), distinguish the claim(s) from alternate or opposing claims, and create an organization that establishes clear relationships between the claim(s), counter claim(s), reasons and evidence."

Figure 18.2 Standards and Indicators

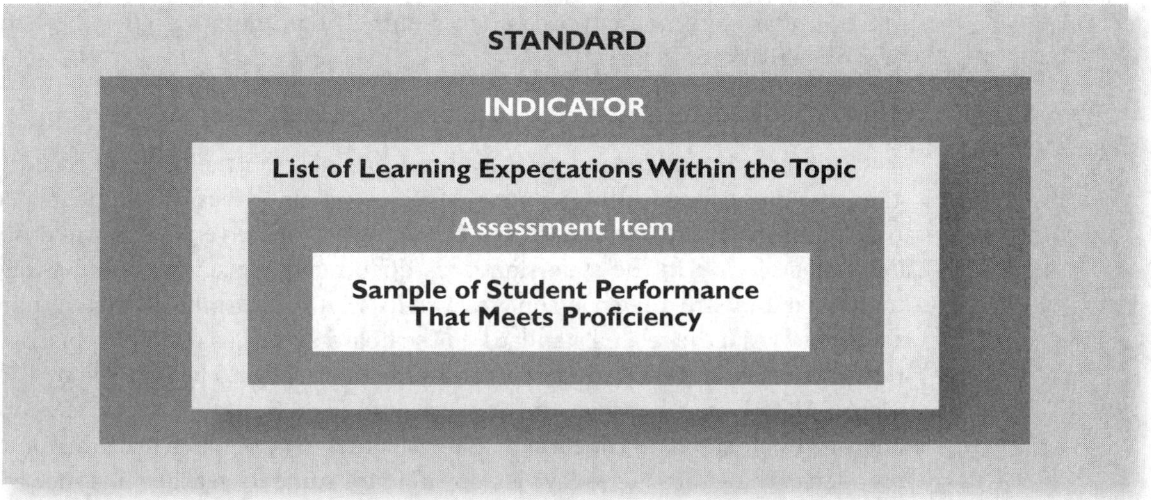

There is nothing wrong with these standards at all. But to plan lessons that enable students to meet them, requires the content analysis from a planning conference as described on pages 482 through 485. The objectives that a teacher comes up with for a given lesson serve the purpose of breaking down the general statements of state standards into an appropriate outcome that is measurable for each student at the end of a particular lesson. In other words, they break down the large objective in the state standards into the smaller pieces of learning that their particular students need to master en route to the bigger objective. For example, the Michigan second-grade content expectation is, "For unit fractions from 1/12 to 1/2, understand the inverse relationship between the size of a unit fraction and the size of the denominator; compare unit fractions from 1/12 to 1/2." No one can create a single lesson that enables students to do that. Today's lesson may have as its objective an understanding that students need first in order to comprehend the inverse relationship described in the Michigan content expectation. Perhaps the prior understanding they need is this: "Students will be able to explain that the denominator in fractional notation tells us how many equal pieces the whole is divided into."

Perhaps more significantly, our own class observations have shown us that many students don't yet realize that they can't compare two fractions unless the two fractions are describing the same whole. That's a common misunderstanding. So today's objective needs to focus on that, and that understanding isn't in the state standards at all. Understanding the developmental sequence of how students learn mathematical concepts is the focus of the Ongoing Assessment Project (OGAP) of the Consortium on Policy Research in Education at the University of Pennsylvania Graduate School of Education (www.ogapmath.com). Similar concept analysis is often required to pinpoint exactly where today's objective should lie.

Note that daily lesson objectives derive from a teacher's ongoing assessment of what students understand and need to learn next on the route to meeting standards prescribed for their course. Most lesson objectives should be related to accomplishing a state standard, but the objective for a given lesson will probably not be found in the state standards documents. Teachers should always know what standard a given lesson is related to. That is why some districts require teachers to write the related standard on the board as well as the daily objective. That practice is supposed to exert a discipline on teachers to be sure the two are related. All too often, however, the standard written on the board, accurately copied from a state standards document, is too abstract to be of much use to anybody in understanding the fit of today's lesson either for students, teacher, or a supervisor who visits. It's a meaningless act of compliance. Teachers need to know the relation of today's objective to the standard they are working on all right, but the most important alignment is that the objective of the day be on target for the needs of the students.

HOW ADMINISTRATORS AND COACHES CAN SUPPORT CLEAR LESSON OBJECTIVES

Use a Planning Conference to analyze the content to be taught for the relationship of the ideas, their hierarchy, sequence, the prior knowledge required to do the tasks assigned, and the most important and worthwhile "take-aways" for the students.

Video: Planning Conference

Example 1: Content Analysis Video

The Planning Conference video shows what this kind of analysis looks and sounds like. One of us is asking Emelia Jordan about the content of her lesson on the respiratory system for about 10 minutes, and following the nine guidelines listed in Table 18.2. The point is to be disciplined and converse about the content before going into the actual lesson and its activities.

Things to Note:

▲ Don't start with "What are you going to do?" or "What are the student activities?" In fact, resist all questions about the lesson, grouping, timing, and student activities until the discussion of content and objectives is complete.

Table 18.2 Nine Guidelines for Conducting a Content-Focused Planning Conference

Guidelines	**Quotes from the video**
1. Dive right into the content.	"What content will you be focusing on?"
2. Directly examine the actual materials that will be used to teach the content.	"Is there a chapter in the book that goes with this content?" "What materials will you be handing to the students?"
3. Focus on the key concepts that the teacher wants the students to take away from the lesson.	"What are the most important things that you want them to understand?"
4. Delve deeply into the meaning of the content, with particular focus on the key concepts. (It is okay to admit you do not understand the material here as your struggle more than likely reflects student struggle and allows the teacher to get clearer about the content.)	"Can you explain that a little further?" "What exactly do you mean when you say 'process'?" "I'm not sure I understand . . ."
5. Break the concepts down hierarchically. First, identify what prior knowledge students must have to be successful in the new task. Then break the current task down into steps—what must be understood first in order to understand the complete concept?	"So what would students need to know from prior experience in order to be ready to move forward?" "How would you break this concept down into parts?" "Which part of this concept do you think students need to understand first?"
6. Have the teacher state the objective (Big Idea) in kid-friendly language exactly as he/she plans to say it to the class, and have the teacher explain how he/she plans to display the objectives.	"How will you present the objectives to the class?" "Say it out loud now just as if you were talking to the class." "How will you present the information? On the board? PowerPoint?"
7. Ask the teacher how he/she plans to track student progress and understanding.	"How will you know if students are understanding or not?" "Will you have an assessment?"
8. Summarize. Have the teacher summarize exactly what he/she wants the students to learn. Summarize the accomplishments of the conference thus far.	"So if you were to go around and interview the students at the end of the day, what would you want them to tell you to show they really understood?" "So far, I think we have really gotten clear on the con tent and defined the objectives, which are . . ."
9. Now you are ready to jump into the activities. Make sure the activities relate directly to the objectives and that they do not require students to deal with too many variables.	"OK, so now what are you going to have the students do?"

- ▲ Make sure the objectives identified are worthy objectives. Do not allow objectives to focus on anything but content and make sure that the selected objective is really worthwhile.
- ▲ Make sure to focus on specific definitions, avoid generalities, and avoid such language as "stuff" and "things."
- ▲ Focus on understanding versus the mechanics of completing a task or operation.

The following is a list of things the teacher should bring to the meeting:

Basic Level

- ▲ Ask the teacher to bring all the materials that he/she plans to use, including books, worksheets, homework, and assessments.
- ▲ Ask the teacher to prepare the objective in kid-friendly language.

More Advanced

- ▲ Ask the teacher to break the concepts up in a hierarchical order.
- ▲ Ask the teacher to bring any examples of prior student work that might be relevant.

Example 2: Content Analysis Video

Video: Content Analysis

Notice which of the guidelines are followed by the peer in the conference (in this case, Jon Saphier) in the video. The result of this brief content-analysis conversation is that Ms. Jordan plans a much better lesson, and all the ideas come from her. She realizes that "respiration" is a system that consists of six sub-processes and makes a chart that shows how they relate to each other.

Then as she goes through the 3-day lesson sequence, she continually points out to students where they are in the development of the process. Of course, she makes a point of highlighting the confusion that comes out in the planning conversation, namely that "respiration" is a chemical reaction in the cell, in fact, in all cells of the body.

Content analysis is a large gap in teacher preparation and professional development that has significant negative consequences for learning. Content analysis is not the same as content knowledge. You can't know what respiration is without taking apart the sequence and relationships of the concepts within the respiratory system so as to make them clear and accessible to learners.

Example 3: Concept Map Video

Concept maps represent a visible representation of content analysis. In this video of a high-functioning grade-level PLC (Professional Learning Community), check out the concept map these fifth-grade teachers construct and then use to isolate what they will reteach to their students.

Videos: Concept Map, Content Analysis

Example 4: Content Analysis Video

This is another example of content analysis. Learning the meaning of fractions and how to do mathematical operations with them is a benchmark in mathematics. Failure to understand these operations beyond application of rote algorithms becomes a serious obstacle to progress in algebra in eighth grade and beyond. So it is important for teachers dealing with student understanding of fractions to understand the hierarchy of concepts that makes up this constellation of understandings.

Planning Conferences

Also available on *The Skillful Teacher* website at www.RBTeach.com/TST7 are scripts and sample dialogs that illustrate Planning Conferences in a number of different disciplines.

This chapter has been about the significance of clear thinking about objectives and how such thinking creates an objective that can serve as the control tower to lesson planning. In the next chapter, we spell out the dimensions of how such planning should proceed.

CHAPTER QUICK GUIDE

Twelve Steps for Developing a Clear Objective:

1. Identify the most worthwhile objective.
2. Determine whether students have adequate prior knowledge.
3. Compose the objective in mastery language.
4. Post the objective.
5. Communicate the objective in student friendly language.
6. Check for understanding.
7. Tell the students the steps to meet the "Learning Target."
8. Get the students to understand why the "Learning Target" is worth learning.
9. Establish the criteria for success you would take as evidence of mastery.
10. Have students self-evaluate according to the criteria for success.
11. Return to what the objective is at least once during the lesson and again at the end.
12. Provide for thinking-skill objectives that the students might have to learn.

To check your knowledge about Lesson Objectives, see the exercises on *The Skillful Teacher* website at www.RBTeach.com/TST7.

CHAPTER

19

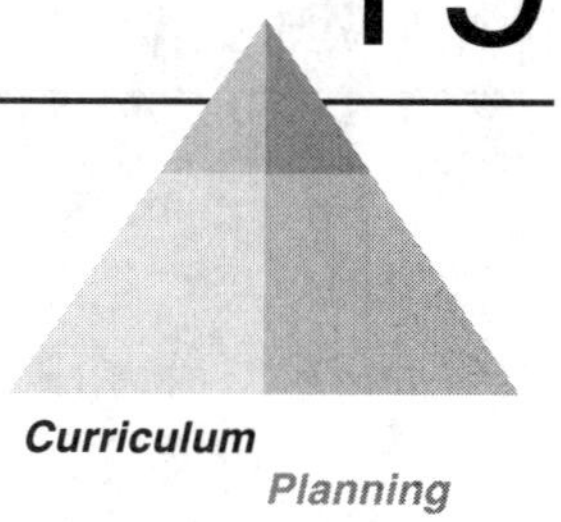

Curriculum: Planning

This chapter is about planning lessons, the small daily packages of crafted instruction within units. Well-designed units are still only general blueprints to what a teacher will do tomorrow with the 30 students in front of her. Good planning skills for daily lessons stand behind good teaching.

To learn about the important teacher knowledge base about unit design, see the excellent work of Wiggins and McTighe (2005) on backward planning. Instructional coaches, department chairs, and administrators often find they get more payback from planning conferences that focus on identifying worthwhile objectives and doing content analysis (see Chapter 18) with teachers than from observations with feedback. This will be true when the teacher's growing edge is related to clarity and issues of curriculum content.

Good planning skills for daily lessons stand behind good teaching.

CURRICULUM UNITS, LESSON, AND SPONTANEOUS TEACHING SKILLS

The centerpiece of planning is the lesson—the planned time period when students engage content through experiences that teachers have designed. A lesson plan is the detailed implementation scenario that specifies what the teacher does and what the students are expected to do during a bounded chunk of time devoted to a particular mastery objective.

It may take more than one class period to complete a lesson. Therefore, certain elements of the lesson, like activating student current knowledge, may take place on Monday, and most of the feedback on student work may be observable on Tuesday. These two class periods, as a package, may comprise a complete lesson on, say, the separation of powers in the U.S. government. That lesson, in turn, is part of a unit on the U.S. Constitution.

The design and overall construction of the unit may be in the district curriculum guide, but the actual plan for individual lessons probably is not (and should not be) in the curriculum guide. Designing lessons and crafting student work is the teacher's job, and curriculum guides and other district materials are supposed to be helpful resources for how to do so. Good curriculum specifies the "what" of teaching, which should include the big ideas and enduring understandings students are expected to take away from units of instruction.

Curriculum documents may also specify other agreements about instructional approaches, like an agreement that students will be writing about their interpretation of mathematical ideas. But it is teachers who plan the "how" of lessons that need to be designed in advance for each day. Then during lessons, teachers make spontaneous moves that weren't planned at all (and couldn't have been) but are drawn mindfully from their repertoires of skills like "probing a student's thinking" to understand why a student is confused.

FIVE KINDS OF THINKING FOR LESSON PLANNING

What we emphasized in the previous chapter on "Lesson Objectives" was the primacy of starting with a worthy mastery objective in one's planning. Having done that, all five questions in Figure 19.1 are important. The reason these circles are nested in a concentric way is to show the following relationships. No one can teach a thinking skill objective without having some content for the students to apply it to, so a teacher who is teaching to a thinking objective almost always has a mastery of knowledge or skills objective too. That is why the thinking circle in the diagram in Figure 19.1 includes the "mastery of knowledge and skills" circle. But the reverse is not necessarily true. A teacher can be teaching for mastery of knowledge without necessarily aiming to teach a particular thinking skill.

Similarly, the way in which the other circles in Figure 19.1 are nested shows the overlapping relationship of different kinds of teacher cognition during planning. For example, one can think "coverage" without having any activities for the students to do, but there cannot be activities without having some content the students are dealing with. To give another example, a teacher can have activities without any clear notion of what she wants students to learn. But she cannot have a true mastery objective without having both something for the students to do (activity) and some content on which to do it. Thus the mastery of knowledge and skills circle contains the other two.

What do we know about how planning actually takes place in American classrooms? There are five kinds of thinking relevant to lesson planning. Each of the five has an important place in planning, but if any one becomes an exclusive mindset, the instruction that results can have significant gaps for students. We now expand on the five kinds of teacher thinking.

Figure 19.1 Key Questions in Lesson Planning

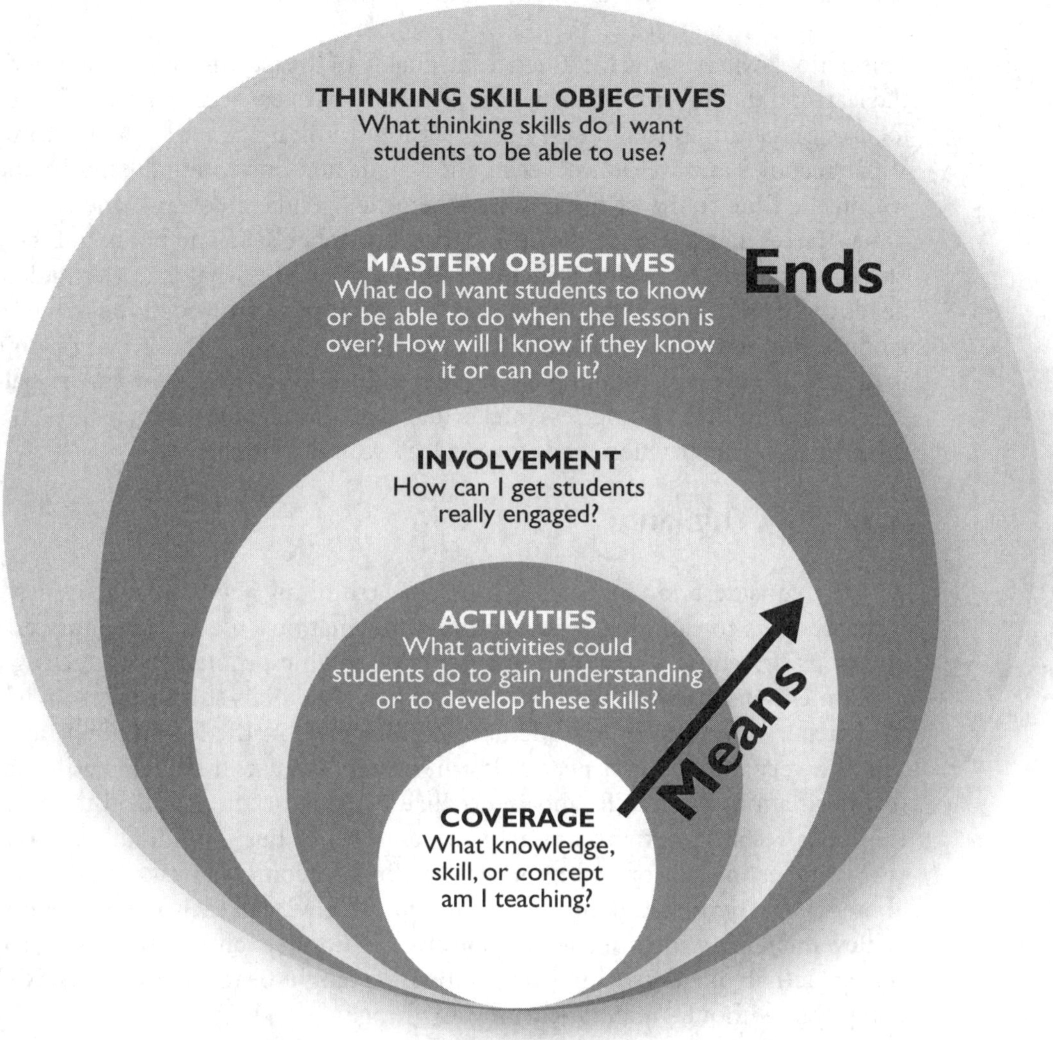

Thanks to Deb Reed for pointing out the Means/Ends relationship

1. Coverage Thinking

One kind of thinking during lesson planning is what content or skill is to be addressed or "covered" in the lesson (an event in history, French Impressionist art, converting fractions to decimals, the preterite tense, dribbling a basketball, the biography of a particular writer, two-part harmonies, and so on). When a teacher is thinking about coverage, she is thinking in terms of *her* part in the lesson. She is going to present, describe, explain, demonstrate, or cover identified information, events, procedures, or processes. As central as this concern is to any lesson, there is a danger when our planning stops here or when we think of what we are covering as the objective of the lesson (e.g., "My objective tomorrow is to cover the material on gas attacks in World War I").

This outlook will negatively influence the quality of the teaching and consequently the learning that takes place. A teacher who confuses coverage with an objective focuses on getting through everything without thinking about student learning. What becomes important is covering the agenda and presenting the information within the time frame of the lesson. When the agenda is covered, the lesson is done. The teacher has taken the information out of her head and put it "out there." She is not necessarily doing it in a way that is guided by what is in the students' heads before she starts. And she doesn't know if it passed through the nether regions of "out there" into students' heads when the lesson is over. When planning is driven by coverage thinking alone, we tend to do minimal—or superficial—checking for understanding, less intellectual exploration, and less integration with other learning. Instruction tends toward lecture and recitation.

2. Activity Thinking

Another consideration in designing lessons is thinking about what activities we want students to do, such as researching information on a website, answering questions, watching a film, building a model, solving problems, conducting an experiment, discussing a reading, and so forth. The focus shifts now from what the teacher will do to how students will participate in the lesson. Once again, this is a very important aspect of lesson design; what will students do to take in information, process it, and internalize it? This becomes a liability only if the focus rests on activities alone—students being busy—without examining the activities in light of an important learning outcome or weighing decisions about what activities students will do in terms of how well each activity supports achievement of an intended lesson objective. Without such a focus, it is possible that an activity is not teaching what should be taught or that the activity can be completed without students' learning anything.

"Write a story," for example, may be the activity for after lunch in a primary-grade room. To get the children involved (make the activity more fun, more attractive, more motivating), the teacher has textured wallpaper pieces they can use to make covers for their "books" and is going to help them bind their books. The quality of stories ranges from complete plots with beginnings, middles, and ends to random pictures with no text at all. While binding each book, the teacher asks the children about their stories; some make comments, some don't. The teacher is focusing on the binding and keeping the flow of students moving. An observer in the class sees no evidence that there is any particular feature the teacher is looking for in the stories. She is making an effort to be positive about some aspect of each child's work but appears to be looking for nothing in particular. The real goal is just that the students produce stories of any quality and make books to put them in. This is activity thinking in isolation from other important planning concerns. The teacher might not have intended that, but no other conclusion is supportable from the observation.

When teachers' prime planning concern is about activities, they miss opportunities to underline the critical learnings, make connections between learnings for students, and check and evaluate student learning. A teacher thinking in terms of activities is concerned more with what students are doing rather than with what they are learning. Sometimes this confusion shows up in assessment. Criteria for success might focus more on the visual appeal or mechanics of the product versus the content substance that indicates achievement of important learning outcomes.

3. Involvement Thinking

Another important concern in lesson planning is to get all students engaged in the learning experience. This can be accomplished in many ways: using examples that are relevant to students (a lesson on the court system for eighth graders that features a case of police shutting down a party—kids are arrested for transporting beer even though they did not actually drink it); causing movement, interaction, and exchange of opinion among students; or presenting discrepant events that arouse curiosity. When a teacher plans how information will be presented or activities are shaped and varied to accommodate a variety of learning styles, differing levels of background knowledge, or degrees of readiness, we see the most complex level of this aspect of planning, and the effects show up in the classroom. There is strategic consideration about how to present and have students process information in a variety of modalities, whether students should do activities individually, in pairs, in small groups, or as a whole class; there is often choice and variety available to students. We see evidence of this kind of thinking when teachers design differentiated learning experiences for students. The idea is to make the experience inviting and accessible to all students, provided that all of the concerns and decisions about student engagement are in relation to a particular learning outcome for the lesson.

Here again, if student involvement or engagement becomes the dominant concern without being considered in light of a clear learning objective, things will look very different. When a teacher says, "My objective tomorrow is to get all students to react personally and say what they'd do if they invented a horrible weapon. Would they turn it over to the government?" He is confusing involvement thinking with real learning objectives. There is no learning outcome implied. Success will be measured by whether or not students participated, rather than by what new learning has occurred or is in evidence.

Or consider the following scenario of a teacher talking about a lesson: "My students love to do word searches, so I make up one with their spelling words in it, and they do it for seatwork. They really have fun with them. They really got into that word search today!" But when we ask how it helped students learn to spell the words, the answer is, "I'm not sure. I assigned it because I thought they'd like to do it, and they do." As it turns out, there is no evidence that word searches improve students' ability to spell the words they find. It may improve their ability to scan complex data fields for visual information. And some may develop systematic searching strategies for finding the words more efficiently, but this was not the objective. Students who learn systematic search strategies are learning it randomly and incidentally, not through any deliberate actions of the teacher or following the directions given.

Students have to be engaged with activities that are carefully designed to lead to desired learnings.

Studies of teacher planning (conducted by having teachers think aloud) have shown that activity thinking and involvement thinking have tended to dominate planning. Planning lessons that are engaging for students is important; it is a good thing to do. But student engagement is not enough for learning. They have to be engaged with activities that are carefully designed to lead to desired learnings.

If we think of a learning experience as a journey students will take, then coverage, activity, and involvement thinking are like planning the details of the trip—the scenic roads, stops along the way, possible alternate routes, what vehicles to use, how to make it interesting, and so on—without being sure where you're going. However, the next two kinds of thinking (determining and articulating the objectives or student learning outcomes) are of the highest order of importance in lesson design. To continue the metaphor, the mastery objective identifies the *END* of the trip. Hence, it needs to be determined before decisions are made about the *MEANS*—what to cover, what activities students will do, and how things will be designed to maximize student involvement.

4. Mastery Thinking

If the objective is mastery of the spelling words, then the teacher will do something that should increase the likelihood that the students will spell the words correctly. Perhaps they will quiz each other in pairs and then make a list of the words they missed and go through a practice routine of seeing, saying, writing in the air, and retesting, over a 10-minute period. Then clearly there is a mastery objective at work for the students.

Perhaps a teacher says, "My objective for tomorrow is for students to be able to distinguish between rational, amoral, and moral reasons for political decisions from the list of positions we will generate in class." If he focuses on student learning, there will be lots of checking to see what students know, perceive, or can do. When the goal is mastery, timetables are flexible, and what's important is that students learn well, even if less material is covered.

When teachers plan with a focus on mastery objectives they ask themselves certain questions: (1) "What exactly do I want students to know and be able to do when this lesson is over?" (2) "How will I know they have learned it, that is, what will I take as evidence the objective has been met?" Thus thinking clearly about objectives also means thinking about formative assessment and how to gather the data today that will enable us to determine where student learning is in relation to the targeted objective.

5. Generic Thinking Skills

A fifth kind of thinking about objectives is practiced by teachers who, in addition to aiming to teach concepts, information, and skills, wish to develop particular thinking skills in students at the same time. Let's go back to the word search. Suppose you want students to learn something about systematic search as a strategy. That's the kind of skill we use to look through a collection of nuts and bolts for a particular size, or scan a map for Maple Street and know at the beginning only that it's somewhere on the page.

Video:
Explicit Teaching of Thinking Skills

A teacher who wants students to learn strategies for systematic search would certainly talk about how different children were going about looking for the words. Examples would be comparing approaches and strategies, giving names to the different strategies, listing them on the board, asking students where else they could use these strategies or what other kinds of tasks would be good places to try them out (transfer), and so forth. This teacher has a generic thinking objective: to develop a thinking skill apart from any particular content knowledge.

Consider a seventh-grade social studies class working on a chapter about Bedouins of the Arabian desert. There's a lot of information in the chapter—facts and concepts galore. But their teacher wants them to learn more than facts. She wants them to learn about hierarchical relationships—not just relationships in Bedouin life, but the nature of hierarchical relationships in general, how to find them and represent them. So she adds something to the assignment, asking them to identify key terms from the chapter and make a diagram that shows their relationships to one another. Now something more is required. Figure 19.2 shows two diagrams that students might draw.

Note the different kinds of thinking behind these two diagrams. The first has terms arranged subordinately according to size. The Murrah is one of many

Figure 19.2 Diagrams for Learning About Hierarchical Relationships

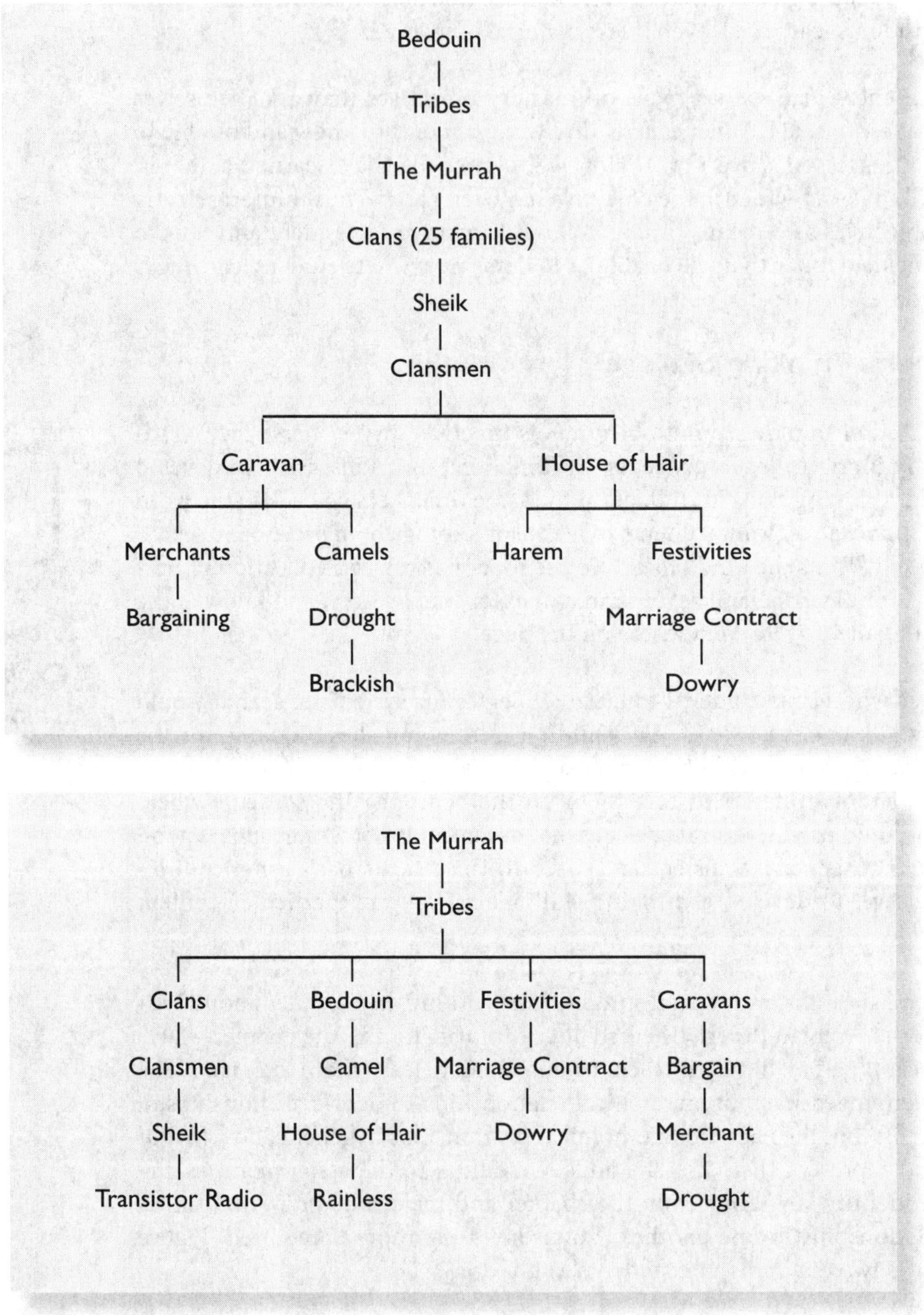

tribes. Each tribe (Murrah included) is composed of clans of about 25 families, and each clan is headed by a sheik. Each family is organized around a patriarch and inhabits a "house of hair" (a Bedouin dwelling) with a harem. Then the relationships shift to category groupings.

The second diagram shows relationships that are random and nonlinear. The diagram seems to have been created by free association rather than consistent application of some particular kind of logic.

Now students compare their diagrams in small groups and explain the kind of relationships their connecting lines represent. They talk to each other about their thinking and later in a total class discussion will develop, in particular, what hierarchical or subordinated relationships mean using their examples. The teacher will use those words (*hierarchical, subordinated*) because the objective for this and for the upcoming series of lessons is that they become able to do that kind of thinking, whether it's around Bedouins, sports, or computer programming. The objective here goes beyond mastery of content, though it includes that. It aims to develop a particular thinking skill.

There are literally dozens of thinking skills that may be targeted and taught simultaneously with and through academic content. But it takes consciousness and intentionality to ensure that improving students' thinking capacity or skills is the focus of a learning experience. When we bring this lens to lesson design we ask ourselves, "What thinking skill or processes could I teach or reinforce in this lesson and how might I engineer activities and assignments so that kind of thinking will be an instructional focal point?"

TEACHER THINKING AND LESSON PLANNING

We want to make the case that there are pitfalls when coverage, activity, or involvement thinking dominates planning. Since the real goal of coverage thinking is to get through material, such teaching is predictably characterized by more teacher talk, more lecture, and less checking for understanding.

Activity thinking or coverage thinking is not good enough if one never gets as far as mastery thinking in preparing for lessons.

Activity thinking tends to produce classes where students are often busy, sometimes working in groups. There may be good record-keeping systems on student completion of tasks and assignments, but activity thinking, when it dominates, tends to produce classes where students are clear on neither what is to be learned nor the criteria for quality work. Involvement thinking adds higher energy and more fun, but classes may look essentially the same as those that are activity based. Table 19.1 describes what lesson objectives sound like for each

Exhibit 19.1 Key Questions Involved in Lesson Planning

1. What thinking skills do I want students to be able to use? How will I know if they can do it?
2. What do I want students to know or be able to do when the lesson is over?
   How will I know if they know it or can do it?
3. How can I get students really engaged?
4. What activities could students do to gain understanding or to develop these skills?
5. What knowledge, skill, or concept am I teaching?

kind of thinking. A full Taxonomy of Generic Thinking Skills is available on *The Skillful Teacher* website at www.RBTeach.com/TST7.

PDF

Taxonomy

In previous chapters, we presented repertoires and argued that all behaviors in a repertoire can be good if they are an appropriate match to the student, situation, or curriculum. The repertoire argument needs to be modified, however, to be valid for the five kinds of thinking about objectives. Activity thinking or coverage thinking is not good enough if one never gets as far as mastery thinking in preparing for lessons. On the other hand, fully developed planners —teachers who have clear images of what they want students to know and be able to do—still have to identify content for coverage. They still have to invent or find activities that could logically lead students to master the intended learnings. Good planners, in fact, ask the key questions listed in Exhibit 19.1 involved in *all five* kinds of thinking, but they start by thoroughly answering the mastery question: "What do I want students to know or be able to do? How will I know if they know it or can do it?" Teachers who are logical, linear, and analytical like to start with a statement of the mastery objective and proceed deliberately to develop assessment criteria and criterion tasks. Then, they identify activities and materials that fit in with this objective.

Many of us have "neat" activities or materials we love to use or think will be highly engaging for students. But this is a dicey place to start the planning process, because there is a tendency to warp the objective to fit the activity we love. There may be a need to give up certain engaging activities we are attached to, if they do not directly help students learn something they are supposed to be learning.

Each of us in teaching, in looking back at a class we taught or observed, ought to be able to infer a clear statement of what students were supposed to be able to do at the end. And that "something" needs to be connected to the standards of our state and part of the curriculum our school or district is committed to.

Table 19.1 What Objectives Sound Like for Each Kind of Thinking

Thinking	Sample Language Used	Purpose
1. Generic Thinking: centered on ways that children function intellectually.	"Analyze relationships between concepts and diagram them hierarchically."	For students to express or develop a certain kind of thinking skill.
2. Mastery Thinking: centered on what children will learn in the way of new information or skills.	"Be able to describe to each other the principal causes of World War I." "Measure distance using scale on the map."	For students to be able to know or do something specific.
3. Involvement Thinking: centered on how children will react.	"After giving a dramatic reading of the story, I'll solicit their opinions and get them involved in a discussion."	For students to be visibly involved–at least to participate actively and at best to be excited and have fun.
4. Activity Thinking: centered on what children will do.	"They'll look at the video, then make a map of the South, then answer the questions at the end of the chapter."	For students to finish certain tasks.
5. Coverage Thinking: centered on what the teacher will do, what agenda to get through.	"First, I'll discuss the heat of reaction; then I'll go over endothermic reactions, entropy, enthalpy, and then review valences."	To mention or get students to mention ideas.

TWENTY-ONE PLANNING DECISIONS

This is what skillful teachers do beforehand as they are planning their lesson:

1. Check-in with the big ideas of the unit.
2. Articulate the mastery objectives for themselves after digging deeply into the content.
3. Decide how to communicate objectives to the students.
4. Decide what evidence would demonstrate mastery of this lesson objective.
5. Analyze evidence about previous student learning (perhaps do an error analysis of yesterday's quiz or homework) so they know where to focus.
6. Plan pacing and subgrouping.

7. Pick materials, models, examples, stories, and cases to use.

8. Anticipate confusions, especially language and vocabulary meanings, and identify requisite prior knowledge students might not have.

9. Design and choose learning experiences.

10. Check that learning experiences are logically linked to the intended learning.

11. Decide how to collect evidence of learning during or concluding this lesson.

12. Plan how students will make their thinking visible and public.

13. Plan how to get students to summarize.

14. Plan how to get students' minds in gear at the beginning.

15. Predict how much time will be needed for each task or activity, and plan other environmental variables (space, management routines) that may need to be arranged.

16. Plan the effective effort strategies that may be employed or taught.

17. Plan how to diversify for different learning styles.

18. Plan certain key interactive moves like an opening question.

19. Decide who may need assistance or extensions during the lesson and provide for it.

20. Plan what extensions and challenges will be provided for students who are ready for them.

21. Plan how and when to explain the homework and its connection to today's lesson.

We expand on each of these points and look at planning decisions a teacher could conceivably make. These steps are important for planning any class regardless of whether it's a literature discussion in AP English, second graders circulating at math learning stations, a seventh-grade earth science lab, or whole-class direct instruction in the U.S. Constitution.

Don't get the idea that if one doesn't go through all 21 decisions, the planning is poor. In certain situations, some decisions are not applicable. In primary grade literacy, for example, in a guided reading group with three first graders on book "D," there is no decision about materials. The leveled books are the materials. Checking for understanding is continuous as children read, and objectives may be slightly different for each of the three children. A teacher conducting lessons based in curricula that use inquiry models of teaching might not start by clarifying objectives for students (though they would be developed at some point later). For example, for the first lesson or two on representative government there is no "evidence from yesterday" about how much progress students have made toward mastery (though there might be a pre-assessment to find out what they already know or think they know about representative government).

The decisions that follow are divided into two sets. The first 13 are basic and indispensable decisions for any lesson planning. The second set of eight decisions is important too, but these topics are at a finer level of specificity. Good planning allows quite a bit of flexibility about the order in which a teacher addresses these issues and, as we have noted, not all of them need to be addressed for certain lessons. In general, the decisions don't have to be addressed in a linear fashion in the order presented. This should reassure nonlinear thinkers who hate lists and recipes. The first five decisions, however, are so important for getting focus in one's teaching and getting student results that we are going to ask even the creative-random among us to think these through thoroughly before going on with your planning.

The Thirteen Basic, Indispensable Planning Decisions

1. Check-in with the curriculum, the standards you're working on, and particularly the big idea (enduring understanding) that's on the table to be sure the lesson you're planning connects explicitly to it.

2. Dig into the content to examine its nuances and central ideas. Articulate the most worthwhile mastery objective of this lesson (or series of lessons) to yourself fully. Say exactly what the students will know or be able to do, or do better, at the end of the lesson.

3. Plan how to communicate the objective to the students with unmistakable clarity in language they will understand. How are you going to get them clear about what they're trying to learn? Will you generate essential questions and criteria, give exemplars, or share assessments you will be using?

4. Decide what evidence you will use as confirmation of student mastery. They may not meet it tomorrow, but having this end in mind is the fulcrum of good planning.

5. Give careful attention to the evidence from yesterday (or whenever else is relevant) about who "has it" and who doesn't. Also, look carefully at those who have it so you know when they're ready for an extension or deepening activity.

6. In light of the evidence from yesterday's work (or from your pre-assessment if this is the first lesson in the series), plan the pace and grouping or subgrouping if appropriate for differentiation of instruction. This includes the size of the bite (how big an increment of learning) you will aim for in this lesson. It also includes whether you need to do some preteaching for some students and some reteaching for some students who didn't get it yesterday. It means coming up with extensions and challenges for those who got it quickly.

7. Pick materials, including exactly what manipulatives, pictures, diagrams, pieces of text, equipment, and media will best make the learning accessible to the students.

8. Anticipate confusions, especially about vocabulary and concepts to be used, and preteach if necessary. Anticipate misconceptions, and plan how to surface them and contradict them.

9. Choose student learning experiences, such as the following:

   - ▲ Instructional strategies you will use (e.g., demonstration, modeling, thinking aloud, mini-lecture with graphic organizer). Pay particular attention to how you can embed reading strategies in your routines for engaging text.

   - ▲ Tasks, exercises, and activities the students will do.

   - ▲ Hooks that will engage student interest.

   - ▲ The sequence of student tasks and teacher-guided strategies within the lesson most likely to develop the concept, skill, or understanding.

   - ▲ How to preteach essential vocabulary or concepts that some students may lack.

10. Check that doing the task will logically lead to learning the intended skill or concept.

11. Decide when and how you will gather the evidence of student learning during or after the lesson.

12. "Plan how students will make their thinking and understanding public" (West & Staub, 2003, p. 13). See "Making Students' Thinking Visible" in Chapter 11, "Clarity."

13. Select a strategy for getting students cognitively active in summarizing and assimilating their new learning.

The Eight Implementation Detail Planning Decisions

14. Decide how you will get students' minds in gear for this lesson at the beginning, activate their prior knowledge, and find out what they already know.

15. Arrange the environmental variables (space, routines that may need to be preplanned or taught) and how much time you predict will be needed for each task or activity.

16. Choose the effective effort strategies you may explicitly teach or that you may ask students to use (e.g., student self-evaluation, use of "effective effort rubric").

17. Decide specific interactive moves you should make (key steps in directions, key questions to ask, cues to give, connections to past learning) "to make sure important ideas are being grappled with and will be highlighted and clarified" (West & Staub, 2003, p. 12).

18. Decide how to diversify for different student learning styles.

19. Decide how much support, cuing, and help students may need while doing the work, including deployment of other people who may be in the room.

20. Decide "what extensions or challenges you will provide for students who are ready for them" (West & Staub, 2003, p. 12).

21. Choose homework and how and when to explain it and what it's for.

THE FINER POINTS ABOUT THE BASIC AND INDISPENSABLE DECISIONS

Although most of these decisions may seem relatively straightforward, some further discussion and concrete examples may help to clarify the importance of giving each thoughtful attention during planning.

Decision 1: *Check-in with the Curriculum, the Standards, and the Big Idea*

A big idea or enduring understanding is something important to connect the learning to that is motivating.

You could do a good lesson on consonant digraphs in second grade and get away without connecting it to a big idea. The same is true with density in eighth-grade science or separation of powers in eleventh-grade U.S. history. Most of us who are veterans have taught our way through the decades without making connections to big ideas. But our students would have been better off if we had kept big ideas in mind and made explicit connections for them when appropriate.

The big idea in the second-grade lesson may be a theme we're pursuing all year long: "You can get tools for figuring out any word you don't know, and this year we're filling in our tool box so you'll be able to sound out any word!" Perhaps in your curriculum, the word is *strategies*, and the big idea is that "we're learning to be strategic readers. As readers, we're in charge, and we have lots of different strategies to reach for if we don't know a word." So in today's lesson, digraphs are explicitly connected to phonic clues, a strategy different from the one the class worked on yesterday (which was reading the whole sentence and skipping the unknown word to see if that enabled the children to guess).

Another example is about how the Constitution designs separation of powers of the three branches of government into the working of our republic. Teaching how that operates and why (checks and balances) is a standard U.S. history objective. This learning (and, in fact, most other teaching points, regardless of academic discipline) becomes more compelling and more interesting to students if they see it as connected to something that's bigger and inherently important. That's what a big idea or enduring understanding is—something important to connect the learning to that is motivating. One possibility of a big idea for the separation of powers might be, "It takes vigilance to preserve the balance of powers our founding fathers built into the Constitution. Every few decades you can find an episode in history where an interest group tries to assert its power by strengthening one of the branches above the others. So far, we've managed to counter those campaigns, but it hasn't been easy." A big idea like that stimulates a strong reason for students to understand the operation of separation of powers because they're going to be asked to use it to analyze historical episodes that could have derailed the U.S. democracy and perhaps analyze current efforts to swing power to one branch.

Decision 2: *Dig into the Content and Articulate the Mastery Objective for Yourself*

"What do I want students to know or be able to do? How will I know if they know it or can do it?"

Compose the objective in mastery language so you yourself know what student performance ("will be able to do") you would take as evidence of mastery. Mastery objectives start with the learner as the subject: "Students will be able to . . ." followed by an action verb (e.g., make, list, describe) that can be observed (see Chapter 18, "Lesson Objectives").

The next step for planning a lesson is thinking deeply about the content to be learned today. What the students are supposed to be learning is usually listed at a high level of abstraction in the standards document of the school district (or state) and the list of learning expectations for the course. But to plan a lesson that works for the children today, we need to be much more specific than that.

Before we think about assessment, student activities, metacognition, differentiated instruction, designing questions, or student motivation, we must look at the materials in the curriculum at a finely grained level to find out what the content is that the students are supposed to learn. Maybe it's a skill, a concept, a body of information (facts), or a combination of these. But first, we must determine exactly what it is supposed to be and express this in concrete and precise language.

So get the book, the lab manual, the novel, or the problem set that the students are going to engage today, and examine it in detail. Here are some examples from different grade levels and subject areas:

Video: Planning Conference

Example 1: Elementary Mathematics

First-grade students are asked to fill in blanks in number patterns.

The first one is, "2, 4, ____, 8, ____, ____. What is the rule?"

The second one is, "The rule is to go back four each time: 34, _____, 26, ____, 18, ____, _____ " There is a number line on the page to help them.

A student who can count by 2s may see that the first example is a pattern of counting by 2s, and then might just swing into using that memorized pattern to fill in the blanks. Is that what you, the teacher, want this exercise to be about—

applying memorized counting by two patterns? If so, that would be fine. But perhaps, the learning is supposed to be about number lines and how to use them as a visual tool for understanding addition. The rule is "add two" with each increment, and that means jumping two spaces on the number line. Are you sure your students know how to apply repetitive rules to adding on a number line? Do they need any instruction or practice before you turn them loose for independent work? What exactly is the most developmentally appropriate idea mathematically and the most important learning for the students to get out of this?

What about the second task on the sheet: a subtraction model. That means going to the left on the number line, "backward" on the number line, decreasing in value. But the numbers in the task, though going down in value, go from left to right on the page, "increasing" direction on the number line, which is the opposite of how one would go on the number line to carry out subtraction. Will that be confusing? Do you expect the students to use the number line to get their answers, counting back four units with each move? Are you using the terms *addition* and *subtraction* yet? What vocabulary is appropriate for where the students are in their learning? What does a student have to know in order to do this second example? Should you do the second example at all today?

These are the kinds of questions we need to ask ourselves about the content before planning other aspects of the lesson. The starting point is looking at the actual materials to see what the learning objective should be for the students, given what they know and what the next step for them should be.

Example 2: Seventh-Grade Science

The textbook chapter is full of information about the interaction of ocean waves and landforms, including the names of many landforms that get created (for example, spit, headland). There are also terms that pertain to the processes that ocean movement cause (erosion, deposition), and there are terms related to these processes (sediment, glacial moraine). So amid all this information, what is the most important learning that students walk out the door with?

We have to do a close reading of the chapter ourselves to answer that question. Such a close examination of the text reveals that the main point is that waves alter land and that affects peoples' lives. Everything else in the chapter is about different aspects of the phenomenon: ways that happens, what the landforms look like, and the names of these different forms. But the main thing is for the students to understand that the ocean with its waves and currents is constantly altering the shape of the coastline and that these changes have consequences for human and animal life. If the activities of the lesson are not designed so every student walking out the door could say that in his or her own words, then the lesson hasn't been properly planned.

The next step after formulating a clear statement of the mastery objective is to communicate it to students. This is not a simple package handled by writing an objectives sentence on the board (though there's nothing wrong with that). It's fine to tell the students what the mastery objective is, but just telling them doesn't mean they understand it (or care about it). The essential questions and enduring understandings that are embedded in good curriculum help with "Why should I care?" For example, we may be studying the separation of powers to answer the larger question, "Is the Supreme Court taking over the legislative function, and is that OK?" When Grant Wiggins said, "Assessment is the Trojan horse of school reform," he meant that through assessment, students (and families and everyone else too) finally "get" what you really wanted them to learn. Therefore, giving the students the assessment (yes, the test) in advance gets people really clear about what the learning is supposed to look like.

Communicating what you really want students to know or be able to do includes explicitly showing them the performance task you expect them to do at the end of the instruction, ideally with a list of criteria, exemplars of products that are done well, and rubrics for scoring the exemplars. It may also include having students develop their own criteria or having them analyze "not yet" examples, since we all get clearer about what something is by also knowing what it is not (see Chapter 18, "Lesson Objectives"). In addition, it will include checking for understanding of the objective and "unpacking" it at the beginning of the lesson as described in Chapter 18. That is to make sure they understand the vocabulary in the objective and the outcome it aims for.

So far, we have advocated planning explicitly how to (1) make a clear statement of objectives, (2) show the assessment task, (3) give criteria, (4) share exemplars, and (5) explain rubrics. Having all these ready up front would be the fullest way to communicate objectives to students in a no-secrets classroom. You don't need all these, of course, when the learning targets are small. If students are learning the skill of using latitude and longitude to locate a place on the globe, they don't need a rubric. But many student products assigned (essays, lab reports, stories, oral reports) could have all five of these elements available for students. Math and science problems—that exemplify the skills students are responsible for—can be given to students in advance along with solutions worked out just as you want them to be able to do on the assessment.

If you expect the students to explain what powers each branch of government has and how they check and balance one another, you wouldn't give them the whole exemplary essay that answers the question in text. You would tell them the aspects of checks and balances you want them to be able to comment on and not leave them to guess. For example, "Be able to explain how the legislature uses the confirmation process and the budget process to influence the court; show an example of how the court tests the constitutionality of legislation and can overturn it; be sure to explain how influence is exerted in at least one significant way between each of the following: legislative on executive, legislative on judicial, executive on legislative, executive on judicial, judicial on executive, judicial on legislative."

Choosing and communicating objectives in primary-grade literacy and numeracy looks a little different. If you're doing guided reading with three first graders on a book at the "E" level, you are working on a developmental continuum with each of the three children. Your records identify different skill elements to focus on with each child. Maisha is ready to work on fluency and reading with more natural speech rhythm; John is ready to master sound blending with "e" and "i" words; Darcy is ready to master the voice changes signaled by periods and commas. Notice we haven't said "Maisha needs . . ." or "John needs . . ." It's not that they're needy; it's that they are mastering the skills of reading that are next for them developmentally. They're all reading the same book, seated with you at the same time. As each child reads, you give cues and small pieces of instruction in line with what skills they're developing: "Now, Darcy, pay attention to the comma in the sentence coming up; I bet you'll be able to make it sound just like talking!" Note the expression of confidence in her.

Decision 3: *Plan How to Communicate the Objective to the Students with Unmistakable Clarity*

Check back to Chapter 18, "Lesson Objectives," for points on student-friendly language and check for understanding of the objectives on pages 471 and 472.

Decision 4: *Decide What You Will Take as Evidence of Student Mastery*

What's the test item or performance that, if a student could do it successfully, you would take as evidence of mastery? It may be as simple as looking over a student's shoulder and seeing her set up a three-step word problem correctly after reading it. It could be hearing a student explain to you how the executive branch exerts influence over the judiciary through the appointment process. The point is this: it is extremely important for us as teachers to get this performance in mind clearly before we begin a lesson. This performance becomes the anchor for everything else we do in the planning process. Thus when we get to designing learning experiences, we will ask, Would question X or activity Y likely lead students to be able to do this performance?

Having envisioned specifically what performance we want from each student, we are much more likely to assess the children frequently and use those data as feedback for them and for ourselves about the effectiveness of the instruction. Both kinds of feedback are essential to successful teaching, and both have their origin in the planning of lessons.

Decisions 5 and 6: *Analyze Evidence and Plan Pace and Grouping*

When planning a lesson, we should consult data from the students' performance yesterday (or whenever we last got data). This information will help us decide about our pace for the class tomorrow. Obviously, if our students show on the quiz (or in the learning logs) that they don't understand what the purpose of the executive branch of government is, we will not move forward with the judiciary. More likely though, we discover from the evidence that a few students don't get it and the rest do. That's the way it is with most things taught at any given time. So now in our planning we have to design something so that the four students, who are still foggy about the executive branch and its powers, can get clear.

Before generating options for how to handle this situation, consider the attitude this step represents. We are saying that if four students didn't show evidence of understanding what they were doing in today's class, it is our responsibility to come up with a plan tonight so they will understand by the end of tomorrow (or soon). We can't say, "I taught it; they just didn't learn it" and move on with the rest of the class, leaving four students with this gap or move on with the hope that it will become clear to them through ensuing activities. We have to plan something to happen for them that will make it clear, and if possible, plan it for tomorrow. That's what teachers are for. That is what professional decision-making and diagnostic expertise are all about. That's what knowing how to reach diverse learners is all about. If all the job entailed was being a content expert and going through the material, then anyone who knows the material could teach. But if making sure the students learn the material is what the job is about, then the job requires professional expertise about planning and teaching. That is the position that stands behind these pages on planning skill.

One option is to set up the class in groups for the first 15 minutes debating whether the executive, particularly the president, has the authority to launch a punitive military strike against a country that has been proven to sponsor a terrorist group against the United States. While the groups are debating the question and coming to a position, you could take aside the four students who still have confusion about the purpose of the executive and reteach yesterday's lesson in a different way, with diagrams and frequent checking for understanding of each of them.

Another option is to make an appointment with the four students at the beginning of class to see you for supplementary instruction during X block, which the school has reserved for tutoring and extra help: "Evidence from yesterday's quiz shows me you four need another go around from me on the executive branch. We didn't get it done yesterday. I'm sure you can master this information, but I must have 30 minutes with you all together during an X block. Does it work better for you today or tomorrow?" Notice the positive attribution statement in this language and the joint assignment of responsibility for the teaching and learning between teacher and students.

Here is a third option. All year you have been working on a climate of mutual help and community building in the class. Thus students who have received feedback that they're struggling with a concept can ask for help from their peers. Asking for and giving help has become a valued and praiseworthy behavior in the class and become scheduled into the rhythms of class routine. So at the beginning of tomorrow's class, you say, "Okay, before we start, does anybody want help with any of yesterday's material?" Three of the four hands go up: "Who's willing to give them a briefing [the term the class has adopted for peer tutoring] at lunch or some other time today?" Hands go up; the students who ask for help pick someone, as is the class routine. You thank and praise all who have entered this process, quickly by name, including the volunteer helpers who weren't picked.

While this is going on, you walk past Jerome, who didn't raise his hand for help but should have, and gently say, "What about you, Jerome?" "I'm goin' to ask my Dad tonight," he replies. How you respond to Jerome depends on the context variables: whether it's good Jerome will ask his dad, whether Jerome is an isolate and you're trying to build connections between Jerome and others in the class, and all sorts of other possibilities. The point here is not how to handle Jerome, but that you have a deliberate plan you decided to implement the night before to deal with what the evidence told you—that four students don't get it yet.

There are many options besides these three, and no argument is made that these three are superior to others. We are making the argument, however, that a teacher has to come up with something to deal with the situation and that doing so is part of planning the night before.

Decision 7: *Pick Materials*

This is the favorite part for many of us. In fact, some us like to start planning here because we have materials we love to use, materials the students have enjoyed in the past, and materials we think are engaging and clear. Beware! This is a habit that can lead to engaging activities that are unconnected to what the students are supposed to be learning.

Maybe, you have a great case study you like to use when you study pollution in earth science. You've never seen a better one. And you love to show the movie *A Civil Action* to drive the point home about corporate responsibility as a wrap-up. But does the case study help you make the main point of the unit—that proactive environmental cleanup has social costs as well as social benefits?

You could use the case to make that point if you had some additional data to go with it. That is, you may find a place for your favorite materials in this series of lessons you're preparing, but start with the mastery objective and the evidence you would take that students had mastered it. Then go back and see if your favorite materials still fit or if they can be modified to fit the objective more precisely.

Decision 8: *Anticipate Confusions*

When planning lessons, it is enormously helpful if the teacher's experience base allows him or her to predict what will be difficult or confusing for students about upcoming concepts or skills. Teachers use those predictions to develop something particularly clear or vivid for explaining that concept, warn the students in advance that this is particularly hard (thus they should ratchet up their focus and attention), do something to surface the confusion explicitly and explicitly contradict it, or tailor materials and the tasks students are asked to do to address that confusion.

Student confusions are often rooted in their different understandings of the words and terms used. For example, in the primary grades when students are given a set of seven tiles and a set of four tiles and asked how many more there are in the larger set, there is a confusion that prevents them coming up with 3 as the answer. It's a language confusion. They tend to focus on the word "more," identify the bigger set, which has more, and count how many are in it. Thus they give the answer 7. We have seen teachers design excellent activities for students that nevertheless don't do the job, because they didn't anticipate this kind of confusion.

One meaning of "how many more" in a mathematical question is "how many extra in the bigger set if you match up the two sets one to one." Failure to use that language—or in some way address the language confusion of the children—delays the learning and causes confusion that is evident despite an otherwise excellent design for materials and tasks. Anticipating this confusion might have led to a different sequence of activities (like saving the introduction of the subtraction algorithm for later) and different language in the directions to the students with the task.

Decisions 9 and 10: *Design Learning Experiences That Are Logically Linked to the Intended Learning*

Planning the minute-to-minute unfolding of learning experiences in some detail is a vital component of teaching skill.

The next aspect of lesson planning is the design of student learning experiences. Schlechty (2000) says that the center of teaching skill is the work we create for students to do. That is congruent with what Ralph Tyler (1949) said long ago when he pointed out that learning proceeds from what the students do, not what we do. But what the students do derives from the tasks we set for them and the preparation (instruction) we give them for those tasks. A learning experience is more complex than just designing tasks for students, although it includes the tasks. It is smaller than a lesson because a lesson can shift gears and contain several learning experiences. Every time the activity changes, the learning experience changes. Typically, a good lesson changes activity structure every now and then so as not to bore students.

A learning experience may be the teacher presenting, a Q&A session, a demonstration, student group work, and all manner of cognitive activities and formats. In this stage of planning, a teacher may choose a strategy to help students understand, like developing a graphic organizer of photosynthesis or doing a think-aloud with an approach to problem-solving in math. And interspersed with these activities is a sequence of tasks for students: solve this problem; respond to this inference question; compare notes with your neighbor; determine the most important variable, defend your choice; make a table of data; or come up with a topic sentence. The design of the students' cognitive experience in a lesson is under our control. Clearly, doing that well has a tremendous influence on children's opportunity to learn. Thus planning the minute-to-minute unfolding of those learning experiences in some detail is a vital component of teaching skill.

Let's start with student tasks. We select or make them up for students to do, some during the lesson, and some afterward for homework. The key question is, "Is the doing of the task likely to lead students to learn the learning?" This is not a trivial question.

Let's say that students are asked to trace a map of Africa, fill in the names of the countries, and color it in. This is part of a unit on Africa. Some outcomes a teacher might reasonably want in the unit are for students to be able to name African countries if they are shown an outline of the shape without the name, identify which countries have coasts and which are inland, estimate the relative size of African countries in relation to each other, and explain the relationship between the country's location and water supply to its climate and growing season. Any of these might be worthwhile goals, but none of them will be realized by drawing an attractive map. There is nothing wrong with each student going home with an attractive, accurate map of Africa, but additional events and assignments must be planned if they are to learn something.

If we want students to be able to name the countries, then we make up a game where that is required. If we want students to know which countries are inland, then we have them highlight these countries on the map in a certain way and memorize a list. If we want them to know the relative sizes of the countries, then we have them estimate how many cutouts of given countries can fit inside a to-scale cutout of, say, the United States and construct a table of comparisons from smallest to largest. If we want them to understand the placement of the country on the continent in relation to climate and growing season, then we have them color in the map by topological features and write sentences about the patterns of crops and closeness to the equator. It should be logically conceivable that the doing of the task assigned to students could (though not necessarily by itself) lead them to the intended learning. Our point is this: look carefully at the activities you select for students to do in relation to the mastery objective and ask yourself if doing that task is connected to the precise learning you're aiming for. Fun activities do not ensure worthwhile learning.

Look carefully at the activities you select for students and ask yourself if they are connected to the precise learning you're aiming for.

Decision 11: *Decide How and When to Gather Evidence of Student Learning*

Each lesson should produce data we can use to decide how many students "have it," who doesn't, and who is ready for moving ahead. If we don't have data of some kind to look at as we're getting ready to plan, then there was a hole in our planning or implementation yesterday.

Decision 12: *Decide How Students Will Make Their Thinking and Understanding Public*

The sequence of activities should include a way for students to be talking, writing, and interacting with each other around the content of the class in such a way that they can respond to one another and the teacher has access to their thinking. If we have internalized the principles of "Making Students' Thinking Visible" (see Chapter 11, "Clarity"), this will be built into how we structure student interaction for robust talk.

Decision 13: *Plan How to Get Students Cognitively Active in Summarizing*

The "Summarizing" section in Chapter 11, "Clarity," describes the significance of this behavior. The planning implication is simply that time needs to be provided for it to occur, and the actual mechanism for summarizing may require some preparation.

THE FINER POINTS ABOUT IMPLEMENTATION DECISIONS

These decisions are slightly less critical than the ones above, but they can often determine the success of a lesson.

Decision 14: *Get the Students' Minds in Gear*

This item means choosing and using an activator (see Chapter 11, "Clarity"). No lesson hinges on doing or not doing this strategy. It is particularly useful, however, when starting a new topic like "taxes" or "weather," because it can surface many misconceptions we can deal with later.

Decision 15: *Decide How Much Time Will Be Needed for Each Task or Activity*

Do a fast-forward time-lapse mental movie in which you imagine the activities playing out. Will they fit in the time allotted? If necessary, plan other environmental variables (space and routines) so that they will.

Decision 16: *Plan the Effective Effort Strategies That May Come into Play*

This is an uncommon element in lesson planning. We have included it because teaching the students how to exert effective effort is a commitment of ours personally, and we think it should be in the background all the time, waiting for opportunities to be included in any lesson (these strategies are profiled in Chapter 14, "Expectations"). Suffice it to say here that we should scan those ideas often during lesson planning to see which ones can be included today, especially strategies like student self-identification of errors and self-correction.

Decision 17: *Plan Interactive Moves*

This includes planning your questions so as to guide thinking appropriately. A related question is what mediating we have to do as teachers so the students can take advantage of the available learning by doing the task. For example, if we want students to be aware of the proximity of the African country to the equator and its effect on climate, we could have students draw the equator on the map at the beginning. Then we might say, "Now as you're drawing in countries, figure out how you'll record in a separate data table how far they are from the equator.

Later, I'm going to ask you to show some connection between their location and their crops and growing season. Who wants to predict what we may find?"

Questioning Skills

These moves cue the students about a line of inquiry that they will be pursuing about geography, climate, and crops. It also gets a few predictions out for the students to be thinking about as they're working on the map: "Mr. Rodriguez, I think the countries close to the equator will have a lot of desert and grow crops only close to rivers." Without some deliberate structuring for students' cognition while working on the map, they may produce a great map without any cognition at all related to what you want them to know. Students can trace and label a perfectly beautiful map while at the same time socializing. Good planners decide in advance on structuring moves that increase the percentage of student attention and cognition that is spent on the desired learning.

A number of the Clarity moves (like activating students' current knowledge or explicitly telling students the reason for the activity they're doing) fit here. Of particular importance is planning the questions to ask so as to guide thinking along productive paths and stretch the thinking of all students to higher levels. (For more detail on this, see the document "Questioning Skills" for Chapter 11 on *The Skillful Teacher* website at www.RBTeach.com/TST7.)

Decision 18: *Plan How to Diversify for Different Student Learning Styles*

The simplest and most practical level of diversification is the set of variables we've laid out in Chapter 20, "Differentiated Instruction." If you have all the above issues under control, then it is time to see how you can vary perceptual mode, grouping structure, and so on to match and stretch student learning preferences. To go deeper into this topic, explore McCarthy (1987b), Gregorc and Ward (1977), Dunn and Dunn (1978), and Tomlinson (2014).

Another potential decision (we call it 18a) is to plan how and when to check for understanding. Acknowledging that this is often done on the fly, it may be helpful to flag a check-in point during planning to make sure we stop and get some data from all the students about how clear they are. Such a point would be where we're shifting gears or subtopics, and failure to understand the previous topic would ruin a student's understanding of what you are about to explain in the next 5 minutes. For example, in automotive class you've just finished explaining the four-stroke cycle of a piston in the internal combustion engine. You're about to explain the significance of spark plug timing, that is how close to top dead center of the compression stroke the plug fires. But if the students have any confusion about what is happening in the compression stroke and that the valves are all closed, thus holding in the gas-air mixture, they won't understand the significance of spark timing at all. You'd better stop here and check for understanding. Wiliam (2015) calls these questions "hinge" questions. For an interesting "how to article" on hinge questions see Fletcher-Wood (2013).

Decision 19: *Decide How Much Help an Individual Student May Need and from Whom*

This item is related to planning pacing and grouping. If you have aides, paraprofessionals, or volunteers in the room, this is where we plan who is deployed with whom.

Decision 20: *Plan Extensions or Challenges for Students Who Are Ready for Them*

Some students will get the instruction quickly and be left sitting on their hands unless we plan an extension activity that will stretch them. This activity needs to be one that they can do with help from peers or on their own since we will be working with those who don't get it yet at this time.

Decision 21: *Plan Homework*

In the era of the "flipped classroom," homework is often watching/listening to a teacher presentation that would previously have been delivered in class. Input of information or presentation and demonstration is the purpose. There should be no argument about how worthwhile this kind of homework is as long as the presentation or demonstration is clear and the content is on target for the students.

On the other hand, debate abounds about traditional homework, whether to give it, and if so, how much. However, we do not derive much wisdom from the research (Cooper, 2008) because such research has been unable to account for whether the assignments are worthwhile, that is, whether they have quality and appropriateness. We described how these features operate in Chapter 12, "Principles of Learning." Let's examine the elements of these two criteria for being worthwhile:

1. **Appropriateness:** This is the easier of the two criteria to investigate. It simply asks that the students have adequate prior knowledge to do the assignment, and that it is not so easy that it does not advance or deepen their learning.

2. **Quality:** If homework causes practice with something that benefits from practice, like speaking or reading a foreign language, that would

meet the standard of quality as long as it was effective practice. What makes practice effective? It should have the following qualities:

- Massed
- Smallest unit that has meaning
- Short bursts
- Frequent sessions
- Overlearning

For details on these five elements, see Chapter 12, "Principles of Learning."

If homework asks students to apply a skill that is at their growing edge, it is worthwhile. It is not worthwhile if it asks for application of a skill they have mastered long ago or that is over their heads. Other homework assignments can apply and deepen skills. They can call for students to manipulate information and practice high-level thinking. Here are a few examples:

- Make a bulleted list of arguing points from two editorials that take opposite positions on who should be our next U.S. senator.
- Draw a graphic organizer of the chapter we discussed in class today in the science textbook, in such a way that you show the important ideas and how they relate to each other.

The position we take here is that it is good to assign homework if the homework is *good*—useful for practice and learning and worthwhile in the thinking it provokes. For example, "Read Chapter 3 in the text" or "read the next short story in the anthology" as prep for class discussions would be better if there were something specified for students to read for (e.g., "Decide on the tone the author adopts and what words or phrases leads you to that conclusion.") Another worthwhile addition to the "read" assignment would be to apply a particular skill of literate readers that the class has been working on. For example, "Identify points with the most convincing evidence and be prepared to say why the evidence is convincing."

Many ELA teachers, especially in elementary school, require students to read a certain number of minutes nightly from a trade book that is at their level. The rationale here is that readers improve by reading. While there is certainly support for the proposition that more independent reading correlates with reading achievement and academic success (Cullinan, 2000), it is quite possible that students who choose to read more are those already best at it and those who enjoy reading most. We would urge consideration of reading level and student interest in shaping these nightly requirements for reading at home.

So should we assign homework? Only if it's good homework. Good homework has the following characteristics:

- ▲ Students understand how it is connected to their learning.
- ▲ It advances the students' understanding of a concept.
- ▲ It generates fluency with a skill or ability to apply a skill in a more difficult or different context.
- ▲ It gives students the background information they need for upcoming in-class work.

But beyond its quality, plan how you're going to explain to students the connection between today's class and tonight's homework.

PLANNING, CLARITY, AND EXPECTATIONS

Planning is a carefully executed cognitive scenario, really a set of cognitive tasks in an extended scenario. It is not intuitive or easy, and not to be done hastily, but clearly it can be learned and coached, though often not developed sufficiently in teacher preparation. Good planning draws on—and is related to—many of the concepts developed in Chapters 11, "Clarity," and 14, "Expectations," and is described in Exhibit 19.2.

Much checking for understanding ("Clarity") is not generally planned in advance, though it is often wise to identify certain benchmark moments for checking. Successful teacher checking is broad and deep and springs spontaneously from the teacher's repertoire during interactive teaching. This chapter is about the elements that show up during a lesson that do *not* spring spontaneously from an acquired repertoire in the way "Attention" and "Momentum" moves do or checking and unscrambling do.

A virtuoso may make sensitive and skillful moves on the fly during instruction, but if these moves are not done within a well-designed plan for students, learning is limited. Consider an analogy to sports. A virtuoso player may dazzle us with his or her performance in one part of the field, but unless there is a game

Exhibit 19.2 Relationships Between Planning, Clarity, and Expectations

Planning Decisions	Clarity Move	Expectations Arena
1. Recall big idea		
2. Articulate mastery objective for today		
3. Plan how to communicate objective	Communicating objective	
4. Envision evidence you'll take as a sign of achievement of objective mastery	Criteria for success	
5. Analyze evidence from recent student work		
6. Plan pace and subgrouping		Grouping and "reteaching loop"
7. Pick materials		
8. Anticipate confusions	Anticipating confusions	
9. Identify presentation strategy and student tasks	Explanatory devices	
10. Check match of student task with objective		
11. Plan how and when to gather evidence of student learning	Checking understanding	Calling on and responding to students
12. Plan how students will make their thinking public	Making thinking visible	
13. Plan how to get students to summarize	Summarizing	
14. Plan how to get students' minds in gear	Activating knowledge	
15. Plan space, time, routines		
16. Plan effective effort strategies		Six Attributes of effective effort
17. Plan interactive moves (cues, questions)	Explicitness, questioning	
18. Plan how to diversify		
19. Plan student assistance		
20. Plan extensions and challenges		
21. Plan homework: what, why, and connections to today	Making connections	Feedback and grading structures

A big part of the skill of successful teachers is knowing how to plan all of the elements of sound instruction.

plan that is solid and appropriate, the team won't win despite its talented players. The teacher in a classroom is like a player-coach. She is on the field interacting with individual students, making plays, and making a difference. But the teacher is also responsible for the conditions of the game: the quality of the learning experiences designed for the students; the careful attention to data about current student performance that will underlie teacher choices; the careful planning of questions, groupings, and the series of tasks for students; the quality and frequency of feedback that has been engineered for the students that day; and the structures and systems that build student confidence and promote effective effort. All of these aspects of students' experience unfold every day, and the more design and thought that are behind them, the better the learning will be. A big part of the skill of successful teachers is knowing how to plan these and other elements of sound instruction. Planning happens off the field, the night before.

CHAPTER QUICK GUIDE

Twenty-One Planning Decisions

1. Check-in with the big ideas of the unit.
2. Dig into the content and articulate the most worthwhile mastery objective.
3. Plan how to communicate objectives to the students.
4. Decide what evidence would demonstrate mastery of this lesson objective.
5. Analyze evidence about previous student learning (perhaps yesterday's quiz or homework) so students know where to focus.
6. Plan pacing and subgrouping.
7. Pick materials, models, examples, stories, and cases to use.
8. Anticipate confusions, especially language and vocabulary meanings, and identify requisite prior knowledge students might not have.
9. Design and choose learning experiences.
10. Check that learning experiences are logically linked to the intended learning.
11. Decide how to collect evidence of learning during or concluding this lesson.
12. Plan how students will make their thinking visible and public.
13. Plan how to get students to summarize.
14. Plan how to get students' minds in gear at the beginning.
15. Predict how much time will be needed for each task or activity and plan other environmental variables (space, routines) that may need to be arranged.
16. Plan the effective effort strategies that may be employed or taught.
17. Plan how to diversify for different learning styles.
18. Plan certain key interactive moves like an opening question.
19. Decide who may need assistance or extensions during the lesson and provide for it.
20. Plan what extensions and challenges will be provided for students who are ready for them.
21. Plan how and when to explain the homework and its connection to today's lesson.

To check your knowledge about Planning, see the exercises on *The Skillful Teacher* website at www.RBTeach.com/TST7.

NOTES

CHAPTER 20

Curriculum
Differentiated Instruction

Curriculum: *Differentiated Instruction*

The main point of this area of performance is to enable you to survey the activities you offer to students so that you can describe them in a new way. This new way may give you a fuller picture than you have had before of what students are experiencing in your class, or it may give you a picture of what they are not experiencing, that is, the characteristics your learning experiences do not have. This information could lead you to make one of the following statements:

▲ "That's fine. It's okay not to have these features. What I'm doing is really on target for this curriculum, and those wouldn't be."

▲ "Well, there are some things I'm not doing that would be good to do. I'd like to do them, but there's just so much time. I think I'll put them on the back burner for now and look into adding them when things slow up a bit."

▲ "Well, there are a few things I hadn't thought about much before. They'd be really good, and I'd like to try them now."

Being effective with differentiated instruction is a developmental level for teachers who are already proficient with other foundational skills.

The point is that you should be able to look at your teaching, or that of someone else, and see more than you have before and then make some decisions based on your new understanding. You may come away from this chapter newly aware, or perhaps reminded, of some important things that you can design into students' experiences that match the students. In *The Differentiated Classroom* (2014), Carol Ann Tomlinson explains "that it's about choosing the strategy that will work best for a given learner at a given time" (p. 102). This is what we mean throughout this book by "matching."

This area of performance is constructed from the students' point of view. We ask first, "What are students experiencing in their environment? What are the attributes of the activity? What is it like from the students' angle to be doing this?" Then we ask, "So what? What difference does it make? Of what importance is what students are experiencing on this particular attribute? What does it mean about their overall school learning?" This enables us to make choices, because the shape of the learning experience is, after all, something we control as teachers.

TYPES OF DIFFERENTIATION

"Differentiation" has many meanings. It can mean students are studying different material at the same time. This may be because of student choice (see "experts" in Chapter 16, "Classroom Climate"). While their topics may be different (e.g., one student is becoming an expert on elephants, another is becoming an expert on race cars), the criteria for success for their reports will be the same.

Reteaching or extension groups is another form of differentiation (see the "Scholar's Loop" in Chapter 14, "Expectations"). Students are working in groups on different concepts or skills with the teacher taking charge of one group. Students who need support with a concept or skill are in one group and students who need extension work with new challenges are in another group. Ongoing formative assessment during instruction produces the information about which students have which needs. The management of grouping, choice of materials, and determination of tasks requires a level of planning beyond total group instruction that follows a pacing guide. It is, however, the most important focus for differentiation to bring all students to high standards.

The movement of the last decade for Response to Intervention (RTI) is based on this value. RTI groups children across classrooms within a grade level to focus on a particular skill. It takes constant communication between the teachers to regroup based on data. Married to this communication and assessment pattern must be the commitment to getting all students to proficiency. This will mean accelerating some students who are behind. Without this value, RTI could degenerate into permanent tracking in an elementary school.

Reteaching and extension groups are forms of differentiation that must be powered by a desire to accelerate the learning of students who are behind, not a strategy to reduce curriculum demands for "low" performing students. Thus the belief system that "Smart is something you can get" transforms how teachers implement differentiated instruction. Differentiation becomes a tool for implementing the growth mindset, not an adjustment for "low" performing students.

Research on the effects of differentiation is weak (Hattie, 2012). Our hypothesis is this: being effective with differentiated instruction is a developmental level for teachers who are already proficient with other foundational skills. If the objectives are not appropriate for the students and they don't understand them to begin with, differentiated instruction can't possibly have an effect. Differentiation also fails in the absence of ongoing formative assessment to give a teacher accurate information about students and their level of mastery. Differentiated instruction cannot be expected to boost achievement if students do not believe they can achieve or that it is worth their while to do so.

So professional development on differentiated instruction should be postponed until teachers have demonstrated proficiency on the "Big Rocks" of objectives, assessment, and student motivation. This chapter is of particular use to teachers who want to make instruction more interesting and varied for students. The variables to follow could be matched to students' learning style, as many (Dunn & Dunn, 1978; Gregorc & Ward, 1977; McCarthy, 1987a; Tomlinson, 2014) have recommended over the years, but even without a focus on matching these variables can be deliberately manipulated to make learning more active, more varied, and more interesting.

ANALYZING LEARNING EXPERIENCES

We analyze a student's learning experience almost as if it were a real, tangible thing, like a rock. It isn't tangible, but it is real and has describable attributes as a rock does. Supervision, for example, is an attribute with three possible values (or options): independent, facilitated, or directly supervised. Which are students experiencing right now? They may be closely and directly supervised right now and independent later in the day. Their learning experience may change based on this attribute, and when it does it's a different learning experience.

A learning experience takes place over a time span with a beginning, middle, and end. It can be quite short—a matter of minutes—or extend to hours. When it changes on significant attributes, it's a different learning experience.

This kind of analysis yields a full and accurate picture of what the student is experiencing in a planned activity. We can look at activities over a period of time and see what patterns and ranges are built into these experiences. Then we can decide if the range is appropriate. Are we ever giving students a chance to work cooperatively, for example, or is it always competitive or individualistic? Which sensory input channels are stimulated? Do we ever use the kinesthetic channel? What is the balance between concrete and abstract in our teaching? This area of performance provides a set of questions with which to survey our teaching periodically and see if we are offering what we want to offer. Finally, this area of performance gives some sharp-focus lenses to look at matching and adjusting learning experiences for individual students or groups.

THIRTEEN ATTRIBUTES OF DIFFERENTIATED INSTRUCTION

In the following sections, we describe the attributes of Differentiated Instruction one by one and lay out the possible forms each may take. You may choose to profile yourself as you go, noticing which of the options characterize learning experiences you offer and then deciding if those choices are broad enough and appropriately matched to your students.

1. Sources of Information

Definition

You can examine learning experiences to determine whether the information the students are working with is *conventional*—from conventional sources such as a text, a reference book, you, or some other source that gives the information to them—or *constructed*—meaning that the students constructed the knowledge through some process of their own, such as observation, experiment, interview, deduction, induction, application of logic, discussion, debate, or questioning.

Looking something up is always a conventional source of information. The student's own initiative, objective, and choice of learning experience may be behind the act of looking up, for instance, design features of an airplane, but the source of the information is still conventional.

Significance

It is significant to know whether students are ever challenged or put in positions where they are able to use their own resources as active agents for the generation of knowledge new to them, as opposed to receiving information that has been assembled, organized, or digested for them. Neither source of information is better than the other, but they are clearly different in their effects on the learner. If teaching uses either source to the exclusion of the other, we are led to ask whether learners have sufficient balance in their educational program.

2. Resources

Definition

Students may use any one or more of the following resources in the course of their work:

▲ A text

▲ The teacher

▲ Peers

▲ Families

- ▲ Interviews with outside people (other than family, teachers, or peers)
- ▲ Observation
- ▲ Audiovisual material
- ▲ Online services or electronic sources
- ▲ Reference books
- ▲ Their own imaginations or experiences

This attribute is an index to the breadth of resources brought to bear on the student's learning experience and can tally a simple count of how many are used.

Significance

Over the course of a student's education, we would expect all of the resources listed to be used. In any one course, grade, or class, you would ask which resources and how broad a range were appropriate and desirable, and compare that with the reality. In examining an individual student's educational experience, you could usefully ask how many of these resources were brought to bear across different courses and evaluate the fit of the operating range of resources to the intentions of the program.

3. Personal Relevance

Definition

On this attribute, learning experiences are found to be *contrived, simulated,* or *real.* The degree to which the learning experience relates to aspects of life that have personal meaning to the students is indexed here. Does it connect to their real world outside school?

Doing a workbook page containing problems of adding money in the form $124.35 + 3.50 = ? would be judged as contrived, since calculating the answer on a workbook page is not connected to the students' world of experience outside school. But if the class has set up a model store selling grocery items (or anything they might find in a real store), and the students are buying items using play money (or even real money), then this activity simulates real experiences from the students' lives. If the class takes a trip to a supermarket and spends money it has made through some project to buy supplies for a party, and they collect, purchase, pay for the items, and get change, then the activity is judged real: it is integrated, connected, and related directly to the real world.

Contrived in this sense does not have a negative connotation. Much of learning and knowledge construction is contrived in that it does not simulate or reproduce the reality outside school, nor could it. It is impractical for almost all of us to learn about the history of India by visiting historic Indian sites (though that would be nice). And aspects of historical study necessarily require reading books and other contrived (versus real) experiences to proceed effectively with the learning. There is no general value implied in this attribute that real learning experiences are superior to contrived ones. Students do not have to leave school on a field trip to enter the realm of real learning experiences either. The act of painting is real no matter where one does it. Painting is painting and not a simulation of painting, whether or not one does it in school or in an art studio. The same applies to creative writing or other aesthetic work of any kind. Having a debate is a real experience between the debaters and not simulated just because it is not taking place in a court of law or a legislative chamber. Many experiences in school are inherently real for students. Settling a dispute with another student over how to share materials is a real experience in which students play a deliberate role and act as mediators according to certain designs.

Significance

Many educators believe it is important that as many learning experiences as possible connect to students' real world of meaning—their world of experience outside school. One school of learning theory holds that such learning experiences are more effective, more powerful, and more lasting in effect (Dale, n.d.). The student, it is said, has a context in which to embed the new information and because of its relevance to his personal life is more impelled to attend to and participate in what's going on. This then guarantees a level of involvement on the part of the student with the learning experience that will maximize learning. To people of this persuasion, it is important to know how much realness is characteristic of learning experiences being offered. Early childhood educators and open classroom educators are especially interested in this attribute of learning experiences (Bussis, Chittenden, & Amarel, 1976).

Regardless of one's beliefs about the learning theory of personal relevance, it is a distinction we can make among learning experiences. It produces data to bring to an analysis of teaching-in-action in comparison with teaching's intentions. We can look at curriculum designs to see where and how often opportunities for realness exist and how appropriate such experiences might be to the content and the learners. We can evaluate the efficiency of a curriculum in terms of the balance among contrived, simulated, and real experiences that is best for accomplishing the objectives of the instruction in the time allowed.

4. Type of Interdependence

Definition

Johnson and Johnson (1987) first set out a three-point typology for learning experiences: *cooperative, competitive,* and *individualized* (they don't use the term *learning experiences;* they say *goal structures*). A learning experience specifies the type of interdependence existing among students—the way in which students will relate to each other and the teacher. One might say they have taken a specific aspect of the social climate—that aspect related to competition and its presence, absence, or opposite—and defined it in detail:

> When students are working together to find what factors make a difference in how long a candle burns in a quart jar, they are in a cooperative goal structure. A cooperative goal structure exists when students perceive that they can obtain their goal if and only if the other students with whom they are linked can obtain their goal. Since the goal of all the students is to make a list of factors that influence the time the candle burns, the goal of all the students has been reached when they generate a list. A cooperative goal structure requires the coordination of behavior necessary to achieve their mutual goal. If one student achieves the goal, all students with whom the student is linked achieve the goal. When students are working to see who can build the best list of factors influencing the time a candle will burn in a quart jar, they are in a competitive goal structure. A competitive goal structure exists when students perceive that they can obtain their goal if and only if the other students with whom they are linked fail to obtain their goal. If one student turns in a better list than anyone else, all other students have failed to achieve their goal. Competitive interaction is the striving to achieve one's goal in a way that blocks all others from achieving the goal. Finally, if all students are working independently to master an operation in mathematics, they are in an individualistic goal structure. An individualistic goal structure exists when the achievement of the goal by one student is unrelated to the achievement of the goal by other students; whether or not a student achieves her goal has no bearing upon whether or not other students achieve their goals. If one student masters the mathematics principle, it has no bearing upon whether other students successfully master the mathematics principle. Usually there is no student interaction in an individualistic situation

> since each student seeks the outcome that is best for himself regardless of whether or not other students achieve their goals. (Johnson & Johnson, 1987, p. 7)

Johnson and Johnson have an observation checklist with a series of yes-no questions for classroom organization, student-student interaction, and teacher-student interaction. The outcome scores of the checklist are three percentage figures for the three possible goal structures. There is a recognition that a learning experience will rarely be exclusively cooperative. From the percentage figures of Johnson and Johnson's observation checklist, one could make a statement about the dominant quality of the learning experience along the attribute of competition.

An important body of research literature has emerged on the effectiveness of cooperative learning for cognitive as well as affective ends. This is accompanied by a technical literature on how to do cooperative learning. At least five forms of cooperative learning are developed and available for teachers to try (Figure 20.1). They are arranged in the order of the demands they place on students for interaction and communication skills (from least demanding on the left to most demanding on the right).

If you want to rate yourself on this attribute, you will want to be able to look at a single learning experience and characterize its dominant quality: cooperative, competitive, or individualistic. For example, in certain science lab courses we have observed, groups of students worked together sharing apparatus, ideas, and information as they performed a common experiment. This we considered significant cooperation. At the same time, these students were recording experimental results in individual notebooks the teacher graded separately.

Different groups of students were at different places in the sequential programmed curriculum. Some were working alone, either because no one else was at the same place as they or because they wanted to work alone (which the teacher allowed). Students took tests individually when they felt ready. Individual pretest feedback was given by the teacher to students and tests were graded individually. This was significant evidence for calling the learning experience individualistic. In this lab course, there were no observed instances of students' comparing test scores in a competitive way, though in interviews teachers cited cases where that happened. Indeed, even if we had observed students' comparing scores, it wouldn't necessarily merit a judgment of competition as a value of the learning experience on this attribute since what one student earns on the test has no bearing on the score of any other student. It could be argued that

Figure 20.1 Formats for Cooperative Learning

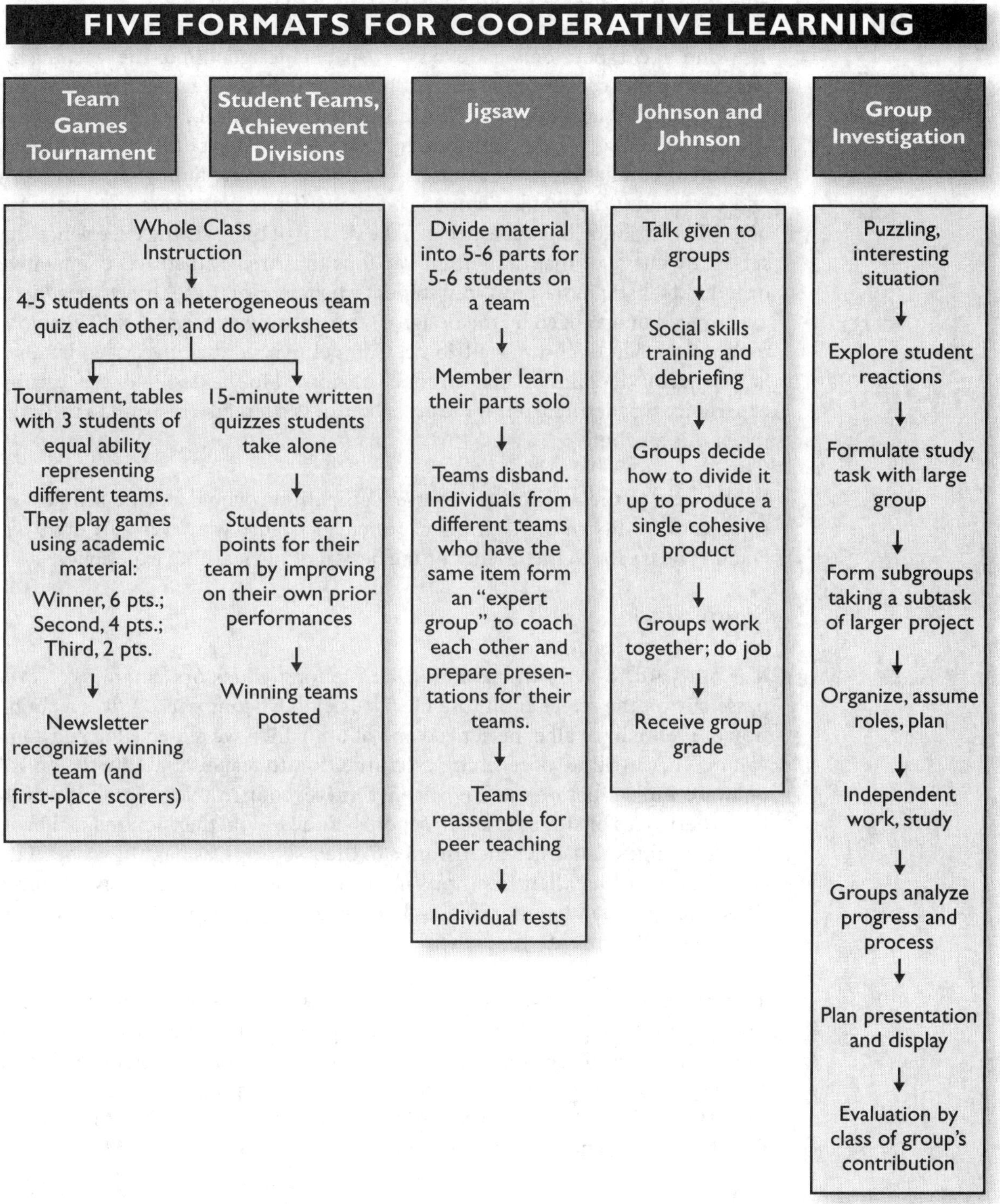

comparing test scores reflects competitive qualities inherent in humans, and the culture, in the process of testing itself ("Whadjaget?").

The kind of competition we looked for was one designed into the learning experience by the teacher or the curriculum—something like a team game, a contest for speed or accuracy involving a group of students, or a recitation period where a student gives right answers in competition with peers. Many competitive forces emanating from students themselves, peers, family, or the culture and community may affect student behavior. These forces are not examined here. This attribute looks at aspects of the design of the learning experience that set up, by virtue of that design, interactions that are competitive, cooperative, or individualistic in nature. Only students' behavior of these three types that is encouraged or arranged by the design of the learning experience will enable us to make a judgment on this attribute. Competitive, cooperative, or individualistic behavior of children that cannot be attributed to the design of the learning experience that comes from some other source is deemed irrelevant to the judging of this attribute.

In the case of the science lab course, competition would not be scored as a significant quality of the learning experience because whatever of it there was couldn't be traced to the teacher or the design of the learning experience.

Significance

It is not hard to get a discussion started among educators, families, or even passersby on the street about the merits or evils of competition. It is a condition of life we have all experienced and about which we all have formed some values. This attribute of teaching calls attention to teachers' ability to control, in aware and deliberate ways, how competitive, cooperative, or individualistic the experiences of students are in schools. Educational decision makers bring different values and different histories to their settings, as has always been the case. But whatever their decisions about the shape of learning experiences, these decisions can be informed and deliberate, if made by professionals who know the full implications of their acts.

This attribute provides tools for surveying your own teaching to see how much cooperation or competition you are putting into students' experiences. It also offers resources for getting the balance you want. Despite the "era of cooperative learning" (1960s to 1980s) having come and gone, it is striking that John Hattie's (2012) meta-analysis of the literature concludes that it is a powerful intervention, and gives it an overall effect size of .41!

Matching

There is matching if the teacher differentiates deliberately among groups or individuals as to the competitive, cooperative, or individualistic quality of learning experiences.

5. Degree of Supervision

Definition

Students may be directly supervised by a teacher who checks on what and how everybody is doing, may be independent and responsible for their own work, or the teacher may facilitate their work by being available as a resource person and occasionally intervening with suggestions, recommendations, or stimulating questions (Dunn & Dunn, 1978). As we reflect on the learning experiences we design, the number of these three possible conditions present in our teaching—*supervised, facilitated,* or *independent*—can be counted.

Significance

A limited range on this attribute—for example, a teacher who always supervises all learning activities—excludes certain kinds of learning in a classroom. The breadth or narrowness of range on this attribute is something we can look at for its nurturant effects on students, that is, the effects on them of living in an environment of that kind. We can then ask if that is what we intend. And we can, of course, compare this range of supervisory modes and the nurturant effects attached with the goals of the curriculum.

Matching

Teachers who discriminate among students on how much supervision they require or can tolerate so as to maximize their performance are matching the amount and kind of supervision they provide to the characteristics of students.

Jane flourishes if left to work independently much of the time, checking in occasionally for conferences with the teacher. Working under direct supervision for the bulk of the day unnecessarily limits her learning experiences. But Moira can't seem to get herself organized. She'll have several false starts and then may socialize away her morning if she is not directly supervised in her work. Her teacher provides much direct supervision for her and much independence for Jane. The same kind of distinction can be made for subgroups of the class and would enable us to conclude "yes" for matching on supervision.

6. Self-Expression

Definition

Students may or may not be given the opportunity to express something of themselves in a learning experience. If they are given such an opportunity, the self-expression may be delivered through drawing, creative writing, performing, speaking, or building or construction of some sort. Merely to respond or recite is not to express one's self as meant here. Expressing oneself means expressing something that is unique to the individual or expressing some standard information in a way that encourages students to bring something of themselves to the expression.

An assignment to diagram mitosis for biology (though different students will embellish the product to different degrees) is a prescribed product that has the student express mitosis, not himself or herself. An assignment to represent the *1812 Overture* in paint is also prescribed but frees the student to express things unique to him or her that are stimulated by the music. A recitation question asking a student to summarize Turner's frontier thesis does not allow self-expression as would a question asking a student to say how he would have responded to the offer of free western land had he been alive a hundred years ago.

Significance

The significance of this attribute relates to the value placed on self-expression by those responsible for the educational program. Data on the attribute enable us to raise the attribute as an important and perhaps overlooked aspect of learning experiences over which program designers and teachers have control. And as before, we can compare realities with intentions, where intentions about self-expression have been considered by program designers and made explicit.

Matching

We may look to see if the ways in which we encourage expression of the self also allow differences in ways students can best do that expressing. If matching were present, one would see not only a range on this attribute but also negotiation or direct planning of students' activities where they were asked or permitted to express themselves in ways different from other students.

7. Degree of Abstraction

Definition

Learning experiences can be scored as *concrete, representational* (iconic), or *abstract* (Bruner, 1966). Concrete means manipulative—students are touching or seeing real objects that are integral to the learning experience. Iconic means representational—a picture, image, or other facsimile of real objects—is embedded in the materials with which the learner is interacting. Abstract means symbolic words or thoughts are the stuff of which the learning experience is made without support from facsimiles or concrete objects.

Significance

We can compare the range of levels of abstraction offered to the nature of the content and make judgments concerning appropriateness. Similar comparisons can be made in consideration of the age and learning style of the students. We might expect to see teachers of young children designing more concrete experiences than at other grade levels. But it has been acknowledged for several decades in learning style models that reliance on concrete models and examples is highly useful for many learners, no matter what the age.

Matching

Because students of the same age are often at different levels with regard to their ability to process abstract information, we might expect a teacher to discriminate among students and adjust the level of abstraction of the learning experiences offered to characteristics of individual students. Conrad Toepfer (1981) and others have applied these insights to the typical middle school curriculum and found that much of it demands formal operational thinking of students, a kind of thinking that, according to their statistics, only 12% of American youngsters are capable of at age 12. Toepfer makes a strong case that teachers who match the level of thinking to the students' capacity for abstract thinking, especially in the plateau period of 12 to 14 years of age, make a huge difference in school failure rates. He and his colleagues recommend testing students for their level of thinking (onset of concrete operations, concrete operations, initial formal operations, established formal operations) and accommodating instruction to the stage. Intelligence, he points out, is different and uncorrelated to stage thinking. Super-bright youngsters go through the same Piagetian stages of growth and in about the same proportions per given age as students of average and below-average IQ.

This attribute of learning experiences bears a hard look if we are to meet the needs of all students at all ages, stages of development, and learning style orientations.

8. Cognitive Level

Definition

In Chapter 11, "Clarity," we discussed questioning and Bloom's (1956) Taxonomy (and Anderson and Krathwohl's [2001] update of that Taxonomy) as a framework for designing questions requiring different levels of thinking. We can examine learning experiences to see what cognitive level of performance they ask of students. We can also look across learning experiences we offer to identify the range of thinking embedded in them and count the number of levels for which evidence can be produced.

Significance

Researchers have long investigated the number of higher-level questions teachers ask students in verbal interactions. The research implies that the more higher-level questions used, the better, and studies have attempted to correlate the proportion of higher-level questions with student achievement (Winne, 1979a). However, large doses of high cognitive levels may be quite inappropriate for students who have not worked through lower levels with the same material. When we considered the Models of Teaching area of performance in Chapter 13, we saw that for certain models (e.g., Taba's) it is the order in which cognitive operations are demanded of students that is important, not the raw amount at any level.

Focusing on the cognitive level embedded in learning experiences offered by a teacher enables us to collect data on the range offered. Any predominance of one or two particular levels will prompt us to ask, "Why?" If a teacher or a curriculum has some specific thinking objectives in mind, we can compare intentions with reality.

Matching

Tailoring or adjusting learning experiences on the same or similar material—so that the cognitive level demanded is different for different students—is evidence that we are differentiating cognitive level across students. The danger in such differentiation is if we deny to low-skill students the opportunity for higher-level thinking. This pattern appears when one holds low expectations for students derived from impressions of their lower innate ability. Thus instruction becomes more drill oriented and less interesting for these students, deepening their cycle of failure and their subsequent rejection of school itself.

The point here is to be aware if we are limiting the involvement of certain students with experiences from the higher levels of Bloom's taxonomy. We can differentiate learning experiences appropriately for different students in many ways, including pace. But we should look for ways to offer the full range of cognitive levels to both high- and low-skill students.

9. Structuring

We have all heard people refer to students who need a high degree of structure. We have often wondered exactly what is meant by that *structure* and discovered, not too surprisingly, that people mean different things, such as the student has to be closely supervised or the task has to be broken down into small pieces and the student told exactly what to do, when, and how. We find out how structuring is being handled when we give directions. We would have called this section "giving directions," except that giving directions is only one way that activities get set up. Sometimes students are asked to set procedures, and sometimes teachers and students negotiate what to do and how. One way to analyze differences in instruction is to examine how much and where these different kinds of structuring are occurring: by the teacher (high structure), negotiation (moderate structure), or students (low structure). Another question to ask is whether we differentiate among students along this attribute of who structures activities; that is matching.

When teachers give directions, they often structure (that is, make decisions and give instructions about) the content to be worked on, the procedures to follow, the behavior to do (for example, "write," "discuss," "compare," "listen"), the form of student products, and the point of closure (signaling when it's over). Content, behavior, procedures, products, and closure are the five components of structuring. Exhibit 20.1 identifies each of these aspects of a learning experience and the choice points one has for either increasing or decreasing the degree and kind of structure embedded. Thus the degree of structure in a learning experience is largely a matter of whether or not decisions are being made and who is making them.

Content

Content means information or objects dealt with at the item level. Who decided, introduced, or is responsible for the presence of the particular items students are working with? Making reliable assignments of responsibility here requires being clear on the unit of analysis. Just how big or small is an item?

Exhibit 20.1 Who Decides the Structure?

	No one decides	**Student decides**	**Negotiation**	**Teacher decides**
	Low Structure →		→ *High Structure*	
1. Content				
2. Behavior				
3. Procedures				
4. Products				
5. Closure				

Adapted from Ann Berlak.

Table 20.1 provides some examples. At the most general level, the teacher is almost always responsible for content. In the example where students debate the pros and cons of busing, the teacher probably (though not necessarily) introduced the subject. The teacher is responsible for the topic—the area being treated—but clearly that is above the item level. If teachers are responsible for the responses the students are producing in that they ask factual or leading questions, then they are responsible for the content. But if the students are bringing in information not directly tied to the teacher's questions, items, or objects that could not be the only reply to the question or the lead-in of the teacher, then the students are responsible for the content at the item level (though perhaps not the general topic).

What can be said about a discussion where the teacher starts off being responsible for the content, say, a recitation, and then switches to more open-ended exploration of the same material, and all within the same discussion: "And now what would you have done in General Lee's position? Do you think he did the right thing? Can you justify your position?" Here the responsibility for content has shifted from teacher to students, and an important attribute to the learning experience has changed. We will be interested in knowing what other attributes of the learning experience have changed.

For individual learning experiences, we can note who is responsible for the content at the item level. Across learning experiences, we can note which of these parties are responsible if we survey a number of lessons: teacher, student, or negotiation.

Table 20.1 Examples of Who Decides the Content?

Activity	Item	Responsible Party
1. Recitation or review of Civil War battles with teacher leading questioning in chronological order, seeking identification and sequence.	Pieces of information elicited from students	Teacher
2. Teacher says, "Read this book and answer the questions at the back."	The book, the questions	Teacher
3. Teacher says, "Pick a book you'd like to read, and summarize it verbally for me." Although the use of time is structured by the teacher in this item and the behavior and writing are also structured, the content—what is operated on, written about—comes from the student.	The book	Student
4. Teacher suggests, "Use the blocks to make a model of the store we visited." Although the student controls the shape of the product, what the store will look like, the item on which he is operating—blocks—and the model of a store were directed by the teacher. If the student were free to represent the store in any medium he chose (paint, clay, or something else), then the behavior would have been attributed to the student as the shape of the product, but the content would still be the teacher's decision about what to represent.	Model of store	Teacher
5. Class discussion about the pros and cons of busing to integrate public schools, with the teacher serving as facilitator and clarifier, not taking a stand, trying to get students to show their positions.	Arguments, positions, and evidence for positions	Students
6. Following a discussion of movies, students form interest groups to study selected aspects of movie production: special effects, casting, script writing, shooting schedules. Students nominate themselves into groups, and teacher mediates which groups may form and the membership.	Special effects, casting, shooting schedules, script writing	Negotiated

Behavior

To determine who has structured the student behavior within the learning experience, the question to ask is what verb describes what the student is doing. Who is responsible for that operation (verb) being the operation: the teacher, the student, or is it negotiated? The student is reading, writing, summarizing, responding verbally, building, or painting. Who chose that? These are questions to ask of individual learning experiences. Then when we look across learning experiences and note our range on structuring of behavior, we ask how many of the three possibilities we've exercised or none at all. It may be that we have a behavior in mind for the learning experience but fail to state it. This is of no consequence if the behavior is obvious or understood by the students. For example, "doing" a page in a workbook is understood to mean, "Follow the directions on the page," which almost always calls for a written response in a blank or on a line. On the other hand, if the behavior is not clear to the students or we didn't fully think it out ("What do we do, Mr. Jones?"), then we could conclude "none" here. For example, "Do the next chapter in your book," may mean, "Read and answer the questions at the end," "Read only," or "Read for the general idea." Unless some routine has been established for what "reading a chapter" means, we could conclude this is "none" on structuring behavior.

Procedures

Procedural moves set the details of who and how—for example, dividing a class into teams for a spelling bee, giving directions for a worksheet exercise, and describing the procedure in a concept attainment game. Included in this category are the negotiations, which may go on at some length, when students are given the opportunity to decide how they want to go about studying a given content area. Procedures may come from the teacher or from the students, or they may be negotiated. Which are the following?

- ▲ "We are going to divide the class into three groups. John, Gary, and George will be in group 1."
- ▲ "First we're going to do worksheets. Then I want you to write down the items that were difficult, and when you've done that, we'll discuss those items."
- ▲ "We're going to go around the circle here, and each of you will tell us something you read about Hemingway and I'll write it on the board."
- ▲ "How shall we do this? Shall everybody participate?"

- "John has suggested that we invite the editor of the newspaper to speak. Do you agree that this is a good way to begin our study of journalism?" (Joyce, 1969).

It may be that we have some procedures in mind for the learning experience but fail to state them. In that case, there is no structuring of procedures. If we say, "Work on your folders, boys and girls," and within each folder there is a structuring of procedures for each child in the form of a note ("Charlie, do the first two worksheets and then bring them to me for checking"), then the procedures are structured by the teacher. But if it is unclear what the procedures are to be because we have failed to state them or think them out and don't explicitly ask students to make decisions about procedures, then one might conclude "none."

Products

Who determines the form of the tangible products: teacher, student, or both together (negotiated)?

- Teacher: "I'll tally votes here on how many thought the Civil War represented progress versus setbacks." The tally is the product.

- Student: Any creative or expressive activity (painting, creative writing) makes a student responsible for the form of the product.

- Negotiated: "How shall we represent the data from our poll?" Students and teacher negotiate a form, perhaps deciding on bar graphs.

Closure

How will the student know when the learning experience is over? The end point can be defined in terms of time, quantity of material completed, or a certain kind of product being produced. Who determines these limits: teacher, student, or both together?

For certain experiences, closure is inherently determined by the student (examples are a painting or creative writing—except where the teacher says, "Write a four-page story"). For others, it is clearly teacher determined ("Do the first three lines of problems"). But if closure is not inherently or explicitly delegated to the student, then failure to state it may lead us to conclude "none" on structuring of closure. The key questions are, "Which ways do we have for structuring closure to learning experiences?" and, "Are they used appropriately?"

Teachers who hand out folders containing pages of new worksheets and expect students to begin working are evidencing "none" for structuring of procedures and closure—and they often experience the consequences of that lack of structuring.

Matching

One reason teachers treat students differently with regard to structure is learning effectiveness (Colarusso & Green, 1973). Jane may be capable of designing her own procedures for collecting data from her science experiment, whereas Fred needs the teacher to structure procedures to maximize the benefit he gets from the experience. A certain group of students may be quite capable of picking their own reading material, whereas another is not (content).

But another reason might have to do with long-range goals. Some teachers have as a goal helping students become more independent, self-motivated learners. This means moving gradually from higher to progressively lower structure. Such a teacher takes students where they are and provides the degree of structure necessary for learning to proceed efficiently. If this happens to be high structure, so be it. Over time, the teacher introduces negotiation of certain attributes, say, procedures and closure, with some students. Over the course of the year, more and more students become involved in more and more decision-making about their learning as they show they are ready.

We feel that understanding structuring (and accountability) is the key to understanding the erratic record of open classrooms in the 1960s and 1970s. Those that worked were in control of structuring and matched it to the students in the class. Those that didn't offered too little structure to students who were unprepared to deal with it. The physical look and arrangement of the room, open versus traditional, is usually no clue to the level of structure and the degree of appropriateness for different students. Whole populations of students may be matched to a level of structure, or structure may be differentiated across different individuals and groups within the same class. Few American visitors to British infant schools in the early 1960s perceived the high degree of structure and accountability built into students' working routines, despite the open, child-centered, and apparently effortless flow of constructive activity (Berlak, Berlak, Bagenstos, & Mikel, 1975).

A robust line of research developed by David Hunt and his associates since 1966 has established the better learning that results when students experience a degree of imposed structure matched to their level of development. Numerous instruments are available for determining whether a student is suited to a high- or low-structure treatment (Hunt, 1971; Hunt & Sullivan, 1974; Rich &

Bush, 1978). The possibilities we have sketched for who does the structuring—teacher, negotiated, or student—correspond to Hunt's ratings of high, moderate, and low degrees of imposed structure.

10. Grouping and Interpersonal Complexity

Definitions

Students may work alone, with a single peer, with a group of peers, with the total class, in a dyad with the teacher, with other adults (the principal, a visitor, a family member), or in a small group with the teacher. Any one or more of these possible combinations may characterize learning experiences over the course of a day or week. Each individual learning experience may have its own grouping. First, one can simply count the number of groupings evidenced to index a teacher's range.

Significance

Characterizing the groupings in our teaching allows us to ask about what kinds of interpersonal complexity are consistent with the objectives of the curriculum. It also allows us to see how much congruence there is between intentions and reality. Notice we have replaced the word *grouping* with *interpersonal complexity.* This is because there is more to say about a group than how many people are in it.

It is also important to know what kind of interaction they are having with one another. Six students and a teacher may be answering recitation questions in a small group; these students have no interaction with each other and only simple interactions with the teacher as they give direct factual answers. Thus the interpersonal complexity is low. In that same group, however, the teacher may invite students to respond to or extend, interpret, or refute other students' answers. Students may begin speaking directly to one another without the teacher as intermediary between every student utterance. The teacher may still moderate the discussion and call on people, but the interpersonal complexity is now moderately complex and no longer simple. If the students are freely interacting with each other and create their own conversational rules and agendas as they go, the interpersonal complexity is high.

In a curriculum stressing social objectives—say, cooperation, listening to each other, or mutual respect—we would expect to see learning experiences with groups of students, dyads, and other combinations that brought students together without exclusive teacher direction. Whatever the themes of the curriculum, the types of interpersonal complexity displayed enable us to describe an important and real part of the learning environment and ask questions about the effect of those patterns on students' learning. Taken from the perspective of curriculum as planning, interpersonal complexity is a design feature of learning experiences that a teacher can tailor to the nature of the objectives and the needs of the learners.

Matching

In studying our teaching, we can determine whether we discriminate among students in the kind of interpersonal complexity designed or allowed for in learning experiences (Colarusso & Green, 1973). Mehmet works well in large groups but tends to act out or be silly in small-group instruction. He does have a few peers with whom he seems able to work effectively. He allows these students to help him and can work cooperatively with them when he has to deal with them only one at a time. So we engineer teacher–Mehmet and peer–Mehmet learning situations as often as possible (while also working on his difficulties with being in groups) to maximize his productive learning time in the class. We have matched the interpersonal complexity in his learning experiences to observed characteristics of Mehmet.

Better learning results when students experience a degree of imposed structure matched to their level of development.

We observe that this class attends poorly in a large group. So while making attention an objective for them, we make sure they have as many individual and small-group work situations as possible. That is a decision to match the needs of this particular class.

Ms. James notices her English class does not handle the high level of interpersonal complexity she encourages; they seem alternately to flounder or to attack each other when discussing the readings. She reduces the interpersonal complexity to moderate and increases her role as mediator. They prove quite capable of handling high-level literary analysis but require less interpersonal complexity than last year's class.

Where teachers show different patterns of grouping and interpersonal complexity for different children, we can note matching on this attribute. How about the possibility of a mismatch? What would it look like so that we could defend such a judgment? Probably, the learning experience isn't going well. A mismatch means that something is wrong, and when something is wrong, we expect to see symptoms—usually disruptive behavior or inattention. Students are experiencing difficulty under these conditions, and we must be able to attribute this difficulty to inappropriate grouping or interpersonal complexity rather than to other causes (students' emotional issues, inappropriate work, poor transition). How might an observer help to distinguish such causes?

Repeated observations over a long period of time might enable an observer to see groupings that were consistently successful for a certain student and others that were consistently unsuccessful. If the students were frequently placed in these failure settings, the observer could attribute mismatch to the grouping or interpersonal complexity. This would put the observer in the position of knowing, through repeated observation, something the teacher did not. Although such a situation is conceivable, a single observation is rarely enough to produce it. More likely, the observer would be in a position to problem-solve with the teacher, exploring what the cause of the problem might be.

11. Information Complexity

Definition

"Students who are low in conceptual level (CL) are less capable of processing information in a complex way and less capable of dealing with information in a responsible fashion; students higher in CL are more capable of processing information in a complex way" (Hunt, 1971). It sounds simplistic, but it is not. The conceptual level of students is not the same as intelligence or ability. Often two youngsters who are both quite bright are different in conceptual level. What does it mean to process information in a complex way? We define three levels of information complexity:

▲ **Level 1—Low Complexity:** Information is linear and direct. One thing leads to another. Qualities of the learning tend to include remembering, sequence, performance, concepts, and skills. Learners are not asked to consider alternatives or make distinctions between points of view or such things as people's feelings or orientations. They have difficulty developing concepts on their own but can learn them receptively without difficulty.

▲ **Level 2—Moderate Complexity:** The notion of alternatives appears. Students are asked to make distinctions and differentiate sources, points of view, courses of action, and possible explanations. They can assimilate the idea that there is more than one possible explanation for a phenomenon. Comparison and contrast enter the picture. Students can develop their own concepts from data.

▲ **Level 3—High Complexity:** Students can consider several alternatives. Their ability to differentiate and distinguish increases and develops into the ability to see the relationships between different points of view or different explanations.

Significance

Clearly, there is a developmental quality to these three levels (e.g., five-year-olds are usually not ready to describe the relationships of different points of view). Thus this attribute reminds us to look at students and check if we are challenging them appropriately with the complexity of their tasks. It further challenges us to ask if they are ready to move toward the next level. And finally, it prompts us to differentiate among students within a class and adjust their work appropriately.

Hunt's (1971) developmental model considers what we have called separately structuring, grouping/interpersonal complexity, and information complexity all at once. These are three facets of conceptual level that correlate with one another. For example, a student who is low in conceptual level (as measured by Hunt's paragraph completion test) will function best with a high degree of imposed structure, simple dynamics in groupings, and low information complexity. Conversely, a student high in conceptual level learns best with low structure, more complex grouping interactions, and more complex information processing. The research supporting the effectiveness of this matching has been quite striking and quite consistent. It has proved applicable for adults as well as children and has been used successfully as a way to form classroom and instructional groupings (Gower & Resnick, 1979; Rich & Bush, 1978).

12. Sensory Channels

Definitions

This attribute of learning experiences is about the *perceptual modalities* and *motor expressions* students are called on to use as they engage new information or ideas and then make a product or express what they know. Sensory input channels may include one or more of the following: *visual, auditory,* or *tactile/kinesthetic.* Motor expressions that students exercise in the context of the learning experience may be *large motor muscles, small motor,* their *voice,* or nothing at all. Finally, the design of the learning experience may call for student output in the form of talk, writing, or performance of an observable skill.

Significance and Matching

Matching students' optimum input and output channels is often cited as one way to individualize learning experiences for different students. Dunn and Dunn (1978) make a strong case for it. To the degree to which this is taking place, we would expect to see similar or identical objectives being worked on by students through input and output channels adjusted for their characteristics.

A count can be made of how many channels are used for input of information to students in learning experiences: visual, auditory, and tactile/kinesthetic. Regarding how students act in learning experiences (student output), the number of channels from among the following can be counted: talk, writing, or performance of some kind (such as drawing, building, manipulating, acting out motorically). Regarding motor use, one can record how many of the following muscle groups are used by students: large motor, small motor, voice, or passive (no motor).

A tradition of authors from Jensen (2008) to Susan Griss (2013) has clearly established the advantages of movement in the classroom for attention and cognition. They are well worth considering.

One might use data about these three attributes of learning experiences to evaluate how active the learning was and how that level of physical activity fit goals for the learning program or for the needs of the students. But more likely, the greatest significance of these data will be raising our awareness of the range we can create and the potential for matching that the range will offer.

Simply seeing a variety of perceptual channels operating differentially across students does not prove matching. To support a "Yes" judgment on matching, there must be evidence that a particular mode is being used with a particular student or group of students and that there is not just random variety. Such evidence might be provided by a teacher remark or a systematic assignment system for directing certain students to a learning experience with a dominant perceptual mode different from other learning experiences being offered around the same objective to other students.

13. Scale

Definitions

Sometimes the scale of objects, print, or models used in learning experiences has been *enlarged* or *reduced.* The scale of materials used can be either of these two, or it can be *normal,* that is, as normally found. This attribute begins by a simple count of how many of these three possibilities are present.

Significance

Like all the other attributes, scale is an attribute of a learning experience that affects the interaction of the learner with the environment, and that environment is under the control of the curriculum designer and the teacher. It can be controlled to effect. Examining this attribute of teaching brings it to consciousness and provokes questions about whether all the opportunities for scale manipulation in learning experiences have been taken. For example, by miniaturizing into models, we can bring concepts from the abstract to the iconic level to good effect for students who don't function well abstractly. Whole outdoor physical environments (a stream, a town, a valley) can be captured in paint on giant sheets of cardboard (3 feet by 4 feet) and unfolded around the periphery of a classroom to simulate the environment of the stream. By enlarging worksheets or other standard school tasks onto giant plastic-covered boards or using giant felt or plastic numbers, a teacher can provide variety to the conduct of otherwise standard learning experiences.

Matching

When we see the scale of an object adjusted for use with a particular student or students, we can conclude "Yes" on matching for scale. This can be particularly important for primary children for whom size of print and number of items on a page can be confusing.

CHAPTER QUICK GUIDE

Thirteen Attributes of Differentiated Instruction

1. Source of Information	conventional	constructed		
2. Resources	text	family	audiovisual	reference books
	teacher	interviews	online services	imagination
	peers	observation	electronic devices	experience
3. Personal Relevance	contrived	simulated	real	
4. Type of Interdependence	competitive	individualized	cooperative	
5. Supervision	supervised	facilitated	independent	matched
6. Self-Expression	no	yes	matched	
7. Degree of Abstraction	concrete	representational	abstract	
8. Cognitive Level	recall	analysis	synthesis	
	comprehension	application	evaluation	
9. Structuring	none	teacher	student	negotiated
Content				
Behavior				
Procedures				
Products				
Closure				
10. Grouping and Interpersonal complexity	low	moderate	high	matching
11. Information Complexity	low	moderate	high	matching
12. Sensory Channels				
Student input	visual	tactile/kinesthetic	auditory	matched
Student motor use	large motor	small motor	voice	passive
Student output	talk	writing	performance	matched
13. Scale	normal	miniaturized	enlarged	matched

To check your knowledge about Differentiated Instruction, see the exercises on *The Skillful Teacher* website at www.RBTeach.com/TST7.

NOTES

CHAPTER 21

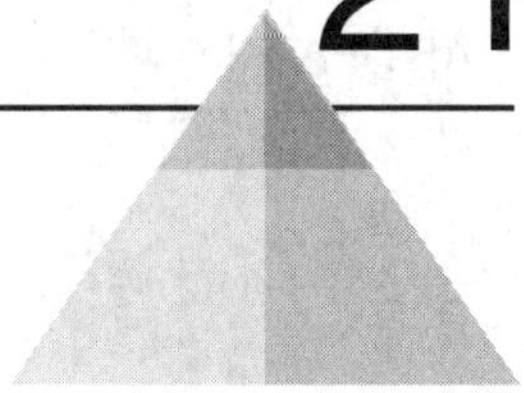

Curriculum: Assessment

Grant Wiggins (1993) once said that assessment was the Trojan horse of school reform. What he meant, we believe, is that if we did assessment properly and lined up all the soldiers it would take to do it well, we would open the gates to the rest of the army of improvement efforts waiting outside the city. Another way of looking at it is certain changes have unusually large ripple effects into other practices, and good assessment is one of them.

The primary purpose of classroom assessment is to increase student achievement.

The view of what good classroom assessment is has undergone radical changes since the late 20th century. We have shifted from the notion of using tests primarily as mechanisms to sort and grade students to using assessment to accomplish the following:

1. Inform instruction.

2. Gather data about what students know prior to beginning instruction (pre-assessment).

3. Continually gather data about how well students are understanding during instruction (formative assessment).

4. Adjust instruction and reteach, when necessary, in an effort to ensure that all students can be successful in the end (summative assessment).

We have shifted from designing and administering tests after completing instruction to designing assessment tasks before we develop the instructional plan. We have shifted from having students "guess what will be on the test" to making criteria for success and assessment of learning public, precise, and understood by students prior to instruction. While in the past tests had been something done to students, we now see the need to make students partners in the assessment process by developing criteria with students, student self-assessment, student error analysis, student use of feedback, and student goal setting. We have shifted from an "every teacher for himself" orientation to conviction about the importance of common interim schoolwide assessments developed and used by all teachers who teach the same content. The primary purpose of classroom assessment is to increase student achievement rather than to simply measure it for reporting purposes.

Assessment that is designed to increase student achievement is crafted to accomplish three goals:

1. Motivate students to want to do better.
2. Give students useful information they can use to do better.
3. Inform teachers' reteaching plans so students can do better.

There are other reasons for doing assessment besides helping students learn more. And some of them are valid. Table 21.1 summarizes 12 purposes of assessment. In this chapter, we focus on numbers 3 through 7: assessment as a vehicle for increasing student achievement. This means focusing on classroom assessment as done by teachers on a daily and weekly basis. Thus we begin with the question, What is it that a teacher needs to know about classroom assessment?

The foundation for productive classroom assessment is teachers of the same content agreeing on the most important learning standards for the course or semester (Reeves, 2004). This is the starting point for a chain of events that leads to good assessment. Without it, students don't receive cohesive schooling because what they learn will depend on their teachers' idiosyncratic choices. The logical next step among these same colleagues is to develop common interim assessments that can be used to measure student progress and make instructional adjustments.

Many of our colleagues who have had experience with this in the field, among them Rick DuFour at Adlai Stevenson High School in Illinois and Jamey Verrilli and Paul Bambrick-Santoyo at North Star Academy in Newark, New Jersey, report that common assessments across teachers who teach the same content, given quarterly and schoolwide, are a powerful lever for elevating student achievement if teachers examine the students' responses closely and do error analysis to plan reteaching. How these meetings can be structured to maximum effect has been described thoroughly by Marshall (2006).

With long-term (course, semester, or yearly) learning goals established and quarterly assessments designed, we have laid the foundation to support ongoing and productive daily and weekly classroom assessment.

Table 21.1 Twelve Purposes of Assessment

1. To make summative statements about:	How well students have done overall in meeting course or unit objectives
2. To certify students as:	• Competent in a field of knowledge • Competent in a field of practice • Eligible for promotion
3. To signal clearly:	• Knowledge is important • The criteria and standards for quality work
4. To make instructional decisions about:	• Where to start students with instruction • Which skills are mastered • Which skills or subskills to reteach to which students
5. To give feedback to students about:	Students' strengths, weaknesses, and interests
6. To give feedback to teachers about:	• The effectiveness of instruction • The effectiveness of curriculum
7. To report progress to families and communities	Any or all of the above
8. To elevate the curriculum so as to provide meaningful, higher-level thinking tasks for all students	
9. To sort, rank, or compare students for:	• Honors and rewards • Admissions into programs with limited enrollment
10. To norm students or groups of students for:	• Comparative achievement in relation to national groups • Comparative achievement in relation to other populations
11. For placement in:	Courses, grades, or levels
12. To predict success in:	A course, school, or a job performance

TWELVE COMPONENTS OF GOOD CLASSROOM ASSESSMENT

Prior to planning assessment, of course, the teacher articulates lesson and unit objectives that are worth learning, shares with students what the objectives are and why they are worth learning, and clarifies them daily for students in a form comparable with statements such as, "You (students) will demonstrate that you are able to . . . by . . . ." This gives students something to aim for and the teachers a footing for evaluating their learning experiences. These actions set the stage for assessment planning and implementation.

Exhibit 21.1 Twelve Components of Classroom Assessment

1. Determine the assessment task
2. Communicate the standards of performance
3. Assess prior knowledge
4. Frequent data collection and record-keeping by the teacher
5. Frequent high-quality feedback to students
6. Student self-assessment
7. Student record-keeping about progress
8. Frequent error analysis by the teacher
9. Error analysis by the students
10. Planning and implementing reteaching
11. Goal setting and action planning by students
12. Reporting systems on student progress including three-way conferences

To accomplish the three goals (to motivate students to want to do better, to provide them useful information and support so they can, and to inform teachers' reteaching plans), classroom assessment must be composed of multiple components carried out in a sequence by students and teachers. Twelve components of good classroom assessment are enumerated in Exhibit 21.1.

To begin with, all successful assessment requires a clear understanding by both teachers and students of the learning expectations behind it, the criteria for success, and the expected level or standard of performance. Components 1 and 2 address these concerns. Classroom assessment itself starts at component 3, and each of the remaining components brings students more closely into the game.

Putting It All Together

Figure 21.1 represents the ideal role of assessment in a 24-hour cycle of teaching and learning in any class. The cycle starts on the left with "Assessment and Teaching." The intent is to show that these two activities are not separate. A thorough teacher is always assessing and recording how students are doing with new learning (and doing so on the fly) while teaching. What does a teacher need to make all of these components happen? A commitment to do the following:

Figure 21.1 Cycle of Teaching and Learning

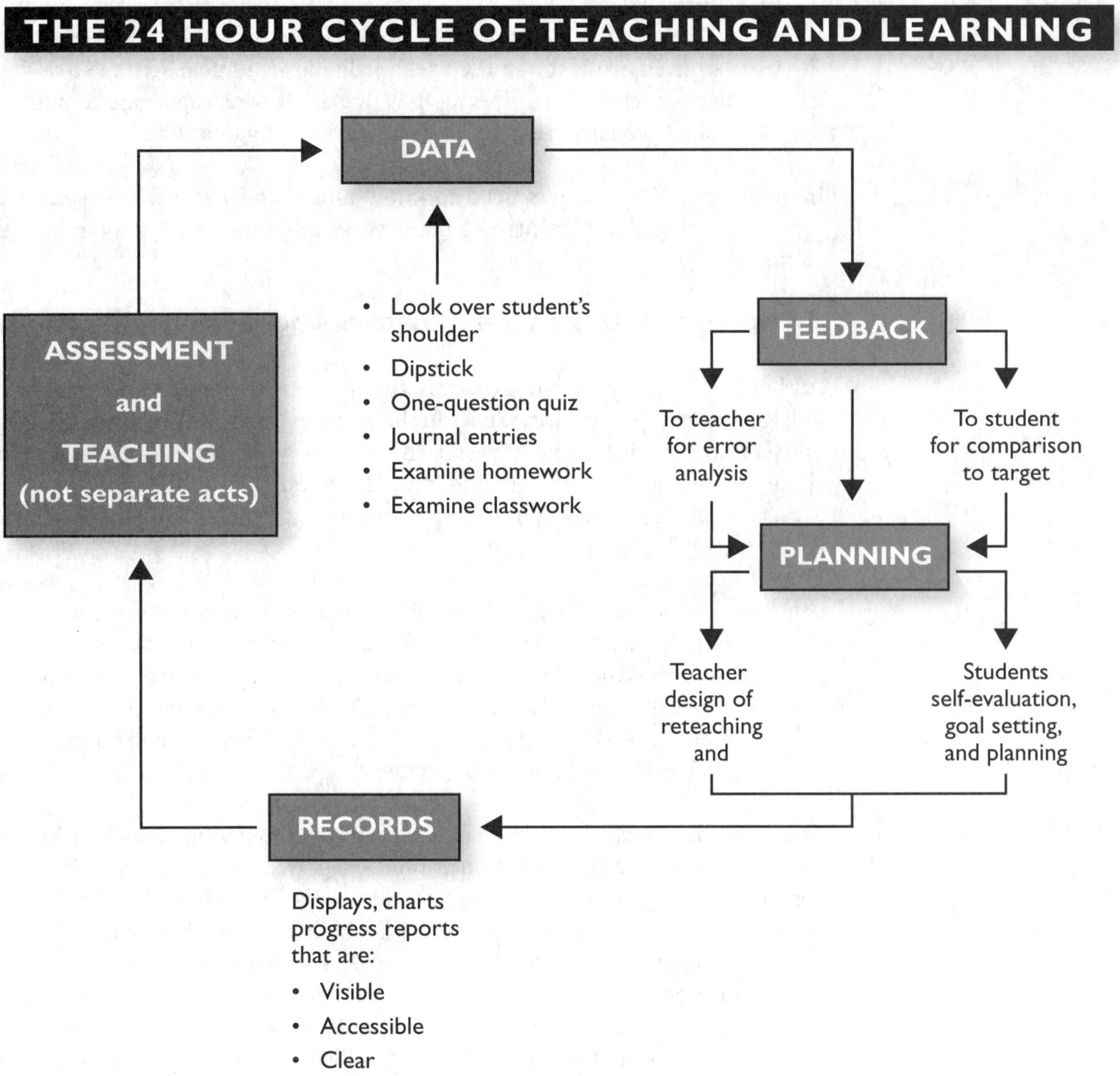

▲ Use assessment to inform teaching on a daily basis. This means teachers need to become expert at data analysis and, most particularly, item-level error analysis so as to design precise and timely reteaching for students who didn't "get it" the first time around.

- ▲ Use assessment to inform students on what they need to do to improve their own learning (i.e., feedback systems that generate daily, useful information).

- ▲ Create mechanisms for student self-evaluation and goal setting so assessment practices can promote positive emotional engagement, and "so students can experience winning streaks" (Stiggins, 2005).

In summary, what teachers need to know most is how to use assessment to inform teaching and learning on a daily basis and to use assessment as a motivation for students.

Component 1: Determine the Assessment Task

Authenticity is a key idea in the assessment movement because authentic tasks amalgamate complex performances in the same way real-life problems do. Wiggins (1993) says that authentic assessment "conveys the idea that assessments should engage students in applying knowledge and skills in the same way they are used in the 'real world' outside of school" (as cited in Marzano, Pickering, & McTighe, 1993, p. 13). He adds:

> Assessment is authentic when we directly examine student performances on worthy intellectual tasks . . . engaging and worthy problems or questions of importance, in which students must use knowledge to fashion performances effectively and creatively. The tasks are either replicas of or analogous to the kinds of problems faced by adult citizens and consumers or professionals in the field. (p. 229)

Thus a worthwhile assessment task has a student applying skills and knowledge in realistic, complex situations, and is integrated as closely as possible with something the student would have to do in the world outside school. What will be assessed will not be just subskills like the ability to decode words with short "a," balance chemical equations given valences and quantities, or the knowledge of facts or even comprehension of "the causes of the Civil War" as an isolated measurement. Rather, what will be assessed is the ability to perform complex tasks that require higher-order thinking skills and the integration of knowledge. In other words, tasks that are authentic because they are direct models or simulations of what people have to perform in the real world. In performing these complex tasks, of course, each of us must draw on our knowledge of subskills and facts, but they are put to use in service of a larger task that is realistic.

Jamentz (1993) offers the following criteria as a checklist for analyzing assessment tasks created for children:

- Does the task spark students' interest and motivation?
- Does the task require students to construct meaning?
- Does the task encourage demonstration of important habits of mind?
- Does the task encourage multiple modes of expression?
- Is the task free from arbitrary constraints?
- Does the task measure progress over time?
- Does the task require collaboration with others?
- Is the task a representative challenge, emphasizing depth rather than breadth of response?
- Does the task explore and identify hidden strengths?
- Does the task genuinely assess learning and effort rather than native talent?
- Do the standards for the task cover a wide range of knowledge, skills, and habits of mind considered important to the subject area or, if interdisciplinary, those that transcend a single discipline?
- Are the standards for good performance clear to students before they engage in the task?
- Are the standards for the task appropriately weighted?
- Are the standards for the task in harmony with shared school, district, state, or national goals?
- Does the task match the scoring framework?
- Is the task multidimensional, allowing for a single performance to be strong in some areas and weak in others?
- Is the assessment structured to provide prompt and useful feedback to the teacher and student?

- Does the task provide built-in opportunities for students to practice, rehearse, and retake it? (p. 29)

We think the first three characteristics on the list are particularly important. The anchor of the process for developing authentic assessments is getting clear on what we really want students to know or be able to do. Notice that the analytical criteria set out in "The Rubric in Exemplars" (see Exhibit 21.6) in the next section pertain to high-level thinking, problem-solving, and communication skills. This does not mean that lower-level skills like mastering calculation skills, times tables, and the like are disregarded, but the value (and thus the assessment) is clearly keyed to reasoning strategies the writers believe are important to using math in life. These choices of higher-level, problem-solving skills thus guide the kinds of tasks that will be created.

Generating authentic assessments of complex student performances is an important capacity for teachers to master.

Authentic assessment tasks are a far more valid measure of educational effectiveness than traditional paper and pencil assessment if we view education as the preparation of young minds for successful living. And they are more motivating to students. Teachers who design authentic assessments find it a creative process that benefits from a high level of interaction with peers and often with students, too. Once they have discussed what they want students to know or be able to do, teachers then cast around for (or create) tasks that conform to as many of the criteria as possible.

Having piloted the assessment tasks, a group of teachers developing rubrics typically sit down with a large collection of student products. They quickly sort the student work into four piles representing poor, fair, good, and excellent levels of performance by examining the products with little or no discussion or analysis, and grouping ones that seem at about the same level of performance. Placing a sample in a category is done by the sense of how the product strikes the teacher. Then comes the most important part of the process, which carries the most inherent staff development meat for teachers. Going over student work samples in detail, the teachers describe in writing the characteristics of each category and thus produce the first draft of their rubric.

It will be important to remember that as we leave the era of the No Child Left Behind legislation, developing higher-level thinking and problem-solving abilities is elevated in importance. Thus generating authentic assessments of complex student performances will remain an important capacity for teachers to master.

Component 2: Communicating the Standards of Performance

To give students a concrete image of what the words in the objective mean and what meeting standards looks like, students need to see, hear, and understand the standards (or criteria) by which their work will be assessed. Performance standards and criteria for success should be public, precise, prior, printed, and presented in models of exemplary work:

- "Public" means there are no secrets: students (and families) know exactly what will be the basis for evaluating the work.
- "Precise" means naming the qualities or characteristics that need to be present in their work and explaining or describing them in sufficient detail such that students understand what each means and can determine whether or not and where each characteristic is present in a given piece of work.
- "Prior" means sharing this information with students when the assessment task is described at the beginning of the class, course, or unit of study and before they begin to work toward achievement of an objective. This enables students to focus on what is important during the learning experiences and to participate in assessing whether they are building the foundations for success in the end.
- "Printed" means written down for students to refer to as they participate in learning experiences and invest effort in an assessment task.

What is written might be a simple bulleted list of what must be addressed in a lab report or characteristics of an effective oral presentation. For more complex assessment tasks that assess multiple objectives or will be practiced several to many times over, criteria might be communicated in a performance task list or a rubric. A performance task list (Exhibit 21.2) spells out the component parts of the task and assigns either a "yes" or "not yet" rating scale or a certain number of overall points that each component is worth, indicating the relative importance of each component to the final piece of work. A rubric (Table 21.2) specifies, in matrix form, the qualities or components on which a piece of work will be assessed and the specific indicators of proficiency—novice, practitioner, expert, or below standards, meets standards, exceeds standards—that might be demonstrated in each component of the work. As is true of most everything else in teaching, these options represent a repertoire of ways for representing criteria, from simple to more complex, and the option we choose for individual tasks is a matter of matching the complexity of the format to the nature and

Exhibit 21.2 Formats for Communicating Criteria for Success: Bulleted List and Performance Task List

BULLETED LIST: Summarizing a Historical Conflict

Your summary should include three paragraphs, each of which:

- *Begins with a claim:* names an event that was a contributing cause to the conflict and names the parties involved and time frame of the event.
- *Is supported by evidence: contains* 2-3 sentences explaining how/why that event was a contributing factor.
- *Concludes with an impact statement that is clearly connected to the conflict:* As a result . . .

PERFORMANCE TASK LIST: Delivering a Speech

Speaker ____________ Date ____________
Topic ____________ Run time ____________

PREPARATION/STRUCTURE	Possible Points	Self	Teacher
• Engaging, inspirational topic	______	______	______
• Gained attention and interest	______	______	______
• Clear introduction of central idea	______	______	______
• Indication of subject's value	______	______	______
• Logical outline/order	______	______	______
• Vivid, distinct main points	______	______	______
• Sufficient support material	______	______	______
• Well-structured conclusion	______	______	______
DELIVERY AND STYLE			
• Voice quality: clarity and audibility	______	______	______
• Rate of speech	______	______	______
• Use of eye contact	______	______	______
• Use of gestures	______	______	______
• Relaxation, confidence	______	______	______
• Sincerity, investment	______	______	______
• Use of visual aids	______	______	______
OVERALL			
• Held audience interest	______	______	______

Adapted and reprinted with permission from Gerry Speca, April 2007.

Table 21.2 General Science Lab Rubric

	4	3	2	1
FORMAT				
Title page	Contains title, name, date, course, period, teacher.	Has title and name. Missing one other.	Has title and name. Missing two others.	Missing title, name or more than two others.
Sequence	Logically sequenced: question, hypothesis, test, material, procedures, data, analysis/conclusion. All are present.	Only one category missing or out of sequence.	Two categories missing or out of sequence.	More than two categories missing or out of sequence.
REPRODUCIBILITY				
Hypothesis	Clear explanation of purpose; provides context.	Gives correct purpose with some framework.	Declares purpose that is correct.	Purpose is incorrect.
Design	Clear step-by-step description of experimental procedures; labeled diagrams/drawings of devices used in experiment.	A step-by-step description missing one key detail; diagrams/drawings included not labeled.	Step-by-step description missing not more than two key details; devices used are mentioned but not shown.	Description lacks more than two key details; not mention of devices used to carry out experiment.
ACCURACY				
Units	Units are used correctly and consistently throughout the report.	Units generally used correctly in most of report.	Units used only in parts of report.	Units rarely used or generally incorrect.
Data Manipulation	Calculations are clearly laid out. Math correct. Figures display data correctly; all variables labeled.	Few calculation errors. Figures correct; variables unlabeled.	Calculations contain errors. Figures correct; no labels or legend.	Math not shown. Figures display data incorrectly.
CONCLUSION				
Framework	Restates hypothesis, supports or refutes it and explains role of test in making decision.	Restates hypothesis and supports or refutes it.	Supports or refutes hypothesis without restating it.	Does not address hypothesis.
Evidence	Uses data powerfully as evidence.	Uses data to support statements.	Refers to data in the body of the report as support.	Does not use data to support arguments.
Logic	Conclusion logically follows from data.	Conclusion is logical but not thoroughly defended.	Conclusion is logical but poorly defended.	Conclusion is incorrect.
Context	Discusses scientific implications of experiment.	Cites a use for the work. Makes proposals for further investigations.	Describes work as useful but supplies no supporting evidence.	Provides no statement about relevance.

Adapted from Access Excellence at The National Health Museum, 2007.

complexity of the task. A more detailed discussion of how to design rubrics appears later in this chapter.

"Presented in models of work" means that students see concrete models (pieces of work) that exemplify the standard of performance and criteria for success they are expected to achieve. These models—commonly referred to as exemplars—should be accompanied by a concrete explanation of how and why the exemplar meets the standards: "You should be able to do one that has these qualities!" The qualities are named specifically and pointed out in the exemplar. Or once standards and criteria have been identified, students examine sample pieces of work and participate in identifying where, and if, those qualities appear. If exemplars are unavailable, criteria must either be presented and explained to students with a check for understanding or the students must help to generate criteria for proficient work with the particular assignment.

This same thinking applies to communicating images of good work for units of study, major projects, and year-long goals. At the macro level, students and families might be given sample products that represent benchmarks of progress for a whole year in, say, reading and writing. Three samples that the Mather Elementary School in Boston uses to communicate standards for good work by the end of particular grade levels are shown in Exhibit 21.3. When standards and criteria are public, precise, prior, printed, and presented in models of good work, we are offering students a comprehensive package to support them in focusing their effort effectively.

Video: Co-Creating Criteria for Success

The Relation of Rubrics to Exemplars and Criteria

Rubric, or scoring rubric, is the name given to the most detailed and comprehensive tool used to communicate criteria for success. Note that it is the criteria that are the central feature. Rubrics are communication devices for criteria. They break out different levels of quality to which the criteria have been met by student performance. They replace grades with specific information about a student performance. Usually in matrix form, a rubric identifies categories that define and describe the important components of the work to be produced. In a well designed rubric, each component is accompanied by a progression of quality indicators (usually four) that contain precise descriptions of what levels of performance need to be met to demonstrate levels of proficiency (novice to expert) within that component. Exhibit 21.4 shows an example of a rubric for scoring an essay.

The qualities to be assessed—that is, the components of a good essay—are organization, sentence structure, usage, mechanics, and format. Each is written down the left-hand side of the matrix. Each quality (component) has three paragraphs spelling out three different levels of performance. In between are two blank spots for

Exhibit 21.3 Sample Exemplars for Communicating Standards

Writing - The material below is what an average kindergartener should be able to write by the end of the year

Reading and listening - The passage below, from *In a Dark Dark Wood-* by June Meiser and Joy Cowley, is the level that a student at the completion of kindergarten should be able to listen to with good comprehension. Other books that kindergarteners should be able to understand include: *Caps for Sale, Farmer in the Dell, Blueberries for Sal, If You Made a Million, Stone Soup, The Hungry Crocodile,* and *Why Mosquitoes Buzz in People's Ears*:

In a dark dark wood, there was a dark dark path. And up that dark dark path, there was a dark dark house. And in that dark dark house, there was a dark dark stair. And up that dark dark stair, there was a dark dark room. And in that dark dark room, there was a dark dark cupboard. And in that dark dark cupboard, there was a dark dark box. And in that dark dark box there was a ghost!

Source: Reprinted with permission. Excerpted from Curriculum Exemplars for Writing and Reading. Mather Elementary School, Boston, Massachusetts, 1994.

Exhibit 21.3 Sample Exemplars for Communicating Standards (continued)

Writing - The piece below is the level expected of an average student at the completion of the second grade.

My Pet by Cathal Doherty
I have pet parrot. His name is Tweety. I like to chase him around. It is grey and white. It talks funny and it tickles you. We play together. It is fun to have a pet.

Reading - The passage below, taken from *City Mouse and Country Mouse* by Aesop is the level that a student at the completion of second grade should be able to read with accuracy, fluency, and comprehension. Other books that second graders should be able to read include: *Amelia Bedelia, Angel Child, Dragon Child, Blueberries for Sal, If You Made a Million, Stone Soup, The Hungry Crocodile,* and *Why Mosquitoes Buzz in People's Ears*

The rugs were beautiful bright colors. In each room were beautiful chairs and tables and lights. Best of all was the kitchen. Country Mouse ran up and down everywhere. Everything in the kitchen was shining and bright. There, right in front of his eyes, was a mountain of food.

Exhibit 21.3 Sample Exemplars for Communicating Standards (continued)

Writing - The piece below is the level expected of an average student at the completion of the fifth grade.

The Wolverine

I wake up screaming. Pain in my head so intense I can't put a name to it, can't fight it, can't run away from it. I don't even know where I am. I'm in some kind of cave? Images flash through my brain. Memories, a jungle, a girl, then a fight that I thought I won. I was wrong. Still fighting with my brain the pain unbearable like a million white hot needles digging into my skull. I'm beyond reason, beyond hope when that happens I turn animal.

The animal in me fights back pushing back at the needles. The strain takes its toll. I feel the darkness closing in. I thought I was dead only I'm not. I hear voices shouting then the lights come on! What I see in the mirror can't be real, but my senses tell me it is. I feel hard-packed dirt at my feet and sweat sliding down my back. I hear the buzzing of insects and crackling of fire. I see a beast out of hell, eyes blazing with arms like tree trunks. I still think I'm dreaming then reality sinks in. Boom! Aagh! I'm a wolverine.

Reading - The passage below, taken from *Island of the Blue Dolphins* by Scott O'Dell, is the level that a student at the completion of fifth grade should be able to read with accuracy, fluency, and comprehension. Other books that fifth graders should be able to read include: *Bridge to Terabithia, Roll of Thunder, Hear My Cry, Sarah, Plain and Tall, Stone Fox, Vampire Bat Girls' Club, Witch of Banneker School, Shiloh,* and *The Land I Lost.*

A short distance beyond the dune, near the cliff, I saw the pack of wild dogs. There were many of them and they were moving around in a circle.

In the middle of the circle was Ramo. He was lying on his back, and had a deep wound in his throat. He lay very still.

When I picked him up I knew that he was dead. There were other wounds on his body from the teeth of the wild dogs. He had been dead a long time and from his footsteps on the earth I could see that he had never reached the cliff.

Two dogs lay on the ground not far from him, and in the side of one of them was his broken spear.

I carried Ramo back to the village, reaching it when the sun was far down. The dogs followed me all the way, but when I had laid his down in the hut, and came out with a club in my hand, they trotted off to a low hill. A big gray dog with long curling hair and yellow eyes was their leader an he went last.

It was growing dark, but I followed them up the hill. Slowly they retreated in front of me, not making a sound. I followed them across two hills an a small valley to a third hill whose face was a ledge of rock. At one end of the ledge was a cave. One by one the dogs went into it.

scoring a student's work if it seems to fall between two descriptions. This arrangement yields a five-point scale for each quality. Notice also that some components are weighted more than others: organization is six times as important as format.

Exhibit 21.4 Rubric for Scoring an Essay

	1	2	3	4	5	6
Organization	Little or nothing is written. The essay is disorganized, incoherent, and poorly developed. The essay does not stay on topic.		The essay is not complete. It lacks an introduction, well-developed body, or conclusion. The coherence and sequence are attempted, but not adequate.		The essay is well organized. It contains an introductory, supporting, and concluding paragraph. The essay is coherent, ordered logically, and fully developed.	X6
Sentence Structure	The student writes frequent run-ons or fragments.		The student makes occasional errors in sentence structure. Little variety in sentence length or structure exists.		The sentences are complete and varied in length and structure.	X5
Usage	The student makes frequent errors in word choice and agreement.		The student makes occasional errors in word choice and agreement.		The usage is correct. The word choice is appropriate.	X4
Mechanics	The student makes frequent errors in spelling, punctuation, and capitalization.		The student makes occasional errors in spelling, punctuation, and capitalization.		The spelling, capitalization, and punctuation are correct.	X4
Format	The format is sloppy. There are no margins or indentations. Handwriting is inconsistent.		The handwriting, margins, and indentation have occasional inconsistencies–no title or inappropriate title.		The format is correct. The title is appropriate. The handwriting, margins, and indentations are consistent.	X1

Note: The numbers in the right column indicate the weighting scheme.
Adapted from Archbald, D., and Newmann, F. M. Beyond Standardized Tests: Assessing Authentic Academic Achievement in Secondary School. Reston, Va.: National Association of Secondary School Principals, 1988, p. 11. For more information on NASSP products and services to promote excellence in middle level and high school leadership, visit www.principals.org.

After examining this matrix, students and families know what the teacher is looking for and what the standards for good work are. And they will know even better if a sample of a well-done essay is provided with notes pointing out how and where each quality is manifested. There are many print and internet resources available today for collecting sample rubrics to assess a wide range of products, performances, content, and skill areas. As is true of all available resources, we have to be judicious, informed consumers and select the best or fine-tune those that don't quite measure up. In other words, we need to look for exemplars of good rubrics. So what would we look for in selecting a rubric or what would we strive for in designing our own? Here are some guidelines we have found to be useful.

The best instructional rubrics accomplish the following:

- ▲ Address all relevant content and performance objectives.
- ▲ Address different skills as separate criteria and assess them independently of one another.
- ▲ Include gradations of quality (novice to expert) within each criterion.
- ▲ Describe each gradation in specific detail, thus making obvious what differentiates one level from another.
- ▲ Fit on one piece of paper.
- ▲ Are easy to understand and use by both teacher and student.
- ▲ Are accompanied by examples of student work that exemplify the levels described in the rubric.
- ▲ Are always a work in progress.

Rubrics can be used as formative or summative assessment tools. When used as formative tools, rubrics enable students to self-assess and receive feedback on which level of proficiency is demonstrated in their work within each criterion in the moment. The feedback and the quality indicators can be used by students to determine where to invest their effort in improving the work and achieving higher levels of quality or proficiency. A rubric used in this way becomes a feedback mechanism that provides guidance about how to incrementally improve performance. Used as summative tools, rubrics clearly define the target for students and provide them with specific feedback on why they achieved a

Exhibit 21.5 Rubric for a Cross-Curricular Sixth Grade Exhibition

GOAL

Student will communicate accumulated knowledge through creative and analytical writing.

EXHIBITION

Using class notes, individual research, literature, and information from audio-visual presentations, students will write a letter to their family describing a trip to an assigned culture by including information on the following aspects of this culture:

- Art, architecture, literature
- Government
- Inventions and technology
- Social, economic, and political systems
- The daily lives of the common people
- Religion and ethical beliefs
- Importance of geography in the development of this culture
- Why this culture fell or declined

EXPECTATION

Guidelines:

- Correct grammar, spelling, capitalization, and punctuation must be used.
- Letter will be written in class.
- Final copy of the letter will be typed on school computer word processing program.
- Student will use appropriate note-taking skills and be able to organize ideas in proper outline format.
- Student is able to research notes to communicate knowledge creatively, establishing tone, point of view, and setting.

Model: Student letter is attached.

Adapted from Penny Knox, Oak Creek Elementary School, Irvine, California.

particular score or grade on a piece of work. If they should do that type of work again, the feedback on the rubric can serve as a resource for goal setting on the next piece of work.

Exhibit 21.5 is an example, developed by Penny Knox at Oak Creek Elementary School in Irvine, California, of a cross-curricular sixth grade exhibition and the rubric that accompanies the project. In this case, the teacher and students use the rubric for both formative and summative assessment purposes. The project gets scored four times on each criterion. Three times are labeled "Practice Date" (formative assessment) and the final (summative) assessment is simply called "Exhibition." This reflects a design in which students produce the final product (write the letter) three times and get detailed feedback each time on the quality of their work. The teacher can use the data to determine where reteaching needs to occur for some or all of the students. And the students can use the feedback to focus their effort on improving specific skills or in developing more background knowledge prior to the final exhibition. In this school, the children take the product home for one of the practice trials and work with their families to apply the scoring rubric to the child's product. This is a particularly effective way to inform and involve families in the education of their children.

Exemplars

The complement to a good rubric is a set of samples of actual student work that exemplify the different cells of the rubric, accompanied by explanations of why each sample exemplifies the level of quality claimed for it. Exhibit 21.6 is a rubric found on www.Exemplars.com, a website that publishes collections of benchmark mathematical tasks, designed by K–12 teachers, with actual student work produced for each task. A benchmark task is one that calls for students to display a variety of competencies thought to be important. Such tasks aren't given every day but are saved for assessing student progress at certain key junctures. The rubric is used to score student products as Novice, Apprentice, Practitioner, and Expert. An accompanying narrative explains how and why the samples exemplify one of the four levels of the rubric.

Video: Creating Criteria for Successful Exemplars

Exhibit 21.6 *The Rubric in Exemplars*

Levels	Problem-Solving	Reasoning and Proof	Communication	Connections	Representation
Novice	No strategy is chosen, or a strategy is chosen that will not lead to a solution. Little or no evidence of engagement in the task is present.	Arguments are made with no mathematical basis. No correct reasoning nor justification for reasoning is present.	No awareness of audience or purpose is communicated. Little or no communication of an approach is evident. Everyday, familiar language is used to communicate ideas.	No connections are made.	No attempt is made to construct mathematical representations.
Apprentice	A partially correct strategy is chosen, or a correct strategy for only solving part of the task is chosen. Evidence of drawing on some relevant previous knowledge is present, showing some relevant engagement in the task.	Arguments are made with some mathematical basis. Some correct reasoning or justification for reasoning is present with trial and error, or unsystematic trying of several cases.	Some awareness of audience or purpose is communicated, and may take place in the form of paraphrasing of the task. Some communication of an approach is evident through verbal/written accounts and explanations, use of diagrams or objects, writing, and using mathematical symbols. Some formal math language is used, and examples are provided to communicate ideas.	Some attempt to relate the task to other subjects or to own interests and experiences is made.	An attempt is made to construct mathematical representations to record and communicate problem-solving.

Source: Reprinted with permission. www.Exemplars.com.

Exhibit 21.6 The Rubric in Exemplars (continued)

Levels	Problem-Solving	Reasoning and Proof	Communication	Connections	Representation
Practitioner Note: The practitioner must achieve a correct answer.	A correct strategy is chosen based on the mathematical situation in the task. Planning or monitoring of strategy is evident. Evidence of solidifying prior knowledge and applying it to the problem-solving situation is present.	Arguments are constructed with adequate mathematical basis. A systematic approach and/or justification of correct reasoning is present. This may lead to: 1. Clarification of the task. 2. Exploration of mathematical phenomenon. 3. Noting patterns, structures and regularities.	A sense of audience or purpose is communicated. Communication of an approach is evident through a methodical, organized, coherent, sequenced, and labeled response. Formal math language is used throughout the solution to share and clarify ideas.	Mathematical connections or observations are recognized.	Appropriate and accurate mathematical representations are constructed and refined to solve problems or portray solutions.
Expert Note: The practitioner must achieve a correct answer.	An efficient strategy is chosen and progress toward a solution is evaluated. Adjustments in strategy, if necessary, are made along the way, and/or alternative strategies are considered. Evidence of analyzing the situation in mathematical terms, and extending prior knowledge is present.	Deductive arguments are used to justify decisions and may result in more formal proofs. Evidence is used to justify and support decisions made and conclusions reached. This may lead to: 1. Testing and accepting or rejecting of a hypothesis or conjecture. 2. Explanation of phenomenon. 3. Generalizing and extending the solution to other cases.	A sense of audience and purpose is communicated. Communication at the practitioner level is achieved, and communication of arguments is supported by mathematical properties used. Precise math language and symbolic notation are used to consolidate math thinking and to communicate ideas.	Mathematical connections or observations are used to extend the solution.	Abstract or symbolic mathematical representations are constructed to analyze relationships, extend thinking, and clarify or interpret phenomenon.

Behind all the mathematical tasks in the Exemplars collection are analytical criteria for good performance: problem-solving, reasoning and proof, communication, connections and representation. These criteria serve as guidelines for creating good tasks as well as for scoring student work on the tasks.

A fine set of samples in different academic areas compiled by Exemplars (www.exemplars.com) is available on *The Skillful Teacher* website at www.RBTeach.com/TST7. These samples show the kind of thoughtful analysis it takes to apply a rubric properly. Though these samples are for mathematics content, similar collections can be assembled for any discipline and any skill or concept within the discipline. Making those collections of exemplars is, in fact, exactly what we are advocating that teams of teachers do.

Establishing Scoring Reliability

The last step in constructing good rubrics is establishing reliability across teachers in scoring student work samples. Reliability means that the rubrics are sufficiently clear and the teachers are sufficiently in agreement about the meaning of the levels of performance that different teachers would score a given work sample in the same way. This high level of reliability is established when teachers practice scoring students' work samples together, compare results, reconcile differences through discussion, and continue to practice until they are "reliable" in their scoring or until they have fine-tuned the language in the rubric to ensure common interpretation of criteria. One writer notes that

> The conversation about standards inevitably stumbles over the degree to which standards should be explicitly stated. Is it enough to say student work should demonstrate "attention to detail"? Or should we describe the type and amount of detail we expect? There is little doubt that the latter provides students and teachers better guidance for planning teaching and learning, but capturing and agreeing on the former can be a significant step. (Jamentz, 1993, p. 38)

If teachers take the time to work through to consensus on what the items in a rubric really mean and come up with exemplars of each level of performance, they can be clear with students about intended learnings. Even better, they can produce more precisely designed learning experiences whose activities are more likely to enable students to learn what they want. To summarize, the sequence for developing a rubric goes like this:

1. Establish criteria for success.

2. Identify and spell out levels of performance.

3. Construct authentic tasks.

4. Select and display exemplars.

5. Establish reliability across teachers in scoring student work.

Well-designed rubrics and clear criteria in advance are essential for communicating the three messages of expectations: "This is important. You can do it. I won't give up on you." Without clear criteria for comparing student work, there is no way to make feedback full and informative enough for low-performing students. And without adults who take the time to give this full feedback, along with help to use it, students too easily can conclude they are incapable. It is not fair to students who do not have a clear image of what quality looks like to ask them to guess. They certainly won't figure it out from being told repetitively that they are not making the grade.

Without clear criteria for comparing student work, there is no way to make feedback full and informative enough for low-performing students.

Collaborative planning time for groups of teachers is required for the process we have described. In fact, what we are really trying to do is develop a professional culture in which teacher analysis of student work is expected and valued (California Assessment Collaborative, in Jamentz, 1993). Principals and department chairs play a key role in communicating that message through what they say, model, and facilitate through scheduling, use of meeting time, and the resources they make available to teachers for this work of building rubrics. The administrator as a "school culture builder" (Saphier & King, 1985) plays a crucial role in the development of authentic assessments and in building the capacity of teachers to use the assessment process to improve instruction.

Involving Students in Establishing Standards

Students can play a big part in developing criteria for the products they are about to create and, in the process, become clear about the goals and be motivated to meet them. Involving students in the process of identifying important standards of performance can eliminate the student complaint that got Chris Gustafson (1994) started on her assessment project. A student said to her after class one day, "I don't understand why I got this grade." Chris decided to get her students involved in defining standards at the beginning of a unit on immigration:

> I handed out a list of topics and asked the students to select one. The next day students who had chosen the same project formed groups that would write a grading standard by which their projects would be evaluated. I explained that a project completed as described on the project sheet [which she had provided] would receive a C. Each group was to

> decide what they would need to add to my criteria in order to receive a B or an A. As an example, we set a grading standard together for a writing project. That gave me a chance to discourage responses that were too ambitious: everyone's journal did not have to be typed, but more than a half page of writing on each sheet would be required, and so on.
>
> After writing the journal grading standard as a class, each group decided what [their particular] projects would have to include to receive a B or an A. I took all their suggestions and typed one grading standard for each project. The next day, I handed each person his or her group's grading standard sheet. Now, before students even began the project, they knew how it would be evaluated.
>
> This time, when I took the projects home, each one had a grading standard attached to it. And what a difference that made: because my students didn't have to guess what to do to get a high grade, they were more successful; our high standards resulted in better projects; and although I still made comments, evaluation was easier. Parents could also see exactly how the evaluations had been done. The process was open to all, and the students had had a part in creating it. (Gustafson, 1994, p. 22–23)

Component 3: Assessing Current Knowledge Before Instruction

Prior to introducing a new skill, topic, or concept, some type of pre-assessment can yield data about where students are in relation to where we want them to be. A ninth-grade life science teacher uses an Anticipation Guide containing true/false statements about photosynthesis (including some commonly held misconceptions) to determine what students believe to be true based on prior experience. A third-grade teacher asks students to write "the number that represents three thousand and forty-two" and to label what each digit stands for, and uses several more examples like this to gather data about student understanding of place value. An art teacher asks students to draw a picture that includes some objects in the foreground, on the horizon, and off in the distance to assess students' level of understanding and skill with perspective drawing. What is common to all three of these is that they happen prior to instruction and are used as data sources to inform how the topic will be introduced and pursued and to determine the need to differentiate some aspects of instruction or form flexible skill groups along the way. Assessing prior knowledge gives us essential information about what background knowledge to teach, to whom, and how long to spend on it so that our students can learn the intended curriculum. And as the above examples show, it doesn't have to take much time.

Component 4: Frequent Data Collection and Teacher Record-Keeping

Once instruction is underway, there must be ongoing data collection to keep students on track and support them in investing their effort effectively. It is not enough to say, "I am always assessing my students" unless you have some daily data record that shows you actually did so. The data can come from looking over students' shoulders as they work: walking around with a class list while students are learning to use certain commands in a software application or solving one long division problem, checking off names of students who demonstrate mastery while making notes about types of errors that caused you to intervene and offer guidance. Data might come from listening to students read aloud one on one, or from asking a well-planned combination of recall and comprehension questions of many students during whole-class instruction to get information about which students not only recognize halves and quarters, but also know they always have to be comparing the same whole for fractional equivalents to be valid.

The main point about collecting assessment data is that it is ongoing and we must use the information to inform our teaching.

Certain kinds of data collection and error detection can happen very quickly using whiteboards and posing a series of examples with the same multiple-choice set of answers to ascertain understanding. You've just reviewed the spelling and uses of "their," "they're," and "there" and want to determine whether or not students got it. You project a sentence on the wall ["I want to be ________ in the morning."] and ask students to write the correct spelling on their whiteboards and show their response on the count of three. After a series of 10 or so examples, you have noted where there is still uncertainty and confusion and will use the data to decide what to review and with whom. Other sources of data about student mastery might come from analysis of products students have produced in a class or from written student responses to a one-question quiz: "Based on the discussion so far, what do you think were the most important causes of the Civil War?"

The main point about collecting assessment data is that it is ongoing and we must use the information to inform our teaching: to determine who "has it," who doesn't, where students are in relation to the objective, and what reteaching needs to occur with whom.

Record-Keeping

Records can take the form of checklists and profiles, logs, journals, and anecdotal records, or portfolios. What is important is that the form of the record be appropriate for the assessment methodology and a good fit for the content or skill being assessed.

Teachers who prefer checklists and profiles have traditionally used checklists in the elementary grades to track student skill acquisition, such as mastering multiplication tables, mechanical writing skills, or developmental levels of literacy. The checklist in Exhibit 21.7 represents a record-keeping device in which a check signals the student's developmental point on a particular behavior.

Checklists represent the idea that important academic behaviors develop over time and can be assessed along a continuum from emerging to fully developed. Although most developmental checklists are found in the areas of reading and writing, many districts have created them for other areas, including mathematics and science competencies. Checklists are useful components in assessment because they summarize in compact form a student's level of skill acquisition and allow teachers, students, and families to see on the same form the next target skill. Teachers who share these checklists with students must be careful not to overwhelm them. Certain children may interpret a sea of empty check boxes as a huge and unattainable roster of things to be learned and throw up their hands up in despair.

Checklists are useful components in assessment because they summarize in compact form a student's level of skill acquisition.

Logs, Journals, and Anecdotal Records of student performance are often best recorded in records of some sort that are easy to create, access, and interpret. These records may capture observations of anything from student social behavior to comments on their class participation or skill at interpreting books read. Hill and Ruptic (1994) describe systems that use triple ring binders, folders, file cards, computers, sticky notes, and mailing labels.

The more repetitive the comments become, the more a teacher may be inclined to move to a checklist. It is more efficient to write a behavior once and check off when a student can do it. The more individual or idiosyncratic the comments, however, the more useful an anecdotal record is. Exhibit 21.8 shows two sheets that allow individual, original entries. The record forms in Exhibit 21.9 are designed as checkoffs for skills displayed but still allow space for anecdotal comments.

Behind the choice of which record form to use must be clear teacher thinking about what is being assessed. The design of the recording instrument should meet the criteria of ease of use, clarity, accessibility, and appropriateness.

On another note, "data walls" have become popular as a form of teacher record-keeping that makes student results visible and public. In New York City, Kinnari Patel displays the current levels and recent changes in students' reading levels for all the students in grades K–3 on a board in the teachers' lounge (Figure 21.2). Across the top of the display, the big letters represent the reading level of the student's current book. Students' names are on sticky notes and are placed

Exhibit 21.7 Assessment Checklist

READING	***First Noticed***	***Developing***	***Independent***
(Motivational)			
• Expresses a desire to own or borrow books			
• Recommends books or stories to other people			
• Keeps a book close by to be read in spare moments			
• Chooses books at an independent reading level			
• Develops preferences for different genres and for specific authors and illustrators			
(Listening)			
• Listens for increasingly longer times to stories read aloud			
• Listens to stories without interrupting and takes turns in responding			
(Conventions of Print)			
• Understands more complex punctuation during story reading (e.g., quotation marks, period after abbreviation, and so on)			
• Continues to build on knowledge of sight words			

Exhibit 21.7 Assessment Checklist (continued)

(Linguistics)	***First Noticed***	***Developing***	***Independent***
• Uses all cuing systems in a balanced and integrated way when working out unknown words in a story (e.g., context, picture, and letter/sounds cues)			
• Self-corrects when reading			
• Uses a variety of strategies when in difficulty (e.g., reads on to the end of the sentence, starts sentence again [the rerun strategy], substitutes a word that makes sense for an unknown word and reads on, and so on)			
• Rereads for additional information, clarification, or pleasure			
• Reads familiar material aloud expressively to enhance meaning			

Adapted from The Cambridge Handbook of Documentation and Assessment: Child Portfolios and Teacher Records in the Primary Grades. Edited by Lynne Hall, Lynn Stuart, and Brenda Engel. University of North Dakota, Grand Forks, February 1995.

Exhibit 21.8 Two Examples of Anecdotal Records

ANECDOTAL RECORDS for Susan

12/17 Had to go home w/mom; crying right at 8:45 – called her to take her home – "big fight" Mom/Dad re work	12/18 Home again at 8:45 Back at 9:30 to "help do things for others" after calming down	1/4 Crying again during "Attendance" job... difficult goodbye w/Mo Stress connected w/ Dad's lay-off and holidays	1/7 Tearless, normal start Even Able to take redirects at writing (off task) calmly
1/11 Very helpful getting Tory caught up after long illness. Good teacher shows how t then does own work side-by-side ready to assist "student"	1/21 Having trouble finishing SACAJAWEA She can read it, but it is a real challenge and seems not to hold her interest. Rdg level/maturity level issue?	2/1 "I'm not sure I want to do these tubs again" Offered options: Latin cubes ★ Estimating! recording w/ >< = + chose this	2/2 Working on chapter book of her own autobiography – 4 chapters so far
2/12 Good compromising in problem solving activity w/ Theo, Trent and Alanna	3/1 Author's circle for her autobiography; planning to use comments/questions for revision		

Exhibit 21.8 Two Examples of Anecdotal Records (continued)

ANECDOTAL RECORDS for Cindy's Conference Group (teacher)

Alice	Brad	David	Dylan
1/19 Beginning to read more difficult (Nate the Great) chapter books competently w/minimal help. Hard work, but can do it!	1/11 Talked about getting off the video game words and stretching yourself. Me exasperated about his being stuck in the mire of copying w/Harry. Took it well—contrite, agreed w/me, made commitment to do more	1/15 Needing to go to the bathroom a lot. He also noticed this—said he would speak to his parents	1/15 Serious about taking responsibility for his own learning. Stayed in at recess to finish. Only took 5 minutes. Well done
Elizabeth	Harry	Jeri	Kathleen
1/12 Off the wall all AM! Popping up and down, interrupting, off task, noises and other sounds, repeated redirections necessary. Respectful behavior discussed	1/17 Writing story about "Baseball Diamond Mystery" w/Andy—Prominent swastika has it all over it and drawing of what looks like Hitler... nothing said yet, but watching this	1/8 W/Kleenex reading Annie Sullivan. "This is sad" "Do any more people die?" Talked about whether to continue—it's okay to cry/feel sad w/books	1/11 Finished "Kathleen" were her book. Nudged to correct the few misspelled words—1st time.
Lawrence	Mandy	Michael	Nancy
	1/12 Really pleased. First day to bring lunch packed at home rather than buying school lunch. "I made it myself!"	1/17 Making a book about fishing trip w/lift-up flaps showing fish + names of them	
Paul	Randy	Ricky	Susan
1/15 Went to Lawrence's on the bus, but Mom still came by at the end of the day... to check on him?	1/19 On time every day this week... maybe we've licked the tardiness problem?		1/11 Very helpful getting Tory caught up after long illness. Good "teacher", shows how to, then does own work side-by-side ready to assist "student"
Thomas	Tory	Vince	Zoey
			1/13 Shocked and wanted to share with me what she was reading about M L King Jr..

Exhibit 21.9 Two Examples of Check-Off Record Forms

Reading Conference Record

Student________________________

	Date: 12/8	Date: 12/17	Date:	Date:	Date:	Date:
	Title: Two Little Dogs (G)	Title: Sleeping Out (F)	Title:	Title:	Title:	Title:
Level Appropriate	Instructional Frustration ✓	Instructional Independent				
Strategies: Whole idea						
Picture clues	✓					
Pattern						
Sight Words	✓	✓				
First letter						
Decodes	✓	✓				
Context clues	✓	✓				
Skip /return						
Rereads	✓	✓				
Reads Fluently		✓				
With Inflection		✓				
Literal Comprehension	✓	+				
Interpretive Comprehension	✓	+				
Strategy Taught	contractions context	contractions speech marks				
Comments	door's = door is that's gate's won't = will not don't = do not isn't = is not I noticed you used context to self-correct over (after) the (they)	It's = it is what's = what is she's = she is Ways to show speech: word bubbles speech marks (quotation marks)				

CODES: + consistently
✓ sometimes

Source: Hill, B. C., & Ruptic, C. Practical Aspects of Authentic Assessment. Norwood, Mass.

Exhibit 21.9 Two Examples of Check-Off Record Forms (continued)

READING CONFERENCE RECORD

Name ______________________

Date and Title	Miscues & Comments book » said	Skills/Strategies Taught	Fluency	Comprehension Factual	Comprehension Inferred
10/19 The Witch's Christmas	with → witch wreath → w very → every	wr = r Look at pictures	✓	+	✓
10/21 The Enormous Egg	me → my s/c when → than →	what makes sense?	–	✓	✓
10/26 scary stories	many miscues Read to Demo Dan! picked book from library · proud	syllables -oi	–	✓	✓
11/2 The Return of the 3rd Grade Ghostbusters	enough check → jack discovered how he could "read" periods →	gh = ph context expression	+	+	✓

CODES: + = Very Good
✓ = Average
– = Needs Improvement

Figure 21.2 Data Wall

Source: Kinnari Patel, principal, Explore Charter School, Brooklyn, New York

in the column under their reading level. Thus, there is a big, visual display of the spread in each class and a way to compare the spread and levels between classes at the same grade level.

Whenever a student moves up a level, the teacher moves that student's sticky note and writes the previous level's letter and the date of move-up on the back of the note. Thus, at any time, an observer can turn over any student's sticky note and see how many levels he or she has moved through this year and on what date each move took place. This is a clear way of identifying which students are making progress and which are not.

When a teacher moves a student's sticky note, it leaves a gap in the column it came from. The gaps at the end of each day show the principal, Ms. Patel, where movement has occurred. She then moves up sticky notes to fill in any gaps in any column so that the next day if any gaps appear, she is informed visually that a child in a given class has moved up a level in reading. This form of recordkeeping enables different teachers of the same content and grade level to compare notes on how students are doing. It also provokes questions early on about why certain students are moving slowly or are stuck.

Component 5: Frequent High-Quality Feedback to Students

In chapter 14, "Expectations," we quoted Bellon, Bellon, and Blank (1991), "Academic feedback is more strongly and consistently related to achievement than any other teaching behavior. This relationship is consistent regardless of grade, socioeconomic status, race, or school setting" (p. 277). We think this robust finding, consistent over the 20 years since their statement (Hattie, 2012), has two parallel explanations:

The act of self-assessment should be an act of learning.

1. Good feedback gives students the precise cognitive information they need to improve performance.

2. The fact that a teacher takes the time and trouble to give useful feedback is inherently a message of caring and wanting the student to succeed. And the language a teacher uses while giving feedback can explicitly embed confidence in the student and encouragement as well. It sounds like this, "You took apart the first two hard word problems carefully and accurately. This one has one extra step. I bet if you go at it with that in mind, you'll see just what to do." Since feedback can play such a positive role in student motivation, we have chosen to put the detailed text and the how-tos of this vital teaching skill in Chapter 14, "Expectations."

The same logic could be applied to "Student Self-Assessment" and "Student Record-Keeping," the two sections that follow. We kept them in this chapter, however, in order to keep the 12-point framework about skillful and comprehensive assessment intact.

Component 6: Student Self-Assessment

The act of self-assessment should be an act of learning. Popham (2006) states, "There are enormous instructional payoffs in making students active, assessment informed partners in the learning process" (p. 14). This requires that students be continually self-assessing and reorienting their efforts as a result of examining their own work, feedback from peers, and feedback from teachers. And it has implications for both skills and dispositions we need to cultivate in students.

Videos: Peer Assessment 1, 2, & 3

Earlier in this chapter, we described some of the skills and conditions involved in being "assessment informed." Students must have a clear understanding of performance standards and criteria for good work and know how to apply those standards to work samples (their own or those created by others). They need to know how to analyze the nature and cause of their errors, search for clues on how to correct their errors, decide how to reorient their efforts, and chart a course of action (set goals). They need to receive specific and ongoing feedback and use the feedback to set goals. We need to teach students how to do error analysis and also the techniques of goal setting (see Chapter 12, "Principles of Learning," for more on goal setting).

If students are to be "active, assessment informed" partners, there are also dispositions we need to cultivate. Students need to understand and accept that when they first start to learn something, they're probably not very good at it. Stiggins (2005) says, ". . . while they're learning, it's got to be OK not to be good at it at first. We don't want the word 'failure' coming into play." We want students to see that errors are opportunities for learning, not confirmations of stupidity; that learning is a process—a steady accumulation of knowledge and skill over time—not an event; that achievement occurs along a continuum of incremental progress; that the continuum is not a scale of worthiness or smartness but rather it indicates where they are in the moment in relation to a goal they are working to achieve; that assessment tells them where they are in the journey and what they need to do next, not how good they are as students. We want students to develop an understanding that they aren't supposed to understand everything the first time around; that it is perseverance, quality, and care that lead to achievement; that they have plenty of ability to achieve the goals we set for them, but consistent effort and effective strategies are necessary ingredients that make the recipe for success; that good students solicit help and get lots of feedback on their work and use the feedback to improve their performance. Well beyond assessment, these represent beliefs that we consider to be life liberating because they reorient some counterproductive negative assumptions like mistakes are a sign of weakness, good students can do it by themselves, the faster you learn something the smarter you are, and only a few who are smart can achieve at high levels (see Chapter16, "Classroom Climate," for more on this topic).

Component 7: Student Record-Keeping About Progress

Beyond teaching students how to do error analysis and goal setting, another way to build student confidence and ownership of learning is through record-keeping and making their performance and progress visible, accessible, and clear to them. Rick Stiggins (2005) makes the point that properly done, this builds "positive emotional engagement" of students with academic work. "It feels good to succeed," says Stiggins. "When the human brain experiences success, it feels good and we're wired to want more. The trick is to take advantage of students' intrinsic love of self-improvement and give them a scaffold they can ascend, step by step." As part of a list of strategies for making assessment "a vehicle to deepen learning and to reveal to students their developing proficiencies . . . ," Stiggins and Chappuis (2005) recommend several practices that illustrate the way in which teaching students the processes of self-assessment simultaneously reinforces some of the above-mentioned dispositions:

> A teacher arranges items on a test according to specific learning targets and prepares a "test analysis" chart for students, with three boxes: "my strengths," "quick review," and "further study." After handing back the corrected test, students identify learning targets they have mastered and write them in the "my strengths" box. Next, students categorize their wrong answers as either "simple mistakes" or "further study." Then stu-

> dents list the simple mistakes in the "quick review" box. Last, students write the rest of the learning targets represented by wrong answers in the "further study" box.
>
> Students review a collection of their work over time and reflect on their growth. "I have become a better reader this quarter. I used to . . . but now I . . ."
>
> Students use a collection of their self-assessments to summarize their learning and set goals for future learning: "Here is what I have learned . . . Here is what I need to work on . . ." (p. 15)

Linda Hunt, teacher at Bonny Eagle High School in Standish, Maine, made visible records of student progress, error analysis, reteaching, and goal setting all an integral part of her everyday work with students. She tracks class progress on a test-retest cycle. While individual student scores are not identifiable in the public chart, the number of students scoring at each level is. Linda uses the charts to identify and plan with students what concepts are tripping them up and involves the students in planning where and how reteaching needs to take place. Reteaching (often using peers) and test retakes are normative practices in her class; retakes occur only after reteaching and the highest grade a student gets on a retake replaces any lower grade on the same material. When it comes to self-assessment, the important thing is that she starts with posting the data and having students participate in analyzing trouble spots and identifying focus areas for reteaching.

Linda displays the results of tests and retests on a leaf and branch chart. The top scoring students do not elect to retake the test. Their scores, if added to a second chart, would put almost all the scores in the top three ranks. All but one of the bottom range scores from the first test have been dramatically improved. Another chart shows an item analysis of the questions on the first test and enumerates how many students missed that item. The class has used this chart to identify concepts they want retaught and to set individual goals.

A third chart records possible actions students are going to take individually. In their personal notebooks, they pick a strategy to pursue and make a commitment to it. So in Ms. Hunt's self-assessment mechanisms, we see the juncture of two arenas from Chapter 14, "Expectations": "Retakes and Redos" and "Grading Practices" with the public display of student data on tests, both for the positive purpose of student motivation. In this class, effective effort is rewarded, and the assessment practices are used to do so.

At this point, we return to our beginning premise in Figure 21.1: teaching, assessment, and learning are intricately intertwined; "a good assessment makes a good teaching activity, and a good teaching activity makes a good assessment" (Shavelson, Baxter, & Pine, 1992, p. 22); and high-quality assessment for learning is an ongoing cycle that involves teachers and students working as partners in the processes of ongoing data collection, feedback, and error analysis.

Component 8: Frequent Error Analysis by the Teacher

Our most powerful reteaching begins when we analyze the errors of those students who did not show mastery and design reteaching based on understanding the student thinking that led to the error. There are five key questions to ask when doing error analysis. They are worded here for a team of teachers who are analyzing errors together, though they could just as easily be used by an individual teacher.

1. What might the students have been thinking to make this error?
2. How can we find out which of our hypotheses is right?
3. What different reteaching strategies could we use to fix this?
4. How will we plan and manage tasks and time in the period to get fifteen minutes for reteaching a few times a week?
5. How can the team help?

What follows is an excerpt from a "think aloud" error analysis session between a pair of colleagues looking at the test item in Exhibit 21.10 and the data on how 99 students responded to this item. Thirty-nine students had the correct answer (B) and 60 didn't. The numerical tally was generated by Kim Marshall, at the time the principal of the Mather Elementary School in Boston.

> **Teacher A:** "Twenty-seven students incorrectly chose answer C. What might they have been thinking to pick that one?"
>
> **Teacher B:** "Perhaps they did not know that they need to zero a linear object on a ruler when measuring its length. That is quite common in elementary children. And rulers don't help, since many rulers place the first hash marks for measuring one quarter inch inward from the physical edge of the ruler."

Teacher C: "So maybe the problem is the children don't know they have to put the beginning of the object at the exact zero point on the ruler and that zero point might not be the physical left-end point of the ruler."

Teacher A: "Or maybe they were just careless and didn't look carefully enough to notice that the truck in the picture was placed at 3 inches instead of 0."

Teacher C: "Or maybe some children are making a mixture of both these two errors."

Teacher A: "So for reteaching we will need to think about what fixit strategies we could use for tomorrow . . ."

Teacher B: "And they should be quite different depending on which error the student was making."

Teacher A: "Let's work out what to do for the children who don't know or don't remember to zero the object on the ruler. We could make up some pretend rulers on oak tag where the first hash mark was at different distances in from the edge. We could cue the kids that they had to zero the object (say we will have different size blocks for them to measure) and tell them that it won't be easy to do because these are 'trick' rulers."

Teacher B: "We could say you have to measure each object with a different one of the trick rulers and have the kids pass the rulers and the objects around the circle."

Teacher A: "Maybe put kids in groups of five . . . "

The scenario continues while these teachers analyze the thinking of children who answered C and D. (D is the "best" error. Can you tell why?) And the conversation moves to how to gather data about who made which types of error and how to manage the reteaching. This think-aloud could also be a teacher looking at her own data and thinking by herself. But imagine the power if teachers had regular collaborative opportunities with dialogue like this to examine data and plan how to reteach a concept! Prior to reteaching, the teacher (or the team of teachers) will do a little data gathering with the students to see which of their hypotheses about the cause of the error is true. That can be done in minutes by simply asking a few children to think out loud about how they did the problem. This is also a golden opportunity for the teacher to share with students how she or he went about error analysis in preparation for teaching students, and how students can do the same with their own work.

Exhibit 21.10 Fourth Grade Mathematics Question

Use the diagram below to answer question 19.

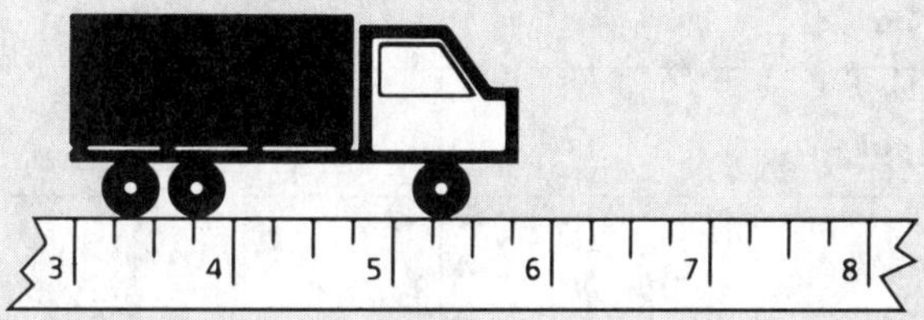

19. How long is the truck?

A. 5 3/4 inches	27	Mather School student responses to this question.
B. 2 3/4 inches	39	
C. 5 1/2 inches	27	
D. 2 1/2 inches	6	

Adapted from Massachusetts Comprehensive Assessment System: Release of Spring 2001 test items.

Component 9: Error Analysis by Students

Teaching students how to do error analysis is a fundamental skill in effective self-assessment and is one of the most significant ways in which we can make assessment an act of learning.

Examine the record in Exhibit 21.11 created by Deborah Levitsky for her eighth-grade team. Weekly quizzes are returned to students the day after the quiz and students fill in their score. Then students have to identify which problems they got wrong and do a form of error analysis in the third box down, as they attempt to analyze the types of errors or confusion their incorrect responses represent. Exhibit 21.12 contains a record filled in well by a student after a quiz on adding fractions, followed by an example of a record filled in poorly.

The negative example in Exhibit 21.12 is negative because the student hasn't figured out what is different about the ones he got wrong from the ones he got right. In the positive example, the student has looked closely at the problems she got wrong to see what is throwing her off. A fourth box could be added asking the student what he or she is going to do to learn the item, fill the gap, or prevent the error in the future.

Exhibit 21.11 Test Record

Name:	**Date _____**	**Date _____**	**Date _____**	**Date _____**
What was your score, as a fraction? (e.g., 8/10)				
Which problems did you get wrong? (Give the number for each.)				
What caught your eye? OR What did you notice? OR What concept did you have problems with?				
Plan for improvement				

Adapted from Deborah Levitsky, New Leaders for New Schools.

Exhibit 21.12 Student Self-Assessment

Name: Positive	**Date _____**	**Name: Negative**	**Date _____**
What was your score, as a fraction? (e.g., 8/10)	7/10	What was your score, as a fraction? (e.g., 8/10)	7/10
Which problems did you get wrong? (Give the number for each.)	#4, 6, 9	Which problems did you get wrong? (Give the number for each.)	#4, 6, 9
What caught your eye? OR What did you notice? OR What concept did you have problems with?	Getting the common denominator when the numbers are big	What caught your eye? OR What did you notice? OR What concept did you have problems with?	Adding fractions
Plan for improvement	Come for extra help in G Block	Plan for improvement	Work harder

Adapted from Deborah Levitsky, New Leaders for New Schools.

As the negative example in Exhibit 21.12 suggests, students need to be taught how to analyze errors effectively and may need side-by-side coaching by their teacher to really internalize the skill. In fact, whole-class lessons in error analysis are a necessity and are very productive when introducing this kind of self-assessment mechanism. A class activity can be students doing error analysis in pairs or in small groups. They help each other identify what went wrong when something went wrong. Teachers can make instructor answer books available in class for students to use after they do exercises or tasks. After checking their responses against the answer books, students have to explain their errors; when they do so, they can get full credit for the item.

Making error analysis the focus of a whole class lesson tacitly sanctions errors as normal.

Making error analysis the focus of a whole-class lesson tacitly sanctions errors as normal and error analysis as a critical vehicle for identifying where we need to focus future effort to improve performance. Thus student self-assessment and error analysis are a direct manifestation of the belief that effective effort is the key to success.

Component 10: Planning and Reteaching

Our exploration of assessment thus far underscores how dramatically the job description of teachers has changed. It used to be that teachers would teach and then assess which students learned what was taught. In addition, they would grade students to differentiate who learned the most. Then, the class would move on to the next topic.

Now, the purpose of assessment is different. A fully committed teacher sticks with all the students until they reach proficiency—at least in literacy and mathematics—and strives to accelerate the learning of students who enter behind in academic attainment. This is both a moral and a legal imperative whose requirements stem from law (No Child Left Behind), moral conscience, our democracy's promise of equal opportunity, and economic necessity to compete successfully in the "flat world" (Friedman, 2005). Therefore, the prime purpose of assessment is to inform instruction in order to bring all students to proficiency. Thus skills and concepts that students didn't get the first time around must be retaught. Thoughtful error analysis sets the stage for meaningful and productive reteaching with those students.

In an era when teachers are feeling pressure to cover curriculum, keep up with pacing guides, and prepare for standardized high-stakes tests, reteaching creates an additional challenge: how to afford the time to reteach and manage reteaching with one group while those who "got it" are productively engaged in meaningful work. Here are two examples from secondary teachers:

> In her eleventh-grade American history class after a 20-minute discussion of a current Supreme Court case, Ms. G takes aside five students who showed confusion in yesterday's quiz. They don't understand how some analysts think the Court is tacitly legislating morality. At yesterday afternoon's team meeting with the other history teachers, she got the idea of making an analogy to a family situation where parental rules get interpreted by other care givers. While she is trying this out, the rest of the class is in groups preparing briefs they would use in arguing before the Court on the case she and they have spent the first 20 minutes explicating. They are going to hand in a flowchart of how their arguments flow logically and indicate what evidence and precedents they would cite.

The prime purpose of assessment is to inform instruction in order to bring all students to proficiency.

An earth science teacher describes another scenario:

> In my earth science class we have been watching sections of Al Gore's movie, *An Inconvenient Truth*, as part of our study of global warming. I am also using it as a way to show how powerful visual displays can make data more real for audiences. I gathered from yesterday's class discussion that a few students don't really understand why two particular graphs are different ways of representing the same data on temperature change. This is a problem, because these two graphic forms will come up many times over the coming year. Everybody needs to be fluent with them. I have gotten an idea from my science teammates about how to use an animation feature of PowerPoint to show side by side how the two templates could be tracking the same data. While I try this with the three students who are confused, the rest of the class will use a data table from Gore's book to construct a graphic display they think would be persuasive. They can choose from among four forms used in the film or another one if they can justify it. Pairs will make class presentations in the final 15 minutes of class.

Although we believe that nothing will be as effective as reteaching another way by the students' own teacher (who knows the students, the content of the work, and what was done before), settings outside regular class hours—extra help blocks, tutoring centers, Saturday school, and homework help centers—can and should be created for students to fill in missing ideas or skills from recent classes.

The commitment to reteaching and to making it an integral part of classroom life is a poignant reminder of where professional knowledge and beliefs intersect. As a professional community, we have to believe that all students are capable of reaching proficiency and that it is our most important work to continue to figure out how to make that possible for all students. Only then will we be tenaciously motivated to invest our creative and collective effort to develop the management and instructional skills requisite for in-class reteaching and to tackle the institutional obstacles (schedules, isolation of teachers, and so on) that stand in the way of making it feasible. Note that in both previous examples, the teacher got the idea for a reteaching strategy from colleagues. Helping each other plan reteaching strategies and useful short activities for the rest of the class is high-leverage use of common planning time among teachers. It is the penultimate indicator of a high-functioning professional learning community.

Component 11: Goal Setting and Action Planning by Students

It's one thing to set a goal and another to set a goal in such a way that you will work hard on it and attain it. Both the motivational and the technical planning aspects of goal setting are explained at length in Chapter 12, "Principles of Learning."

Component 12: Reporting Systems Including Three-Way Conferences

Videos: Student-Led Conferences

The final component of good classroom assessment is three-way conferences with students, teachers, and families that are led by the students. The steps above prior to this one lay the groundwork for student-led conferences, because they develop a great deal of student involvement through participation in generating criteria, student self-assessment, error analysis, and goal setting. As Rick Stiggins says in his excellent book, *Student-Involved Assessment for Learning* (2005), "We cannot simply plug in student-led parent conferences in a traditional teacher centered assessment environment, where students have little idea what the expectations are or how they are doing with respect to those targets. . . . We must set students up to succeed at conferences or such conferences are not worth conducting" (p. 350).

Stiggins goes on to describe what it takes to make these conferences productive. The early steps include tasks described previously: ensuring that learning expectations are public and clear to everyone and that they are aligned with assessments and helping students self-assess and build collections of quality work (portfolios) that represent their progress.

He recommends sending portfolios or parts of portfolios home periodically, before three-way conferences, to keep families informed of student progress and invite parent-student conversations. As conference time approaches, have a conference with each student to review their assembled portfolio of products and help them become articulate about how these products compare with the criteria for this kind of work as well as their analysis of what they need to work on next. Role-play a good and a bad student-led conference with the entire class. Develop criteria for a good one. Make students responsible for inviting participants and for following up on the invitation so that all are informed. Gregory, Cameron, and Davies (2001) give a sample of a useful letter to send home explaining the purpose of these student-led conferences to families. They also give additional useful guidelines for conducting the conference.

It is now part of the conventional wisdom that children do better when their families are positive partners with the school in their children's education.

"When the event happens, make sure students welcome all participants, handle introductions, review the objectives of the meeting, coordinate meeting events, . . . and summarize results" (Stiggins, 2005, p. 353). Thus preparing students to lead the conference is not time lost to instruction, but an episode of instruction itself. Stiggins also recommends soliciting a follow-up written review of the experience from the family—perhaps a questionnaire—to help them suggest future learning targets for their child. And he also recommends a debriefing with the students about the experience by writing about it or having large group discussions. Chapter 13 on this topic in Stiggins's book is well worth reading. It includes tips on how to make these student-led conferences practical in high schools and middle schools by only doing one quarter of the class each quarter of the school year, having "substitute" adults available for students without a parent or guardian to show up, and other creative ideas for managing the logistics and timing of such conferences. Conferences such as these can be powerful motivators for students to focus on their learning goals.

Another important topic is the form of written reports that go home to families. Numerical and letter grades do not give much information. They represent non-specific indicators of their children's performance against some unknown set of criteria. Worse, they represent a ranking of their children in a normal distribution curve; that kind of a grade reports only how well the student has done in relation to others in the class with no reference to actual learning at all.

Reports to families should be varied to include portfolios, checklists, rubrics, and anecdotal comments. This kind of information-rich report can build the support and involvement of families in their children's education unavailable in any other way. It is now part of the conventional wisdom that children do better when their families partner with the school in their children's education. They cannot do this without information about what their children are supposed to be learning and about what quality work should look like. Similarly, feedback and reporting generated through authentic assessment give families specific information and cues about what and how to help their children. No system of letter grades can build this kind of home-school partnership that is now known to be so important for successful schooling.

One of the forces, commonly cited as standing in the way of eliminating number and letter grades, is that colleges demand grades for their admission process. High schools can't abandon class rank and letter grades, it is argued, because the colleges demand them. Is this really true? Alfie Kohn (1995) reported over 20 years ago:

> I wrote letters to the Dean of Admission at Harvard and Brown and said, "What would you do if you got an application from a student who went to a school where there were no grades given at all (much less those unbelievably pernicious additive things like Honor Societies and class ranking), where there was only a sheaf of qualitative assessments of the kid? Would you consider such an applicant?" And both Harvard and Brown wrote back and said, "We not only would, we do." In fact, the guy from Brown added that such a student would probably be at a relative advantage because we would have a lot more information about that student than they would with a 3.6 (what the hell does that mean?). Now at state schools it becomes more problematic, to be sure. At least let's pull the plug on this pseudo argument that says, "We have to continue to destroy kids' interest in learning because the colleges demand it." It's more complicated when you look up close.

Another force to preserve letter and number grades is that they are easily manipulated into summative figures that can be used to compare the effectiveness of schools and districts by magazines, newspapers, and political interests. There is not, at the moment, a great call from families for anecdotal reports or for the use of rubrics. Many families are satisfied by the simplicity of the letter grading system because they are used to it, and because it appears to answer their bottom-line question: "How is my child doing?" Letter grades allow short answers like, "Doing well" (my kid is getting an A), "Fair" (my kid is getting Bs), "Poor" (my kid is getting Cs or Ds). Those kinds of data also invite quick and easy responses by families, such as rewards or praise for doing well and punishments, restrictions, or injunctions to buckle down for not doing well. But this kind of reporting also excludes them from involvement in their child's education in any substantive way. Only through examination of real samples of their child's work in comparison to models of what he or she is supposed to be producing (with specific criteria for what is expected) can they see exactly how to help.

Side by side with this call for authentic reporting is the reality of family time in a society with many single-parent and two-job families who want to be able to digest information about their children's progress quickly. This factor calls for reporting systems that do not overwhelm families with mounds of rubrics and samples, so teachers should select key products at important benchmarks to share with families and illustrate the criteria for quality work concisely and compactly. This effort will be rewarded by more support from families in helping students master what is important. In describing what reports look like that meet these standards of being informative but time efficient for teachers and for families, Wiggins (1996) writes:

> Over time what matters is whether Johnny can make discernible progress toward authentic standards, irrespective of the grades teachers are most comfortable giving. But a single score, like a single grade, is inadequate feedback. A more helpful report would disaggregate performance into its many separate elements: Susan is thorough and accurate at laboratory work, though weak on tests; she is very conscientious and accurate in her homework problems. Jamie's lab work is spotty but indicative of understanding; he does extremely well on tests; and his homework, when done, is excellent—but it isn't always turned in on time, and careless mistakes are made in it. (p. 142)

He then goes on to present models of such reports that could disaggregate performances. In the process, he distinguishes three kinds of data they would provide for each performance element: achievement levels, work quality, and progress.

> Achievement levels refers to exit-level standards of performance. Work quality refers to the caliber of the products produced, at any level (thus allowing us to make the apt kind of distinction made in diving, figure skating, and music competition: degree of difficulty vs. quality points). Progress is measured backwards from exit standards. Progress would thus be charted along multiyear continuums so that a 3rd grader would know how she was doing against 5th grade and (sometimes) 12th grade standards, just as we find in such performance areas as diving, chess, and band. (p.144)

He then provides an excellent example from Victoria, Australia (Exhibit 21.13). Note that the heavier the shading, the more frequently the student performs at that level. This format allows families and students to see at a glance the upper limits of what a student can produce and the range of performance level he or she usually does produce. Immediately below these shaded bands of levels are compact statements of the student's progress relative to the class and overall quality of care and thoroughness in the work. To the right is a summary of the types and number of assignments that were given and a profile of strengths and weaknesses (disaggregating the elements of performance). All of this information is laid out on one page and is visually clear.

Exhibit 21.13 Language Arts Report

Student: John Doe

Level of Performance: Writing: semester (2/93–6/93)

A	B	C	D	E	F	G	H	I

shading is proportional to frequency of scores

Level of Performance: Writing: year (9/92–6/93)

A	B	C	D	E	F	G	H	I

shading is proportional to frequency of scores

Progress in Writing: 4/5 (Good, relative to class)

Quality of Work Products: 3/5 (Satisfactory; slightly below average)

Consistency of Work Product Quality: 2/5 (Well below average of class)

Class Data: Writing

Class Range: Writing 5/93

A	B	C	D	E	F	G	H	I

Class Performance: Writing 5/93

1. criteria scores (average of scores on all five leading criteria): 3.6 (out of 5)

2. most difficult criterion: "revision leading to polished work": 2.6 (out of 5)

Work This Quarter

4 stories, poems
6 analytic papers
1 formal research paper
reflection journal

Writing Profile

Genres of writing
strength: persuasive
weakness: analytic
most progress: description

Critieria scores
strength: vitality of ideas (3.6)
weakness: mechanics (2.3)
greatest gain:
focus (2.4 → 3.2)

Each criterion is judged using a 5-point scale:
5 = top score

Score in parentheses = student's average score

Please refer to exemplar book for samples of student papers for each level of performance and quality of work, summary of the six genres of writing and five criteria used in scoring, and description of performance.

Exhibit 21.13 Language Arts Report (continued)

ENGLISH PROFILES IN WRITING

Writing Band A	
Uses implements to make marks on paper.	Explains the meaning of marks.
Copies "words" from signs in immediate environment.	Writing shows understanding of difference between print and picture.
Writing Band B	
Holds pencil/pen using satisfactory grip.	Writing shows use of vocabulary of print.
Writes own name.	Use of letters and other conventional symbols.
Writing Band F	
Narratives contain introduction, complication, resolution in logical order.	A range of vocabulary and grammatical structures.
Complex sentences—principal and subordinate clauses: use of both active and passive voice.	Understanding of the difference between narrative and other forms of writing.
Corrects most spelling, punctuation, grammatical errors in editing others' written work.	Consults available sources to improve or enhance writing.
Writing Band H	
Vocabulary shows awareness of ambiguities and shades of meaning.	Organization and layout or written text is accurate and appropriate for purpose, situation, and audience.
Meaning is expressed precisely.	Figurative language, such as metaphor, is used to convey meaning.
Edits and revises own work to enhance effect of vocabulary, text organization, and layout.	Edits and revises others' writing, improving presentation and structure without losing meaning or message.
Writing Band I	
Writes with ease in both short passages and extended writing on most familiar topics.	Uses analogies, symbolism, and irony.
Extension beyond the conventions of standard English writing in a skillful and effective way.	Structures a convincing argument in writing.

Adapted from Wiggins, G. "Honesty and Fairness: Toward Better Grading and Reporting." In T. Guskey (Ed.), 1996 ASCD Workbook. Alexandria, VA.: Association for Supervision and Curriculum Development, 1996, pp. 173–174. The Association for Supervision and Curriculum Development is a worldwide community of educators advocating sound policies and sharing best practices to achieve the success of each learner. To learn more, visit ASCD at www.ascd.org.

As a backup to the report form itself is a page that explains the meaning of the nine bands (levels) of student performance. And there is also a background booklet for families, developed by the district, that shows by example what the nine levels mean. It contains performance samples of work at each level, rubrics, and sample teacher comments on the work samples. Thus Wiggins develops a set of criteria for good reporting systems well worth attending to:

- ▲ Disaggregate performance into its elements (not, for example, calling "language arts" one global entity).
- ▲ Report separately students' achievement level, work quality, and progress.
- ▲ Are based on clear descriptions of what each level of performance means, including booklets for families that spell out quality performance with examples at different levels.

Creating such reporting systems takes considerable effort and time, especially for such steps as creating the background booklet with good examples of performance at each level plus teacher comments highlighting the way in which each paper or sample illustrates the level. Good reporting systems to families, however, can create their own market. Until people have experienced something new and useful, they don't know they want it. The better it is, the more they come to feel they can't do without it. Some critics may see this position as naive, believing more cynically that the majority of people will always cling to the easier way—the traditional grading system. It is our belief, however, that families are likely to want the extra data to help their children perform well and achieve at higher standards. These data will be available only when assessment and reporting systems spring from authentic roots.

VALIDITY AND RELIABILITY

Now we come to the topics of validity ("Is the assessment assessing what we really want to measure?") and reliability ("Would the assessment give the same result or score if we administered it again to the same subjects?"). For complex performance assessments, validity is a particularly important issue as teachers design assessment tasks. Any assessment task requires a range of student behaviors, perhaps reading or listening to directions or gathering information from sources that require more or less initiative and perseverance, then acting cognitively on the information, then representing the output of that cognition in writing, speaking, or other expressive forms. The more complex the assignment is, the more it resembles a chain where any weak link can cause a break.

Complexity is an asset when assessments are used as opportunities for teaching and learning. But a "mastery/not yet" benchmark assessment—an assessment used to signify attainment of some important level of learning for students—must be sure not to contain confounding variables of student performance that are off to the side of what we want to measure. For example, assignments containing a great deal of essay writing to assess science knowledge are good as learning experiences yet may obscure the data on what the student really knows about, say, using microscopes.

The following questions need to be answered satisfactorily if assessments are to be technically sound. The questions include checks (where applicable) on criteria, sample size, objectivity, reliability, and validity:

- Are pre- and post-test measures taken? Student behavior should be assessed before instruction begins to see if students already know the material or part of the material.
- Is assessment repeated at some future date after the end of instruction to measure the permanence of the learning?
- Is the sample of items big enough (sufficient questions on each area) so that chance error doesn't mask what students really know or can do?
- Is the assessment administered objectively, without bias, distractions, or confusion to individuals?
- Are assessments scored or judged accurately?
- Is the assessment reliable?
- Is the assessment device appropriate to students with diverse learning styles, and does it thus represent multiple intelligences? Are assessments culturally responsive?

Methods of Data Gathering on Student Learning

Fleming and Chambers discovered in 1983 that short-answer paper-and-pencil tests at the fact level dominated assessment in American schools at all levels, K–12. And Goodlad's (1984) data revealed that recitation structures—cycles of teacher questions and student answers, a form of ongoing oral assessment—accounted for over 80% of all lessons observed. And 80% of the questions in these recitation lessons were at the fact-and-recall cognitive levels (Cotton, 1988, 2000). It seems from more recent studies that nothing has changed (Shingles, 2015.)

Though the preponderance of lower-level questions is a problem, it is not that there is anything inherently wrong with assessing students' knowledge of facts, or in doing so orally; it is surely one kind of data we want to gather from time to time. Rather, it is the pervasiveness of those limited practices—and the relatively superficial nature of the data they yield—that is troubling. Like every other area of teaching examined in *The Skillful Teacher*, there is no one right or best way to gather data about student learning; there exists a repertoire of methods for doing so and that is what we explore here. It is the responsibility of every teacher to develop a wide repertoire of ways to assess student learning because it enables assessment of various types of learners and learning styles. But more than that, it enables matching assessment format to the cognitive level of objectives being assessed, and aligning assessment practices with the demands of 21st century curricula. These demands include knowing how to use knowledge and skills, thinking globally and critically, applying knowledge to novel situations, analyzing information, communicating, collaborating, solving problems, making decisions, using technology as a tool for learning, functioning as a productive contributor within an organizational setting, and using all of these skills to understand and address global issues (Saltpeter, 2003). Obviously, more than paper-and-pencil short-answer tests, essays, and written reports are needed, though these will remain part of our map.

There is no one right or best way to gather data about student learning; there exists a repertoire of methods for doing so.

We are going to describe a number of assessment devices and the kind of learning for which each is appropriate. Each device has a place, including short-answer tests, essays, and written reports. But teachers must now have the capacity to design and use a much wider range of assessment devices because they will be aiming squarely for the kinds of learning the devices measure. Figure 21.3 identifies the repertoire of assessment devices and shows their relationships.

Tests

Short Answer

There is a place for short-answer tests (fill in the blank, true or false, multiple choice) in educational practice, but it is much smaller than the place it once held. Though they are not "authentic," short-answer quizzes where students respond with right answers—facts on timed tests, a series of recall questions involving content knowledge, and so on—enable us to gather data about whether students have basic foundation knowledge or mastery of certain skills. Short-answer quizzes can be appropriate whenever students need feedback on their factual knowledge to identify what to study. Short-answer quizzes can also be oral, a much-neglected medium. Short-answer oral quizzes can allow students' assessment to be individualized, and they can also be given by

Figure 21.3 Assessment Devices for Gathering Data on Student Learning

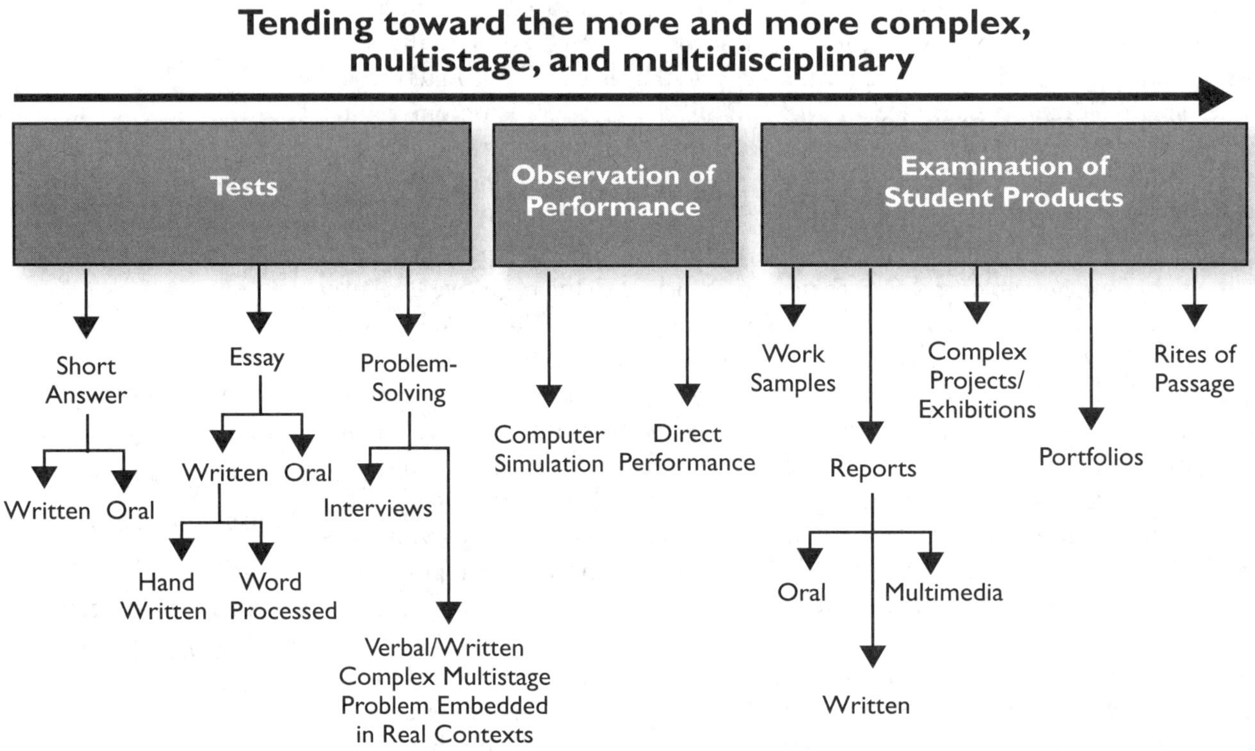

students to one another. Then benchmark certification quizzes can be given by the teacher when students declare themselves ready for certification (e.g., ready for the multiplication fact mastery test on tables). When the characteristics of good assessment are applied to short-answer quizzes, students know what the criteria for success are (e.g., completing the pack of math flash cards in 60 seconds, knowledge of all the states and capitals without error). Perhaps they keep track of their own progress and use the data on each set of results to plan what and how to study next to reach the criteria.

Essays

An essay test is a highly verbal task, performed orally or in writing, that asks students to do higher-level thinking using information acquired over a period of time. The thinking task may ask students to take and defend a point of view, provide specific evidence, or show relationships of cause and effect between events or conditions and actions or outcomes. Essays should continue to play a significant role in assessment, but paper and pencil essays are only one format. There are new questions in the literature these days about the reliability of handwritten essays in an era when many students are accustomed to using the computer as their primary writing tool. There is speculation and a growing body of research that being required to handwrite essay responses creates a handicapping condition that interferes with student expression. Increased use of keyboard technology may alleviate this problem, but oral presentations could also be used much more frequently, and student performance could be assessed on the same criteria of organization, evidence to support claims, sentence structure, and so forth. Samara (2005) presents the following product guide for oral reports:

- Introduction—speaker introduced; topic described; impetus for project explained; expected outcomes discussed.
- Beginning—topic described in general terms; major points outlined; audience involved.
- Middle—major points supported with details; intermittent summarizations; transition statements link major points; audience involved with content.
- Summary—major points reviewed; call to action/ask for acceptance of concepts/beliefs/positions.
- Body language—sustained eye contact with each member of the audience; formal posture; natural gestures/expressions, clear/well-paced voice.
- Use of visual aids—to support major points; intermittent use; limited. (p. 9)

This guide could be used by teachers, students, or both as criteria for giving feedback to students on their performances. It would also be a formative guide for students in preparing their oral reports.

Problem-Solving Tasks

Complex problems embedded in real-life situations can be found in many current development efforts at national, state, and district levels. Exhibit 21.14 is an example drawn from the National Assessment of Educational Progress Pilot Study of Higher-Order Thinking Skills Assessment Techniques in Science and Mathematics (NAEP, 1987).

Exhibit 21.14 Problem-Solving Assessment Task

Triathlon: Interpreting Data

Students are required by this paper and pencil task to examine data about five children competing in three athletic events and decide which of the five children would be the all-around winner. Students must devise their own approach for computing and interpreting the data and explain why they have selected a particular "winner." Students must be careful in their interpretation, because the lower scores are better in the 50-yard dash, while the converse is true in the frisbee and weight lift.

Student Assessment Sheet

Joe, Sarah, Jose, Zabi, and Kim decided to hold their own Olympics after watching the Olympics on TV. They needed to decide what events to have at their Olympics. Joe and Jose wanted a weight lift and frisbee toss event. Sarah, Zabi, and Kim thought running a race would be fun. The children decided to have all three events. They also decided to make each event of the same importance. They held their Olympics one day after school. The children's families were the judges and kept the children's scores on each of the events.

The children's scores for each of the events are listed below:

Child's Name	Frisbee Toss	Weight Lift	50-Yard Dash
Joe	40 yards	205 pounds	9.5 seconds
Jose	30 yards	170 pounds	8.0 seconds
Kim	45 yards	130 pounds	9.0 seconds
Sarah	28 yards	120 pounds	7.6 seconds
Zabi	48 yards	140 pounds	8.3 seconds

Record Findings: (A) Who will be the all-around winner?

(B) Explain how you decided who would be the all-around winner. Be sure to show all your work. Account for Findings:

Account for Findings:

____

____

____

Adapted from Archbald, D., and Newmann, F. M. Beyond Standardized Tests: Assessing Authentic Academic Achievement in Secondary School. Reston, VA.: National Association of Secondary School Principals, 1988, pp. 15–16. For more information on NASSP products and services to promote excellence in middle level and high school leadership, visit www.principals.org.

Tasks like these tend to be engaging to students because of their personal relevance. But they also go beyond traditional word problems. This one demands that students invent some sort of protocol for converting performances in the three events to individual scores of some kind. No such protocol or guideline is given in the problem; the student has to create it. A student might decide to assign points for first-place finishes, second-place finishes, and so on and then add up the totals for each competitor (being careful to have most points for first place and not assigning a score of 1 to first—unless the lowest point total would be the winner, another piece of sophisticated thinking). At another level, a student might create a weighting scheme for actual results in the events, regardless of what place someone finished in the event. In either case, explaining the solution is as important as the actual answer.

This sort of item assesses a range of student capacities. In this case, they need the ability to read and interpret a table of data, analyze the scores, and interpret them into rank order for each event, and invent a scoring rule for comparing overall performance and to explain that rule.

Observation of Performance

Assessment of performances gathers data on students in the act of doing something—solving a problem, conducting a science experiment, doing a drawing—and thus avoids the possible mediating effects of language skills called for in traditional tests. The data are as much about how the student was performing the operation as about the final results.

Direct Observation

Direct observation of student performance allows teachers to observe exactly what they want to assess without injecting confounding variables into the process as written tests usually do. Suppose you want to know if students understand what variables in science really are. In addition, you want to know if they can apply that knowledge to designing and carrying out an experiment that controls the variables and uses consistency and preciseness to reach a conclusion. Then you might design a task like the following. Shavelson, Baxter, and Pine (1991) cite a task where students have to figure out which of three brands of paper towels will hold the most water. To do that task, students take samples from each of the three rolls of paper towel, making sure the samples are the same size; saturate each with water, making sure they are completely saturated; then measure how much water each saturated towel holds, either by weighing or squeezing out the towel and measuring the volume of water squeezed out (a slightly less reliable method since the towels may be unequal in how much water they retain). If there is only one scale to do the weighing, the student has

Direct observation of student performance allows teachers to observe exactly what they want to assess without injecting confounding variables into the process as written tests usually do.

Exhibit 21.15 Paper Towels Score Form

Paper Towels Score Form

Student ______________________ Observer__________ Score ____

1. Method for getting towel wet
   A. Container — Put towel in/pour water in/ 1 pitcher or 3 beaker/glasses
   B. Drops
   C. Tray (surface) — Towel on tray/pour water on; Pour water on tray/put towel in
   D. No Method

2. Saturation
   A. Yes B. No C. Controlled (same amount of water–all towels)

3. Determine Result
   A. Weigh towel
   B. Squeeze towel/measure water (weight or volume)
   C. Measure water in/out
   D. Count # drops until saturated
   E. Irrelevant measurement (i.e.. time to soak up water, see how far drops spread out, feel thickness)
   F. Other

4. Care in saturation and/or measuring Yes No A little sloppy (+/-)

5. Correct result Most Least

Grade	Method	Saturate	Determine Result	Care in Measuring	Correct Answers
A	Yes	Yes	Yes	Yes	Both
B	Yes	Yes	Yes	No	One or Both
C	Yes	Controlled	Yes	Yes/No	One or Both
D	Yes	No or Inconsistent		Yes/No	One or Both
F	Inconsistent or	No and Irrelevant		Yes/No	One or Both

Adapted from Shavelson, R. J., Baxter, G. P., and Pine, J. "Performance Assessment in Science." Applied Measurement in Education, 1991, 4, p. 353.

to be sure excess water from the previous weighing is removed before weighing the second towel.

For such tasks, it is relatively simple to develop a protocol—that is, a form with places for an observer to record checks or scores—that records how well the student did on various dimensions of the task (equal size samples, completeness in saturation, care in measuring and weighing, recording of results). An example of a score form is shown in Exhibit 21.15. "Moreover," say Shavelson, Baxter, and Pine (1991), "the scoring scheme should capture the procedure used and could thereby characterize performance in terms of both processes and outcomes" (p. 351).

Doing large-scale standardized assessments of large numbers of students on activities such as the paper towel task is expensive and time consuming compared to paper-and-pencil tests. Rooms have to be set up with stations for each task, and a trained observer has to score individual students as they rotate through the stations. Despite the cost, Shavelson and Baxter's own research has made it clear that such performance assessments yield valid and reliable measurement results. They also point out, however, that

> performance tasks vary on a number of factors, especially knowledge domain specificity and requirements for students to monitor their own performance as they proceed on a task. Some are inherently more difficult than others. More importantly, some students perform well on one task and others perform well on another task. Consequently, a number of assessment tasks are needed to generalize, with any degree of confidence, from students' performance to the science domain of interest. (p. 358)

This sort of assessment provides such a direct and realistic measure of the thinking skills students should be learning that it remains valuable for states to sample populations of their students on an annual basis. This sampling will give a reliable statistical report card on how well particular districts are doing in developing the skills and work habits that are valued, even if expense prohibits assessing all children by direct observation in the near future.

Individual teachers can use direct observation of performance much more in assessing their own students, and not only in science. For example, in a math class how many times does a teacher have to observe a student doing a complicated long division problem successfully to know the child can do long division? Maybe twice. And he or she can record mastery on a checklist. Suppose you have a student who thinks aloud as she does a word problem. How many such problems do you have to witness the student solving to know that she follows orderly steps like these: identifies the real problem, searches to separate relevant from irrelevant data, and identifies the operation that is called for by the problem? Probably, not very many.

Computer Simulation

To simplify and make more efficient the observation of student performance, most performances can be converted into computer simulations in programs that record all student responses for us to examine later. Some applications give to students direct content-related feedback on their responses: for example, an electric circuit application that either brightens or dims a bulb depending on where students place resistors in a circuit. Others are branching programs that channel a student to an instructional segment about the concept or skill if the student has made an error.

Our point is that we want computer-based applications in any content area to give us as teachers a flow of information about what our students know and don't know, can do, or can't do. And there are many programs that enable that.

Edutopia (www.edutopia.org) keeps an updated list of high-quality sources for these programs in science, including free sites. Check out Eric Brunsell's (2014) blog post "Ten Websites for Science Teachers" at https://www.edutopia.org/blog/websites-for-science-teachers-eric-brunsell.

If one Googles "free [fill in the subject] teaching resources," a plethora of options shows up. Replace "science" with any subject or even topic (e.g., punctuation) and a similar cornucopia is revealed.

Examination of Student Products

Notebooks

An alternative way to get direct data on student performance is through notebooks in which students record their actions and thinking. Students are asked to use the notebooks while they conduct hands-on investigations. Shavelson (Shavelson, Baxter, & Pine, 1991) praises this methodology because it is inexpensive and "provides an opportunity for students to express themselves in writing, an important skill in doing science and a way of integrating curricular areas" (p. 352). Furthermore, trained teachers can score the notebooks rapidly. The student's capacity to write clearly becomes a confounding variable if the assessment target is purely related to scientific thinking.

Reports: Oral, Written, and Multimedia

A report is a vehicle for showcasing language and communication skills. Students who already have these skills will be able to show them off. Students who are less proficient in language and the organization of ideas will have less to showcase. Before producing a report, the student must record and organize information and then plan how to present it, which means planning the sequence and deciding on the inferences, conclusions, and hypotheses that will be in it. Studies of writers show that the writing, drafting, and revision process itself produces some of the steps above.

Report writing, like other forms of creative writing, is not the orderly process one might think. "I write what I know to find out what I think," said Henry Glassie (1982) in *Passing the Time in Ballymenone,* an anthropological study of Irish village life. Thus a teacher who examines and responds to a student's report is examining the student's thinking and communication skills as well as assessing how much understanding there is of the information studied in prepa ration for the report. One of the reasons a report is a productive assessment device is precisely that it orients both teacher and students toward developing communication skills. A teacher is implicitly stating an objective to improve research, organization, and communication skills when assigning a report.

A report is supposed to be a way for students to show they have internalized a body of knowledge and can do something intellectual with it beyond reciting facts. Thus reports typically ask students to go beyond information and do any one or several of the following operations: make inferences, give conclusions supported by appropriately selected evidence, make reasoned and supportable predictions or hypotheses, give opinions, surface assumptions, and sometimes make original connections. These thinking operations can be called for and successfully produced by primary-grade children given appropriate experiences and guidance. Thus the nature of the report assigned makes the report, as assessment, a potential vehicle for teaching organization and thinking skills. Getting ready to produce the report should therefore be an "episode of learning" (Wolf, LeMahieu, & Eresh, 1992).

A report is supposed to be a way for students to show they have internalized a body of knowledge and can do something intellectual with it beyond reciting facts.

Report writing is not something students are born knowing how to do or learn to do by being assigned the task. Teachers are obligated to teach students how to produce reports, and that means breaking down the task into component parts. The link between assessment and the teaching of report writing is the model of good performance provided at the beginning and the explicit analysis of those good products with the students: "What about this good report we are looking at makes it a good report?"

One of the reasons a report is a productive assessment device is that it precisely orients both teacher and students toward developing communication skills.

Similarly, if the report is oral or multimedia, videos of former students delivering good reports or a preserved exemplar of an excellent multimedia report need to be presented to students and analyzed for their good points. Analysis means showing exactly where examples of criterion behaviors occur, for example: "See how this sentence summarizes the main points of the previous four paragraphs? That's what I'm looking for in your reports when I say 'summary sentences' on your criteria sheet. Can anyone find a sentence like that in the second section of the paper?" Here is an example for a multimedia report: "Notice how she uses the music to set a mood at the beginning before saying any words, but then brings music back with the jazz piece when the mood she wants is different. Be looking for music that fits with your message in a similar way." The teacher-student dialogue might go like this:

> **Teacher:** "What did you notice about this student's use of visual material?"
>
> **Student:** "I noticed that for every main idea there was a different visual—either a chart or a picture—to go with it."
>
> **Teacher:** "Right, and that's something I'll be looking for in your reports too. But the visuals have to be a good fit with the point you're making. How were these a good fit?"
>
> **Student:** "Well, when she had a chart with the words, it wasn't really a good fit. It was just having the words printed neatly and using different colors. But when she had the picture of the riot, that was a good fit to show how violent the reaction to the draft really was!"

Exhibitions

An exhibition is a complex project that displays the student's capacity to perform a set of higher-level thinking skills that the school thinks are important. The sixth-grade project developed by Penny Knox (Exhibit 21.5), in which students write a letter describing a culture, is an exhibition. It takes the students all year to gather the knowledge and skills required to do it well. All students are expected to do it, and the criteria for success are clearly spelled out in a rubric. In addition, they have several trial runs at the final product before they produce the version that "counts." In the vision of high school articulated by Ted Sizer's Coalition of Essential Schools (http://essentialschools.org), an exhibition is both a gateway to graduation and a target for the student's four years of high school. Each student must present an exhibition, and it must meet minimum standards if that student is to graduate.

An exhibition also serves as a powerful stimulus to faculty dialogue about what these skills for graduation should be. The list almost always includes higher-level thinking and communication skills as with the item: "Can state assumptions and argue a point of view with clear evidence." Graduation targets like these push across departmental boundaries and cause teachers to plan within their disciplines for how they can teach for them. They also increase interdepartmental communication and open the door for integration of curriculum. Thus "graduation by exhibition" becomes a genuine force for bringing a school together and shaping practices around certain core outcomes it wants for students (Saphier & D'Auria, 1993).

When an exhibition is required for graduation, its magnitude and complexity vary from school to school. Sid Smith and his faculty moved English High School in Boston a significant step forward when they instituted an exhibition requiring all students to write a two-page position paper on a controversial issue of their choice. "It formed the basis of English High School's commitment to decide what its students must know and be able to do to earn their high school diploma. It was the start of the school's effort to require all its students to publicly demonstrate their skills and knowledge" (McDonald, 1993, p. 17). That an exhibition requirement applies to all students for graduation and that it is assessed by competency rather than by grades and numbers makes it a lever for raising standards for all. It also makes schools gauge both the strength of their belief that all students can achieve to a high level and their determination to get them there.

If a position paper is a start on the process of developing graduation by exhibition, the multiple exhibitions collected in a portfolio that are required for graduation from Walden III High School in Racine, Wisconsin, represent maturity. Archbald and Newman (1988), drawing on the student handbook written by Tom Feeney, a teacher at the school, summarize the exhibition requirements in Exhibit 21.16.

Requiring a wide-ranging portfolio of this magnitude takes years of faculty collaboration on developing the topics, standards, scoring rubrics, and procedures for students to navigate their way to successful completion. A school that has thought out graduation requirements this far and expressed them in terms of performance knows what it stands for. It is also clear that to prepare students to succeed on these assessments requires substantial integration and coherence between departments. Such is the promise of the authentic assessment movement.

Portfolios

What makes portfolios an important tool is that students do a self-assessment and choose what goes into their portfolio.

A portfolio is a "purposeful collection of student work that tells the story of a student's efforts, progress, or achievement in a given area" (Stiggins & Conklin, 1992, p. 36). Portfolios provide the database for teachers to continue exploring and refining successful performance directly with students. They also provide a tangible bank of products over time that ideally reveal how far students have come. Thus they become a credible record of progress that can provoke "wow!" responses from families and students alike in a way grades or compliments never could.

> The feature that defines a portfolio and differentiates it from a folder or collection of work is the selection mechanism. Based on the purpose or purposes, pieces are included to demonstrate progress toward a stated aim. A portfolio is a subset of all work done; something must be rejected for it to be constructed. (Mitchell, 1992, p. 107)

What makes portfolios an important tool is that students do a self-assessment and choose what goes into their portfolio. A crucial role for the teacher is to pose questions that students use to select items for inclusion. Ruth Mitchell (1992) supplies one set of questions that might be used in having students reflect on a selection:

1. Why did you select this particular piece of writing? (Why does this piece stand out from the rest of your work?)

2. What do you see as the special strengths of this work?

3. What was especially important to you when you were writing this piece?

4. What have you learned about writing from your work on this piece?

5. If you could go on working on this piece, what would you do?

6. What kind of writing would you like to do in the future?

7. Now that you have looked at your collection of writing and answered these questions, can you identify a particular technique or interest that you would like to try out or investigate in future pieces of writing? If so, what is it? (p. 110)

Exhibit 21.16 Exhibition Requirements at Walden III High School, Racine, Wisconsin

The portfolio. The portfolio, developed during the first semester of the senior year, is intended to be "a reflection and analysis of the graduating senior's own life and times." The following are its requirements:

1. *A written autobiography,* descriptive, introspective, and analytical. School records and other indicators of participation may be included.
2. *A reflection of work*, including an analysis of the significance of the work experiences for the graduating senior's life. A resume can be included.
3. *Two letters of recommendation* (at minimum) from any sources chosen by the student.
4. *A reading record* including a bibliography, annotated if desired, and two mini-book reports. Reading test scores may be included.
5. *An essay on ethics* exhibiting contemplation of the subject and describing the student's own ethical code.
6. *An artistic product or written report* on art and an *essay on artistic standards* for judging quality in a chosen area of art.
7. *A written report analyzing mass media*: who or what controls mass media, toward what ends, and with what effects. Evidence of experience with mass media may be included.
8. *A written summary and evaluation of the student's coursework in science/technology, a written description of a scientific experiment* illustrating the application of the scientific method, an analytical essay (with examples) on social consequences of science and technology, and an essay on the nature and use of computers in modern society.

The Project. Every graduating senior must write a library-research-based paper that analyzes an event, set of events, or theme in American history. A national comparative approach can be used in the analysis. The student must be prepared to field questions about the paper in the overview of American history during the presentations, which are given in the second semester of the senior year.

The Presentations. Each of the above eight components of the portfolio, plus the project, must be presented orally and in writing to the ROPE committee.

Six additional oral presentations are also required. However, there are no written reports or new products required by the committee. Supporting documents or other forms of evidence may be used. Assessment of proficiency is based on the demonstration of knowledge and skills during the presentations in each of the following areas:

9. *Mathematics knowledge and skills* should be demonstrated by a combination of course evaluations, test results, and worksheets presented before the committee, and by the ability to competently field mathematics questions asked during the demonstration.
10. *Knowledge of American government* should be demonstrated by discussion of the purpose of government; the individual's relationship to the state; the ideals, functions, and problems of American political institutions; and selected contemporary issues and political events. Supporting materials can be used.
11. *The personal proficiency demonstration* requires the student to think about and organize a presentation about the requirements of adult living in our society in terms of personal fulfillment, social skills, and practical competencies and to discuss his or her own strengths and weaknesses in everyday living skills (health, home economics, mechanics, etc.) and interpersonal relations.
12. *Knowledge of geography* should be demonstrated in a presentation that covers the basic principles and questions of the discipline, identification of basic landforms, places, and names and the scientific and social significance of geographical information.
13. *Evidence of the graduating senior's successful completion of a physical challenge* must be presented to the ROPE committee.
14. *A demonstration of competency in English* (written and spoken) is provided in virtually all the portfolio and project requirements. These, and any additional evidence the graduating senior may wish to present to the committee, fulfill the requirements of the presentation in the English competency area.

Adapted from Archbald, D., and Newmann, F. M. Beyond Standardized Tests: Assessing Authentic Academic Achievement in Secondary School. Reston, VA.: National Association of Secondary School Principals, 1988, pp. 24–25.

These questions show how portfolios set the stage for goal setting as well as self-evaluation. The last question is actually asking the student to set a goal.

Portfolios also enable a powerful form of parent involvement. They can be sent home periodically with students, and families can be asked to read them thoroughly. Then they are asked to write back (or communicate in some other way) what they noticed, enjoyed, or were concerned about in their child's work. Kathryn Howard uses the form in Exhibit 21.17 to invite families to participate in portfolios in her eighth-grade writing course.

Through the examination of student work, teachers are drawn into authentic and productive conversations about teaching that comprise true collegiality.

The concept of involving students in self-evaluation and goal setting makes portfolios desirable vehicles for student development in any subject area, including math and science. Knight (1992) and others show how having students save their best tests, best labs, and other best pieces that show forms of their mathematical and scientific knowledge can provoke the kind of self-examination and goal setting that goes with being an effective student.

Developing a climate of self-examination and reflection does not come without its costs. One author writes:

> Portfolios are messy. They demand intimate and often frighteningly subjective talk with students. Portfolios are work. Teachers who ask students to read their own progress in the "footprints" of their works have to coax and bicker with individuals who are used to being assessed [by others]. Halfway through the semester, at least a half dozen recalcitrants will lose every paper or sketch they have ever owned. More important, teachers have to struggle to read and make sense of whole works and patterns of growth. Hence, hard questions arise: "Why bother? What comes out of portfolio assessment?" The immediate answer lies in integrity and the validity of the information we gain about how and what students learn. (Wolf, LeMahieu, & Eresh, 1992)

Judith Warren Little once commented in an audiotaped interview (Sparks, 1993) that the most powerful form of staff development might be to put a group of teachers in one room with samples of student work. Her point was that in comparing and debating the merits of actual student performances, teachers refine their concepts of standards. In addition, teachers inevitably get hooked into discussions about which learning experiences to use to develop specific student capacities.

It has been our experience that in these situations, teachers go on to invent learning experiences together. Through the examination of student work, teachers are drawn into authentic and productive conversations about teaching that

Exhibit 21.17 Parent Portfolio Review and Reflection

Student ________________________________
Reader ________________________________
Date ________________________________

Please read everything in your child's writing folder, including drafts and commentary. Each piece is set up in back-to-front order, from rough draft to final copy. Further, each piece is accompanied by both student and teacher comments on the piece and writing process. Finally, the folders also include written questionnaires where students write about their strengths and weaknesses as writers.

When you have read the folders, please talk to your children about their writing. In addition, please take a few minutes to respond to these questions:

- Which piece of writing in the folder tells you most about your child's writing?
- What does it tell you?
- What do you see as the strengths in your child's writing?
- What do you see as needing to be addressed in your child's growth and development as a writer?
- What suggestions do you have that might aid the class's growth as writers?
- Other comments and suggestions?

Thank you so much for investing this time in your child's writing.

Adapted with the permission of the Free Press, a division of Simon & Schuster, from Kathryn Howard in Testing for Learning: How New Approaches to Evaluation Can Improve American Schools, by Ruth Mitchell. Copyright © 1992 by RuthMitchell, p. 112.

comprise true collegiality. Portfolios of student work provide the raw material in organized form for this kind of collegial sharing, refining, and curriculum development. Thus it is reasonable to assume that use of student portfolios can encourage more collaborative work among teachers. It would certainly be a useful practice in schools that are seeking to develop a collaborative culture.

REFLECTING ON ASSESSMENT

Many prominent thinkers in the assessment movement (Wolf, LeMahieu, & Eresh, 1992; Zessoules & Gardner, 1991) use the phrase "assessment as a moment for learning" to convey the point that assessment should be integral to planning lessons, not end points. Others have made the point that assessment is an occasion for learning. This is because when students are given a challenging problem they are able to see relationships and connections that were not obvious to them before. The learning that takes place is a function of the interaction between the student(s) and the task or the students and each other. It does not take place because the teacher is actively mediating the students' thinking (Baron, 1989).

Those are the beliefs behind "assessment as a moment for learning," and they are reflected in the following statements:

> Less noticed is that tests routinely fail to inform learning. The efficient collection of data about a sample of student performance for an outside audience has come to dominate over the first audiences and obligations for assessment: to make students and teachers acute critics of the quality of work and able discussants of what should count as excellence. . . . Students infrequently have the opportunity to make use of what they learn from earlier performances to inform a second try. In essence, rarely are school assessments the occasion for making public the standards and strategies for doing good work. Yet all we know regarding the generation of worthwhile work tells us that it requires incubation, revision, collaboration, and the public display of and debate about failure, risk, and excellence.
>
> The implication for the redesign of current testing is that a major portion of school based assessment should be conceived as an episode in which students learn how to write or experiment, or do research, using the power of assessment to push them along the "zigzag path" that Magdeline Lampert cites in her presentations to her students at the University of Michigan. In more specific terms, assessment ought to:
>
> • Be live: that is, conducted in the face and threat and promise of serious and ongoing work of consequence for the student.
>
> • Take the form of a series of iterative episodes of work followed by time for personal reflection and the gathering of responses from peers, mentors, and judges.
>
> • Allow an individual ways and time for making use of the resulting chorus of opinion so as to make it possible to decide what in the criticism is apt, and what misses the mark.
>
> • Permit that individual to plow the fruits of critique and reflection back into his or her final response [or next try]. (Wolf, LeMahieu, & Eresh, 1992)

These recommendations imply that teachers must create the time and place in class for students to critique one another's work—and not just writing. They apply as well to dinosaur fact sheets produced by third graders, geometry proofs of tenth graders, and science experiments of fifth graders. This collaboration and critique is characteristic of a "portfolio culture, that is, a setting where there is frequent and public discussion about what makes for good work and a clear sense that good work takes a long time to emerge." It thus becomes incumbent on teachers to create frequent opportunities for these public discussions about good work.

In these discussions, "students have access to the criteria that will be used to score their work and those criteria are explained, even debated" (Wolf, LeMahieu, & Ereshe, 1992). The point is that they learn about capacities like the ability to pose an interesting problem. Modern assessment puts the teacher, not the testing company, in charge because assessment is built systematically into instruction. Because what is assessed is students' evolving and improving process, not just one-time performances, the data collected are about process and strategy as well as product. Student self-assessment is at the core.

In a tenth-grade geometry class, for example, each student is assigned different proofs for homework. Twice a week at the beginning of class, students show their proofs to a partner, who reads the proof and critiques it according to the criteria of logical order, completeness, and readability. Readability includes neatness and whether abbreviations and references can be understood. The teacher periodically models how to do these critiques with proofs at the board; students change partners each day when they critique each other.

In another classroom, the teacher uses self-evaluation to collect data about eighth graders' ability to play different roles in discussion groups (for example, summarizing, stating issues, breaking tension). She has told the students she is collecting the self-evaluations to see whether they have increased their ability to play multiple roles and so that she can identify students who need more help. Each role has been explained and modeled by the teacher, and students have practiced them in structured exercises. Now students are asked to participate supportively in a new group discussion. In their self-evaluation, they are to record what role or roles they see themselves as having played and the roles played by every other member of their group. They have succeeded when they can claim three or more different roles and the majority of their group supports their claims. One instance of role-appropriate behavior is enough to claim that role. The teacher meets with students who play fewer than three roles and has them pick an additional one to try in the next discussion. Students who claim more roles than their group testifies to are asked to write examples of the unsupported roles, which the teacher may accept as evidence. In her grade book, she keeps a checklist of students who meet the criteria. For comparative purposes she has her own observational records of which roles individuals played before instruction.

Self-evaluation can also yield added dividends of more student involvement, more awareness of criteria, and better discrimination of quality. Waters, MacMullen, and Glade (1992) have students periodically isolate their best work from the collections in their writing folders. As they explain, "The making of this collection provides students with an ongoing opportunity to review and analyze their best work, choose what best represents him or her, establish a sense of progress, [and] establish a base line from which to move ahead." It also creates the groundwork for individual teacher-student conferences around the collection. Such conferences are unmatched opportunities for involving students in goal setting and helping them generate ownership for their own learning.

TEACHING TEAMS AND ASSESSMENTS

The objective is not fully conceptualized until its assessment is defined.

It is rare in teacher training for candidates to study the design of assessment instruments. Yet we are arguing here that the kind of thinking that goes into the design and creation of assessment instruments (whatever their form—written tests, performances, exhibitions, essays, or something else) is the foundation of good instruction. Put another way, the detailed conceptualization, design of assessment criteria, and assessment tasks enable teachers to "plan backward" (Sizer, 1992, p. 102). The design of effective learning experiences flows from thinking that starts with the students' point of view and flows from clarity about what teachers want the students to know and be able to do at the end of the experience. Thus the clearest articulation of the objective appears in the assessment task and its criteria for success. In fact, the objective is not fully conceptualized until its assessment is defined.

From this perspective, then, expanding the ability to design different kinds of high-quality assessment tasks is essential to the professional teacher. If teaching is not a profession but rather a trade that any competent person can do with a year of basic training, then we can let others make the decisions and do the design work on assessments. But if we are a profession, we must develop the capacity to design and continually refine our own assessments based on changing students and changing curricula.

STANDARDS

On observing the proliferation of the use of standardized tests in 1920, the noted journalist Walter Lippmann (1920) wrote: "We will breed generations of students and educators who don't believe that those who begin weak can ever become strong." He was right.

The clearest articulation of the objective appears in the assessment task and its criteria for success.

Standardized tests are designed to produce normal distributions, not to represent standards that all students could reach. Normal distributions, by definition, must always have a lower half, and within the lower half there must always be a bottom stanine. Lippmann accurately foresaw that the design of standardized testing inevitably led to sorting, and that sorting would produce losers (bottom-scoring students), who would form permanent low opinions of their own intellectual capacity. The structure of the assessment system and the view of unevenly distributed intellectual gifts behind it was inherently incompatible with success for all and, in fact, damned many to a permanent intellectual underclass.

Authentic assessment might have given Lippmann heart, for here he would have seen a form of testing where everyone can be winners. The location and the look of the finish line—standards clearly laid out for all to see—and periodic feedback and self-evaluation can allow all students to self-correct and chart a course to success.

The authentic assessment movement went into seclusion as the press for high standardized test scores from the No Child Left Behind law washed over the nation. We have much work to do before No Child Left Behind becomes the force for equity that some of its authors hoped for. When this equity goal is back on center screen, so will be the commitment to developing thinking skills in all our students and the connection to authentic assessment.

Authentic assessment provides the map for children to identify the learning targets and track their progress toward the standard. They will take advantage of such a map, however, only if they believe errors are opportunities for learning as opposed to confirmation of their inadequacy (Dweck, 1991). Authentic assessment is philosophically aligned with mastery learning because it encourages sustained effort to reach criterion levels of performance. Coupled with teachers who send high and positive expectations to students, one would now have designed an environment where the structures of the school are consistent with a belief in all students' capacity to learn to a high level. If we really want to prepare all students for the demands of this century, nothing less than this marriage will do.

WHAT'S NEXT?

The gap between the assessment practices we advocate here and the practices found in most schools is about the size of the Grand Canyon, and to close this chasm takes extensive teacher planning time, usually in grade or department groups. Our advice is to start slowly as individuals with natural partners (say, the teachers in a high school who teach biology) and to work simultaneously with administrators to devote allocated meeting time to instructional topics—for example, comparing student work samples for quality. Here are some other useful steps that can be begun immediately:

1. Make a special effort to present students with clear criteria for success and models of good performance for each important topic and assignment. Take the time to help the students understand exactly what about the models of good performance makes them good.

2. Get students involved regularly in self-evaluation and peer feedback using the criteria for good performance.

3. Review which methods of assessment and record-keeping devices you are using. Stretch for diversifying and expanding the repertoire. Do you use one-minute interviews or oral presentations as a way of finding out if students have mastered objectives? Do you use direct observation and checklists as a way to record student progress where appropriate?

4. Explore the possibilities of exhibitions across grades or for graduation as ways of bringing it all together for students.

5. Develop and refine portfolios as comprehensive collections of authentic student performance including self-evaluation.

The liberator for authentic assessment will arrive when teachers and administrators devote planning time to compare samples of student work and develop clear exemplars that define what they believe to be the most important student learnings.

CHAPTER QUICK GUIDE

The Three Goals of Assessment:

1. Motivate students to want to do better.
2. Give students useful information they can use to do better.
3. Inform teachers' reteaching plans so students can do better.

The Twelve Purposes of Assessment:

1. Make summative statements
2. Certify students
3. Signal clearly what is important
4. Make instructional decisions
5. Give feedback to students
6. Give feedback to teachers
7. Report progress to families and communities
8. Elevate the curriculum so as to provide meaningful, higher-level thinking tasks for all students
9. Sort, rank, or compare students
10. Norm students or groups of students
11. Placement
12. Predict success

Twelve Components of Classroom Assessment:

1. Determine the assessment task
2. Communicate the standards of performance
3. Assess prior knowledge
4. Frequent data collection and record-keeping by the teacher
5. Frequent high-quality feedback to students
6. Student self-assessment
7. Student record-keeping about progress
8. Frequent error analysis by the teacher
9. Error analysis by the students
10. Planning and implementing reteaching
11. Goal setting and action planning by students
12. Reporting systems on student progress including three-way conferences

To check your knowledge about Assessment, see the exercises on *The Skillful Teacher* website at www.RBTeach.com/TST7.

NOTES

CHAPTER 22

Curriculum
Overarching Objectives

Curriculum: Overarching Objectives

Many of you reading *The Skillful Teacher* came into teaching because you had something in particular you wanted to give to students. You had a passion for it, and you built everything you did around it. You had an overarching objective.

Maybe what you wanted was that your students would leave you loving books and believe that books have something of value for them. Maybe you wanted your students to be critical thinkers who could size up situations with care and be deliberate in their decisions. Maybe you wanted your students to know what it is like to walk in someone else's shoes, to develop empathy for other human beings. No matter what else you were teaching, that overarching objective was always in the back of your mind and somehow visible in your choice of teaching as a profession.

Not all teachers have overarching objectives, but those who do stand out from the crowd. Overarching objectives are those big-picture outcomes for students that, if a teacher has them, shape core practices and account for much of what we see that is effective in their classrooms. These are teachers who have asked themselves, "What do I most want for my students? When they leave me at the end of the year, what is the most important thing I want them to carry away from their learning experience?" These overarching objectives may not show up in unit or lesson plans, but they permeate everything the teacher does. They show up in interactive behavior and decisions about learning experiences.

Overarching objectives are stated in sentences like these: when my students leave me at the end of the year,

- They will know how to work effectively in groups.
- They will have the motivation and the skills to be lifelong learners.
- They will be slow to judge and adept at critical thinking.
- They will know how to confront without hostility and resolve conflicts without rancor.

- ▲ They will understand the balance of life on the planet and be willing to do their part to preserve it.

- ▲ They will understand and appreciate the differences between people in the world—differences of color, culture, language, thinking style—and respond with tolerance and inclusion rather than with prejudice and exclusion.

This list is meant to exemplify the concept of overarching objectives, not be an all-inclusive or a recommended list. Although one may value all these statements, it is rare that an individual will be seen in practice to stand for more than one of them. If you stand for an objective, it permeates your practice and influences everything you do. It is always in the back of your mind and serves as a backboard against which you make all your decisions. A person can have only a few overarching objectives at this level of commitment—usually one and maybe two or three at most. Otherwise, one becomes simply too diffuse in one's efforts and makes little progress on any front.

Individual teachers who have overarching objectives may give lasting gifts to their students. It would also be possible for teams of teachers or teams within a larger school to have an overarching objective in common and achieve even more by virtue of their consistency and congruence with one another. Beyond that, it would be possible for a whole school to share an overarching objective and create an environment so supportive and total in its commitment as to be an incredible engine for change. In such places, the objective becomes a beacon for structuring arenas throughout the school that go well beyond individual classroom practices—arenas like the cafeteria, school reward systems, faculty meeting time, extracurricular activities, or student government. We have written elsewhere in detail about the process of creating such a school (Saphier & D'Auria, 1993). It is not easy or quick, but it can be done. In this chapter, however, we focus on the classroom dimension of overarching objectives.

How does a teacher go about pursuing an overarching objective in his or her own classroom? How does it influence interactive teaching, his or her choices of strategies from the other areas of performance of skillful teaching? How does it influence the way a teacher treats curriculum if the overarching objective is unique to that teacher and is not part of the curriculum as written?

INTERACTIVE TEACHING

The overarching objective becomes an instruction set, a charter, a guidance system for which items to pluck from the repertoires of each area of performance. The overarching objective highlights certain areas of performance themselves. Because we will run only one overarching objective through an exercise in which we will highlight only one set of choices, it is our hope that readers, singly or in groups, will repeat the following exercise for different overarching objectives that represent their personal commitments.

Example: Suppose a teacher has an overarching objective that students leave at the end of the year with an appreciation of human differences so that they not only tolerate differences but embrace them. This teacher will be particularly active with the Classroom Climate (Chapter 16) area of performance. Developing community among the students with acceptance and inclusion (Strand 1) will be particularly important to this person. This teacher will also want to recognize differences in learning style among students and have the students themselves understand how learning styles influence behavior and students' reaction to different kinds of tasks (Strand 3). Thus this teacher might explicitly teach the students about learning style, their own and others, and be explicit about calling for the students to value and honor the differences between themselves and their peers.

Models of Teaching (Chapter 13) that bring students together in groups and teach them how to work well with those different from themselves will be prized by this teacher. Thus Group Investigation—Johnson, Johnson, and Holubec's (1988) version of cooperative learning with social skills training—and Slavin's (1990) Student Teams and Academic Divisions (STAD) will be valued. Certain strategies from Clarity (Chapter 11) that bring students together with peers will be used often, because this teacher will see them as an opportunity to bring students from different backgrounds into joint work situations where they need and can help one another. This teacher would tend to choose strategies like "Round the Clock Learning Buddies" and numerous other activators and summarizers.

Classroom Routines (Chapter 9) might be structured with content that emphasizes the human differences theme. For example, a daily news routine may highlight events from around the world where racial or ethnic differences have been respected or disrespected. Students could be expected to bring in clippings or articles for posting on a bulletin board and later discussion in the class. Routines might be created for students to get help from one another where peers with different strengths—art, organization, video editing, writing—were available to help with projects and assignments.

The Personal Relationship Building (Chapter 15) area of performance would be important to this teacher. The teacher's desire to value differences would require, as a foundation, that each student felt acknowledged and valued personally by the teacher. This teacher would rank high on the application of fairness, respect, and active listening with all students, especially those who might be different—physically or mentally disabled, learning disabled, or racial minorities.

CURRICULAR CHOICES AND MATERIALS

In addition to choices like those within areas of performance previously mentioned, an overarching objective will influence choices of curriculum units and materials and how the teacher deals with the materials.

A teacher who has respect for human differences as an agenda might be expected to highlight issues of race in social studies or in literature and deal with them in a way that forces students to think. For example, characters or episodes in *Huckleberry Finn* can be placed on a grid as they come up during the novel and be discussed in terms of racist or anti-racist behavior (Figure 22.1). One of the revelations in this exercise is that there is no such thing as "passive anti-racist" behavior. Being passive in the presence of racism and disapproving without speaking or acting supports and perpetuates the racism.

These discussions would not replace others but would be woven throughout the unit on *Huckleberry Finn* by a teacher who had an overarching objective pertaining to human differences. Both the racist and anti-racist actors and actions in this book could be addressed within a context of understanding and dismantling racism. The stories and novels a teacher chooses for students is an obvious place to locate an overarching objective. Whether it be courage, perseverance, respect for difference, or any other character trait, excellent bibliographies can be found to aid in the selection of books.

Overarching objectives that pertain to attitudes and habits of mind tend to show up in specific skill lessons and units. For example, if the overarching objective is love of learning and the skills to pursue one's own questions, the teacher is likely to teach interviewing skills explicitly to children because interviewing is a major way to find out what one wants to know. This same teacher is likely to make

Figure 22.1 Forms of Racist and Anti-Racist Behavior

	Racist Behavior	Anti-Racist Behavior
Active		
Passive		

Adapted from Beverly Daniel Tatum and Andrea Ayvazian. Mount Holyoke College, South Hadley, Massachusetts.

it a high priority that students learn how to use library and internet resources. These skills are in direct support of the overarching objective and might not have entered the curriculum at all but for the big picture objective. The larger point here is that a teacher's overarching objective may easily have direct implications for the skills that the teacher chooses to emphasize or teach at all.

Five Classroom Realities

Overarching objectives may be understood and classified through a set of lenses set forth by Gower and Scott (1977). They describe five realities—social, personal, moral, political, and information processing—present in any classroom (or, for that matter, any other human interaction) at all times. These five dimensions could be used to classify overarching objectives teachers may have for students. Objectives may be primarily social in nature (for example, students learn to resolve conflicts nonviolently) or moral (respect for human differences). These objectives can be aimed at personal development (students become risk-takers) or political outcomes (students become active environmentalists). Finally, these objectives may aim to develop certain thinking skills or ways of processing information that students use whatever the content they're studying (for example, they will be able to restrain the rush to judge and will exercise critical thinking skills).

Another way to use these five lenses from Gower and Scott (1977) is to analyze the classroom realities that teachers create on each of the dimensions from an inductive point of view. Even without a deliberate overarching objective in any of these five categories, a certain reality for students in each of the five dimensions is created in every classroom by every teacher. Each has attributes, and each can be described. Switching gears now from the prescriptive and intentional (overarching objectives) to the descriptive and perhaps unintentional, let us examine these five realities, which form a hidden but describable curriculum in every classroom in every school.

1. Social Reality

What is the social reality in a class at any given moment? Social reality has to do with the way people interact. We can inquire into group dynamics, norms, roles, expectations, and interpersonal transactions from any one of a number of points of view. But the point remains that at every moment there is a social reality present, whether or not we attend to it. It has been constructed or allowed to develop and can be described. Its form may or may not be a deliberate creation of the teaching. A group of students working together cooperatively on a group project constitutes a very different social reality with respect to norms, roles, and interpersonal transactions from the same group working with a teacher as director.

2. Personal Reality

Every one of us has a personal reality, at any moment, that consists of how we are feeling and reacting. Our hopes, fears, dreams, and goals, which we carry with us at all times, are touched to a greater or lesser degree by the events of the moment. Each student in a classroom, at every moment, has a personal interior state of feeling. That state is complex, changeable, and real. Each individual's feelings at the moment are the personal reality for him or her. When we seek to understand or provide for personal reality in the classroom, we are examining the changeable, interior, personal world of individuals and their feelings of well-being.

3. Moral Reality

We enter the moral dimension in a classroom when we ask about the concepts of right and wrong, duty, justice, and obligation, that are embedded in curriculum materials, teacher behavior, class norms and procedures, and students' judgments and choices. Such concepts exist, function, and can be described and analyzed in any class, whether or not the teacher is aware of and deliberate about them. Sometimes in more recent curriculum packages, moral considerations are taken up head-on in learning experiences (Lickona, 1972, 1991; Shaftel & Shaftel, 1967).

4. Political Reality

The political dimension of reality has to do with power, influence, and control. When we examine this dimension, we ask questions like, Who has power? How is influence exerted? On whom, by whom? How are decisions made? Who influences the course of events and their form? How does one person (the teacher or a student) get another to behave in a certain way? Who decides what will be done next? What are the students learning in this class about their role in relation to power?

5. Information Processing Reality

The information processing reality in schools has to do with academics. How is information dealt with? How is it presented, acquired, received, manipulated, and used? The answers are quite different when one contrasts a discovery orientation with an advance organizer orientation, or a Socratic discussion with a laboratory experience, or programmed instruction with self-directed research.

The nature of each of these five realities can be described for a given class period. In addition, one could comment over time on how much variance there was within each of the five dimensions. By variance, we mean the range of ways to be on one dimension, the number of different realities observable over time when the classroom is examined through a particular dimension's lens. The social reality of a class may remain constant, such as always one large teacher-directed group; or it may have two social realities: a large teacher-directed group and a large democratic discussion group with emphasis on interpersonal transactions. This distinction is not one that would be picked up by the attribute interpersonal complexity of learning experiences. One may see a variety of social realities over a class day or week or year. If the teacher ceases being a direct-skill lesson leader and becomes an equal participant and facilitator in a discussion of, say, states' rights, the social reality within a small group changes.

Moral reality may be invariant. Community norms and expectations that students do their work (the good, duty, obligation) are maintained and enforced by the teacher without discussion. A different moral reality may be observed at different times, as when children consider ethical issues as a learning activity, or when groups are permitted to problem solve with the teacher acting as a mediator.

Emphasis Within Dimensions

The hidden curriculum can be seen as those social, personal, moral, and political learnings that accrue to students as a result of the environment in which they function, in both the classroom and the broader school at large. These learnings may be built in unconsciously, or they may be deliberate and orchestrated by the teacher. Either way, they are happening and in all five dimensions.

When they are deliberate, we find teachers who can talk explicitly about their ideas of social curriculum, personal or psychological curriculum, and, less often, moral curriculum and political curriculum. These people may be so clear as to have an overarching objective related to that dimension and curriculum to go with it. This curriculum may evince itself in explicit learning experiences or, more subtly, in intentional aspects of the learning environment the teacher constructs or allows to exist (for reasons he or she attributes to social goals or moral goals). Emphasis in any dimension usually manifests in awareness, deliberateness, and objectives for that dimension. As we observe teaching and interview teachers about their teaching, we find that we can identify dimensions that are being emphasized in the design of the learning environment or in personal interactions with certain students.

We commented before that there is some describable reality on each dimension at all times, regardless of the teacher's awareness or deliberateness about what it is. When a dimension is emphasized, even if it has only one form, it means that the dimensional reality figures prominently in learning experiences and one would expect the teacher to be able to say why. For example, some teachers may provide a high frequency of negotiation and choices by students because they have a philosophical commitment to developing student ownership and influence (a commitment from the political dimension). If we observe students in frequent debate, stating and defending positions on issues with the teacher as facilitator and clarifier, we would expect the teacher to have something to say about getting students to be independent thinkers, or critical thinkers, or effective speakers, or some such goal.

MATCHING DIMENSIONS TO NEEDS OF CLASSES OR INDIVIDUALS

Although they stop short of forming overarching objectives, many teachers pursue personalized objectives for particular students that are outside the formal boundaries of their academic agendas. These goals could be from any of the five dimensions and could show up in individual choices or interactions. They are, in fact, usually highly personalized moves and reflect a high level of matching.

For many teachers, these moves are quick and spontaneous. Although it often takes probing to get people to even remember they did them, the moves may come from deep and consistent wells. Experienced and well-developed teachers may have many such individual objectives from the five dimensions for different students.

If a teacher has a social goal for a child, that teacher wants the student to develop or increase some particular interpersonal capacity or insight. "Well, I stopped and asked Jane how she saw the issue because I wanted her group to hear her thinking. She's too shy to offer it on her own and needs an opening. I want to help raise her status in her group." This teacher has a social goal for the student.

If a teacher has a personal goal for a student, that teacher wants the student to develop some personal capacity or inner strength. "Jimmy, I'd like you to see if there is any pattern to the ones you got wrong. If there is, how about setting a goal and checking it out with me before lunch?" This teacher has a personal objective for Jimmy to learn how to self-analyze and set goals.

If a teacher has a moral goal for a student, that teacher wants the student to learn something about justice, right, duty, or obligation. Charmaine has several students sent to her today for help during the 90-minute period. The teacher has arranged in advance with Charmaine by negotiation that she, who is skilled at analyzing and setting up word problems, will be willing to help others in this difficult problem set. This arrangement is not an attempt to boost Charmaine's self-esteem. Her self-esteem is already at the point of arrogance. The teacher is systematically trying to help Charmaine develop a sense of responsibility for the success of others. This is an example of a moral objective.

When a teacher has a political goal for a child, that teacher wants that student to learn something about power or influence. Mrs. James has had Peter read a chapter on mediation during the class study of the labor movement. She has asked him to conduct a mock mediation in front of the class in which he explicitly models the mediation skills in the chapter. Later, when Peter gets into one of his frequent high-pitched arguments with a classmate that he usually wins by bullying, Mrs. James intervenes and says, "Peter, let's mediate. Coach me through the steps." She does this frequently over the first term in an attempt to teach Peter an alternative way to exert his influence in a dispute.

Notice that in these examples, some of the teachers' actions were spontaneous, as in the case of Jane and the goal to increase her status in the group. Others were deliberate and planned, such as the last example with Peter. What all the examples share in common, however, is individualized thinking about objectives for the child's growth. These objectives are in realms that include academic and thinking skills, but also go beyond into other dimensions.

In the teaching ranks of our schools, there are thousands of unheralded virtuosos of the five dimensions profiled in this chapter. These people make subtle and deliberate on-the-fly moves with individual students. These moves are keyed to social, personal, moral, and political objectives that rarely show up in lesson plans but are alive as perceptual filters the teachers use to catch teachable moments with particular students. These teachers are complex thinkers who can and who do address multiple objectives simultaneously.

Understanding this aspect of sophisticated teaching may give observers a new lens for inquiring into those quick little comments and moves that teachers make almost in passing with individual students. This lens can serve as a foundation for interesting questions in conferences as observers help teachers debrief and interpret the complex reality of interactive classroom teaching.

For teachers, this chapter may provide a frame for thinking about their students, one by one, and for sorting through the multiple ways their teaching can match the needs of individuals.

CHAPTER QUICK GUIDE

Five Classroom Realities:

1. Social
2. Personal
3. Moral
4. Political
5. Information Processing

An Overarching Objective Reflects Area of Performance Repertoires:

- ▲ Classroom Climate
- ▲ Models of Teaching
- ▲ Clarity
- ▲ Routines
- ▲ Personal Relationship Building

To check your knowledge about Overarching Objectives, see the exercises on *The Skillful Teacher* website at www.RBTeach.com/TST7.

NOTES

Reference List

Aaronson, J., Zimmerman, J., & Carlos, L. (1999). *Improving student achievement by extending school: Is it just a matter of time?* San Francisco, CA: WestEd.

Ainsworth, L., & Viegut, D. (2006). *Common formative assessments*. Thousand Oaks, CA: Corwin Press.

Alexander, M. (2012). *The new Jim Crow: Mass incarceration in the age of colorblindness*. New York, NY: The New Press.

Algozzine, B., & Douville, P. (2004). Use mental imagery across the curriculum. *Preventing School Failure: Alternative Education for Children and Youth, 49*(1), 36–39.

Alvarado, A., Elmore, R., & Resnick, L. (2000). *High performance learning communities project: Final report*. Pittsburg, PA: Learning Research and Development Center.

Ancess, J. (2003). *Beating the odds: High schools as communities of commitment*. New York, NY: Teachers College Press.

Anderson, L .W. (1983). Policy implications of research on school time. *School Administrator, 40*, 25–28.

Anderson, L. M., & Krathwohl, D. R. (Eds.). (2001). *A taxonomy for learning, teaching and assessing: A revision of Bloom's taxonomy of educational objectives*. New York, NY: Longman.

Archbald, D., & Newmann, F. M. (1988). *Beyond standardized tests: Assessing authentic academic achievement in secondary school*. Reston, VA: National Association of Secondary School Principals.

Arlin, M. (1979). Teacher transitions can disrupt time flow in classrooms. *American Educational Research Journal, 16*(1), 42–56.

Armbruster, B. B., Anderson, T. H., & Ostertag, J. (1989). Teaching text structure to improve reading and writing. *The Reading Teacher, 43*(2), 130–137.

Arnold, J. (1987). Simone was out of control and so was I. *Learning, 16*(4), 44–45.

Aronson, E. (1978). *The jigsaw classroom*. Thousand Oaks, CA: Sage.

Asher, James J. (2003). *Learning another language through actions* (6th ed.). Los Gatos, CA: Sky Oaks Productions, Inc.

Aspy, D., & Roebuck, F. N. (1977). *Kids don't learn from people they don't like*. Amherst, MA: Human Resource Development Press.

Atkins-Burnett, S., Xue, Y., Nicholson, J., Bickel, D. D., & Son, S-H. (2003). Creating a system of accountability: The impact of instructional assessment on elementary children's achievement test scores. *Education Policy Analysis Archives, 11*(9).

Ausubel, D. P. (1963). *The psychology of meaningful verbal learning*. New York, NY: Grune & Stratton.

Ausubel, D. P. (1968). *Educational psychology: A cognitive view*. New York, NY: Holt.

Barbe, W. B., & Milone Jr, M. N. (1980). Modality. *Instructor, 89*(6), 44–47.

Barell, J. (2003). *Developing more curious minds*. Alexandria, VA: ASCD.

Barklay, R. A. (1995). *Taking charge of ADHD.* New York, NY: Guilford Press.

Baron, J. (1989). Performance Testing in Connecticut. *Educational Leadership, 46*(7), 23–25.

Battistich, V., Solomon, D., Kim, D. I., Watson, M., & Schaps, E. (1995). Schools as communities, poverty levels of student populations, and students' attitudes, motives, and performance: A multilevel analysis. *American Educational Research Journal, 32*(3), 627–658.

Beesley, A., & Apthorp, H. (Eds.). (2010). *Classroom instruction that works: Research report.* Denver, CO: Mid-continent Research for Education and Learning (McRel).

Bellon, J. J., Bellon, E. C., & Blank, M. A. (1992). *Teaching from a research knowledge base: A development and renewal process.* Upper Saddle River, NJ: Pearson Education.

Bennett, B., & Smilanich, P. (1994). *Classroom management.* Ontario, Canada: Bookation, Inc.

Berger, R., Rugen, L., & Wooden, L. (2014). *Leaders of their own learning.* San Francisco, CA: Jossey-Bass.

Berlak, A. C., Berlak, H., Bagenstos, N. T., & Mikel, E. R. (1975). Teaching and learning in English primary schools. *The School Review, 83*(2), 215–243.

Berliner, D. C. (1990). What's all the fuss about instructional time? In M. Ben-Peretz & R. Bromme (Eds.), *The nature of time in schools: Theoretical concepts, practitioner perceptions.* New York, NY: Teachers College Press.

Black, P., & Wiliam, D. (1998). Assessment and classroom learning. *Education Assessment: Principles, Policy, and Practice, 5*(1), 7–74.

Black, P., & Wiliam, D. (2004). The formative purpose: Assessment must first promote learning. *Yearbook of the National Society for the Study of Education, 103*(2), 20–50.

Bloom, B. S. (1956). *Taxonomy of educational objectives book 1: Cognitive domain.* New York, NY: Longmans.

Bloom, B. S. (1974). Time and Learning. *American Psychologist, 29*, 682–688.

Bloom, B. S., & Krathwohl, D. (1956). *Taxonomy of educational objectives: The classification of educational goal.* New York, NY: Longmans.

Boesenecker, A. (2011). *Preparing effective verbal and visual presentations.* Retrieved from http://www.american.edu/sis/undergradresearch/upload/Preparing-Effective-Verbal-and-Visual-Presentations.pdf.

Bomer, R., Dworin, J., Semingson, L., & Semingson, P. (2008). Miseducating teachers about the poor: A critical analysis of Ruby Payne's claims about poverty. *TC Record, 110*(2).

Book, C. L., & Galvin, K. M. (1976). *Growing Together: Classroom communication.* Columbus, Ohio: Merrill.

Borko, H., & Putnam, R. (1995). Expanding a teachers' knowledge base: A cognitive psychological perspective on professional development. In T. Guskey & M. Huberman (Eds.), *Professional development in education: New paradigms and practices* (pp. 35–66). New York: Teachers College Press.

Brookfield, S. (1990). Using critical incidents to explore learners' assumptions. *Fostering critical reflection in adulthood: A guide to transformative and emancipatory learning*, 177–193.

Brookhart, S. M., & Moss, C. M. (2014). Learning targets on parade. *Educational Leadership, 72*(2), 28–33.

Brooks, J. G., & Brooks, M. G. (1993). *The case for constructivist classrooms.* Alexandria, VA: ASCD.

Brophy, J. (1981). Teacher praise: A functional analysis. *Review of Educational Research, 51*(1), 5–32.

Brown, A. L. (1989). Analogical learning and transfer: What develops? In S. Vosniadou & A. A. Ortony (Eds.), *Similarity and analogical reasoning.* Cambridge: Cambridge University Press.

Bruer, J. T. (1993). The mind's journey from novice to expert. *American Educator, 17*(2), 6–15.

Bruner, J. (1966). *Toward a theory of instruction.* Cambridge, MA: Harvard University Press.

Bruner, J. (1979). *The process of education.* Cambridge, MA: Harvard University Press.

Bugelski, B. R. (1971). *The psychology of learning applied to teaching.* Indianapolis: Bobbs-Merrill.

Bulgren, J. (1991). *Teaching concepts: Concept diagramming and the concept of teaching routine.* Lawrence: Institute for Research in Learning Disabilities, University of Kansas.

Bulgren J., Deshler, D., Schumaker, J., & Lenz, B. (2000). The use and effectiveness of analogical instruction in diverse secondary content classrooms. *Journal of Educational Psychology, 92*(3), 426–441.

Bussis, A. M., Chittenden, E. A., & Amarel, M. (1976). *Beyond surface curriculum: An interview study of teachers' understandings.* Boulder, CO: Westview Press.

Butler, D. L., & Winne, P. H. (1995). Feedback and self-regulated learning. *Review of Educational Research, 65*, 245–281.

Cabello, B., & Terell, R. (1993). Making students feel like family: How teachers create warm and caring classroom climates. *Journal of Classroom Interaction, 29*, 17–23.

Caldwell, J. H., Huitt, W. G., & Graeber, A. O. (1982). Time spent in learning. *Elementary School Journal, 82*(5), 471–480.

Canter, L. (2006). *Classroom management for academic success.* Bloomington, IN: Solution Tree.

Canter, L., & Canter, M. (2001). *Assertive discipline: Positive behavior management for today's classroom.* Bloomington, IN: Solution Tree.

Centers for Disease Control and Prevention [CDC]. *ADHD Data & Statistics.* Retrieved 2017 from https://www.cdc.gov/ncbddd/adhd/data.html.

Chance, P. (1992). The rewards of learning. *Phi Delta Kappan, 74*, 200–207.

Chappuis, J. (2014). Thoughtful assessment with the learner in mind. *Educational Leadership,* 71(6), 20–26.

Charney, R. S. (2002). *Teaching children to care: Classroom management for ethical and academic growth, K–8.* Turners Falls, MA: Northeast Foundation for Children.

Chavez, R. (1984). The use of high-inference measures to study classroom climates: A review. *Review of Educational Research, 54*, 237–261.

Clarke, J. H. (1991). *Patterns of thinking.* Needham Heights, MA: Allyn & Bacon.

Coates, T. (2016). *Between the world and me.* Waterville, ME: Thorndike Press, a part of Gale Cengage Learning.

Colarusso, C. A., Green, P. P., & Bucks County Public Schools, Doylestown, PA. (1973). *Diagnostic educational grouping with strategies for teaching program.* [Washington, D.C.]: Distributed by ERIC Clearinghouse, http://www.eric.ed.gov/contentdelivery/servlet/ERICServlet?accno=ED075751

Conant, E. H. (1973). *Teacher and paraprofessional work productivity.* Lexington, MA: D.C. Heath.

Connolly, P., & Vilardi, T. (1989). *Writing to learn mathematics and science.* New York: Teachers College Press.

Conyers, M., & Wilson, D. (2014, May 20). Brain movies: When readers can picture it they understand it [Blog Post]. Retrieved from https://www.edutopia.org/blog/brain-movies-visualize-reading-comprehension-donna-wilson

Cooper, H. M. (1979). Pygmalion grows up: A model for teacher expectations, communication and performance influence. *Review of Educational Research, 49*, 389–410.

Cooper, H. M. (2008). Does homework improve academic achievement?: If so, how much is best? *SEDL Letter, 20*(2).

Costa, A. (1985). *Teaching for intelligent behaviors.* Orangevale, CA: Search Models Unlimited.

Costa, A. L. (1985). *Developing minds.* Alexandria, VA: ASCD.

Costa, A., & Kallick, B. (2000). *Habits of minds series.* Alexandria, VA: ASCD.

Costa, A. L., & Kallick, B. (Eds.). (2008). *Learning and leading with habits of mind: 16 essential characteristics for success.* Alexandria, VA: ASCD.

Cotton, K. (1988). *Classroom questioning.* Portland, OR: Northwest Regional Educational Laboratory.

Cotton, K. (1989). *Educational time factors.* Portland, OR: Northwest Regional Educational Laboratory.

Cotton K. (2000). *The schooling practices that matter most.* Portland, OR, and Alexandria, VA: Northwest Regional Educational Laboratory and the ASCD.

Culatta, R. (n.d.). *Dual coding theory (Allan Paivio).* Retrieved from http://www.instructionaldesign.org/theories/dual-coding.html.

Cullinan, B. E. (2000). Independent reading and school achievement. *School Library Media Research, 3*(3).

Cummins, J. (1986). Empowering minority students: A framework for intervention. *Harvard Educational Review, 56,* 18–36.

Cummins, J. (2001). *Negotiating identities: Education for empowerment in a diverse society.* (2nd ed.) Los Angeles: California Association for Bilingual Education.

Cummins, J. (2009). *Basic interpersonal communicative skills and cognitive academic language proficiency.* Retrieved from University of Toronto webpage: www. iteachilearn. com/cummins/ bicscalp. html.

Cummins, J., Baker, C., & Hornberger, N. (2001). *An introductory reader to the writings of Jim Cummins.* Buffalo, NY: Multilingual Matters Limited.

Curry, J., & Samara, J. (1994). Workshop handouts at the NSDC Annual Conference.

Curwin, R. L. (2003). *Making good choices: Developing responsibility, respect, and self-discipline in grades 4–9.* Thousand Oaks, CA: Corwin Press.

Curwin, R., & Mendler, A. (1999). *As tough as necessary: Countering aggression, violence, and hostility in schools.* Alexandria, VA: ASCD.

Curwin, R. L., Mendler, A. N., & Mendler, B. D. (2008). *Discipline with dignity: New challenges, new solutions.* Alexandria, VA: ASCD.

Cushman, K. (2003). *Fires in the bathroom: Advice for teachers from high school students.* New York: New Press.

D'Angelo, K. (1983). Precise writing: Promoting vocabulary development and comprehension. *Journal of Reading, 26*(6), 534–539.

Dale, E. (n. d.). *Cone of learning.* Unpublished paper. University of Ohio.

Daniels, E. (2005). On the minds of middle schoolers. *Educational Leadership, 62*(7), 52–54.

DeGrandpre, R. (1999). *Ritalin nation: Rapid fire culture and the transformation of human consciousness.* New York: Norton.

Delpit, L. (2006). *Other people's children: Cultural conflict in the classroom.* New York: New Press.

Deng, B. (1992, Feb). *A multilevel analysis of classroom climate effects on mathematics achievement of fourth-grade students.* Unpublished paper, (ED 348 222).

Dishaw, M. (1977). *Descriptions of allocated time to content areas for the AB period.* San Francisco: Far West Laboratory for Educational Research and Development.

Dishon, D., & O'Leary, P. W. (1998). *A guidebook for cooperative learning.* Holmes Beach, FL: Learning Publications.

Dodd, A. W. (1995). Engaging students: What I learned along the way. *Educational leadership, 53*(1), 65–67.

Dreikurs, R., & Cassel, P. (1972). *Discipline without tears: What to do with children who misbehave.* New York: Hawthorn Books.

Dreikurs, R., & Grey, L. A. (1986). *A new approach to classroom discipline: Logical consequences.* New York: HarperCollins.

Dreikurs, R., Cassel, P., & Kehoe, D. (1990). *Discipline without tears* (2nd ed.). New York: Penguin Group.

Duffy, G., Roehler, L., & Rockliffe, G. (1986). How teachers' instructional talk influences students' understandings of lesson content. *Elementary School Journal, 87*(1), 3–16.

DuFour, R., DuFour, R., Eaker, R., & Karhanek, G. (2004). *Whatever it takes: How professional learning communities respond when kids don't learn.* Bloomington, IN: National Educational Service.

Dunkin, M. J., & Biddle, B. J. (1974). *The study of teaching.* New York: Holt.

Dunn, R., Griggs, S. A., Olson, J., Beasley, M., & Gorman, B. S. (1995). A meta-analytic validation of the Dunn and Dunn model of learning-style preferences. *The Journal of Educational Research, 88*(6), 353–362.

Dunn, R. S., & Dunn, K. J. (1978). *Teaching students through their individual learning styles: A practical approach.* Upper Saddle River, NJ: Prentice Hall.

Durlak, J. A., Domitrovich, C. E., Weissberg, R. P., & Gullotta, T. P. (Eds.). (2015). *Handbook of social and emotional learning: Research and practice.* New York: Guilford Publications.

Dweck, C. S. (1975). The role of expectations and attributions in the alleviation of learned helplessness. *Journal of Personality and Social Psychology, 31*, 674–685.

Dweck, C. S. (1991). Self-theories and goals: Their role in motivation, personality, and development. In R. Dienstbier (Ed.), *Nebraska Symposium on Motivation. 38*(3), pp. 199–235

Dweck, C. S. (1999). Caution: Praise can be dangerous. *American Educator, 23*, 4–9.

Dweck, C. S. (1999). *Self-theories: Their role in motivation, personality and development.* Philadelphia: Taylor and Francis/Psychology Press.

Dweck, C. S. (2002). Messages that motivate: How praise molds students' beliefs, motivation and performance (in surprising ways). In J. Aronson (Ed.), *Improving academic achievement.* Orlando, FL: Academic Press. pp. 61–87

Dweck, C. S. (2007). The perils and promises of praise. In Scherer, M. (Ed.). *On Formative Assessment: Readings from Educational Leadership (EL Essentials).* Alexandria, VA: ASCD. pp. 66–75.

Dweck, C. S. (2008). *Mindset: The new psychology of success.* New York: Random House Digital, Inc.

Dyer, K. (2016, May 24). Teach. Learn. Grow [Blog Post]. Retrieved from https://www.nwea.org/blog/2016/take-three-55-digital-tools-and-apps-for-formative-assessment-success/

Eaton, J. F., Anderson, C. W., & Smith, E. L. (1984). Students' misconceptions interfere with science learning: Case studies of fifth-grade students. *The Elementary School Journal*, 84(4), 365–379.

Easley, J. A., & Zwoyer, R. (1975). Teaching by listening: Toward a new day in math classes. *Contemporary Education, 57*(1), 19–25.

Ebbinghaus, H. (1885). *Memory.* Trans. H. A. Ruger & C. E. Bussenius (1913). New York: Teachers College, Columbia University.

Egan, G. (1975). *The skilled helper.* Monterey, CA: Brooks/Cole.

Ellsworth, P. C., & Sindt, V. G. (1994). Helping 'aha' to happen: The contributions of Irving Sigel. *Educational Leadership, 51*(5), 40–44.

Emmer, E. T., & Gerwels, M. C. (2006). Classroom management in middle and high school classrooms. In C. Evertson & C. Weinstein (Eds.),

Handbook of classroom management: Research, practice and contemporary issues. Mahwah, NJ: Erlbaum.

Engel, B. S. (1977). *Informal evaluation.* Grand Forks: University of North Dakota Press.

Evans, W., & Bechtel, D. (1996). *Extended school day/year programs: A research synthesis.* Philadelphia: Laboratory for Student Success at Temple University.

Evertson, C. (1982). Differences in instructional activities in higher and lower achieving junior high English and math classes. *Elementary School Journal, 82*(4), 329–350.

Eylon, B., & Linn, M. C. (1988). Learning and instruction: An examination of four research perspectives in science education. *Review of Educational Research, 58*, 251–301.

Fadel, C., & Lemke, C. (2008). *Multimodal learning through media: What the research says.* San Jose, CA: CISCO Systems. Retrieved from http://www.cisco.com/c/dam/en_us/solutions/industries/docs/education/Multimodal-Learning-Through-Media.pdf.

Ferguson, R. F., Phillips, S. F., Rowley, J. F., & Friedlander, J. W. (2015). *The influence of teaching: Beyond standardized test scores: Engagement, mindsets, and agency.* Retrieved from http://www. agi. harvard. edu/publications.php.

Finkelstein, E., & Samsanov, P. (2008). *Powerpoint for teachers: Dynamic presentations and interactive classroom projects (grades K-12).* San Francisco, CA: Jossey-Bass.

Fisher, C. W., Filby, N. N., Marliave, R. S., Chaen, L. A., Dishaw, M. M., Moore, J., & Berliner, D. C. (1978). *Teaching behaviors, academic learning time and student achievement: Final report of phase IIIb, beginning teachers evaluation study.* Technical Report V1. Sacramento: Commission for Teacher Preparation and Licensing.

Fisher, D., & Frey, N. (2012). Making time for feedback. *Educational Leadership*, 70(1), 42–47.

Fleming, M., & Chambers, B. (1983). Teacher-made tests: Windows on the classroom. *New Directions for Testing and Measurement (Testing in the Schools), 19*, 29–38.

Fletcher-Wood, H. (2013, August 17). Do they understand this well enough to move on? Introducing hinge questions [Blog Post]. Retrieved from http://improvingteaching.co.uk/2013/08/17/do-they-understand-this-well-enough-to-move-on-introducing-hinge-questions/

Flower, A., McKenna, J. W., Bunuan, R. L., Muething, C. S., & Vega, R., Jr. (2014). Effects of the Good Behavior Game on challenging behaviors in school settings. *Review of educational research, 84*(4), 546–571.

Fogarty, R., Perkins, D., & Barell, J. (1991). *How to teach for transfer.* Palatine, IL: Skylight Publishing.

Fordham, S., & Ogbu, J. U. (1986). Black students' school success: Coping with the burden of "acting white." *Urban Review, 18*, 176–206.

Fouché, J. (2015). Predicting Student Misconceptions in Science. *Educational Leadership, 73*(1), 60–65.

Fraser, B. J. (1986). Two decades of research on perceptions of classroom environment. In B. J. Fraser (Ed.), *The study of learning environments.* Salem, OR: Assessment Research.

Fraser, B. J., & Fisher, D. L. (1983). Student achievement as a function of person-environment fit: A regression surface analysis. *British Journal of Educational Psychology, 53*, 89–99.

Fraser, B. J., Malone, J. A., & Neale, J. M. (1989). Assessing and improving the psychosocial environment of mathematics classrooms. *Journal of Research in Mathematics Education, 20*, 191–201.

Fraser, B. J., & O'Brien, P. (1985). Student and teacher perceptions of the environment of elementary school class rooms. *Elementary School Journal, 20*, 567–580.

Frattura, E. M., & Capper, C. A. (2007). *Leading for social justice: Transforming schools for all learners*. Corwin Press.

Frick, R. (1987, Jan. 28). Academic red shirting two years later: The lessons learned. *Education Week*, p. 20.

Friedman, T. (2005). *The world is flat. A brief history of the 21st century*. New York: Farrar, Straus, & Giroux.

Friedrich, G. W., Galvin, K. M., & Book, C. L. (1976). *Growing together.. classroom communication*. Columbus, Ohio: Merrill.

Fry, W. (2000). Role of laughter. In E. Jensen (Ed.), *Brain-based learning*. San Diego, CA: Brain Store Publishing.

Fulwiler, T. (1987). *The journal book*. Portsmouth, NH: Boynton/Cook Publishers, Inc.

Gagné, R. M. (1992). *The essentials of learning for instruction* (4th ed.). Hinsdale, IL: Dryden Press.

Gamoran, A. (1992). Is ability grouping equitable? *Educational Leadership, 50*, 11–17.

Gardner, H. (2006). *Multiple intelligences: New horizons*. New York: Basic Books.

Garza, R. (2009). Latino and white high school students' perceptions of caring behaviors: Are we culturally responsive to our students? *Urban Education, 44*(3), 297–321.

Gay, G. (2000). *Culturally responsive teaching: Theory, research and practice*. New York: Teachers College Press.

Gershenson, Holt, & Papageorge. (2016). Who believes in me? The effect of student–teacher demographic match on teacher expectations. *Economics of Education Review, 52*, 209–224.

Glasser, W. (1965). *Reality therapy*. New York: HarperCollins.

Glasser, W. (1969). *Schools without failure*. New York: Harper-Collins.

Glasser, W. (1986). *Control theory in the classroom*: New York: HarperCollins.

Glasser, W. (1998). *The total quality school*. New York: HarperCollins.

Glasser, W, & Dotser, K. L. (1998). *Choice theory in the classroom*. New York: HarperCollins.

Glassie, H. (1982). *Passing the time in Ballymenone* (Vol. 74). Philadelphia: University of Pennsylvania Press.

Glickman, C., Gordon, S. P., & Ross-Gordon, J. M. (2007). *Supervision and educational leadership: A development approach*. Needham Heights, MA: Allyn & Bacon.

Goldstein, L. S. (1998). More than gentle smiles and warm hugs: Applying the ethic of care to early childhood education. *Journal of Research in Childhood Education, 12*(2), 244–261.

Good, T. (1980). Classroom expectations in pupil-teacher interactions. In J. McMillan (Ed.), *The social psychology of school learning*. Orlando, FL: Academic Press.

Good, T. L., & Brophy, J. E. (2000). *Looking in classrooms* (8th ed.). NY: Longman

Goodlad, J. A. (1984). *Place called school*. Princeton, NJ: McGraw Hill.

Gordon, T. (1974). *T.E.T.: Teacher effectiveness training*. New York: Peter H. Wyden.

Gordon, T., & Burch, N. (2003). *Teacher effectiveness training: The program proven to help teachers bring out the best in students of all ages*. New York: Three Rivers Press.

Gordon, W. J. J. (1973). The metaphorical way of learning and knowing. Cambridge, MA: Porpoise Books.

Gore, A. (2006). *An inconvenient truth*. New York: Rodale.

Gorski, P. (2006). The classist underpinnings of Ruby Payne's framework. *Teachers College Record, 12322.*

Gould, S. J. (1982). *The mismeasure of man*. New York: W. W. Norton & Company.

Gould, S. J. (1996). *The mismeasure of man*. (Rev. ed.) New York: W. W. Norton & Company.

Gower, R. R., & Resnick, H. (1979, August). *Theory and research: Evaluation results.* Washington, DC: U.S. Office of Education.

Gower, R. R., & Scott, M. B. (1977). *Five essential dimensions of curriculum design.* Dubuque, IA: Kendall Hunt.

Graham, S. (1985). Teacher feelings and student thoughts: An attributional approach to affect in the classroom. *Elementary School Journal, 85,* 91–104.

Graham, S., & Barker, G. (1990). The down side of help: An attributional-development analysis of helping behavior as a low-ability cue. *Journal of Educational Psychology, 82*(1), 7–14.

Greene, R. W. (2008). *Lost at school.* New York, NY: Scribner.

Greenwood, C. R. (1991). Longitudinal analysis of time, engagement and achievement in at risk versus non-risk students. *Exceptional Children, 57,* 521–535.

Gregorc, A., & Butler, K. A. (1984). Learning is a matter of style. *Vocational Education Journal, 59*(3), 27–29.

Gregorc, A. F. (1985). *Inside styles: Beyond the basics.* Maynard, MA: Gabriel Systems.

Gregorc, A. F., & Ward, H. B. (1977). A new definition for individual. *MASSP Bulletin,* 20–26.

Gregory, A., & Weinstein, R. S. (2008). The discipline gap and African Americans: Defiance or cooperation in the high school classroom. *Journal of School Psychology, 46*(4), 455–475.

Gregory, K., Cameron, C., & Davies, A. (2001). *Conferencing and reporting.* Merville, BC: Classroom Connections International.

Griss, S. (2013, March 20). *The Power of Movement in Teaching and Learning.* Retrived from http://www.edweek.org/tm/articles/2013/03/19/fp_griss.html

Gustafson, C. (1994). A lesson from Stacey. *Educational Leadership, 52*(2), 22–23. ASCD.

Haertel, G. D., Walberg, H. J., & Haertel, E. H. (1981). Socio-psychological environments and learning: A quantitative synthesis. *British Educational Research Journal, 7*(1), 27–36.

Hahn, A. L., & Garner, R. (1985). Synthesis of research on students' ability to summarize text. *Educational Leadership, 42*(5), 52–55.

Hambacher, E., & Bondy, E. (2017, April). Culturally relevant critical teacher care in elementary classrooms. Presented at the American Educational Research Association. San Antonio, TX.

Hammond, D. (1985). *Wordsplash.* Rochester, MI: Oakland University.

Hammond, Z. (2015). *Culturally responsive teaching and the brain: Promoting authentic engagement and rigor among culturally and linguistically diverse students.* Thousand Oaks, CA: Corwin Press.

Hannaford, C. (2005). *Smart moves: Why learning is not all in your head.* Arlington, VA: Great River Books.

Harrison, A. F., & Bramson, R. M. (1982). *The art of thinking.* New York: Berkeley Books.

Hattie, J. (2009). *Visible learning: A synthesis of over 800 meta-analyses relating to achievement.* New York: Routledge.

Hattie, J. (2012). *Visible learning for teachers: Maximizing impact on learning.* New York: Routledge.

Hattie, J., & Timperley, H. (2007). The power of feedback. *Review of Educational Research,* 77(1), 81–112.

Haystead, M. W., & Marzano, R. J. (2009). *Meta-analytic synthesis of studies conducted at Marzano Research Laboratory on Instructional Strategies.* Englewood, CO: Marzano Research Laboratory.

Heath, S. B. (1983). *Ways with words.* Cambridge, England: Cambridge University Press.

Heimlich, J. E., & Pittelman, S. D. (1986). *Semantic mapping: Classroom applications.* Newark, DE: International Reading Association.

Henderlong, J., & Lepper, M. R. (2002). The effects of praise on children's intrinsic motivation: A review and synthesis. *Psychological bulletin, 128*(5), 774.

Herrnstein, R. J. & Murray, C. (1994). *The bell curve: Intelligence and class structure in American life.* New York: Simon and Schuster.

Herron, J. D. (1975). Piaget for chemists. *Journal of Chemical Education, 52*(2), 146–150.

Hilgard, E. R., & Bower, G. H. (1966). *Theories of learning.* New York: Appleton-Century-Crofts.

Hill, P., & Ruptic, B. (1994). *Practical aspects of authentic assessment.* Norwood, MA: Christopher-Gordon Publishers.

Hiller, J. H., Fisher, G. A., & Kaess, W. (1969). A computer investigation of verbal characteristics of effective classroom lecturing. *American Educational Research Journal, 6*(4), 661–675.

Howard, J. (1990). *Getting smart: The social construction of intelligence.* Lexington, MA: The Efficacy Institute.

Howard, J. (1995). You can't get there from here: The need for a new logic in education reform. *Daedelus, 124*(4), 85–92.

Howard, J., & Hammond, R. (1985). The hidden obstacles to Black success-rumors of inferiority. *New Republic*, 193(11), 17–21.

Hudgins, B. B. (1977). *Learning and thinking: A primer for teachers.* Itasca, IL: F. E. Peacock.

Hunt, D. E. (1971). *Matching models in education.* Ontario, Canada: Ontario Institute for Studies in Education.

Hunt, D. E., & Sullivan, E. V. (1974). *Between psychology and education.* Hinsdale, IL: Dryden Press.

Hunt, J. M. (1961). *Intelligence and experience.* New York: Ronald Press.

Hunter, J., & Csikszentmihalyi, M. (2003). The positive psychology of interested adolescents. *Journal of Youth and Adolescents, 28*(1), 1–26.

Hunter, M. (1967a). *Motivation.* El Segundo, CA: Theory Into Practice Publications.

Hunter, M. (1967b). *Reinforcement.* El Segundo, CA: Theory Into Practice Publications.

Hunter, M. (1967c). *Retention.* El Segundo, CA: Theory Into Practice Publications.

Hunter, M. (1967d). *Teach more—faster.* El Segundo, CA: Theory Into Practice Publications.

Hunter, M. (1971). *Teach for transfer.* El Segundo, CA: Theory Into Practice Publications.

Hunter, M. (1977, March). *Improving the quality of instruction.* Paper presented at the ASCD Conference, Fifth General Session, Houston.

Hunter, M. (1982). *Mastery teaching.* El Segundo, CA: Theory Into Practice Publications.

Hyerle, D. N., & Alper, L. S. (2011). *Student successes with thinking maps: School-based research, results, and models for achievement using visual tools.* Thousand Oaks, CA: Corwin Press.

Inamullah, H. M. (2011). A study of lower-order and higher-order questions at secondary level. *Asian Social Science, 7*(9), 149.

Irving, D. (2014). *Waking up white, and finding myself in the story of race.* Cambridge, MA: Elephant Room Press.

Jacobs, H. H. (1997). *Mapping the big picture.* Alexandria, VA: ASCD.

Jamentz, K. (1993). *Charting the course: Toward instructionally sound assessment.* San Francisco: California Assessment Collaborative.

Jensen, A. (1969). How much can we boost IQ and scholastic achievement. *Harvard Educational Review, 39*(1), 1–123.

Jensen, E. (2000). *Brain-based learning.* San Diego, CA: Brain Store Publishing.

Jensen, E. (2008). *Brain-based learning: The new paradigm of teaching.* Corwin Press.

Johnson, D. W., & Johnson, R. T. (1987). *Learning together and alone* (2nd ed.). Upper Saddle River, NJ: Prentice Hall.

Johnson, D. W., & Johnson, R. T. (1995a). *Teaching students to be peacemakers*. Edina, MN: Interaction Book Company.

Johnson, D. W., Johnson, R. T., & Holubec, E. J. (1988). *Advanced cooperative learning*. Edina, MN: Interaction Book Company.

Johnson, D. W., Skon, L., & Johnson, R. (1980). Effects of cooperative, competitive, and individualistic conditions on children's problem-solving performance. *American Educational Research Journal, 17*(1), 83–93.

Johnson, M. S. (1976). I think my teacher is a . . . *Learning, 4*(6), 36–8.

Jones, F. H. (2013). *Tools for teaching: Discipline • instruction • motivation*. Santa Cruz, CA: Frederic H. Jones & Associates, Inc.

Joos, M. (1967). *The five clocks*. New York: Harcourt Brace.

Joyce, B., Calhoun, E., & Hopkins, D. (2002). *Models of learning: Tools for teaching*. Philadelphia: Open University Press.

Joyce, B. R. (1968). *A guide to the teacher-innovator: A program to prepare teachers*. Washington, DC: American Association of Colleges for Teacher Education.

Joyce, B. R. (1978). *Selecting learning experiences*. Washington, DC: ASCD.

Joyce, B. R., Clark, C., & Peck, L. (1981). *Flexibility in teaching*. White Plains, NY: Longman.

Joyce, B., & Showers, B. (1986). The evolution of peer coaching. *Educational Leadership, 53*(6), 12–16.

Joyce, B., & Weil, M. (1986). *Models of Teaching* (3rd ed.). Upper Saddle River, NJ: Prentice Hall.

Joyce, B., & Weil, M. (2003). *Models of Teaching* (7th ed.). Upper Saddle River, NJ: Prentice Hall.

Joyce, B., & Weil, M. (2014). *Models of Teaching* (9th ed.). Upper Saddle River, NJ: Prentice Hall.

Kagan, S. (1997). *Cooperative learning*. San Juan Capistrano, CA: Kagan Cooperative Learning.

Kagan, S., Kagan, M., & Kagan, L. (2015). *59 Kagan Structures*. San Clemente, CA: Kagan Publishing.

Kallison, J. M., Jr. (1986). Effects of lesson organization on achievement. *American Educational Research Journal, 23*(2), 337–347.

Katz, L. (1992). *Five keys to successful implementation of the whole* [audiotape]. Presentation to the Association for Supervision and Curriculum Development, New Orleans.

Keene, E. O., & Zimmerman, S. (1997). *Mosaic of thought: Teaching comprehension in a reader's workshop*. Portsmouth, NH: Heinemann.

Kennedy, M. (2016). Parsing the practice of teaching. *Journal of Teacher Education, 67*(1), 6–17.

Kerman, S. (1979). Teacher Expectations and Student Achievement. *Phi Delta Kappan*, 60(10), 716–18.

Kerman, S., Kimball, T., & Leslie, M. (1980). TESA: Teacher Expectations and Student Achievement. *Phi Delta Kappa.*

Killen, R. (2006). *Effective teaching strategies: Lessons from research and practice*. Australia: Cengage Learning.

King, A. (1990). Enhancing peer interaction and learning in the classroom through reciprocal questioning. *American Educational Research Journal, 27*(4), 664–687.

Kitzmiller, E. M. (2013). "You Can't Control Me!" Cultivating authority in a struggling urban high school. *Teachers College Record, 115*(12), n12.

Kleinfeld, J. (1975). Effective teachers of Eskimo and Indian students. *School Review*, 83, 301–344

Knight, P. (1992). How I use portfolios in mathematics? *Educational Leadership, 49*(8), 71–72.

Kobrin, D. (2004). *In there with the kids: Crafting lessons that connect with students*. Alexandria, VA: ASCD.

Kohn, A. (1995). *From degrading to degrading: Basic questions about assessment and learning* [Audiotape, 953213]. Alexandria, VA: ASCD.

Korinek, L., & deFur, S. H. (2016). Supporting student self-regulation to access the general education curriculum. *TEACHING Exceptional Children, 48*(5), 232–242.

Kounin, J. (1970). *Discipline and classroom management*. Austin, TX: Holt.

Krasnow, J. (1993). The social competency program of the reach out to schools project. Wellesley, MA: Wellesley Centers for Women.

Kreidler, W. J. (1984). *Creative conflict resolution*. Glenview, IL: Scott Foresman.

Ladson-Billings, G. (1995). Toward a theory of culturally relevant pedagogy. *American Educational Research Journal, 32*(3), 465–491.

Lafferty, J. C. (1992). *The subarctic survival situation*. Plymouth, MI: Human Synergistics.

Lampert, M. (1990). When the problem is not the question and the solution not the answer: Mathematical knowing and teaching. *American Educational Research Journal, 27*(1), 29–63.

Lantieri, L. (2001). *Schools with spirit: Nurturing the inner lives of children and teachers*. Boston, MA: Beacon Press.

Lapp, D., Fisher, D., & Grant, M. (2008). "You can read this text—I'll show you how": Interactive comprehension instruction. *Journal of Adolescent & Adult Literacy, 51*(5), 372–383.

Leinhardt, G., Zigmond, N., & Corley, W. M. (1981). Reading instruction and its effects. *American Educational Research Journal, 18*(3), 343–361.

Lemov, D. (2017). How knowledge powers reading. *Educational Leadership, 74*(5), 10–16.

Levin, J. R. (1993). Mnemonic strategies and classroom learning: A twenty-year report card. *The Elementary School Journal, 94*(2), 235–244.

Levin, J. R., McCormick, C. B., Miller, G. E., Berry, J. K., & Pressley, M. (1982). Mnemonic versus nonmnemonic vocabulary-learning strategies for children. *American Educational Research Journal, 19*(1), 121–136.

Lewis, B. V. (1979).Time and space in schools. In K. Yamamato (Ed.), *Children in time and space*. New York: Teachers College Press.

Lickona, T. A. (1972). *Strategy for teaching values*. Pleasantville, NY: Guidance Associates.

Lickona, T. (1991). *Educating for character*. New York: Bantam Books.

Linsin, M. (2014, March 22). How to use music to make routines more fun and effective [Blog post]. Retrieved from https://www.smartclassroommanagement.com/2014/03/22/how-to-use-music-to-make-routines-more-fun-and-effective/

Lippmann, W. (1920, July 21). Is Harding a Republican? *New Republic*.

Luiten, J., Ames, W., & Ackerson, G. (1980). A meta-analysis of the effects of advance organizers on learning and retention. *American Educational Research Journal, 17*(2), 211–218.

Ma, L. (1999). *Knowing and teaching elementary mathematics: Teachers' understanding of fundamental mathematics in China and the United States*. Mahwah, NJ: Erlbaum.

Mackenzie, A. A., & White, R. T. (1982). Fieldwork in geography and long-term memory structures. *American Educational Research Journal, 19*(4), 623–632.

Mager, R. R. (1962). *Preparing instructional objectives*. Palo Alto, CA: Pearson.

Mahoney, J. (2003). What matters: A classroom odyssey. *Phi Delta Kappan, 85*(3), 235–238.

Mamchur, C. (1990). But . . . the curriculum. *The Phi Delta Kappan, 71*(8), 634–637.

Marshall, K. (2006). *Interim assessments: Keys to successful implementation*. New York: New Leaders for New Schools.

Marzano, R. J. (2003). *What works in schools: Translating research into action.* Alexandria, VA: ASCD.

Marzano, R. (2004). *Building background knowledge for academic achievement.* Alexandria, VA: ASCD.

Marzano, R. (2009). The art & science of teaching/teaching with interactive whiteboards. *Educational Leadership, 67*(3), 80–82.

Marzano, R. (2010). The art and science of teaching/representing knowledge nonlinguistically. *Educational Leadership, 67*(8), 84–86.

Marzano, R. J. (2000). *A new era of school reform: Going where the research takes us.* Aurora, CO: Mid-Continent Research for Education and Learning.

Marzano, R. J. (2003). *Classroom management that works: Research-based strategies for every teacher.* Alexandria, VA: ASCD.

Marzano, R. J. (2003). *What works in schools: Translating research into action.* Alexandria, VA: ASCD.

Marzano, R. J., & Haystead, M. (2009). *Final report on the evaluation of the Promethean technology.* Englewood, CO: Marzano Research Laboratory.

Marzano, R. J., Kendall, J. S., & Gaddy, B. B. (1999). *Essential knowledge: The debate over what American students should know.* Aurora, CO: Mid-Continent Regional Educational Laboratory.

Marzano, R. J., & Pickering, D. J. (2010). *The highly engaged classroom.* Solution Tree Press.

Marzano, R. J., & Pickering, D. J. (2013). *The highly engaged classroom.* Bloomington, IN: Solution Tree Press.

Marzano, R. J., Pickering, D. J., & McTighe, J. (1993). *Assessing student outcomes.* Alexandria, VA: ASCD.

Marzano, R. J., Pickering, D. J., & Pollock, J. E. (2001). *Classroom instruction that works: Research-based strategies for increasing student achievement.* Alexandria, VA: ASCD.

Marzano, R. J., & Riley, A. (1984). *Unpublished data.* Aurora, CO: Mid-Continent Regional Educational Laboratory.

Maslow, A. (1962). *Toward a psychology of being.* Princeton, NJ: Van Nostrand.

Matsumura, B. L. C., Slater, S. C., & Crosson, A. (2008). Classroom climate, rigorous instruction and curriculum, and students' interactions in urban middle schools. *The Elementary School Journal, 108*(4), 293–312. http://doi.org/10.1086/528973

Mayer, R. E. (1989). Models for understanding. *Review of Educational Research, 59*(1), 43–64.

McAdams, D. (2006). *What schools can do: Reform governance for urban schools.* New York: Teachers College Press.

McCarthy, B. (1987a). *The 4MAT system.* Barrington, IL: Excel.

McCarthy, B. (1987b). *The 4MAT workbook: Guided practice in 4MAT lesson and unit planning.* Manchester, UK: Excel.

McCarthy, B., & McCarthy, D. (2005). *Teaching around the 4MAT® cycle: Designing instruction for diverse learners with diverse learning styles.* Thousand Oaks, CA: Corwin Press.

McDonald, J. P. (1993). *Graduation by Exhibition: Assessing Genuine Achievement.* Alexandria, VA: ASCD.

McGee, L. M., & Richgels, D. J. (1986). Teaching expository text structures to elementary students. *Reading Teacher, 38*(8), 739–748.

McNeill, J. D. (1984). *Reading comprehension: New directions for classroom practice.* Glenview, IL: Scott, Foresman.

Meisels, S. J. (2003). Impact of Instructional Assessment on Elementary Children's Achievement. *Education Policy Analysis Archives,* 11, 9.

Mendler, A. N., & Curwin, R. L. (1983). *Taking charge in the classroom*. Reston, VA: Reston Publishing Co.

Mendler, A. N., & Curwin, R. L. (1999). *Discipline with dignity*. Alexandria, VA: ASCD.

Mitchell, M. (1993). Situational interest: Its multifaceted structure in the secondary school mathematics classroom. *Journal of Educational Psychology, 85*(3), 424–436.

Mitchell, R. (1992). *Testing for learning*. New York: Free Press.

Moos, R. H., & Moos, B. S. (1978). Classroom social climate and students' absences and grades. *Journal of Educational Psychology, 70*(2), 263–269.

Morrow, L. M. (1985). Retelling stories: A strategy for improving young children's concept of story structure and oral language complexity. *Elementary School Journal, 85*, 646–661.

Murray, H. G. (1991). Effective teaching behaviors in the college classroom. In J. Smart (Ed.), *Higher education: Handbook of theory and research*. New York: Agathon Press.

Myers, I. B., & McCaulley, M. H. (1985). *Manual: A guide to the development and use of the Myers-Briggs type indicator*. Palo Alto, CA: Consulting Psychologists Press.

New England Association of Schools and Colleges. (2011). *Standards for Accreditation*. Retrieved from http://cpss.neasc.org/standards.

Newmann, F. M. (1993). Director's overview. *Issues in Restructuring Schools, 5*(2).

Newmann, F. M., & Wehlage, G. G. (1995). *Successful school restructuring*. Madison: University of Wisconsin.

Nicholls, J. G. (1978). The development of the concepts of effort and ability, perception of academic attainment, and the understanding that difficult tasks require more ability. *Child Development, 49*, 800–814.

Nicholls, J. G., & Burton, J. T. (1982). Motivation and equality. *Elementary School Journal, 82*(4), 367–378.

Novak, J. D. (1991). Clarify with concept maps: A tool for students and teachers alike. *Science Teacher, 58*(7), 45–49.

Nunnery, J. A., Butler, E. D., & Bhaireddy, V. N. (1993). *Relationships between classroom climate, student characteristics, and language achievement in the elementary classroom: An exploratory investigation*. Paper presented at the Annual Meeting of the American Educational Research Association, Atlanta.

Nuri-Robins, K., Lindsey, R. B., & Lindsey, D. B. (2012). *Culturally proficient instruction: A guide for people who teach* (3rd ed.). Thousand Oaks, CA: Corwin Press.

Nuthall, G. (2005). The cultural myths and realities of classroom teaching and learning: A personal journey. *Teachers College Record, 107*(5), 895–934.

O'Sullivan, R. (2005). Raising children in an age of Ritalin. *The Journal of Andrology, 26*(3), 302–303.

Oakes, J. (1985). *Keeping track: How schools structure inequality*. New Haven, CT: Yale University Press.

Oakes, J. (1995). Two cities tracing and within-school segregation. *Teachers College Record, 96*(4), 681–690.

Ondaatje, M. (1979). *There's a trick with a knife I'm learning to do*. Toronto: McClelland and Stewart.

Ormrod, J. E. (2004). *Human Learning* (4th ed.). Upper Saddle River, NJ: Pearson Education.

Osborne, R., & Freyberg, P. (1984). *Learning in science: The implications of children's science*. Portsmouth, NH: Heineman.

Paivio, A. (1971). *Imagery and verbal processes*. New York: Holt, Rinehart & Winston.

Palincsar, A. S. & Brown, A. L. (1984). Reciprocal teaching of comprehension-fostering and comprehension-monitoring activities. *Cognition and Instruction, 1*(2), 117–175.

Paris, D. (2012). Culturally sustaining pedagogy: a needed change in stance, terminology, and practice. *Educational Researcher, 41*(3), 93–97.

Paris, S., Wasik, B., & Turner, J. (1991). The development of strategic readers. In R. Barr, M. Kamil, P. Modenthal, & P. D. Pearson (Eds.), *Handbook of reading research*. New York: Longman.

Park, C. (1956). The bay city experment . . . As seen by the director. *Journal of Teacher Education, 7*(2), 101–110.

Pauk, W. (1974). *How to study in college*. Boston: Houghton Mifflin.

Payne, R. (2005). *A framework for understanding poverty* (4th ed.). Highlands, TX: aha! Process, Inc.

Pearson, P. D., & Gallagher, M. C. (1983). The instruction of reading comprehension. *Contemporary educational psychology, 8*(3), 317–344.

Perkins, D. (2003). *Making thinking visible*. Seattle, WA: New Horizons for Learning.

Perkins, D. (1995). *Outsmarting IQ: The emerging science of learnable intelligence*. Simon and Schuster.

Perkins, D. N., & Unger, C. (1989). *The new look in representations for mathematics and science learning*. Paper presented at the Social Science Research Council Conference, Computers and Learning, Tortola, British Virgin Islands.

Perrone, V. (1991). *Expanding student assessment*. Alexandria, VA: ASCD.

Peterson, P., & Swing, S. (1982). Beyond time on task: students' reports of their thought processes during classroom instruction. *Elementary School Journal, 82*(5), 481–491.

Pfeiffer, J. W., & Jones, J. E. (1974). *A handbook of structured experiences for human relations training*. La Jolla, CA: University Associates.

Polanyi, M. (1966). *The Tacit Dimension*. New York: Doubleday.

Popham, J. A. (2006). Tale of two test types. *Principal, 85*(4), 12–16.

Popham, W. J., & Baker, E. L. (1970). *Systematic instruction*. Upper Saddle River, NJ: Prentice Hall.

Pradl, G., & Mayher, J. S. (1985). Reinvigorating learning through writing. *Educational Leadership, 42*(5), 4–8.

Prensky, M. (2007, March 9). Simulation nation: The promise of virtual learning activities [Blog Post]. Retrieved from https://www.edutopia.org/simulation-nation

Pressely, M., Borkowsky, J. G., & Schneider, W. (1987). Cognitive strategies: Good strategy users coordinate metacognition and knowledge. *Annals of child development, 5*, 89–129.

Randolf, C. H., & Evertson, C. M. (1995). Managing for learning: Rules, roles, and meanings in a writing class. *Journal of Classroom Interaction, 30*(2), 17–25.

Reardon, S. F. (2013). The widening income achievement gap. *Educational Leadership, 70*(8), 10–16.

Reeves, D. B. (2002). *Making standards work: How to implement standards-based assessments in the classroom, school, and district* (3rd ed.). Denver: Advanced Learning Press.

Reeves, D. B. (2004). *Accountability in action: A blueprint for learning organizations* (2nd ed.). Englewood, CO: Advanced Learning Press.

Reinhart, S. C. (2000.) Never say anything a kid can say. *Mathematics Teaching in Middle School, 5*(8), 478.

Resnick, L. (1995). From aptitude to effort: A new foundation for our schools. *Daedalus, 124*(4), 55–62.

Responsive Classroom. (2015). *The first six weeks of school*. Turners Falls, MA: The Center for Responsive Schools, Inc.

Reyes, M. R., Brackett, M. A., Rivers, S. E., White, M., & Salovey, P. (2012). Classroom emotional climate, student engagement, and academic achievement. *Journal of educational psychology, 104*(3), 700–712.

Rich, H. L., & Bush, A. J. (1978). The effect of congruent teacher-student characteristics on instructional outcomes. *American Educational Research Journal, 15*(3), 451–458.

Ritchhart, R., Church, M., & Morrison, K. (2011). *Making thinking visible: How to promote engagement, understanding, and independence for all learners*. Hoboken, NJ: John Wiley & Sons.

Rivera-McCutchen, R. L. (2012). Caring in a small urban high school: A complicated success. *Urban Education, 47*(3), 653–680.

Roberts, M. A. (2010). Toward a theory of culturally relevant critical teacher care: African American teachers' definitions and perceptions of care for African American students. *Journal of Moral Education*, 39(4), 449–467.

Rodriguez, L. F. (2005). Yo, mister! *Educational Leadership, 62*(7), 78–80.

Roger, T., & Johnson, D. W. (1988). Cooperative learning: Two heads learn better than one. *Transforming Education: Awakening the Full Human Potential... in Everyone.* Langley, WA: Context Institute, 34–36.

Rogers, D. M. (1987). *Classroom discipline: An idea handbook for elementary school teachers*. New York: Prentice Hall Professional Technical Reference.

Rolón, C. A. (2003). Educating Latino students. *Educational Leadership, 60*(4), 40–43.

Rosen, R. (2017). *Between play and the quotidian: Inscriptions of monstrous characters on the racialised bodies of children*. Race Ethnicity and Education, 20(2), 178–191.

Rosenberg, M. B. (1999). *Nonviolent communication: A language of compassion*. Del Mar, CA: PuddleDancer Press.

Rosenshine, B. V. (1981). How time is spent in elementary classrooms. *Journal of Classroom Interaction, 17*(1), 16–25.

Rosenthal, R., & Jacobson, L. (1968). *Pygmalion in the classroom*. New York: Holt.

Rothstein-Fisch, C. & Trumbull, E. (2008). *Managing diverse classrooms: How to build on students' cultural strengths*. Alexandria, VA: ASCD.

Rowe, M. B. (1983). Getting chemistry off the killer course list. *Journal of Chemical Education, 60*, 954–956.

Rowe, M. B. (1987). Wait time: Slowing down may be a way of speeding up. *American Educator, 11*(1), 38–43, 47.

Russell, D. (1980). *Teaching decisions and behaviors for instructional improvement*. Talk given at the ASCD Convention, Atlanta, GA.

Ryan, M. (1987, Jan. 18). Students who act up. *Parade Magazine*, p. 10.

Sagan, C. (1980). *Cosmos*. New York: Random House.

Salpeter, J. (2003). 21st century skills: Will our students be prepared? *Technology And Learning, 24*(3), 17–29.

Samara, J. (2005). *Teachers serving teachers: The curriculum project*. Presented at the Raising Student Achievement Conference, St. Charles, IL.

Saphier, J. (2005). *John Adams' promise: How to have good schools for all our children, not just for some*. Acton, MA: Research for Better Teaching.

Saphier, J. (2017). *High expectations teaching*. Thousand Oaks CA: Corwin Press.

Saphier, J., & D'Auria, J. (1993). *The core value process: Bringing vision to school improvement*. Carlisle, MA: Research for Better Teaching.

Saphier, J., & Haley, M. (1993). *Activators: Activity structures to engage student thinking before instruction.* Acton, MA: Research for Better Teaching.

Saphier, J., & King, M. (1985). Good seeds grow in strong cultures. *Educational Leadership, 42*(6), 67–74.

Sarason, S. (1996). *Revisiting the culture of the school and the problem of change.* New York: Teachers College Press.

Scheerens, J., & Bosker, R. (1997). *The foundations of educational effectiveness.* New York: Elsevier.

Schlechty, P. (2000). *Shaking up the schoolhouse.* San Francisco: Jossey Bass.

Schunk, D. H., & Gaa, J. P. (1981). Goal-setting influence on learning and self-evaluation. *Journal of Classroom Interaction, 16,* 38–44.

Schutz, W. J. (1967). *Expanding human awareness.* New York: Grove Press.

Seigle, P., & Macklem, G. (1993). *Social competency program.* Wellesley, MA: Stone Center.

Shaftel, G., & Shaftel, F. (1967). *Role playing for social values.* Upper Saddle River, NJ: Prentice Hall.

Shavelson, R., Baxter, G., & Pine, J. (1991). Performance assessment in science. *Applied measurement in education, 4*(4), 347–362.

Shavelson, R., Baxter, G., & Pine, J. (1992). Performance assessments: Political rhetoric and measurement and reality. *Educational Researcher, 21*(4), 22–27.

Shaw, V. (1992). *Community building in the classroom.* San Juan Capistrano, CA: Kagan Cooperative Learning.

Sheets, R. H., & Gay, G. (1996). Student perceptions of disciplinary conflicts in ethnically diverse classrooms. *NASSP Bulletin, 80*(580), 84–94.

Shepard, L. (2005). Linking formative assessment to scaffolding. *Educational Leadership, 63*(3), 66–70.

Shernoff, D., Csikszentmihalyi, M., Schneider, B., & Shernoff, E. (2003). Student engagement in high school classrooms from the perspective of flow theory. *School Psychology Quarterly, 18*(2), 158–176.

Schifter, D. (1996). *What's happening in math class?* (Vol. 1). New York: Teachers College Press.

Shingles, R. (2015, January 30). A Guide to Bloom's Taxonomy. [Blog Post]. Retrieved from http://ii.library.jhu.edu/2015/01/30/a-guide-to-blooms-taxonomy/

Shockley, W. (1992). Society has a moral obligation to diagnose tragic racial IQ deficits. *Shockley on eugenics and race: The application of science to the solution of human problems,* 212–218.

Short, D. & Echevarria, J. (2005). Teacher skills to support English language learners. *Educational Leadership, 62*(4), 8–13.

Shulman, L. (1986). Paradigms and research programs in the study of teaching: A contemporary perspective. In M. C. Wittrock (Ed.), *Handbook of research on teaching* (pp. 3–36). New York, NY: Macmillan.

Shulmand, M., & Meckler, E. (1994). *Bringing up a moral child: A new approach for teaching your child to be kind, just and responsible.* New York: Doubleday. Copyright © 1985, 1994 by Michael Schulman & Eva Mekler.

Sizer, T. R. (1992). *Horace's school.* Boston: Houghton Mifflin.

Slavin, R. (1986). *Using student team learning.* Baltimore: Center for Research on Elementary and Middle Schools, Johns Hopkins University.

Slavin, R. (1988). Synthesis of research on grouping in elementary and secondary schools. *Educational Leadership, 46,* 67–77.

Slavin, R. (1990). *Cooperative learning: Theory, research, and practice.* Upper Saddle River, NJ: Prentice Hall.

Slavin, R. (1993). Ability grouping: On the wrong track. *College Board Review, 168,* 11–17.

SMART Technologies, Inc (2004, April). *Interactive whiteboards and learning: A review of classroom case studies and research literature*. Paper Retrieved from http://peremarques.pangea.org/pdigital/es/docs/Research%20White%20Paper.pdf

Smith, L., & Land, M. (1981). Low-Inference Verbal Behaviors Related to Teacher Clarity. *Journal of Classroom Interactions, 17*(1), 37–42.

Sommer, R. (1969). *Personal space: The behavioral basis of design*. New York: Prentice Hall.

Sparks, D. (1993). Dennis Sparks interviews Judith Warren little on professional development in school reform [Audiotape]. Oxford, Ohio: NSDC.

Stallings, J. (1980). Allocated academic learning time revisited, or beyond time on task. *Educational Researcher, 9*, 11–16.

Stanford, G. (1977). *Developing effective classroom groups*. New York: Hart Publishing Co.

Stanley, S., & Greenwood, C. (1983). How much opportunity to respond does the minority disadvantaged student receive in school? *Exceptional Children, 49*(4), 370–373.

Stanton-Salazar, R. (2001). *Manufacturing hope and despair: The school and kin support networks of U.S. Mexican youth*. New York: Teachers College Press.

Steele. C. (2010). *Whistling Vivaldi*. New York: W. W. Norton & Company.

Stephenson, J., & Watrous, B. (1993). The morning meeting repertoire: A collection of ideas that work. *Responsive Classroom, 5*(2), 8.

Stiggins, R. (2005). *Student-involved assessment for learning*. Upper Saddle River, NJ: Pearson.

Stiggins, R., & Chappuis, J. (2005). Using student involved classroom assessment to close the achievement gap. *Theory into Practice, 44*(1), 11–18.

Stiggins, R., & Conklin, N. (1992). *In teachers' hands: Investigating the practices of classroom assessment*. Albany, NY: State University of New York Press.

Stigler, J. W., and Hiebert, J. (1999). *The teaching gap: Best ideas from the world's teachers for improving education in the classroom*. New York: Free Press.

Stronge, J. H. (2002). *Qualities of effective teachers*. Alexandria, VA: ASCD.

Sue, D. W., Capodilupo, C. M., Torino, G. C., Bucceri, J. M., Holder, A., Nadal, K. L., & Esquilin, M. (2007). Racial microaggressions in everyday life: Implications for clinical practice. *American psychologist, 62*(4), 271.

Sugai, G., & Horner, R. (2006). A promising approach for expanding and sustaining schoolwide positive behavior support. *School Psychology Review, 35*, 245–259.

Swap, S. (1974). Disturbing classroom behaviors: A developmental and ecological view. *Exceptional Children, 41*(3), 163–172.

Sylwester, R. (1995). *A celebration of neurons: An educator's guide to the human brain*. Alexandria, VA: ASCD.

Taba, H. (1962). *Curriculum development: Theory and practice*. Orlando, FL: Harcourt.

Tasker, R. (1981). Children's views and classroom experience. *Australian Science Teachers' Journal, 27*(3), 33–37.

Tatum, B. D. (1994). Teaching white students about racism: The search for white allies and the restoration of hope. *Teachers College Record, 95*(4), 462–476.

Tatum, B. D., & Ayvazian, A. (1994). *Forms of Racist and Anti-racist Behavior*. South Hadley, MA: Mount Holyoke College.

Tomlinson, C. A. (2014). *The differentiated classroom: Responding to the needs of all learners*. Alexandria, VA: ASCD.

Thompson, J. (2007). *The first year teacher's survival guide: Ready to use strategies, tools and activities for meeting the challenges of each school day.* San Francisco, CA: Jossey-Bass.

Tindal, G., & Parker, R. (1987). Direct observation in special education classrooms. *Journal of Special Education, 21*(2), 43–58.

Tishman, S., Perkins, D., & Jay, E. (1995). *The thinking classroom.* Needham Heights, MA: Allyn & Bacon.

Tobin, K. (1985). *Wait-time in science—necessary but insufficient.* Paper presented at the annual meeting of the National Association for Research in Science Teaching, French Lick Springs, Indiana.

Toepfer, C. F., Jr. (1981). *Brain growth periodization research.* Washington, DC: ASCD.

Tomlinson, C. A. (2004). *How to differentiate mixed ability in mixed ability classrooms.* Alexandria, VA: ASCD.

Torff, B. (2011). Teacher beliefs shape learning for all students. *Phi Delta Kappan, 93*(3), 21–23.

Toshalis, E. (2015). *Make Me! Understanding and Engaging Student Resistance in School.* Harvard Education Press. 8 Story Street First Floor, Cambridge, MA 02138.

Traver, R. (1998). What is a good guiding question? *Educational Leadership, 55*(6), 70–73.

Triandis, H. C. (1989). The self and social behavior in differing cultural contexts. *Psychological review,* 96(3), 506.

Tyler, R. (1949). *Basic principles of curriculum and instruction.* Chicago: University of Chicago Press.

United States National Commission on Excellence in Education. (1983). *A nation at risk: The imperative for educational reform.* Retrieved from http://www2.ed.gov/pubs/NatAtRisk/risk.html.

United States National Education Commission on Time Learning. (1994). *Prisoners of time: Report of the National Education Commission on Time and Learning.* Retrieved from http://www2.ed.gov/pubs/PrisonersOfTime/index.html.

U.S. Bureau of Labor Statistics. (2016). *Employment projections program.* Retrieved from http://www.bls.gov/emp/ep_education_training_system.htm.

U. S. Department of Education, National Center for Education Statistics (1999). TIMSS (Trends in International Mathematics and Science Study). Retrieved from http://timssandpirls.bc.edu/timss1999.html.

U. S. Department of Education, National Center for Education Statistics (2003). *TIMSS (Trends in International Mathematics and Science Study).* Retrieved from http://timssandpirls.bc.edu/timss2003.html.

Ullucci, K. (2009). "This has to be family": Humanizing classroom management in urban schools. *The Journal of Classroom Interaction, 44*(1), 13–28.

Valenzuela, A. (1999). *Subtractive schooling: Issues of caring in education of U.S. Mexican youth.* Albany: State University of New York Press.

Van Edwards, V. (2015, August 25). 20 hand gestures you should be using [Blog post]. Retrieved from http://www.huffingtonpost.com/vanessa-van-edwards/20-hand-gestures-you-shou_b_8034618.html.

Van Houton, R. (1980). *Learning through feedback.* New York: Human Sciences Press.

Van Manen, M. (1991). *The tact of teaching: The meaning of pedagogical thoughtfulness* (SUNY series, the philosophy of education). Albany: State University of New York Press.

Van Merriënboer, J. J. (1997). *Training complex cognitive skills: A four-component instructional design model for technical training.* Englewood Cliffs, NJ: Educational Technology Publications.

Velasquez, A., West, R., Graham, C., & Osguthorpe, R. (2013). Developing caring relationships in schools: a review of the research on caring and nurturing pedagogies. *Review of Education,* 1(2), 162–190.

Walberg, H. (1997). *Uncompetitive American schools: Causes and cures.* Washington, DC: Brookings Institute.

Waters, F., MacMullen, M., & Glade, J. (1992). *Intelligent learning.* Unionville, NY: KAV Books.

Webb, N. M. (1982). Student interaction and learning in small groups. *Review of Educational Research, 52,* 441–445.

Weiner, B. (1972). *Theories of motivation: From mechanism to cognition.* Chicago: Markham.

Weiner, B. (1974). *Achievement motivation and attribution theory.* Morristown, NJ: General Learning Press.

Weiner, B. (1985). An attributional theory of achievement motivation and emotion. *Psychological Review, 92,* 548–573.

Weiner, B. (1996). *Human motivation: Metaphors, theories and research.* Thousand Oaks, CA: Sage.

Weinstein, C., Curran, M., & Tomlinson-Clarke, S. (2003). Culturally responsive classroom management: Awareness into action. *Theory Into Practice, 42*(4), 269–276.

West, L. & Staub, F. C. (2003). *Content focused coaching: Transforming mathematics lessons.* Portsmouth, NH: Heinemann.

Whisler, J. S., & Marzano, R. J. (1988). *Dare to imagine: An Olympian's technology.* Aurora, CO: Mid-Continent Regional Educational Laboratory.

White, B. (2009). *Mama makes up her mind: And other dangers of southern living.* Boston, MA: Da Capo Press.

Wiggins, G. (1993). *Assessing student performance: Exploring the purpose and limits of testing.* San Francisco: Jossey-Bass.

Wiggins, G. (1996). Honesty and fairness: Toward better grading and reporting. In T. Guskey (Ed.), *ASCD Yearbook,* (pp.141–177). Alexandria, VA: ASCD.

Wiggins, G. (2004). Assessment as feedback. *New Horizons for Learning, 10*(2).

Wiggins, G. (2011). Giving Students a Voice: The Power of Feedback to Improve Teaching. *Educational Horizons, 89*(4), 23–26.

Wiggins, G. (2012). Seven keys to effective feedback. *Educational Leardership, 70*(1), 10–16.

Wiggins, G., & McTighe, J. (2005). *Understanding by design* (2nd ed.). Alexandria, VA: ASCD.

Wiliam, D. (2015). Designing great hinge questions. *Educational Leadership, 73*(1), 40–44.

Wilt, J., & Watson, B. (1978). *Relationship Building Activities.* Waco, TX: WORD.

Winne, P. H. (1979b). Aptitude-treatment interactions in an experiment on teacher effectiveness. *American Educational Research Journal, 14*(4), 389–410.

Winne, P. H. (1979a). Experiments in relating teachers' use of higher cognitive questions to students' achievement. *Review of Educational Research, 49*(1), 13–49.

Winne, P. H., & Marx, R. W. (1982). Students' and Teachers' View of Thinking Process for Classroom Learning. *Elementary School Journal, 82*(5), 493–518.

Withall, J. (1949). Development of a technique for the measurement of socio-emotional climate in classroom. *Journal of Experimental Education, 17,* 347–361.

Wolf, D., LeMahieu, P., & Eresh, J. (1992). Good measure: Assessment as a tool for educational reform. *Educational Leadership, 49*(8), 8–13.

Wolfe, P. (2001). *Brain matters: Translating research into classroom practice.* Alexandria, VA: ASCD.

Wong, H. & Wong, R. (2009). *The first days of school: How to be an effective teacher* (4th ed.).

Mountain View, CA: Harry K. Wong Publications, Inc.

Wood, C. (1994a). *Yardsticks.* Greenfield, MA: Northeast Foundation for Children.

Wood, C. (1994b). *The responsive classroom.* Greenfield, MA: Northeast Foundation for Children.

Wood, C. (1999). *Time to teach, time to learn: Changing the pace of school.* Greenfield, MA: Northeast Foundation for Children.

Wormeli, R. (2009). *Metaphors and analogies: Power tools for teaching any subject.* Portland, ME: Stenhouse Publishers.

Writers' Express. (2006). *Teacher's guide to commenting on polished pieces.* Somerville, MA: Writers' Express.

Yager, S., Johnson, R., Johnson, D., & Snider, B. (1986). The impact of group processing on achievement in cooperative learning groups. *Journal of Social Psychology, 126*(3), 389–397.

Yeh, S. (2006). High-stakes testing: can rapid assessment reduce the pressure? *Teachers College Record, 108*(4), 621–661.

Zahorik, J. A. (1996). Elementary and secondary teachers' reports of how they make learning interesting. *The Elementary School Journal, 96*(5), 551–565.

Zessoules, R., & Gardner, H. (1991). Authentic assessment: Beyond the buzzword and into the classroom. In V. Perrone (Ed.), *Expanding Student Assessment* (pp. 47–71). Alexandria, VA: ASCD.

Zimmerman, B. J., & Marinez-Pons, M. (1990). Student differences in self-regulated learning: Relating grade, sex and giftedness to self-efficacy and strategy use. *Journal of Educational Psychology, 82*(1), 51–59.

Subject Index

Symbols

4MAT 431
24 Operating Principles 257

A

Abstractions 15, 16
Academic discipline 3, 4, 8
Academic learning time 88, 101
Academic routines 110–111
Academic vocabulary 198, 201, 202, 210
Accountability 2
Accountable Talk 255
Achievement gap 1
Acknowledging moves 52
Acknowledging students 392
Activator 205, 206, 208, 209, 210
Activators (Saphier & Haley) 209
Active participation 286
Activity Thinking 490
ADD 98
ADHD 98
Adult Professional Culture 5, 9, 13
Advanced Organizer Model 296
Advance notice 65
Alerting moves 51
Allocated time 82, 83, 84, 103
Analogies and Metaphors 214
Anchoring Table 244
Anecdotal Records 574, 577, 578
Anticipating confusions 211
Anticipation 66
Anticipation Guide 208
Anti-Racism Continuum 36
Application in Setting 269
Areas of performance 11–13
Arenas for expectations messages 332
Assessment
  Exemplars 561–563, 567
  Problem-Solving 602
  Twelve Purposes of 551, 619
Assessment Devices 600
Attention 55–57
  Moves 47
  Repertoire 56
Attitude of Positive Expectancy 139
Attitude toward errors 348
Attribution Retraining 379
Attribution Theory 315, 325, 326, 327
Awareness Training Model 301

B

Behavior
  Disruptive or inattentive
    Causes 123–124
  In effective organizations 5, 8
  Off-task 151, 152
Behavior Modification 189
Beliefs
  Deep collaboration 2, 22, 27
  Professional knowledge 3, 7, 10, 13, 21, 22, 27, 34
  Racism. *See* Racism
  Seven knowledge bases 22
  Teacher efficacy 24
  Teaching knowledge and skill 21
  The learning environment we create 23
Bell Curve of Innate Ability 322
Bias 34
Big Idea 201
Bloom's taxonomy 250
Brain research 43
"Brights" 333, 334
Broken Squares Activity 415
Brown vs. Board of Education 25

C

Calling on Students 333
Caring 389, 390, 403, 404, 136
Casual register 236
Challenge, balance 46
Challenging Students 188
Charlie Brown syndrome 205
Charlotte Danielson's Framework for Teaching 17
Checking for Understanding 248, 472

Checklists 457, 574, 575
Check-Off Record Forms 579, 580
Classroom Assessment 551, 552, 619
Classroom Climate 176
  Community and mutual support 409
  Influence and control 409
  Risk-taking and confidence 409
Classroom procedures 111
Classroom Reality
  Information Processing Reality 627
  Moral Reality 626
  Personal Reality 626
  Political Reality 627
  Social Reality 626
Classroom space
  Centers 74
  Circle 73
  Clusters 74
  Perimeter 74
  Rows 74
  Ten recommendations 77
  Twos 73
  "U"s 74
Close Confusers 279
Cognitive Behavior Modification 189
Cognitive connections 87, 205, 237, 266, 456
Cognitive Empathy 247
Cognitive Level 534
Coherent Curriculum 458
Collaborative for Academic, Social, and Emotional Learning (CASEL) 178
Collectivism 117
Common Core 1, 2
Communicating Value 393
Communications
  With families and community 5
Community building 412, 416
Compare and Contrast 245
Comprehensiveness 12, 14
Concept Attainment Model 297
Concept Map 485
Concrete-Semiabstract-Abstract Progression 269
Conflict Resolution Skills 417
Consequences 144
  Hierarchy of escalating 150
  High impact 171
  Last resort 175
  Medium 156
  Small 151
Constructivist Teaching 434
Content 535, 536, 503, 537
Content analysis 3, 4, 8, 482–484
Content-specific pedagogy 3, 4, 8
Contiguity 280
Cooperative Learning 529
Coverage Thinking 489
Criteria for Success 204, 332, 350, 384, 388, 472, 474, 355
  Bulleted List 558
  Performance Task List 558
Crosswalk 17
  Charlotte Danielson's Framework for Teaching 17
  David Rose's Universal Design for Learning 17
  Kim Marshall's Teacher Evaluation Rubrics 17
  Massachusetts Model System for Teacher Evaluation 17
  Robert Marzano's Teacher Evaluation Model 17
Cueing
  Minimal and Progressive 231
Cultural blindness 32, 39
Cultural competence 33, 39
Cultural destructiveness 32, 39
Cultural improficiency 32
Cultural incapacity 32, 39
Culturally pre-competent 33
Culturally relevant instruction 36
Cultural proficiency 33
  Six stages 33
Cumulative Review 280
Curriculum
  Agreements of 443–446
  Elements of 446
  Topics 446
Cycle of Teaching and Learning 553

D

Data collection 573
Data Wall 581
David Rose's Universal Design for Learning 17
Degree of Abstraction 533
Degree of Guidance 281
Degree of Supervision 531
Demonstrating fairness 400
Designing for Cognitive Impact 269
Designing for Motivational Impact 274
Desisting moves 48–50
Dipsticking 251
Direct Instruction 89
Disruptions
  Body language of meaning business 134, 153
  Causes 123

Consequences 144
Eliminating 134
Downtime 47

E

Educational Contract 173
Educational Games 231
Effective Effort 6, 24, 25, 26, 27, 324, 379
Attributes of 380
Efficient management systems 99
Effort-Based Ability Theory 322, 325, 388
Emotional State 45
End Without Closure 287
Engaged time 85, 87, 101
Enlisting Moves 52
Error Analysis
By Students 587
By the Teacher 585
Essays 600
Evaluation 355
Every Student Succeeds Act (ESSA) 1, 2
Exhibitions 608–609
Expectations
Four Kinds 317
Expectations, Four Kinds 317
Explanatory Devices 213
Explicitness 238
Extension groups 522

F

Feedback
Areas of effective 321
Feeling Tone 287
Filler moves 62
Follow-up question 341
Foreshadowing 247
Formative Assessment 247, 263, 265, 378, 493, 522, 549, 567
Framing Reteaching 332, 367
Framing the Learning 196

G

Generic pedagogy 3, 5, 8
Generic Thinking Skills 493
Gestures, Demonstrations, and Modeling 215
Get acquainted activities 411
Gifted students 375
Giving assignments and tasks 349
Giving Feedback 350
Giving Help 345
Goal Setting 274
Grades 371
Graphic Organizers 222–225
Greeting 411, 412
Group Dynamics 416
Group Identity 414
Grouping 373, 541
Group Investigation 623
Group Investigation Model 304
Growing Lilies in the Desert, 7
Growth Mindset 315, 322, 330, 331, 388
Guess My Category Activity 288
Guess what's on the teacher's mind 177
Guidance
Degree of 281

H

Hidden curriculum 108
Hierarchical relationships 494
Hierarchical relationships diagram 494
High Expectations 323, 330, 332, 378, 388
High Expectations Teaching
10 Arenas of Classroom Life 332
Attitude Toward Errors—Persevere and Return 388
Calling on Students 332, 333, 388
Feedback 320, 321, 332, 333, 350, 351, 353, 354, 355, 364, 380, 383, 384, 388
Giving Help 332, 345, 388
Grades 371, 388
Grouping 332, 373, 376, 388
Positive Framing for Reteaching 366, 388
Redos 388
Responding to Students' Answers 388
Retakes 370, 371, 388
Tasks and Assignments 332, 349, 388
Tenacity 332, 347, 369, 370, 371, 388
High-expertise teaching
Knowledge 3
High Success Time 88
Home Contact 139
Homework 514
Housekeeping routines 108–109
Humor 392, 126, 397, 403

I

Implicit Bias 34, 37
Incrementalist Theory 322, 325, 388
Indicators 458, 481
Individual differences in learners 3, 5, 8

Individualism 117
Inductive Thinking Model 293, 298, 299, 308
Information Complexity 543
Information processing teaching model 301, 309, 311
Innate ability 322, 324, 326, 327, 329, 330, 331, 365, 379
Inquiry Training Model 299
Instructional time 84, 89, 99, 100
Intelligence 35
  Bell curve 24, 25
Interactive Teaching 623
Interactive Whiteboards 226
Interdependence 414
Intrusion, moves for 64
Involvement Thinking 491
Isolation of Critical Attributes 270
Itinerary 200

J

Jigsaw activity 414
John Adams' Promise 7

K

Kim Marshall's Teacher Evaluation Rubrics 17
Knowledge bases for high-expertise teaching 3
Knowledge of Results 276
KWL Chart 206

L

Laughter, benefits of 46
Learning strategies 308, 382, 428
Learning Style 430
Lesson Flexibility 65
Life-liberating beliefs 330, 378, 384, 420, 425
Life-limiting beliefs 384, 420, 423, 439
Logical Consequences 189

M

Making Students' Thinking Visible 246, 248, 255, 259, 261, 266
Massachusetts Model System for Teacher Evaluation 17
Mastery Language 469
Mastery Thinking 492
Matching 12, 235, 337, 531, 532, 533, 534, 540, 542, 544, 546, 628
Mazes 234
Meaning 271
Measures of Effective Teaching (MET) project 1
Mental Engagement 237
Mental Imagery 227–229
Microaggressions 34
Mnemonics 281
Modeling 272
Modeling Thinking Aloud 216–219, 219
Models of Discipline 188–189
Moves 15, 16
Myers-Briggs 431
Mysteries exercise 416

N

No Child Left Behind Act (NCLB) 1
Nondirective Teaching Model 303
Nonreport 431, 432, 433
Normalizing Errors 422
Notebooks 606

O

Objectives
  Communicating 198
  Stated, lived, worthy 466, 467
Observation 457, 603
Open and thinking, 276
Operant conditioning 278
Operating Principles 257
Overarching Objectives 621–623
Overlapping moves 61

P

Pacing 93, 100
Paper Towels Score Form 604
Patterns 15, 16
Patterns of Instruction 305
  Direct Instruction 306
  Lecture 305
  Recitation 306
PBIS 189
Peer coaching 309, 310
Perceptual Modes 284
Performance Task List 558
Persistence 320, 333, 397, 398
Personal Influence 189
Personal Relevance 525
Physical Models 220
Physical movement 46
Planning Conference 482–484
Portfolios 610–613
Positive Behavior Interventions and Supports (PBIS) 189
Practice 282
Practice sessions 282
Pre-Assessing 209

Presentation Software 230
Principles for Attention and Engagement 286
Principles of Learning 268
Privacy 75
Problem-Solving Skills 417
Professional Knowledge 5
Progressive Differentiation
  Geometry Concepts 296
Provisioning moves 60
Pygmalion in the classroom 26, 315, 334, 335

Q

Questioning skills 265
Questions 13, 233, 239, 240, 250, 253, 265

R

Race to the Top 1
Racism , 26, 29, 34, 36, 37, 18, 39
Readiness to Receive 204
Reality Therapy 189
Realness 402
Recitation 306
Record-Keeping 573
Redos 371
Re-education 156
Reinforcement 277
Reliability 597
Repertoire 12
Report
  Language Arts 595
Reporting Systems 591
Reports: Oral, Written, and Multimedia 607
Resistant students. *See* Challenging students
Resources 524
Respecting students 400
Responses to student answers 276
Response to Intervention (RTI) 522
Responsibility building 414
Responsive Classroom 178
Restorative Discipline 189
Retakes 371
Reteaching 332, 366, 367, 388, 522, 589
Rhythm 93, 100
Risk-Taking 419
  Five Beliefs 420
Robert Marzano's Teacher Evaluation Model 17
Role Plays 231
"Round the Clock Learning Buddies" 623
Routines
  Culture 116
  Elements of effective 116
  Self-assessment 115
  Teaching 113
Rubric
  Cross Curricular Sixth Grade Exhibition 566
  Exemplars 568–569
  Science Lab 559
  Scoring an Essay 564
  Spot Check 200

S

Safety and operational routines 109
Say-Do 283
Scale 545
Second Language Learners 202, 204, 214, 215, 234
Self-Awareness Training 189
Self-Expression 532
Sensory Channels 544
Sequence and Backward Chaining 286
Seven knowledge bases 22
Similarity of Environment 288
Simulations 231
Skillful teacher
  Definition 10
Skillful Teacher Framework 11
"Slows" 333, 334, 408
Smart is something you can get 332, 522
Social Contract 139
Social Skills 110, 416, 476
Sort Card activity 210
Sources of Information 524
Speech Patterns 233
Standards 113, 200, 309, 316, 317, 318, 328, 330, 388, 617
  Communicating 318
Standards and Expectations 316, 328
State Standards 477
Stereotypes 25
Stereotype threat 35
Stop My Teaching 427
Structure 536
Structuring 535
Student Agreement 172
Student friendly language 471
Student influence 426
Student interests 403
Student ownership 426
Student record-keeping about progress 583
Student self-assessment 582, 588
Student Teams and Academic Divisions (STAD) 623

Subdividing moves 66
Summarizers 264
Summarizing 74, 89, 100, 116, 217, 225, 179, 262, 263, 264
Summative assessment 453, 549, 565, 567
Synectics Model 301

T

Taboo exercise 137
Taxonomy. *See* Bloom's taxonomy
Teacher comments (Writers' Express) 357–362
Teacher Effectiveness Training (TET) 189
Teacher traits 392
Teaching Teams 616
Technical Principles of Design 279
Tenacity. *See* Persistence
Ten Jobs of Teaching 6
Test Record 588
Tests 599
The Class 30
The Important Questions of Teaching 13
Therapeutic Models of Discipline 189
The Scholar's Loop 367
Thinking Skill Objectives 474
Three-way conferences 591
Time allocations in school 82
Time audits 91
Time on Task 85
Time-out 167
Tracking 374, 375, 377
Transfer 272
Type of Interdependence 527

U

Unscrambling confusion 253

V

Vagueness 234, 235
Validity 597
Visual Representations 220
Vividness 289

W

Wait Time 337, 338, 339
White privilege 37
Winning moves 54
"Withitness" 61
Wordsplash 207
Work habits and procedures 109–110

RBT Professional Development Programs

Research for Better Teaching, Inc. (RBT) offers a portfolio of professional learning opportunities in the areas of teaching, school leadership, and the effective use of student data. The programs listed below are a sample of the many programs RBT delivers on-site in schools or districts. Customized professional development experiences, on-site coaching, or consulting in these topics to meet specific needs may also be requested. For more information about these and other opportunities to partner with RBT, please visit www.RBTeach.com or email info@RBTeach.com.

SKILLFUL TEACHING

Studying Skillful Teaching: Promoting Motivation, Learning, and Achievement (SST)

The Studying Skillful Teaching program is RBT's cornerstone program for building teachers' capacity – the knowledge and skills as well as the courage and conviction – to promote students' motivation, learning, and increased achievement. It is based on the belief that teaching is a process of decision-making; and that skillful teachers never stop learning through experimentation, data analysis, study, and collegial sharing about what works best for their students. This reflective dialogue is consistently rated by our clients as an invaluable asset for building common and coherent language among their educators.

High Expectations Teaching (HiEx)

This program teaches what it looks like and sounds like when a teacher acts authentically from a growth mindset. Participants will learn how to choose language, develop classroom structures, and use effective instructional strategies to motivate all students, but particularly to get low-performing, low-confidence students to change their stereotypes about themselves.

Making Student Thinking Visible (MSTV)

This online program equips teachers to create robust talk environments where students talk more than teachers and at a high level of thinking. When skillfully applied, these skills build students' social skills, classroom climate, and high levels of engagement in meaningful ways across grade levels and content areas. Features RBT founder and president, Jon Saphier, with commentary by Lucy West.

Foundations in Teaching (FIT)

Beginning teachers need practical skills so that they can be successful in their first years of teaching. This program focuses on three major areas: an introduction to the belief in the growth mindset that says "smart is something you can get through effective effort"; classroom management and climate, emphasizing the elements that need to be in place for a classroom to run smoothly and productively; and the development of clear learning objectives as the anchor for creating daily lesson plans.

SKILLFUL LEADERSHIP

Analyzing Teaching for Student Results (ATSR)

This is a program for leaders on how to improve classroom teaching and learning. Reflecting the national shift towards learning-focused supervision and evaluation, the Analyzing Teaching for Student Results (ATSR) program helps leaders zero in on the impact of teaching decisions on students. During the program, participants examine high-leverage teaching strategies and use both a common language and a concept system about teaching to support any state framework. The seven-day curriculum provides multiple opportunities for participants to develop keen observation and analytical skills that will support teachers in building their own capacity to impact students' learning. It includes an on-site co-observation with the instructor for each participant.

Coaching for Sustainable School Improvement (CSSI)

This program prepares coaches to play the vital role of improving instruction by working with individual teachers to hone their practice, providing just-in-time professional learning opportunities tied to teacher and school goals, and strengthening a collaborative professional culture. Features the use of classroom video in the coaching relationship and incorporates the work of leading coaching expert, Jim Knight.

The Skillful Leader: Taking Action to Improve Ineffective Instruction (TSL)

One of the most challenging aspects of teacher evaluation systems is how to improve the quality of instruction by underperforming teachers. Knowing how to support these teachers, often rated "needs improvement" or "unsatisfactory", is a source of ongoing frustration. In this practical program, participants will learn to identify and assist individuals whose current instruction is not positively impacting student growth and outcomes. Sample strategies and approaches from the book by Platt and Tripp, *Strengthening Teacher Evaluation: Taking Action to Improve Ineffective Instruction*, aka *The Skillful Leader III* (2014).

SKILLFUL LEADERSHIP *(cont.)*

Social Emotional Learning: Planning for Sustainable Systemic Implementation (SEL)
Social emotional learning (SEL) is rightfully at the top of most districts' agendas these days. After all, "Emotions are everywhere" and have a profound influence on student learning. This is a program for district-level planning teams. RBT has reviewed the SEL field and identified 12 different approaches in the field. They can be viewed in progressive levels of complexity and sophistication. Adopting a good SEL program is a good start, but is not enough. Most programs focus on only one of the 12 approaches, and a district must develop a comprehensive plan to meet the needs of their students. In this program, participants will be introduced to the 12 approaches and they will begin to review the current status of their school/district's implementation of each of the twelve. Then they will begin to develop a clear, comprehensive SEL plan, all through the lens of high-expertise teaching.

How to Build Strong Adult Professional Culture: The Essential Ingredient for School Improvement (APC)
This is a program about the everyday behaviors of school leaders who successfully build strong Adult Professional Cultures (APC). It is a program for principals, assistant principals, team leaders, and instructional coaches, and very much for central office personnel who interact with school leaders. Our learning at RBT, supported solidly by research, is that there will be no sustainable improvement in student results and no elimination of the achievement gap until leaders and teachers succeed in making strong certain norms of behavior between adults.

Differentiated Conferencing (DC)
The Differentiated Conferencing program instructs supervisors and coaches on how to develop the knowledge and skills to conduct meaningful and actionable conversations with teachers who are at different levels of professional maturity. It helps them build their capacity to have effective conferences with teachers at five different levels of development. Participants will develop a repertoire of skills to apply in situations from non-directive to directive and even to particularly difficult conversations. Supervisors and coaches grow their conferencing skills and match their clients with just-right approaches.

SKILLFUL DATA USE

Coaching High-Impact Teacher Teams (TEAMS)
High-impact teacher teams build their collective expertise in the practices that matter most for increasing student achievement: they clarify learning goals, they plan for and infuse formative assessment practices throughout their instruction, they analyze results based on pre-established success criteria, and they take timely, targeted action to provide feedback, re-teach, and extend learning. In short, they use data frequently and in-depth to make sure that each student succeeds. The program includes on-site or virtual follow-up.

Data Coaching: Unleashing the Power of Collaborative Inquiry (DATA)
This program is for Data Coaches and school/district leaders of Data Teams to learn how to lead a structured process of collaborative inquiry that increases professional community, effective uses of data, and student achievement. Based on *The Data Coach's Guide to Improving Learning for All Students: Unleashing the Power of Collaborative Inquiry* (Corwin Press, 2008) by Love, Stiles, Mundry, and DiRanna.

See www.RBTeach.com for further details on programs, including schedule, pricing, and registration, or contact us at info@RBTeach.com or +1 (978) 263-9449.

RBT Publications and Products

SKILLFUL TEACHING

The Skillful Teacher: The Comprehensive Resource for Improving Teaching and Learning (7th ed. 2018)
Updates the last edition with powerful new material and 100+ videos illustrating the skills. Designed for both the novice and the experienced educator, *The Skillful Teacher* is a unique synthesis of the Knowledge Base on Teaching, with repertoires for matching teaching strategies to student needs. Designed as a practical guide for practitioners working to broaden their teaching skills, the book combines theory with practice and focuses on 18 critical areas of classroom performance. A must for instructional coaches and mentors.
by Jon Saphier, Mary Ann Haley-Speca, & Robert Gower

High Expectations Teaching: How to Persuade Students to Believe and Act on "Smart Is Something You Can Get" (2017)
For all the productive conversation around "mindsets," what's missing are the details of how to convince our discouraged and underperforming students that "smart is something you can get." Until now. With the publication of *High-Expectations Teaching*, Jon Saphier reveals once and for all evidence that the bell curve of ability is plain wrong—that ability is something that can be grown significantly if we can first help students to believe in themselves.
by Jon Saphier

Activators: Activity Structures to Engage Students' Thinking Before Instruction (1993)
This book is a collection of classroom-tested, practical activity structures for getting students' minds active and engaged prior to introducing new content or skills.
by Jon Saphier & Mary Ann Haley

Summarizers: Activity Structures to Support Integration and Retention of New Learning (1993)
This book is a collection of classroom-tested, practical activity structures for getting students cognitively active during and after periods of instruction.
by Jon Saphier & Mary Ann Haley

SKILLFUL LEADERSHIP

Transforming Ineffective Teams: Maximizing Collaboration's Impact on Learning: The Skillful Leader II (2008)
This important "Skillful Leader" book arms administrators and teacher leaders with step-by-step strategies to confront and raise the performance of teams and individuals who undermine student learning. The text includes methods of collecting data, strategies for intervention, and tips for hiring and training. Individual and community profiles, together with legal notes, provide practical tools for busy leaders.
by Alexander D. Platt, Caroline E. Tripp, Robert G. Fraser, James R. Warnock, & Rachel E. Curtis

Strengthening Teacher Evaluation: Taking Action to Improve Ineffective Teaching (The Skillful Leader III) (2014)
This work serves as a how-to handbook to accompany the bestselling *The Skillful Leader: Confronting Mediocre Teaching*. Like its predecessor, the book offers dozens of illustrations, new cases, and sample documents plus legal advice to help evaluators confront ineffective instruction. It is a cover-to-cover guide for solving thorny teacher performance problems.
by Alexander D. Platt & Caroline E. Tripp

Beyond Mentoring: Putting Instructional Focus on Comprehensive Induction Programs (2011)
This book emphasizes the critical role of instructional practice in the induction support that is given to new and beginning teachers. Using RBT's model for the comprehensive induction of new teachers, educators are guided through the steps of developing an induction plan for new teachers and integrating the induction program with the district's professional learning community.
by Jon Saphier, Susan Freedman, & Barbara Aschheim

Talk Sense: Communicating to Lead and Learn (2007)
Barry Jentz shows how leaders can build the requisite trust and credibility for improving organizational performance. Typically, leaders "talk tough" to improve performance. When that doesn't work, they "talk nice" (or vice-versa). By learning to "talk sense", leaders can succeed in their efforts to improve performance.
by Barry Jentz

RBT Publications and Products

SKILLFUL DATA USE

The Data Coach's Guide to Improving Learning for All Students: Unleashing the Power of Collaborative Inquiry (2008)
This resource helps Data-Team facilitators move schools away from unproductive data practices and toward examining data for systematic and continuous improvement in instruction and learning. The book includes a CD-ROM with slides and reproducibles.
by Nancy Love, Katherine E. Stiles, Susan Mundry, & Kathryn DiRanna

Laminated Guide: Data Literacy for Teachers (2011)
For every teacher, data coach, and inquiry team. In a fold-out 8.5" x 11" laminated form, ready to be inserted in a notebook, the guide provides a simple framework to help teachers feel comfortable, knowledgeable, and skilled in effectively using a variety of data, including formative assessments.
by Nancy Love

Laminated Guide: The Skillful Inquiry/Data Team (2012)
For every grade level (elementary) or subject-area (middle and high school) team of teachers, plus school and district administrators. In a fold-out 8.5" x 11" laminated form, ready to be inserted in a notebook, this guide provides a proven-effective inquiry process and practical tools to maximize their impact on student achievement.
by Nancy Love

DVD: The Skillful Data Use Series (2012) Volume 1 Collaborative Inquiry: Connecting Data to Results. DVD collection of introductory instructional videos based on The Data Coach's Guide and Using Data to Improve Learning for All provides expert commentary, insights from successful implementations, and views of Data Teams in action.

Posters: Unleashing the Power of Collaborative Inquiry (2009)
Eight full-color, 24" x 36" laminated posters: (1) Using Data 19 Tasks, (2) Building the Bridge, (3) Using Data Diagram, (4) Data Driven Dialogue, (5) Data Triangle, (6) Logic Model, (7) Verify Causes Tree, and (8) Drill Down Deep. Data is power!

OTHER RBT RESOURCES

John Adams' Promise: How to Have Good Schools for All Our Children, Not Just for Some (2005)
Curriculum reform, structural reform, funding reform, organizational reform—all these 20th-century efforts have failed to make a significant dent in the achievement gap and the performance of disadvantaged students, especially in cities and poor rural areas.
by Jon Saphier

How to Bring Vision to School Improvement Through Core Outcomes, Commitments and Beliefs (1993)
This practical guide provides a proven step-by-step sequence for generating consensus among parents and staff about a few valued core outcomes they want for all children. Then it shows how to achieve the concrete outcomes in the areas of school and family life.
by Jon Saphier & John D'Auria